No Labour,
No Battle

No Labour, No Battle

Military Labour During the First World War

John Starling and Ivor Lee

SPELLMOUNT

First published in 2009 by Spellmount,
an imprint of The History Press
The Mill, Brimscombe Port
Stroud, Gloucestershire, GL5 2QG
www.thehistorypress.co.uk

British Library Cataloguing in Publication Data.
A catalogue record for this book is available from the British Library.

ISBN 978 0 7524 4975 3

Printed in Great Britain

Dedication

This history is dedicated to 41790 Private Samuel Slinger 70 Company Labour Corps, killed in action 11 September 1917, and all the other personnel of the British, Dominion and Foreign Labour units.

CONTENTS

Acknowledgements

Twentieth-century military history has been an interest of mine since childhood. I grew up in what could be called a Royal British Legion family. My father had served as an infantry officer during the Second World War and on leaving the Army worked for the Legion, initially at Headquarters and later running Halsey House, Cromer, one of their residential homes. My mother was a member of the Legion's Women Section serving as Chair of both Norfolk and West Lancashire Counties.

My interest in the Labour Corps started early in the 1990s when researching the War Memorial in the Lancashire village of Hesketh Bank. One man, Private Samuel Slinger had served in the Labour Corps. On trying to find out about the Corps 'experts' told me that it was a civilian force, they were the Pioneer Battalions and they were soldiers who worked on the land. The latter, at least, had some truth in it. Finding virtually nothing in the Official Histories I asked an old friend, Ray Westlake, if there was anything published on the Labour Corps. Whilst there was no History, Ray put me in touch with John Starling as someone who was also interested in the Corps.

John and I spoke about our mutual interest and decided to meet up the next time I came down to London. Perhaps fittingly this meeting took place in the cafe at the National Archives, Kew, as we were to spend hundreds of hours researching documents.

From the very start it was clear that this would be not be just two people collaborating on a First World War history, but friends working together on a shared mutual interest.

John and I have different skills that complement each other. He has the patience to spend hours reading and transcribing, often barely legible War Diaries whereas I enjoy researching the political and military environment, contemporary publications and the service records of individual officers and soldiers. Perhaps even more important was the mutual support, without which this history would never have been written.

We decided that in order to ensure a consistent style, one person would produce the text. Although I undertook this task John's input on each section was invaluable, pointing out omissions and suggesting additional information.

Over the years I have received thousands of emails from people tracing an ancestor's service in the Labour Corps, many of whom have added important information about the Corps and helped build up my database of men who served in the Corps. It is not possible to thank all these individuals but I would like to record my appreciation to them and to those who have contacted me through the Great War Forum (www.1914–1918.invisionzone.com/forums) and the Canadian Expeditionary Force Study Group (http://www.cefresearch.com/phpBB2).

There are a number of people who I want to thank personally for their help, advice and support: Samuel Slinger's relatives for his photograph and access to his letters; William Spencer at the National Archives who has an encyclopaedic knowledge of the Archives and has helped uncover obscure references to the Labour Corps; Charles Messenger, who not only asked me to read the draft chapter on Labour in his book, *Call to Arms* but has provided invaluable information on the Entrenching Battalions; Michael D. Robson, in Israel, for assistance on the Egyptian Labour Corps; Christine Liava'a, in Fiji, for assistance with the Fijian Labour Corps; and Margaret Tyler and her husband Kevin C. Dowson for the photograph of the 3rd Alien Company and information about CQMS Wiehl.

Producing this work has been a labour of love and it would not have occurred without the encouragement and help of my wife, Anne. She has never complained even when our holidays in France and Belgium, Turkey, Greece, Israel and Egypt included time spent on research and visits to CWGC Cemeteries. She read the text and made important suggestions on how it could be improved. Most of all she has made sure that I kept to deadlines.

Ivor H. Lee
Banffshire

I was commissioned into the Royal Pioneer Corps in 1977. I have always had an in interest in military history and noticed a number of references to the Labour Corps but also noted there were no formal records. In 1993 I was in command of 187 Company when the Pioneer Corps was amalgamated into the Royal Logistic Corps. One of my tasks in Northampton was to assist in the closure of the RPC Museum. Whilst undertaking this work I unearthed a number of memoirs of the Chinese and Egyptian Labour Corps. At the same time I started to research Pioneer and Labour units at the National Archives, Kew. I first made contact with Ivor Lee following a conversation with Ray Westlake. The last 15 years I have been compiling an archive and trying to construct War Diaries for the various Companies and Groups.

This book would not have been written without the encouragement and help of Ivor. We seem to have complemented each other as Ivor has the ability to find long lost references whilst I have the patience to read masses of semi-legible papers at Kew. A lot of assistance has been provided by The Royal Pioneer Corps Association, the Royal Logistic Corps Museum at Deepcut and William Spencer at the National Archives, all of whom I would like to thank. I am also grateful to Roy Hemington of the Commonwealth War Graves Commission, Professor Richard Holmes, the Defence Academy, who has provided excellent guidance – as well as a marvellous foreword – and Col David Owen of the RASC/RCT Association for their assistance. I should also thank my various work colleagues, who, over the years, have been persuaded to comment on various papers. I should particularly thank Phil Harding who has read the first draft. Most of all I have to thank my wife Deborah for her patience and assistance in reading the text.

John Starling
Oxfordshire

Abbreviations

AAG	Assistant Adjutant-General
ACI	Army Council Instruction
ACL	Assistant Controller of Labour
ADDL	Assistant Deputy Director of Labour
ADL	Assistant Director of Labour
AE	Area Employment
AG	Adjutant-General
ALC	Assistant Labour Commandant
ANZAC	Australian and New Zealand Army Corps
AO	Army Order *also* Agricultural Officer
AOC	Army Ordnance Corps
AOD	Army Ordnance Department
APM	Assistant Provost Marshall
ASC	Army Service Corps
AT	Army Transport
BEF	British Expeditionary Force
Bn	Battalion
BORs	British Other Ranks
Brig	Brigadier General
BWIR	British West Indies Regiment
Capt	Captain
CC	Carrier Corps
CCS	Casualty Clearing Station
CE	Chief Engineer
CIGS	Chief of the Imperial General Staff
C-in-C	Commander in Chief
CL	Controller of Labour
CLC	Chinese Labour Corps
CNL	Controller of Native Labour
CO	Commanding Officer *also* Conscientious Objector
CRE	Commander Royal Engineers
CSM	Company Sergeant Major
CWCG	Commonwealth War Graves Commission
DAAG	Deputy Assistant Adjutant General
DADL	Deputy Assistant Director of Labour
DCL	Deputy Controller of Labour

DCM	Distinguished Conduct Medal *also* District Court Martial
DDL	Deputy Director of Labour
DE	Divisional Employment
DGR&E	Directorate of Graves Registration and Enquiries
DGT	Director General of Transport
DHQ	Divisional Headquarters
DL	Director of Labour
DNTO	Divisional Naval Transport Officer
DORA	Defence of the Realm Act
DOS	Director of Supplies
DSO	Distinguished Service Order
EBD	Employment Base Depot
ECLC	Eastern Command Labour Centre
ELC	Egyptian Labour Corps
FGCM	Field General Court Martial
GG	Garrison Guard
GHQ	General Headquarters
GLC	Greek Labour Corps
GOC	General Officer Commanding
GRO	General Routine Order
GRU	Graves Registration Unit
GS	General Service
HQ	Headquarters
HS	Home Service
IBD	Infantry Base Depot
IGC	Inspector General of Communications
ILB	Infantry Labour Battalion
ILC	Infantry Labour Company *also* Indian Labour Corps
IWB	Infantry Works Battalion
IWC	Infantry Works Company
IWGC	Imperial War Graves Commission
IWM	Imperial War Museum
IWT	Inland Waterways Transport
JLC	Jail Labour Corps *also* Jewish Labour Corps
LC	Labour Commandant
LoC (LofC)	Line of Communication
Lt	Lieutenant
Lt Col	Lieutenant Colonel
Maj	Major
MC	Military Cross
MEF	Mediterranean Expeditionary Force
MID	Mentioned in Dispatches
MLB	Mauritius Labour Battalion *also* Macedonian Labour Battalion *also* Military Labour Bureau
MLC	Military Labour Corps
MM	Military Medal
MSM	Meritorious Service Medal
NA	National Archives

NCC	Non Combatant Corps
NCF	No Conscription Fellowship
NCO	Non Commissioned Officer
NTO	Naval Transport Officer
NWF	North West Frontier
OBE	Order of the British Empire
OC	Officer Commanding
OR	Other Ranks
PB	Permanent Base
PNTO	Principal Naval Transport Officer
PoW	Prisoner of War
PU	Permanently Unfit
QM	Quartermaster
QMG	Quarter Master General
QMS	Quartermaster Sergeant
RA	Royal Artillery
RAMC	Royal Army Medical Corps
RE	Royal Engineers
RFC	Royal Flying Corps
RGA	Royal Garrison Artillery
RLC	Russian Labour Corps
RMLC	Royal Marine Labour Corps
SANLC	South African Native Labour Corps
SCLC	Southern Command Labour Centre
ScCLC	Scottish Command Labour Centre
TW	Transport Workers
UP	United Provinces
WCLC	Western Command Labour Centre
WO	Warrant Officer
ZMC	Zion Mule Corps

LIST OF TABLES

FOREWORD BY RICHARD HOLMES

Seldom has that insufficiently-acknowledged phrase 'no labour, no battle' been more true than in the First World War. There is widespread agreement that it was a gunner's war, but the shells that shaped the conflict (and have left such an enduring mark on the landscape), had to be taken to ports, embarked, shipped to France and other theatres of war and then unloaded, transported to depots close to the front, and finally hauled forward onto the gun positions from which they would be fired. Trench warfare – combat in that obdurate framework of fighting and communication trenches, barbed wire entanglements, command post and reserve positions – depended upon backbreaking work. Roads and railways had to be built and repaired, timber for everything from huts to duckboards had to be felled, sawed and fashioned, and salvage – from discarded rifles to redundant boots – had to be recovered and wherever possible, refurbished for re-use.

The British Army was bigger than it had ever been before, or would be since. It put nearly six million men through its ranks, and in the summer of 1917, when numbers on the Western Front peaked, it had some 1.7 million in that theatre alone. This mighty leviathan gulped down resources: ammunition for its artillery, mortars, machine-guns and rifles; food, fodder and water for its men and animals; fuel for its motor vehicles and aircraft; and what were gently described as 'trench stores' – the wearisome litany of duckboards, sandbags, wire pickets, water pumps, corrugated metal, timber for stakes and revetments, and the half-round 'elephant iron' that made roofed-over sections of trench – for its field defences.

There is no shortage of scholarly work on the acceleration in munitions production, and on the political, social and economic consequences of wholly unprecedented changes in the organisation of British industry and agriculture. Similarly, almost every aspect of the fighting army's life has been explored, from its command structure, to its weapons and tactics and the everyday life of its officers and men. Yet there has been no comprehensive survey of the organisation and use of military labour, even though its numbers were prodigious (at the time of the Armistice the Agricultural Companies alone contained 75,000 men, three-quarters the size of the entire British Army in 2009) and its impact was scarcely less than war-winning.

Of course we can see why. Not only does the topic lack the drama of battle or the controversial decision-making of high command, but, even in an army as inherently decentralised as the British, its organisation was fluid, often eccentric, and its wartime structures soon withered in the pale sunlight of peace: it was scarcely the stuff for aspiring regimental historians. Nor was labour likely to appeal to those who found the war's most definitive expression in the everyday life of its infantry, who sought the vicarious excitement in the achievements of its heroes, or who believed that the whole shocking business could best be understood in terms of 'lions led by donkeys'.

This is the first proper history of military labour in the First World War. It charts the fortunes of the many types of unit involved, from Home Service Labour Companies through Docks Battalions, Pioneer Battalions to companies charged with the exhumation and reburial of the dead, using War Office files in the National Archives to explain the administrative details which illuminate the complex twists and turns of units' organisational lives. It also examines the controversial issue of overseas labour units like the Cape Coloured Labour Battalion, the Fijian Labour Corps and the Chinese Labour Companies. Headstones of the latter's members are a not infrequent sight in Commonwealth War Graves Commission cemeteries on the Western Front, and I can never see one without musing on the vagaries of fate that whisked a man from Shantung to die in Flanders.

Although theirs is evidently a labour of love, the authors do not flinch from difficult issues. When Private Freddie Alberts of the Cape Coloured Labour Battalion was shot for murder, the firing party botched its task though the range was very short and the victim had a white envelope pinned over his heart. The Medical Officer was narrowly missed by the sergeant who administered the coup de grâce with his revolver. Ratu Joseva Sukuna, a Fijian high chief, was commissioned into the Fiji Defence Force but the governor decreed that Europeans need not salute him. He resigned his commission and served as a quartermaster sergeant in the labour corps, eventually returning home to become Speaker of the Legislative Council and later to receive a knighthood. Exhumation squads went about their ghastly work by first looking for grass that was a vivid bluish green, or water that was greenish black or grey, the tell-tale signs of a body near the surface, and groped for identity discs in rotting humanity. A wise company commander emphasised that men behaved much better if reminded that their job was really important because so many men were missing, and 'the greater the stress laid upon the need for identification, the greater the interest the men take in their work'.

Labour units were not immune from the indiscipline that accompanied the slow process of demobilisation: in June 1919, 360 soldiers were tried for disobeying a lawful order when men of the Eastern Command Labour Centre refused to go on parade, though proceedings were eventually halted. The introduction of conscription in early 1916 raised the question of conscientious objection to military service, and the authors are right to emphasise that many local tribunals asked questions, intended to prove whether a man was a genuine Conscientious Objector or not, that doomed him whatever his answer. Many objectors were enlisted into the Non Combatant Corps, whose strength peaked at 3,319, it members serving as part of the Army although they could not be trained to use weapons of any description. Some objectors simply refused to obey orders, and were court-martialled: ten died in custody (one hunger striker died when the tube used to force-feed him sent fluid into his lungs) or shortly after release. There was an undercurrent of what we might term today 'institutional racism'. For instance, black chaplains in South African Native Labour Corps were granted neither rank nor status, and one complained of an attitude by which: 'Black was black, and a boy was a boy, however dressed, educated or entitled.'

There is also much resilience, determination and courage in the story. In 1917 a sergeant earned the Distinguished Conduct Medal (one of the many decorations awarded to members of the Labour Corps) for keeping a vital stretch of road in the Ypres salient repaired 'although driven back by shell fire and gas several times'. When the great German offensive of March 1918 rolled the British right back towards Amiens, 876

Labour Company shifted 2,000 wounded to safety just before the Germans arrived, and 141 Labour Company stuck to its duties at an ammunition dump until it was actually being machine-gunned. Often officers and men of the Labour Corps ran a soldier's risks: in May 1918 three officers and 286 men of 101 Labour Company were gassed. All the officers and 134 of the men died, but the company was hard at work five days later.

Foreign labourers were not afraid to risk their lives: in May 1919 1st Class Ganger Yen Teng Feng was awarded the Meritorious Service Medal for spending four hours in a burning ammunition dump, dragging tarpaulins off stacks of ammunition to drench them with water. Although the men of the Bermuda Royal Garrison Artillery, working as a labour unit on the Western Front, suffered terribly from weather which could scarcely have been less like that to which they were accustomed, in October 1918 a Bermuda RGA detachment near Ypres, offloading ammunition and sending it on to nearby batteries, stuck to their task under shellfire: their lieutenant was awarded the Military Cross.

Many readers will be attracted to the subject because they will have had a relative serving in the Labour Corps. With a strength that peaked at just under 400,000 in early 1918, during the last two years of the war the corps was about the same size as the Royal Engineers and around eight times that of the Foot Guards, although – because its casualties were necessarily fewer – its throughput of personnel was smaller than was in the combat arms. But many members of the corps began their careers as infantrymen, and then re-badged as their battalions became part of the corps, or when they themselves were medically downgraded. At this time in the Army's history all non-commissioned personnel had a regimental number which was exactly that – an identification number issued to them by virtue of their service in a specified regiment or corps. The notion of an 'Army number' issued to a man on joining the Army and remaining with him for the whole of his career (thus providing a good indication of the year of his enlistment) did not arise till later. Thus a relative's First World War service medals, their rim engraved with his name, rank, number and corps, may simply indicate that he was in the Labour Corps, and this will provide little clue as to what he actually did during the war.

This book has an invaluable appendix relating the numbers of British Labour Corps personnel to the battalions or Infantry Labour Companies that were re-badged to form Labour Companies. For instance, a man with a number between 55201 and 55800 will have been a member of 13th Battalion The Queen's Royal Regiment (West Surrey) which formed 93 and 94 Labour Companies. A similar table relates the numbers of men serving in Home Service Labour Companies to their company number and its location: a number between 173141 and 173440 links a man to 315 Company, a works company based at Fovant in Wiltshire.

This painstakingly-researched book will appeal to far more readers than those who are tracing the war record of a great-uncle, for you cannot really understand the way the British Army went about its business during the war without understanding how it used the labour upon which so much depended. The next time you see a Labour Corps headstone in a CWGC cemetery, pause to remember that they also served who plied pick and shovel, often in conditions that we can scarcely guess at, providing service upon which so very much depended.

Richard Holmes

INTRODUCTION

Warfare has always been manpower intensive. Apart from the large number of combatant troops many more personnel, both military and civilian, are engaged to keep
the military force operating. These personnel are involved in the manufacture of
materials, movement of supplies such as ammunition and food/forage, building and
maintenance of camps, mending and cleaning equipment, manning headquarters and
training establishments, recovery of the dead and wounded and many other tasks.

This work is undertaken by soldiers not involved in the fighting, either 'resting' or
actually withdrawn from the line, specialist military units such as logistic or medical
servicemen, 'Camp Followers' such as wives, personnel recruited as soldiers or by
civilian contractors to undertake specific tasks, locally recruited civilians, prisoners
and Prisoners of War. Apart from the military specialists these labourers tended to
be recruited for a specific campaign and were not under unified command.

In 1817 a Corps of Military Labourers was formed for duties in the West Indies, the
men being raised from supernumerary rank and file of the West Indian Regiment.
Eventually fifteen companies of 100 men, under three sergeants and five corporals
(European), were raised and administered by officers of the Quartermaster General's
Department. It was disbanded in 1888 and never served outside the West Indies.[1]

During the Crimean War (1853–56) a Military Works Corps was formed in the
summer of 1855. It consisted of 1,000 Navvies supervised by officers who were
recruited from major Public Works organizations in Britain. Units started to arrive
in the Crimea on 11 August 1855. This Corps did not enjoy a good reputation:

> The Commander of the Forces has frequently noticed the misconduct and idleness
> of the parties of the Army Works Corps attached to this Army. He has just received a
> report that a party of 100 men, employed on Saturday last in loading Railway Stores
> at Balaclava grossly neglected their duty, and performed about one-fifth of a proper
> day's work.
>
> Unless a marked improvement takes place in the conduct and exertions of this
> Corps the Commander of the Forces will lay before the Secretary of State a strong
> report of its inefficiency, with a request that any gratuity which it may be intended to
> give the men on arrival in England may be forfeited.[2]

Despite representations from the Superintendent-General of the Corps the unit
was disbanded.

The first formal establishment for military labour was raised during the Indian
Mutiny, 1857. Independent Pioneer Companies, which were first formed in India

in 1770 to support the Sappers and Miners, were increased to battalion size to provide labour for all military units.[3] These units were retained after the Mutiny, due to the need to build and maintain roads and outposts in underdeveloped regions. Being infantry they were also capable of defending themselves. When not on operations they were encouraged to take up civilian contracts, an example of which was the construction of the 13-mile Matheran Light Railway in 1904 by the 121 Pioneers.[4] Pioneer Battalions proved so successful they increased from two in 1864 to twelve in 1904. The Pioneers Battalions encountered problems during the First World War when emphasis changed from 'infantry with construction skills' to 'construction troops with some infantry skills', which resulted in a clash with the role of the Sappers and Miners. The Pioneer Battalions were disbanded on 10 February 1933.[5]

Civilian contractors were widely used to support military operations. In 1884 Thomas Cook were contracted to move and support the Gordon Relief Column in Sudan. The requirement was to move 18,000 men and some 80,000 tons of supplies to the Forward Base at Wadi Halfa, 793 miles south of Cairo on the Nile. The contractor made use of 27 steamers, some 650 sailing boats and some 5,000 local labourers.[6] A failure in supervision of the contract and a misunderstanding of military requirements resulted in a lack of coal for the steamers and a delay of thirteen days, although the task was completed by November 1884.[7]

The main source of labour for any campaign was the recruitment of local civilians. In mobile operations some civilians moved with the Army, although in most cases this form of labour was static. The Boer War (1899–1902) involved the importation of civilian labour from other nations including India and China. Probably the most famous civilian stretcher-bearer, Mohandas Gandhi, was from Natal's Indian community.[8]

The story of military labour during the First World War does not follow a neat chronological pattern. Decisions regarding the organisation of labour were often made in response to a particular problem. Within a few weeks or months major alterations often negated the original decision. A good example of this was the decision, announced on 13 April 1917, to create Labour Battalions from the Infantry Works Battalions. Over 41,000 soldiers were posted to seven Labour Battalions in order to provide military labour in Britain. Less than two months later, on 5 June 1917, it was announced that men in the Labour Battalions were to be transferred to two newly created units, Labour Centres and Home Service Labour Companies. The Labour Battalions would then cease to exist.

In view of the complex way military labour developed in the different theatres of war this history has been separated into six sections. The first three sections examine the role played by military labour in Britain, France and the other Theatres of War. Within each section the reader will find references to various Dominion and Foreign Labour units, such as the Cape Coloured Labour Battalion and the Egyptian Labour Corps.

The following two sections provide a more detailed history about each of the Dominion and Foreign units.

The section entitled 'Research' has been included to assist family historians researching an ancestor who served in the Labour Corps. There is also a list of the honours and awards made to members of the Corps.

In writing this history we are conscious that there are several references, especially about foreign labourers, that the reader may find offensive. These references come from contemporary records and reflect the views held at the time, not the views of the authors.

Few records were kept at the time and the Official Histories rarely have more than the briefest mention of Labour units. Some original records no longer exist; for example, German bombing in 1940 destroyed the Labour Corps nominal rolls.

In this history, we set out to give the reader a clearer picture of military labour during the First World War. Despite our extensive research, new information on the Labour Corps often emerges. We are always interested in any information that helps build an even better picture of the work of Labour units and welcome contact through www.labourcorps.co.uk.

Labour units during the war were the poor relative of the Army, made up of the old, unfit and foreigners. A majority of the men were non-combatant. At the time, and since, they have not been given the recognition they deserved. Their work may not have been glamorous but can be summed up in four words: No Labour, No Battle.

1   Elliott, E., *Royal Pioneers 1945–1993*, p.10
2   General Order 14 April 1856.
3   MacMunn, *The History of the Sikh Pioneers*, p.3
4   Tugwell, W., *History of the Bombay Pioneers*, p.3
5   ibid p.9
6   See www.thomascook.com/about-us/thomas-cook-history/
7   Barthorp, M., *War on the Nile*, p.99
8   Pakenham, T., *The Boer War*, p.225

SECTION ONE: HOME SERVICE

GOVERNMENT INTERVENTION AND CONTROL

Outbreak of War

During the First World War soldiers stationed in Britain played a major part in ensuring the economy satisfied the needs of both the civilian and military population. In order to understand why and how soldiers played this role it is necessary to consider Government policy and its intervention in both army recruitment and running of the economy during the war.

In 1914 the Liberal Government had been in office for some nine years and pursued policies based upon free trade, social reform, maintaining peace, non-intervention in foreign affairs and preserving the liberty of the individual. The war was to force a change in direction despite attempts to maintain Liberal principles.

Even before war was declared the King issued a proclamation which commanded the people to obey any instructions or regulations issued in the Defence of the Realm. This was followed on 8 August by the Defence of the Realm Act (DORA) conferring on the King in Council power to make regulations during the war. DORA passed through Parliament in one day and was 'in many ways one of the most extraordinary legislative measures ever passed by the British Parliament'.[1] The Act gave the Authorities and its agencies unprecedented rights to control the lives of the nation. It specified a number of acts for which a civilian could be tried by court martial including spreading false reports or communicating with the enemy. In addition it enabled the military authorities to demand all or part of a factory's output and to take possession of any land or building they needed.

The original Act was supplemented on 28 August and 27 November. The 1914 Acts prohibited such things as owning a homing pigeon, trespassing on a railway line or publishing information that would be of benefit to the enemy. As the war went on further Acts introduced a wide range of controls including food-rationing, licensing laws that included determining the times when public houses could be open, employers in key industries being told what to produce and what wages to pay, employees being forbidden to strike or demand higher wages and the introduction of passports and identity cards. Although the original Act gave the authorities the power to direct the lives of the people of Britain, the initial reaction to controlling industry and commerce suggests that the Liberal Government hoped to continue to operate according to their pre-war principles.

It is doubtful whether anyone could have envisaged the tremendous effect the outbreak of war in August 1914 was to have on commerce, industry and agriculture in Britain. On 4 August, David Lloyd George, speaking to businessmen, promised that the Government would 'enable the traders of this country to carry on business as *usual*'.[2] Whether this was meant merely to calm fears of unemployment, inflation and trade collapse or, as has been suggested, also to reflect the wider view that the Navy blockading German ports would bring the war to an early end, is not certain.[3] What is certain is that the Government wanted to ensure trade was kept as close as possible to pre-war levels. The following day Lord Kitchener was appointed Secretary of State for War. Two days later he informed the Cabinet that Britain had to be prepared for a war lasting several years with an army of millions. Taking millions from the labour force and a long war meant that the concept of business as usual would not work; but as will be seen, this does not appear to have been accepted by the Government until the spring of 1915 at the earliest.

Enlistment and industry

The declaration of war saw huge numbers of men clamouring to enlist. On 7 August 1914 Kitchener called for the first 100,000 volunteers to join the Army. In mid-August stories of German atrocities in Belgium started to appear in the press and at the end of the month news was received of the British retreat from Mons. By the end of August nearly 300,000 men had enlisted in the Army, a month later that number had expanded to over 750,000, a third of the total number of men who enlisted within the first year of the war. Numbers alone do not present a full picture of what was a complex situation. The majority of these men enlisted in the period between 25 August and 15 September 1914, with more men enlisting in the first four days of September than the 130,000 who enlisted in October. This was not only a drain on the civilian labour force but also created major logistical problems. At the time there were only enough barrack places for about 175,000 men and the munitions industry was equipped to supply an Army of 100,000 men, not one of a million or more. The Army of 1914 was based on their previous experiences of numerous small colonial wars, in today's jargon 'low intensity operations'.

Industry, terrified by the possible loss of overseas markets, reacted by cutting nearly 500,000 jobs by the end of August so that despite military recruitment, unemployment rose sharply in August and September 1914. The situation was considered so grave that the Prince of Wales and the King made two national appeals for money to prevent distress caused by unemployment. The Engineering Employers and Trades Unions met on 19 August to discuss ways of overcoming rising unemployment. However, in the words of the Chancellor of the Exchequer: 'By September, 1914, these fears were dispelled, for the dislocation of work in certain directions brought about an actual dearth of labour.'[4]

Although unemployment grew during the first two months of the war large-scale unemployment soon became a thing of the past, to be replaced by a shortage of labour in industry. One of the primary areas of concern in 1914 was the loss of skilled workmen in the engineering industry since they were required in both ordnance factories and armament works and no measures were taken to restrict the recruitment of these men. Whilst the Government may have been concerned about the loss of skilled engineers, a study of recruitment in 1914–1915 showed that the situation affected all areas of industry and commerce.

Despite the high levels of unemployment in Britain before the war, recruits came from all occupations and backgrounds. It has been suggested that the popular concept of a 'rush to the colours' is inaccurate and that the initial recruits tended to be the young, those without commitments, the unskilled, the unemployed and the desperate.[5] This was not the view expressed in 1923 by Wolfe, who stated that the difficulty was not to find the first 100,000 men but to choose the most suitable: 'The first rush was universal. All classes, and … all types of industry gave equally.'[6] In reality there were differences in enlistment rates between the different sectors and also in different industries within the same sector. It has been suggested that in August 1914 it was the commercial sector that was affected more than agriculture, manufacturing or transport.[7] Unfortunately, at the time the government did not keep ongoing statistics of the loss of labour from each industry, although from October 1914 onwards it did carry out a number of sample surveys. In July 1915 it estimated that some 20 per cent of labour in manufacturing industries had enlisted, varying from 16 per cent of the textile sector compared to 24 per cent of the paper and printing sector. What is true is that all sectors of industry and commerce were to be affected by the major loss of workers.

The Board of Trade survey found that during the first twelve months of the war almost 1,250,000 men enlisted from manufacturing industries, 20 per cent of the total male labour force for the sector. Although the comparable figure for agriculture was only 120,000 men, this represented 15 per cent of the male labour force and, of course, had a major impact on what was a manual labour dominated industry. Figures do not exist for enlistment from the transport, commerce or public services sectors for the period up to July 1915. However, Board of Trade statistics for July 1916, 1917 and 1918 show that the highest proportion of enlistment came from the commercial sector, followed by manufacturing, public services, transport and agriculture.[8]

By April 1915, around 36 per cent of the male population of London of military age had joined up, a similar figure to the agricultural county of Westmoreland (35 per cent), and the industrialised county of Lancashire (34 per cent).[9] An ad hoc approach to enlistment meant that by July 1915 the electrical engineering and chemical and explosive industries had lost almost a quarter of male employees. The coal mines, iron, steel and engineering industries lost about one-fifth of their labour.

At a local level the creation of 'Pals' Battalions often had a major effect on labour supply in the area. Lord Derby, the War Minister, is generally credited with the creation of the Pals battalions, units formed in one business or industry or from one locality. Although Derby announced the idea on 24 August 1914, it was originally discussed at the War Office almost two weeks before and the first Pals battalion, the 10th (Stockbrokers) Battalion, Royal Fusiliers began recruiting on 21 August.[10] Over 140,000 men were to be enlisted in 144 Pals Battalions, each unit drawn from a specific area, industry or from men with a common interest.[11] Often the creation of a Pals Battalion merely served to heighten the problem of the loss of labour. When, for example, the North Eastern Railway Company raised their own Pals Battalion, the 17th Northumberland Fusiliers, at the end of September 1914, the company was to lose a further 1,000 workers in addition to the 2,000 or so employees who had already enlisted. As a recruiting tool it was a brilliant idea but what was not realised was the effect that the removal of large numbers of the labour force from specific locations would have, or as was to be seen after the carnage on the Somme on 1 July 1916, on the lives of whole communities.

Popular sentiment fuelled by the media in response Lord Kitchener's call to arms and Lord Derby's Pals battalions saw large numbers of skilled workers swelling the ranks of the Army. Among the volunteers who joined prior to January 1915 were some 10,000 skilled engineers, 160,000 miners and 145,000 from the building trades.[12] Although the Government realised that the men industry needed for the war effort were enlisting, solving the problem was not easy. Some skilled men were sent back to work in their industries but the Army did not want to give the impression that they did not need men. At the same time the concept of conscription was, in 1914, an anathema to the Liberal Government and politicians saw the levels of enlistment at the time as proof that compulsion was not necessary.

Government action during 1914 suggests that their primary concern was to ensure Kitchener obtained his army of 1,000,000 men. The planning and organisation of the war during its initial phase appears to have been carried out in a reactive rather than a proactive manner. The War Office, for example, altered the minimum height requirement for recruits four times between August and November 1914. It was raised from 5ft 3in to 5ft 6in on 11 September to try to cut down the number of recruits. As a result 10,000 men who had been enlisted were sent home on arrival at their Army establishment. However, a fear that Kitchener's Army of 1,000,000 would not be achieved resulted in the height requirement being reduced to 5ft 4in on 23 October, and on 14 November, two days after Kitchener obtained the permission to increase the Army by a further 1,000,000 men, down again to 5ft 3in.

By the end of July 1915, 2,008,912 men had enlisted, creating a major drain on the labour market.[13]

Badging

By the end of 1914 the Army had grown by over 1,000,000, but there was almost no intervention to stop men in vital industries enlisting in the period up to the end of 1914.

There was some attempt to avoid the loss of vital workers by the Railway Executive Committee as early as 4 September 1914 when they announced that railway and canal workers could only enlist if their employer certified that they could be released. The War Office, in a notice sent to recruiting officers in September 1914, supported this decision. Evidence suggests that many men simply failed to name their employer on enlisting or that recruiting officers 'overlooked' the order.

In September 1914 the munitions company Vickers suggested the idea of issuing a badge to men employed on vital production work to protect them from the recruiting sergeant but this 'was not favourably considered' by the Government.[14] It was not until the end of 1914 that this idea was taken up quite vigorously by the Admiralty in order to protect men involved on production for them. The War Office's reaction to badging, however, was less enthusiastic and it was not until March 1915 that badges were issued to its own workers in the Royal Factories and to some employed by contractors. In May 1915 the War Office informed recruiting offices that certain skilled munitions workers should not be enlisted but the individual employer was to be the arbiter of whether the man was skilled or not.

Despite the Army expanding at a much greater rate than the Navy, between December 1914 and May 1915 the War Office only issued about 80,000 badges compared to some 400,000 issued by the Admiralty.

Voluntary enlistment or conscription

From almost the outbreak of war the Government considered the question of conscription versus voluntary enlistment. As early as 25 August 1914, Kitchener was suggesting to the House of Lords that unlike Germany and Austria, Britain would rely on a voluntary system of enlistment but with the proviso that it produced the soldiers needed. As a result of his speech Asquith informed the House of Commons that the Government was not considering conscription. By Christmas it was apparent that the war would be a long, drawn-out struggle, requiring huge resources of both men and munitions. However, the number of men enlisting dropped from an average of 220,000 a month between August 1914 and January 1915 to less than 88,000 in February 1915.[15]

The Government's view was that there was no need for conscription, and in March Asquith denied the need for the issue to be investigated. A month later Lloyd George, then Chancellor of the Exchequer, told the House of Commons that the Government did not think that conscription would mean a more successful outcome of the war.

Spring 1915 was a difficult time for the Liberal Government; the shell crisis in March, disagreements within the War Cabinet and growing concerns within the Conservative opposition at the lack of progress in the war. At the same time wives of soldiers serving in France, supported by the Northcliffe Press, began to voice their anger that they had to survive on minimal allowances whilst single men stayed at home earning relatively good money working in safe jobs. The Northcliffe newspapers were also critical of Kitchener and War Office incompetence. All these factors led to the downfall of the Liberal Government and the establishment of Asquith's Coalition Government on 19 May 1915.

As soon as Asquith had resumed his seat after informing the Commons of the Government reorganisation, General Sir Ivor Herbert rose and urged the Government to undertake a census and registration of the male population as preclusion to conscription. His speech was followed by one after another of the Conservative backbenchers expressing their party's policy, and supporting his suggestion.

The Conservative members of the Cabinet took up Herbert's proposal for a national registration scheme, a view actively supported by Northcliffe's newspapers. On 29 June the Government introduced the National Registration Bill, stating that its purpose was to secure knowledge of the forces the country possessed; 'Opposition to it, based mainly on the presumption that it was a preliminary to conscription, came from a small group of Liberal and Labour Members.'[16] When the results of the register were collated it was found that there were some 5,000,000 men of military age not serving with the forces, of whom about 1,800,000 were not in vital occupations or medically unfit. The Government, however, still resisted any move towards conscription.

The War Cabinet pressed Asquith for a committee to investigate both the manpower situation and the financing of the war. Reluctantly Asquith agreed to the establishment of this committee in August 1915. Kitchener was to tell the committee that his minimum requirement was for 70 full-strength divisions and that he felt this would require some form of compulsion. Lloyd George, now Minister for Munitions, in a complete about turn from the view he had expressed as Chancellor of the Exchequer in April 1915, now supported conscription. He told the committee:

> You will not get through without some measure of military compulsion or compulsion for military service. The longer you delay the nearer you will be to disaster. I am certain you cannot get through without it.[17]

On 2 September the committee issued its report to the Cabinet in which it called for 100 rather than 70 divisions and said that, whilst the men were available, the drop in recruiting demonstrated they could not be obtained through a voluntary system. Although the committee's report was not published it was an open secret that the Cabinet was divided in its view on conscription.

By 28 September Asquith pleaded with the House of Commons for an end to the conscription controversy on the grounds that the Cabinet had given it careful consideration. However, the next day a secret meeting took place between the Labour MPs, Asquith and Kitchener. At this meeting Kitchener put forward his views for conscription through ballot, whilst Asquith left many feeling that he would resign if the Cabinet insisted on conscription.

On 8 October Lord Kitchener laid before the Cabinet a memorandum that stated: 'The voluntary system, as at present administered, fails to produce the number of recruits required to maintain the armies in the field.'[18] Despite this there were still members of the Cabinet who opposed compulsory recruitment, some arguing that it was impracticable because the volunteers already enlisted would be unwilling to serve alongside pressed men.[19]

The Cabinet devised a final test of the voluntary system. On 5 October Lord Derby was appointed Director of Recruitment and asked to plan a new recruitment drive using the returns of the National Register.[20] Under the 'Derby Scheme' Recruiting Officers carried out a personal canvas of every man on the register who was asked to attest – to pledge himself to join up when called for service. The men were classified by marital status and age. The Derby Scheme also introduced local tribunals to hear applications for exemption or requests to be moved from one group to another. As part of the scheme married men were given the undertaking that they would not be called up until all the single men had been enlisted. A point emphasised on 2 November 1915 when Asquith told the House of Commons:

> I am told by Lord Derby that there is some doubt among the married men who are now being asked to enlist as to whether they may not be called upon to serve, having enlisted, while younger unmarried men are holding back and not doing their duty. Let them disabuse themselves of that notion at once. So far as I am concerned, I

would certainly say that the obligation of the married men to enlist is an obligation which ought not to be enforced, and ought not to be held binding on them unless and until we can obtain, I hope by voluntary effort, and as a last resort by other means, as I have stated, the unmarried men.[21]

Lord Derby handed his report to Asquith on 20 December. It showed that 60 per cent of married men had attested, secure in the knowledge that they would not be asked to fulfil their promise until all the single men had been called up. For single men, however, the number who had put themselves forward was only half the 2,179,231 eligible. It was estimated that when the men who were in 'starred' occupations or medically unfit were taken into account, the Army would only get some 340,000 through the Derby scheme. As Lloyd George said:

> In face of these figures, it was obviously impossible to pretend that Mr Asquith's pledge to the married men had been fulfilled. Over a million single men had refused to attest, and the policy of recruiting them compulsorily was the inevitable sequel.[22]

On 21 December Asquith asked Parliament to approve increasing the Army by another 1,000,000 men. He did not reveal Lord Derby's findings, saying that he had only had time to glance at the report the previous evening. Within a few days casualty figures were released that showed almost 530,000 British soldiers had been killed, wounded or were missing.

It was now obvious that voluntary enlistment could not produce the number of recruits required. Following heated discussions in the Cabinet on 27 and 28 December – which resulted in Sir John Simon, the Home Secretary, resigning in opposition to compulsory conscription – a Military Service Bill was laid before Parliament on 5 January 1916.

Under this Bill, unmarried men and widowers without children or dependants between the ages of 18 and 41 faced compulsory enlistment. The Bill completed its path through Parliament by 27 January during which exemption on the grounds of conscience was added to the Bill although the wording of the clause did leave the way open for a man to be called up for non-combatant service.[23]

During February, single men who had attested under the Derby Scheme were called up and on 1 March single men who had not already joined up were automatically considered as having enlisted for the duration of the war. In Lloyd George's words:

> So ended the first round. But the issue could not rest there. Forces were at work which, with a march as inevitable as destiny, pressed the nation forward into a complete system of compulsory service.[24]

On 21 March Sir William Robertson, Chief of the Imperial General Staff, declared that the infantry serving abroad were 78,000 men and the Territorial Divisions in Britain, 50,000 below establishment and that of the 193,891 men who had been called up under the Military Service Act, 57,416 had failed to appear. On 15 April the Army Council informed the Cabinet that by the end of June it was estimated that there would be a deficit of some 179,000 men. Parliament met in secret sessions on 25 and 26 April when it was suggested that if, within five weeks, 65,000 married men had not been encouraged to enlist then compulsion would be sought. An attempt by the Government to introduce limited extensions to the Military Service Act on 27 April was withdrawn in view of the opposition, to what was seen as a half-hearted measure.

Lloyd George introduced the Military Service (General Compulsion) Bill to Parliament on 3 May 1916.[25] Only 36 MPs opposed the Bill at its second reading and on 25 May it received the Royal Assent. Compulsory conscription now applied to all men aged 18 to 41 and men who had been rejected as physically unfit could now be re-examined.

Three further Military Service Acts were to be passed as the war progressed. The third Act (April 1917) called for the examination of Home Service Territorials and those who had previously been rejected for service. It also introduced a new schedule of protected occupations. The fourth Act (January 1918) enabled the re-examination of men who had been exempted on occupational grounds. The final Act (April 1918) was to be the most drastic – lowering the minimum age to 17 and raising the maximum to 55. It also extended conscription to Ireland, the Channel Islands and the Isle of Man.

Munitions Supply

In one area of military supply, munitions, it was poor quality work and a failure to produce the quantity required that led to a national scandal in the spring of 1915. Between 25 August and 29 September 1914, the War Office ordered as many artillery pieces as it had in the previous ten years. The armament factories were asked to produce quantities far in excess of their possible output and had no alternative but to sub-contract the work. The change on the Western Front from a mobile war, which relied on mobile guns firing shrapnel shells, to a static, trench based war, with reliance on heavy guns firing high explosive shells was to exacerbate the problem. High explosive shells were more dangerous to manufacture than shrapnel shells and required a skilled workforce. Armaments were being produced without the usual quality controls and in factories that had little or no experience of producing munitions, resulting in poor quality shells that failed to explode or exploded in the barrels of the guns.

Quality was not the only problem; the manufacturers could not produce shells in the quantities required by the Army because so many skilled workers had enlisted. During the first five months of the war, the Board of Trade Labour Exchanges arranged for some 18,000 workers to be supplied to the munitions industry, however, by January 1915 this number was still some 6,000 short.

On 20 April 1915, Asquith, on advice from Kitchener, stated that there was no shell shortage. However, as early as 11 February 1915 Field Marshal French's Chief of Staff advised the First Army Commander, General Haig, against the copious use of shells in his planning for the forthcoming battle of Neuve Chappelle. After the battle the shortage of munitions continued and the artillery was limited to using seven shells a day rather than the thirty or so considered necessary. Following the failure of the British attack at Festubert, a report by Colonel Reppington, the War Correspondent, was to appear in *The Times* on 14 May headed: 'Need for

Shells: British Attacks Checked: Limited Supply the Cause.' In the article he stated the failure of the attack was firmly laid at the lack of high explosive shells. The 'Shell Scandal' sealed the fate of Asquith's Liberal Government and on 25 May he announced the formation of Coalition Government.

Kitchener, having responsibility for the munitions failure, had become a liability to the Government but his public popularity meant that his role as Minister of War was secure. The Government did, however, move responsibility for munitions production from Kitchener to Lloyd George who became head of the new Ministry of Munitions. The appointment of Lloyd George did not lead to a change of policy: 'The government's action was in keeping with its response to every previous crisis in this war: the Ministry of Munitions was yet another ad hoc solution devised at the eleventh hour.'[26]

Lloyd George's first act as Minister of Munitions was to introduce a Munitions Bill, which became law on 9 June and brought under the Ministry's control any establishment where munitions were manufactured. Workers in controlled establishments could not leave their employment without a leaving certificate from their employer. The Munitions Act saw lockouts and strikes outlawed, gave the Ministry powers to regulate wages and to overrule trade union rule and custom which tended to restrict output. However, resistance to the Act meant that two important trades, the miners and cotton workers, were expressly excluded from these controls.[27]

In general, Government policy throughout 1915 was one of non-intervention rather than a coordinated approach to solving the needs of the home and the fighting fronts.

Railways

One of the best illustrations of the 'Business as Usual' policy was in relation to the railway network during 1914–1915. Recognising that the railways were vital to the war effort the Government had taken control of them on the day war was declared, although this control was exercised by an Executive Committee comprised of managers of a number of railway companies. Government intervention in the running of the railways was kept to a minimum so, in effect, an industry that was vital to the logistical operation of the war was still organised by the various private companies.

Four days after war was declared the Railway Executive Committee issued their first announcement to the public, warning them, 'in consequence of the European war crisis the regular passenger train and boat services usually run by the railway companies may be considerably curtailed or interrupted'.[28]

Passengers were issued tickets that allowed them to use any route possible rather than being restricted to a specific railway company. By 17 August 1914 newspapers informed the public that the railways were once again operating normally. A week later the ticket ruling was revoked only to be reintroduced in a piecemeal fashion as the war progressed. During 1914 travel to and from the Continent continued under as near normal conditions as possible. Tickets could still be bought for all places in Italy, Spain and Switzerland and for French destinations other than those on the *Nord* and *Est* systems.

Services such as sending luggage in advance of a journey were commonly used pre-war but suspended in August 1914, presumably because the Army requisitioned the horses used to move luggage. It was reinstated by October the same year. During the Christmas period of 1914 railway companies not only put on extra trains, as in previous years, but offered excursions so that relatives and friend could visit the troops at their UK camps.

As 1915 progressed so did the demands to move soldiers and their resources throughout the country on the rail network. Clearly this was to have an effect on non-military traffic, with trains cancelled or withdrawn. Dining and sleeping cars and some of the cheap fares, like those to race meetings and agricultural shows, were withdrawn. When the Racing Industry complained about the withdrawal of the special fares on race days they were reinstated by the railway companies. Just before Easter 1915 the Railway Executive announced that the excursion trains and most of the cheap fares were being suspended because they needed to run more goods trains to move military supplies. However, full employment meant the public could afford to pay full fares and these changes appear to have had little affect on the custom of going away at Easter. Some lines even saw a boom in 1915, as travel to the Continent became more difficult. The Brighton line, for example, saw an increase in first class travel as the town replaced France and Switzerland as a holiday destination.

When war was declared there were almost 1,400,000 goods vehicles on the country's rail network. In theory this was more than enough stock to meet the needs of both civil and military users. However, half of this stock was privately owned and could only be loaded on the owner's instructions. In addition, much stock was only used to transport goods one way, having to return empty. It was not until July 1915 that the companies agreed that 'foreign' wagons might carry return loads on the way back to their own lines.

It was also quite common for industry working for the Government to order far more raw materials than they needed to ensure that they had enough to meet delivery dates. Since most companies did not have enough storage space for these materials it was decided to store them in loaded railway wagons in sidings. This not only took wagons out of the system, but as railway companies were only paid when the wagon was unloaded, deprived the carriers of payment for weeks at a time.

Government departments were the worst for tying up stock by poor planning when moving munitions, as the following examples illustrate. On one occasion seven truckloads of grenades were sent from Birmingham to Chesterfield for inspection. When the inspector rejected them they had to be returned to Birmingham, a journey of some 124 miles.[29] Woolwich Arsenal, on receiving a request for munitions, would often place it in a wagon by itself. As a result two or more wagons, each only partially full, were often used rather than combining their loads. It was common practice for a wagon to be loaded for a journey of a mile or less rather than use horse transport.

The problem became so acute that in November 1915 a joint Railway and Government Ministry committee was set up to consider ways to improve the use of goods wagons. This committee was to prove effective and reduced the number of wagons detained from 5,000 in January 1916 to 900 six months later. However, these improvements were, in the main, achieved through cooperation rather than regulation.

Agriculture

Agriculture, a labour intensive industry, saw 15 per cent of its permanent workers enlist by July 1915. It was an industry where, at harvest time, the permanent work-force was supplemented by thousands of casual workers. By 1915 the majority of the casual workers were either already serving in the forces or being employed in other industries, earning far more than they could as farm labourers. A system was intro-duced whereby soldiers based in Britain could be released for agricultural work when required. There was, however, no Government direction for farmers about which crops or animals should be raised.

The Government made arrangements to buy sugar in the West Indies and to build up a reserve of wheat in 1914 but would not make any financial arrangements to encourage farmers to produce more. Instead patriotic appeals were made to the industry to undertake a 'plough up' campaign. Wheat acreage increased but it is questionable whether this was through farmers' patriotism or the realisation that prices would go up and improve their profits. The effect, however, was to lead the Government to believe that non intervention was the correct policy.

Concern about rising prices as a result of German submarine attacks on British shipping led, in June 1915, to the Government establishing a committee under the chairmanship of Viscount Milner. Milner was asked to consider the future course of food production with particular reference to the harvest of 1916 and beyond. Within a month Milner had produced an interim report recommending a move to more wheat production for which farmers would receive a guaranteed price and the establishment of local committees who would liaise between the individual producer and the Board of Agriculture.

Milner's proposals had the backing of Lord Selbourne, President of the Board of Agriculture, but the Government rejected the guaranteed price option following discussions at the Cabinet meeting on 4 August 1915. The Government did agree to the creation of the County Agricultural Committees. Milner's final report, which appeared in October, put forward a number of suggestions including the need to retain skilled labour on the farms and a continuation of the policy of releasing soldiers for agricultural work.

The 1916 wheat harvest was both smaller and of a poorer quality than the previ-ous year. By July 1916 food prices were 61 per cent above the level they had been at the start of the war. Non intervention was no longer an option, and in November milk became the first commodity to come under a controlled price. In the months ahead fixed maximum prices were established for almost all agricultural products and regulations about their sale and distribution introduced.

It was the appointment of David Lloyd George as Prime Minister in December 1916 that signalled the real change in Government policy. Powers taken under DORA allowed the Government to decide upon land use and which crops were to be grown. To implement this policy small Executive Committees were to be formed by each of the County War Agricultural Committees.

The local Committees, most of which had been established by the end of January 1917, had a maximum of seven members, made up of farmers and landowners or agents, appointed partly by the County Council and partly by the Board of Agriculture. Intervention was now a fact, for as Ernle says:

The powers vested in the Committees were drastic. Where grass-land could be more profitably used in the national interest as arable, they were empowered to require it to be broken up, or to enter and plough it up themselves. Notices were to be served on occupiers specifying the grass fields to be ploughed, or the acts of cultivation to be executed, which the Committees considered necessary for the increase of food production.[30]

Farmers had no right of appeal and could, if they failed to comply with the order, be fined or even imprisoned. The Board of Agriculture recognised that their existing structure would not be suitable to support the Local Committees so a new branch, the Food Production Department, was formed on 1 January 1917.

The importance of the Food Production Department cannot be over emphasised:

> ... charged with the novel functions of collecting and distributing labour, machinery, implements, fertilisers, feeding-stuffs, and other requisites of the industry and of assisting Committees to enforce their orders. It was designed to serve as a clearing house for the requirements of individual farmers, notified through their Executive Committee. It became the pivot of the campaign. Its services were invaluable and multifarious.[31]

The Military Services Act of January 1916 introduced conscription. Although farmers were given exemption from military service under the Act, the same did not apply to their sons or employees. It was, of course, possible for a farmer to apply to the local tribunal for exemption of a son or employee on the grounds that they were essential workers and initially at least, most applications were approved. There were, however, wide variations in the way individual tribunals approved or rejected applications for exemption.

For an industry that was labour dependant the loss of workers to the armed forces was potentially catastrophic and was only to be solved by the use of soldiers, prisoners of war, schoolboys and women. Chapter Four covers the vital role that soldiers played in agriculture during the war.

1   Hammerton, Sir J., *A Popular History of the Great War*, p.71
2   French, D., *British Economic and Strategic Planning 1905–1915*, p.92
3   ibid, p.92
4   NA MUN 9/34 p.1. The Chancellor also explains how during the first weeks of the war many measures were taken to provide against growing unemployment including a Cabinet Committee of the Prevention and Relief of Distress which instigated schemes to start public works to alleviate distress and employers being prepared to reduce overtime, introduce night shifts and to work short time. At the same time State insurance of shipping was introduced in an attempt to maintain overseas trade.
5   Hughes, C., 'The New Armies' in Becket and Simpson (eds), p.103
6   Wolfe, H., *Labour Supply and Regulation*, p.13
7   Becket, I., 'The Nation in Arms 1914–1918' in Becket and Simpson (eds), p.9
8   Dewey, P., 'Military Recruiting and the British Labour Force During the First World War' in *The Historical Journal* 1984, Vol 27, p.203–205
9   NA CAB 37/128/30 'Notes by the Secretary of State for War', Appendix 2
10 Simkins, P., *Kitchener's Army*, p.83
11 Pals Battalions were enlisted from towns like the Accrington Pals (11th East Lancashire), specific industries like the West Yorkshire Wool Textile Pioneers (21st West

Yorkshire) and from groups with similar interests like the 1st Football Battalion (17th Middlesex). See M. Middlebrook, *Your Country Needs You* p.63–84

12 Hughes 'The New Armies' p.102

13 NA CAB 25/95, 'Enlistment for the Regular Army and Territorial Force August 1914–November 1918'

14 ibid MUN 9/34 p.4 'Words of the Chancellor of the Exchequer'.

15 From February to December 1915 monthly enlistment averaged 100,000 with a low figure of 55,000 in December 1915.

16 Lloyd George, D., *War Memoirs of David Lloyd George*, p.430

17 ibid, p.432

18 ibid, p.433

19 Lord Curzon was so incensed by this suggestion that he arranged for the idea to be posed to a number of officers and men in France. He was able to report that these fears were without foundation and that the men in France felt that those who would not enlist should be called to service.

20 The National Register had categorised men between the ages of 18 and 41, into four groups. Group 1 were those in essential civilian occupations. Group 2, men in trades and occupations from which a few could be spared, Group 3 those trades where a large proportion could be spared and Group 4 the 'unstarred' men who could be spared for military service.

21 Quoted in Lloyd George, War *Memoirs of David Lloyd George*, p.435

22 Lloyd George, p.436

23 'In the case of exemption on conscience grounds, may take the form of an exemption from combatant service only, or may be conditional on the applicant being engaged on some work which in the opinion of the Tribunal dealing with the case is of national importance.' Quoted in Boulton, D., *Objection Overruled*, p.91

24 Lloyd George, p.437

25 Sir William Roberson wrote to Lloyd George on 2 May 1916 'The great thing is to get the Bill, and for it the Empire's thanks are due to you – alone.'

26 DeGroot, G. J., *Blighty,* p.77

27 A few weeks after the Munitions Act was passed a serious strike broke out in the South Wales coalfields. As a result the Government used their powers to include the mining industry under the provisions of the Munitions Act.

28 Hamilton, *Britain's Railways in World War* 1, p.37

29 ibid, p.66

30 Ernle, *English Farming Past and Present* p.403

31 ibid, p.403

MILITARY LABOUR IN BRITAIN

The War Office's initial response in August 1914 to the logistical demands made by the rapid increase in the number of soldiers was to carry on as usual. If more uniforms were needed, the answer was to expand orders with the civilian manufacturers; if more armaments were needed, expand orders with armament firms.

Using tents, requisitioning schools, village halls and sports clubs as well as billeting men in private houses, hotels and boarding houses initially solved the problem of accommodating 1,000,000 soldiers. There was some recognition that these were short-term solutions when on 12 August 1914 the Army's Directorate of Fortifications and Works was asked to submit plans for a standard hutted camp that could house a battalion. Two days later these plans were submitted and by 17 August the Army Council had accepted them and instigated building programmes. Contracts were given to private contractors like Messrs A. N. Coles of Plymouth who built Rugeley Camp on Cannock Chase, Staffordshire, with accommodation for 20,000 men.[1] Building these camps was not without problems. There was a shortage of labour, of seasoned timber and of galvanised sheets. The weather was also a problem; between mid-October 1914 and mid-February 1915 southern England saw rain on 89 out of 123 days. This turned many of the tented camps into fields of mud, increasing the demand for the completion of the hutted camps and often holding up work in progress.

During the last three months of 1914 Sick Returns show that over 29,000 in the Salisbury Plain area were reporting sick each month. A major factor was the bad weather and poor quality of the tented camps. Over 1,500 soldiers developed pneumonia, 301 dying of the disease by the end of January 1915. Discontent among recruits in the training camps increased during November 1914 culminating in strikes in a brigade of the 22nd Division at their camp at Seaford.[2] Despite all these problems and the need to complete the camps, during 1914 and 1915 the War Office does not appear to have made any use of building workers now in the Army to assist with the work. Even with large numbers of potential labourers under their command, the War Office believed building camps for soldiers was the function of private contractors, who, through having to use unskilled workers, often produced poor quality work.[3]

During the first few months of the war the Army released some men to carry out skilled tasks in the engineering industry, notably in ordnance production. There was a concern at the War Office that releasing men from the front could be interpreted as the men being surplus to military requirements.

By January 1915 about 300,000 soldiers were permanently stationed in Britain, many of whom were medically unfit for service overseas. Even when those employed on Home Defence and Regimental duties were excluded, there were always thousands of men who could be made available for short-term, non-military duties. Government departments, local authorities and civil contractors were able to employ soldiers to work on Government contracts if there was not enough local civilian labour and their employment did not interfere with training or military duties.[4] Civilian employers were responsible for paying the men at the local civilian rate and for the cost of conveying the men from their camp to their place of work. In theory, no soldier could be employed for more than two months but it appears this limit was not always adhered to. An example is the building of the Officers' Club at Catterick Camp. The project was a civilian one with the building funded by private donors. Soldiers from the camp, however, undertook the work. As a Treasury paper explains:

> It should be explained that by arrangement with the military authorities at Catterick, owing to the scarcity of civilian labour in the district, soldier labour then available in the Camp was employed in the autumn and winter of 1916 upon the construction, the donors paying the working pay.[5]

Liverpool Dock Battalion

Little has been written about the Liverpool Docks Battalions despite their major role in Liverpool Docks from 1915 until the end of the war. The most comprehensive work is an article written by Keith Grieves in 1982 and much of this section is based upon his work.[6]

The outbreak of war saw the east coast ports virtually closed to international cargo traffic because of the danger from German raiders. The south coast port of Southampton became a military port, transporting men and supplies to France. As a result, the vast majority of international trade had to come through the west coast ports and Liverpool in particular.

Liverpool port soon became so congested that by 11 January 1915 there were 44 steamers waiting to berth. By 1 March several large vessels, including some with perishable goods, had been waiting over a month to berth. The problem of this huge increase in shipping was exacerbated by working practices at the port, a shortage of dock labour and industrial unrest.[7]

In an attempt to overcome these problems and as 'an experiment in the military organisation of a vital war industry', in March 1915 the War Office authorised Lord Derby to raise a battalion of dock labourers, to be called the '1st Dock Battalion' Liverpool Regiment, to work on the Mersey.[8] It was made up of dock labourers already members of the National Union of Dock Labourers (NUDL) who were attested and placed under military law for home service. Although there was no upper age limit and no medical examination for prospective entrants, the initial enthusiasm for the scheme amongst the Mersey dockers meant that the men were generally of a reasonable medical standard. Men in the Battalion were paid according to the appropriate civilian wage with an additional military pay of one shilling a day.

There is no doubt that Lord Derby, who in 1914 had raised five battalions of the Liverpool Regiment, saw the Battalion as one way that men could help the war effort. He is quoted as saying:

> I have always had it in my mind that there were many then working in the Docks, who, unable to enlist owing to age, would still be glad to put on His Majesty's uniform and be employed as soldiers but in a civil capacity.[9]

James Sexton, NUDL General Secretary, enthusiastically supported the scheme which was in contrast to most Trade Union leaders who were opposed to the idea of military law being applied to industry.[10]

Initially the Battalion consisted of three companies, each with 1 sergeant, 10 corporals and 114 other ranks. Lord Derby became their Commanding Officer with a Captain Ronald Williams as the Adjutant, responsible for allotting men to their work.[11] Support from the NUDL can be seen in the appointment of the President, Vice-President and an official of the Union as the sergeants for the three companies.

On 3 June 1915, Lloyd George, the Minister of Munitions, made a famous speech in Manchester, in which he argued for both increased mobility and more state control of labour.[12] The next day he visited Liverpool where he inspected the Dock Battalion describing them as 'a new experiment in the mobilisation and organisation of labour'.[13]

Whilst the Dock Battalion received the support of the NUDL the same was not always true for other dockworkers. A union meeting on 18 April 1915, which was intended to explain the purpose of the Battalion, had to be disbanded before any speeches could be made. Members of the Battalion were insulted on their way to work, and in June a dock labourer was fined 40 shillings by the magistrates for having used obscene language towards the Dock Battalion. Grieves suggests that it was incidents like these that made Lord Derby wary of any plans to extend the scheme.[14]

Within the trade union movement there was a fear that the Battalion could be used for strike breaking. On 19 February 1915 the Isle of Man authorities had used troops to unload a ship held up by a strike at the port. At the end of the month an industrial strike in Northampton had been broken by the introduction of 'blackleg' labour from the ASC.[15] In addition, the Dockyard Battalion had been formed two weeks after an unofficial weekend strike had taken place at Liverpool and Birkenhead Docks. During this strike Lord Kitchener had sent, through the NUDL, an appeal to the strikers in which he had written that if 'this appeal has no effect I shall have to consider the steps that will have to be taken to ensure what is required at Liverpool being done'.[16] So when the Dock Battalion was established there was a perception that it could and may be used for strike breaking.

Lord Derby stated, on the establishment of the Dock Battalion, that it would follow Trade Union rules and not be used as a strike breaking force. However, in June 1915 when employers in Liverpool faced a possible strike he wrote: 'I had arranged to put the Dock Battalion in to do the work if it had been required.'[17] Derby's personal record indicates that whilst he did not intend to use the Battalion as a strike breaking force it would have been easy for it to be used in this way.

The creation of the Dock Battalion does not seem to have had a significant affect on reducing the congestion at the Port. In June 1915 the MP for West Toxteth told the House of Commons that since April an average of 60 vessels a day waited for berths. The Battalion continued to expand and had a nominal establishment of 1,400 men. In December 1916 a second battalion was formed and the force appears to have reached its maximum size in September 1917 when the two Battalions had a total strength of 1,859.

The Dock Battalion had been formed to be independent of the civilian labour force at the Liverpool Docks. In Liverpool one difficulty was in determining government and non-government work and there were several disputes arising from the allocation of work. Dockers were able to claim exemption from military service but as the Army's demand for more men increased in 1917 the Port Labour Committees had to review the civilian workforce and removed many exemption certificates, thus allowing men to be called up.[18] As the civilian labour force decreased, the Liverpool Committee began to oversee the control of all labour working in the port. This was to have an effect on the independence of the Dock Battalion, which, as Grieves says, 'ceased to act on its own and no longer operated independently of civil labour during the last eighteen months of the war'.[19]

The War Office had concerns, as early as September 1915, that the Dock Battalion was not financially viable because of the irregular employment pattern of the men. In January 1918 the Treasury also made reference to the high financial cost of the unit to which the new adjutant, Captain Lemonius remarked that

> ... whatever the strength of the Unit may be it is impossible to employ the whole of it continuously owing to the fact that the work comes in rushes, and under these circumstances it is absolutely necessary to incur some expense in retaining a reserve.[20]

Serving in the Dock Battalions did not exempt men from being called up for front line service, a process known as 'Combing Out'. Between December 1917 and January 1918, 53 men from the Battalions joined front line units. In January 1918 the Battalion adopted the same policy as the Port Labour Committee by combing out men under 26, the age being increased to 31 in March 1918. Men who had enlisted in the Battalion before 15 October 1915 were exempt from this. Records for November 1918 show the Battalion strength as 1,586 which means that it had lost about 300 men from its peak in September 1917.

If, as Grieves suggests, the Dock Battalion was an experiment in military organisation it was not to be repeated. Lord Derby did, late in 1915, suggest the formation of dock companies of 250 men formed under military law. The companies would be centrally located and sent to ports in their area when required. Although the War Office did not take up this proposal they did create the first of the Transport Workers' Battalions in March 1916 (see page 41).

Munitions Work

The Shell Crisis of the spring of 1915 brought to the attention of the authorities the need to supplement civilian labour where necessary. On 16 September 1915 ACI 139 established a register of serving soldiers skilled in munitions work. This register was to be completed 'in view of the great shortage of skilled labour and the urgent need of increasing the supply of skilled men competent to manufacture munitions of war'.[21]

To identify these men 24 representatives of the Ministry of Munitions, under the guidance of a Major Scott, visited Army bases. These representatives consisted of ten skilled investigators from the Labour Exchange and fourteen MPs who volunteered to assist in the selection process. By 20 October 1915 Scott was able to report to Sir H. Llewellyn Smith at the Ministry that a total of 27,367 soldiers were available for munitions work. Further scrutiny reduced this number by about half, as Llewellyn Smith was to comment 'the net result then of scouring the Army in the United Kingdom will be to add 15,000 men to the available force of skilled Munition Workers'.[22]

Whilst the Army appeared to be supporting this move to enable soldiers to work in munitions, there was concern at the War Office that they may lose essential men. The War Office therefore decided that men in the RFC or employed as artificers in cavalry, yeomanry, the RA, RE, ASC or AOC were not to be included on the list.

Major Scott's report on the release from the Colours of men serving in Britain for munitions work for the period up to November 1915, states that some 1,500,000 men were paraded and addressed. Of these, 106,000 volunteered and 40,132 were provisionally selected.[23] At the same time it was clear that the system was not working effectively. The Officer Commanding Aldershot Command wrote to munitions firms regarding some 76 soldiers he had been informed were being employed on munitions work. The replies he received indicated that some of the men had already been returned to military duty and that the firms had no knowledge of some of the soldiers. As a result he had no idea where seventeen men on his strength were being employed.[24] This problem led to the Army enquiring how all soldiers temporarily released for civil employment were situated and whether they were employed on munitions work. The Army also wanted to know whether those men who had changed employers had done so with military or Ministry of Munitions sanction.

Officers in charge of records were instructed to record the present addresses of employers where men were working and that 'men who cannot be traced should be proceeded against as absentees or deserters'.[25]

Although ACI 139 of 1915 established a register of skilled men it appears that the Army did not always provide the type of men the munitions firms required, as an account of the soldiers employed at the Chilwell Factory[26] during May 1916 demonstrates:

> By the middle of May a labour Battalion had arrived at Chilwell but military regula-
> tions meant that the departments in which the soldiers worked had to be organised
> into a three eight hour shift system. This resulted in further labour being required to
> maintain the output. Amongst these soldiers were men of the South Wales Borders
> who apparently (for religious reasons) declined to work on Sundays. Lord Chetwynd
> was not too impressed as a whole with his labour Battalion, he considered them to be
> 'of miserable physique and of heavy drinking habits' (the Battalion did, at this time,
> include two epileptics, a lunatic and several coronary cases!).[27]

The scheme did not cover all the skills required by the munitions factories, notably toolmakers and coppersmiths, so a request was made to Field Marshal French to look for suitable men serving with the BEF. French agreed with the proviso that the total number of men selected did not exceed 2,000. Between December 1915 and April 1916 Major Scott interviewed 17,140 men serving in France; of these 1,996 were sent to Havre for practical workshop testing and 1,732 finally selected.

The Release from the Colours scheme was to end in January 1917. In April Mr Kellaway (Parliamentary Secretary, Ministry of Munitions) reported to the House of Commons that on 10 April there were between 45,000 and 50,000 soldiers still engaged in the manufacture of munitions.

Works and Labour Companies and Battalions

On 18 December 1915 the War Office stated that: 'Labour is urgently required to assist in making and mending roads in and around camps, for current repairs to hut-ments, and other similar duties.'[28]

They therefore formed as a 'tentative measure' one Infantry Works Company (IWC) in each of the six Regional Commands. These companies had a strength of 1 officer, 3 sergeants, 2 corporals and 100 men, all of whom were unfit for service overseas.

Men called up for service were given a medical examination and classified in one of four categories:

1. General Service
2. Field Service at Home

3. Garrison Service (a) Abroad (b) at Home
4. Labour (a) (Roadmaking, entrenching, works companies etc.)
   (b) Sedentary work, clerks.[29]

Men in category 4 were sent to the IWCs. The first of these companies were formed in January 1916 in the Royal Fusiliers, Middlesex, Wiltshire and Somerset Light Infantry Regiments, a total of some 380 men. By April 1916 the number of companies had grown to 19 (1,920 men) and the War Office announced that further companies were to be formed.[30]

The growth in numbers created administrative difficulties and in order to overcome this the War Office announced that the General Officer Commanding

> … may attach to their headquarters staff a regimental officer not below the rank of major who will be charged with the duty of co-ordinating and regulating the supply of men for employments, working parties, fatigues and labour throughout the Command.[31]

This was the first instance of the creation of a staff post specifically to administer demands for labour.

The need for labour in France led to the formation in Britain of Infantry Labour Battalions (ILB), from men fit for service overseas, in February 1916. Forming these battalions took precedence over IWCs and men already in IWCs were medically examined to determine if they were fit enough to serve overseas.

From 22 March 1916, men called up for service were classified as fit for service at home or overseas. Those fit for home service were posted to an IWC, those fit for overseas to an Infantry Labour Company (ILC). The original ILCs had the same strength as IWCs, 106 all ranks. Labour Battalions were formed by bringing together ILCs in the same Command (see page 88).

As units formed specifically for service overseas ILCs and ILBs did not play a major role in Britain. The 17th and 18th (Labour) Battalions, Royal West Surrey Regiment were the exception. Formed at Crawley in November 1916 they remained in Britain and were transferred to the Labour Corps in June 1917 when they became Eastern Command Labour Centre (ECLC).[32]

It appears the original intention was for the 17th and 18th Royal West Surrey Regiment to be used in France. In December 1916 the GOC in France was informed by the War Office that these two Battalions would not be sent to France, their place being taken by the 1st, 2nd and 3rd ILCs, Royal West Surrey Regiment, each of which would have a strength of 536 all ranks.[33]

From 1 June 1916 medical categories were reclassified as Classes A to E:

Class A – Fit for general service
Class B – Fit for service abroad other than general service
Class C – Fit for home service only
Class D – Temporarily unfit for service
Class E – Unfit for service and not likely to become fit for 6 months.[34]

Classes B and C were further subdivided,

(i)   In garrison or provisional units

(ii) Labour units, or on garrison or regimental outdoor employment

(iii) Sedentary work as clerks, storemen, batmen, cooks, orderlies, and sanitary duties.

A man was classified as (ii) if he was 'able to walk to and from work a distance not exceeding 5 miles, see and hear sufficiently for ordinary purposes.'[35]

Carpenters and blacksmiths were the only skilled trades incorporated in the IWCs on their formation in January 1916. This changed in June 1916,[36] when men in medical categories B and C with a variety of skilled trades serving in Infantry Depots or Reserve Battalions, were transferred to IWCs so the Chief Engineer of the Command could make use of them.[37] With so many more men being transferred to Works Companies, an Infantry Works Battalion (IWB) was set up in each Command to receive both the tradesmen prior to their allocation to an IWC and other recruits, including drafts for service in the Labour Battalions overseas.[38]

Many IWBs organised companies by trade so that men with similar skills such as bricklayers, carpenters and masons served in the same company. Agricultural labourers were in a separate company and another company would contain the clerks, cooks, policemen, tailors and shoemakers.

One unique feature of these battalions was that a man could be made an NCO almost on recruitment. It has been claimed that one of the first IWBs had a CSM who had been in the Army for six weeks, a sergeant with three weeks service, a corporal with one and a lance corporal with just six hours service. Although it has not been possible to verify this, it is known that master builders and other specialist tradesmen were rapidly promoted to senior NCOs.

Men in these battalions were among the lowest medical category capable of serving in the Army and often nearer to 40 than 30 years of age. They came from widely different backgrounds as a contemporary article noted:

Every Works Battalion is a strange mixture. Thrown together in the same hut or tent is the independent gentleman and the man who, a few weeks ago, sold newspapers on a street corner; the mild bespectacled-looking man, who strolls into the canteen and play Chopin on the piano, is a chum of a man who is entered on the books as an organ-grinder. There are men who talk half a dozen languages, and others who cannot write their names, but they are all doing their bit.[39]

Their work varied greatly and included road construction, harvesting, hay-baling, coal-heaving, moving stores and cleaning camps. A difficulty facing all battalions was that requests for men were usually made on a daily basis, often several requests arriving at different times during a day. These would be passed to the CSM who would order a parade, pick the men required and dispatch them to undertake their work. As a result there could be several parades a day and men were often sent to undertake tasks for which they did not have the skills or physical capability. There is no doubt that many, if not most, of these men would not have been in the Army had there not been such an urgent need for labour.

By the beginning of August 1916 there were 13,912 men serving in IWCs throughout Britain.[40] IWCs were organised on a regimental basis, some 30 regiments having at least one IWC. As the number of men in Works Companies and

Battalions grew so did the problems of maintaining fluidity of labour. In November 1916 an administrative change was introduced in an attempt to overcome these problems. IWCs in a command were affiliated to the Works Battalion of that command and renumbered to the battalion.[41] There appear to have been two exceptions to this: the Royal Irish Rifles who retained their IWC and the Royal Fusiliers who retained five IWCs.

By February 1917 there were over 10,000 men serving in some 112 IWCs and 40,000 men in seven Infantry Works Battalions. These men were to be transferred to the Labour Corps following its creation in April 1917.

Transport Workers Battalions

If the creation of the Liverpool Dock Battalion ensured a regular supply of labour for that port, the same was not true for the other ports and docks throughout Britain, where shortage of labour was a common occurrence. A solution to the problem was sought through the creation of a flexible unit that could quickly be sent to any port that required men. The creation of a civilian force of this kind was unthinkable to the Government so the answer lay in the creation of a military unit, a Transport Workers' (TW) Battalion.

In February 1916 the Admiralty informed the Port and Docks Authorities, that approval had been given for the formation of a special Battalion of Transport Workers for duty at ports in the Britain.[42] The authorities were notified that the men were to be stationed as a complete unit inland and detailed for work where and when needed, for a minimum of 5 days, and only when there was insufficient civilian labour at the port. The Dock Employers paid the men at the local rate and provided protection under the Workmen's Compensation Accident Scheme in case of accident or death.

The Battalion, designated the 16th (TW) York and Lancaster Regiment, was formed with its HQ at Colsterdale in Northern Command. Although an Army Battalion, its officers were re-commissioned from the Royal Navy Volunteer Reserve following liaison between the War Office and Admiralty. The other ranks of the Battalion were found from men in provisional battalions who were willing to transfer. The men should, where possible, have been familiar with the work they would be required to undertake. The Battalion was commanded by a lieutenant colonel, with seven officers and had three companies, each 212 men strong.

Men joining the Battalion were discharged from their current regiment and re-attested. Their terms of service stated that they were enlisted for service in Britain only. Whilst they were soldiers and therefore subject to military law, they were not issued with arms. One important aspect of their conditions of service was that they 'may be required to work any reasonable hours day or night and at any jobs that may be required'.[43]

The 16th York and Lancaster Regiment was to be the only TW Battalion until December 1916 when the War Office decided to form a similar battalion in each of Eastern, Scottish, Southern and Western Command.[44] These four battalions were: the 12th (TW) Battalion, Bedfordshire Regiment (HQ at Croydon); 16th (TW) Battalion, Cameronians (Scottish Rifles) (HQ at Paisley); 15th (TW) Battalion,

Worcestershire Regiment (HQ at Swindon); and 15th (TW) Battalion, South Lancashire Regiment (HQ at Bebbington).

The men were selected from Home Service units and the Royal Defence Corps who were of medical category B(i) or B(ii) or C(i) or C(ii) and been employed in dock work in civil life.[45] The new battalions had an establishment of nineteen officers, seven warrant officers, 47 sergeants and 1,030 rank and file, divided into five companies.

Four further TW Battalions were to be formed during 1917. The 17th (TW) Battalion Cameronians (HQ at Hamilton) in February 1917; 13th (TW) Battalion Bedfordshire Regiment (HQ at Croydon) in March 1917; 16th (TW) Battalion Worcestershire Regiment (HQ at Bristol) in March 1917; and 16th (TW) Battalion South Lancashire Regiment (HQ at Prescot) in April 1917.

A further battalion, the 17th (TW) Battalion South Lancashire Regiment (HQ at Bidston) was formed in May 1918 specifically for work on the canals in the Midlands and north-west England. Their role extended beyond loading and unloading canal boats to operating the Army's own boats and working alongside civilian boatmen on canal barges.

The terms of enlistment of the men in TW battalions meant that they could not serve overseas or be transferred to other units. As a result Army records show that by January 1918 three of the battalions contained a small number of medical category A men, presumably men originally classed as B(i) or B(ii) who had been reclassified A. The Army's demand for men in 1918 meant the terms of enlistment were altered, allowing men to be transferred to other units. Surprisingly, the number of category A men also increased, so that by November 1918 of the 16,375 men in these battalions some 1,476 were category A (9 per cent of the total strength).

By the end of the war the battalions had increased in size from their nominal strength of 1,103 men to an average size of 1,630. They varied from the 17th South Lancashire with a strength of 1,082 men, to the 15th South Lancashire, with a strength of 1,875.

Regimental histories make little reference to TW Battalions, the one exception being the history of the South Lancashire Regiment, which devotes four pages to the Regiment's 15th, 16th and 17th Battalions.[46] The 15th Battalion, formed at Kinmel Park in December 1916, and under the command of Lieutenant Colonel R. H. Keane, was employed primarily at the Birkenhead and Bootle Docks until it was disbanded in March 1919. The 16th Battalion, formed at Prescot in April 1917, was employed at the docks at Liverpool, Salford, Birkenhead and Barrow-in-Furness until disbanded in August 1919. In May 1918 the 17th Battalion was formed at Bidston in Cheshire specifically for work on the canals, which linked the industrial works in the Midlands with the ports in north-west England. The Battalion supplemented the civilian personnel engaged in canal transport. The work of the Battalion included operating locks and road bridges, driving motor barges, and loading and unloading the barges.

Returns show men employed on 'Agriculture' and 'Farming' as well as dock and canal work.[47] Agriculture presumably included men working in the vegetable production area at the Battalion Headquarters. It has not been possible to ascertain whether the term 'Farming' was also used for men working in a battalion's agricultural area or for men attached to agricultural companies.

Employers requiring labour would make a request to a Battalion's Commanding Officer. Each battalion would have groups of men working in numerous different locations within their area.[48] Whilst this provided fluidity of labour it also resulted in men from more than one battalion working in the same port at the same time. In August 1917, for example, men from the 16th South Lancashire, 12th Bedfordshire, 13th Bedfordshire and 15th Worcestershire Regiments were all working at the same time at Newhaven docks. At times large numbers were employed at one location. As an example, almost 800 from the 15th Worcestershire Regiment were employed at Southampton and 700 from the 16th South Lancashire Regiment in Manchester. An analysis of the work of the nine battalions for the period from August to October 1917 shows that they accounted for a total of 557,952 days work, a reflection of the large numbers of men employed by the TW Battalions.

The War Cabinet decided, in April 1918, that the total strength of the TW Battalions should be increased from 10,000 to 15,000 men with a view to the men being used not only at docks, on the canals and railways, but also in steel works. Although the extra men were enlisted it has not been possible to find any record of them being employed in steel works.

In August 1918 Sir Norman Hill, Chairman of the Port and Transit Executive Committee, asked for an increase of a further 5,000 men if 'the flow of essential traffic through the ports and over the railways and canals is to be maintained during the coming Autumn and Winter'.[49] Sir Auckland Geddes, Director of the Ministry of National Service, saw no necessity to increase the strength of the battalions and turned down this request. However, Hill's request appears to have met with agreement at a higher level, as on 2 November 1918 the Army ordered the formation of two further battalions, the 19th and 20th Cameronians. They are mentioned in the Regimental History: 'Four Transport Workers battalions were raised in the Regiment – the 16th, 17th, 19th and 20th. They were disbanded as soon as the purpose for which they had been created was accomplished.'[50]

The battalions continued in existence until the summer of 1919.[51] The role they played is best summed up in the words of the Regimental History of the South Lancashire Regiment:

> No inspiring story can be written about the activities of the 15th, 16th and 17th Battalions, but officers and men played an essential part behind the scenes in maintaining the links in the chain that connected their comrades on the various battle-fronts with the factories and other sources of supply in the United Kingdom.[52]

Conscientious Objectors

Following the passing of the Military Service Act of January 1916 voluntary enlistment gave way to compulsory service. Prior to this Act there were examples of men who objected to bearing arms serving in non-combatant roles such as the Quaker's Friends Ambulance Unit.

Under the Act a man could object to bearing arms on religious, moral or political grounds. The role played by Conscientious Objectors (COs) from 1916 onwards and the way the authorities dealt with them is a complex story, with men doing military service in non-combatant roles, undertaking civil work for the Home Office, being posted against their will to the Army, being taken to France and sentenced to death under military law, being sent to civilian prisons having been convicted of a military offence, and dying as a result of the conditions in which they were imprisoned or accommodated.

In view of this complexity the role played by C. O.s has been included in a separate section (see page 198).

Middlesex Regiment – Alien Battalions

In June 1916 the decision was made that enlisted naturalized Britons of German, Austrian, Hungarian, Bulgarian and Turkish parentage would be appointed to the Middlesex Regiment rather than be able to serve in any regiment or corps as had been the practice.[53] At the same time men of alien parentage serving in the Army, like Private Albert Wessel, who had already seen service in France with the Royal Fusiliers, were to be transferred to an Infantry Works Battalion of the Middlesex Regiment.

Two Middlesex Regiment Battalions, the 30th and 31st, were created as receiving depots for aliens who had been called up or transferred from existing units. These Battalions provided detachments that were employed on permanent military work within Southern and Eastern Command and eight companies who served in France.

The 30th Battalion moved from Crawley to Reading in September 1916, its headquarters located at 315 Oxford Road. The 31st Battalion moved from Mill Hill to Sevenoaks in 1917 and to Reigate, Harpenden and Croydon in 1918. It has not been possible to identify how the men in the two Battalions were employed.

Early in 1917 the Army made the decision to send Alien Companies to serve in France. This decision led to questions being raised in the House of Commons about whether the men had been told they were only to serve in Britain (see page 208).

In February 1919 concerns were raised in the House of Commons by Colonel Josiah Wedgwood, MP for Newcastle-under-Lyme, that the men in the Alien Battalions had been told that as the sons of alien enemies they would be the last to be demobilised. He asked the Secretary for War whether 'the money spent on keeping up this battalion in England is spent for the protection of this country or as a disciplinary charge?'[55] He was assured the men were being treated in the same way as other soldiers who were eligible for demobilisation.

Prisoners of War

Prior to 1916 all enemy PoWs were brought to Britain and accommodated in camps. Under the Geneva Convention PoWs could be employed, but not on 'war work'. A list of the prisoners with their civil occupation was updated weekly and this enabled the committee which oversaw PoWs, to send men with the correct skills to an area where there was a demand for their services. There was a general detention camp at Alexandra Palace and a number of what became known as 'Parent' camps throughout the country including Frith Hill near Aldershot, Handforth in Cheshire, Shrewsbury and Dorchester. Affiliated to these Parent camps were smaller

Working camps, which accommodated between 75 and 1,000 men. Some Working camps only existed whilst there was a need to employ PoWs in the area whereas others were permanent.

Both types of PoW camp had a permanent establishment of British officers and NCOs and German NCOs who helped enforce discipline. The British were drawn from men serving in Home Command and the Royal Defence Corps. No evidence can be found of other ranks in the Labour Corps being used to guard PoWs although Labour Corps officers are known to have commanded PoW camps in Britain.

Many PoWs were employed in agriculture. The very nature of the work meant that almost as many guards as PoWs were required. For some time this proved a difficulty for the authorities but a solution was found by attaching PoWs to Labour Corps agricultural companies, the members of which acted as guards.

PoWs were employed by the War Office, the Home Office, the Ministry of Munitions, the Board of Agriculture and by civilian contractors. They were employed in a variety of tasks including building hospitals and barracks and on road and railway maintenance. The numbers employed depended on the requirement of the employer as the following examples illustrate:

6 PoWs employed receiving and sorting war salvage at the War Office's Salvage Depot at Birmingham.

413 PoWs working, under military supervision, at the RAF Camp at Orford Ness, Suffolk.

90 PoWs were employed at Boot Depot at Southall, which was in reality a dumping ground for old Army Boots. Their work was grading, sorting, mending, sewing and stretching the 350,000 pairs of odd boots stored there.

At times PoWs were employed alongside men of the Labour Corps as happened in September 1918 at Wool Station, near Dorchester. The RE were building a railway in the area and their 30 Sappers were supported by 60 Labour Corps privates, probably from 383 Company, and 30 PoWs from the 'Parent' Camp at Dorchester.[55]

1   Whitehouse, C. J. and G. P., *A Town for Four Winters*, p.4
2   Simkins, P., 'Soldiers and Civilians' in Becket and Simpson, p.171
3   Crawford, T., *Wiltshire and the Great War*, p.25
4   NA WO 293/4 ACI 707 – 1 April 1916
5   ibid NA T 1/12314
6   Grieves, K. B., The Liverpool Dock Battalion Military Intervention in the Mersey Docks 1915–1918 in *Transactions of the Historic Society of Lancashire and Cheshire* pp.139–158
7   Between August 1914 and January 1915 8,000 dockers from the Mersey Docks joined the Army. According to the *Liverpool Echo*, 13 January 1915, this amounted to one quarter of the dock's labour force.
8   Grieves, p.139
9   From the Derby Papers at the Liverpool Record Office quoted in Grieves p.143
10 James Sexton was a supporter of the war effort and his union took a view that they should support the government and avoid industrial action during the hostilities. David Lloyd George was later to suggest that it was only though support from Sexton that the scheme was made possible.
11 Lord Derby was to remain the Battalion's Commanding Officer throughout his time at the War Office where he was to serve as Director of Recruiting, Under

Secretary of State and Secretary of State for War. He resigned from the latter post in April 1918 becoming British Ambassador in France although continued as CO of the battalion.

12 Following his Manchester speech Lloyd George gave consideration to the mobilisation of labour in the munitions industry and had several meetings with trade union leaders. When the trade unions indicated that such a move would be met with vigorous opposition the plan was dropped in favour of the voluntary enlistment in the munitions industry of skilled men (the King's Munitions Corps).

13 *The Times,* 5 June 1915 quoted in Grieves p.146

14 Grieves, K., p.148

15 Troops were also used to break strikes during April 1915 at Foden's motor works, Sandbach and by joiners in Edinburgh.

16 *The Times,* 22 March 1915 quoted in Grieves p.142

17 Quoted in Grieves, p.148

18 Whilst dockers were exempt from military service there was considerable variation in the way certificates were issued and their withdrawal. Some ship owners were accused of using the system to ensure they got the labour they wanted. Examples exist of Trade Unions complaining that too many of their older men could not get work because of young men with exemption certificates. Examples of the various problems experienced during 1917 can be found in the NA documents NATS 1/1060 and NATS 1/1061.

19 Grieves, K., p.155

20 From the Derby Papers at the Liverpool Record Office quoted in Grieves, p.150

21 NA WO 293/3 ACI 139 – 16 Sep 1915

22 ibid MUN 9/18

23 ibid MUN 5/69/323/101

24 ibid WO 293/3 ACI 184 – 17 Nov 1915

25 ibid

26 The national shell filling factory at Chilwell, Nottinghamshire was the largest such establishment in Britain where over 19 million shells were filled 1915–18

27 Haslam, M. J., *The Chilwell Story* 1982, p.20

28 NA WO 293/3 ACI 205 18 Dec 1915

29 ibid WO 293/3 ACI 269 24 Dec 1915

30 ibid WO 293/4 ACI 864 24 Apr 1916 – the companies were formed in six Commands. Six in Scottish, 16 in Northern, 3 in Western, 21 in Southern 23 in Eastern and 11 in Aldershot Command.

31 NA WO 293/4 ACI 861 22 Apr 1916

32 James, *British Regiments 1914–1918,* p.44

33 NA WO 95/31 The letter sent to the GOC on 12 December 1916 stated: 'I am commanded by the Army Council to inform you that the formation of the 17th and 18th Battalions, The Queen's (Royal West Surrey) Regiment has been cancelled.' Although both James and Wylly (History of the Queen's Royal Regiment) both state that the two Battalions were formed in November 1916.

34 ibid WO 293/4 ACI 1023 19 May 1916

35 ibid

36 ibid WO 293/4 ACI 1218 18 June 1916

37 The trademen were blacksmiths, bricklayers, carpenters and joiners, engine drivers, fitters, glaziers, linesman, masons, metal workers, painters, plasterers, plumbers, stokers, switchboard attendants and wiremen.

38 June 1916 saw the creation of five Works Battalions – the 23rd Battalion King's Liverpool; 13th Battalion Devonshire; 10th Battalion Royal Scots Fusiliers; 29th Battalion Middlesex and 25th Battalion Durham Light Infantry Regiments. A sixth the

24th Battalion King's Liverpool was also formed and appears to have been renumbered as the 27th (Works) Battalion. A seventh, the 33rd Battalion Middlesex Regiment was to be formed in January 1917.

39 *The Record* A Labour Corps Magazine Vol 1 No 1 p.11
40 NA WO 73/102
41 ibid WO 293/5 ACI 2173 18 November 1916
42 ibid ADM 1/8448/32
43 ibid WO 293/4 ACI 498 5 Mar 1916
44 ibid WO 293/5 ACI 2269 6 Dec 1916
45 The qualifying trades included dock labourers, lighter men, barge men, carters and motor drivers, warehouse men, stevedores, and port railway men.
46 Whally-Kelly, Captain H. pp.265–268
47 NA NATS 1/403
48 Locations of Transport Workers Battalions October 1917 – see page 352
49 NA NATS 1/299 Transport Workers Policy
50 Story, H. *History Of The Cameronians Scottish Rifles 1910–1933*, p.385
51 NA WO 293/10 ACI 374 18 June 1919
52 Whally-Kelly, Captain H. ICH DIEN, p.268
53 NA WO 293/5 ACI 1209 17 June 1916
54 Hansard, 24 February 1919
55 NA NATS 1/1330

THE LABOUR CORPS IN BRITAIN

By the early part of 1917 there were some 80,000 men serving in 30 Labour Battalions and 120 Infantry Labour Companies in France, and over 100,000 men in Britain. It was apparent that they could not be satisfactorily administered unless brought together in one corps. On 21 February 1917 a Royal Warrant[1] sanctioned the creation of the Labour Corps, its organisation outlined in ACI 611. The object was to obtain 'more fluidity in utilizing the services of men in Infantry Labour and Works Units, and to simplify administrative work'.[2]

Administration

Administration of the Corps and the appointment of officers was dealt with by the War Office department AG 12. Formed on 19 April 1917 under Lieutenant Colonel Wetherall, the department's staff consisted of two Deputy Assistant Adjutant Generals (DAAG), two former soldier clerks, two soldier clerks and one female clerk. By January 1919 its staff had increased to one DAAG, two staff captains, one former soldier clerk and eleven soldier clerks. AG 12 dealt with all administrative matters, including weekly and monthly returns relating to both British and foreign labour, the Middlesex Alien Battalions and Companies, the Non Combatant Corps, the Transport Workers Battalions and The Liverpool Docks Battalions. The Corps Records Office and Pay Office were located in Nottingham.

Lieutenant Colonel Wetherall noted, in December 1918, that the speed with which the Corps was formed created difficulties:

The Labour Corps with its Record and Pay Offices was then somewhat hastily formed and the sudden transfer of thousands of men, many of whom had already been transferred several times and whose documents had not kept pace with them, led to a serious state of affairs and very nearly to a breakdown in the Record and Pay Offices.

To have been successful the formation of the Corps should have been carried out very much more gradually but the desire to get a 'move on' outweighed other considerations.[3]

The creation of the Corps was a huge administrative task with men being issued new numbers, identity discs, cap badges and shoulder titles.[4] During May and June 1917 almost 190,000 men had to be issued with new regimental numbers. Each unit was issued with a block of numbers for the NCOs and other ranks. As many labour units were operating above strength, more numbers were provided than a company's nominal strength. The men were issued with their new number; a record of this together with any unused numbers was sent to the Record Office.

ACI 611

The initial thinking outlined in ACI 611 was that the Labour Corps would be made up of five different types of unit. Two of these were Labour Companies, and Labour Group Headquarters for service overseas (see page 105). The other three were the Depot Labour Companies, Home Service (HS) Labour Companies and the Labour Battalions based in Britain.

A Medical Board examined men in HS and Depot Companies every three months. Men classified 'A' were transferred to infantry battalions; men classified B(i), B(ii), C(i) and C(ii) were available for labour duties in Britain and overseas.

The identification of a man's unit was shown by his shoulder title, Labour and Depot Companies having the letters LC preceded by the company number, Group Headquarters just LC and Battalions, LB. This was later rescinded.

The 'Royal Arms' replaced regimental cap badges although the ACI noted that it would be some time before this could take place. The new badges came into general use during August 1917 but the loss of a regimental connection proved to be unpopular with both officers and men. Private Pearce of 77 Company recorded a typical view that he 'disliked the successor, a rather large crude Royal coat of arms'.[5] This badge was retained for the remainder of the war although it is not uncommon to see photographs of labour units in which both officers and men are wearing regimental badges. The Corps was finally granted its own badge[6] in October 1918 and these were issued from early December onwards.[7] However, even in 1919, it was common to find regimental badges being worn alongside the rifle, pick and shovel badge of the Labour Corps.

Depot Labour Companies

These were formed from the Depot Companies that already existed in Home Service Commands. Their function was to provide drafts for labour companies overseas, to receive men returning from overseas and to provide working parties in Britain with the proviso that these men could be recalled at short notice if required for drafts. Two Depot Companies were formed in each of Scottish (Blairgowrie), Northern (Strensall, York), Western (Oswestry), Eastern (Thetford) and Southern (Plymouth) Command numbered 295–304 Companies. Men transferred to these companies were issued numbers in the range 122,641–128,640. Commanded by a captain or major, its HQ staff consisted of a subaltern, a CSM and thirteen ORs. Under the HQ were four platoons, each commanded by a subaltern with one sergeant and 120 men.

In June 1917 ACI 897 announced that the Depot Labour Companies were to change their title to Reserve Labour Companies.[8] Four days after the war ended it was announced that the Reserve Companies would cease to exist as independent units at the end of November, and the men were transferred to the Command's Labour Centre.[9]

Works Companies

The existing Infantry Works Companies (IWC) were combined to form the Home Service (HS) Labour Companies. Although the original idea was that two IWCs would be combined to form one HS Company, in reality two or more companies were formed from a number of IWCs. For example, the 32 Durham Light Infantry IWCs formed fifteen HS Companies, numbered 344–358.

A total of 54 HS companies were formed, numbered 305–358, the men in them being issued numbers in the range 170,141–186,240. HS (Labour) Companies were renamed HS (Works) Companies in June 1917.

Commanded by a major or captain each company had two subalterns, a CSM, six sergeants and 243 other ranks. The men in these companies were primarily skilled tradesmen and were allotted to work for the RE where their skills could be utilised. The tasking of HS Labour Companies was determined, not at Command level, but at the War Office by the Director of Fortification and Works. The companies did not keep War Diaries so there is little information about their work. In general they were used to help the Engineers maintain and build military facilities including airfields (310 Company at Yatesbury and 329 at Orford Ness), roads and railways (312 Company at Bulford), hospitals (315 Company at Fovant), Ordnance Depots (336 Company at Woolwich) and hutting (352 Company at Catterick). 338 Company is one of the few companies for which some records exist. In November 1918 it was supplying detachments to the RH & RFA School of Instruction at Shoeburyness and the RE and RGA Signalling Training Depot at Chatham and Thames Haven.[10]

From July 1917 until January 1919 an average of 13,000 men were employed monthly in HS (Works) Companies. Numbers dropped to 3,500 by April 1919 and 891 by October, the last recorded data on HS Works Companies.

Labour Battalions

In April 1917 there were nine Works Battalions in Home Command providing working parties for both military and civil use. Whilst the two Middlesex Alien Battalions (30th and 31st) were not transferred to the Labour Corps the other seven (the 23rd and 27th King's Liverpool, 13th Devonshire, 10th Royal Scots, 29th and 33rd Middlesex and 25th DLI) became the 1st to 7th Labour Battalions, Labour Corps. The men were numbered from 128,641–170,140.

Commanded by a lieutenant colonel, administration was undertaken by a head-quarters consisting of four more officers, three warrant officers, four sergeants and two batmen. The basic unit of the battalion was a company consisting of a captain or major as its OC supported by a subaltern, a CSM, two sergeants and 249 other ranks. The number of companies varied according to the number of other ranks posted to the battalion. The smallest two Battalions, the 27th King's and the 33rd Middlesex both had a strength of 2,000 men and the largest, the 29th Middlesex, almost 13,000 men.

With over 40,000 men serving in seven Labour battalions it was soon clear that this structure did not provide the fluidity of labour the authorities wanted. Within two months plans to break up the battalions into smaller companies were put in place.

Expansion and Change

Major changes to the Corps announced in a four week period from 23 May 1917 suggest that initial planning of the Labour Corps had been undertaken too quickly and without sufficient thought. The changes that occurred are outlined in brief below, each of these changes being considered in more depth later.

Employment Companies were added to the Corps on 23 May with the publication of ACI 837.[11] There were four types: Divisional and Area Employment Companies, for service overseas (see page 118); Home Service (HS); and Depot Employment Companies, in Britain. This ACI also announced the shoulder title for all men would be LC.

On 5 June ACI 897 announced that Depot Companies were to be entitled Reserve Companies and HS (Labour) Companies became HS (Works) Companies. Men in the Labour Battalions were transferred to two new units, the Labour Centre and, the previously used name, the HS (Labour) Company. Agricultural companies were added to the Corps with the publication of ACI 924 on 12 June.[12]

The basic structure of the Corps was completed on 20 June 1917 when ACI 985 brought the RE Labour Battalions and the ASC Labour Companies, both of which served overseas, into the Labour Corps (see page 113).[13]

HS (Employment) Companies

The Employment Companies were formed from men who were employed on command, garrison or regimental duties. A total of 59,000 NCOs and men were transferred to HS Employment Companies between July and August 1917. Although 240 company numbers (450 to 689) were allocated to the HS Employment Companies only 200 were formed. Later some unused company numbers were allotted to Agricultural Companies.

The Employment Company consisted of a major or captain as OC, a subaltern, a CSM who also acted as CQMS, one orderly room clerk, one batman and 270

NCOs and other ranks. A list of the men and the trade for which they were best suited was maintained by each company. The recognised trades were:

Batman	Cook	Telephone Operator	Sanitary duty
Orderly	Clerk	Storeman or Caretaker	Shoemaker
Policeman	Butcher	Loader and brakeman	Salvage
Laundry	Tailor	Bath and Drying room	Traffic Control
Regimental Institute (included running Cinema, Theatre and Canteens)			

Table 1: Recognised Trades for Employment Companies

HS Employment Companies consisted of men of the lowest possible medical categories in order to release fitter men for posting to companies overseas.[14]

From August 1917 until February 1919 an average of 50,000 men were employed each month in HS Employment Companies with a peak of almost 67,500 in November 1917. These men were employed at Recruit Distribution Battalions, in Command Depots, at Enteric Depots, Dysentery Depots and Military Convalescent Hospitals. They were not, however, used at Infantry, Cavalry, RE or RA Depots or for MGC, Brigade of Guards, Household Cavalry, Tank Corps, ASC, AVC, AOC or RAMC units, all of which had to provide their own men for regimental employments.

The number of men employed at any establishment was dependant on the number of men catered for at the place of work. This ranged from 11 men for a unit of less than 750, to 42 for a unit over 2,250 strong. There are no surviving records for these companies so it is not possible to identify exactly where an individual company or detachment was employed. Occasionally a soldier's record will contain a report that gives some idea of where he was employed. An example is 162392 Private James Tarr who was a member of 687 HS Employment Company, employed at The Prince of Wales Hospital for Officers, Marylebone. On 4 September 1917 Private Tarr's body was found, with a fractured skull and spine, in the well at the bottom of a lift shaft. The lift was used to move coal to the various floors of the hospital. Following a post mortem, which recorded his death as accidental, his body was buried at Brookwood Military Cemetery.

Depot Employment Companies

In each of the eight Home Commands a Depot Employment Company (Companies 359–366) was formed in order to provide drafts for overseas Employment Companies. They received new recruits, men transferred to the Labour Corps and personnel returning from overseas employment companies.

Commanded by a captain or major, its headquarters consisted of a subaltern, a CSM, a CQMS, four sergeants, six corporals and two batmen. A company was divided into four platoons, each commanded by a subaltern, with one sergeant and three corporals.

In June 1917 ACI 897 announced that the Depot Employment Companies were to change their title to Reserve Employment Companies. Four days after the War ended it was announced that the Reserve Companies would cease to exist as independent units at the end of November, and the men were transferred to the Command's Labour Centre.

Labour Centre

ACI 897 established a Labour Centre in each Home Command at the same station as the Reserve Labour and Employment Companies. Companies overseas were associated with a centre in Britain, which provided reinforcements. If a man was returned to Britain as no longer fit to serve overseas, he would be posted to the appropriate centre before transfer to a HS Company or discharge.

Command	Location of Labour Centre	Associated Overseas Companies (June 1917)
Scottish	Blairgowrie	1 to 15, 225 to 255 and 771 to 785
Northern	Stensall Camp, Yorks January 1918 to Ripon	16 to 55, 256 to 265 and 786 to 800
Western	Park Hall Camp, Oswestry November 1918 to Prees Heath	56 to 92, 266 to 275 and 801 to 815
Irish	Gough Barracks, The Curragh February 1918 to Clandboye October 1918 to Newtonards	182 and 183, 711 to 750 and 851 to 870
Eastern	Thetford January 1918 to Sutton	93 to 132, 276 to 285 and 816 to 830
Aldershot	Blenheim Hutments, Aldershot	184 to 224, 286 to 294 and 831 to 850
Southern	Eggbuckland Plymouth October 1918 to Fovant	All Group Headquarters, 152 to 181 and 700 to 710
London District	158 City Road	133 to 151 and 751 to 770

Table 2: Locations of Labour Centres and Associated Companies.

Some men, like 299149 Private John Cairns, found that after a period in Britain they were declared fit enough to return to France. Cairns, 716 Company, returned on medical grounds on 14 April 1918. He joined Irish Command Labour Centre and following a medical board he was returned to France on 5 June to join 723 Company.

The centre was an administrative unit commanded by a lieutenant colonel. For most centres the HQ staff consisted of six officers, eight NCOs ranging from sergeant to sergeant major, and four clerks. There were three exceptions: Irish Command, which had only three officers, Aldershot and London District, each with four officers. The HQ administered 1,000 men and for every 500 additional men an extra CQMS and clerk were attached.

New recruits to the Labour Corps were posted to a centre and then moved to either a reserve company prior to drafting or a HS company. Each centre received weekly demands for men from overseas. Those selected were notified to the AAG's department who informed GHQ overseas of the likely date of arrival and arranged for their embarkation. HS Companies placed demands for men through the local Labour Centre, and upon allocation the Records Office were informed of those posted.

HS (Labour) Companies

The original Home Service Labour Companies were, under ACI 897 of June 1917, renamed Works Companies. At the same time several new companies were formed, the men for which came from the labour battalions.

Commanded by a major or captain, with a subaltern and a CQMS, the number of NCOs and other ranks varied according to the number in the company. The ACI did not lay down the nominal strength of a HS Company although it did state: 'every endeavour should be made to form each company on a basis of 500 men'.[15] Between July 1917 and February 1919 a total of 27 HS Labour Companies were formed (company numbers 367–393) with an average size of 357 all ranks.

HS Labour Companies were used to undertake the unskilled work needed to support the Army. This included labouring tasks associated with building camps, airfields and military railways, loading and unloading stores and other equipment and jobs such as repairing ammunition boxes returned from France. The labour companies also provided working parties for civilian firms, contractors and government departments such as the Admiralty, Ministry of Munitions and Road Board. Companies were located at each of the Labour Centres and at important military establishments including 377 at Rugeley Camp, 378 at Catterick, 385 at Devonport, 387 at Woolwich and 393 at Pembroke Dock. The Companies did not keep war diaries so little is known about their employment. One exception to this is 374 Company, which provided labour for the construction of the military railway at Porton Down, Wiltshire.

When HS Labour companies were formed, men in ILBs who were already employed on civil work or attached to the ASC Forage Branch, continued with their employment. Instead of joining a Labour company they were posted to the Labour Centre of the command in which they were being employed. The ILB ceased to exist once all the men in it had been posted to a HS Company or Labour Centre. This change appears to have taken some time. An example is 331677 Private George Dickinson who was transferred, not to a Labour Centre, but to the 1st Labour Battalion on 12 July 1917 where he remained for nine days before being posted to 740 Company. This indicates that 1st Battalion was still in existence over a month after the changes had been introduced.

Agricultural Companies

Agricultural Companies had been formed in February 1917 but were almost permanently short of men. Under ACI 924 of 12 June 1917 these companies were transferred to the Labour Corps which provided a greater pool of labourers.[16] In theory men could easily be moved wherever needed in Britain, although evidence suggests that movements tended to be within the same command area. Perhaps more importantly, a single administrative organisation made it easier to move men between agricultural and military work as required.

With the approach of the 1917 harvest almost 15,000 more men were allocated to agricultural work from both Labour Corps units and Home Defence units. In previous years these men had returned to their units once the harvest was complete. In

1917 it was decided that all these men would be transferred to the Labour Corps and either remain in agricultural companies or be posted to general labour companies.[17]

Operation of the systems for reinforcement

In theory, a man joining a Labour Centre would normally be posted direct to a reserve company while he waited for a posting to a company either in Britain or overseas. Personnel working in agricultural companies, forage units or with civil contractors did not pass through a reserve company but were still administered by the Labour Centre HQ. In practice this system was not always applied, as the following three examples show:

> 266092 Private J. O'Neill was transferred to Western Command Labour Centre (WCLC) on 4 July 1917 and posted on the same day to 549 HS Employment Company. He remained with this company until posted back to WCLC on 20 January 1918 where he remained until discharged through ill health on 23 April.

> 392957 Private E. Cadman joined Eastern Command Labour Centre (ECLC) on 14 November 1917 only to be posted to 363 Reserve Employment Company three days later and to 576 HS Employment Company after a further four days.

> 503179 Private S. Robinson joined ECLC on 10 December 1917. It was not until 13 April 1918 that he was posted to 301 Reserve Labour Company where he remained until 30 November. He returned to ECLC only to be sent seven days later to 589 HS Employment Company.

Men could be moved between companies without passing through a Labour Centre.[18] An example of this can be seen in the service record of 189418 Private A. Hayes who was transferred from 17th Gloucestershire Regiment on 19 May 1917 to Southern Command Labour Centre (SCLC) and posted that same day to 304 Reserve HS Labour Company. On 1 June he was posted back to SCLC. In civilian life Hayes had worked on a farm and it is possible that for the next six months he was employed in the centre's own vegetable garden. On 28 December 1917 Hayes was posted to 424 Agricultural Company, transferring on 6 April 1918 directly to 627 Agricultural Company and back to 424 on 28 March 1919 before being discharged in June. Both these companies worked in the Worcestershire Regiment's Depot vegetable garden in Worcester.

An ACI published in September 1917 suggests that men were being transferred to the Labour Corps because their original unit considered them difficult or unwanted.[19] The ACI pointed out that no man in medical category A, B(i) or C(i) could be transferred to the Labour Corps without War Office sanction and only then if the man was over age or possessed some special qualification required by the Corps. It also pointed out that B(ii) and C(ii) men with technical qualifications were not to be transferred to the Corps. B(iii) and C(iii) could only be transferred if capable of undertaking sedentary work and not if the intention was for them to be discharged.

The War Office believed that too many men were being transferred to the Labour Corps on medical grounds alone. A man's previous civil work was not taken into account when deciding his suitability for a particular corps or unit:

> e.g., a B(ii) navvy is more suited for a Labour Unit than the RAMC, and similarly a B(ii) man of light physique, but a fair standard of education, such as a shop assistant, would be more use as a RAMC Hospital Orderly than in a Labour Unit.[20]

The instructions were that men should only be posted to the Labour Corps if they were medical category B(ii) or C(ii) and over 25 years of age (19 in the case of Irish recruits). That a man should have no defect which made it impossible for him to handle a pick or shovel although men capable of lighter work such as batmen or orderlies could be posted to Employment Companies. In order to meet the large demand for agricultural labourers men in categories B(ii) and C(ii) with agricultural experience were to be posted to agricultural companies.[21]

The distinction between category B and C was to be abolished in October 1917, with the new Class B being men not fit for general service but fit for service at home or overseas as determined by a medical board.

Trade qualifications and pay scales

On 22 July 1917, ACI 1183 stated that a man being transferred from one corps to another on medical grounds, or to meet the needs of the Army, was entitled to retain his special rates of pay.[22] Special rates of pay applied to skilled tradesman. However, there appears to have been uncertainty about trade payments for those working in Britain. This was finally clarified on 6 September 1917, in ACI 1375, which stated that tradesmen serving in the HS Works Companies would receive trade pay if they passed the ordinary RE tradesmen's tests, although such additional pay was not available if they were employed on civilian work.[23]

The RE carried out trade tests but it was not always possible for a man to attend a course in order to take his proficiency test. Early in 1918 it was decided that men with specialist skills including lithographers, photographers, printers and surveyors, who had previously served in the RE, could be assessed on their qualification reports and receive trade pay until they were re-tested.[24]

In August 1918 it was announced that a new Labour Corps unit, the Army Trade Test Centre was to be formed at Woolwich. The Centre, which was to have an establishment of 222 all ranks, would enable the Labour Corps to carry out trade tests rather than having to rely upon the services of the RE.[25]

Personnel already employed at Woolwich, who would be required to run the Trade Test Centre, were to be transferred to the Labour Corps. Although formed in August, the first indication of Labour Corps soldiers being employed at the centre appears in November 1918 when the unit's strength was 2 officers, 2 WOs and 141 other ranks.[26] By February 1919[27] the strength was 1 WO and 79 ORs and the last reference to the Test Centre is July 1919[28] when the strength was 10 sergeants and 61 other ranks.

Discharge Centres and Clearing Office

Although by the end of September 1917 the basic structure and administration of the Labour Corps had been established, little thought appears to have been given to how it would deal with men due to be discharged on medical grounds. It appears that these men were posted to the centre associated with their company to await discharge. As a result the centres became congested, and in February 1918 discharge centres were established in London District and Southern, Aldershot and Scottish Command. Centres were established in the other four commands a month later. The eight centres dealt with about 600 officers and men each month from February 1918 to May 1919, after which the monthly average dropped to around 200.

By October 1918 the number of Labour Corps personnel being returned from overseas to hospitals in Britain due to sickness or wounds had become so great that a new way of dealing with their administration had to be devised. These were men who were expected to return to service. Rather than the Labour Centre dealing with their administration, it was decided to create a clearing office that was located in Nottingham.[29] When a man was discharged from hospital he was granted leave, at the end of which he would be posted to the Labour Centre in the command in which his home address was situated, or if this centre had no accommodation, the nearest one. It was expected that a soldier would receive a posting order within two days of completing his leave period. In December 1918, the clearing office administered 7,000 men. Numbers peaked at 16,800 men in May 1919. During its 26 months in existence the clearing office administered an average of 5,200 men a month.

A transfer centre was established in Eastern Command although it only appears to have been in existence for one month in July 1918.[30] Its strength comprised a WO, five sergeants and eighteen other ranks. There is, however, no information about its function.

Additional units and administrative changes

There were two new HS units added to the Labour Corps during 1918. In April two Russian Battalions, were created.[31] Numbered the 8th and 9th Labour Battalions they were located at Sevenoaks and Pembroke Dock. The 8th Battalion received recruits from the London District and Eastern and Southern Command and the 9th from Northern, Western and Scottish Command. The main function of these two battalions was to provide manpower for companies, four of which were to serve in France. In addition to the men in France an average of 2,000 served in these units in Britain between May 1918 and January 1919. There are no records of the British employment.

Four days after the war ended, it was announced that the HS Reserve Companies would cease to exist as independent units at the end of November 1918, and the men transferred to their command's Labour Centre.[32] ACI 39 of 17 January 1919 directed that no further men would be transferred to the Labour Corps for regimental employments in Britain.[33]

During January 1919, salvage companies were formed for duty at the British salvage depots.[34] Instructions were given for the immediate formation of one section at Wavertree, Liverpool, three at Regent's Canal Docks and four at Southall. According to the ACI, when sufficient sections had been formed in a command to warrant the formation of a headquarters, the War Office was to be notified so that they could issue a company number. No evidence can be found of new companies being formed early in 1919 so it is possible that existing Labour companies may have been used for this role.

In April 1919 it was announced: 'As no units of the Labour Corps were included in the Armies of Occupation at Home it is necessary to dispose of all Labour Corps personnel serving at home.'[35] The work being undertaken by HS Companies was to be reviewed, and reports sent to command headquarters who would decide when they could be disbanded. By October most HS Works, Employment and Agricultural Companies had been disbanded, the exceptions being 348 Works Company at York, 412 Agricultural Company at Backworth and four Employment Companies (771 at Aldershot, 231 at Ripon, 252 at Clipstone Camp and 512 at Nottingham). These companies, with the exception of 512, ceased to exist in November 1919. 512 Company continued until October 1920, presumably servicing the records and clearing offices in Nottingham. There was also an unnumbered HS Employment Company formed in London District that operated between January and March 1920.

The first Labour Centre to close was Scottish Command in September 1919. Five other centres were to close by February 1920 (Irish Command in November 1919, London District in December 1919, Southern and Western in January 1920 and Northern in February 1920). Eastern Centre was the last to close in January 1921. The Discharge Centres operated until March 1920 although records indicate that there were still 61 men, presumably too ill to be discharged, technically posted to a Discharge Centre in June 1920.

The Records and Pay Office at Nottingham was closed on 25 March 1921 with the instruction that any future enquiries should be referred to the Army Pay Office at York.[36] The final War Office announcement regarding the Labour Corps occurred on 3 December 1924 with the cancellation of ACI 611 of 1917, the ACI that had created the Labour Corps.[37]

From its creation in April 1917 until the end of the war the average strength of the Labour Corps in Britain was 160,000. An analysis of the records shows that the percentage of men in each type of company remained fairly static throughout this time, with about 17 per cent at Labour Centres, 10 per cent in HS Labour Companies, 37 per cent in HS Employment Companies 6 per cent in HS Works Companies and 30 per cent in Agricultural Companies.

Life in UK units

With no HS units keeping War Diaries, little is known about individual companies. However, there is some information about two Labour Corps centres, Southern Command Centre at Eggbuckland, Plymouth and the Scottish Command Centre (ScCLC) at Blairgowrie.

In Southern Command a Labour Corps monthly magazine called *The Record* was started in December 1917. Edited by Second Lieutenant E. Rayner it was intended to, in his words, 'provide good edifying literature to our hard-working comrades of the Corps'.[38] *The Record* was available for a subscription of 12/- a year including postage. It is not known how long this magazine was in existence; the Imperial War Museum holds copies of the first three issues but to date no other issues have been found. As with most regimental magazines it contains a mixture of articles. It features reports on the work, origins and organisation of the Labour Corps, a diary of a six day visit to Labour Companies in France, some items of general interest and many humorous articles.

The magazine also gives an idea of some of the social and sporting events undertaken by men at Southern Command Centre. These include a visit on 8 November 1917 by the 'Pros and Cons', a Concert Party from the Derriford, Convalescent Camp, 364 Company's own Concert Party, the 'Woodford Khaki Boys', performed at the Town Hall, Kingsbridge on 28 November in aid of the V.A. Hospital, Collapit Creek and on 11 December at the Globe Theatre, Royal Marines Barracks, Plymouth. Sporting activities include matches between the football teams of the Centre, 303 and 304 Companies and the Royal Defence Corps from Laira. There was also a billiards match between the sergeants at the Centre and those of 303 Company.

Links with the community included the farmers from the Saltram Estate arranging a Boxing Day concert and supper for the men from the camp at Harwicke. A payday collection by 379 Company, who were employed at Southampton Docks, which amounted to £8 5s, was donated to Dr Barnardo's Homes.

In the case of ScCLC it is the local newspaper, the *Blairgowrie Advertiser* that gives an idea of life at the Centre. The paper had a weekly item about events at the camp and links with the local community. Many of the entries are merely a report about the weekly tea and sacred concert held at the Public Hall canteen. These articles were clearly written to boost morale and included an address given by Reverend John Guthrie from South UF Church. He praised the men of the Labour Corps:

> Some of them had been at the Front already and met with misfortune – something had happened to them and they were now in the Labour Companies. They were apt to be disappointed and feel they were of no use. They had been in the thick of the fray, in the hottest corner of the fighting, and now they were here. They were of use still, and he wanted to tell them straight out that if they were faithful in doing their work even as they were, they would be doing their country as great a service as in winning the Victoria Cross (applause).[39]

Reverend W. D. Niven, who had previously served as a chaplain in France, gave a similar address:

> … one thing he had learned in France and Belgium, and that was how worthy of honour and respect the Labour Corps is … the first Labour Corps they saw in France did not give them a very good impression. The Corps was standing at a roadside leaning on their pick and spade, and their most serious work seemed to be smoking. He discovered afterwards the reason for that – many of them were conscientious objectors. They had, at least, conscientious objections to working. Soon, however, his Battalion's ideas on the subject

were changed, for they afterwards saw what the Labour Corps was composed of, and they saw amongst them men with three or four wound stripes and with a row of medals on their breast, which showed that they had already done their brave duty for King and country in the fighting ranks. They were, however, sorry to see men who should never have been in France at all – men who were sticking at it in spite of their physical weakness and disability but who were showing a splendid and worthy example not only to their own comrades but to all men in the fighting line. The Labour Corps gained enormously in the respect of the fighting men when it was known the kind of work they were doing, and when they saw the danger to which they were exposed when working under shell fire and bombs. The spirit of courage and resolution they were showing and the enormous debt the fighting ranks owed to the Labour Corps, were noteworthy.[40]

The paper also reported occasions when men at the centre were presented with bravery awards. An example of this was the presentation of the MM to 129798 CQMS H. Sumner by the OC of the centre, Lieutenant Colonel William Rose-Black in September 1918.[41] CQMS Sumner had originally joined the Army in 1885 and, at the age of 43 when war was declared, he joined the National Reserve and was posted to 13th King's Liverpool. He transferred to the 23rd Works Battalion King's Liverpool, which became the 1st Labour Battalion, Labour Corps. On 19 May 1917 he arrived in France joining 226 Company, the Divisional Employment Company for 29 Division. Whilst with this company he was wounded three times and also gassed on 30 November 1917. The *Advertiser* reported that he was awarded his MM following an incident in the Cambrai area:

> When the enemy broke through or tried to break through armed only with a big shovel and nothing else, did excellent work not only in helping his men to get back safely, but he retarded the progress of the enemy by assisting the artillery.[42]

Eleven days after this report appeared, on 18 September 1918, CQMS Summers was discharged as no longer physically fit for war service.

Not all reports about individual soldiers concerned awards for bravery. There were also reports of men who died whilst serving at the Centre. When 40681 Private Smith was accidentally killed, the paper reported:

> The body of Private Charles Smith, Labour Company, who was harvesting at Foss Home Farm, Pitlochry, was on Sunday found in the Tummel. He had been missing since 28 October. It is supposed he had fallen in the flooded water on returning from a visit on the opposite side of the water. He was aged 30 and belonged to London.[43]

Many entries refer to sporting activities including a bowls match between four officers and local civilians,[44] and a mixed doubles tennis tournament organised by Lieutenant Steele.[45] References to football matches are frequently found, including a 'Football match in fancy dress between teams of 296 Company and the NCOs of the Expeditionary Draft for Chinese Labour Corps, presently attached to Labour Corps'[46] and the match played on 26 October 1918 between Dundee Hibernian and the Labour Centre Garrison XI. Played in aid of Labour Corps Comfort Funds, the Garrison XI beat Dundee Hibs by 5 goals to 4.[47] The other social events that frequently appear in the paper are concerts and dances arranged either for or by the men at the Centre, 296 Company's 'Erich Entertainers' being praised for their professionalism.[48]

One officer at Scottish Centre, Captain William Steele, CO of 296 Company, appears to have played an important part in both supporting and organising social events. In June 1917 he is described as 'the popular and genial CO of the Company'.[49] Promoted to captain in November, he was given a complimentary dinner by the officers of his company at the Queen's Hotel, Blairgowrie. In January 1918 he promoted a concert that raised £29 12s 2d to fund the supply of tobacco to soldiers and sailors serving abroad. In November 1918 he organised a matinee performance at the Pavilion Theatre, Glasgow that was made up of both soldiers from the Centre and professional artists from the D'Oyle Carte Company, at which nearly £400 was raised for the Labour Corps Comforts Fund.

One social event of particular note took place on 17 August 1918 when a fete was held at Blairgowrie House to raise funds for the Labour Corps PoW Fund. Attended by over 4,000 people, the fete, together with a collection amongst the men of the Labour Corps serving in Scotland, raised a total of £2,687 3s 5d for the fund.

Discontent and Strikes

The reports in the *Blairgowrie Advertiser* emphasize the important role played by the Labour Corps in France and tend to give the impression that the men at the centre spent their time at concerts, playing sports and fitting in well with the local community. This was not always the case. On 9 December 1918 five soldiers in the Railway Hotel asked for whisky but were told that only beer was available. They claimed that civilians were being sold whisky and in the argument that ensued the hotel keeper and two civilian policemen were assaulted. As the men were being taken to the Police Office a number of other soldiers set upon the police. The *Advertiser* reported that: 'Some 200 or 300 soldiers gathered about the Police Office, and great threats of violence were used to the Police and the crowd smashed the fanlight windows.'[50]

With the situation deteriorating, Police Inspector McPherson contacted the Labour centre and five or six officers came from the centre. However,

> ... they were unable to control the crowd. Their orders were disobeyed and ultimately the Officers had to take shelter in the Police Office. In order to save further riotous conduct Inspector McPherson liberated the men in the cells.[51]

The men later appeared in the Sheriff's Court where four were sentenced to 60 days and one, Private William Ogilvie, to three months in prison.

A similar incident took place on 10 January 1919 at Stirling when men in 459 Agricultural Company demonstrated about the delay in demobilising them. Two soldiers were arrested for 'horseplay in the streets', which resulted in others storming the Police Office and securing their release. The military authorities had to send out a picket in order to restore order. The two men appeared in court the following day, one being sentenced to two months in prison and the other fined £2.[52]

The delays in demobilisation led to disturbances throughout the Army. Nearly 50 incidents took place during January and February 1919, one involving a Labour Corps company. On 9 January the men in 562 HS Employment Company at Heaton Park, Manchester went on strike. Four men representing the company met with the colonel in charge of the base and put their grievances to him. They complained that they had all served overseas, many being either wounded or ill through service and that they were being maintained in the Army whilst men who had been recruited more recently had already been discharged. In addition, there were complaints about the poor quality of the food they were receiving. The *Manchester Guardian* reported that the colonel sent a special messenger to the War Office with a report of the incident although it is not known what action, if any, was taken.[53]

The most serious incident involving the Labour Corps took place at the ECLC at Sutton in June 1919. *The Times* reported that during the second week in June a committee of five soldiers, calling themselves delegates, had been formed to complain that they should be demobilised and not be posted to France.[54] Following a demonstration at the camp on Saturday 21 June, a battalion of the Cheshire Regiment and one from the Welsh Regiment were sent to place the camp under armed guard. The following day a detachment of regular soldiers with fixed bayonets and a machine-gun were positioned outside the railway station. At the camp the men were ordered to leave their tents, armed guards fetching out those who refused. Eighteen hundred men were then marched under armed guard to the railway station where they were placed on trains to Canterbury and Dover, the guard being called to those who refused to board.

As a result of the refusal to leave their tents some 360 ringleaders were charged with resisting lawful authority, not going on parade when it was their duty to do so and not using their best efforts to resist a mutiny. On 22 June at the Drill Hall, Sutton, these men were brought before Courts Martial presided over by Brigadier General Anley. The prosecution evidence was that the men in camp had been ordered to parade at 6.30 am and when they refused they were given until 7.25 am to change their minds. During this time officers and NCOs went through the camp and men who agreed to parade were marched away. Those who refused were rounded up by men from the Cheshire and Welsh Regiments and put under arrest. In defence the men claimed that they were not the men who had refused to parade, some of them stating that they had not heard the call to parade. Initially, 40 men were acquitted of all charges. However it was virtually impossible to distinguish which of the other 320 men had been guilty and which innocent. In view of this the GOC Eastern Command decided that 'rather than any innocent men shall suffer with the guilty, the proceedings shall be abandoned' and all 320 were released.[55]

1   NA WO 123/59 AO 85
2   ibid WO 293/6 ACI 611 13 April 1917
3   ibid WO 162/6
4   During the First World War a soldier was issued with a regimental number and if transferred to another regiment or corps issued with a new regimental number.

5 IWM Reference 74/62/1
6 The Pioneer Corps on its formation in 1939 adopted the Labour Corps badge.
7 NA WO 293/9 ACI 1093 5 Oct 1918
8 ibid WO 293/6 ACI 897 5 June 1917
9 ibid WO 293/9 ACI 1275 15 Nov 1918
10 ibid WO 33/904
11 ibid WO 293/6 ACI 837 23 May 1917
12 ibid WO 293/6 ACI 924 12 June 1917
13 ibid WO 293/6 ACI 985 20 June 1917
14 ibid WO 293/ 6 ACI 850 25 May 1917
15 ibid WO 293/6 ACI 897
16 ibid WO 293/6 ACI 924
17 ibid WO 293/7 ACI 1545 12 Oct 17
18 ibid WO 293/6 ACI 924
19 ibid WO 293/7 ACI 1396 10 September 1917
20 ibid WO 293/7 ACI 1479 27 Sept 1917
21 ibid WO 293/7 ACI 1479
22 ibid WO 293/7 ACI 1183 27 July 1917
23 ibid WO 293/7 ACI 1375 6 September 1917
24 ibid WO 293/8 ACI 034 11 Jan 1918
25 ibid WO 293/9 ACI 882 9 Aug 1918
26 ibid WO 73/108
27 ibid WO 73/110
28 ibid WO 73/110
29 ibid WO 293/9 ACI 1117 23 Oct 1918
30 ibid WO 73/108
31 ibid WO 293/8 ACI 414 19 April 1918
32 ibid WO 293/9 ACI 1275
33 ibid WO 293/10 ACI 39 17 Jan 1919
34 ibid WO 293/10 ACI 59 26 Jan 1919
35 ibid WO 293/10 ACI 252 11 Apr 1919
36 ibid WO 293/12 ACI 175 17 March 1921
37 ibid WO 293/15 ACI 699 3 Dec 1924
38 *The Record,* Dec 1917 p.1
39 *Blairgowrie Advertiser* 28 Apr 1917
40 ibid 2 Feb 1918
41 His name appears as Summers in the *Blairgowrie Advertiser.*
42 *Blairgowrie Advertiser,* 7 September 1918
43 ibid, 2 Nov 1918
44 ibid, 9 June 1917
45 ibid, 16 June 1917
46 ibid, 22 September 1917
47 ibid, 2 Nov 1918
47 ibid, 22 Dec 1917
49 ibid, 30 June 1917
50 ibid, 28 Dec 1918
51 ibid, 28 Dec 1918
52 Rothstein, *The Soldiers Strikes of 1919,* p.63
53 ibid, p.61
54 *The Times,* 23 June 1919
55 ibid, 21 July 1919

SOLDIERS AND AGRICULTURE

Of all the industries in Britain which used military labour during the war, agriculture not only involved the highest proportion of men, but also had military units established specifically to serve its needs. From the first use of soldier volunteers to aid the harvest in 1915 there were to be over 75,000 soldiers serving in agricultural companies by the end of the war. Although soldiers were not used in agriculture until 1915, the problems the war caused for food production due to the loss of both acreage and labour were apparent from the first days of the war.

The loss of land, horses and men

Two of the initial problems faced by agriculture were the loss of land and of animals. Within days of the declaration of war the military began to requisition land and property throughout the country for use as military camps and training areas, and later to build aerodromes and munitions factories. Some counties, like Wiltshire, where by the end of 1914 an additional 100,000 soldiers were encamped, were particularly badly affected. This led to complaints, typical of which was that of an East Sussex farmer made in January 1915, that he had not only had 100 acres of his arable land commandeered by the Army and turned into rifle ranges and trenches, but his farmyard turned into a sea of mud and no offer of compensation made.[1]

In 1914 the horse was an essential part of British agriculture, providing the power needed for ploughing, carting and harvesting and as the primary mode of human transport. It was also essential as a beast of burden for the Army who requisitioned farmers' horses. By June 1915 the Army had obtained approximately 70,000 heavy horses, some 8 per cent of those in use in agriculture, and 25 per cent of saddle horses.[2] Although the Government arranged that for the rest of the war, the majority of Army horses were obtained from overseas, it was not until 1918 that the number of horses available for use on farms would match that of 1914.

By the end of 1914 this labour intensive industry had seen more than one in eight of its permanent workers enlist in the armed forces. Just as importantly, agriculture also lost a high percentage of its essential casual workers to the forces, or to other industries which paid higher wages. In February 1915 the *Farmer and Stockbreeder* pointed out that the wet winter coupled with the shortage of labour meant farmers could not respond to the call to grow more grain.

In April 1915, at a meeting of the National Farmers' Union Executive Committee, it was suggested that the Army Council should be approached with a view to using soldiers to help with the next harvest. On 10 June the Under Secretary for War informed Parliament that consideration was being given to releasing soldiers to help with the hay and corn harvests.

Soldiers as farm workers

A month later, on 10 July, Army Council Instruction 84 was published, which defined the harvest season in England and Wales as 15 July to 15 October 1915 and said that soldiers in Britain could volunteer to be granted leave for up to four weeks to help with the harvest.[3] Similar ACIs for Scotland and Ireland were published on 26 July and 11 August respectively. Whilst recognising the need for additional labour for the harvest, the Government was not, at this time, willing to send soldiers to do this work, but relied upon men volunteering or on farmers requesting that their sons or workers be given furlough for harvest work.

Although farmers applied to the Employment Exchange for soldier labour they were responsible for meeting the man on his arrival at the local railway station and for paying him the going rate for the work. From the Army's point of view the scheme had the advantage that they did not have the cost of the man's wages and keep at a time when he was not needed for official duties. In October 1915 the scheme was extended to cover the winter period, and in January 1916 the Army decided that soldiers who were convalescing at depots or hospitals could be temporarily employed on agricultural work in the area where they were located.[4]

The Army Council had originally stated in July 1915 that 'only men accustomed to farm work will be sent'[5] and for the autumn and winter cultivation period that 'only men accustomed to work with farm horses will be sent'.[6] However, restrictions were imposed and men who were armed, being trained with arms or preparing to go overseas could not be released for agricultural duties. This meant that the soldiers undertaking farm work did not always have relevant experience. There was apprehension amongst farmers that the soldiers would not be suitable for farm work and that employing them may mean they would be unable to retain their permanent employees. This often meant that farmers did not apply for soldier labour.[7]

Payments to soldiers

As with all circumstances where soldiers were used for civilian work it was the responsibility of the civilian employer to cover the cost of the employment. The rate of pay for the 1915 harvest varied according to the part of the country where the soldier was employed.

Area	10 hour day without lodging	10 hour day with lodging	Overtime per hour
East Anglia, East and West Ridings of Yorkshire[8]	6s	4s 6d	6d
Other areas in England and Wales[9]	5s	3s 6d	5d
Scotland[10]	5s 6d	4s	6d
Ireland[11]	4s	2s 6d	4d

Table 3: Rates of Agricultural Pay for 1915 Harvest

Similar arrangements were made to provide soldiers for the autumn and winter cultivation in 1915 in England, Wales and Scotland with reduced rates of pay.[12] A further supply of soldier labour for agriculture was approved on 12 January 1916 when it was agreed that soldiers who were convalescing from injury or illness could be used for civilian work.[13]

Farmers complained that in many cases the rates of pay meant that soldiers were receiving as much as skilled civilian farm workers although many were only undertaking unskilled tasks. This was a disincentive to farmers who would have preferred to employ civilian labour if it were available. Soldiers who were married and living away from home were also entitled to separation allowances and this was another cause of discontent with both farmers and agricultural workers. In Monmouthshire, for example, a soldier with three children earned a wage of 25s a week with an additional separation allowance of 25s 6d a week. A civilian labourer in similar circumstances received a total of 28s a week in wages and allowances.[14] It was not until the summer of 1918 that separation allowances were stopped for soldiers who were living at home. Farmers also complained that the soldiers worked shorter hours than civilian workers and were provided with the clothing needed for their work. Paying the men also involved additional work for the farmer.

As the war progressed, the lack of civilian agricultural labour resulted in an increase in their rates of pay. It was not until 1917 that there was a serious attempt to tackle the problem of civilian and military rates of pay. The Food Production Department was formed in January 1917; their remit included the creation of a coherent scheme for the deployment of soldiers to agricultural work. To overcome the question of the difference in wages, it was decided that soldiers should be paid the civilian rate for the area in which they were employed, this being set by the local County War Agricultural Committee. One anomaly was that for harvest work the old scheme remained in place, with the War Office continuing to fix minimum rates.

When a soldier was employed on civilian work he was not available for military duties and his Army pay was deducted on those days that he was paid for farm work. An additional deduction of 3s 6d a day was taken from his farming wages and was paid directly to the Army, by the farmer, to be credited to their funds.[15] A similar attitude was taken with regard to soldiers injured whilst in a farmer's employment. In such cases the soldier had no claim to an Army pension but was dealt with under the Worker's Compensation Act. The farmer, as the employer, was responsible for insuring the soldier.

Where men were given agricultural furlough to work their own farms they were, in effect, paying themselves and the Army decided that in such cases no Army pay or allowances should be credited.[16]

Recruitment Tribunals

During 1915, farmers, in common with other employers throughout the country, were increasingly concerned about the loss of skilled workers and in the summer of that year the Government and Army Council agreed that recruiting officers should be discouraged from inducing skilled men to enlist. In reality this policy was easy to formulate but more difficult to enforce. As a result, in the autumn, the Army Council agreed to the formation of local tribunals to hear applications by employers against the enlistment of men essential to the war effort.

The tribunals played an even more important role after the Military Services Act, which introduced conscription, had passed through Parliament in January 1916. Although farmers were given exemption from conscription the same did not apply to their sons or employees. It was possible for a farmer to apply to the local tribunal for the exemption of a son or employee on the grounds that they were essential workers and, initially at least, most applications were approved. There were, however, wide variations in the way individual tribunals approved or rejected applications for exemption.

1916 – Army needs against agricultural needs

In 1916 the Army Council appeared to recognise the need for change in the arrangements for soldier labour in agriculture. By the spring of 1916 the agricultural industry had lost almost 25 per cent of its labour to the forces, and the Army was enlisting many more men in preparation for the forthcoming attack on the Somme. Food production was further hampered by the fact that the winter of 1915–1916 was one of the wettest and coldest for many years. Despite this, the Government was still unwilling to direct labour to agriculture and farmers were still losing their most able men to the armed forces.[17]

The Army Council introduced two changes on 25 January 1916. Firstly, it decided that soldiers allocated to farm work need not have previous agricultural experience, and secondly, it allowed farmers who lived near a military base to apply directly to the Commanding Office for labour for a period of up to six days. This change was seen as a way of allowing farmers to obtain military labour quickly when the weather was fine. However, the first change frequently resulted in inexperienced men being sent to farms and farmers would often return them as unsuitable.

On 24 May the Army Council issued another instruction that up to 10 per cent of trained men in home defence units, and all other men serving at home, could be sent for agricultural work. One restriction was that soldiers in home defence units could only be used as long as they could be brought back to their base within 24 hours. They also pointed out to Commanding Officers that they had no right to refuse to send eligible and willing men to work on the land.[18] As a result of this instruction Army officers were appointed in each county or district to liaise closely with a local civilian representative, nominated by the County War Agricultural committee and the local Employment Exchange.

In reality the Army Council failed to meet the demand from farmers for soldier labour. During June 1916, for example, applications were made for 13,391 soldiers to assist with farm work whereas the Army only supplied 3,795.[19] The Board of Agriculture protested to the War Office about the discrepancy between the numbers required and the numbers supplied. The War Office agreed to increase their allocation of men to 14,000 by the end of July. This was considered unsatisfactory and the matter was discussed at the Cabinet meeting on 1 August, when it was decided that more men were needed if the harvest was not to be lost. The War Office initially agreed to release a further 12,000–15,000 men but within a few days withdrew this offer only to reinstate it a few days later. Despite agreeing to this extra allocation, the War Office never matched the demand for soldiers to work on the land during 1916. The was due to administrative problems between the War Office and the Board of Agriculture, the reluctance of the Army to release men, and the demand by farmers for specific men. In the period 12 August to 3 October 1916 the Army supplied a total of 16,690 men for agricultural work, less than 60 per cent of the 28,805 requested by farmers. Significantly, almost half of the men (7,679) released by the Army had been specifically requested by name, being either farmers' sons or former employees. The War Office reported that almost 1,500 of the men sent for agricultural work during the summer of 1916 were so bad that farmers refused to keep them.

Government Intervention

It was David Lloyd George's appointment as Prime Minister, in December 1916, that brought about a change in Government policy on food production. Powers taken under the Defence of the Realm Act allowed the Government to decide upon land use and which crops were grown. To implement this policy small Executive Committees were formed by each of the County War Agricultural Committees.

The local committees, most of which had been established by the end of January 1917, had a maximum of seven members, farmers and landowners or agents, appointed partly by the County Council and partly by the Board of Agriculture.

> The powers vested in the Committees were drastic. Where grass-land could be more profitably used in the national interest as arable, they were empowered to require it to be broken up, or to enter and plough it up themselves. Notices were to be served on occupiers specifying the grass fields to be ploughed, or the acts of cultivation to be executed, which the Committees considered necessary for the increase of food production.[20]

Farmers had no right of appeal and could, if they failed to comply with the instructions, be fined or even imprisoned.

The need to bring more land into production required an increased number of farm workers. The War Office, however, was at the same time calling for the enlistment of a further 30,000 farm labourers into the Army. Due to these conflicting requirements the War Cabinet, meeting on 23 January 1917, discussed the possibility of soldiers from the Home Defence forces being used for service overseas, but these men were not fit enough for front line duties.

Formation of Agricultural Companies

If the Army was to get its extra 30,000 farm labourers, fit young men, then it would have to provide replacements to work in agriculture. The War Office solution was to make use of men of low medical categories, already serving in the home forces, and created the Agricultural Companies.[21]

These companies were to be commanded by a captain or major, supported by two subalterns and two NCOs and have a strength of 250 other ranks, including men for clerical duties to deal with the applications for labour. The initial companies were formed from the soldiers already being employed by the Board of Agriculture. The Army was eager to ensure that the men placed in these companies would be soldiers surplus to their immediate needs, and specifically excluded men who were serving in home defence units and those enrolled as Army Reserve Munition workers.

Ernle's view is that these men were 'unaccustomed to Agricultural work, and physically unfitted for service in the Army'.[22] Whilst it is certainly true that the majority had little or no agricultural experience, the fact that they were unfit for overseas service should not be confused with fitness to serve in the Army. These men were generally in medical categories C(ii) or C(iii) and whilst the classification C(iii) was intended for sedentary roles such as clerks or orderlies, C(ii) was for men who were fit to serve in home service labour units. Additionally, as was found in other labour units later in the war, the physical condition of many men improved as a result of their new lifestyle.

The original intention was to provide 11,500 men in 46 agricultural companies. By July 1917 only 8,159 men were serving in agricultural companies, although a month later, at the start of the harvest, this had risen to 12,722.[23] One reason for the delay appears to be that companies could not be formed until there were officers to command them and men could not be allocated to the companies until they were formed. 138 officers were required but the vast majority of these could not be taken from the existing home service units, so instructions were issued that the officers should be obtained, if possible, from local retired officers.[24] Men selected to serve in the agricultural companies were transferred to the depot of the regiment at which the company was to be stationed.

By the beginning of March 1917 the first of the Agricultural Company men were working, but in order to meet the demands for spring ploughing some 12,500 men of the home defence forces were sent on temporary 'Agricultural furlough' until the end of April 1917. However, it was found that less than 3,000 of these men could plough.[25] The ploughing season was in danger of becoming a complete failure, so on 12 March all skilled ploughmen, some 18,000 men serving in Britain, were ordered to return to their depots, and sent on Agricultural furlough. These skilled ploughmen were, in the main, Category A men and fit for service in front line units. To meet military needs these men were recalled to active service in May, before ploughing had been completed, but at the same time the 'Agricultural furlough' for the remaining men was extended until 25 July.[26]

The system of providing soldiers for agricultural duties was different in Scotland, where in January 1917, the National Service Department (Scotland) (Agricultural Section) was established. It was 'charged with the duty of ascertaining definitely the exact nature and amount of Labour necessary to enable Agriculturalists to comply with the demands made on them by the Board of Agriculture'.[27]

A distribution centre was established at Tollcross School, Edinburgh, where soldiers were sent, classified as skilled ploughmen, horsemen, general farm workers, lambing shepherds, stallion leaders, cattlemen, milkers and dairymen, orramen and farm labourers, and between January and July 1917 some 12,000 soldiers passed through this centre on their way to agricultural work.

The thorny question of agricultural workers being enlisted had arisen again during April 1917 when a deputation from the War Agricultural Committees met with the Prime Minister. As a result the Army Council agreed with the Board of

Agriculture and the War Agricultural Committees that in England and Wales the number of men taken from agriculture would not exceed the 30,000 that had already been agreed by the Cabinet. In addition, in the case of men employed full time on farm work, no man with a current exemption would be conscripted, nor would any man below category A unless agreed by the local agricultural committee.[28]

As early as April 1917 it was estimated that for a successful 1918 harvest an additional 3,000,000 acres of land would need to be brought into production. This would require about 80,000 more soldiers. By June 1917 the Cabinet had agreed that the country could manage with an additional 2,500,000 acres and that the number of soldiers could be reduced to 50,000, half of whom would be skilled workers. The plan was that soldiers would be released at the rate of 5,000 a week starting 7 July 1917. If this timetable was followed all 50,000 would be released by early September. Once again there was conflict between the need for more men in France and the supply of soldiers for British agriculture, and by December 1917 the number of men released for agricultural work was less than 35,000.

Agricultural Companies become part of the Labour Corps

On 22 February 1917 a Royal Warrant was published establishing the creation of the Labour Corps.[29] The Army Council published the details of this new Corps on 13 April 1917 although no mention was made of agricultural companies.[30] However, in June the Army Council, probably in an attempt to meet the requirements of the War Cabinet, created the Labour Corps' Agricultural Companies.[31] Initially these were formed from the existing Regimental Agricultural Companies. They were allocated company numbers 403–449 inclusively.

When the men were transferred to these new agricultural companies they ceased being a member of their previous regiment and became a member of the Labour Corps. As was the policy at the time, soldiers on transfer to another regiment were issued with a new regimental number. Unfortunately, German bombing in 1940 destroyed company records. However, research suggests that the men transferred to these Labour Corps Agricultural Companies in June 1917 were allocated numbers in the range 230,000–290,000.

The Army used the creation of these new companies as an opportunity to make some changes to their composition. Each company headquarters consisted of two officers, a CSM, a sergeant and ten privates, including one batman, one storeman, one orderly, one cook, two sanitary men and four clerks (privates or females). If possible one clerk should have knowledge of accounts. The company still had 250 private soldiers (labourers).

Although each company had a headquarters, this was little more than an administrative office. The men in the company would either live at home or on the farm where they worked, only dealing with the company HQ over issues of pay or leave. The Officer Commanding an agricultural company could have men spread over hundreds of square miles and have little or no contact with them.

The Army Council stated that the soldiers should, as far as possible, consist of men who had knowledge of agriculture. Any man who was unsuitable for work on the land was withdrawn and posted to the Labour Corps Centre once a suitable replacement had been found. Should a man's medical classification improve to category A he would be posted to a reserve infantry battalion. Recruits to the Labour Corps, up to medical category B(ii), with relevant experience would be posted to the agricultural companies. The Army was at last recognising that the agricultural companies needed men with agricultural skills and the physical capability to undertake the work.

Further agricultural companies were created in October 1917.[32] Initially formed using men from home service units who were skilled ploughmen, had agricultural experience or were already working as farm labourers. As the demand for more men increased, the likelihood of finding sufficient experienced agricultural workers reduced. Later ACI 1545 introduced a system whereby men who had worked on the harvest could be tested to determine if they possessed enough skill for them to be transferred to agricultural companies.[33] ACI 1395 stated that men being posted to agricultural companies should, where possible, be sent to a part of the country where they worked in civil life.[34]

The War Cabinet was concerned about the poor physical condition of many of the men serving in the agricultural companies. At a Cabinet meeting in November 1917, Sir Auckland Geddes referred to the 'large number of men technically in the Army, and wearing uniform, who were of no military value, and were not part of the Home Defence Force'.[35] He suggested that recruiting for agricultural companies should cease and that they should be gradually disbanded. Lord Derby said that maintaining agricultural companies was of great importance to the production of food and expressed a concern that if these men were set free they would 'leave agriculture and enter munitions work where the wages were so much higher and conditions so much easier'.[36] Lord Derby's view prevailed, and the number of agricultural companies was to increase throughout 1918.

Recognising that there could be times when the men in a particular company were not needed on farms, permission was given for them to be temporarily used for other military work within the command, provided they were available for immediate recall by the War Agricultural Executive Committees. These men were prohibited from being sent to work in munition firms. In theory, a structure was in place that could provide a permanent supply of military labour with the skills needed to complete the vast majority of tasks required of them.

1918 – Manpower Shortages

During the early part of 1918 the Army instructed that a survey of the men in agricultural companies be carried out since there were concerns that they were being employed on non-agricultural work. The results in Scotland showed that about 10 per cent of the men were employed in what the War Office considered non-agricultural work. The Officer Commanding an agricultural company would be under considerable pressure to supply labour in his area and there must have been many occasions when it was easier and perhaps expedient to agree to a request for what may not have been strictly agricultural work. However it is difficult to understand how men could have been allowed to work in road making, as carpenters, in car work and as chauffeurs, all of which appeared in the War Office survey.

The results of the survey caused some concern, particularly as it came at a time, following the German Offensive of March 1918, when the Army required more men for overseas service. There is evidence that soldiers employed on agricultural work were being withdrawn for other duties.

Although fertilizer production does not appear in the list of agricultural work it was the employment of agricultural company soldiers by a fertilizer company that resulted in the secretary of the company writing to the Secretary of State for Scotland on 22 May 1918 complaining about 'a serious grievance connected with the withdrawal from our works of soldiers released from the colours in order to increase and expedite the output of Fertilizers'. In his letter he stated: 'We were loaned eleven of these men by the Commanding Officer of an Agricultural company' and that it was impossible to replace the men withdrawn.[37] On 26 June, the Ministry of National Service made a request to the War Office that men in agricultural companies who were at present mixing fertilizers or making or repairing machinery, should not be withdrawn on the grounds that it would seriously interfere with the production of food in Scotland. The War Office turned down the request explaining that it had been agreed that men in agricultural companies should only be employed directly on agricultural work.

On 30 May 1918 the secretaries of the Black Isle, Easter Ross and Tain Farmers Clubs all wrote to the Secretary of State for Scotland expressing concern that 70 men from the agricultural company at Inverness, who were waiting to be sent to farms, were being recalled for other duties.

On the 18 June 1918 the Army felt it necessary to tell the General Officers Commanding the home service units to carry out medical inspection of all men in agricultural companies whose medical category had not recently been ascertained. This raised concerns that more men were to be withdrawn, although the Army did say:

> It is not intended to withdraw any men from their employment at present, until further instructions are issued, even if raised to category 'A', and this should be made perfectly clear to farmers and to agricultural committees.[38]

At the same time the Board of Agriculture Scotland told the Under Secretary of State for Scotland that upwards of 15,000 extra men were needed for the 1918 harvest. This figure included replacements for the 5,500 already withdrawn from agricultural companies for other military duties.

Whilst they hoped for some 5,000 workers from the Women's Land Army, men discharged from service, War Agriculture Volunteers, schoolboys and Irish labourers, this still left a deficit of about 10,000 men. Eight days later the Secretary of State was informed by the Ministry of National Service that the War Office had said there was very little hope of supplying soldiers for harvest work in England and Scotland because of the military situation.

Evidence from service records suggests that during 1918 men returning from overseas, whose medical condition meant they were likely to be demobbed, were almost certainly transferred to one of the Labour Corps agricultural companies. At times this was for only a few weeks, whether they had any agricultural experience or not.

In January 1919 the Army allowed any agriculturist serving in Britain to be attached to one of the agricultural companies, pending his demobilisation. This resulted in over 12,000 men being sent to their former employers on agricultural furlough.

During 1919 demobilisation started to have an affect on the number of soldiers employed in agriculture. By April 1919, 54,000 agricultural workers had been released but there were still almost 25,000 men working in agricultural companies. When the suggestion was put forward that the agricultural companies should be disbanded, the Government was greeted with protests from farmers who maintained it would be impossible to replace them. On 16 April the Leader of the House of Commons declared that it was impossible to keep men in the Army if they were not required for military reasons. By early May, bad weather had caused a late sowing season and the Government had to change its policy, allowing 20 per cent of the members of agricultural companies to be temporarily retained. 'It was ironical that farmers, who had greeted the formation of the agricultural companies with derision, should prove in the end such enthusiastic advocates of their retention.'[39]

Month	1917	1918	1919
January		46,284	73,980
February		46,403	63,091
March		52,326	41,035
April		58,432	24,224
May		61,537	19,816
June		64,527	17,349
July	8,159	65,840	7,342
August	12,722	66,882	4,608
September	12,472	68,191	3,001
October	13,101	69,057	325
November	15,907	75,087	
December	31,034	74,855	

Table 4: Strength of the Agricultural Companies 1917–19

Local concerns

There was official recognition of the importance of the role of the agricultural companies in food production during the war:

> It would have been utterly impossible in 1917 to carry on farming at all without a large supply of soldier labour, and this position is now very much emphasised by the additional ground which has been ploughed up.[40]

At local level, however, there were numerous complaints from farmers that the men sent to them from the agricultural companies were of little or no use. A frequent complaint concerned the poor physical condition of the men. Farmers grumbled that they were being asked to keep infirmaries.[41]

In Herefordshire, among the soldiers sent to work on the land, were men who in civilian life had worked as a lift attendant, bricklayers' labourers, ships' painters, brass polishers, needle makers, chocolate makers, cabmen, ladies' tailors, and musical conductors. From the Loughborough area of Leicestershire it was bitterly observed that very few soldier labourers had any idea how to work with horses 'and it is an exception to get a soldier who can milk. They are poor substitutes for the skilled men taken from the land'. In that district the value of work performed was calculated in the ratio of three soldiers to two ordinary agricultural labourers.[42]

There were also fears in some rural areas that there would be an increase of radical social views and ideas brought in by these men. At Drayton St Leonard in Oxfordshire three men stationed there in the spring of 1918 were classed as 'Socialists from the towns', who were stirring up 'the muddy water and [giving] the people courage to protest against, e.g. bad housing conditions'.[43] There is also evidence that some members of the agricultural companies illegally maintained their contributions to the Farmworkers Union.[44]

The soldiers did not always welcome having to work as agricultural labourers. In Holland, Lincolnshire one group of men refused to stay in the sheds that were offered to them as sleeping quarters, and in Caernarvonshire a farmer was frankly informed by one unwilling recruit that he would 'rather be in France than on a farm'.[45]

Dangerous work

Despite agricultural companies being made up of men of low physical condition they were asked to carry out some of the most physically demanding and dangerous work undertaken by the Labour Corps in Britain. At the time agriculture was not only a labour intensive industry but also one in which accidental injury or deaths were quite common. The following two cases are examples of soldiers who met their deaths whilst members of agricultural companies.

241273 Private Frederick Francis was a 32-year-old single man, a member of 425 Agricultural Company, which had its HQ in Guildford, Surrey. His home, however, was Tivetshall St Margaret, Norfolk and he was employed at a local farm. On 20 September 1917 he met with an accident at Tasburgh where his employer, Mr Archie Wright, Lodge Farm, Tivetshall, had sent him. The cart horse he was driving took fright at a traction engine and ran away, throwing Francis off the tumbril. He was found unconscious at the side of the road and died from injuries to his lungs and liver whilst being taken to hospital.[46]

528724 Private Waugh served in the 3rd Battalion Scottish Rifles where he lost a finger on his right hand and was transferred to the Labour Corps on 31 July 1917. Private Waugh was a gardener by trade and came from Thornhill, Dumfries. He was a member of 460 Agricultural Company whose HQ was at Ayr. On 12 January 1918 he started work at Home Farm, Crawfordton, Dumfries and on 19 February he was one of three men felling an ash tree at the farm. In his evidence to the Procurator Fiscal, James Brown, the Factor for the Estate, described how the three men had cut about half way through the tree when it fell backwards. 'It struck him right up his back as he was running. He was pinned to ground face downward, hardly any bleeding. He was not alive. He never moved. It was not more than four seconds from the time I spoke to them till he was lying quite dead.'[47]

Ploughmen and Tractor Drivers

There were some specialist skills, like that of ploughmen and tractor drivers, that were not to be found amongst the majority of the men in the agricultural companies. Even though soldiers with these specialist skills were required by the agricultural committees there is evidence that they were being withdrawn for military service elsewhere. During the spring of 1917 the Lancashire Executive Committee had the services of 1,301 Army ploughmen but these were withdrawn in May.

Due to the shortage of ploughmen, in the autumn of 1917 the Army gave three months agricultural furlough to some 1,500 skilled ploughmen serving in France.[48] There is, however, doubt about the exact number of men who actually returned to Britain.

In September 1917 the first training school for horse-ploughmen was set up by the Food Production Department. Eventually some 30 of these schools were established and over 4,000 soldiers trained.[49] During training the men were paid 21s a week but this rose to the local rate for ploughmen once qualified.

On 29 January 1917, 898 MT Company, ASC was established at Mossley Hill, Liverpool with the primary purpose of receiving motor tractors that the Government had purchased from America. As drivers were needed for these tractors the Food Production Department set up schools to train drivers. Men with knowledge of petrol engines or experience of driving motor vehicles spent two weeks at the training school and a further two weeks on a farm, working alongside an experienced tractor driver. These schools trained 4,093 men as tractor drivers and a further 200 in the use of steam-ploughs and threshing machines.[50] As far as can be ascertained, the tractor drivers and steam-tackle operators were part of the ASC and never transferred to the Labour Corps.[51]

The Forage Department

The Forage Department's role was to bale hay and straw for use by the Army in Britain and overseas. As the Army increased in size during 1914 and 1915 so did the problem of supplying it, both at home and overseas, with forage and other farm produce. In France local supplies of hay soon became inadequate to meet the Army's needs and supplies had to be sent from Britain.

In November 1915 the decision was made to form a Forage Department within the ASC. This Department had its HQ at 64 Whitehall Court, London SW1, and was made up of eight companies, six stationed in England and one each in Scotland and Ireland.[52]

Records show that in June 1916 recruits medically classified as C(ii), and having some agricultural knowledge, were selected to work in the Forage Department.[53] By September 1916 more manpower was urgently required and the Army Council decided to increase the Forage Department by some 2,500 men.[54] The men, all of whom were medical category B(ii), were initially taken from the Infantry Works Battalions and then from other units, with the exception of the RAMC.

The Forage Companies were to remain part of the ASC, until disbanded on 1 July 1920. However, from 12 June 1917, only replacements for Labour Corps men attached to the Forage Companies were allowed.[55]

The Forage Companies worked in teams of twelve and would move from farm to farm baling the hay and straw that had been purchased by the Army, and transporting it to railway depots. Their work was physically demanding, repetitive and had to be carried out in all weathers. On a good day a team could bale as much as ten tons of hay. Despite the harsh conditions and hard work the men in these companies were amongst those of the lowest physical category.

Working alongside the Forage Department was a Women's Forage Corps, their numbers reaching a peak of 6,000. These women, who wore khaki and green uniforms with ASC badges and the shoulder title 'FC', were used for clerical duties and the whole range of tasks involved in gathering forage. It has been suggested that in the latter stages of the war women were undertaking most of the duties of the Forage Department.[56]

1   Horn, P., *Rural Life in England in the First World War* p.86
2   ibid, p.90
3   NA WO 293/3 ACI 84 10 Jul 1915
4   ibid WO 293/4 ACI 78 12 Jan 1916
5   ibid WO 293/3 ACI 84
6   ibid WO 293/3 ACI 1345 14 Oct 1915
7   Horn, p.94
8   NA WO 293/3 ACI 84
9   ibid
10 ibid WO 293/3 ACI 227 26 July 1915.
11 ibid WO 293/3 ACI 104 11 August 1915.
12 In England and Wales the men were paid 4s a day (2s 6d without board), in Scotland 4s 6d or 3s.
13 NA WO 293/4 12 January 1916.
14 Horn, p.98
15 NA WO 293/5 ACI 1597 15 August 1916
16 ibid WO 293/5 ACI 1973 16 October 1916.
17 Middleton, T. H., *Food Production in the War* p.141
18 NA WO 293/4 ACI 1056 24 May 1916. Although these instructions potentially increased the number of soldiers available for agricultural work the army insisted that soldiers in Home Defence units could only be used as long as they could be brought back to their base within 24 hours. In addition they would not allow men being trained or preparing to go abroad to be used. Even more importantly they would not allow men who had recently been called up to be used for agricultural work as 'as it is presumed that if he had been indispensable his case would have come before the local tribunal with the view to exemption being granted.'
19 NA CAB 42/17/1 Cabinet meeting, 1 August 1916
20 Ernle, *English Farming Past and Present* p.403
21 NA WO 293/6 ACI 259 13 February 1917
22 Ernle, p.125
23 NA WO 73/106
24 ibid WO 293/6 ACI 259
25 Ernle, p.126

26 NA WO 293/6 ACI 801 17 May 1917
27 ibid NATS 1/640
28 ibid WO 293/6 ACI 731 5 May 1917
29 ibid WO 123/59 Army Order 85 22 February 1917.
30 ibid WO 293/6 ACI 611 13 April 1917
31 ibid WO 293/6 ACI 924 12 June 1917
32 ibid WO 293/7 ACI 1395 10 Sep 1917
33 ibid WO 293/7 ACI 1545 12 Oct 1917
34 ibid WO 293/7 ACI 1395 10 Sep 1917
35 ibid CAB 23/4/287 War Cabinet 29 November 1917.
36 ibid
37 ibid NATS 1/640
38 ibid
39 Horn, p.110
40 Report of the Board of Agriculture and Fisheries on Wages and Conditions of Employment in Agriculture, 1919, Vol. IX, 236.
41 Ernle, p.125
42 ibid, pp48–49
43 Horn, p.105
44 Mansfield in *Norfolk & Suffolk in the Great War* Ed. Gerald Gliddon p.79
45 Horn p.105
46 NA WO 363/F969
47 ibid WO 363/W528
48 Dewey, P. E., *British Agriculture in the First World War* p.116. At the Cabinet meeting of 12 December 1917 the number was given as 1,000 men and the time as 2 months NA CAB 23/4, 296
49 According to Dewey p.116 the men received two weeks training whereas Horn p.104 says it was of three-week duration.
50 Montgomery, *Labour Supply*, pp.35–40
51 When additional Agricultural Companies were formed in September 1917 from men currently undertaking agricultural duties but not in Agricultural Companies the men of 898 Company ASC were specifically excluded. (NA WO 293/7 ACI 1395)
52 Young, M., *Army Service Corps 1902–1918* pp.83–4
53 NA WO 293/4 ACI 1305 30 June 1916
54 ibid WO 293/5 ACI 1812 17 Sep 1916
55 ibid WO 293/6 ACI 924 12 June 1917
56 Horn, p.111

Section Two: France and Flanders

1914–15 LOCALLY CONTROLLED LABOUR

On 7 August 1914, three days after the declaration of war, the first British troops arrived in France. These men, members of the Army Service Corps, were tasked with setting up a supply base at the Ports of Entry at Havre, Rouen and St Valery. The commandants of the bases were also to establish three rest camps so that when the infantry started to arrive on 14 August the infrastructure was in place to receive them.

Civilian Labour

Setting up these supply bases and camps relied not on troops brought from Britain, but in line with Army policy, on French civilians.

The policy adopted in 1914 was clearly outlined in the 1909 Field Service regulations, which stated:

> Civilian labour will be hired or requisitioned for unloading and stacking supplies wherever possible. Military labour will not be used for this service if civilian labour is available, or unless military labour can be provided without interfering with the fighting efficiency of the troops.[1]

As early as 1912 the French had agreed to provide civilian labour to assist the British Army's supply routes in the event of a war in Europe. It was, for example, French civilians that set up the tented camp at Rouen prior to the arrival of the BEF.[2]

Local French and Belgian labour was employed at the Ports and Depots. In May 1915 the Army Ordnance Department (AOD) Depot at Havre was employing 6 Belgian men and 50, presumably French, women. They were also employed to assist the Royal Engineers (RE) in the repair of roads and preparation of defences. One of the best examples of this is the work of Temporary Captain L. Delphin, RE, the first officer to be awarded an honour for labour duties. As the citation for his Military Cross states:

> For conspicuous energy in raising, practically unaided, in the district of Bethune, a labour corps from the refugee and local population. He carried out valuable work

with this corps in the preparation of defences, and worked with it for many weeks under shell fire during the spring and summer of 1915.[3]

Whilst the policy of employing local labour had proved successful in places like India and Africa where native labour was both cheap and plentiful, there were some at the War Office who recognised that the same would not be true for a war in Europe because the local population was liable to be called up for military service.

In September 1915 the British GHQ in France, concerned that French men were being withdrawn to serve in their Army, wrote to the War Office suggesting that Belgian refugees living in Britain be recruited for roadwork in France. GHQ had the support of the Belgian Legation for this plan. The men were allocated to the RE and employed by the director of works.

Army Service Corps

On 4 August 1914 it was announced that two Army Service Corps Labour Companies were to be established, each of 536 all ranks commanded by a sub-altern, to work in the supply depots at the three French ports used by the BEF. Recognising the need for experience of moving supplies, 36 civilian foremen and 60 gangers were enlisted to be the sergeants and corporals in these companies.[4]

Number 1 Labour Company ASC was formed on 24 August, and under the command of Captain R. W. Day, arrived in France two days later for service at Havre and Valery.[5] Number 2 Labour Company, commanded by Captain N. P. R. Copeland, was stationed at Rouen and arriving on 31 August. According to the war dairy of the Inspector General Communications (IGC) the establishment of these first two companies was different from the later ASC Labour Companies in that in addition to ASC soldiers they included 232 and 130 CWG respectively.[6] Although the diary does not specify what CWG stands for it appears likely that they were civilian workers. One other ASC company, 5 ASC Labour Company, which arrived on 9 October 1914, under the command of Lt J. Dixon, comprised 212 men and a shipwright, presumably another civilian. By April 1915 a further seven ASC companies were serving in France, including 6 Labour Company who worked specifically for the AOD.[7]

The number of ASC Labour Companies continued to increase during 1915, until there were 29 stationed in France, one in Britain and three in Salonika. The last company to be formed, on 31 January 1916, was 32 Labour Company ASC. Four of the companies were disbanded in March/April 1917, the remainder transferring to the Labour Corps in June 1917.

The Labour companies helped ensure the movement of supplies from the docks to the front, but the organisation for unloading the ships was outside their control. This was the responsibility of the Naval Transport Officer who relied on French civilian labour to undertake the task. Unfortunately, the irregular supply of civilian labour meant ships could not always be turned around as quickly as they would have liked.

Lack of communication between the Navy and the Army led to further problems. In November 1914 the Navy ordered ships to divert to Boulogne but failed to inform the Army of this change with the result that the stores were offloaded and remained at the dock. The Inspector General Communications informed the Navy that in future ships were only to be diverted with his agreement.[8]

To solve the problem of irregular civilian labour the Navy turned to the Army, who, in December 1914, recruited stevedores and dock labourers and formed two ASC companies for service at the French ports. The two ASC (Naval Labour) Companies were supplemented by fatigue parties from the troops at the base, and in theory, should have solved the problem of a quick turnaround of ships. However, problems often arose over the use of these Companies as

> ... they were under the control of the local ASC officers and Army staffs, and the Naval Transport Officers found great difficulty in obtaining the parties they required, whilst the personnel were frequently changed.[9]

To the fighting soldier these Labour companies were seen, at best, as having an easy life and, at worst, as shirkers. There was even a rumour that these men were civilians who were paid four times that of the man at the front and that they were 'a lot of hardy ruffians who used to be escorted to and from their work by a military escort to prevent them running amok in the town'.[10]

In 1914 requests for supplies, other than ammunition, food and forage, were made at divisional level and sent to the War Office. The supplies were packed so that on arrival in France they were unloaded directly onto divisional trains. Initially, French civilians were used to assist in this work and by the end of 1914 the British employed some 900 women and 300 men. As the strength of the Army increased a decision was made to establish depots in France where supplies could be stored before issue to units. Whilst this meant that supplies could be quickly distributed to wherever they were needed, it also resulted in a greater demand for sorters, packers and labourers. In January 1915 the IGC estimated that this would require a labour force of between 5,000 and 6,000.[11]

At the beginning of October 1915 it was decided that ASC Labour companies should be used to discharge RE materials from ships. As a result one company would be stationed at each of Boulogne, Havre and Rouen and two at Calais.

To fulfil all the tasks expected of the ASC at the ports, bases and depots a total of 38 companies would be required, but there were only 22 operating in France. On 8 November the War Office agreed to send two additional ASC Labour companies for every three divisions despatched overseas. In January 1916 they were still nine short of the estimated requirement.

British Civilian Labour

In addition to French and Belgian civilians, some British civilian workers were employed to support the Army in France. The part played by these British civilians is far from clear, with only the briefest reference to them in Army records. The IGC felt that there were some roles being undertaken by serving officers that could be undertaken by civilians and on 6 November 1914 the IGC asked the Secretary of State for 42 civilians to replace officers on the Lines of Communications (LoC).[12] On 9 May 1915 the War Office instructed that all British civilians employed by the

Army Ordnance Department should be returned to Britain and replaced by trained men, although no reason was given.[13]

Perhaps the most important use of British civilians was at Boulogne. As a port it had limited space and railway access. This soon led to congestion and difficulty in offloading ships. It was decided that the General Manager of the South Eastern and Chatham Railway Company, Mr F. H. Dent, should oversee the running of the port using both British and French labour. On 13 January 1915 he wrote to the IGC that mixing British and French contractors was a disadvantage and that he intended to operate the port using French and Belgian civil personnel.[14] This led to a period of correspondence between the IGC and Mr Dent over the Boulogne port. The War Office agreed, on 26 February 1915, that the S. E. & C. Railway Company should take over the whole working of the port so far as British traffic was concerned.[15] The company cleared new stacking areas, built additional railway sidings, erected new hangars, and even loaned seven of its small shunting engines for use at the port.

The system of contracting work at the port of Boulogne, to a civilian company, had its problems. The French authorities complained that the contractor was paying labourers at a higher rate than normally paid in France. There were also some concerns that commercial practices did not always match military needs. In June 1915, for example, GHQ wrote to the Director of Supplies (DOS) complaining that the tonnage of ammunition required at the front for a 24-hour period could not be supplied, and said that a further 400 men were required for this purpose. As a result the DOS immediately transferred an ASC company from Calais to Boulogne to supplement the contractor's labour. Because of these problems the idea of using a private contractor to run a port was not adopted for any of the other French ports and as Henniker, in the Official History, says:

> On further consideration, however, the conclusion was come to that it was inadvisable to entrust the work altogether to civilian management and labour. The work being done was quite different from the ordinary transit of goods through a port in peacetime. The supply trains for the front were loaded in detail in the dock area and the handling of ammunition in particular required technical knowledge, while the army services demanded more elaborate checking of stores off ship, into warehouses, and on to rail than is needed for commercial traffic merely in transit.[16]

Railway Companies

On arrival at the ports men and supplies were transported to depots and the front using the French and Belgium railway systems. On 15 August 1914 the 8th (Railway Company) RE landed at Havre to assist in railway maintenance.[17] Although this skilled company brought its own light tools it was expected to work alongside French civilian labour. More skilled labour was required and, on 26 September, the IGC requested that 10 Railway Company RE be sent to France, but this was rejected by the Secretary of State for War. It was thought the French had sufficient skilled railway workers and that Belgian, French and Italian civilians could provide the unskilled labour required.

As the months progressed civilian labour became scarce because of French conscription and it was decided to provide dedicated labour from the ASC. Captain A. H. Hartshorn was appointed OC of 1 Railway Labour Company ASC at Aldershot on 6 January 1915 and three days later the Company, consisting of three officers and 210 other ranks left for Havre. On arrival in France one section, of an NCO and 25 men, remained at Havre, the rest of the Company going to St Omer. Within a short time other sections were sent to Bailleul, Steenwerck, Caestre and Strazeele. The Company continued to grow throughout 1915 and by August had a strength of four officers and 505 men. In October 1915 2 Railway Labour Company was created. On 29 March 1916 the two companies were renumbered 33 and 34 Railway Labour Companies ASC and both placed under the command of Major Hartshorn. They continued in existence until June 1917.[18]

RE Companies

The role of the RE was to provide the buildings, workshops, roads and bridges needed to support the Army in France. Within the Lines of Communication Brigadier General A. M. Stuart, the Director Works, commanded them. Initially Stuart's staff comprised Colonel Hemming (Deputy Director), Colonel St John (Assistant Director) and 35 officers. Within a short time many of these officers were used to replace RE casualties in other RE units. By the end of August 1914, Stuart had at his disposal 20 and 29 Fortress Companies RE, each consisting of 3 officers and 100 men. Shortly afterwards 49 Fortress Company was placed under his command but almost immediately both 20 and 49 companies were transferred to the front to work under the Engineer Advisor at GHQ. Initially, French civilians provided unskilled labour, but after the German advance on Paris, this was withdrawn as the French mobilised their reserves. Stuart encountered problems owing to a lack of personnel, with officers, supervisory staff and labour being withdrawn for other duties.[19]

In February 1915, in an attempt to improve the situation Stuart divided the communications area into northern and southern works areas. Colonel Huskisson, from his HQ at Boulogne, controlled the northern area covering Calais to Etaples; Stuart, assisted by Colonel Hemming, controlled the southern area. Each area contained works districts, controlled by an Assistant Director of Works, which were located in Rouen, Calais, Boulogne, Etaples, Abbeville, Dieppe, Havre and Marseilles.

In March 1915 six Territorial RE Fortress Companies were sent to France and placed at Stuart's disposal but he still lacked the unskilled labour required.[20] On 3 August 1915 the War Office took the decision to form eight RE Labour Battalions from enlisted men with labouring experience. Labour Exchanges were asked to submit the names of suitable men to local recruiting offices who, after medical examination, passed their names to the Aldywch Labour Exchange, London which acted as the central agency. It was the Labour Exchange that identified experienced gangers or foremen who were to become the battalion warrant officers and NCOs. On arrival in France several men were found to be unfit for heavy labouring work.

The 5th Labour Battalion appears to have had particular problems whilst still in England:

> The officer appointed adjutant arrived at Southampton on 19 August. He located his men, 800 of them aged 35 to 50, at a recently pitched tented camp. They were in civilian clothes, had come from all over the country and, not knowing the gangers who had been included in their number, were totally leaderless. Apart from their tents, they had neither uniforms nor equipment; nor did they have any food. The adjutant managed to feed them with iron rations of bully beef and biscuits and began to attempt to get them in some sort of order. During the next couple of days the commanding officer and quartermaster arrived, and uniforms for the men were made available. More and more men also reported, until there were 1,200, 150 men over establishment. Luckily, the weather remained fine. On 25 August, nine other officers arrived, recently gazetted civil engineers, who had to be sent to obtain uniforms for themselves. Not until the following day did the battalion begin to receive its equipment, but it was a desperate race against time since it was due to embark for France on the afternoon of the 28th. Before this took place, many men had to be dragged out of public houses and guards placed on them. The battalion then spent two days at Le Havre, before facing a twenty-two-hour train journey to Belgium. Nevertheless, in a little over two weeks since its inception the battalion was carrying out its first tasks behind the Front, road repairs and constructing concrete machine-gun posts.[21]

The 1st Labour Battalion RE arrived at Havre on 22 August 1915 with four more battalions arriving over the next six days. The Director of Works wrote to the War Office on 3 September pointing out that eight battalions would be needed to undertake defences and works, and requested a further eight be formed for work on the roads.[22] His letter pointed out that he was unable to find any additional French or Belgian labour and that those currently employed could be withdrawn at any time by their Governments.[23] He suggested that it might eventually be necessary to increase the number of battalions required for roadwork to one for each corps. The War Office agreed to the formation of a total of twelve RE Labour Battalions, eleven of which were to serve in France and one in Salonika.

A further request to extend the number of RE Labour Battalions in France to sixteen was sent to the War Office on 30 October. Support for more men came from the Commander-in-Chief, who, on 27 November, informed both the War Office and Lord Derby that although sixteen RE Labour Battalions had been promised, only eleven had been sent to France. The five 'missing' battalions were vital for work on the lines of communications and he would be willing to accept Russian, Italian or Belgian labour. To support his case he pointed out that a lack of labour meant the British Army was unable to use all berths available for offloading ships. The War Office, replying on 19 December 1915, rejected the request because all labour was employed extending munition factories. They added additional battalions would be formed once personnel became available.[24]

In September 1915, 600 Belgian workers were recruited in England and allocated to the Director of Works to provide unskilled labour. These men could be used on the roads, for defences and in workshops that were outside the zone of shellfire.

Pioneer Battalions

A further attempt to overcome the shortage of unskilled labour was made in December 1914 when the War Office informed the General Officers Commanding the divisions, that each of the divisions of Kitchener's New Army would have a pioneer battalion. The pioneer battalions were to be, first and foremost, fighting infantry but with specific skills in road making, entrenching and demolition.

In January 1915 the War Office issued further details of the duties expected of the pioneer battalions. These included technical work on railway embankments, felling trees, bridging and constructing wire obstacles. It was intended that each battalion would have a RE officer and NCO attached to them to oversee the technical side of their work although in reality this did not happen. The role of the pioneer battalions was to provide 'organized and intelligent labour' for the Royal Engineers but it was stressed that they would remain fighting infantry.

It was left to the commanders of the New Army divisions to ascertain which unit would be best suited to form their pioneer battalion. Men in the designated pioneer battalions who did not possess the necessary skills could be transferred to a different battalion.[25] If a commander could not identify a suitable battalion in his division it was possible to arrange for one to be transferred from another division where there was spare capacity. Officers for these New Army pioneer battalions were found from serving officers with field engineering experience and civilians with an engineering background. Other ranks in pioneer battalions received 2d a day more than the corresponding rank in an infantry unit, and wore a distinctive badge to indicate they were pioneers.

In early 1915 it was a relatively easy task for commanders to identify pioneer battalions for the first three of Kitchener's New Armies since they were still being created and preparing to go overseas. By April 1915, pioneer battalions were on the establishment of each of the 9th to 26th Divisions, with the exception of the 10th (Irish) Division.[26] All of these divisions, with the exception of the 9th (Scottish) Division had battalions nominated from within their existing formation.[27]

The first four pioneer battalions, with the 9th, 12th, 14th and 18th Divisions, arrived in France in May 1915. The next four with the 15th, 17th, 19th and 20th Divisions arrived in July, and six more with the 21st to 26th Divisions in August. Finally, the 11th Battalion Hampshire Regiment, the pioneer battalion with the 16th (Irish) Division, arrived in France in December 1915.[28] Although the pioneer battalions did not have an RE officer attached to them, much of their work was carried out on the instructions of the divisions' Commander of RE. When in the trenches they were used to improve the trenches, ensure the light railway system was in good working order and, following an attack, repair and strengthen captured trenches. When the division was pulled back for a rest the pioneers were used for a wide variety of tasks including road and rail repairs, improving billets and even assisting local farmers with their harvests.

GHQ in France was slower to adopt the idea of pioneer battalions despite pressure from the War Office, and it was not until July 1915 that they decided to provide each Regular and Territorial division with a pioneer battalion. GHQ looked initially to the Territorial Force already in France as a source for these battalions. However this was not regarded favourably by many of the territorial battalions or their corps commanders. IV Corps, for example, pointed out to Second Army HQ that neither of the two Territorial battalions in the 6th Division, being made up of clerks and shopkeepers from London, would make suitable pioneers[29]. Using the Territorial battalions as pioneers in Regular divisions would mean they were separated from their Territorial division. To overcome this GHQ decided that territorial battalions considered as suitable for conversion to a pioneer battalion would serve with the territorial divisions and that new Army battalions would be used to support the regular Army divisions. By the end of 1915 both the New Army and Territorial divisions had pioneer battalions although the same was not true for most of the regular Army divisions.

There were, however, to be some exceptions to the rule that Territorial battalions would only serve with the territorial divisions. One example is the 4th Battalion Coldstream Guards, which was formed specifically as a Territorial Pioneer Battalion at Windsor Castle on 17 July 1915, and by 15 August had joined the Guards Division in France.

The 1st/5th Battalion Cheshire Regiment had been a front line unit since February 1915 but having established a good reputation for digging work, became 5th Division's pioneer battalion in November 1915.[30] The conversion to a pioneer battalion was not always welcomed; as Captain Thomas Heald of the 1st/5th Cheshires put it, 'we did not join to dig for others'[31] and as George McGovern, a former officer of the Battalion said, 'They will cease to exist as a fighting unit and become the scavengers of the brigade.'[32]

For one territorial battalion, the 1st/5th Black Watch, the move was from pioneer to infantry battalion. The battalion had arrived in France on 2 November 1914, being transferred to 24th Brigade, 8th Division eleven days later. They were converted to the Division's pioneer battalion on 8 October 1915. In January 1916 they were transferred to the 51st Highland Division, their parent division. The 51st Division already had a pioneer battalion, the 1st/8th Royal Scots, so the Black Watch Battalion reconverted to an infantry battalion.[33]

The 17th Northumberland Fusiliers had even more changes to their role. Formed at Hull in September 1914 from employees of the North Eastern Railway Company it had, in the words of the company magazine a 'signal honour in being selected as a "pioneer" battalion' in January 1915.[34] In June it became the pioneer battalion of the 32nd Division. It remained with the 32nd until 19 October 1916 when it was converted into railway construction troops and attached to GHQ.[35] On 2 September 1917 it rejoined the 32nd Division as the pioneer battalion. Within ten weeks it had returned to GHQ as railway construction troops where it remained until 31 May 1918 when it joined the 52nd Division as its pioneer battalion.

Additional Military Labour

Both the RE and ASC could call upon infantry soldiers who were behind the lines to provide unskilled labour when it was needed. This meant that frequently, when the men were supposed to be resting or training, they were being used for labouring tasks. Captain J. C. Dunn, 2nd Battalion Royal Welch Fusiliers, described how they were used when in reserve during 1915:

September 4th – The Battalion, in reserve and now in Bethune, had to find large work-ing-parties daily. No one got much rest during September. There were fatigues for everyone, whether in or out of the trenches.

September 8th – Hundreds of men paraded early every morning, marched some miles for a fatigue and marched back, arriving about 7 in the evening. One man said he'd been on fatigue for nineteen consecutive days including Sundays, hadn't had his shirt off and was covered with lice.[36]

To the infantry soldier, being used as casual labour was often seen as even worse than being in the trenches: 'Having worked for six days on communication trenches, and come to look forward to the front line as a place of rest, we took over the front on a wet day following a wet night.'[37]

There was a tendency for the employing unit to demand more men than required for the task:

Off-loading stores at the Docks and loading trains for the front were the chief jobs. Because the RE indented for too many men, parties of 150 to 200 were often detailed when 75 would have been more than enough, the glut got in each other's way and delayed the work.[38]

The shortage of casual labour became so great during the summer of 1915 that even the Cavalry Corps was used to assist in the building of defences. In July 1915 entrenching battalions were formed and provided a source of labour that could be used to dig trenches and undertake repair work behind the front line.[39] In total some ten entrenching battalions, with an establishment of 20 officers and 1,000 men, were formed at the Infantry Base Depots (IBD).

Entrenching battalions helped avoid overcrowding at the IBDs, and by enabling new arrivals from Britain to be employed close to the front line, prepared men for trench warfare. Men from the entrenching battalions could be transferred to front line units at any time, so neither the number of men available nor continuity of labour could be assured. 11th Entrenching Battalion, for example, was down to 2 officers and 25 men in July 1916; by October its strength was 25 officers and 895 men.[40]

Men in the entrenching battalions often showed little interest in their work. As the CRE of 37 Division noted, the men 'changed almost daily, neither the officers nor men have time to arouse the slightest interest in their work'.[41]

Entrenching battalions remained in France until 1917.[42] Casualty levels at the start of Third Ypres meant it was impossible to maintain them and they were dis-banded. They were reformed in February 1918.

Summary

During the first half of 1915 little consideration appears to have been given to the number of men needed to support the Army at the front. The Army in France had increased from 270,000 men at the end of 1914 to 464,000 by 1 April 1915. There was a lack of infrastructure in place to support them.[43] To address this problem it was vital that the tasking of labour was coordinated efficiently.

The major problem was the lack of an overall tasking authority and limited cooperation between the different employers. If, for example, there was a high demand for dockyard stevedores the manpower came only from the ASC Labour Companies, and not from any under-utilised RE. Similarly if the RE needed extra labour they were unable to call upon any spare ASC men.

In June 1915 the IGC decided that 'as Base Commandants will claim they cannot be spared',[44] each of the bases should use the same weekly return so that there was a baseline to use when men were required for duties elsewhere.

With the arrival of the New Armies, from May 1915, numbers rose rapidly to 986,000 by 1 December. These large increases of men led to subordinates increasingly asking the IGC for more labour in order to fulfil their requirements. On 18 September, for example, the IGC recorded that the 2,040 labourers at Boulogne handled an average of 1,878 tons daily but the base commandant was expecting to increase throughput to over 3,000 tons a day and was requesting an extra 1,700 men.[45]

Despite the creation of ASC and RE Labour units, the pioneer battalions and the use of the infantry fatigue parties, the Cavalry Corps and civilian labour, it was noted that throughout 1915, 'The lack of unskilled labour had from the beginning been the cause of great difficulties.'[46]

1   Field Service Regulations (1909) Part II p.35
2   NA WO 95/4116
3   *London Gazette,* 2 October 1915
4   The concept of enlisting civilian workers into specific units to undertake a specialist labour role was to be used again later in the war when the Liverpool Dock Battalion was formed (see page 34).
5   Young, M., *Army Service Corps* pages 56 and 236.
6   NA WO 95/3951
7   These nine Labour companies served at Le Havre, Rouen, Abancourt, Boulogne, Dieppe, Abbeville, Dunkirk and Marseilles.
8   NA WO 95/3950
9   Blumberg, General Sir H., *Britain's Sea Soldiers* p.450
10 Burgoyne, G., *The Burgoyne Diaries* p. 123 quoted in Messenger, *Call To Arms* p.215
11 NA WO 95/3951
12 ibid WO 95/3950 The IGC requested 20 engineers, surveyors and architects for the Director of Works, 10 civilians to replace Assistant Military Landing Officers and 12 to replace Railway Transport Officers.
13 ibid WO 95/3956
14 ibid WO 95/3952
15 ibid WO 95/3953
16 Henniker, A., *Transportation on the Western Front* p.92
17 ibid p.53
18 According to Michael Young 33 Railway Company was disbanded on 15 June 1917 and 34 Railway Company absorbed into the Labour Corps. It has not been possible to determine which Labour Corps Company it became.
19 Subordinate staff included foreman of works, mechanics, inspectors of RE machinery, clerks and draughtsmen.
20 The Royal Engineers Fortress Companies were renamed Army Troops Companies later in 1915. Army Troops Companies worked on the construction of defences accommodation and route communications. In addition, they ran corps workshops and

parks, built positions for heavy guns and worked on water supply, frequently in forward areas.

21 Messenger, C., *Call To Arms,* p.223

22 NA WO 95/28

23 On 18 September 1915 the French Government decided that their labour would only work on roads south of the line Hazebrouck–Lille–Orchies–Valenciennes–Maubeuge placing more pressure on the labour needed by the British north of the line.

24 NA WO/95/3963

25 At least 50 per cent of a Battalion's strength should be men with experience of working with a pick and shovel. The other 50 per cent should have specialised skills such as bricklayers, joiners or metal work and, at the same time, the ability to dig trenches.

26 The 10th (Irish) Division was not to have a Pioneer Battalion until June 1915 when the 5th Royal Irish Regiment was converted to a Pioneer Battalion. The Battalion was to land at Suvla Bay in August 1915.

27 The 9th Seaforth Highlanders was formed as a K3 battalion and attached to the 9th (Scottish) Division, a K1 Division, on December 1914, becoming its Pioneer Battalion in February 1915.

28 The delay for the 16th (Irish) Division was caused by the loss of several of its units to the Guards Division whilst undergoing training in Britain.

29 Messenger, p.217

30 ibid, p.217

31 Wolff, *Subalterns of the Foot* quoted in Messenger, p.217–218

32 Wolff, quoted in Messenger, p.217–218

33 Despite the 51st Division being the 1st/5th Black Watch's parent division they were only to remain with the division until 29 February 1916 when they were transferred to the 39th Division only to be amalgamated with the 1st/5th Battalion to form the 4th/5th Black Watch.

34 Quoted in Mitchinson, *Pioneer Battalions in the Great War,* p.6

35 Mitchinson on page 113 says that when it was decided in 1916 to convert the Battalion from its pioneer role a rumour spread amongst the men that they were being 'downgraded into a Labour Battalion' but it was announced, 'it would be officially converted to a Railway Pioneer Battalion.'

36 Dunn, Captain J. C., *The War The Infantry Knew,* p.146

37 ibid, p.166

38 ibid, p.147

39 NA WO 95/3958

40 Messenger, p.222

41 Mitchinson, p.216 Note 4

42 In 1917 two Entrenching Battalions were formed in Salonika but both had been disbanded by June 1918

43 NA WO 95/3954

44 ibid WO 95/3954

45 ibid WO 95/3960

46 Barker Brown, *The History of the Corps of Engineers* Vol V, p. 543

1916 ARRIVAL OF LABOUR UNITS

If a lack of unskilled labour was a feature of the first seventeen months of the war, the same was not true for 1916. During the year the number of unskilled labourers increased from about 50,500 to 82,000 in addition to 20,000 Prisoners of War.

Infantry Labour Battalions

With an Army at almost one million strong in January 1916 the demand for
unskilled labour to support them was a concern for GHQ. On 15 January a committee was set up to determine the requirement for unskilled labour. Employing
organisations indicated an immediate demand for at least 5,000 men. At the end
of the month the C-in-C wrote to the War Office pointing out that not only was
the demand for labour increasing daily but also the only option available was to
use men in reserve, which severely interfered with their training. It was impossible
to employ any more French labour, and the Belgian Government had withdrawn
nine companies of Belgium Travailleurs who had been working for the British. He
suggested recruiting men over 40 years of age, as labourers did not need to be of the
same medical fitness as the fighting soldier. The War Office response was that one
more battalion was being raised but it was not expected to be in France for some
time and there were 3 pioneer battalions in Britain that, on arrival in France, could
be used for unarmed labour duties.[1] GHQ informed the 2nd Army on 20 February
that these three battalions would be sent to them as soon as they arrived, only to
be told four days later by the War Office that the pioneers were not being sent to
France, but retained in Britain for training.

On 23 February[2] the War Office announced that in three commands, Northern,
Western and Eastern,[3] a labour battalion was to be formed from men fit for labour
service abroad. Commanded by a lieutenant colonel each battalion was made up
of four companies of 250 men. Forming these battalions was to take precedence
over the Infantry Works Companies (IWCs) that were also being formed for use
in Britain, and men already selected for these were examined to determine if they
were medically fit for service overseas. At the beginning of March the first three
battalions, the 12th Battalion West Riding, the 33rd Royal Fusiliers and the 18th
Cheshire Regiment, were formed.[4]

On 16 March GHQ was informed that the labour battalions should be ready
within fourteen days. GHQ instigated a number of measures in an attempt to
ease the labour situation until they arrived. These included making use of surplus men from ammunition parks, supply columns and field ambulances to unload
stores from trains and barges. Horse transport was used instead of motor transport
to reduce wear and tear. Armies were reminded they should make efficient use
of labour by ensuring employers were allocated the minimum number of men
required to complete the task and that employers surrendered labourers once the
task was completed.

March 1916 was to be a month of rapidly changing decisions at the War Office.
During the month the creation of five more battalions was announced.[5] Initially,
two were formed, one each in Scottish and Southern Command.[6] On 22 March
home commands were informed that any man called up for service who was cat-
egorized as fit for labour would be deemed as fit for service at home or overseas.
Those in the latter group were formed into Infantry Labour Companies (ILCs),
which would 'eventually be formed into Labour battalions for service on the
Continent on Lines of Communication'.[7] On 29 March it was announced that
a further three battalions were to be formed in Northern, Western and Eastern
Command.[8]

It was soon realised that the eight battalions already raised would not be sufficient to meet the requirements in France, and on 24 April it was announced that in future, home commands would form suitable recruits into labour battalions. The organisation of these battalions appears to have been left to each command who were required to inform the War Office when a battalion had been formed and the regiment to which it belonged. The War Office then allotted a number to it.[9] This opened the way for the formation of many more labour battalions and is well illustrated by the following examples:

> In Southern Command, between May and July 1916, seven Labour Battalions, the 12th and 14th Devonshire, the 12th Duke of Cornwall's Light Infantry, and the 10th, 11th, 12th and 13th Royal Berkshire were formed.[10]
>
> The 10th Berkshire Regiment was formed on 9 May at Cambridge Barracks, Portsmouth by combining the 2nd, 3rd, 6th, 8th and 9th ILCs Berkshire Regiment with the 2nd, 3rd, 9th and 10th ILCs Wiltshire Regiment. When these Companies were combined 866 men were found to be fit for service in the Battalion, 96 were discharged as unfit and 154 reclassified as category 'A' and transferred to infantry units. 150 men from the 11th ILC Royal Warwickshire Regiment brought the Battalion up to strength on 15 June.[11]
>
> In Scottish command the 19th Royal Scots was formed at Blairgowrie, Perthshire on 12 April by combining two ILCs from the King's Own Scottish Borders and the Argyle and Sutherland Highlanders with two IWCs from the Royal Scots and Royal Scots Fusiliers. There are no indications that men from any other sources were used to form the 19th Royal Scots yet its strength when it arrived in Le Havre on 18 May was 11 officers and 1034 other ranks.[12] This suggests that both the ILCs and IWCs operated well in excess of their establishment of 100 other ranks.

Whilst forming, labour battalions were recruited until they were 25 per cent over strength. A medical board then determined who would serve in the battalion overseas. For example, the 19th Royal Scots recruited over 1,200 men. When the battalion left for France 228 men were transferred to the 12th Black Watch who were recruiting as a labour battalion. Similarly, before the 12th Black Watch left for France 126 men were transferred to the 14th Scottish Rifles. From March to July 1916 no fewer than 23 labour battalions were formed. Most arrived in France within four weeks of being formed.

The 12th West Riding Regiment illustrates the speed of deployment and the work undertaken in France. Raised at Middlesborough on 10 March they left Southampton on 1 April arriving in Havre the next day, and by 3 April were building a new railway from Bergues to Poperinghe.[13] The Battalion lost their first man on 8 April when Private Valentine Anderson died from meningitis. On 8 June two companies moved to the Somme where they were joined by the rest of the Battalion in early July. The Battalion's Diary records they remained on the Somme until January 1917 working at Meaulte, Trones Wood, Fricourt, Longueval and Aveuly during which they came under shell fire and gas and aircraft attacks which resulted in the deaths of two officers and fifteen other ranks.[14]

Permanent Base

Permanent Base (PB) men were classified as unfit for front line service and were re-examined monthly by medical boards. Some were temporarily classified PB due to wounds, whilst others were long term PB, for example, due to their age. They provided unskilled labour on both the LoC and in Army areas during 1916. In March the AG complained that too many men in France were classified as PB and that many could be returned to Britain to work in munitions, which would free up fit men for service in France.

By 1 April 1916 almost 1,500 PB men were employed on the LoC and a further 2,000 in the Army Areas, although Army commanders estimated that they needed twice this number. The IGC and AG agreed to increase the number of men allocated to the Armies to 3,100. There were, however, differences in opinion between the IGC and Army commanders over how they should be employed. The IGC determined that they should be employed on non-military duties that were 'detrimental to the fighting spirit and efficiency of the able bodied soldier if continued for a long period'.[15] He determined that duties as guards, traffic control and temporary fatigues could be done by fit men without detriment whereas duties such as hospital orderlies, baths, laundry, sanitation and canteens were suitable for PB men only.

The need for PB men was particularly acute in the First Army, which occupied an area with many mining towns where a large number of refugees from the battle areas were living. The 1,000 PB men allocated to the First Army was 500 less than they estimated was required and another 258 men were allocated on 27 May after a request for more PB men was made as

> ... the municipal authorities in these towns are hampered by a large increase of population and by a dearth of labour and lack of funds, and, consequently the whole of the sanitation and scavenging in these towns devolves on the troops.[16]

At the beginning of June the War Office suggested returning PB men to Britain and replacing them with Garrison Battalions. The IGC did not support the idea, pointing out that most PB men were employed in small detachments and that about 3 per cent were declared fit and returned to their unit each month.

With the attack on the Somme the number of PB men on the LoC rose from 1,427 on 1 June to 16,000 on 25 July. When the Third Army had difficulty finding enough stretcher-bearers in order to load the wounded on to ambulance trains it requested 300 men be allocated to them. This request was rejected by the IGC on the grounds that he did not believe it would be an economic use of limited resources. By September it was recognised that there was a need for a better way to control tasking of PB men and the C-in-C decided to form a battalion of over 4,000 with permanent staff at the Employment Base Depots (EBD) at Havre, Rouen, Etaples and one of over 2,000 at Calais. In addition, at each Army HQ an officer was appointed to administer PB men in the area.

A PB man would be sent to the EBD with a medical classification from 1–7, or, as Permanently Unfit (PU), the latter being returned to Britain. The classes which determined a man's fitness to undertake a role, being:

1 Batmen
2 Cycle Orderlies
3 Graves Registration Units (mostly for digging)
4 Light fatigues
5 Escorts with PoW Companies
6 Stretcher bearers
7 Heavy Fatigues

GHQ wanted to ensure that PB men surplus to legitimate requirements were not retained by the units to which they were attached. In February 1917 all units on the LoC had to submit returns showing the number of PB employed.

ANZAC soldiers were paid more than British soldiers and it was considered uneconomical to keep them in France if they could not undertake the duties for which they enlisted. Instructions were given in February 1917 that all ANZAC Corps PB men should be sent to England to be returned to Australia or New Zealand.[17]

The record for Etaples EBD in March 1917 illustrates the number of PB men being dealt with. During the month it received 1,688 men classified from 1 to 4, 1,546 class 5 to 7 and 54 PU. At the time the strength of the battalion was 8,679, of whom 2,596 were at the depot, the remainder being employed according to their classification.[18]

Port Labour

Unloading supplies at the ports was a perpetual problem, in part caused by the dual management system in operation. Unloading ships was the responsibility of the Principal Naval Transport Officer (PNTO) who had two ASC (Naval) Labour Companies that reported directly to him. These companies were supplemented by French labour employed by him and paid for by the Admiralty.

Once goods were unloaded they became the responsibility of the Army. At each port there was a Labour Superintendent who received a daily statement of the requirements for the following day. He then arranged with the Base Commandant for the labour to be supplied from any available enlisted labour, PB details or civilian labour. The problem with this system was that there were daily fluctuations in the labour required and it was not uncommon for shortages to occur.

In January the French Mission complained that local labour was being monopolised by the Army or by British contractors who paid higher rates than usually paid in France. They also reminded the British that in 1912 it had been agreed that labour would be brought from Britain for all the ports. The IGC's official response was that the French Government had agreed to local labour being employed and that wage rates were agreed locally with the port authorities. The French threatened to remove all French labour at the ports unless the rates of pay were standardised. The IGC wrote on 16 February: 'French Labour can no longer be depended upon.'[19] However, his wish to replace it was not possible. In an attempt to improve the situation, the French stipulated that no more civilian labour should be engaged except with the formal consent of the *Commissaire Regulateur* of the port and produced rates of pay that it was suggested the British should use. Initially, the wage rates only applied to male labour but by August 1916 this was extended to female labour. This appears to have improved matters and civilians continued to be employed at the ports.

At the end of February the two ASC (Naval) Labour Companies were renumbered 35 and 36 ASC Labour Company (Naval) and allocated to the Admiralty, reporting directly to the PNTO, although under Army discipline. These 1,100 men were insufficient to satisfy the needs of the PNTO although his request in March for more naval companies was rejected. He was informed that 4, 5 and 6 ASC Labour Companies were composed of stevedores, and were available. However, there was no guarantee that any request from him for additional men would be found from these companies.

In June the PNTO suggested the naval companies be transferred to the Royal Marines. The IGC supported the idea but, being shore based, wanted the base commandant to be responsible for their discipline.[20] Discussions in both France and Britain about whether these companies should remain part of the Army carried on throughout 1916. In the end it was decided that they should become part of the Royal Marines and on 2 February 1917 the two ASC companies were transferred to the newly formed Royal Marine Labour Corps (RMLC).

In Britain the Liverpool Docks Battalion had helped relieve the difficulties at the port. The Battalion's help was sought in April 1916 and Lieutenant Colonel R. F. Williams and Captain Tattersall of the Battalion, together with Master Stevedore Marsh and Master Porter Robertson arrived to reorganise the ports. They started at Rouen but William's lack of military experience and tact brought no improvement. He was sent to Havre where he had even less success. Within a month Marsh and Robertson returned to Britain, saying that they would not work with Williams.

The IGC sought advice from a War Office Commission, which was examining how the ports were operating. Its president informed him: 'Lieut-Colonel Williams was worse than useless, in fact he went as far to say that it was positively dangerous to keep him out here; that he has completely upset everybody at the Ports, and instead of improving things he would do harm.'[21] This view was supported by the other two members of the Commission. The IGC ordered Williams to return to Britain on 16 June and as no other suitable employment could be found for him he relinquished his commission seven days later.

Non Combatant Corps

The introduction of conscription resulted in the announcement on 10 March of the formation of the Non Combatant Corps (NCC).[22] Each company, commanded by a captain or subaltern with two sergeants and six NCOs, drawn from existing units, had 94 privates.[23] The men held exemption certificates, wore uniform, were subject to military law and trained in squad drill but could not be armed or train with arms of any description. They could be employed in road making, hutting, timber cutting, quarrying, sanitary work, loading and unloading ships and vehicles and digging as long as they were not employed in the firing line. Unlike most labour units the majority of men were category A and officers were instructed that they were not to be given work which was lighter than, or more congenial than, tasks given to men of British labour companies in the same locality.[24] One of the first companies to arrive in France was the 1st Eastern Company who were allocated, on 22 April, to the Director of Works for employment in the quarries at Rinxent.[25] In an effort to reduce the amount of shipping needed to import timber and stone, plans were made to source these materials in France. The NCC was seen as an ideal source of labour for this work. On 23 April Haig wrote to the War Office:

> I am of opinion that, if the Non Combatant Corps is made available in sufficient numbers, the solution to the labour problem on the Lines of Communication may not only be found, but the labour at present lent to the Director of Works by Armies for the production of stone and timber needed by them will be able to be released for work elsewhere, where it is urgently wanted.[26]

He went on to indicate that the number required would be 16,050, which included 1,100 skilled artisans and tradesmen. However the total strength of the NCC in Britain and France never exceeded 3,300 and it is questionable whether his use of the term 'Non Combatant Corps' was intended to include not only those men who had rejected conscription but also those in Army labour units. There is the possibility that at the time, Haig did not realise the difference between the NCC and normal labour units.

In all, almost 800 members of the NCC were to serve in France most of whom were educated and generally proved to be good workers. Initially some educated men were attached to other units as clerks, but on 23 May the Adjutant General instructed that men in the NCC were to be employed in manual labour and not to be used for clerical work.

The fighting soldier tended to despise COs who were considered cowards and shirkers, the NCC being known as the 'No Courage Corps'. At times, men of labour battalions were mistaken for COs and treated to abuse and ridicule. However, as Captain Thomas relates in June 1916, on one occasion, a member of a labour battalion showed that he was willing to fight:

> But what annoyed the men more than all was being referred to as Conscientious Objectors (one Battalion we met pathetically asked if we fought with bananas). At Meaulte one private showed his willingness to fight by fairly knocking out a gunner who contemptuously referred to him as a 'Conchie'; a gallant deed for which he was first arrested by the MP and then liberated and complimented by our sporting Colonel.[27]

Their refusal to handle ammunition restricted how they were employed. There are, for example, reports of men refusing to push a truck because it contained ammunition. If a man refused to obey an instruction he was charged under military law but returned to Britain to serve his sentence in a civilian prison. On completion of his sentence there was a possibility that he would then be allowed to undertake work of national importance in Britain. This decision by the Government resulted in GHQ expressing concern that it actively encouraged men to be insubordinate.

The NCC companies were employed in Army Areas but could not be used in the danger zone. With a company comprising 100 men they were often used for isolated work where it would have been difficult to send a detachment of coloured labour, who it was believed, would have required special accommodation and more supervision.

Preparation for 1 July

With preparations underway for the forthcoming offensive on the Somme, the need for unskilled labour became more important: 'The railways were inadequate; the roads in the area behind the front where the troops would have to be concentrated were few and indifferent.'[28] Accommodation and water supplies for 400,000 men and 100,000 horses for a minimum of seven weeks had to be provided. Some 50,000 miles of cables had to be buried, 50 miles of new railway laid and hundreds of miles of roads and existing railway repaired and improved.

On 11 March the IGC was informed by the War Office, that German PoWs should be retained in France rather than sent to Britain and that consideration was being given to them being used in forests and quarries and on loan to the French at ports. The response from the French and British military was not favourable to the idea and Haig wrote to the War Office saying that he had 'reluctantly come to the conclusion that PoWs could not be profitably employed in France'.[29] Despite Haig's comments the decision to use PoWs in France was confirmed and they began working in the rear area. Whether this was an efficient use of labour is questionable because PoWs had little incentive to work hard supporting the Allies war effort and they required guarding. At Havre 700 PoWs began employment on 6 April accompanied by 140 escorts. A second group of 500 who arrived on 16 April had 100 escorts.

The newly formed labour battalions were to play an important part in preparing for the Somme Offensive. By 12 May seven battalions had arrived in France of which five were used in the forward area to move stores and ammunition and assist with the road and rail work. Although not used in the trenches they were employed within the range of German guns. The 12th West Ridings moved to the Somme on 8 June to work on the Meaulte to Maricourt Line, suffering their first deaths from enemy action on 16 July when shelling resulted in Lance Corporal Jevons and Privates Pearson and Horner being killed, and seven others wounded.

On the LoC 22,000 men were employed each day during May. Almost 12,000 in ASC companies, 4,000 in labour battalions, RE labour battalions or the NCC, 1,100 in the Naval Companies and almost 2,000 French and Belgian civilians. Of the remainder, over 1,000 were reinforcements waiting to be sent to infantry units and there were nearly 1,500 PB men.

In the forward areas the divisional infantry pioneer battalions and men being 'rested' from the trenches supported the engineers. One of the most successful commanders on the Somme, Ivor Maxse, complained that the men in his 18th Division were used as labour to build and repair roads and railways whenever out of the trenches prior to 1 July when they should have been training. The problem for GHQ was that there was insufficient labour so the experience of the 18th Division was repeated throughout the British sector.

The 14th Northumberland Fusiliers, for example, opened up nearly 2,000 yards of fire and communication trenches during the night of 23/24 June. The 18th

Northumberland Fusiliers laid over 2,000 yards of trench tramways, dug gun pits, dugouts and observation posts and repaired communication trenches during a six week period prior to 23 June.[30]

Coloured Labour

A possible solution to the manpower problem lay in the employment of coloured labour. Military units of coloured personnel were already being used as labourers. The C-in-C was offered the Bermuda RGA. On accepting them he asked the War Office for details of the heavy guns on which they were trained so it appears that they were being considered as fighting troops. Arriving in France in June 1916 they were attached to the British RGA on the Somme but used at the ammunition dumps to move shells rather than operating guns. A month after their arrival the decision was taken to bring two battalions of the British West Indies Regiment (BWIR) from Egypt to France, and to recruit the Cape Coloured Labour Battalion.

During May 1916 the C-in-C accepted the offer of a battalion of Canadian Negroes. The battalion, No. 2 Construction Battalion was authorized on 5 July 1916 and its 19 officers and 605 other ranks left Canada for Europe at the end of March 1917.[31] Being under strength, its status was changed to a company on arrival in France and it was attached to the Canadian Forestry Corps.

Coloured civilian labour had not yet been recruited, although as early as March 1916 the War Office suggested bringing Egyptian labourers to France. At the War Committee meeting on 11 April the President of the Board of Trade reported that although schemes for recruiting Egyptians to work in France had been satisfactorily arranged in Egypt, it had been impossible to overcome the objections of local authorities in France.[32] It was almost a year before Egyptian labour came to France.[33]

The idea of using Chinese labour was first raised on 11 July when the War Office suggested to the IGC that there were a number of unemployed Chinese, experienced in port work, in Britain who could be employed in France. The idea was rejected on the grounds that there would be difficulty in housing and feeding them.

The decision to use coloured civilian labourers in France was based on the need to relieve unfit military personnel in France so they could be deployed for work in Britain. As the Director of Organisation, Major General Woodward, emphasised at a conference held at GHQ on 12 August:

> Tribunals are keeping back a lot of men because there are insufficient for land and for certain trades. The War Office are naturally opposed to this, but must make some return of men to England either to work on land or for trade purposes in order to relieve men of fighting age in order that we may get reinforcements.
>
> If we can show the Government that we are doing all we can to give back men, the Secretary of State will have a strong lever to induce the Tribunals to tighten up the 'exemptions' and to 'debadge' many now exempted.
>
> We want men unfit for service to release fit men. Unless we do this, drafts will go down. You will not get the drafts necessary to keep up the strength of the Army.[34]

Woodward went on to suggest using black and Chinese civilian labour in order to release men back to Britain. In reality the use of Chinese labour had already been approved by the War Office and communicated in a letter to the Colonial Office six days earlier:

> The Secretary of State for War has agreed to the principle of the employment of Chinese Labour for work in France and in other theatres of war in order that the British labour now being employed in France be released for work at home to mitigate the existing shortage of men in agriculture and industries.[35]

The IGC, AG and QMG argued that the French would not support the employment of Chinese by the British; that Chinese who could not read English should not be employed at the ports or loading stores at railheads; and they could not be employed on roadwork, as they would be working in areas that could be shelled by the enemy. The IGC went as far as to say: 'If I am asked what I can spare to be replaced by Chinese labour, I shall say not one.'[36]

Woodward also informed the conference that arrangements were in hand for 10,000 Africans, in five battalions, commanded by Colonel Pritchard, to be sent to France. The first battalion of the South African Native Labour Corps (SANLC) arrived in France on 20 November 1916 despite the view of the IGC that 'black men would die like flies in the winter'.[37]

The IGC, AG and QMG suggested the proposals could endanger the maintenance work being undertaken and that unless the Tribunals and Trade Unions at home

> … would agree to release a corresponding number of men for active service at the front, no steps should be taken to replace by Chinese and Black labour, those men now working on the LoC in France who are not fit for the front.[38]

The French gave their approval for Chinese to be employed, as long as they were subject to Military Law, on 1 September 1916. Recruiting commenced in China with the first contingent of the Chinese Labour Corps (CLC) arriving on 19 April 1917.

The SANLC Commander, Colonel Pritchard, arrived in France before his men in order to clarify the conditions under which they would be housed, fed and employed. This was done at a conference held at GHQ on 23 October 1916. It was at the insistence of the South African Government that the men should be segregated from other troops and housed in barbed wire compounds.

A similar conference took place on 29 December 1916 preceding the arrival of the CLC. The arrangements put forward by Colonel Fairfax, their Commanding Officer, were far less stringent than those proposed for the SANLC. Compounds would only be used in the rear areas and the Chinese would manage their own catering and camp discipline without the need for British guards. Fairfax explained to the conference that the Chinese generally gave no trouble, drunkenness being almost unheard of.

With the ever increasing demand for labour the decision was taken in the autumn of 1916 to bring another civilian labour force, the Indian Labour Corps, to France, although the first contingent did not arrive until April 1917.

Forestry

A small RE unit was formed at the end of 1915 specifically to exploit the forest of Nieppe. As with other labouring tasks, infantry detachments were used to support the RE company. A detachment from the Guards Pioneer Battalion, the 4th Coldstream Guards, worked in the Clairmarais Forest near St Omer from 3 March until 1 July 1916. Lieutenant Blacker, who commanded the detachment, describes how men were taught by French *Gardes Forestiers* to fell trees for military use, which included the fascines used in muddy areas to form rough tracks or primitive roadways.[39] Blacker does not describe how the men were selected to undertake this type of work but does explain that he had been chosen to command the detachment as he had been buried by a shell explosion in February. In view of this it is likely that the Coldstream Guards selected men who were temporarily unfit for front line service.

Five forestry companies were formed during 1916. By May, 1,300 civilians and 1,400 soldiers, primarily ASC, were supporting these skilled companies, producing 15,000 tons of timber each month. GHQ estimated that by November 10,000 men would be needed in order to produce 54,600 tons a month.[40]

One solution was to send Canadian lumbermen, who were being employed in forests in Britain, to France. In June, Colonel Alexander McDougall, who had been responsible for bringing the first forestry unit to Britain, paid a four day visit to see the work being undertaken in France. By August there were 73 Canadians working in the forests and in September the 1st Canadian Forestry Company was formed from the 101 Squadron, Canadian Remount Depot and McDougall arranged to equip and send 250 men to work in France.[41] The creation of a Canadian Forestry Corps was approved on 7 November 1916 and McDougall was appointed its CO.[42] (See page 255)

Although the members of the corps were skilled forestry workers they required the support of unskilled labour. Roads and light railways had to be built in the forests to move equipment, wood and the charcoal which was being produced. Labour units, working under the supervision of the RE, also built accommodation and medical facilities. The Labour Corps, the NCC, Middlesex Alien Companies, Indian, Chinese, South African and PoWs all worked in the forests.

The arrival of the labour battalions in 1916 enabled some relief for infantry detachments. The 14th Cameronians arrived in France on 24 July 1916. Two days later they were in tented accommodation at St Saens and began four months' work in Eawy Forest, near Dieppe. The battalion, which did not move into hutted accommodation until September, appears to have earned a good reputation for their work. In November, three companies were moved to the Crecy Forest where they remained until May 1917, the fourth company joining them from Eawy in March. The 12th South Staffords arrived in France on 28 July and two days later started two months work in the Caudebec Forest.

In September 1916 three PoW Companies, 5, 16 and 20, comprising men with forestry or other appropriate skills were employed in Rinxent Forest. 16 Company was moved in October to the Brotonne Forest where it appears to have remained until the end of the war. The other two companies remained at Rinxent, where, during an air raid on 4 September 1917, nine escorts (guards) and 39 PoWs were killed with 13 escorts and 40 PoWs wounded. Ensuring PoWs did not escape when working in forests was a difficulty for the authorities and a reward of 25 Francs was given to any French man who captured an escaped prisoner. The Report on Labour in the BEF says that it was not until different scales of escorts were introduced in June 1918 that this problem was solved, although prisoners escaping from companies working in forests continued to be reported until the end of the war.

The first contingent of the SANLC arrived in France on 20 November 1916 and was immediately sent to Eawy Forest where a camp had been made ready for them. They quickly learnt the skill of felling trees and earned great praise from their employers. The Report on Labour in the BEF noted that, of all the tasks undertaken by the SANLC, forestry was the one that they were the most successful and interested in. The contingent remained at the work until March 1917 when they were replaced by PoW companies.

A further five forestry companies were formed during 1917–18. Once again these were supported by unskilled labour units. After their arrival in June 1917 a number of Indian Labour Companies were sent to forest areas where they were used both for forestry and charcoal production. Three companies, the 76 (Kumaon), 27 (Lushai) and 28 (Lushai) were noted for undertaking particularly good work.[43] However, not all companies were as successful; 49 (NWF) Company, sent to Blavincourt Forest in August 1917, had to endure poor conditions living in tents with only one blanket per man. It was discovered that a number of men in the company were opium eaters and they had to be evacuated.

A number of CLC companies were sent to work in forests, including 8, 67 and 68 CLC Companies at Le Parc in September 1917. In January 1918 it was decided to form three specialist Chinese 'Forestry' Companies, 115, 128 and 135, comprised of skilled men. Each company had 60 sawyers, 2 masons, 2 plumbers, 2 shoemakers, 2 tailors and 1 tinsmith. In addition, skilled blacksmiths, fitters, platelayers and engine drivers were provided if requested by the employer.

Allocation and use of labour

By the end of August 1916 each Army, the Railway Directorate and the Director of Works (LoC) had labour allocated specifically to them.

The labour allocated to the IGC was 'pooled' to enable it to be used where needed on the LoC, on roadwork, at the railheads and dumps. The details of this allocation can be found on page 354.

Using labour efficiently

The way labour was organised and distributed for work during 1916 led to problems related to a lack of overall control and the inefficient use of men.

In Army Areas men were required to work as sanitary squads and to provide services – under the control of the Town Major – for soldiers resting from the front. These services included the provision of canteens, baths and cinemas. Whilst some PB men were used, many men were those who were resting before going back to the front. As a result, soldiers were not being rested properly. Additional problems were that men undertook work they did not wish to do or for which they did not have the skills. The men allocated to a particular task frequently changed and so they did not acquire the relevant skills. The problems were exacerbated when a division left its area since it sometimes took the PB men attached to it. On 21 July 1916 instructions were issued that PB men would not move with the division they were supporting but would remain with the Town Major.

The IGC had the perennial problem that a unit or depot, having been allocated men for a particular task, was reluctant to release them when the task was completed. The attempt by the IGC to re-deploy the men was invariably met with the cry that 'they were needed and could not be spared' even when there was no work for them to do. It was common practice throughout 1916 for men to be given a new task by the unit to which they were allocated without reference to a higher authority. As a result, men were frequently employed on trivial and, at times, unnecessary work, whilst labour could not be found for more important tasks.

Following labour returns submitted to GHQ at the beginning of August the QMG wrote to all Armies on 27 August pointing out that as much as 6 per cent of the labour allotted to road maintenance was being used on sanitation, water supply at Corps HQ, traffic control, baths, hutting, workshops or miscellaneous duties. His letter stated that 'labour which is allotted to Armies for a specific purpose will not be diverted to other tasks without reference to GHQ'.[44]

There was often a lack of supervision by officers, which resulted in wasted manpower. Much of the work was undertaken by small detachments of men being supervised by a junior NCO. Frederick Voigt, who served in a RE Labour Battalion, describes a working party where, by mid morning, only a small number of men were working, the majority resting behind a stack of timbers. It was only after a corporal appeared on the scene that 'the wearisome, monotonous trudge began again'.[45] This was to slow and then stop altogether when the corporal left. Work resumed again when a sergeant appeared and ordered them to work. Meanwhile, the sergeant in charge of the party had not been seen for much of the day, spending it in an improvised shelter in front of a fire drinking tea. He only emerged when an officer appeared in the afternoon.

Employers frequently failed to supply sufficient information about the work for which they needed labour. As a result men could arrive for work without the correct tools or bearing tools that were not required. Voigt describes how they were made to march to a task carrying shovels only to find that they were not required since the job was to carry sleepers across a railway line and restack them.

At the railheads a lack of coordination between the different branches resulted in men sent to unload trains finding the train was not due for several hours. Sometimes they were ready to cross-load a train only to find the wagons or vehicles they were supposed to transfer the goods onto had not arrived. Situations like these resulted in 'the dumping of ammunition and supplies in stations, thereby blocking them for other purposes'.[46] Similar problems occurred at the ports where the discharge of ships was constantly delayed by numerous factors including 'the lack of experienced supervision of the labour employed'.[47] Once unloaded a shortage of railway wagons meant stores had to be, temporarily at least, kept on the quay or in transit sheds.

By August 1916 the situation at the ports and on the railways was grave. Sir Eric Geddes was appointed to investigate transport arrangements, both in Britain and

France, for the BEF, and brought a fresh view to the question of the movement of supplies. The traditional approach had been based on the quantity of ammunition and stores needed to maintain a division. Geddes looked at the total tonnage that had to be moved between different points and the most appropriate mode of transport. Following his investigation transportation services in the BEF were co-ordinated under one authority. Geddes was appointed Director General of Transport with the temporary rank of major general. Whilst not directly addressing the issue of unskilled labour, Geddes' investigation did lead to the decision that labour units should not be permanently attached to particular services.

Control of unskilled labour at the main bases was far from satisfactory, with some men being under the control of the Labour Superintendent, some the Naval Transport Officer (NTO), and some the Director of Supplies. Some labour was permanently attached to specific tasks and some was pooled for tasking as required. On 27 September 1916 the Base Commandant at Havre proposed appointing an officer at the base to command working parties. These parties would be formed into a labour corps in order to create a more efficient organisation. The proposal was accepted as a trial by the IGC with the role of the Labour Superintendent being retained and working directly under the Base Commandant. ASC Labour Companies at the port, which were previously tasked by the Assistant Director of Supplies, would now come under the OC Labour Corps. The NTO arranged for the Naval stevedores to come under the OC Labour Corps for the purposes of discipline and interior economy. The IGC was anxious that as few changes as possible should be made to permanent working parties as many of them had become accustomed to specific areas of work. He also expressed his hope that the Base Commandant would 'bring the various Heads of Departments together, and explain to them how necessary it is that this scheme should be tried, and that we hope they will work together to ensure its success'.[48]

The Base Commandant at Havre was instructed to report to the IGC after the scheme had been in operation for two weeks. It appears the Havre experiment met with success, as on 24 October the QMG announced 'the formation of a Labour Corps at Rouen, Calais and Boulogne'.[49] He pointed out that changes being considered for the LoC included the idea of a labour corps.

In November the War Office suggested replacing 1,264 ASC labourers at the ports with two labour battalions, the 17th and 18th Royal West Surrey. In response, the QMG pointed out that a 1,000 strong battalion was unwieldy for use at a port where small detachments were needed. He suggested re-forming the battalions along ASC company lines, a company consisting of 5 sections, each 100 strong. Approval of his request was received on 12 December with three Infantry Labour Companies (ILCs), 1st, 2nd and 3rd ILC Royal West Surrey Regiment, arriving in France early in 1917.

Labour Directorate

By the end of October 1916 unskilled labour had grown to some 800 officers and 78,000 other ranks with further men scheduled to arrive in France. This labour was made up of 11 RE battalions, 30 Infantry Labour battalions, 29 ASC companies, 2

ASC Naval companies, 2 BWIR battalions, the Cape Coloured Labour Battalion, the Bermuda RGA, 2 SANLC battalions, 8 NCC companies and 47 PoW companies. Not only did they vary in size from the 100 strong NCC company to the 2,000-strong SANLC battalion but there were also restrictions on where and how some units could be employed. When these issues were considered in conjunction with the problems of the various transportation services, the decision was made to form a general pool from which all services would be supplied 'in accordance with the relative urgency of their requirements at any particular time'.[50] This pool of labour would be under the command of the Directorate of Labour and Lieutenant Colonel Evan Gibb was 'pulled out of relative obscurity as an Assistant Quartermaster General at GHQ' to be the first Director of Labour on 26 November 1916.[51]

Gibb, originally commissioned into the West India Regiment in 1898, had served in the ASC since 1899 including service in the Boer War where he had been awarded the DSO. From the outbreak of the First World War he served as DAQMG, becoming Assistant Director of Transport in November 1914 and AQMG in 1915. His work at GHQ meant he 'had the right experience to fight his corner successfully'.[52]

On 6 December, Gibb, as Director of Labour, was promoted to brigadier general giving a clear signal of the importance of the role. Gibb remained in post until February 1918 when he became controller of salvage, his wartime career ending in 1920 as the last GOC of the forces in France and Flanders.

The decision to form the Directorate was transmitted to the War Office for approval and followed on 15 December by further proposals suggesting the formation of a labour corps in France.[53] The way had been set for unskilled labour to be organised efficiently so that it would undertake the tasks required although this would not be achieved for some time.

1 NA WO 95/3965
2 ibid WO 293/4 ACI 420 23 February 1916
3 Men from Scottish command being allocated to Northern command and Southern and London District to Eastern.
4 NA WO 293/4 ACI 504 5 March 1916
5 The 12th Duke of Cornwall's Light Infantry, 19th Royal Scots, 34th Royal Fusiliers, 22nd West Yorkshire and the 19th Cheshire Regiment.
6 NA WO 293/4 ACI 593 17 March 1916
7 ibid ACI 625 22 March 1916
8 ibid ACI 680 29 March 1916
9 ibid WO 293/4 ACI 864 24 April 1916
10 Southern command comprised of the Royal Berkshire Regiment, the Duke of Cornwall's Light Infantry, the Devonshire Regiment, the Somerset Light Infantry, the Dorset Regiment, the Hampshire Regiment, the Wiltshire Regiment, the Oxfordshire and Buckinghamshire Light Infantry, the Worcestershire Regiment and the Royal Warwickshire Regiment.
11 NA WO 95/4174
12 ibid WO 95/4178
13 ibid WO 95/430
14 ibid
15 ibid WO 95/3967
16 ibid WO 95/3568

17 ibid WO 95/83
18 ibid WO 95/4186
19 ibid WO 95/3965
20 ibid WO 95/3969
21 ibid WO 339/36095
22 ibid WO 123/58 Army Order 112 Formation of the NCC 10 March 1916
23 Privates in the Non-Combatant Corps could only be promoted to acting NCOs
24 NA WO 107/37 Report on Labour. Appendix C
25 ibid WO 95/3967
26 ibid
27 Thomas, T. C., *With A Labour Company in France,* p.4
28 Edmonds, J., *Official History 1916 Vol.* 1, p.271
29 NA WO 95/3966
30 Mitchinson, K., *Pioneer Battalions,* p.74
31 Ruck, C., *The Black Battalion*
32 NA WO 95/3967 CAB 37/145/28
33 ibid WO 95/3967 WO 95/3969
34 ibid WO 95/3967 WO 95/31
35 ibid WO 95/3967 WO 32/11345
36 ibid WO 95/31
37 ibid WO 95/31
38 ibid WO 95/31
39 Blacker, J., *Have You Forgotten Yet?,* pp. 89–104
40 NA WO 95/30
41 Bird, C. & Davies, W., *The Canadian Forestry Corps,* p. 35
42 On 2 April 1917 a Forestry Directorate was set up at GHQ under McDougall who
   was promoted to Brigadier-General.
43 NA WO 107/37 Report on Labour, p.42
44 ibid WO 95/30
45 Voight, F., *Combed Out,* p. 41
46 Henniker, A., *Transportation on the Western Front,* p.181
47 ibid, p.182
48 NA WO 95/3971
49 ibid WO 95/3971
50 Henniker, p.497
51 Young, p.190
52 Messenger, p.230
53 NA WO 95/83

1917 GROWTH AND DEVELOPMENT

The twelve months from January 1917 was to be a watershed in the history of military labour in France. With the creation of the Labour Directorate unskilled labour was brought under one administrative regime. The Directorate was not without problems as it had to deal with a huge increase in manpower. During the year, British labour increased from 82,000 to 150,000, PoWs from 20,000 to 70,000 and coloured labourers from 2,800 to 145,000. The Directorate also had to cope with officers and men often unfit for the task in hand, with employing services that saw labour as their personal troops. They also had to meet the demands for support for three major offensives, at Arras in April, Flanders from July to November and Cambrai in November.

The Labour Directorate

The War Office approved the formation of the Labour Directorate on 11 January 1917. At GHQ the Director of Labour (DL) Brigadier General Gibb, was supported by a colonel as Deputy Director, three lieutenant colonels as Assistant Director (ADL) and three captains, Deputy Assistant (DADL).

The Directorate at GHQ, which worked under the instructions of the QMG, was divided into three branches: Distribution and Allotment of all unskilled labour; Personnel, Appointments and Posting of Officers; Technical questions, including statistics, methods of increasing output and equipment of Labour units.

At each Army HQ and on the LoC, HQ was a lieutenant colonel as ADL and at each corps HQ and base port a DADL. As the work grew changes were made on the LoC by dividing it into three areas (north, central and south) each with an ADL and DADL. Corps HQ had a DADL (captain) but as he was part of the 2nd Echelon he remained in situ when the corps moved.

On 5 January the QMG sent a letter, which defined the duties of the ADL and DADL:

> These Officers will act as the advisers, on Labour matters, of the Commanders of the Formations to which they are posted, dealing on their behalf with the allotment and distribution of Labour with a view to its proper employment and economical work-ing and forecasting future requirements subject to the proviso that Labour allotted for work under a department will during working hours be distributed and controlled directly under the orders of this Department.[1]

Three Classes of Labour

In his letter the QMG confirmed the decision that had been taken on 19 December 1916 to divide labour into three different classes:

1   Technical units such as railway companies, operating sections, and repair units.
2   Specialised units such as railway construction units, special road construction units and special quarry units.
3   Unskilled units comprising all units not included in 1 and 2.

It was also agreed that technical and specialised units were to be administered and controlled by the departments under which such units normally worked and not under the control of the Labour Directorate, which would control unskilled labour. It had already been established that the technical and specialised units were not suf-ficient in themselves to do all the work required, and needed supplementing with unskilled labour. However, the amount needed to supplement these units depended on the tactical situation and therefore it would have been uneconomical to perma-nently attach unskilled labour to them.

The distinction between skilled and unskilled labour was not as clear as these classes suggest. Between the technical unit and the most unskilled unit, there was a marked difference, but for those continually employed on labour duties, there was no such thing as really unskilled abour. Ideally it would have been more efficient for each service to have its own labour, selected for its aptitude for the special work required, and always kept on the same work. But as the needs of each service varied, it was more economical for the force as a whole that labour should be pooled and transferred from one service to another as required. As labour was re-allocated there was a time of 'low efficiency' whilst new skills were learnt.

Within the units under the control of the Labour Directorate a number of skilled companies were formed and attached to technical or specialised units. PoW companies comprising skilled workers were employed in forestry, quarrying and at RE and Transport workshops and AOD repair shops.

Amongst the first Chinese to arrive in April 1917 were 450 certified skilled tradesmen and by the end of 1917 this number had increased to 4,726. There were also a number of Chinese who had previous experience of railway maintenance. As a result 21 skilled companies were formed for work, which included port construction (1, 4 and 6 Companies), railway maintenance (112 Company) and at tank workshops (51 and 69 Companies).

Whilst British labour units were not formed into skilled companies some were used primarily for one type of work, thus increasing their efficiency. The 14th Cameronians, for example, were used for forestry work from their arrival in France in July 1916 until May 1917. The formation of employment companies (May 1917) and artizan companies (September 1917) made use of a limited number of skilled tradesmen.

Dividing labour into skilled and unskilled brought with it problems that had not been anticipated. The use of the term 'unskilled' was taken by many to infer that no skill was needed to work in a labour unit. As General Wace was to record:

> It took time to get it recognised that Labour Officers for example, needed certain qualifications, and the failure to recognise that 'Unskilled Labour' had a special purpose to fulfil which needed special qualifications, made the building up of a Labour 'esprit de corps' a difficult matter.[2]

A further difficulty was that some specialised units saw the supervision and instruction of unskilled labour by officers, NCOs or even sappers as their responsibility and that the role of the labour officer and NCOs was purely in respect of discipline. 'This misunderstanding was in time overcome, but it did harm while it lasted.'[3] The misunderstanding can be traced directly to a memo issued by the QMG on 5 January 1917, which stated, 'labour allotted for work under a Department will, during working hours, be distributed and controlled directly under the orders of that Department'.[4] The problem was that many employers took this to mean that the labour unit was a reinforcement of their own units. It became common practice for labour units to be split up and shifted about without any reference to the units' chain of command. The 14th Devonshire Regiment recorded in March 1917 their companies were spread over a large area with detachments being continually moved.[5]

One Directorate but different units

A major difficulty facing the Directorate was the variation in the size of the units under its control. The South African Native Labour battalions were 2,000-strong, and the RE and Infantry labour battalions 1,000. The ASC labour companies and PoW companies were both about 500 strong and the NCC 100 per company. By January 1917 no reinforcements were being sent to the RE Labour battalions and their average strength had dropped to 600 all ranks.

It had already been found that the 1,000 strong battalion was too large a unit for labour purposes. The battalion had to be split into detachments, which were often scattered over a wide area, to the great detriment of both discipline and organisation. The ASC companies had proved themselves to be a far more convenient size and so it was decided that labour units would be organised into companies of 500 all ranks, consisting of four platoons.

Whilst this smaller unit gave more flexibility it brought with it other problems for the Directorate. Army regulations meant that the OC of a labour company was recognised as a commanding officer, which gave him the authority to exercise the full powers of punishment laid down in paragraph 493 of King's Regulations. This gave him the right to deal with a case summarily and award punishments including loss of pay, extra duties or Field Punishment Numbers 1 and 2. However, many of these newly appointed officers, particularly those that arrived with coloured labour units, had neither the experience nor military background that would have been expected of commanding officers. As a commanding officer, reference to a superior authority about discipline or administration would have to be made to the corps commander in Army areas or the Area or Base Commandant on the LoC. To change this would have meant a change in King's Regulations, so Labour Group Headquarters were created, which both solved this problem and aided the administration of labour units.

Group Headquarters

Commanded by a lieutenant colonel supported by an adjutant, a quartermaster, a warrant officer, orderly-room sergeant and twelve other ranks, labour units in an area came under the direction of the Group Headquarters which was responsible for discipline and administration. Where the group contained non-British labour units, an interpreter clerk for each nationality was added to the headquarters. The Group Headquarters acted as the channel of communication between individual companies (usually between 4 and 20) and a higher authority; it was responsible for the administration, billeting, state of accommodation and supplies for the units within the Group. It also had responsibility for the efficiency of the work undertaken by units in the Group and ensuring men received training in, for example, the use of anti-gas appliances.

The creation of the Group enabled the Directorate to put in place a senior officer who could support and advise the inexperienced OC of a company. It was with regard to discipline when the powers given to the Group Commandant were important. If the OC of a company decided an offence was one for which he could not issue a sufficient punishment then he had to refer it to the Group for the commandant to decide whether he could deal with the case himself or to apply for a court martial. The Group commandant was also given the authority to restrict the punishment awarded by the OC of a company to seven days field punishment or forfeiture of pay.

In creating the Group Headquarters the Directorate had, in reality, created a difficulty for itself in Army Areas. Most corps commanders wanted one officer responsible for all matters relating to labour in his corps and the obvious person was the DADL. However, DADLs at corps only held the rank of captain, and not technically a staff officer. As such they experienced difficulties when called upon to issue orders to the lieutenant colonels commanding the labour groups. Difficulties between the two often arose over matters of discipline referred by the Group commander to corps, particularly as the DADLs had been chosen for their ability to organise and distribute labour rather than dealing with the discipline of a force that could be as large as 20,000 men.

Although this difficulty began to appear during the spring of 1917, it was not until March 1918 that a new administrative system was implemented to overcome the problems.

Infantry Labour Companies (ILCs)

The experiences on the Somme in 1916 had highlighted the need for the fighting man to be prepared for an offensive rather than being used as labour, and prior to the Arras offensive demand was made early in 1917 for more ILCs to be sent from Britain. They began to arrive mid-February and by the end of the month 23 ILCs, 75 officers and 11,296 men, had arrived in France. The real increase was to occur the following month when a further 96 ILCs, 348 officers and 45,005 men, were to arrive. So great was the number of men arriving through Boulogne that on 15 March it was decided that only 500 men a day would be allowed to go on leave to Britain until all the labour units had arrived in France.[6]

It was common for an ILC to be created and sent to France within two or three weeks. The story of 5 ILC King's Liverpool Regiment illustrates the part played by the ILCs. Created at Oswestry on 13 February from men 'hastily gathered in drafts from other units or freshly called up from civil life'.[7] When on 25 February it was to be sent to France, 30 men were drafted in from the 23rd (Works) Battalion King's Liverpool to make up the company to full strength. The company arrived at Folkstone rest camp the following day where 18 men had to be isolated due to measles, the remaining 3 officers and 478 men arriving in France on 27 February. The men came from a wide variety of occupations including a baker, a labourer, a farm worker and an innkeeper with ages ranging from 21 to 40. A few, like 20-year-old Private J. White from Manchester, formerly 9 South Lancashire, had seen service earlier in the war but many, like Private J. Armstrong a 39-year-old labourer from Liverpool, had only been called up for service on 13 February. What they all had in common was they were medically unfit for service in the front line.

Arriving in France the company was sent to Aveluy only to find that they should have been taken to Albert and had to march the two miles to their billets. Even worse was to occur twelve days later on 13 March when they had to march seven miles to Albert where they were taken by train to Doullens and then marched another two miles to Grouchies only to find that nobody was expecting them.[8] At the end of March the company was taken by bus to Arras where they were employed at the ammunition dump repairing roads, and for the Town

Commandant clearing roads and sanitary duties. With the formation of the Labour Corps the company became 70 Company Labour Corps.

In August they were moved to Poperinghe where they were employed in the forward area. Unarmed and under constant threat from German artillery and aircraft the Company was employed on road maintenance, loading and unloading ammunition, drainage and ditching and in provided ten men to casualty clearing stations. It was on 11 September that thirteen members of the company were killed whilst marching to work. One of these men was 41790 Private Samuel Slinger whose death was reported in the *Southport Guardian*.[9]

> The following is an extract from a letter received by his parents from his commanding officer, Captain A. L. Evans: 'I am sorry to have to send you bad news of your son, Private S. Slinger, of the company under my command. I very much regret to say that he was killed yesterday by enemy artillery fire while marching to work with his section. A shell dropped by the side of the road and caused a number of casualties. Your son was one of the most willing and best workers in my company. His comrades deplore his death, as he was very much liked, and in conveying to you my sympathy, in your sad loss I can speak for all who knew him.'[10]

The Company was to remain in the Poperinghe area until October 1918, working primarily on roads and defences and at the ammunition dumps. They quickly earned themselves a good reputation for their work, as a letter from the Chief Engineer of XVIII Corps dated 30 September 1917 testifies:

> I would like to thank you, your officers and men for the very good work they have done on my forward roads under trying conditions. They have, in my opinion, materially contributed to the success of our last operations and although they have had a good many casualties I feel that these sacrifices have been made in a good cause. I wish you all a quieter time and hope you will work with me again.
> Signed Brig H G J L Lotbinere.[11]

From Poperinghe they were moved to Menin where they remained until January 1919 when they were disbanded, with most of the men joining 732 Company to undertake work at the docks.

Middlesex Alien Companies

The decision to create Middlesex Regiment battalions from naturalized Britons whose parents were enemy aliens was announced in June 1916 in ACI 1209.[12] By August, two battalions had been formed and were employed on military labour tasks in Britain.

The need for labour led, early in 1917, to the decision to send Alien companies to France. The 1st (Alien Company) Middlesex Regiment, 4 officers and 493 other ranks, arrived in France on 6 March 1917. Three more companies, the 2nd, 3rd and 4th Companies, were to arrive later in March and during April, bringing the number of men to almost 2,000. A further four companies were to arrive during

1918, the 5th and 6th Companies in April, the 7th in July and the 8th in December, bringing the total number of men to almost 4,000.

The war establishment and scale of clothing and equipment for the Middlesex (Alien) Companies were the same as those for the British labour companies. As with the NCC companies, they were administered by the Labour Directorate and employed as part of a labour group although they were not to become part of the Labour Corps. The decision not to transfer the Alien companies to the Labour Corps being made, not by GHQ in France, but by the War Office.[13]

Men from Alien companies sent to their base depot were not retained for any length of time and were either returned to their own unit as soon as possible or returned to Britain. Similarly, new arrivals from Britain were sent on to their company within a day or two. No man in an Alien company could be transferred or posted to another unit or branch of the service without special War Office authority.[14]

Unlike men in the British Labour Corps the majority of those in Alien companies were medical category A and, as General Wace recorded, 'were excellent workers'.[15] As men with parents who were enemy aliens there were severe restrictions placed upon where and how the companies could be employed. In June 1917, for example, when half of the 4th Company were working in Nieppe Forest, the Labour Directorate reminded officers that 'being Aliens they should not be split up but all employed in one place'.[16]

Good officers create good units

When the labour battalions were being formed during 1916 the officers and men were drawn from those deemed as 'Fit for Labour' on the LoC. The men of the 19th Cheshires, for example, were 'drawn from all units in the Western Command, and included cotton spinners and factory hands from the Midlands, farmers from the country towns, and miners from South Wales'.[17] Although the battalion had only two weeks training in Britain before being sent to France, the majority of its officers and men had seen prior service, albeit in Britain, in the Army.

Amongst the officers selected to serve in labour units were men who had already seen service in France and returned to Britain due to injury. Lieutenant Cecil Fowke, Border Regiment, had returned with shell shock in June 1916. After four Medical Boards, in October he was declared unfit for general service but fit for light duties with the regiment's reserve battalion. Posted to the 22nd (Labour) Battalion Cheshire Regiment on its formation, he arrived in France with them on 16 December. From arrival in France until May 1917 the battalion was primarily used on railway work between Arques and Berguette and between Doullens and Arras. In May (now 65 Company Labour Corps) they were moved to the Poperinghe area. Employed on the light railways in the Ypres Salient the company was often working within the range of German guns, and on 19 June six men were killed by shell fire. Whilst the company was employed in this area Cecil Fowke's shell shock returned. He returned to Britain on 12 July where after several more Medical Boards he joined Western Command labour centre in November 1917 and later served with 540 HS Employment Company at the PoW Camp, Chepstow.

The speed with which the labour companies were created and formed at the start of 1917 meant that, initially at least, many of the officers of labour units had neither the military experience nor skills needed for their role. Whilst many were to prove to be good officers others were less successful. William Forgan, a civil engineer, applied for a commission in February 1917. A month later he was commissioned into 3 ILC Seaforth Highlanders based at Blairgowrie. Sent to France in April he was posted to the 1st ILC, Seaforths (12 Company Labour Corps) near Arras. By June the company was located in the Dickebusch area working primarily on both broad gauge and light railways, dangerous work that attracted attack from German heavy guns. How these attacks affected the officers of this company is not known. However, on 9 August the company CO, Captain Ripon, was found guilty at a FGCM of drunkenness and sentenced to forfeiture of seniority and a severe reprimand. A month later Second Lieutenant Forgan was to face a FCGM charged with conduct to the prejudice of good order and military discipline and drunkenness. Acquitted on the first charge he was convicted of drunkenness and sentenced to dismissal. On 9 October the sentenced was commuted to a severe reprimand although 'the Council further decided that the officer was to be called upon to resign his commission, adjudging him unfit to hold H.M.'s commission'.[18]

In a letter to the War Office on 22 October, William Forgan explained that in February he had been invited to take up the duties of a 'Technical Officer' and only to be employed in giving technical advice. When he arrived in France he found that there were no 'Technical Officers' and 'in spite of the fact that I never had any army training was sent as a discipline officer to join the 12th Lab Coy at the Arras Front. I found that from the want of training I was quite unfitted for these duties and the physical strain was too much for me so that my health broke under it.'[19] He went on to ask that he be relieved of his commission or placed where his technical knowledge could be used. Second Lieutenant Forgan resigned his commission on 16 November 1917.

Age does not seem to have been a barrier to a man being appointed as an officer with a labour unit. Herbert Cunningham Clogstoun arrived in France with the Indian Labour Corps on 23 August 1917. A former policeman and farmer in India, aged 60 years and 7 months, he was to command the 55th (Khasi) Company from October 1917 until May 1918. He went on to serve as an instructor at the Indian Base Depot and in 1919 for the India Office in London.

Another of the successful older officers was Roger Pocock. Aged 49 when war was declared, Pocock had already had an incredible life as an adventurer and writer, which included service in the Canadian North-West Mounted Police in the 1880s, spending six months riding from Canada to Mexico and service in an irregular unit during the Boer War. In December 1904 he initiated the Legion of Frontiersmen, a patriotic, armed volunteer auxiliary force that both trained for war and hunted for German spies. Although Pocock's link with the Legion ended at an acrimonious general meeting in 1909, the organisation prospered and was reportedly 17,500 strong by August 1914.[20]

Pocock tried to enlist when war was declared but was rejected because of his age, in addition to being both shortsighted and physically impaired. After many attempts he succeeded in enlisting, was promoted to corporal and became an orderly-room clerk. Through a legion contact he was appointed quartermaster sergeant, then lieutenant of the Warwickshire Territorial Royal Horse Artillery in 1915. In late

December 1916 he was ordered to Taunton to become one of the platoon commanders of 1 ILC Hampshire Regiment (later to become 178 Company, Labour Corps). Pocock describes how after three days the officer due to command the company arrived only to be found to be unsuitable and Pocock was promoted to captain and in command of the company.

Pocock was both fiercely patriotic and an unconventional officer. He wrote about his experience as CO of 178 Company in an article he subtitled 'A Chronicle of Heroic Crocks'. To Pocock it was a privilege to serve: 'For young and able-bodied men it was their right to serve in the fighting line, but for us of the Labour Corps – the aged, the disabled, the wreckage of the Army and of the nation, it was a privilege to be allowed within the danger areas.'[21] He described his company as 'an amazing mixture of volunteers up to 70 years of age, of conscripts drawn from sedentary life, of Jews from the slums and gypsies from the highways, roughs, tramps, company directors, public entertainers, pavement artists, navvies – rich, poor, destitute, but all of us alike, rated unfit.'[22]

Despite referring to his men as 'the dregs of England put to the test of war'[23] his prime concern was for them rather than 'the "base wallahs" at Boulogne with plenty of decorations and no manners'.[24] When one of his men committed an offence that could have resulted in the death sentence he showed an unconventional approach to justice. He arranged for the man and the his friend to be left with the company's sergeant major for 40 minutes during which summary justice was applied:

> Honour was satisfied, and there were black eyes and broad grins when I resumed the trial, inflicting such ferocious punishment that I was afterwards hauled over the coals for tyranny. But the mutineers, a gang of Birmingham pugilists, had become my devout allies, enforcing discipline.[25]

Prior to the attack at Messines Ridge the amount of work asked of the company resulted in all four platoons becoming exhausted. Once again Pocock's unconventional approach emerged and he created and personally led a fifth platoon for night work made up of 'officers and clerks, sick, lame, and lazy, cooks, guard and prisoners'.[26]

During the battle of Messines Ridge, due to a staff officer's blunder, the company's camp was located in full view and range of German guns. Without permission he moved them behind Kemmel Hill:

> I could afford to be cashiered for cowardice in the field and would rather be shot outright than allow my men to be massacred because a fool had blundered. A succession of these gentry came about me, chill in their manner, pointing out the enormity of my conduct. I told them to go and see the camp I had abandoned, barely in time before it was destroyed.[27]

The Arras Offensive

The Arras Offensive, which began on 9 April, was to be the first test of the new labour organisation. Most of the ADLs and DADLs were appointed during

February and March and, as such, had not had time to settle into their role. The first difficulty they had to overcome was making employers understand that labour was not permanently allotted to them nor was it within their prerogative to allocate it to another task without reference to the Directorate.

A second difficulty that had to be overcome was the inefficient use of labour. It was common for employers to request far more men than were required for the task. On 3 February 1917 the Third Army DQMG sent a memo to all services and departments pointing out that there were many examples of faulty allotment of tasks by employers. He cited examples of 100 men being allocated to a task for which only 50 were required and the 'remaining 50 were left to sit about in the cold with nothing to do' and of ten men allotted to unload a truck when only four men could work on it at a time and of too few tools being available for the number of men being employed.[28]

Both the weather and a lack of suitable equipment added to the difficulties labour units were to face. The hard frost experienced in VII Corps area at the end of January resulted in roads quickly becoming damaged and unsuitable for vehicles; the Corp's DADL recording on 1 February that 'Practically all work has stopped. Picks & shovels are so blunt that work clearing drains cannot proceed quickly.'[29] The ADL of the Third Army noted that, on 15 February, the 22nd Cheshires were asked to undertake rail cutting at Authieule with blunt tools and on 3 April that 5 and 6 Northamptonshire ILCs, had 'no respirators, helmets, oilskins or orders'.[30]

A further difficulty related to both the numbers of labour troops arriving in France and the experience and capabilities of both officers and men. At the beginning of 1917 there were some 25,000 men employed on labour in the Third Army Area, of which 6,000 were in labour battalions and the remainder supplied by fighting formations. By the middle of February the number of fighting troops used for labour had risen to 23,000. General Haldane, commanding VI Corps, estimated that he employed in excess of 4,000 men in and around Arras, the majority of men being taken from his four divisions and not from labour units.[31]

As ILCs arrived in France they were allocated to the sectors where they could be used to replace fighting troops. Their work included constructing three railway lines, turning existing single track into double track, the connections between the lateral and the light railways and the construction of a network of forward light railways. On 10 March ten companies were allotted specifically to this work – three in VI Corps, five in VII Corps and two in XVII Corps. In the Third Army area the 6 ILBs were supplemented by 34 ILCs so that by the opening of the battle the number of fighting men being used for labour had reduced to 2,000. By the end of the battle on 15 May there were 37,000 men in labour units in the Third Army Area being entirely administered by the ADL, Third Army, assisted by three DADLs.

Creation of the Labour Corps

The formal announcement of the creation of the Labour Corps was published as Army Order 85 on 21 February 1917.[32] The detail of how the Corps would be organised, both in Britain and overseas, was published in ACI 611 on 13 April.[33]

ACI 611 announced that labour companies, with a total strength of 500, were to be formed from the labour battalions and ILCs. Two companies were formed from each battalion so, for example, the 19th Royal Scots became 1 and 2 Labour Companies and the 14th Scottish Rifles became 3 and 4 Companies. Each ILC formed one Labour Company with, for example, the King's Liverpool Regiment's 27 ILCs becoming 66–92 Companies. The companies were numbered 1–203,[34] the men in them being issued with a number in the range 1–121,800.[35] The labour battalion's HQ personnel were used to form 42 Labour Group Headquarters, being issued with regimental numbers 121,801–122,600.[36] In reality these instructions merely formalised the arrangements that the Directorate had already put into place.

Although details of the ACI were issued to Armies on the day it was published, many transfers to the Labour Corps only began to be put into place from the beginning of May. The 6th Labour Group recorded that the change of numbers would operate from 13 May 1917 when, for example, 3 ILC Devonshire became 168 Company and 2 ILC Hampshire became 179 Company.[37] Service records show a similar pattern for men already serving in France. Edward Blower's, for example, records his transfer from 37079, 3 ILC Lincolnshire Regiment, to 24664, 42 Company Labour Corps as taking place on 9 May 1917.

Two British labour units were not transferred to the Labour Corps, the Middlesex Alien companies and the NCC, but like foreign labour units, they were administered by the Labour Directorate.

Base Depot

In producing ACI 611 the Army Council appears to have neglected to consider the whole picture with regard to unskilled labour in France. Whilst establishing the structure of the labour company and its administration through the group, no reference was made to employments in Army Areas or on the LoC. In addition, consideration does not appear to have been given to the mechanism to deal with men arriving in France or those being returned to Britain.

These oversights were to be rectified with the publication of ACI 837 on 21 May.[38] The ACI created the Labour Corps Base Depot at Boulogne to receive men arriving from or returning to Britain. Commanded by a lieutenant colonel the Depot's staff comprised an adjutant, a quartermaster, a RSM, a RQMS, 11 clerks, 8 sergeants, 2 batmen and 66 other ranks for general duties. The Base Depot also received for transfer to the Labour Corps men from infantry and other non-technical units who having been discharged from hospital were medically classified as lower than A but fit enough to serve in France.

General Labour Companies

By April 1917 many labour battalions were operating above their nominal strength of 1,000, and surplus men were allotted to the C-in-C to form the companies 184 to 200. With insufficient numbers to form all fifteen companies additional men were found from two sources:

1   Men classified as PB, for example, number 9 Permanent Base Company, forming 197 Company.
2   Bantams who were already being used as labour, for example, 193 Company being formed primarily from the 17th West Yorkshires and 195 from Bantams attached to the 36th Royal Fusiliers.

The 12 RE labour battalions and 24 ASC labour companies, whilst being administered by the Labour Directorate, were not transferred to the Labour Corps on its formation. This was to change with the publication of ACI 985 on 20 June, the RE battalions becoming 700–711 Companies and the ASC companies 712–735 Companies.[39] Men previously in these units who had already been returned to Britain were also transferred to the Labour Corps unless there was a specific request to retain a man in either the RE or ASC.

From June 1917 onwards only one other general labour company would be formed in France. In April 1918 it was decided that Russians and other aliens should be withdrawn from fighting units become labour troops. These men were not to be employed at ports, near important depots, in tank areas or in forward areas. Initially it was decided they should be sent to the Middlesex Regiment Base Depot at Etaples and that Russians would be formed into a separate labour company. It appears that this presented the authorities with administrative difficulties, so the decision was changed and these men were placed in either 160 Company or, in the case of any dissatisfied Russian, into a separate section of 1 Scottish Company NCC. There is no explanation of why these two companies were chosen, although it appears that there were disagreements at GHQ about the use of these men, with the QMG favouring their move to the NCC company. With the War Office deciding on 8 June 1918 that the Russians would not have restrictions placed upon where they worked, a Labour Corps Company (991) was formed from both Russians and Rumanians who had been withdrawn from the front, such as 581966 Private J. Zokas, as well as from Russians already serving in the Labour Corps, like 273859 Private A. Citron. The Company was sent to the 3rd Army Area where it was employed on the LoC at Le Ponchel.[40]

Life and work in General Companies

The life and work of individual companies is poorly documented in War Diaries. Until the formation of the Labour Corps several of the labour battalions and ILCs did keep their own diary but these ceased by May 1917. From then onwards there are few company diaries, as instructions were given that they did not have to be kept. References in higher level diaries tend to focus on where companies were located rather than the work undertaken or the conditions in which the men worked.

Official Histories also make few references to the work of labour companies and when they are mentioned it is in general terms rather than individual companies. In preparation for the attack at Vimy Ridge in April 1917 eight companies (67, 89, 91, 92, 100, 113, 122 and 139) some 4,000 men worked with Canadian and RE units installing gas and smoke canisters. The only reference in the Official History to this labour is 'Labour Companies of the Royal Fusiliers, King's, Queen's and Northamptonshire Regiments,'[41] whilst the Canadian and RE units are listed by name.

For a Corps that accounted for over 11 per cent of the Army in France at the Armistice there are comparatively few works written by officers and men. Private Theodore Stewart[42] (6 Company), Corporal J. Cumming Morgan[43] (8 Company) and Captain Roger Pocock[44] (178 Company) all wrote articles that were published in the 1920s and 1930s. One thing that is common is the danger that these unarmed, old and unfit men faced:

> The delusion existed, and probably still exists, that no labour companies were ever nearer the line than twenty miles. But when I tell you that the company to which I belonged – originally half of a Scottish labour battalion – was for last seventeen months of the War never at any moment out of range of Jerry's guns, and that when he did get us he got us with his biggest guns and with his high-velocities, from which there was no dodging, and that during the struggle for Passchendaele in the autumn of 1917 our company were awarded a Military Cross, a D.C.M., and eight M.M.'s – well we must have been within hearing distance, anyway.[45]

Unarmed labour companies were, on occasions, required to go forward into the trenches as part of their maintenance role at Ypres. Stewart's company had to

> … fill sandbags in the rear and carry them forward for the reconstruction of damaged parts of the front line and other trenches. It was then that one realised that one was 'in amongst the real stuff'. Now the weird 'ping' of bullets through the air and the 'whistling' of shells with their succession of 'krupps' brought home to one the real character of modern warfare.[46]

An account of Company life can be found in two books, privately published in 1920, by Captain John H. Pedley[47] (67 Company) and Captain Thomas C. Thomas[48] (58 Company).

Pedley had attempted to join up in 1914 but was rejected because of his age. Commissioned in 1915 into the 6th Essex he served in London District until January 1917 when, following the Silvertown Explosion, he managed to convince the War Office to send him to a labour company in France.[49] Pedley joined 168 Company in June 1917 before being promoted to captain and becoming OC 67 Company in September. His first task with 67 Company was to maintain the Menin Road, the company being shelled each day whilst working and bombed and shelled nearly every night. In these conditions Pedley 'had great difficulty in keeping the men in a contented state, as they were at work all day and had to keep on the move most of the night dodging shells and bombs'.[50] Keeping the men fit for work was vital; during December 1917 when the cold and wet conditions caused problems with trench foot Pedley made the men rub their feet with whale oil, and held frequent foot inspections.

Too often the work of the Labour Corps was not recognised. When the Bailleul Ammunition Dump was set on fire by shelling, Pedley's company cleared it despite shells burning furiously and exploding. However, whilst a staff major and the Ordnance officer in charge of the dump were awarded the MC, the Ordnance sergeant major the DCM, and four other ranks of the Ordnance MMs 'not a single award was made to any of my officers or men, although we did the majority of the work, as there were very few Ordnance men employed on the dump'.[51]

When the 19th (Labour) Battalion Cheshire Regiment was formed in March 1916, Captain Thomas was placed in command of 'C' Company, which was to become 58 Company Labour Corps in May 1917. Thomas earned a reputation as an excellent officer but refused promotion, preferring to remain as OC 58 Company. His efforts were rewarded with both an OBE and MC, the citation for the latter stating:

> Near Courtrai, from the 19th to 23rd October 1918, he displayed fine leadership, and made excellent dispositions of his company, which was engaged in converting meter gauge to light railway 60cm track under considerable enemy shell fire and without proper tools for this work. Chiefly owing to his personal effort and example his company completed the 5½ miles of track required for corps ammunition supply by a voluntary effort of 11½ hours work under hostile shell fire.[52]

In the preface to his book Thomas explains that it was not written as a war book but rather

> It is but a plain record, written as a souvenir for the members of a company for whom I have the greatest admiration and respect, with the hope that it will bring back to their memory the days we spent together, when time will have effaced all recollection of the bad days we had and we remember only the good.[53]

This, perhaps more than anything else, sums up the respect and affection this officer had for the men in his company. Although 58 Company continued to exist until August 1919 the decision that demobilisation would be for individuals rather than companies clearly affected Thomas. He ends his book in December 1918:

> My hopes of taking my Company back to England and breaking up there were doomed to disappointment. Individual demobilisation has been ordered, and the company will be gradually shrinking smaller and smaller as the well known faces leave us. Therefore with the wish that we shall some day meet together again, I bring my diary to a close with the end of the year.[54]

The 19th Cheshires maintained a War Diary until April 1917.[55] After this, references to 58 Company are to be found in GHQ, Army, Corps and Labour Group Diaries.[56]

For much of their time 58 Company worked on railway construction and maintenance and developed a reputation as an efficient and skilled unit. This was not the case for most companies who were used for a variety of different roles. Arriving on 14 March 1917 the 11 ILC King's Liverpool Regiment (76 Company) were sent to unload ammunition at Fosseux Loop railhead. At the time the company was described as 'lacking in discipline or any knowledge of military requirements. Naturally the men are helpless and of poor physique. In one case I found a hut which was to be occupied the next day, used as a latrine by the men who were to occupy it.'[57] During the next three months they were to be used for railway and road maintenance before being moved to Wailly in July where they salvaged ammunition. The Company Commander considering the task 'very dangerous and not at all suited to labour' and complained that it was being carried out without sufficient skilled supervisors.[58] They remained in the Wailly area until the end of

October 1917 unloading stores and ammunition at the railhead, at the ammunition dump, on salvage work and building huts. During the Battle of Cambrai they were used on the roads, to build and repair bridges, lay water pipes and build defences. Twelve months after being described as having no military discipline and poor physiques, they were commended at the time of the German offensive for handling '11 tons of ammunition per man during 14 hours' at a forward ammunition dump and railhead and for their work building defences.[59]

Death or injury whilst at work was common amongst labour companies. Often the cause was enemy shelling, as was the case when 57 Company were shelled on 23 July 1917. During shelling three men were killed and eight wounded, including 33876 Sergeant C. Bessler who was awarded the MM for his actions.

> Though wounded in the chest from shrapnel, he continued on duty until after daylight, encouraging the men in their work. He also, after the working party was marched off, organized a burying party and collected the remains of those killed, and saw them buried. He collapsed from his wound later and was taken to hospital.[60]

Some of the most dangerous work occurred when ordnance was set alight by shelling. On 11 August 1917 152 Company were employed at the salvage dump in Elverdinghe Chateau when two shells set it on fire. Most of the company scattered because of the fire. The company commander, Captain Cohen, was trapped by the fire and 90615 Corporal Walker 'at the imminent risk of his life, dashed into the flames and rescued Captain Cohen'.[61] Despite his efforts Captain Cohen died of his wounds. Lieutenant Wellings, Privates 128375 Haley, 90613 Pople and 91054 Webb of 152 Company were also killed. For his actions Corporal Walker became one of the 24 members of British labour companies awarded the DCM.

Accidents also accounted for a large number of injuries and death as men were often working either with or among unexploded ordnance. On 18 October 1917 a party from 109 Company were filling sand bags with rubble. 382271 Private C. Timmins was killed when he placed his shovel into a heap, which concealed a number of grenades. His shovel caused them to explode, killing him.

As Pedley pointed out, danger of injury or death did not only present during the working day. Shelling and air raids on camps were commonplace. The camp of 187 Company was shelled on the night of 21 July 1917, resulting in the deaths of three men and another seven being buried by debris. Seven of their colleagues obtained shovels to dig them out. For these actions 111750 Sergeant Holmes was awarded the MM and the others MID. One of the most serious attacks occurred on 18 August 1917 at the camp occupied by 48 Company, which resulted in 17 men being killed and 58 wounded.

Life in a labour company was equally as difficult as that of a man on the front line. The infantry soldier remained in the front line for a few weeks followed by rest and training in the rear area. Labour companies worked for six days out of seven and remained in one location, often within the range of German guns, for weeks or even months. Thomas recounts how 58 Company moved to Ypres on 31 May 1917:

> From now on, over a period of twelve months, until we were withdrawn from the salient in May 1918, our work was carried out to the accompaniment of bursting

shells and bombs. Scarcely a day passed without one or more parties being shelled off and the number of narrow escapes were legion.[62]

It is difficult enough for a professional soldier to live and work in a danger zone for months at a time. So one can only imagine what it must have been like for the Labour Corps comprised of 'men of low medical category, untrained to arms and unaccustomed to discipline'.[63] In order to help maintain discipline and divert men's attention from the horrors and dangers around them, sporting and social activities formed an important aspect of their life when not working.

By far the most popular sporting activity was football, although in the Ypres Salient the pitch could and did come under shellfire:

> On one particular day, during an exciting match, one team were making a great attack when a shell pitched near. They dropped like one man, but the unfortunate goalie, jumping up to save a shot, failed to get down quickly enough and was outed. We arrived half an hour later to find a goal post smashed and a huge hole just alongside. This was promptly filled up, the post mended, and the match played; but somehow or other the goalie at that end did not play up to his reputation, showing signs of nervousness.[64]

58 Company had a particularly good football team, they played 38 matches, won 28, lost 2 and drew 8, with a goal record of 174 for and 13 against. Matches were played against both Labour Corps and Infantry Battalion teams. One can only imagine the reaction of a Guards team when they were beaten by a labour company especially when 'least in stature, "Tiny" Whitehead, that great little player, who in a memorable match against the Coldstream Guards, surprised their right back by running between his legs and scoring'.[65]

Other sports included athletics and cricket. Playing cricket in the Salient was also difficult owing to an absence of turf and an outfield that was always full of shell-holes and within the range of German guns. Companies also organised their own concert parties: 'Our concert party was one of the most prominent features of the company.'[66] Concert parties would include sketches, recitations, songs, comedians and inevitably a female impersonator. The importance of sport and entertainment cannot be underestimated in helping these men maintain some form of normality:

> All this sport and amusement helped us all to forget for a while the monotony and danger of our lives, and in this we were helped by the wonderful sense of humour possessed by the men themselves. No situation was ever too serious to be made the subject of a joke, and many and varied were the yarns told of one another round the braziers from time to time.[67]

The other important aspect of life was maintaining contact with home. Letters home were censored so gave no idea of the man's location or the conditions in which he lived and worked. It was occasionally possible to get a green envelope, which enabled a man to send a letter that bypassed the company's censor. Content in green envelopes was restricted to family matters and they could be examined at the base depot. Men often took the risk of including details of where they were in green envelopes such as 'and landed here at Crouy Tuesday evening'.[68]

At Christmas the Corps produced and sold its own Christmas card.[69] The profit from the cards (£248 10s 6d) being used to send items to benefit Labour Corps men being held prisoner by the Germans. A second card was produced and sold in 1918 with a further £505 1s being raised. As the war had ended the money was used to create a fireplace, mantelpiece and seats as permanent memorial to the Labour Corps at the Union Jack Club in London.[70]

Employment Companies

The growth of the Army and the formation of schools, baths, cinemas, canteens and other institutions meant that the demand for men for employments always exceeded the number of PB men available. This meant that the fighting soldier had to be used when not in the trenches, at a time when he should be either resting or training. The number being used had grown to such an extent that, at times, it was difficult to accurately identify the fighting strength of units.

In March 1917 the Directorate suggested to the War Office that low category men be sent to France to form employment companies. At divisional level there were already men being used permanently for employment duties, primarily on salvage. Initially, the War Office agreed to send a Headquarters (2 officers and 5 other ranks) together with 104 men to add to those already being employed at divisional level to create Divisional Employment (DE) companies. The 4th DE Company was the first to arrive on 17 May and immediately sent to the 4th Division. The following day the 7th DE Company arrived, becoming the 2nd Division's company. More groups were to arrive during the next three weeks at the end of which DE companies had been formed in 18 of the 50 divisions.

Outside divisions the same core group did not exist. The fighting men on extra regimental employment constantly changed and both the administration and supervision of PB men was inconsistent. Additionally, labour units were frequently being misused on employments.

The solution to the problem, announced in ACI 837, was the creation of two new Labour Corps units – the Divisional and the Area Employment company, both with an establishment of 2 officers and 273 other ranks. At the same time the QMG sent out a circular to all employers saying that labour company personnel were not to be used on employments and that until Employment companies were formed all employments were to be found from PB men.

Divisional Employment Companies

With Divisional Employment companies becoming part of the Labour Corps the existing unit numbers were in danger of being confused with company numbers announced in ACI 611. The decision was made to use company numbers 204–254 for DE companies, and those already in place renumbered. The 1st Division's company changed from the 6th DE Company to 204 Company Labour Corps and the 4th Division's renumbered from the 4th DE Company to 207 Company. Forming 50 DE companies was to take from the end of May until the middle of July. The last company to be formed was 223 DE Company of the 36th Division on 21 July. The Guards Division also had their own company which was formed from men of the Guard's regiments and was not included in the Labour Corps

On 16 September 1917, additional DE companies were formed for the three cavalry divisions (771, 772 and 773 Companies). Two more DE companies (984 and 985) were to be formed in April and May 1918 when 52nd and 74th Divisions arrived in France from Palestine.

DE companies were permanently attached to a division and would move with that division. Located at divisional HQ their role was to run the various divisional institutions such as baths, laundries, canteens, recreation rooms, entertainment and stores. The company also undertook clerical duties, general construction and repair duties, salvage, and sanitation duties as well as providing men as cemetery wardens, caretakers and guards for storage areas. Amongst the regular tasks that the company had to undertake was unloading supply trains. For this work to be carried out efficiently it was recognised that men had to be in good physical condition and so the company was allowed to have up to 40 A men, the remainder being B(i).

As shown below, a definitive establishment was drawn up for DE companies to ensure that each company had men with the skills required for their specific role.

Canteens	10	Orderlies, DHQ	16
Cooks, DHQ	6	Entertainments	12
Cooks, Brigade Headquarters	9	Salvage	50
Band	30	Sanitary	16
Train loaders	75	General duties	17
Clerks, DHQ	8	Shoemakers & Tailors	5
Clerks, Brigade HQ	6	Baths	8
Clerks, R.A. HQ	2		
		Total	270

Table 5: Duties performed by personnel of DE Companies.

Corps and Army Employment Companies

Following the publication of ACI 837 on 21 May 1917, company numbers 255–294 were allocated to Area Employment (AE) companies. These companies were not expected to have to carry out duties as arduous as those employed at divisional level and so for service in an AE company men were graded medical category B(i) or lower.

As early as December 1916 it had been suggested by the Director of Labour that all PB should come under his direct control but objections from other services meant that this was not implemented when the Directorate came into force. There were only a limited number of men in France that the Directorate could transfer from general labour units to AE companies, so initially, companies had to be created in Britain and sent to France.

The Directorate decided that companies would be used in two different ways. Some would be allocated to an Army Area or on the LoC where they would be included within a Labour Group and could be moved to wherever needed. Corps and Army Headquarters would have a company permanently allocated to them and, like DE companies, moved with the formation to which they were attached. At both Corps and Army HQs a definite establishment of specialists such as cooks, clerks and orderlies was drawn up to ensure that men with these skills were posted to these companies.

Companies 256–260 were appointed as the employment companies for the 1st–5th Armies respectively. Their role was to carry out regimental employments as required and provide guards. Almost half of the men in the employment company allocated to Army HQ were employed as cooks, clerks or orderlies.

Canteens	4
Cooks	28
Clerks	30
Orderlies	70
Guards	36
General duties	90
Sanitary	12
Total	270

Table 6: Establishment of an Army HQ Employment Company.

It was decided that the needs of a Corps HQ could be met with a smaller establishment of 1 officer and 119 ORs and the War Office approved this in June 1917. The corps employment companies were numbered from 261–277. Companies 261–274 for I–XV Corps respectively and 275–277 for XVII, XVIII and XIX Corps.

Commanded by a captain or subaltern, administration of the company was carried out by a CQMS and an orderly-room clerk. The establishment for the remaining 117 men is shown below.

Canteens	4
Cooks	11
Clerks	14
Orderlies	24
Police	8
Butchers, tailors, shoemakers	8
General duties	35
Sanitary	12
Batman	1
Total	117

Table 7: Establishment of a Corps HQ Employment Company.

The first company to be taken on strength at Corps HQ was 261 at I Corps on 1 August.[71] The remainder arrived during August and early September with, for example, 275 Company taken on the strength of XVII Corps on 9 September.[72] An examination of the records indicates that most of these companies arrived at their Corp HQ with around 94 other ranks. There is, however, no indication when they achieved their full strength or where the additional men came from.

Area Employment Companies

In addition to the companies allocated by ACI 837 to Divisional, Corps and Army headquarters a further eighteen companies were created for both Army Areas and on the LoC. The first eleven of these, 736–746 were to arrive in France between 28 and 30 July 1917.

The demand for men to undertake employments far exceeded the number available in these companies and so a new dual system of operation was instigated. Some employments were being undertaken by Labour Corps Employment companies under the direct control of the Directorate and some by PB men who were provided from the employment base depots.

At company level a list was kept showing the employment for which the men in the company were best suited. The list covered some seventeen different types of employment as shown below.

Batmen	Policemen
Cook	Butcher
Storeman or Caretaker	Regimental Institute
Sanitary duty	Salvage
Orderly	Loader and Brakesman
Clerk	Bath and Drying room
Tailor	Laundry
Shoemaker	Traffic control
	Telephone Operator

Table 8: Categories of employment in AE Companies.

Keeping a list did not guarantee that the men were capable of undertaking tasks asked of them. 743 Company arrived in France on 31 July and were sent to work at Ghyvelde where it was noted that there were 'very few men suitable for employment except on jobs requiring minimum intelligence'.[73]

In August instructions were sent out by GHQ that all PB men, with the exception of those filling authorised establishment of units, should be transferred to the Labour Corps and formed into Area Employment companies. Armies and the LoC submitted a return to GHQ indicating the number of companies they had formed, at which point they were allocated a company number. Companies were initially formed under the command of Town Majors or Area Commandants until Labour Corps officers could be appointed to command them. In XI Corps, for example, the Bethune (Area) Company, renumbered as 823 AE Company, was formed on 30 August from PB men serving at five towns in the area.[74] Companies created in this way often had far too many men with one type of skill. For example, when 752 Company was formed at Cassel on 18 October over half the men had been employed at the Army School of Signals. This resulted in an additional burden being placed on the Labour Corps administration, having to transfer men to companies where their skills could be utilised.

Although created primarily in order to undertake employments, AE companies were also used for general labour duties if needed or when there was a lack of suitable employment for them. There are numerous examples of AE companies undertaking general tasks in Army Areas, including 281 Company employed on roadwork near Perrone in September 1917 and 293 Company on burial duties in October 1917 at Hamel and Miraumont.

Using employment companies for general duties was even more common on the LoC, particularly at the base ports. A few companies were formed surplus to requirements for employments and it was soon realised that this was wasteful of resources so they were added to the general labour pool. These companies were later amalgamated or converted to general labour companies.

As the AE companies began to undertake their work it was found that the establishment of two officers per Area Employment company was really more than was necessary for the efficient administration of the company and so it was reduced to only one officer, unless a specific request was made for two. By September 1917 there were 90 AE companies on the LoC and in Army Areas. Two months later that number had risen to 230 companies, including the creation of two new types, Artizan and Garrison Guard companies.

Artizan Companies

On 23 May 1917 the QMG had reminded employers that the Directorate was responsible for the distribution and control of unskilled labour and not artizans and that: 'If artizans serving in British labour units are required by the RE for work at their trades, application must be made for their transfer, after the trade test has been passed, to fill a definite authorised establishment.'[75] In August 1917 it was laid down that no tradesman who possessed a skill required by a technical corps should be allowed to remain in a unit in which his skill was not being utilized.[76] On 12 September the creation of AE (Artizan) companies was authorised by the AG. A number of factors are likely to have had a bearing on the decision to create Artizan AE companies.

The principle of skilled companies under the direct control of the Labour Directorate had already been established with the creation of skilled Chinese Labour Corps companies and skilled PoW companies, both of which were entitled to increased pay if classed as skilled. It is likely that among senior officers there was a view that if skilled Chinese and PoWs earned more, the same opportunity should be given to British Labour Corps soldiers, although no evidence can be found to support this theory.

By this time there were many men, like 179220 Private William Hatto, serving in the Labour Corps in France who were skilled tradesmen. Private Hatto, a carpenter, was originally in 336 Company, who were employed by the RE at Woolwich, from 28 April 1917. When AE companies were formed he was sent to France as part of 743 AE Company where he remained until posted to 927 AE (Artizan) Company on its formation in November 1917. He was to remain a member of this company until his death from pneumonia on 10 December 1918. Although William Hatto's skills were used in an Artizan company, tradesmen also served in a number of the general labour companies, which whilst not classified as skilled, had become known for producing good work at a particular task.

The first Artizan companies, (780, 781 and 782) were formed from personnel already serving in the 5th Army Area on 28 September 1917. Companies were formed in the other Army Areas and on the LoC until by December 1917 a total of 24 Artizan companies had been formed. It appears that men who claimed to be tradesmen were posted to a company utilising their skill. In addition to the traditional building trades, they included engine drivers, sign writers, tinsmiths and metalworkers. On posting to a company men were tested to ensure that they had the skill they claimed. Passing the trade test entitled the man to additional pay on the days when he was employed at his trade. Inevitably there was a mismatch of trades, which resulted in the men being moved to other Artizan companies. On 7 January 1918, for example, 834 Company received 6 carpenters from 927 Company, 51 carpenters, 4 fitters and 5 tinsmiths from 936 Company and 5 blacksmiths and 7 fitters from 937 Company.

As with other employment companies men were expected to undertake tasks needed by the company in addition to their trade. In 834 Company, 372133 Private Brodie, a bricklayer, was the company's bootmaker, 108120 Private Davis a mason and chiropodist, 101597 Private Fitcher a painter and haircutter and 91401 Private Freer a painter and butcher. Employment companies were also used for general labouring tasks. Capt C. D. Stoneham, OC of 834 Company, recorded in his Field Service Handbook on 24 November 1917: 'Sgt Hall & Men of No 4 Hut Upper Camp – to move to Albert Station with shovels to unload coal.'[77]

Much of the work was undertaken by detachments with appropriate skills sent where required. Often an NCO, selected for his own trade skill, commanded the detachment. A request for men to work at a Motor Depot in November 1917 saw a detachment made up of two decorators, two glaziers, three painters and a mason being sent from 834 Company. A month later, on 24 December, 927 Company had detachments of men varying in size from 6 to 21 working at two hospitals, on the brigade water tanks, at an auxiliary petrol depot and for the Town Commandant at Arras. If a company did not have sufficient personnel for the task men could be loaned from another Artizan company in the area. When 936 Company required additional bricklayers in order to complete an officers mess they were loaned two by 834 Company.

Garrison Guard Companies

On enlistment a man was given a medical examination which determined the service that he was capable of undertaking. For those not fit enough for general service one alternative was garrison service overseas. The 4th (Garrison) Battalion Royal Welsh Fusiliers, for example, was formed at Bebington in April 1916 and sent to France in June 1916. In France they were used to guard bases, ammunition and store dumps and railway communications. Men were also trained in the use of machine and Lewis guns for anti-aircraft duties. New garrison guard companies were formed following the publication of HQ LoC Circular AH2849 on 28 August 1917.[78] Each company, comprising 3 officers and 223 other ranks, was identified by a letter rather than a number.

In September 1917 the decision was made to transfer the GG companies to the Labour Corps. At GHQ 934 (GG) Company was formed on 20 September[79] and six days later the Director of Labour recorded that Garrison Guard companies were to be transferred to the Labour Corps, becoming AE (Garrison Guard) companies.[80] Existing companies were renumbered, C Company, for example, becoming 908 Company. There were also new companies formed from PB men, two examples being 856 and 916. Initially, 47 companies were formed, 40 being allocated to the LoC and 7 (913–918 and 926 Company) to Army areas. Men in these armed companies were category B(i) and subject to fortnightly examination by the medical officer. If reclassified A the man would be sent to a base depot for transfer to a fighting unit.

There are few existing diaries for the garrison guard companies and they are rarely mentioned in higher level diaries. One of the few exceptions is for A and B Companies. Formed on 20 September 1917 they were renumbered 906 and 907 (GG) Companies three weeks later.[81] Although the diary does not identify whether entries refer to A or B Company it does give an indication of the tasks undertaken. These include guards at No. 1 and No. 2 Military Prison, at hospitals for both British soldiers and German PoWs, providing guards at ASC petrol dumps and at ammunition dumps and escorts for PoW companies.

Further changes to the Garrison Guard companies took place after the German Offensive of March 1918 (see page 146).

Civilian Labour

On its creation the Directorate was charged with the organising and standardising of French and Belgian civilian labour, which by spring 1917 had grown to over 5,000 French and 4,000 Belgian civilians. A large majority of them were employed in the two northern Army Areas and on the LoC in workshops, laundries and on roadwork.

By this point the French had withdrawn almost all able-bodied men from the British Zone for the Army or to work in munitions. They now found there were insufficient men for agriculture and proposed that all civilians working for the British should be withdrawn and replaced by British labour companies. Following discussions it was agreed in June that the British could continue to employ French civilians with the agreement of the authorities in the area.

In XI Corps a French civilian company was formed in May. By September it comprised 775 French civilians and was located at Hersin but there is no indication of how they were employed. The only other reference to this company appears to be in September 1917 when 52 civilians who had been employed by 196 Drainage Company RE were transferred to it. It also appears that it may have been under the direct control of the LC of the Group in which it was located, the LC of 32 Group applying in October to the controller of labour for a French speaking officer to take command of the company.

Foreign and Native Labour

Whilst easing the burden on British units, the influx of native labour during 1917 brought with it other problems for the Directorate.

In preparation for the arrival of the natives the Directorate appointed native advisors with the rank of lieutenant colonel. The South African Native Labour Corps (SANLC) advisor being their commandant Colonel Pritchard; the Indian

Labour Corps (ILC), Colonel Lord Ampthill; the Egyptian Labour Corps (ELC), Colonel Coutts; and the Chinese Labour Corps (CLC), Colonel Purdon. 'With the help of these officers, the Director of Labour was able to study the peculiarities of, and the best way to handle different classes of Native Labour.'[82]

Numbers alone presented administrative and housing difficulties. During 1917 and 1918 almost 180,000 civilian labourers (15,000 ELC, 21,000 SANLC, 48,000 ILC and 95,000 CLC) were employed by the British in France. Added to this were the restrictions placed upon coloured labour. The SANLC were not allowed to leave camp unless accompanied, the CLC not to mix with the Chinese employed by the French and tribal differences amongst the ILC meant that care had to be taken with the make up of individual companies and that rival groups were not made to work together.

The Directorate faced an administrative burden caused by units being recruited on different lengths of contract. The coloured military units used as labour troops, the Bermuda RGA (see page 216), the Cape Coloured Labour Battalion (see page 219), the BWIR (see page 237) and the Fijian Labour Corps (see page 264), were all recruited for the duration of the war. The civilian native units were on different contracts. The ELC (see page 270) was on a six-month contract, the SANLC (see page 223) and ILC (see page 257) for one year and the CLC (see page 297) for three years. The problem was exacerbated by confusion about whether the labourer's contracts ran from the time they were recruited in their homelands, from when they embarked for, or when they arrived in, France. It was this confusion that, in part, caused the strikes and mutinies that occurred in ELC units in September 1917.

In August 1917 the War Office informed GHQ of the dates by which the SANLC would have completed their contract and that it was understood that they should be discharged in Cape Town. Repatriation was due to begin in September 1917 but lack of shipping meant that it was delayed for almost a month. This resulted in unrest among companies at both Abancourt and Rouen on 14 and 16 October. The unrest appears to have been solved without injury and those concerned (5, 6, 7 and 8 Companies) were repatriated by the end of the month. On 4 November the AG decided that those SANLC natives whose contract had come to an end would not be made to work but could sent to a rest camp to await repatriation, a decision that appears to have prevented any further unrest.

Problems relating to the ILC were not only about the length of their contract but also about the conditions under which they could be employed. Conditions varied depending on which district of India they came from. Nagas were told they would not be called upon to fight, but the men fully understood they would be in the danger zone whereas a distinct pledge was given to Santals that they would never be asked to go near dangerous areas. Strikes and unrest over the expiry of the contract began in March 1918 and became so acute that General Sir H. Cox, India Office, visited each company explaining that the lack of ships meant repatriation could not take place. The men were offered a new contract which included a bonus, extra pay whilst they remained in France and the offer of leave in order to visit London and Paris. Most companies accepted these new terms and by October 1918 all but three companies had been repatriated. The three that remained, 78 (Burma), 33 (Bihar) and 85 (Kumaon), had, in fact, been recruited for the duration of the war although this had not been explained clearly by recruiting agents in India. As a result 78 Company was repatriated and the other two agreed to remain and work at Marseilles.

The CLC and ILC, in particular, brought with them many white officers who had little or no military experience. Among the CLC were officers who had been missionaries or merchants in China and were chosen for their knowledge of the language. Consequently, 'only a very few combined the knowledge of Chinese with power to command'.[83]

Each Indian province sent a commandant and assistant commandant with the corps recruited in their area. Although some had previous military experience in India many were civil servants or planters with no military service. These men held a rank equivalent to a colonel or lieutenant colonel. Too senior a rank to command a company, they had to command a group headquarters despite not having the military experience required for such a posting. The Indian 'supervisors', made up of British residents, Anglo-Indians or educated Indians rarely had any military experience but in order to command were commissioned either in the Indian Army or Native Indian Land Force.

In the ELC there were difficulties in finding enough British officers with experience of Egyptians resulting in a number of officers who had neither military experience nor spoke Arabic.

The Flanders Offensives

The Flanders offensive took place from 31 July to 10 November 1917. The contribution labour played in the offensive receives little comment in the Official History. However, its importance can be seen in the build up of labour units. At the beginning of May there were 22 British companies and 7 PoW companies in the 2nd Army Area, by the end of the month there were 55 British companies and by the end of June, 84 companies were employed in the area. The number of companies had risen to 97 by the end of July and 106 by the end of August. These companies, who were employed in the forward area, were found from those employed in the southern Armies and on the LoC.

In addition to the British, PoW companies were used up to 30 kilometres and Chinese up to 16 kilometres from the front. Plans, including preparing PoW cages, were drawn up to move both PoWs and foreign labour forward when the Army advanced to relieve the British companies who would themselves move forward to newly occupied land. This geographical distribution of labour, PoW and coloured labour in the Army back areas, and white labour in the forward zone was to be used for the remainder of the war. It did, however, make it difficult to rest or relieve white labour companies as, with a few AE company exceptions on the LoC and in rear areas, they spent all of their time in forward areas.

Prior to the offensive, companies were tasked to work at both Army and Corps level. At army level companies were allotted specifically to build the new railways, roads and bridges that would be needed as the Army advanced and to Casualty Clearing Stations (CCSs) to provide the extra stretcher-bearers that would be required.

Each Corps was given four or five companies for special corps duties. These duties were: taking over the Ammunition Refilling Points (ARPs) from the Divisional Ammunition Column and moving forward to erect and work new ARPs on the day before the offensive commenced; digging in cables and mending breaks from shell-fire; and responsibility for making and maintaining forward roads. During May and June almost 200 Labour Corps men were killed making and maintaining roads south and north of Ypres. From 'Z day' they were tasked with maintaining forward roads, like the road round Zillebeke Lake, and were prepared to move their camps east of Ypres to take on the roads further east if the advance went well; and working at forward RE dumps unloading materials sent forward from corps dumps.[84]

With almost 48,500 white labour troops involved in the Flanders offensive, moving them without disturbing their work presented a major administrative headache. These were men who were not capable of marching any distance and then undertaking heavy labouring tasks. The light railways and lorries were required for moving ammunition and supplies so companies had to sleep as well as work in areas that were under shellfire. These areas were too far forward for tents, which would have been visible to German aircraft and balloon observers. The unarmed, medically low category and often old men of these labour companies were forced to sleep in bivouac shelters at risk of injury or death from shellfire or bombing.

J. Cumming Morgan described how his company (8 Company) spent three weeks in August living in bivouacs a couple of miles behind Hill 60: 'These "biv-vies" were merely canvas sheets hung over poles and stretched out at each side and pegged down. To get inside one had to crawl on all fours, and into each of them crawled every night to sleep eight weary and generally wet men.'[85]

Throughout August 8, 31, 53 and 151 Companies maintained the road from Shrapnel Corner to Ypres, which included Manor Farm, Zillebeke and Hellfire Corner. Keeping this road, which was subject to frequent shelling, open was vital and as soon as the road was shelled the hole was repaired.

> A squad of men is quickly on the spot with pick and shovel, and the hole is filed up with any mortal thing that can be found stones, beams, bricks, railway lines, sleepers, bits of cars or lorries, wheels, cases of bully, tombstones, dead horses – anything that will occupy space and in a few minutes the traffic moves on once more, and the War goes on![86]

Working during adverse weather and under frequent shellfire, 8 Company earned 7 MMs, an MC and a DCM during July and August. The citation for 1207 Sergeant T. Downie's DCM states:

> For conspicuous gallantry and devotion to duty. He made repeated attempts to fill in shell holes under very heavy shell fire, and eventually succeeded, although driven back by shell fire and gas several times. On numerous occasions he set a splendid example to his men.[87]

The dangers faced by 8 Company were to be faced by many other companies during the offensive and this is reflected in other gallantry awards as the following examples illustrate. Captain H. M. Ellis (143 Company) was awarded the MC 'for devotion to duty in charge of a detachment of men engaged in urgent and hazardous railway work, his conduct throughout infused confidence, steadiness under fire and averted a severe casualty list'.[88]

30018 Sergeant A. Lomas of 51 Company awarded the MM following an incident on 20 August 1917

… whilst in charge of a party of men working on the road between Hellfire Corner and Zillebeke during heavy shelling, (he) secured the safety of his party and assisted the wounded of a party of R.E.s, who were struck by a shell, to the Aid Post at Zillebeke. After this he collected a stretcher-bearer party and returned whilst the shelling was continuing to bring into the Aid Post another R.E. who was wounded, which he did.[89]

On 20 September 1917 a party from 58 Company were detailed to repair several breaks in the light railway line in the Pilkem Ridge area:

The party were under very heavy shellfire from the time the work was started, and one shell blew up one of our guns 10 yards away, and ignited some ammunition lying between the party and the guns, causing the gunners to retire.

Every man in the party showed the greatest coolness and bravery, remaining at work and taking out damaged rails, until a shell burst alongside them and compelled them to retire temporarily. They immediately returned to work, however, and completed the repair.

While still under shell fire, and in great danger from the burning ammunition, the party went to another break close by, and after carrying rails some 2 hundred yards, removed the damaged rails, and placed the others in position, being compelled to complete the bolting up while lying flat on their stomachs owing to the heavy shellfire and their exposed position.[90]

For their action the party's leader 34597 Private W. Riding was awarded the DCM and five others MMs.

Working in such dangerous conditions was not without loss. The men of the Labour Corps may have been unarmed and not directly involved in fighting but this did not stop almost 750 being killed in the Ypres salient by shellfire and bombing during the offensive.

The Flanders offensive was to place a tremendous strain on those companies that had to work and sleep in the shelled area from July until November. With the end of the offensive there was little respite for these companies who were tasked with preparing defences in anticipation of a German offensive that was expected early in 1918. The Directorate did attempt to replace companies which had taken the most strain with ones from other areas but frequently found that employers were not prepared to exchange companies who had worked with them for some time for units they did not know. The failure by the Directorate to insist on such changes taking place almost certainly led to a higher level of wastage through both sickness and exhaustion than should have occurred.

Cambrai

In preparation for the November 1917 operations at Cambrai it was estimated that an additional ten British companies would be needed to support the 3rd Army. However, no labour could be spared from the other Armies with the bulk of British labour still operating in Passchendaele. With all the labour having to be found from within the Third Army ten companies were withdrawn from the DGT Roads, which left the sector without labour on the roads for almost two weeks. Subsequently, Indian Labour companies brought in from outside the area were used to replace British companies at Bus, Fins, Velu and Nurlu, where they were employed on roads.

The plan for the Cambrai offensive involved ensuring the Germans were not aware an offensive was being planned. Labour companies were accommodated in camouflaged tents and shelters, in dugouts or in wooded areas in order to prevent discovery by the Germans, even though they were working within 1,500 yards of the front line.

On 19 November, the day before the battle commenced, each company was issued with details about their role once Zero Hour came. Labour currently on the roads was allocated to the RE Chief Engineer for a period of 48 hours after which they would return to work for the Corps Roads Officer on the Albert–Bapaume Road. It was hoped that the maintenance of secrecy would result in a rapid advance being made in the initial stages of the battle. To support this advance several companies were allocated to the skilled Light Railway companies. The intention was that once the new front line had been established the labour companies would prepare the ground in front of the light railway companies to enable light railway track to be laid to the fighting troops as quickly as possible. The light railway leading to Moeuvres was successfully built under heavy fire as noted in the Report on Labour:

> The approach to the bridges of the Canal du Nord being carried out by Labour personnel within 1,000 yards of the enemy machine guns on the lock at Moeuvres. The average age of the men of this unit was over 50, and previous to the advance the men had been living in dug-outs and had proceeded to their allotted position at dusk the night before under cover of folds in the ground. Owing to the excellent arrangements made by the Company Commander, no casualties were sustained in this operation.[91]

When on 30 November the Germans launched a counter attack, both British and Indian labour units were in danger of being overrun. The most forward of the Indian companies, the 26 (Lushai) and 28 (Lushai) Companies at Nurlu, were marched the seven miles back to Peronne where they remained for 48 hours. 'The orderly way in which they carried out their marches was worthy of all praise.'[92]

Four British companies (63, 80, 107 and 157) at Gouzeaucourt were cut off and became involved in actual operations. At Gouzeaucourt Quarry one company, possibly 63 although it has not been possible to confirm this, defended themselves until relieved by the 6th Battalion Shropshire Light Infantry, and after being relieved, dug trenches for this battalion and carried their ammunition, food, water and wounded.

It was during this action that Major David Watts Morgan (80 Company) was awarded the DSO.[93] David Watts Morgan had, at the age of 47, enlisted as a private on 4 August 1914 in the 10th Welch Regiment. Commissioned in October he was transferred to the Labour Corps in May 1917. He was awarded the DSO 'for his exploits with the 'pick and shovel' brigade at Cambrai in November 1917, when he and his pioneers defended themselves against the German counter-attack until relieved by the Guards.'[94] The citation stated:

> For conspicuous gallantry and devotion to duty. When his camp was heavily shelled with a few NCOs he turned some dug-outs into a temporary dressing station and assisted the wounded in the vicinity. When shelling rendered his position untenable he brought back his men in good order. He displayed great coolness and resource.[95]

60 Brigade's Intelligence Officer, Captain Dugdale, directed another company building the railway line near Gouzeaucourt to reinforce the front where the Germans had broken through. They arrived, by train, in Gouzeaucourt only to find that the Germans had already taken it. Although the exact company cannot be identified it is likely that it was 107 which had 2 officers and 70 other ranks taken prisoner. Another, again unidentified company 'withdrew with the fighting troops and then obtained permission to proceed at night into 'No Man's Land and retrieved their company records and cash'.[96]

Need to reorganise

Arras, Flanders and Cambrai had highlighted weaknesses in the discipline and administration of labour units in the Army Areas. Some of these weaknesses, like the number of officers with little or no military experience and British labour companies consisting of men of low physical category, most of whom had little military training, were hard to rectify.

The main weakness lay in the lack of an organised system of command. ADLs and DADLs were not executive officers, their duties being to advise on labour matters. Labour companies were Corps or Army troops, and as such, the discipline of labour groups came under the Camp Commandant or the OC corps or army troops, whereas their movements and rationing was the concern of the quartermaster branch of the Corps or Army. In practice this separation of distribution and administration could not be maintained. To meet local demands involved almost constant movement of labour units and it was vital for a DADL to know how a company he was allotting a task to would cope with the strain of shellfire and poor conditions.

If the system of administration and discipline was to work it was necessary to review the position of both the ADLs and DADLs with a view to giving them the authority and position required to carry out their task. Such a change could not take place without considering the organisation of labour on the LoC and of the Directorate itself at GHQ.

As the year came to an end the review was underway although the changes it was to initiate would not come into effect until February 1918. In twelve months a Labour Directorate had been formed, manpower for labour had increased from 100,000 to almost 300,000 and units of medically low category men with no military experience had proved their worth in supporting major offensives. Whilst the organisation and administration had not been without problems the foundations had been set for the changes that would turn the Labour Corps into an integral part of the British Army.

1 NA WO 95/33
2 ibid WO 107/33 *Report on Labour* p.6
3 ibid p.6
4 ibid WO 95/33
5 ibid WO 95/430
6 On 4 October 1916 the route coped with 1,200 men a day returning from British.
7 NA WO 95/430
8 ibid WO 95/430
9 Samuel Slinger was 22 years old and worked on his father's farm. He had been called up for service in June 1916 and, as a result of a childhood illness, initially posted to A Works Company of the King's Liverpool Regiment. Samuel Slinger together with seven comrades is buried in Bard Cottage Cemetery, the other five men being buried at Dozinghem Military Cemetery.
10 *Southport Guardian,* 22 September 1917
11 NA WO 95/571
12 ibid WO 293/4 ACI 1209 Disposal of recruits of Enemy Alien Parentage
13 Messenger, p.232
14 The base depot was 'J' Depot, Etaples and not the Labour Corps base depot.
15 NA WO 107/37 p.66
16 ibid WO 95/83
17 Thomas, T., *With A Labour Company in France,* p. 5
18 NA WO 339/95380
19 ibid WO 339/95380
20 The Legion of Frontiersmen formed two battalions during the First World War, the 25th Royal Fusiliers and the Canadian 210th Battalion.
21 Pocock, R., 'My Labour Company at Ypres' in *I Was There Vol 2,* p. 992
22 ibid, p.998
23 ibid, p.998
24 ibid, p.998
25 ibid, p.998
26 ibid, p.992
27 ibid, p.1000
28 NA WO 95/377
29 ibid WO 95/815
30 ibid WO 95/384
31 Falls, C., *Military Operations France and Belgium 1917,* p. 195
32 NA WO 213/59
33 ibid WO 293/6
34 Six companies (95–98 and 201–203) served in Salonika.
35 See page 326–329 and 331
36 There were also two Group Headquarters formed in Salonika.
37 NA WO 95/4173
38 ibid WO 293/6
39 ibid WO 293/6
40 ibid WO 95/83

41 Falls, p.310

42 Stewart, T., 'With the Labour Corps' in *Journal of the Royal United Services Institute 1929* Vol 74 pp. 567–571

43 Morgan, J. C., 'A Labour Company at Ypres' in *True World War 1 Stories,* pp.130–135

44 Pocock, R., My Labour Company at Ypres in *I Was There* ed. Sir John Hammerton

45 Morgan, p. 130

46 Stewart, p.567

47 Pedley, J. H., *Short Account of Some of my Experiences*

48 Thomas, T. C., *With a Labour Company in France*

49 On 19 January 1917 an explosion at a munitions factory destroyed a large part of Silvertown, London killing 73 people and injuring 300.

50 Pedley, p.21

51 ibid, p.31

52 *London Gazette,* 4 Oct 19 page 12341

53 Thomas, p.3

54 Thomas, p.68

55 NA WO 95/571

56 By combining such references with information from the CWGC, the *London Gazette* and Thomas's account a Diary for 58 Company has been compiled – see page 356. NA WO 95/810 22 March 1917

58 ibid WO 95/810 5 July 1917

59 ibid WO 95/83

60 ibid WO 95/384

61 ibid WO 95/969

62 Thomas, p. 25

63 Swinton, E., *Twenty Years After, Supplementary Volume,* p. 777

64 Thomas, p.27

65 ibid, p.51

66 ibid, p.51

67 ibid, p. 52

68 Letter from 105810 Private S Hillier, 177 Company in author's collection

69 See picture section.

70 Unfortunately the Memorial was not maintained when the club was modernised.

71 NA WO 95/610

72 ibid WO 95/939

73 ibid WO 95/929

74 ibid WO 95/886

75 ibid WO 95/34

76 ibid WO 293/7 ACI 1303 22 Aug 1917

77 Item in author's collection.

78 NA WO 95/4174

79 ibid WO 95/4047

80 ibid WO 95/83

81 ibid WO 95/4174

82 ibid WO 107/37 p. 8

83 ibid WO 107/37 p.51

84 'Z Day' – the day an offensive/operation commences

85 Morgan, J. C., p.131

86 ibid, p.132

87 *London Gazette* 30961 18 October 1918

88 NA WO 95/83 26 Aug 1917

89 ibid WO 95/537 17 Sept 1917
90 Thomas, T. p.33
91 NA WO 107/37 p.79
92 ibid WO 107/37 p.80
93 Watts Morgan had started work aged 11 as a pit boy. Through attendance at evening classes he qualified as a mining engineer although never practised becoming secretary to the Rhondda District Miners Federation in 1898. He was elected as Labour MP for Rhondda East in 1918, serving the constituency until his death in 1933.
94 *Oxford Dictionary of National Biography*
95 *London Gazette,* 2 July 1918, page 7888
96 NA WO 107/37 p.80

1918 CONTROL OF LABOUR

During 1918 Labour Headquarters changed from advising on the employment of labour to direct control. This important change allowed the introduction of a more scientific approach to the way units were tasked. The year was also to see the labour organisation tested by the German spring offensives and the mobile war from August onwards.

Cabinet Intervention

During the winter of 1917 Labour Headquarters expressed concern at the loss of native labour due to the repatriation of the Egyptians in 1917 and termination of the South African and Indian labour contracts in 1918. In January 1918 there were some 59,000 Chinese serving in France. Plans for the number of Chinese to rise to 95,000 were already in place. To compensate for the loss of the Egyptian and South African natives it was suggested this should be increased to 150,000 but this never occurred. According to General Wace it was stopped by 'outbreak of bubonic plague in the districts from which the labourers were drawn'.[1] However, War Cabinet papers for January and February 1918 indicate that this was not the real reason.

On 17 January 1918 Sir Joseph Maclay, Minister of Shipping, submitted a memorandum to the War Cabinet in which he suggested that in view of the shortage of shipping, consideration should be given to stopping immediately the transportation of Chinese labourers to France. This would allow an additional 10,000 American troops a month to be brought to France and remove the burden of transporting the Chinese across Canada. He also made the point that he had recently seen these labourers in France and that they were badly supervised with four men doing the work of one. His view was that: 'They were becoming loafers and loungers, and were under no proper control. They were treated as Europeans rather than Asiatics.'[2]

Lord Derby, Secretary for War, whilst agreeing with much of Maclay's criticism about lack of supervision, would not agree to a complete halt to Chinese labourers being brought to France. He suggested bringing those already enlisted and a further 2,000 a month. General Macready, the Adjutant General, agreed that if the demands of France were to be met the importation could not be stopped.

The War Cabinet decided that Maclay, Derby and Sir Eric Geddes, First Lord of the Admiralty, should meet the next day to consider the question of Chinese labour and report back. The Prime Minister decided that he should chair the meeting accompanied by General Smuts. The agenda immediately changed into a discussion about the way the Army organised labour. Derby stated that he had secured the services of Sir Edward Pearson who, with the full concurrence of Haig, was going to France to undertake an investigation and then report on the labour organisation. The Prime Minister, referring to manpower shortages, pointed out 'it was essential, that there should be no idle men in France such as those seen and described by the Shipping Controller'.[3] The AG stated that a new labour organisation was being introduced in France and that it should be allowed a fair trial and suggested that the question of Chinese labour should be held over for a month to see the effect of the new organisation. Despite Derby urging that the transport of Chinese to France should continue, Maclay stated that when another memorandum he was submitting to the Cabinet had been considered 'the importation of Chinese Coolies might be entirely stopped'.[4]

On 30 January Maclay submitted a memorandum in which he stated that the United States Government was being asked to send men to be embodied in the British Army, that there was a good prospect that they would agree to this and that the men would have to be carried in British ships. To do this he would need the ships that were being used to transport the Chinese and that unless the complete suspension of the transportation of the Chinese occurred these ships would be out of position.

The memorandum was considered at the War Cabinet on 19 February. Although Derby attended this meeting the minutes suggest that he was not present when this item was discussed. Maclay stated that he understood Derby 'was prepared to stop the importation of coolies'[5] and the War Cabinet decided 'in the light of this information, that − No more coolies should be shipped from China, on the understanding that the Secretary of State for War agreed'.[6] Following the Cabinet meeting only two further shiploads left China and these were labourers that had already been enlisted. Despite Maclay's attempts in January and February to stop Chinese labourers being brought to France, between January and May 1918, 36,000 Chinese arrived in France to join the 59,000 who had arrived by the end of 1917.

Reports on Labour Organisation

In addition to Sir Edward Pearson's inspection, Sir Frank Baines carried out a second, at the request of Field Marshal Haig. Both visited skilled and unskilled labour and met with officers handling and employing labour, senior officers in charge of the different directorates and those in charge of army areas, depots and ports.

The reports, written in March and June, were both critical of the management of labour in the rear areas. Baines noted that at 'Stores and Base Depots the labour appeared to be working much below normal efficiency and was badly organised.'[7] At the Imperial War Cabinet meeting on 16 August 1918 the Dominion Prime Ministers, based on information received from their own officers, confirmed this criticism.[8] The War Cabinet commended the subject to the British Government with a 'view to such action as may result in a more economical use of the Army's man-power'.[9]

The Reports also recommended that both skilled and unskilled labour should be pooled and under the control of one officer acting under the QMG. More attention should be paid to the use of labour-saving devices and to the layout of depots and stores. Both were critical of the supervision of labour and recommended that labour officers be responsible for ensuring work was completed.

Pearson was particularly critical of the system at base ports where Royal Marine labour had to be supplemented by Army labour: 'The conditions under which the Royal Marine Labour is serving are quite different to those existing on shore. Under the existing arrangement dual control cannot be avoided.'[10] He was 'strongly of the opinion' that all labour should be under Army control and believed this would eliminate dual control and economise it. Pearson recommended that this be tried initially at one port but there is no evidence of it taking place.

In the Report on labour, Wace emphasises that these 'reports were made before the new organisation had really got to work'[11] and that although it was not possible to bring skilled and unskilled labour under one control it was possible to adopt some of the recommendations made by Pearson and Baines.

Reorganisation of the Directorate

On 28 January 1918 the AG wrote to each Army and the GOC LoC informing them that the administration, control and distribution of unskilled labour throughout the Army had been reorganised.[12] Prior to the reorganisation, the Labour Directorate was under the QMG but had to deal with a large amount of administration, which was the concern of the AG's branch. It was therefore decided the part of the Directorate dealing with personnel should be transferred to the AG. The branches, which dealt with the allotment and distribution of labour and with technical matters, remained under the QMG.

The old Labour Directorate therefore ceased to exist. Instead of a Director of Labour, a Controller of Labour (CL) was appointed within the QMG's department. Under him were two Deputy Controllers (DCL) and two Assistant Controllers (ACL). On 11 February, Colonel (promoted Brigadier General October 1918) E. G. Wace replaced General Gibb, who had become Controller of Salvage, as CL.

The Controller, who reported directly to the QMG, was responsible for the allotment and distribution of unskilled labour to the armies and LoC. The CL was empowered to make visits to wherever units under his control were being employed 'and will be given any information he requires as to the numbers of Skilled and Specialised Units under which, or for which, the unskilled labour is working'.[13] Whilst this did not give the CL any authority over skilled units it did mean he was in a better position to determine the labour required by employers and allocate it appropriately.

Administratively the CL was responsible for maintaining records and statistics relating to labour. He had direct access to the DGT and the directors of the various services and departments regarding efficiency of labour and forecasts of requirements. Whilst personnel and discipline came under the AG, the CL, who had direct access to the AG, acted as advisor on postings to labour units and 'on matters affecting administration or organisation of Labour Units observed during inspection which effect the working efficiency of labour'.[14] The controller attended the daily conference of the DQMG, which enabled Labour Control to have an overview of the situation in France, to prepare for future labour needs and also provide the QMG with an accurate picture of the labour available.

Equally important were the changes made in the field. A new post, Labour Commandant (LC), replaced the ADL at Army HQ and the DADL at Corps HQ. Holding the rank of colonel, the LC administered and commanded unskilled labour (including Area Employment, PoW and Civilian labour) within their area. At Corps the post of Assistant DADL became Assistant Labour Commandant (ALC) with the rank of Staff Captain.

The creation of LC as colonel gave the post holder, particularly at corps level, the status commensurate with their role. Prior to the reorganisation, the DADL, who was a captain, had to act under orders from two superiors, the corps commander for Corps services and the ADL for army services employed in his area. After reorganisation it was clarified that the LC at army HQ would command labour within the army troops area and the LC at corps HQ would command labour within the corps area. The one exception was that army HQ could designate certain labour for special work and the army LC would then retain command of them.

Labour was allotted to each army HQ and would then be distributed to Corps and Army Areas. Services and departments requiring labour applied to the HQ of the formation in the area where the work was to be carried out. The LC of the formation would then either allocate labour or inform the employer that their request could not be met. In the case of the latter, the LC or the employer could ask GHQ for additional labour for a specific purpose and period of time.

The Army and Corps LCs were charged with maintaining close contact with the representatives of services and departments in their area in order to assess labour needs. Importantly, the LCs had the authority to inspect unskilled labour and be informed of the numbers of skilled and specialised labour. Once allocated to a group the distribution of personnel to employers was in the hands of the group commander.

The details of the reorganisation, which were set out in GRO 3502 on 3 March 1918, emphasised the importance of the labour officer in ensuring his men were being used economically.[15] Any instances of waste had to be reported immediately to the Formation HQ who had to bring it to the attention of GHQ and the director of the employing service.

Although labour was more static on the LoC there was still a need for the efficient use of the units allocated. Following the reorganisation, three DCL were appointed at LoC HQ and ACLs at the base and administrative area HQs. The ACLs were either a staff captain or major, depending on the amount of labour they had to administer.

Scientific Management

The principles of scientific management of labour originated around the turn of the twentieth century in the USA; its major principles were that materials, manpower, rates of pay and average times needed to perform tasks must be standardised.

In order to establish these standards it was necessary to measure the work under-taken. One of the British Army's advocates of scientific management was Colonel Wace and he surrounded himself with officers who shared his dedication 'to the introduction of efficient methods of direction'.[16]

From February 1917 officers were asked on their daily report to indicate a meas-ure of the work done. However, 'many Labour officers were not sufficiently trained in quantitative measurement to make their estimates of the amount of work done by their Platoon of any value'.[17]

During 1917 both employers and junior labour officers hampered attempts by Wace to collect and analyse the data needed for the introduction of scientific man-agement. Employers claimed that it was unrealistic to insist upon carefully prepared requisition forms or work to predetermined schedules during wartime. Labour Corps officers claimed that labour often had to be used for unforeseen or unas-signed tasks.[18] As a result it was impossible to accurately track labourers and many assignments were not properly reported or assessed.

Opposition to Wace's ideas also came from senior officers within the Labour Directorate. The Commander of the CLC, Colonel Fairfax, sending a memo to the War Office in December 1917, complained that Wace and his staff repeatedly issued complex directions and requested graphs demonstrating job performance.[19] To Fairfax these were unnecessary and actually hampered their work.

The appointment of Wace as Controller in February 1918, together with the increased authority of the LCs and ALCs allowed Wace to insist on a more scientific approach. Labour companies completed returns designed to measure performance and standardise future requirements. Labour officers came under greater pressure to ensure efficient management and discipline

It has been suggested that Wace was not as successful as he would have wished due to

> … jealousy, indifference, or downright opposition from officers who neither cared nor bothered about the way in which labour was deployed; the continual and unex-pected emergencies which the was situation itself manifested; the constant need to refine and defend a system in the middle of difficulties which only officers in the seat of command can fully appreciate.[20]

Despite these factors there is no question that labour during 1918 was far more efficient. The QMG confirmed this in a letter to the War Office on 28 August 1918 which set out the result of the reorganisation of labour. 'The main benefits have been derived in the field of increased efficiency and greater output per man and are mainly due to improved supervision, the introduction of "Task Work" and the use of "Contracting Out".'[21]

Task Work

The principle underlying task work is that the detachment is given a specific time in which to complete the job. The detachment then has a degree of free-dom in planning and executing the work as long as it is completed in the allotted time. As early as March 1916 the C-in-C had reminded armies that task work should be used wherever possible. Resistance to introducing task work resulted in the QMG writing on 22 November 1917 to the heads of all services and departments.

> Task work to a large extent has been gradually introduced in the Abancourt Area with excellent results, and I forwarded herewith for your information a copy of a report compiled by the DADL, Abancourt, clearly showing the advantage both to the 'Employer' and to the Labour Corps personnel when 'task work' is intelligently applied.[22]

Even where task work was adopted, a major problem was that officers often had little or no experience of determining the time and manpower required for a task. This was a particular problem when employers insisted in setting the time. 'The employer who might successively have working for him Chinese, Prisoners of War and British Labour of a low physical category, could not know how much work might be expected of different classes of Labour.'[23]

As the direct control of the labourers undertaking task work passed from the employer to the Labour Corps officer it became the norm for him to instruct his own men and ensure they worked effectively. Even this, during the spring and summer of 1918, was not without problems, as many labour officers did not have the background or experience required. Efficiency improved as officers acquired the skills required to direct their men and officers with technical qualifications such as engineers, architects and surveyors, were posted to labour companies.

Labour Corps officers were supplied with schedules compiled from statistics of completed work. They used these as a guide to allocate time to each task. For example, a British Company unloading a supply train would be expected to move:

Ammunition	1 ton per hour	3 men
General Supplies	1⅛ tons per hour	2 men
Forage	1 ton per hour	2½ men

If the task was entrenching, a British labour company would be expected to excavate 80 cubic feet per man per day in hard chalk, 120 feet in soft chalk, 160 feet in loam and 190 feet in soft sand. These amounts were reduced by 25 per cent if the lift was over 4 feet. Officers were reminded that 'By employing task work and permitting a section, or platoon, to rest for a smoke (except near petrol or ammunition), or cease work, or to return to billets when their own particular piece of work is finished. The spirit of competition thus created has a marked effect.'[24]

Task work was particularly effective with native units. At Dannes, when the SANLC constructed an ammunition depot 'hundreds of thousands of pounds were saved by the alteration from time work to task work under their own officers, while the change enabled the completion of the depot to be effected in time.'[25] The ELC Advisor, Colonel Coutts stated: 'Given proper supervision, and task work, I would back Egyptian Labour against any native Labour in the world.'[26]

It was felt that Chinese labourers would do no more work than they thought was expected of them and would time their effort so that they appeared to be working steadily and well. For this reason task work was seen as particularly suitable for the CLC. Employers often underestimated the physical fitness of the Chinese and would therefore allocate a longer time than required for a task. There were a number of cases of a day's task being completed in so short a time that the employing officer insisted on further work the same day. This led to problems as the Chinese labourer saw this as a breach of faith, their gangers losing face with their men and in consequence losing interest in their work.

Contracting Out

The principle of 'contracting out' to labour officers meant that they took full responsibility for a task including manpower, materials and transport. This worked effectively in many areas, notably at the railheads. There continued to be problems however, with many employers requesting more labour than they actually needed. When labour officers reported this they were often challenged by the employer saying that the number needed was a technical matter and that if the task was to be completed the employer must have the number of men he requested.

In July 1918 the QMG wrote to all Services pointing out that labour officers were not being given enough responsibility by employers and to ensure maximum efficiency: 'In future ... Departmental Officers will, whenever possible, explain to the Labour Officers what is required to be done and leave the latter the decision as to the number of men required and the responsibility of getting particular jobs properly executed and to time.'[27]

The RE's Chief Engineer sent a similar letter to the Army CE saying that wherever possible the RE officer should explain the task to the labour officer, who would ensure that his men complete the work. The main area where labour control faced opposition and difficulties with contracting out was the Docks Directorate. The situation became so acute that a committee of inquiry chaired by Major General Ford, Deputy QMG, was set up in September 1918. The other members of the committee were Colonel Wace, Commodore MacGregor, the PNTO (Principal Naval Transport Officer) and Brigadier General Wedgwood, Director of Docks. Among its recommendations were: Indents for labour would not be reduced by the ACL without agreement of the port's Assistant Director of Docks. The ACL should attend and take a full part in the daily meeting at the port at which shipping and dock work was discussed. Labour officers to be allotted definite responsibilities on the same footing as dock officers.

By the time the recommendations could be implemented the war had ended so it is not possible to judge whether the situation improved.

Civilian Labour

In August 1917 a Civil Labour Bureau was established at Poperinghe. Civilians wishing to be employed were only registered after they had been approved by intelligence and upon receipt of a letter from the local mayor stating they were not required for agricultural duties. Each employee received an identity card on which was recorded their rate of pay.

At the end of 1917 the 5th Army informed Labour Control that they were receiving a large number of applications for work from French civilians. It was decided that, following the success in Poperinghe, similar bureaux would be created in all areas where civilian labour was employed. Their areas of responsibility were based on the French canton or commune boundaries. Arrangements for the Civil Labour Bureaux were outlined in GRO 3907 on 2 May 1918. Officers at the Bureaux were responsible for registering all employees and reporting on the available supply of civilian labour. It was also their task to allot civilian labour to employers and to ensure that arrangements for dealing with accidents and illness complied with French law.

Thirteen Bureaux were opened on 19 June with four more nine days later. By the Armistice a total of 30 had been opened and six more were to be opened by May 1919. One of the few references to the actual work of civilians is in July 1918 when the Civil Labour Bureau located at Roquetoire was employing 2,000 male and female civilians, mainly in the concrete factory.[28]

In his Report on Labour Wace states, 'the part played by Civilian Labour has not been a very important one'.[29] He is critical of the fact that civilian labour was not suitable for the mobile war from August onwards. In his view, 'Labour which cannot be moved at short notice is hardly worth the trouble of organizing'.[30] He does acknowledge that mainly female labour was successfully employed in workshops, laundries and ordnance depots on the LoC.

Foreign and Native Labour

During 1918 Portuguese and Italian soldiers were also used as labour troops. The Portuguese Division had been part of the Allied forces in France from February 1917. Following mutinies in the Portuguese Division and their defeat by the Germans in April 1918 they were withdrawn from the front and used as labour in the Rear Area. There are virtually no references to Portuguese labour troops in British war diaries although there is reference to Portuguese working at cemeteries in their area in September 1917 and a works company in the spring of 1918.

In January 1918 the Italians sent the first of their men to France to be used on defence work. Comprising men unfit for front line service the intention was originally to use the men under French control. When the 5th Army assumed responsibility for a large portion of the French line in February 1918 over 12,000 of the Italians came under British command. The German offensive in March saw Italian labour withdrawn to Abancourt and on 18 April 1918 they were repatriated to Italy.

The contracts of the SANLC and the ILC expired at various times throughout 1918. When a man's contract expired he was repatriated, although as in 1917, a shortage of shipping meant that many remained in France beyond their allotted time. By October 1918 all the SANLC had returned to South Africa and all but two companies of the ILC to India by the end of the year.

Entrenching Battalions

In January 1918 infantry brigades were reduced from four to three battalions due to the shortage of front line soldiers. The army re-formed the entrenching battalions using surplus personnel. Twenty-five entrenching battalions were formed to work on defences in the rear Army Areas and to provide reinforcements. The armies and corps making requests for these units did not have to apply through the labour organisation. The 23rd Manchesters, for example, sent 31 officers and 630 other ranks to the Regiment's 2nd, 11th and 12th Battalions with its surplus personnel becoming part of the 12th Entrenching Battalion. With the German attack in March they provided 20 officers and 500 men as reinforcements for the 7th Royal West Kents.

By the end of May all the entrenching battalions had been disbanded, their men being used to make up for losses. Although no further entrenching battalions were formed, in September 1918 the RE Chief Engineer in the Third Army requested entrenching battalions to assist in transportation. This resulted in the ADL noting, 'yet again he is trying to bypass the established system. There should be only one authority to allot labour within the Army.'[31]

Agricultural Companies

From the outbreak of the war British soldiers had been used to assist French farmers during harvest time if they could be spared from their regular duties. As early as August 1914 there is a record of Grenadier Guards helping the villagers of Grougis to harvest five acres of corn. By 1916 it was decided that more needed to be done to produce vegetables, cereals and fodder in France. The decision in 1916 to retain German PoWs in France provided another source of labour for agricultural work.

As the front line moved forward, land behind the old British line could be re-occupied by civilians and used to grow vegetables. In the autumn of 1916, British troops, together with about 200 PoWs, planted over 1,200 acres of vegetable gardens in and around Marcelcave, Heilly, Poulainville, Saint-Gratien and Mericourt-l'Abbe. There was, however, little planning as to how and where such vegetable gardens should be established. This changed in January 1917 with the attachment of Agricultural Officers (AOs) to each Army and Corps Headquarters. Chosen for their knowledge of agriculture, the AOs consulted local farmers and officials to decide what help was required. The AO then organised working parties from men in the area whilst ensuring their normal training was not affected.

In the 2nd Army, Major S. J. Aubrey-Smith, the AO, initially found that many farmers were suspicious of the capabilities of the men and concerned they would be charged for the labour. By reassuring the farmers that only men with agricultural experience would be used and that there would be no financial cost, he managed to overcome these concerns to the extent that by April 1917 requests for labour outstripped the numbers available. Aubrey-Smith found units unwilling to release men for agricultural duties so PB personnel were used. He encountered problems with men being withdrawn either for front line service if they were fit or for transfer to labour units. To help overcome the problem he arranged for temporarily downgraded front line troops and men being released from hospital to be sent to him.

Throughout 1917 the Labour Directorate supported the work of the AOs by providing labour when requested. Much of this labour came from PoW Companies, with 32, 57, 71, 135, 138 and 148 PoW Companies playing an important role. British labour companies tended to send detachments when required; 48 Company, for example, sent a detachment of eleven other ranks to work for III Corps AO between 1 July and 25 September. When 199 Company was formed from 2 PB Company at the end of September 1917 a detachment of 75 men was allocated to the 3rd Army AO..

In 1917 Dr F. Keeble, from the Ministry of Agriculture, visited France and advised that an area of some 45,000 acres near Roye, south-east of Amiens, be selected for farming operations. Following the appointment of Brigadier General Lord Radnor as Director of Agricultural Production it was decided to form six agricultural companies within the Labour Corps. Each company, consisting of one officer and 169 other ranks, would work a block of 5,000 acres. Machinery, including tractors, cultivators and ploughs, was imported from Britain. It appears that there were difficulties in finding suitable men and by the end of January 1918 only a single company, 50 strong, was in operation.

The idea was that men from front line units should be employed in the six companies.[32] It is possible that a small number of skilled ploughmen and tractor drivers came from front line units but it is more likely that category B men were used. Men like 519189 Private David Samuels who having served with the 9th Battalion South Lancashire Regiment was, by February 1918, unfit for front line service. On 25 February he was sent to the GHQ Farm at Roye and two days later transferred to the 1st Agricultural Company, Labour Corps.

Since only six agricultural companies were formed, each working 5,000 acres, there was a shortfall of labour to work the farm at Roye.[33] This shortage could have been met by using a single labour company (500 men). The Labour Directorate allocated 729 Area Employment Company, 275 strong, to the Director of Agriculture at the end of January 1918. They arrived at Roye on 5 February 1918. Although it has not been possible to confirm, it is likely that a second Area Employment Company, a PoW or a Chinese Labour Company were also allocated to work on the farms at Roye.

Men continued to be posted to the six agricultural companies throughout February and March. 574088 Private Edward Hague was transferred from the Northumberland Fusiliers to the 6th Agricultural Company only five days before the German offensive began on 22 March. The offensive forced the agricultural companies and 729 Company to withdraw to a safer location and the farm was abandoned.

On 28 April 1918 two Area Employment Agricultural Companies (987 and 988) were formed, as the DADL of XI Corps recorded 'from the amalgamation of several Agricultural Companies'.[34] 987 Company appears to have maintained a strength of two officers and 220 men and 988 Company four officers and 430 men. This suggests that total strength of the six agricultural companies formed at Roye had, by the end of March, only totalled around 650 men.

The decision to form the six agricultural companies into two AE Companies was not particularly successful; their large size resulted in each company continually being sub-divided into detachments. On 12 August, 988 had two detachments working in the 3rd Army Area and one each in the 1st, 2nd and 4th Army Areas. In V Corps Area, on 7 September 1918, detachments from both 987 and 988 were sent to Hedauville, northwest of Albert, to assist with harvesting. Although designated agricultural companies, both were used for more general duties when required; 988 unloaded 1,020 tons of ballast and laid 461 yards of new track in XI Corps Area during the last week of May and a detachment from 987 unloaded stores at Pernes railhead on 17 July.

On 16 September, at a conference at GHQ, the Director of Labour and Director of Agriculture discussed the reorganisation of the two AE agricultural companies.[35] As a result of this conference it was decided to revert to six agricultural companies of one officer and 169 other ranks, and on 10 October Companies 1037 to 1042 were formed primarily from 987 and 988 Companies. Each of these companies was allocated to a specific army, 1037 to the 1st Army, 1038 to the 2nd Army, 1039 to the 3rd Army, and 1040, 1041 and 1042 to the 4th Army. These companies were to remain in their army Areas until they were disbanded in August 1919.

The German Offensives

Due to the fall of Russia and the anticipated German offensive, detailed instructions were issued for the conduct of troops in case of attack from December 1917. The 5th Army, on taking over new areas from the French, required an increased number of labour personnel to construct lines of defence. The number of British, foreign and PoW labourers rose from 26,670 on 22 December 1917 to 67,967 on 16 March 1918. A weekly conference between General Hambro, the Army's QMG, and the Labour Commandant dealt with any difficulties they were facing.[36] This close liaison undoubtedly aided the retreat when it came in March as all units were aware of a plan of action. Similar liaison took place in the 3rd Army where some 60,000 men were employed in 66 British Labour companies, 22 Area Employment companies, 16 Indian companies, 7 Chinese companies and 17 PoW companies. Arrangements were three-fold: evacuation of PoW companies, withdrawal of British and foreign labour and the transfer of British, and later foreign labour, to GHQ Defence Lines in the rear area.

The general principle was to treat each labour group as if it were an infantry brigade. For each group a rendezvous point was chosen for Group Headquarters and close to this an assembly point for each company. Company commanders planned routes which avoided the main roads, ration dumps and railheads, to the assembly point. On the instruction 'Concentrate' companies were to move to their assembly points. On the instruction 'Withdraw' the group would move to a designated location in the rear area. Instructions were given that a Company's General Service Wagon was to carry a day's supply of rations and that each man was to wear his great coat and to carry his day's food ration, a full water bottle and a blanket and ground sheet. However, the German advance was so rapid some units were forced to retreat before these instructions could be fully implemented.

Damage to telephone lines made it difficult for army and corps labour commandants and group commanders to keep in touch with the men under their control. A limited number of motorcyclists were used to convey instructions. The labour commandants at army and corps HQs each had four motorcyclists and the group commanders each had two motorcyclists at their disposal. This is a tiny number when it is remembered that a corps labour commandant was responsible for 10,000 to 15,000 men and a group commander for 4,000 to 6,000.

The biggest problem was the lack of transport. Men had to march to the rendezvous points and then to the safer areas, 'which presented a serious difficulty, as their rate of progress was of necessity very slow'.[37] Men had to sleep during freezing nights, in the lanes, roads and mud, in many cases without kit or great coats. Often the Germans were no more than a few hundred yards away from the retreating labour companies. The Labour Corps officers maintained the discipline of the men during these long and often difficult marches, which did much to reduce the number of stragglers.

At Beaumetz, shells landing near the camp of 125 Chinese Labour Company caused panic. The men scattered and had to be rounded up by the Military Police. Not all CLC Companies behaved like this; 139 Company marched 60 miles from Ham to Rosecamps during which time they picked up some sixty stragglers. According to Xu Guoqi, 'during the German Offensive of 1918, companies of the Chinese Labour Corps caught up in the German advance took up picks and shovels to fight the enemy, and many workers sacrificed their lives this way'.[38] Reports of Chinese labour fighting the Germans seem to have originated in the *North China Herald*, however no references to this have been found in war diaries or the Report on Labour so there is doubt over their authenticity.[39] Even the number of casualties is uncertain; the CWGC records show 45 men of the CLC dying between 21 and 30 March 1918. However, 22 of these were killed during an air raid in Calais, which suggests that about 20 died during the offensive.

The Indian labour companies were the most efficient of the foreign labour contingents during the retreat. They were used until they could be relieved by British companies at ammunition dumps at Pozieres and Trones Wood, to erect a Casualty Clearing Station at Aveluy and worked day and night moving supplies at Albert. The 3rd Army Labour Commandant commented, 'no reports were received of stragglers from the Indian Labour Companies and the behaviour of these Units reflected credit on the personnel'.[40]

In V Corps the ILC and their officers earned praise from its Labour Commandant:

> The Indian Labour Troops were excellently managed by their Officers. A particularly fine example was when V Corps Headquarters unexpectedly arrived at TALMAS. That village was at the time occupied by 68th Group comprised of about five thousand Indians. Although orders were not received until midnight, and although the men had been marching for several days, yet within one hour the whole body of men had moved to the next rendezvous. Few incidents of a more impressive nature could be imagined than the almost silent departure in the night of this large body of Indian workers. The hardships of the preceding week appeared to have developed in them a discipline of the highest order.[41]

These words are in complete contrast to that of Colonel R. Temple, Labour Commandant in VI Corps, who commented: 'Coloured Labour in forward areas is a hindrance and not a help during operations.'[42]

Italian officers had not informed their men of the arrangements in case of attack. British officers were assigned to the Italian companies and they were brought to

Bray without panic. However, on 23 March a rumour spread amongst them that the Germans were about ten miles away. All but three Italian companies left the area without permission. They arrived at Amiens only to be turned back in order that they could be brought together for evacuation. The following day the 5th Army was informed that they were to 'evacuate to base forthwith by empty supply and ammunition trains all coloured and Italian labour'.[43] Within three days the Italian, Indian and Chinese labour in the 5th Army Area had been moved to the LoC or were in the process of evacuation.

An emergency camp was set up at Abancourt, under the command of Colonel Newington, to accommodate the units and stragglers that were evacuated from Army Areas. Nearly 30,000 men from British, Italian, Indian and Chinese labour units passed through the camp. The British were refitted and deployed to work on the defence lines. The Chinese moved to their base depot at Noyelles where companies were brought up to strength. The Italians were either handed back to the French or moved to Quevauvillers before repatriation on 8 April. Many of the Indians, coming to the end of their contract, were asked on 29 March whether they would re-engage. To a man they refused and arrangements were made for repatriation, which, due to a shortage of shipping, did not commence until June.

British labour companies were frequently employed close to the fighting, and on 21 March became directly involved. In III Corps

> ... scattered detachments working along the front from La Fontaine to Essigny-Le-Grand and Classtres to Montescourt became involved with the retiring fighting troops and in several cases could not withdraw until after they had jumped into their trenches and assisted in holding off the enemy.[44]

The following examples give an idea of the work undertaken by British companies during the German offensive. On 21 March 150 men of 87 Company and 250 men of 27 Company continued working on the defence line within 800 yards of the enemy. At Noyon 876 Company cleared 2,000 wounded from the CCS. and got away just before the Germans arrived. 141 Company remained at Flavy-Le-Martel ammunition dump and was withdrawn when it had been shelled and brought under machine-gun fire. 159 Company manned the ammunition dump at Abbecourt until the last moment when they arranged for it to be destroyed. The Company then retreated along the canal during which they sustained casualties whilst tearing up and bringing back the light railway line.

One of the strangest sights must have been 41 and 61 Companies who were employed by the Cavalry Division at Guiscard to take charge of the horses and ride them back into Noyon whilst the cavalry held the trenches. Riding horses and carrying the lances they brought them safely back. In general, the British companies were able to retreat according to the previously published instructions. There are two recorded examples of the plans failing:163 Company lost contact with its group when it moved without orders from Pozieres, and when their employer moved 117 and 132 Companies contrary to orders.

A second German offensive, which began in Flanders on 9 April, quickly overwhelmed the 2nd Portuguese Division. On 11 April, Haig issued his famous 'backs to the wall' order that said every position must be held to the last man. Two days later 43 officers and 1,869 British other ranks from labour companies in the 4th Army volunteered to carry arms and took up defensive positions. The offensive continued until 29 April during which labour units worked almost constantly building defences, producing ammunition and food dumps and assisting at CCSs.

On 18 May, in a special order of the day, Field-Marshal Haig acknowledged the part played by the Labour Corps during the German offensives:

> It has been a great pleasure to me to receive many reports on the devotion to duty, endurance and gallant work on the part of the units of the Labour Corps since the commencement of the present battle. These reports have been numerous and are most creditable to all concerned.
>
> I desire to place on record my hearty appreciation of the good work and gallant behaviour of the Labour Corps under most trying circumstances. The discipline and spirit shown by the officers and other ranks of the Corps have enabled them to respond to many unexpected calls on their services in a manner which has been of the greatest value and assistance to the rest of the Army, and has brought distinction and credit on themselves.[45]

The bravery of the men was recognised with the award of over 50 MMs and almost 150 MSMs.

Garrison Guard Companies

With the German offensive in March 1918 there was an urgent need for more men for defence. On 25 March half of 848 Company were sent from Calais, where they had been on guard duties, to help defend Amiens. Returning to Calais on 4 April they became part of the new 199th (Garrison) Brigade, which was formed in VII Corps, in 3rd Army Area, on 6 April.

The Brigade was made up of five provisional guard battalions and the 4th (Garrison) Battalion Royal Welsh Fusiliers. The provisional battalions were made up of nineteen garrison guard companies together with a company from the 1st (Garrison) Battalion Suffolk Regiment. Forming the Brigade took just under two weeks, the garrison guard companies being taken on strength between 18 and 21 April and the Royal Welsh Fusiliers on 19 April. The Brigade was tasked with defending the line between Saulty and Harbarcq, to the south-west of Arras.

Battalion	Forming Units
1 Provisional Guard Battalion	950, 951, 952 & 953 (GG) Companies
2 Provisional Guard Battalion	869, 785, 908 & 909 (GG) Companies
3 Provisional Guard Battalion	894, 935, 848 & 866 (GG) Companies
4 Provisional Guard Battalion	881, 853, 878 & 882 (GG) Companies
5 Provisional Guard Battalion	961, 962 & 934 (GG) Companies + 1 Coy 1st Garrison Bn Suffolk Regt
4th Garrison Bn RWF	

Table 9: Composition of 199 Brigade – April 1918

Taking nineteen companies away from their regular guard duties was to have a knock-on effect. Eighteen new garrison guard companies were formed, from 20 April onwards, from men already in the Labour Corps. One of the first to be formed was 958 Company at Rouen on 20 April where they were used to guard the Petrol Wharf, supply depots and the military prison.

It was decided at the end of May 1918 that the five provisional guard battalions should become infantry garrison battalions. As part of 59th Division they become the 17th (Garrison) Battalion Worcestershire, 25th (Garrison) Battalion King's Royal Rifle Corps, 13th (Garrison) Battalion West Riding, 23rd (Garrison) Battalion Lancashire Fusiliers and 17th (Garrison) Battalion Royal Sussex Regiment.[46]

At the same time it was decided that there was a need to form more infantry garrison battalions made up of category B(i) men serving in the Labour Corps who had previous experience in an infantry unit. These companies, named 'A' to 'X' Garrison Guard Companies, were formed into number 6 to 11 Garrison Guard Battalions. They were to become part of 40th Division on 11 June 1918.[47] They became the 11th Cameron Highlanders, 13th Royal Inniskillen Fusiliers, 13th East Lancashire, 10th King's Own Scottish Borderers, 15th King's Own Yorkshire Light Infantry and the 12th North Staffordshire. Many of the men posted to these battalions were old and unsuitable for front line service, even as was intended, in a quiet sector of the front. The Commander of 119th Brigade recorded that the three garrison battalions under his command were formed after almost half the men had been rejected as unsuitable and replaced by new drafts.[48] On 8 July the War Office decided that the word 'Garrison' would be dropped from the Battalion name.

In June 1918 two new Garrison Guard Companies (986 and 989) were formed. However, within two months the AG had decided that garrison guard companies would cease to exist. On 9 August 1918 the AG's letter No 177/6(M) explained that the companies would either cease to exist, as happened to 912 Company, or, like 917 and 918 Companies, be transferred to the 43rd Battalion, Royal Fusiliers, 'whose strength rose to no less than 49 companies'.[49]

Arming Companies

In the aftermath of the March offensive, on 15 April 1918, the decision was made in both the 1st Army and 3rd Army to arm the Labour Corps as rear defence units. Initially, the idea was to arm all men but so many weapons had been lost this was not possible. Instead, in the 1st Army only companies that had received training in using rifles were armed, whereas in the 3rd Army men with front line experience were drafted into companies already on the defence line, which were then armed. In the event of front line troops being forced to retreat, the armed companies were to defend the line until relieved by infantry units. The primary role of these companies remained labour. 65 Company was armed and sent to Souastre on 16 April for roadwork and did not receive training in using their weapons until 18 May. Two weeks later it lost around 200 men trained on weapons who became 'O' Garrison Company.

The decision to arm Labour companies appears to have been made locally and without reference to GHQ. However, with the creation of 'A' to 'X' Garrison Companies at the end of May, men in armed companies were transferred to the infantry.

The experience in March highlighted the need for Labour companies to be able to defend themselves if they came into contact with the enemy, so orders were issued for the arming of one platoon in each labour company.[50] Later, the training of Lewis gunners provided protection against enemy aircraft. GHQ made it clear these men were not to form a reserve fighting force. Wace is explicit on the benefit of arming labour companies: 'There is no doubt that very considerable moral benefit accrued from arming of labour companies, and an added impetus was given to their esprit de corps.'[51]

Gas Attack

One of the most devastating attacks on a Labour Corps company occurred on the night of 11/12 May 1918. On that night 101 Company was burying cables at Fonquevillers when the area was attacked with both high explosive and gas shells from 7.30 pm until 2.30 am. Initial reports suggested that no men were killed during the attack, although IV Corps Diary refers to 40 officers and possibly 1,400 men being gassed.[52] Among those gassed were three officers (Major R. M. Christie, 2Lt W. Bates and 2Lt F. P. Hazell) and 286 other ranks of 101 Company.

On 12 May 60309 Private H. Chitty was the first of 101 Company to die as a result of the gas. Sixteen more men including 2Lt Bates were to die on 13 May and a further 37 including Major Christie on 14 May. Further members of 101 Company, including 2Lt Hazell, died of the effects of the gas over the next fifteen days so that by 29 May 1918 all three officers and 134 other ranks had died. Within five days of the gas attack the remnants of 101 Company were employed on road-work at Orville and on 18 May received 200 replacements.

Most of the men killed in this attack are buried in St Sever Cemetery Extension, Rouen. It is not known how many of the remaining 150 other ranks may have later died as a result of the gassing.

Russian Companies

In 1917 an Order in Council implemented the Anglo-Russian Convention on Military Service. This meant that Russian subjects living in Britain were liable for military service under the Military Service Act of 1916. On 12 September ACI 1415 announced the intention to form battalions made up of 'Friendly Alien Jews'. In fact the 38th Royal Fusiliers, a Jewish Battalion, was already being formed at Plymouth when the ACI was published. With the Russian Revolution in October, uncertainty arose about the future of the Convention. At the War Cabinet meeting on 23 January 1918 the Director of Intelligence stated that there were some 25,000 Russians, mainly Jews, of military age in Britain of whom 3,000 had been recruited.[53] His view was that these men should either be conscripted or deported to Russia.

By 3 March 1918, when Russia withdrew from the war after signing the Treaty of Brest-Litovsk with Germany, over 1,600 Russians had already been conscripted. Two days later a Russian called Kutchinsky took out a writ against the CO of the 39th Royal Fusiliers, at Plymouth, on the grounds that the Anglo-Russian Convention no longer applied. The War Cabinet discussed the matter on 7 March. They decided that the Secretary for War should fight the case in court; if Kutchinsky was successful there were some 1,600 Russians serving at Plymouth who were likely to cause difficulties about serving in the Army.[54] With the court finding in favour of the Government it was decided on 25 March that the recruitment of Russians would continue. Concerns about recruiting discontented Russians into fighting units resulted in the decision being taken that they would serve in Labour units.

On 19 April 1918 ACI 414 announced the formation of the Labour battalions and companies composed of Russian subjects (see page 289)[55]. Men recruited into these units could not be transferred to any other army corps or regiment without authority from the War Office; nor could they be transferred to other Labour units. Two battalions were stationed in Britain to act as receiving stations for recruits and for men returning from France.

Recruits were generally of poor physique, predominantly from occupations like tailoring, and therefore not used to heavy physical labour. Had these men been enlisted in 1916 or 1917 many would have been rejected as medically unfit for service but by 1918 the demand for labour meant they were accepted. As a result their initial training was concerned with improving their physique, in addition to turning civilians into soldiers. Many spoke either little or poor English and this presented additional difficulties for the non-Jewish officers and NCOs. Due to the extended training it was June before the first Company (1001) arrived in France. Three more Companies 1021, 1002 and 1022 arrived in June, August and December.

The Russian companies are virtually ignored by General Wace in his report, the only reference being:

> The Russian Companies were composed mostly of Russian Jews from the East End of London; the physique of the men was wretched and their efficiency at the start was extremely low. Some of the companies, however, by careful training and by the enforcement of a strict discipline, combined with good rations and a healthy life, improved considerably, and could be relied on eventually to perform a reasonable task.[56]

There is no doubt that the 2000 men who served in France did good service from June 1918 onwards and played a particularly important role in helping to clear the battlefields and create cemeteries following the Armistice. However the reality is that the formation of the Russian companies did not result in the high numbers of additional labourers the War Office wanted in France.

PoW Companies

The relationship between PoW companies and the Labour organisation changed several times during 1917 and 1918. When the companies were created in 1916, each having 400 PoWs, the British officers and escorts were more concerned with discipline and security than efficiency of work. Although the instructions for form-ing the companies made it clear that the role of the escorts was to secure 'both the safe custody of the prisoners of war, and the best results in the quality of their labour', efficiency of labour was a low priority.[57]

Responsibility for the allotment and distribution, but not efficiency, of the com-panies was handed over to the Labour Directorate in January 1917. Labour personnel were attached to the companies but were, at times, misused. In the 3rd Army the DADL pointed out to the AAG, on 28 May, that using labour 'personnel as guards is contrary to instructions and should cease as soon as possible as such guards are not efficient'.[58] Some of the concerns about efficiency were addressed from July onwards when each company had a Labour Corps sergeant and four other ranks attached to it to supervise work. It was the lack of escorts that caused the greatest wastage of PoW Labour. The 5th Army DADL recorded in November 1917 that a shortage of supervi-sion meant that some prisoners were being left in camp when they should be working.

The situation had not improved by February 1918 when Sir Edward Pearson undertook his study of labour. He visited 24 different PoW units and was critical of the way PoWs were being supervised and used:

> This Labour is extremely uneconomical where small parties are required, as, owing
> to the lack of supervision and to the shortage of escorts, larger gangs than the work
> warrants have to be employed. This is a bad principle, as it reacts adversely throughout
> the whole number.[59]

Early in March 1918 the AG signified his intention to post an additional officer to PoW companies, except for those employed in workshops, to supervise the work. The Controller of Labour recommended creating a pool of 250 officers to super-vise work and that each company should have four officers for this purpose, except workshop companies who would have two officers. On 29 April General Routine Order 3884 was published; all officers serving in PoW companies were transferred to the Labour Corps, thus bringing responsibility for efficiency under the control of the Labour Directorate. The final decision rested with the War Office who decided on 12 May that a captain or major would command each company with four other officers to support him. At the same time the number of escorts was revised into three scales depending on the type of work and degree of supervision needed.

PoW companies were still made up of Labour Corps personnel for work super-vision and other personnel for escort duty. The first step to change this came in July 1918 when the escort NCOs and other ranks were transferred to the Labour Corps. Typical of these men was 564875 Private C. Rowen who had been in France since December 1916 with the London Regiment. Wounded at Ypres in August 1917 and gassed at Cambrai in December, he was categorised as B(ii). Posted as an escort to 50 PoW Company at Les Saulx on 26 January 1918 he was transferred to the Labour Corps on 17 July.

The second step addressed the problem of officers having either a security or a supervisory role; every officer should be responsible for both supervision and escort duties. In a final attempt to solve the problem it was announced on 6 August that officers would be titled Company Officers and not Escort Officers or Labour Supervisory Officers.

In London, on 12 August, a meeting was held of the Prisoners of War Employment Committee, attended by both Sir Edward Pearson and Colonel Wace. It was decided the OC of a PoW company could give an increased ration of 2 ounces of edible fat as a reward for increased output, although this was not introduced until October.

Between 8 August and the end of October 168 new PoW companies were formed to accommodate the large numbers of prisoners. Once again, finding sufficient men for supervision of PoW work became a problem and on 22 October it was decided that 5 Labour Corps NCOs would be posted to each company thus reducing the demand for supervision by the employing unit.

At the end of the war it was decided not to create any further PoW companies but rather to increase the strength of each company to 550 men. Restrictions were also removed regarding the work that could be undertaken by PoWs. On 16 November approval was given for them to remove mines and delayed action fuses and on 26 December for them to handle hay.

Despite repatriation and the disbandment of PoW companies, in December the Controller of Labour complained he still did not have enough men for escort duties. In February 1919 it was announced that men from infantry units could be used as escorts, although they were not transferred to the Labour Corps.

A War of Movement

The Labour Corps, which had been formed and equipped for a stationary war, was to face a completely new challenge as a result of the British offensive that began on 8 August 1918. Labour units now played a major part in mobile warfare but were handicapped by insufficient transport. There were attempts to remedy this at corps level where the more forward thinking commanders recognised the importance of labour being in a position to support infantry as it advanced. The commander of V Corps made buses available to move labour units forward whenever required.

Before the offensive, Labour units were working in forward areas preparing land in advance of the skilled Railway Construction Companies. At times this meant that they were operating as far forward as the support trenches. In the Colincamps area companies were working in the open, before the Germans had retreated from the Thiepval Plateau, clearing sleepers and old rails and remaking the railway formation.

For this mobile war a new procedure was adopted whereby a Group HQ was located as close as possible to the fighting line and it would call forward companies as required. This Group and its companies would remain in the area as the British line advanced and a different labour group would leapfrog them and then call up companies under its control. This system ensured that all companies had an equal share of both work and time out of the battle zone.

Many companies became known for their proficiency in particular tasks. The following three examples describe skilled work undertaken by Labour Companies during the final 100 days.

113 Company became so proficient at bridge building that the chief engineer of V Corps made a particular request for the Company to support the Royal

Engineers. In this role they assisted in bridging successively the Ancre, the Canal du Nord, the Escault Canal, the Selle and the Sambre. In addition to this specialised work the Company was also employed on light railway construction, building V Corps HQ and clearing locations. On 26 October, as soon as the infantry had captured the village of Englefontaine, they were brought by lorry to clear the walls and hedges to enable guns to be brought forward. For this action, five men, believed to be 67430 Sgt E. Henderson, 67265 Cpl A. Boon, 382780 Pte W. Heath, 403595 Pte A. Jackson and 67222 Sgt E. I. Lewis, were awarded the MM.

145 Company developed a reputation for constructing and maintaining water points. On 27 September 1918 a small detachment under 2Lt J. O'Connor were building a water point at Equancourt. They completed the task despite coming under heavy shellfire. For their work 364683 Pte A. Ervine and 86714 Pte E. Manton were awarded the MM and 2Lt O'Connor the MC, his citation stating:

> For conspicuous gallantry and devotion to duty. This officer was in charge of a work-
> ing party detailed to construct a water point, which it was important to complete
> quickly. The work took fourteen hours, during which time the party were subjected
> to heavy shell fire, and it was largely due to his coolness and the encouragement he
> gave his men that the task was completed in time.[60]

161 Company, under Captain F. Bawden, who had previous experience in laying mines followed the advance, repairing mine craters and holes in the road: 'Owing to his technical experience the officer was able to detect and remove many enemy mines before they exploded and destroyed communications.'[61]

Labour Superintendents

One of the concerns raised by both Pearson and Baines in their reports was the problem of dual control of Labour. Whilst the system of 'contracting out' helped overcome some of the difficulties, the weakness lay in administering the system. In October 1918 sanction was given for the creation of 100 Labour Superintendents on the Controller's establishment. Fifty-five superintendents held the rank of either major or captain and 45 assistants were either captains or lieutenants. The role of these men was to organise and run labour at ports and depots on the LoC, and in Army Areas, under the ACL. The creation of these posts was in line with Wace's belief in scientific management and he saw the men appointed as potential ACLs.

At the ports the labour superintendent attended the daily employer's conference and was then able to inform the ACL how many men would be required the follow-ing day. In some ports, such as Havre, the employers informed the superintendent of the task, and he determined the number of men required. This 'contracting out' of the work was found to save considerable labour whilst still achieving the task. However, the power of the superintendent to economise labour depended on the amount of responsibility he was given and at some ports and depots his role was seen as little more than advisory.

Wace's Report gives a positive view of the role of labour superintendants but the creation of these posts so late in the war means they were never really fully tested.

Armistice

The work of the Labour Corps did not end with the Armistice. Battlefields had to be cleared, bodies exhumed and reburied and the damage of war repaired. At the same time support had to be proved for the Army of Occupation in Germany. As will be seen, it would be 1921 before the last Labour Corps soldiers returned to Britain.

1   NA WO 107/37 'Report on Labour' p.114
2   ibid CAB 23/5 p.46
3   ibid CAB 24/39 p.495
4   ibid CAB 24/39 p.495
5   ibid CAB 23/5 p.113
6   ibid
7   ibid CAB 24/58
8   The Imperial War Cabinet comprised the Prime Ministers of Britain, Canada, Australia, New Zealand and General Smuts representing the PM of South Africa. This meeting included the Secretary of State for War, Director of Military Operations and Sir Maurice Hankey as Secretary to the War Cabinet.
9   NA CAB 23/44A
10 ibid CAB 24/58
11 ibid WO 107/37 p.21
12 ibid WO 95/37
13 ibid WO 107/37 p.19
14 ibid WO 107/37 p.17
15 ibid WO 107/37 Appendix D
16 Griffin, N.J., *Scientific Management,* p.198
17 NA WO 107/37 p.134
18 Griffin, N.J., p.198
19 NA WO 106/33
20 Griffin p.200
21 NA WO 95/83
22 ibid WO 95/36
23 ibid WO 107/37 p.178
24 ibid WO 107/37 Appendix C
25 ibid WO 107/27 p.27
26 ibid WO 107/37 p.33
27 ibid WO 107/37 p.180
28 ibid WO 95/537
29 ibid WO 107/37 p.127
30 ibid WO 107/37 p.127
31 ibid WO 95/384
32 Maclean, *Farming and Forestry on the Western Front,* p.21
33 ibid, p.21
34 NA WO 95/889
35 ibid WO 95/83
36 Gough, H., *The March Retreat,* p. 9
37 NA WO 107/37 Appendix BB
38 Xu Goughi, *China and the Great War,* p. 143
39 Summerskill, M., *China on the Western Front,* pp. 124–7

40 NA WO 107/37 Appendix DD
41 ibid WO 107/37 Appendix BB
42 ibid WO 107/37 Appendix AA
43 ibid WO 95/83
44 ibid WO 107/37 Appendix CC
45 ibid WO 107/37 Appendix OO
46 ibid WO 95/185
47 ibid WO 95/83
48 Crozier, A., *Brass Hat in No Man's Land,* p. 215
49 Messenger, p.241
50 NA WO 95/39 23 July 1918
51 ibid WO 107/37 p. 208
52 ibid WO 95/726 12 May 1918
53 ibid CAB 25/3
54 ibid
55 ibid WO 293/8
56 ibid WO 107/37 p.40
57 ibid WO 95/31 27 July 1916
58 ibid WO 95/384
59 ibid CAB 24/58
60 *London Gazette,* 10 January 1919, p. 637
61 NA WO 107/37 Appendix BB

1919 SALVAGE, CEMETERIES AND GERMANY

The work of the Labour Corps continued for two years after the Armistice. Its new role included the dangerous work of clearing the battlefields, exhuming and reburying the dead and supporting the British Army of the Rhine in Germany.

Demobilisation

Preparations for returning Labour Corps personnel to Britain to work on the land and in the mines had begun before the end of the war. At the end of August 1918 Labour Groups began to register all men who had been miners before the war with a view to their transfer home to civilian employment in the mines. During October 338 miners returned to Britain from labour companies in II Corps[1] and 214 from XV Corps.[2] It appears that only a few agriculturalists were returned to Britain before the war ended but as soon as hostilities ceased men considered key agricultural workers were returned.

For personnel of the Labour Corps, as with other Army units, demobilisation was based on a number of factors, including the man's industrial skills and his length of service. The decision to demobilise individuals, rather than complete companies, meant that men with key skills were returned to Britain and new men had to be drafted into their company to make up its strength.

For many officers like Captain Thomas, who had served with 58 Company since May 1916, this decision was a disappointment. Thomas wrote:

My hopes of taking my Company back to England and breaking up there were doomed to disappointment. Individual demobilisation has been ordered, and the company will be gradually shrinking smaller and smaller as the well known faces leave us.[3]

The majority of men identified for demobilisation in November and December 1918 served in general Labour companies. By the beginning of January 1919 demobilisation meant that 43 of the 198 companies in France were disbanded. However, because of the need for labour in France the authorities made the decision to retain general companies and disband Area Employment companies. All area employment companies were withdrawn from Army Areas to the LoC on 16 January 1919 and within four weeks, 48 of the 145 Area Employment companies had been disbanded. By May there were only 20 Area Employment companies in France.

With employment companies being disbanded it became common practice for general labour companies to be used for regimental employments. The AG wrote to all Army and Corps commanders on 14 March: 'the use of Labour Corps personnel on Employments is contrary to Labour principles and fighting troops should be used'.[4]

When, due to demobilisation, the strength of a general company fell below 250, the unit responsible for its administration had to decide whether to retain it as a weak company or disband it and send the surplus personnel to other companies.

As officers were released it became increasingly difficult for labour to maintain the administrative structure that had been established during 1918. On 10 February the office of Assistant Controller Labour (ACL) (Central) was disbanded and his responsibilities were passed to the ACL (South). At corps and group level the decision to retain or disband a unit appears to have been made according to the availability of officers. In XIII Corps, for example, 70 Group was disbanded on 10 February 1919 despite five of its companies continuing to exist. In contrast the office of the Labour Commandant (LC) of III Corps closed on 17 March 1919 with the CO of 38 Group assuming the responsibilities of the LC.

On 12 June GHQ instructed each army to disband all labour companies not required for clearing up. Winston Churchill informed the House of Commons on 10 December 1919 that there were 30 Labour companies on exhumation duties in France and two-and-a-half companies working for the RE, dismantling camps and on transport work at Boulogne and Calais. This figure is at variance with Army records, which indicate that at the end of 1919 there were 41 Labour Corps companies serving in France, 24 with the Rhine Army and one in Italy.[5] It has not been possible to identify exactly the work being undertaken by the companies in France, the likelihood being that the vast majority were employed on exhumation and reburial.

Repairing the infrastructure

Following the end of hostilities roads had to be repaired and made safe before the Army could advance to the Rhine. Units like 161 Company often worked well in advance of the infantry. The labour commandant of V Corps reported that labour troops 'in many cases were the first British personnel to come into contact with the inhabitants of the liberated area'.[6]

By the beginning of 1919 clearing the battlefield, salvage and creating cemeteries were the most important roles for labour. As men were demobilised it became increasingly difficult for the Army to find enough personnel to maintain the roads. In the 5th Army the decision was made, on 19 January, to stop using men for road maintenance. By the end of February all Labour Corps personnel employed on roadwork had been transferred to cemetery construction.

At the end of January the French stated that the British were responsible for the maintenance of roads used by British military traffic. However, early in March the British informed the French that British companies would undertake no more roadwork after 15 March 1919. By the end of the month British personnel were withdrawn from work at Dunkirk, Boulogne and Calais to be used for battlefield clearance, salvage and constructing cemeteries.

PoWs

At the end of October 1918 the QMG raised concerns about the loss of skilled and semi-skilled PoWs who would be repatriated once peace was declared. On 9 December GHQ informed the War Office that repatriation would mean a loss of 54 PoW companies employed in workshops. As they were essential for railways, transport and other areas of work it recommended that they be retained until they were no longer required. After consideration, on 2 January 1919, the AG reported that he could not sanction the retention of skilled PoWs, as this was contrary to the repatriation terms laid down in the Peace Treaty.

On 24 November 1918 it was decided that PoWs would be allowed to handle all items of battlefield salvage including unexploded ordnance. At Audruicq and Zeneghem, where British ammunition was being loaded for return to Britain, German PoWs replaced Chinese labourers. They were not, however, allowed to work at Bourbourg, where German ammunition was being handled, in case they booby-trapped a fuse. Consideration was given to transferring the 41,000 PoWs still in Britain to work in France but the QMG rejected this at the beginning of February 1919. Within a few weeks this decision was to be changed, with 20 PoW companies arriving in mid March and by the end of the month 20 officers were sent to Britain to form new PoW working companies.

During 1919 large numbers of PoWs were being used for salvage, exhumation and reburials. Those employed on the exhumation of German dead were given an additional ration of rum on the days they worked (equivalent to half of the British issue), and two ounces of tobacco a week. German PoWs were allowed to dig trenches in British cemeteries but the burials and filling in of the trench had to be carried out by British soldiers. The German PoWs had to be outside the cemetery during the burial service or consecration of the ground.

On 2 July all restrictions regarding the use of PoWs on light railways were removed so that they could be used 'as freely as possible in relief of British troops'.[7] At the end of August instructions were issued that the remaining PoWs should be repatriated and by October 1919 only around 1,500 PoWs were still under British control. By 7 January 1920 the only PoW company still in France was 285 (Polish) Company at Calais and this was repatriated by the end of the month.

Foreign Labour

The demobilisation of British officers and NCOs had a major effect on the work of the Chinese. GHQ recorded on 17 January 'serious reports in loss of efficiency in CLC companies due to the reductions in British NCOs being demobilised'.[8] On 22 January it was decided that, as far as possible, no more British officers or NCOs with the Chinese would be demobilised until the Peace Treaty was ratified. Three days later GHQ decided that if there were surplus British NCOs when a company was disbanded they would be sent to the CLC Depot. In February concern was expressed that the Chinese companies were under-utilised due to a lack of technical supervision. With the disbandment of the Directorate of Forestry in January 1919 a number of Chinese companies were released to work in the ports and to replace PoW companies as they were repatriated. Skilled Chinese labourers who had been employed in the tank workshops were posted to work for the Director General of Transportation.

The Chinese were used extensively on battlefield clearance and at salvage and ordnance depots. Many were injured or killed, particularly when breaking down ordnance. In 23 Ammunition Depot at Bourbourg, on 25 April 1919, six Chinese labourers were killed when German shells they were stacking exploded.

There are several examples of Chinese labourers risking their own lives when accidents occurred. Three labourers were awarded MSMs including 91085 1st Class Ganger Yen Teng Feng of 130 Company, his citation stating: 'On 23 May 1919 at BAILLEUL following an explosion, he worked constantly for four hours removing tarpaulins from stacks of ammunition and drenching them with water.'[9]

Salvage work

Labour units played a full part in salvaging materials that could be reused. The notes for Labour Corps officers stated: 'Units at work on roads and in areas recently occupied by troops will render great service by collecting salvage such as petrol tins, rubber, old tyres, steel helmets, gas helmets, &c., and form a dump at Company H.Q.'[10] With the end of the war salvage had to be undertaken for two reasons. Firstly, to clear the land so that local people could start farming. Secondly, to recover material which could either be used for reconstruction or sold for profit. The most profitable items were rails, piping, copper, brass, aluminium and sound timber from the wooden roads. By 9 December 1918 the 3rd Army had 10,000 men available for salvage work but a lack of transport meant they could not move them forward to where they were needed.

At the beginning of 1919 the Labour Controller visited the 'Devastated Area' to examine how salvage operations were being carried out. He found that procedures varied from area to area, some companies clearing all materials as they moved forward with others clearing general salvage first and then ammunition. In the 1st Army British companies were billeted outside the area and worked inwards, whereas Chinese and PoWs were located in the area and work outwards.

In the 3rd Army there were disagreements between the Labour Commandant and salvage officers over how salvage operations should be undertaken. The LC wanted each company to operate in its own specific area whereas salvage officers wanted all the companies to be concentrated in the east and then move westward. The views of the salvage officers prevailed and their method was adopted but it was not successful, mainly due to the lack of transport. Being responsible for the efficiency of Labour, the LC changed the system so that each company became responsible for clearing a specific area. He also introduced the idea of each company having a section specifically for clearing ammunition and other ordnance.

The idea of salvage being undertaken to enable local people to return to the land changed in May 1919 with the QMG informing the salvage areas that the only reason for keeping British forces in France was to salvage materials and stores that were useful for reconstruction or could be sold. He stated that there was no obligation to the French or Belgians to collect stores, remove dugouts, fill in shell holes and trenches, or remove barbed wire or damaged corrugated iron. Both dud and unexploded shells were not to be collected as such work was 'fait du guerre, and the responsibility of the owner of the soil'.[11] Hand grenades, however, were to be destroyed, with PoWs used, if possible, for this task. Area commanders were reminded to concentrate efforts on the most easterly parts of their area and to ensure that labour was not used for unprofitable work.

In deciding what to salvage the cost of labour and transport had to be taken into account. Each ton of material cost 14s to transport by light railway. In addition there was the cost of manpower at 8s a day for Chinese and 12s a day for British labour. Commanders were urged to make as much use as possible of PoWs until they were repatriated. Although it cost 7s a day to maintain them, this had to be done whether they were working or not, and so PoWs were regarded as free of cost. It was emphasised that white labour should be used as far as possible for sorting, guarding and collecting the most valuable items.

Exhumation and Reburial

At the end of 1915 the French government provided land that would be maintained in perpetuity for British and Dominion war dead. In order to establish cemeteries and record the burials the Directorate of Graves Registration and Enquiries (DGR&E) was established. On 21 May 1917 a Royal Charter established the Imperial War Graves Commission (IWGC). Brigadier General Fabian Ware, the Director of the DGR&E, became its vice chairman. At the end of May 1917 Graves Registration Units were allocated to each Army HQ and to the LoC. Each unit included a surveyor, three clerks, two draughtsmen and a photographer.

To support the HQ units there were 23 Graves Registration Units (GRU), each commanded by a lieutenant with a corporal, 26 cemetery men, a cook and a batman. These units were not assigned to a formation but given a definite area in which they operated as long as they were needed. In December 1917, for example, 1 GRU worked in XIX Corps area, 2 GRU in II Corps and 3 GRU in VII Corps and II ANZAC Corps. In July 1918 men working in these units were transferred to the Labour Corps for administrative purposes. Although they were given Labour Corps numbers, in the range 602800 to 603400, and posted to the Graves Registration Section it appears that they remained under the control of the GRUs. Larger working parties were formed when required, for example on 18 September 1918 a detachment of one officer and 100 men were transferred from the 3rd Army to the 4th Army.

Clearing the battlefield and burying the dead required burial parties from infantry units and support from labour units in addition to the men of the DGR&E. It was one of the most demoralising and unpopular tasks. 372408 Private John McCauley described his feelings when recovering bodies for burial during 1918: 'For the first week or two I could scarcely endure the experiences we met with, but I gradually became hardened.'[12] When bodies were found in water filled shell holes or mine craters he had to feel about in slime and decomposing flesh to search for the man's identity disc so that the body would not be buried as unknown.

By November 1918 the IWGC had details of almost 500,000 men who had been buried and a similar number listed as missing. Initially GHQ asked for volunteers from Labour units to concentrate bodies scattered over the battlefields into properly organised cemeteries. Volunteers qualified for Extra Duty Pay, privates receiving 1s, warrant officers and NCOs 1s 6d and officers 2s 6d a day although this was increased from April 1919.

One of the first Labour Corps companies to volunteer was 68 Company, which was located at Ypres. The company, commanded by Captain G. Crawford, commenced exhumation and burial work at Hooge Crater Cemetery during the second week of January 1919 and continued in this role until disbanded in April 1920.[13]

In January 1919 'speedy clearing up of the battlefields was probably of higher importance, for sanitary and other considerations, than minute accuracy in establishing the identity of the bodies that were found'.[14] The Company received little guidance from GHQ and this, together with pressure to clear the battlefield speedily, led to mistakes being made in the early months of 1919: 'Exhumation Companies, obsessed with the idea that their reputation depended on their concentrating the highest possible number of bodies in the shortest possible time have often paid little or no heed to the essential matter of identification.'[15]

At an inquiry into identification errors in 1920, the Australian Major A. Allen accused some British units of 'chopping men in halves in order to double their body returns'.[16]

Based upon the experiences of 68 Company, Captain Crawford compiled working instructions for exhumation companies in July 1919, which improved working practices and reduced mistakes. These were adopted as standard operating procedure by the DGR&E (see page 371).

It was soon apparent that with demobilisation there would not be enough volunteer Labour Corps units to undertake exhumation and re-burial. On 23 April 1919 at a meeting of the Army Council the AG was asked to prepare a memorandum for the Secretary of State that suggested the formation of a gravediggers' corps, with a limited period of service.[17] Rather than form a new corps it was decided to enlist men into the Labour Corps 'for special duties in connection with the scheme for the exhumation of bodies and the centralisation of military cemeteries in France'.[18]

Enlistment was open to men aged between 17 and 38 of medical category B(i) or lower who were physically capable of the work. For men over 38 the only stipulation was that they could physically undertake the work. Enlistment commenced at the beginning of May and Churchill informed the House of Commons that 2,736 men had enlisted by 24 May.[19] The original idea was that men would be enlisted for one year with 'the engagement in any case terminating on the 30th April, 1920'.[20] However, men were still being enlisted in September 1919, remaining in France beyond April 1920. Service records suggest that the majority of men who enlisted had seen previous service in the Army, often in the Labour Corps. For example, 41-year-old 701054 Private Albert Mogridge, who had enlisted in 1914, served in Salonika with both the Welsh Regiment and the Labour Corps. He re-enlisted on 2 June 1919 and served in 48 Company working on exhumation and reburials until April 1920. Men were paid the normal rate of pay with families receiving separation allowances. Warrant officers and NCOs received an additional 3s a day and other ranks 2s 6d a day on the days when they were employed on exhumation duties.

Having to deal with decomposing bodies was an unpleasant and potentially dangerous task. Each body had to be carefully examined in an attempt to find the identification tag or other form of identity. At times, searching for the identity involved feeling inside a body that had been damaged by shellfire or bullet or where rats had eaten part of the corpse. In 1918 and 1919 examining bodies was particularly unpleasant as little decomposition had occurred and the corpse's flesh often came away when touched.

Exhumation parties also faced the danger of personal injury from rusting equipment and unexploded ordnance. On 20 October 1919 48 Company were searching the Langemark area as part of the concentration at Cement House Cemetery. A detachment from the company, in preparing the midday meal for the exhumation parties, lit a fire in order to boil water. The fire exploded a buried shell killing seven men and injuring a further three.[21]

The living conditions of the exhumation companies was raised in the House of Commons when Major Entwistle, MP for Kingston upon Hull, asked the Secretary for War to investigate the claim by a soldier in 723 Company that whilst employed on exhumation work at Cleury, on the Somme, they had to camp for a fortnight without a groundsheet or blanket, were not able to get tobacco, paper or soap and had not been paid for a month.

For exhumation to be carried out effectively it was important that the company had enough equipment and supplies. On 18 September 1919 the OC of 83 Company, who were working near Bellicourt, complained that they had no canvas despite repeatedly reporting this to the DGR&E. On 22 September the company received twelve bales of canvas, which was used in two days, and they again had to stop work. No further canvas had been received by 7 October when a report was sent to the Labour Commandant for the Cambrai sub-district. Three days later a response was received from the DGR&E Major responsible for the area explaining that there had been a shortage of canvas and that the Company had now been supplied with some and had recommenced work.[22]

Records held by the Commonwealth War Graves Commission indicate a committee was set up in 1920 to investigate a number of mistakes in identification and recording that had occurred when the cemeteries were initially constructed. This was due to the inexperience of the Labour units constructing the cemeteries and poor recording by some of the registration officers. Procedures written by Captain Crawford, OC 68 Company, and adopted by DGR&E in July 1919 rectified these problems. The committee felt that as 68 Company became more experienced fewer errors were made. It noted that

> The 68th Labour Company was the pioneer company in work of this kind, and it was natural that in July 1919, when other companies were in the process of formation its experience should be of particular value to them. It seems to the Committee on the evidence that the value of Mr Crawford's instructions owed much to his realisation of past mistakes and omissions.[23]

60 Company

The Rhine Army included responsibility for the port of Antwerp, which was used for the demobilisation of men and the return of stores to Britain. From 14 February 1919 60 Company undertook sorting and packing of the stores at Antwerp Port. By April they were being employed for five days a week, averaging 80 tons of ammunition a day. This was some 20 tons a day less than expected and the Army considered their work unsatisfactory.

There was clearly dissatisfaction among the men of the Company as their situation was to be raised twice in the House of Commons. On 19 May 1919 William Crooks, MP for Woolwich, asked the Secretary of State for War whether he was aware that the Company was made up of men of poor physical condition who had to rise at 6.30 am, parade at 7.30 am and commence work at 8 am loading, examining, and stacking all calibres of ammunition. He complained that the men had no form of recreation and asked 'whether he will have inquiries made into these complaints with a view of these men being apportioned work more in keeping with their physical strength?'[24] Mr Crooks was informed that the Secretary for War was not aware of the situation and that it would be investigated.

A week later Sir Herbert Nield, MP for Ealing, asked Winston Churchill whether he was aware 'that the band of the 60th Labour Company (late 20th Cheshire Regiment), which is composed mostly of wounded men and men who have been in the trenches, is compelled to work all day and is refused the privilege to practise and play to the troops whilst other regimental bands enjoy such privilege and whether he will take steps to have this grievance remedied and thus remove the dissatisfaction which at present exists among the men?'[25] Churchill's reply was, 'Bands are not authorised for Labour Companies. The personnel of these companies are required for their normal duties.'[26]

Rhine Army

The Labour Corps accompanied the Army of Occupation to Germany, working for the various services and undertaking regimental employments. In Cologne in June 1919, for example, 60 men of 5 Company were working in the bakery, 200 men of 153 Company at the AOC Depot and 100 men of 91 Company at the RE Depot.

During the same month, as men from Cavalry regiments were demobilised it appears that their horses and equipment were kept in Cologne in case reinforcements had to be sent to Germany. Two Labour Companies, 30 and 130, were used to look after the horses and equipment.

In October 1919 there were sixteen general companies, five Divisional Employment companies and three Corps Employment companies employed in Germany. With demobilisation this decreased to two general companies, 48 and 180, and three Divisional Employment companies, 226, 238 and 257 by January 1920. By September 1920 the only Labour Corps representation with the Rhine Army was 257 Company, which remained in Germany until January 1921.

1   NA WO 95/699
2   ibid WO 95/929
3   Thomas p.68
4   NA WO 95/83
5   ibid WO 73/111
6   ibid WO 107/37 'Report on Labour' Appendix BB
7   ibid WO 95/446
8   ibid WO 95/83
9   *London Gazette,* 13 Jul 1920, Page 7443
10 NA WO 107/37 Appendix C
11 ibid WO 95/831
12 IWM DOCS 97/10/1
13 Hooge Crater Cemetery was originally begun in October 1917 with 76 graves. Between January 1919 and April 1920 it was to be enlarged by the concentration of bodies brought from the battlefields of Zillebeke, Zantvoorde and Gheluvelt and from eleven smaller cemeteries. These included 36 bodies brought from Tower Hamlets Cemetery, Gheluvelt and 20 from Menin Road Pillbox Cemetery, Zillebeke There are now 5,923 Commonwealth men buried or commemorated in Hooge Crater Cemetery, with 3,579 burials being unidentified men.
14 CWGC DG R&E48 Report of Committee of Enquiry, 13 January 1921
15 CWGC Revised Instructions quoted in Hodgkinson, P. *Clearing the Dead* p. 50
16 Allen, Major A. evidence given to Inquiry 30/3/1920, quoted in Hodgkinson, P., *Clearing the Dead,* p. 51
17 NA WO 163/24 Minutes of Army Council
18 ibid WO 123/61 Army Order 196 10 May 1919
19 Hansard, 3 June 1919
20 NA WO 123/61 Army Order 196
21 The seven killed were Privates D. Lloyd, J. Bentham, A. Greaves, R. Eyre, J. Byrne, B. Tilley and J. Williams. Initially their deaths were recorded as accidental but later changed to Died of Wounds by the AG
22 IWM Document 5336 Misc 136 (2118)
23 ibid
24 Hansard, 15 May 1919
25 ibid, 22 May 1919
26 ibid. Contrary to Churchill's reply Labour Corps Companies did have Bands as seen in the photograph of 184 Company Band in the picture section.

SECTION THREE: OTHER THEATRES

GALLIPOLI

By late 1914 the Western Front had become a static war and there was a danger that the Russians were about to be defeated by the Germans. In November 1914 the First Lord of the Admiralty, Winston Churchill, put forward a plan to send a naval force through the Dardanelles to threaten Constantinople. He hoped this would force Turkey out of the conflict and bring the war to a swift conclusion.

The War Council decided, on 16 February 1915, to send the 29th Division to Lemnos; to arrange for a force to be sent from Egypt if required; and ordered the Admiralty to prepare transport for moving and landing a force of 50,000 men.[1] On 12 March Kitchener appointed Sir Ian Hamilton to command the Dardanelles military forces. He instructed Hamilton that a full force should be assembled prior to a landing but he should avoid a landing if at all possible. Naval attacks began on 19 February 1915 but on 18 March British and French ships failed to force their way through the narrows and into the Black Sea. The naval campaign having failed the plan was implemented to use the army to capture the Gallipoli Peninsula.

The use of labour in the Gallipoli campaign falls into two main areas: the development of Lemnos and Imbros as bases for the campaign, and Labour supporting the men on the peninsula.

Lemnos and Imbros

When Hamilton arrived at Lemnos on 18 March he noted that it would not make a suitable base for the forthcoming landings due to the lack of wharfs, piers, labour and water. Within an hour of arriving he cabled Kitchener requesting the base for the campaign be Alexandria. Despite his concern, Lemnos, together with Imbros, became the staging point for the Gallipoli campaign. Initially, in accordance with army practice, local civilians were employed to provide labour.

As the campaign developed, locally employed Greeks could not meet the demand for labour. In May 1915 the 2nd and 3rd Egyptian Works Companies arrived at Imbros where they were used to build roads and camps before moving to the Peninsula in August. British troops were also used to provide working parties on the islands. The IGC complained, in August 1915, that the transfer of 1st/4th Essex Regiment to the peninsula deprived the port of Mudros on Lemnos of all military labour and left him without any working parties.[2]

The Peninsula

The authorities recognised that when the invasion took place, support to move stores, ammunition and water would be required. They looked to France where the Indian Mule Corps had provided support for the Indian Division at the Battle of Neuve Chapelle. The battle ended on 13 March and a few days later Captain Alexander, OC 9th Mule Corps, was ordered 'to proceed forthwith to Marseilles in connection with the concentration there of A.T. carts'.[3] On arrival at Marseilles he discovered that the Indian Mule Cart Train, Mediterranean Expeditionary Force was being created for service, to supplement military man-power in the Dardanelles, and he was to command No. 1 Corps. The force consisted of four corps made up of men currently being employed at Marseilles, and those taken from the Indian Division.[4]

Lack of transport meant it was not until 5 April that No. 1 Corps and one troop of No. 2 Corps embarked on two steamers en route to Alexandria.[5] On arrival the Corps was split between duty in Egypt (4 troops) and Gallipoli (7 troops), the latter being transported to Lemnos. At Lemnos they were again split with 3 troops being sent to Helles and 4 troops to the Australians at ANZAC. At ANZAC the mules were initially kept at Brighton Beach but constant shelling meant they had to be moved into the gully behind Walker's Ridge. This became their HQ and was christened 'Mule Gully'. For three weeks the mules were used purely as pack animals but after the Engineers had built a road it was possible, in some areas, to use them with their AT carts. Further mules arrived in the middle of May until there were 600. Limited water supplies meant that no more could be kept in the area. As the weather became hotter some of the wells at ANZAC ran dry. This meant it was not possible to replace mules lost to shellfire. Water storage facilities were built and more mules were brought in until, in preparation for the attack of 6 August 1915, there were almost 2,000 mules in the area.

In March 1915 the Zion Mule Corps (see page 284) was raised in Egypt and arrived on the Peninsula at the end of April. They served in both the ANZAC and British sections earning the respect of the soldiers they supported. They also earned the respect of Sir Ian Hamilton, the Commander at Gallipoli, who wrote 'the men have done extremely well, working their mules calmly under heavy shell and rifle fire, and thus showing a more difficult type of bravery than the men in the front line who had the excitement of combat to keep them going'.[6] They attracted the support of the commanders in the field. In the British sector a request for replacements for men who had been discharged was made on 21 December, only a week before the decision was made that they should be disbanded. The Zion Mule Corps was withdrawn from Gallipoli on 31 December 1915, returning to Egypt where it was disbanded.

The work of both the Indian and Zion Mule Corps at the Third Battle of Krithia was acknowledged in the Official History:

> Special recognition is also due to the infantry transport personnel, the Indian mule-cart drivers and the ZMC for their untiring energy in this action – bringing up ammunition close to the forward positions, and carrying back the wounded under heavy fire.[7]

Egyptian Works Companies were employed at Helles and Suvla. They proved unreliable when under shellfire and in August the Company at Suvla had to be moved back to Mudros. The same problem occurred with Greek Labourers at Suvla, the QMG reporting: 'the Greek Labourers are quick to cease work when shelling commences and it is difficult to get them to start again'.[8] A contingent of 200 Maltese also worked at ANZAC although, due to the heavy shelling, they were not 'well suited for working under the conditions of Anzac'.[9]

By August 1915 troops on the peninsula were heavily engaged in preparing shelters and improving communications before the onset of winter. At the same time Corps Commanders had to provide large parties of men for heavy work at the landing places. The strain on front line troops was relieved to some extent by the use of foreign labour and British ASC and Garrison Battalion detachments. The garrison battalions were primarily made up of men of a lower medical category and in September the QMG commented: 'The Garrison Battalions recently arrived are reported to be anything but robust. It is hoped a proportion of these battalions will be fit for work on the beaches.'[10]

At Helles, in October, detachments from 1st Garrison Battalion Royal Scots provided labour, in addition to some 1,255 Greeks. At ANZAC, between September and November, foreign labour was supplemented at different times by 539 men of the 27th (Labour) Company ASC, 207 men of the 1st Garrison Battalion Essex Regiment, and small detachments from both the Anson Battalion Royal Naval Division and 37th Fortress Company RE.

At ANZAC the labour:

> … was not adequate for the works in hand, especially as winter approached and the weather grew more severe and the work heavier and more pressing. The Egyptians could not work in the cold, and the British labour company consisted of men who, though their spirit evoked the admiration of the other troops, were hardly fitted for the work at Anzac. Recruited in Great Britain from those who were over age or otherwise incapable of more active service, they had expected to be employed in the docks at Alexandria or in similar surrounding.[11]

On 26 November 1915 there was a severe storm, followed by a blizzard and heavy snowstorm that lasted for a few days, resulting in three inches of ice in the trenches. The 29th Division suffered badly with men being frozen to death in the trenches and others suffering severe frostbite. At Divisional HQ the Labour Company, which was made up of unfit or older men, volunteered 'on their own initiative, to hold certain trenches, and so enable the sufferers in occupation to fall back to shelter and warmth. They were allowed to do so, and spent a week at the front without a grumble.'[12]

The Egyptian, Maltese and British Labour Company at ANZAC were evacuated on 11 December 1915. At Helles the Greek Labourers were evacuated on 29 December 1915 and the Indian Mule Corps and British Labour Company by 8 January.

1   On 20 February, Kitchener, without consulting the Admiralty, told the Director of Naval Transport that the Division was not to be sent. It was only on 10 March that he was forced to change this decision. Resultantly the 29 Division did not leave Britain until 16 March.

2   NA WO 95/4266
3   Alexander, Major M., *On Two Fronts* p.119 A.T. – Army Transport
4   Each corps was made up of ten troops, every troop consisting of 108 mules and 50 carts, with 60 drivers. Unlike the Mule Corps in France these corps did not have pack mules.
5   One of the steamers was the SS *Ramazan*, which was later to transport both Alexander's Mule Corps and the Zion Mule Corps from Lemnos to Gallipoli.
6   Jabotinsky, *Story of the British Legion*, p.44 quoted in Watts, p. 46
7   Aspinall-Oglander, Brigadier General C. F., *Military Operations Gallipoli Volume 2*, p.554
8   NA WO 95/4266
9   Bean, C., *Official History of Australia in the War Volume II*, p.835
10 NA WO 95/4266
11 Bean, p.835
12 Swinton, E., *Twenty Years After Volume 1*, p.597

SALONIKA

Salonika is often a forgotten front of the war, where diseases like malaria caused almost three times as many deaths as those caused by battle. The climate was cold and wet in winter, hot and feverish in summer and this alone made the military campaign difficult.

The Balkan Wars

At the turn of the century the Ottoman Empire in Europe stretched from Constantinople to the Adriatic and included Macedonia, Thrace, Salonika and Albania as well as most of the Aegean Islands and Crete. A rising tide of nationalism led to the first Balkan War of 1912, which in reality was four wars, when Bulgaria, Greece, Serbia and Montenegro each declared war on Turkey. Although technically the four were the Balkan League, each undertook their own campaign. The Greek Army, for example, took the city of Salonika one day before the Bulgarian Army arrived. Each country acquired land from Turkey but there were disagreements over their territorial gains.

In 1913 these disagreements led to Bulgaria going to war with Serbia and Greece. Bulgaria was successful against the Serbians but was in trouble at the hands of the Greek Army. Seeing that Bulgaria was weakened, Rumania and Turkey declared war on her on 27 June. Less than a month later the second Balkan War ended and the Treaties of Bulgaria and Constantinople saw new borders being drawn in the Balkans. Bulgaria lost most of the land she had acquired during the First Balkan War, including Macedonia to Serbia and Greece, and Eastern Thrace, which was recovered by Turkey.

The Balkans 1914–15

Serbia's increase in territory and her close ties with Russia were viewed with concern by both Austria-Hungary and Germany. The assassination of the Austrian

Archduke Franz Ferdinand in the Serbian capital Sarajevo on 28 June 1914 led to Austria declaring war on Serbia on 28 July and within seven days the Great War had begun.

In October 1914 Turkey entered the war on Germany's side and looked to regain Eastern Anatolia, territory lost to Russia after the Russo-Turkish War of 1877–78. However, at the Battle of Sarikamis the Russians heavily defeated the 3rd Turkish Army.[1] Turkey also suffered a defeat when they launched an attack on the Suez Canal on 3 February 1915.[2] Following these defeats the German Chief of Staff, von Falkenhayn, tried to impress upon the Austrians the need for success in Serbia, which would give the Central Powers a rail link from Austria to Turkey.[3]

Bulgaria remained neutral in 1914 and both the Allies and the Central Powers tried to persuade Bulgaria to join them. In the autumn of 1915 Bulgaria joined the Central Powers. Two days before Bulgaria mobilized her forces in September 1915, the Greek Prime Minister, Venizelos, invited Britain and France to send troops to Salonika. On 25 September the British and French Governments agreed that an expedition comprising the 10th (Irish) Division and the French 156th Division would be sent to Salonika.

The political situation in Greece was complex, with a pro-Allied prime minister but a pro-German king, who favoured neutrality. The Greek attitude to the British and French force was ambivalent. On 3 October Venizelos assured British and French diplomats in Athens that he was anxious for the arrival of Allied troops while formally reading out a protest that the action breached Greek neutrality. Two days later, on the same day the first French and British troops disembarked at Salonika, Venizelos was forced to resign and Kitchener ordered a halt to the movement of more British troops. After French protests more troops left Mudros for Salonika on 7 October. The reality was that by the time the Allied troops arrived at Salonika, the Serbs, over 200 miles to the north, had already been defeated.

Allies in Salonika

When the 10th Division arrived at Salonika they found a country that had been ravaged during the two Balkans Wars. Malcolm Burr, an Assistant Military Landing Officer, described the scene:

> When the British troops landed in the autumn of 1915, they found a country scarred by the wars of the Balkan States, villages deserted, houses battered, towns destroyed, and many other signs of fighting in a region which had enjoyed the blessings of peace for quite twelve months.[4]

The country's railway system consisted of three single-track lines running in divergent directions from Salonika. The road system was even worse, only two roads, neither of which was capable of supporting heavy traffic, ran from the city. Both roads had to be virtually reconstructed before they could be used for Army vehicles. Other roads were no more than tracks, unable to cope with any form of wheeled transport when it rained or snowed. Faced with this it was necessary to build all the facilities required to support a modern army; piers, roads, bridges and railways all had to be built where nothing existed before.

One of the first tasks the soldiers faced was creating accommodation for themselves and dumps for their stores and equipment. Initially there was plenty of military labour to undertake this task as it was not until 22 October that General Mahon was given permission to send British troops inland from Salonika, and even then his orders meant he was not allowed to cross the Greco-Serbian frontier. A week later, permission was given to send troops into Serbia, and on 10 November the 10th Division took over a section of the front facing the Bulgarian village of Kosturino. These men, battle weary from the heat of Gallipoli, now found themselves in a mountainous region with no roads and facing the winter blizzards; 1,500 men of the Division suffered frostbite. They were evacuated to improvised hospitals south of Salonika during the last week of November.

The decision at the end of October 1915 to send British troops inland from Salonika changed the organisation of British military labour and locally recruited labour.

British Labour

The need for military labour led to the formation in Britain, during October and November 1915, of 25th, 28th and 29th ASC (Labour) Companies who were to serve in Salonika. As with other ASC Labour Companies they were made up of men unfit for front line service through illness or age. Despite this, on arrival in Salonika in November, they were housed in tents and, in the case of 28 Company, not issued with waterproof capes until January 1916.[5] Employed at supply dumps supporting the ASC and AOD, the shortage of labour meant that men were only given one day off in a fortnight.

Illness affected these companies and their work. When 28 Company left Liverpool on 14 November 1915, it comprised 6 officers and 533 other ranks. By February 1916 its strength had dropped to 494, of whom 36 were in hospital. By May 1916 the Company had dropped to 3 officers and 441 other ranks. The cold and wet of the winter was replaced by the heat of the summer with casualties due to heat exhaustion, malaria and dysentery.

British military labour increased in late 1916 with the arrival of the 14th and 15th (Labour) Battalions Queen's Regiment. In January 1917 the ASC Labour Companies appear to have been amalgamated. 29th (Labour) Company ASC was absorbed into the 14th (Labour) Battalion Queen's Regiment as E Company. With the formation of the Labour Corps, on 1 April 1917, the 14th Battalion formed 95, 96 and 201 Companies, Labour Corps and the 15th Battalion formed 97 and 98 Companies. All five Labour companies were badly affected by illness and rarely had their full strength of 500 other ranks. During 1917 and 1918, 95 Company never had more than 336 men. Illness also had a major effect on their working ability; for example, on 8 April 1918, almost the whole company was ill due to malaria.[6] The heat during the summer meant that work was undertaken from 6.30 to 10.30 am and from 4.30 to 7.30 pm to try to avoid the problem of heat exhaustion. Although much of the work involved road and rail maintenance, and employment at stores and ammunition dumps, other tasks included working at hospitals, supervising PoWs, building hangers at aerodromes, hay making and other agriculture.

In November 1917 employment companies were formed in Salonika by transferring 'B' category NCOs and men, who were employed on regimental duties, to the Labour Corps. By the end of the war 21 companies were formed. At the same time four Divisional Employment Companies were formed. Numbered 816 to 819 they were the DE Companies for 22nd, 26th, 27th and 28th Divisions. Agriculture played an important part in the work of these companies. In July 1918, for example, 816 Company issued 8 tons 15 cwt of maize all of which had been grown on land adjacent to Divisional Headquarters by the company.[7]

In February 1918, 20 anti-malarial squads were formed. Each squad was made up of an NCO and two men from the RAMC together with two NCOs and 20 men from either British or Macedonian Labour units. Five British and two Macedonian squads were allocated to each of the 27th and 28th Division areas and six Macedonian squads to the corps area. These squads were used to clear and canalise the water areas, which were breeding grounds for mosquitoes. By June 1918 of the 443 men fit enough to work in 96 Company, 185 were employed on anti-malarial work.[8]

In the days preceding the Battle of Doiran in September 1918 the men of 95 Company, together with Macedonian Labour, were employed on road widening. The task appears to have been a particularly difficult one, the Official History notes they 'had slightly widened and greatly improved the road from Karamudli during the days preceding the attack, but it was still narrow and, into the bargain, steep and winding'.[9] As the British moved forward the Labour Corps was used to assist the RE to repair bridges damaged or destroyed by the retreating Bulgarians: '143rd Field Company RE with 100 men of 96 Labour Company set about repairing, with captured material, the burnt wooden bridge at Gjavato'.[10]

With the Armistice, some labour units moved with XII Corps to Constantinople. The majority of labour companies remained in Salonika and demobilisation began, although by July 1919 there were still 437 men serving in Labour Corps companies. Of these 38 had joined the Army in 1914, 129 in 1915 and 270 were over 37 years of age.

Civilian Labour

In September 1915 the Royal Engineers, responsible for rebuilding the roads, hired Greek refugees to assist. The refugees lived in huts on the edge of the town from which they flocked to work in the morning and back in the evening. This mass movement meant that the already congested road was brought to a complete standstill and the work of the engineers was curtailed. In desperation the Army decided, at the end of October 1915, that these refugees had to be formed into an organized unit. The task was given to Captain Malcolm Burr who was appointed OC of No. 1 Civil Labour Battalion.

The Army could not spare any other British officers or NCOs to staff the battalion and left its creation and organisation to Burr. His first task was to find and appoint officers. With no educated Greeks available and the refugees considered unsuitable,

Burr appointed local Serbians as officers. The refugees were organized into companies of 100 men and women under an overseer, and each company into three gangs under a foreman. Where possible the overseers were educated and spoke both Greek and Turkish. By December 1915 Burr's battalion of Greek labourers had grown to 3,000.

By Christmas 1915 Salonika was the home of 150,000 Allied troops in addition to its 200,000 civilian population. Salonika was now turned into an entrenched base by establishing a 70 mile long defensive line on a radius some 20 miles from the port. As Ward Price, Official War Correspondent with the forces, recorded: 'For the first four months of 1916 the building of the entrenched camp engrossed the energies of the Anglo-French army at Salonica, assisted by a good deal of native labour'[11]

For some five or six miles, on either side of the two roads running out of Salonika, the Army built camps for the men and dumps for stores. Corrugated iron buildings housed the men and their animals. On the Seres road, to distinguish one camp from another, they were known by their distance from Salonika, for example Kilo 6 or Kilo 10.

The two roads were not restricted to military traffic, as Burr described:

> The confusion on them was fantastic. Lorries by the hundred, snorting, rattling, boiling, puffing, drivers swearing, motors hooting, officers gesticulating, dispatch-riders crashing. Greek carts crawling, all on a road far too narrow, the surface honey-combed with potholes of grey slime. To crown it all, in the mornings and evenings every available inch of space was taken by thousands of refugees in tough brown homespuns, with scarlet cummerbunds and ridiculous turbans over their heads and ears, which muffled the sound of the motor horns and drove the drivers to distraction.[12]

The number of civilian labourers continued to grow throughout 1916, including one group of about 1,000 Greek refugees from Kavala who, in October, Burr employed to build a Decauville railway line.

The employment of civilian labour is recorded in the Official History:

> On the Lines of Communication, at the Base, in the docks and in the RE Base Park the fullest possible use had been made of Mediterranean labour. In January 1918 that rationed by the British amounted to over 16,000 Greeks, nearly 2,400 Turks, 2,000 women, and some 2,000 Maltese.[13]

Macedonian Labour
Battalions (MLB)

In April 1917 the decision was made to form the Macedonian Labour Battalions although the name was not used until November. Initially eight battalions were authorised, two in each corps area and four on the LoC. The creation of the MLB enabled a more organised system of labour with personnel registered and officially numbered.

Commanded by a British captain, the Battalion's HQ consisted of four British soldiers (a pay sergeant, two corporal clerks and a batman) and 22 natives (a camp sergeant major who was a Class 1 interpreter, two men equivalent to a sergeant, eight interpreters, six police and five men for camp duties). The rest of the battalion was made up of eight companies, each 120 strong, plus six supervisors, one of whom was a British private who was either a permanent base man or came from a labour battalion. In April 1918 the British establishment increased with the addition of a lieutenant as second in command, and a QMS. A corporal and a private were attached when a detachment of over 100 was being employed.

The battalions were made up of Greeks, Serbs, Turks, Bulgarians and Jews. It is known that at least one battalion, the 7th, was entirely made up of Turkish nationals. From records it appears that there were 24 battalions formed and that their strength was not fixed. The strength of 4th Battalion, for example, varied between 500 and 3,000 whereas the 5th Battalion was between 200 and 800 strong.

In general the labourers caused few problems for the British, although desertions were quite common, particularly during harvest time. In May 1918 about 80 labourers in the 2nd Battalion deserted to work in their own fields. The CO of the 3rd Battalion overcame this problem by taking all the women off road maintenance to enable them to work in their own fields. Desertions occurred when men were employed away from their homes. In May 1917 the 9th Battalion had been formed primarily from labourers from Salonika. Whilst employed at Kopasi over three-quarters of the men absconded in July, within one hour of being paid, despite the fact that they were still owed another seven or eight days' pay.[14]

Uniforms were issued to the labourers in February 1918, those of military age being identified with a blue strap on their collar. Problems between the labourers and the Greek police, seeking deserters from their Army, were common. On 1 July 1918 several men in the 7th Battalion were wounded when Greek police opened fire and attacked them with hammers whilst searching for deserters. Despite being asked not to interfere with work a similar incident occurred four days later. Fifteen deserters were found and removed by the Police. This led to many men deserting from the battalion.[15]

In 1918, as the Allies advanced into Bulgaria, the MLB were not moved to support the Army as 'it was not considered advisable to bring up the 'MLBs, for they were of every race, and the majority of them would probably have got out of hand in Bulgaria.'[16]

Serbian Labour Battalion

The Serbs in the Macedonian Labour Corps established a reputation as hard working and reliable, and in November 1917 groups of Serbs were used to relieve British troops as guards at the Hay Dumps at Salamanli. British officers in the area reported favourably on this work and Captain Malcolm Burr was given orders to detail a few small parties of Serbs, under the name of Serbian Employment Company, for guard duty on dumps, in camps within base area and on lines of communication.

Established as an experiment, Burr was informed that if successful he would be able to create an independent unit. Burr wrote: 'the trial was a success, as I knew it must be, and the thing grew so quickly that before long I had a battalion of Serbs exempt from their own military service by age, some minor physical incapacity, or wound'.[17]

Burr was given command of what was called the 1st Serbian Sentry Battalion, which was independent of the Macedonian Labour Corps. From May 1918 until the end of the war the battalion successfully served at over 70 locations around Salonika. They were particularly good at reducing the theft of stores from dumps.[18]

Maltese Labour

Maltese Labour served in Salonika from September 1916. The first group to arrive included 307 stevedores who were engaged on a three-month contract. They returned to Malta on 26 December 1916 and were replaced by another 238 stevedores. As far as can be ascertained these 545 men were engaged as civilian labourers and were not eligible for a medal.

Two Maltese labour battalions served in Salonika. Although some men re-engaged at the end of their six month contract the majority did not. This made it difficult to provide continuity of labour or make full use of the skilled trades in the battalions. One area where the skills of the Maltese was utilised was in agriculture, growing vegetables for troops and hay for horses.

The Maltese were employed at railheads and supply dumps, to build defences, quarry stone, on road and rail maintenance, and creating channels and clearing scrub as part of the fight against malaria. There is only one record of discontent among the Maltese. A detachment at Karamudli, on 2 June 1918, expressed their discontent that the detachment continued to work even though their contract had expired. The DADL recorded that the Maltese were regarded as the best of all the labourers of any nationality.[19]

Russian Labour Corps

Following the Russian Revolution, the Russian General Yermoloff suggested the Russian troops fighting on the Western Front and in the Middle East be formed into units to fight alongside the Allies. The War Cabinet rejected the idea in December 1917. The Russian Military Attaché at the Italian Army HQ raised the idea again in February 1918 when he suggested forming a Russian Legion to serve under the British. The men would come from the Russian Division serving in France and Salonika.[20] Whilst the idea of a fighting force was rejected it was decided to use the men as Labour units.

In Salonika, on 4 April 1918, seven Russian officers including a Medical Officer and a Priest together with 515 other ranks arrived at Salmanli to form the Russian Labour Corps (RLC). Major Perry commanded the Corps, supported by another British officer and 50 other ranks from 2nd/9th Durham Light Infantry. The men were paraded, formed into four companies and informed that they were subject to British military law. From the beginning there was discontent in the unit since many men did not want to serve under the British. The following day three men considered agitators were handed over to the Assistant Provost Martial (APM).

On 8 April Perry went to Salonika where it was decided that the men would receive pay of 1s 9d a day. At the pay parade the next day a number of the men refused to take the pay, stating that they did not want to stay in Salonika for money but would work for food. Initially the men were used for anti-malaria duties, at the Salmanli Hay dump and to create their own vegetable gardens. Discipline continued to be a problem. On 17 April eleven men were handed over to the APM for refusing to give their names to a British NCO. 1 and 3 Companies refused to take their pay on 24 April and two days later 162 men went on strike and were handed over to the APM.

A new Commanding Officer, Major C. Percy-Rea, arrived on 2 May and had limited success in getting the men to salute him, something they had previously refused to do. Percy-Rea appears to have adopted a firm approach matched by the offer of benefits such as allowing the men to purchase beer after good work. However, strikes continued to be common in the Corps. On 8 May, for example, the Corps refused to work and only went to work after being escorted by armed troops. Four days later the Corps was reorganised into two companies, each commanded by a British officer. If a man refused to obey or threatened a British NCO he faced a court-martial. Seven men were handed between 21 and 28 days Field Punishment No. 1.

The use of strike action appears to have been the norm for these men. As the CO noted, on a day when only fourteen men attended the Divine Service, 'The people appear to be very religious demanding holidays and saints days and going on strike if they do not get them.'[21] On 19 August he offered a day's holiday to those who attended the service and 300 attended.

The Corps was not a success as a working unit. By August 1918, 41 British personnel were required to administer and guard the Corps, which comprised 528 Russians of whom 114 were either absent or in hospital.

1   29 December 1914–4 January 1915
2   The First Suez Offensive began on 28 January although only sporadic fighting took place mainly due to sandstorms until 3 February.
3   Austria's invasion of Serbia started on 12 August 1914. Despite a much larger and better-equipped army their early successes were overturned following a Serbian counter attack on 3 December. By the end of 1914 they had retreated back to Austria-Hungary having lost almost 215,000 men.
4   Burr, M., *Slouch Hat,* p.112
5   NA WO 95/4944
6   ibid
7   ibid WO 95/4827
8   ibid WO 95/4944
9   Falls, C., *Military Operations Macedonia* Vol II, p. 173
10 ibid, p.211
11 Ward, Price., *The Story of the Salonica Army,* p. 59
12 Burr, p.111
13 Falls, C., *Military Operations Macedonia* Vol II, p. 56
14 NA WO 95/4944
15 ibid
16 Seligman, V., *The Salonica Sideshow,* p.187
17 Burr, p.254
18 NA WO 95/4944 30 May 1918

19 ibid WO 95/4826 6 June 1918
20 ibid WO 32/5666
21 ibid WO 95/4994

MESOPOTAMIA

Mesopotamia, which was part of the Turkish Empire, presented a threat to British oil supplies from Persia. To ensure the supply of oil continued, the India Office sent a force to secure the head of the Persian Gulf. By 22 November 1914 the force had captured Basra. Qurna, 50 miles upriver, at the junction of the rivers Euphrates and Tigris was captured in December and a Turkish force was defeated at the Battle of Shaiba in April 1915. With southern Mesopotamia in British hands the pipeline's safety had been secured.

In April 1915 General Sir John Nixon arrived in Basra as the new commander of the forces and, with the support of the India Office, planned further offensive operations that were to prove disastrous. Nixon, who remained in Basra, authorised the 6th (Poona) Division under Sir Charles Townshend to advance on Amara. A fleet of 500 flat-bottomed boats was quickly assembled as the only way forward was by river, and on 3 June an advance force of about 100 men arrived at Amara and persuaded the 2,000 Turks to surrender. Despite a supply line of 150 miles in a country without railways or metalled roads, and shortages of equipment and medical supplies, Nixon decided to push further up the Tigris. At the end of June the 30th Brigade, under General George Gorringe, was successful at Nasiriyeh. The main force, under Townshend, met and defeated the Turks at Kut on 27/28 September 1915. With increasing supply shortages Townshend did not want to advance further but Nixon decided that he should attack Baghdad. Bad weather meant it took Townshend's Division two weeks to march the 40 miles north, reaching Ctesiphon on 22 November. After four days of fighting Townshend had lost over 4,000 men and ordered a retreat, arriving in Kut on 3 December.

Whilst the War Office favoured a retreat further south, Nixon and Townshend decided to remain and hold Kut. On 7 December a Turkish force of 10,500 men besieged the town. After three failed attempts to send forces to relieve Kut in January and April, during which the British suffered 23,000 casualties, the town was without food and supplies. Disease was endemic amongst the men. On 29 April Townshend and his force of about 8,000 surrendered.

The humiliation of Kut changed the British Government's view of the Mesopotamian front. The War Office took control of the Army and in July 1916 General Sir Frederick Stanley Maude replaced Gorringe as commander of the Tigris forces.

During Nixon's time inadequate supply routes and unorganised labour was the norm. When the British had arrived in 1914 Basra 'was a total blank. Roads, lights, telephones, vehicles, housing facilities, civilized conveniences of any kind there were none!'[1] As a port Basra was totally inadequate to handle the level of supplies needed by the Army but Nixon was averse to heavy expenditure improving the port.[2]

The inadequacy of supply routes was highlighted in January 1916 when the lack of shipping meant 10,000 reinforcements and twelve guns could not be sent upstream as part of the force attempting to relieve Kut:

Reinforcements and stores were arriving at Basra faster than they could be sent upstream; accommodation ashore was limited; there was a shortage of labour; and the staff of the Principal Marine Transport Officer was too small; with the result that the congestion at the port was very great.[3]

The British Army suffered difficulties obtaining sufficient civilian labour. As the Official History notes:

The labour question in Mesopotamia was always a difficult one. The local Arabs were unreliable and, although some Persian labour was imported with successful results, the numbers obtained were limited. There were political objections to bringing large numbers of Indian labourers into the country and, when the seriousness of the situation overcame these objections, it was found that Indians themselves were much averse to going to Mesopotamia and large numbers of them refused to embark at the last moment.[4]

In January 1916 Nixon was replaced as commander by General Sir Percival Lake who introduced changes to improve the supply routes. One of his first steps was to order a large extension at Maqil with banks to protect the area from flooding, the building of a wharf and construction of landing places. Recognising the problem of roads made only of earth, he also ordered that 24 miles of metalled roads be built, linking the landing places with stores, depots, camps and the hospitals. 21 and 22 Arab Labour Corps, which had been formed by the Political Department, were used for this work.[5] Despite having to import stone, as none was available locally, most of this work was completed by April 1916.

The movement and supply of troops outside Basra relied upon the rivers but a lack of steamers and tugs was another problem. On 11 March 1916, for example, the 37 steamers and 68 barges available were capable of delivering 300 tons to the troops at the front, 168 tons below the level required.

In March 1916 two Porter Corps[6] arrived from India and a Labour Corps from Egypt to supplement locally employed labour. The Egyptians, however, were of limited benefit, 'declining to work at all in wet weather'.[7] With no central control of labour several departments were competing to attract labour, each paying different rates. Local labour would refuse to work until rates were high enough for them to do two or three days work and then rest for four or five days. As a result shipping was held up and the wharves and jetties congested, while important construction works were delayed due to material and machinery not being off-loaded.

Controller of Native Labour

By August 1916 the labour situation had become so acute that the IGC decided to appoint a Controller of Native Labour (CNL) to control and distribute the labour employed on the wharves at Basra. Captain F. D. Frost MC took up the post on 20 September 1916. Initially Frost, assisted by three army clerks, was responsible for about 4,000 local labourers but the lack of British supervision resulted in poor quality work. To overcome the problem 100 men from the Royal West Kent Regiment were attached to the controller. Most were trained artisans and supervised work relevant to their particular skill. However, in December 1916 these men were recalled to reinforce the front line and replaced by Class B men at the rate of one other rank per 100 'coolies' employed. By October 1917 Frost's department of 40 officers and 340 other ranks were responsible for 18,538 Indians and 39,328 local labourers, employed throughout the occupied territory.[8]

Following his arrival in September 1916, Frost's first task was to ascertain the labour needs of each department operating on the river front. He then met with the Mukhtars (village headmen) of each of the villages along the river. At this meeting he discovered that men from each village were working indiscriminately for the various departments so he instigated a system whereby it was only the men from these villages who could work on the river front, with individual villages allocated to specific departments. The IWT vessel *P.S. 33* ferried 500 labourers from these villages to Basra each morning and returned them at night. Inhabitants of other villages were allowed to work anywhere, except on the river front.

When additional labour was needed at the Base Supply Depot, Maqil, 22 Arab Labour Corps and 2 Porter Corps were permanently allotted, enabling trained gangs of men to be used instead of constantly changing personnel. As the demand for labour increased at the Ordnance Depot, a Kurdish (Persian) Labour Corps known as 24 KLC was formed in October 1916, from Persians living in the Basra area, to replace the Arab labourers. When the IWT required *P.S. 33* to supply the front there was a danger that, without a ferry, the Arab labourers would return to their villages. To ensure this did not happen a work camp was set up for them and they were formed into 23 ALC.

Initially the CNL did not pay or control skilled labour but by the end of 1916 it was found that very large numbers of Arabs, attracted by the higher wages, had moved to skilled labour units. At the same time it was found that many men were taking up work with contractors and were not available to the various departments.[9] As this endangered the whole system of control, the CNL took over all contractors and contracts for labour or construction of any kind.

Following trouble with the labour at Amara in December 1916, which was supplied by contractors, the IGC decided that the CNL should introduce the Mukhtar system as operated in Basra. The move proved successful and 'the dismissal of contractors and starting of the Mukhtars system caused rather an upheaval of labour first, but the local Labour Corps at Amara eventually became the most efficient in Mesopotamia'.[10]

In February 1917 merchants in Basra and Ashar asked the Military Governor 'to reduce the exorbitant rates demanded by coolies working for them who were not under Government control'.[11] The CNL met with the merchants and drew up a scheme whereby civil labour was obtained through civil labour offices operated by his department. Rates of pay were agreed and based on pre-war rates. This civil labour system was later extended to Amarah, Baghdad and Nasiriyah.

During 1917 the CNL's control was extended to Qurna and Nasiriyah and, after its capture, to Baghdad. With control extending beyond the LoC, the department came directly under the Deputy Adjutant General at GHQ and its HQ was moved to Baghdad. By October 1917 the department was responsible for almost 39,000 local labourers throughout Mesopotamia, including those employed by the

Anglo-Persian Oil Company at Abadan. Recruitment was controlled through 47 pay offices that were set up and administered by the department.

Labour Directorate

On 24 October 1917 the department of the CNL was formed into the Labour Directorate. Its role was 'to supervise the raising of Local Labour Corps and Casual Labour, and to advise generally on the distribution of all labour, both Indian and local, with a view to its economical employment.'[12] Frost became Director of Labour (DL) and was promoted to Major. He was further promoted to the temporary rank of Brigadier General on 13 June 1918.

In order to ensure labour was employed as economically as possible, the DL introduced three changes to existing practices. Firstly, labour was placed on work for which it had particular skills. Secondly, corps were concentrated in specific geographic areas. Thirdly, the introduction of payment by piecework, although a shortage of Tally Clerks meant that it was never possible to fully develop the system.

Each Arab Labour Corps was meant to have two British officers but in most cases there was only one. This lack of control resulted in many local corps being over strength in respect of labourers. In April 1918 the Directorate believed that at least one-third of the labour was being wasted. Orders were given that all Corps were to be reduced to their sanctioned strength and that no further casual labourers could be employed. As a result the total local labour was reduced from 61,718 in April to 45,750 in July. The Directorate decided to increase the War Establishment of a corps from two to four officers,[13] the senior officer – the commandant, being supported by an adjutant/quartermaster and two officers called wing commanders.[14] As there was some difficulty obtaining these officers, commissions were offered in the Indian Army Reserve of Officers and to NCOs and men of the Territorial and New Army Units serving in Mesopotamia. The DL noted, 'many useful men were commissioned who had had experience in handling labour before the war'.[15] Tension between the different Arab Labour Corps was a constant problem. The Arab and Kurdish Labour Corps did not work well together nor did the Arab and Indian labourers, and they were, as far as possible, directed to different tasks.

In the two years following the creation of a Controller of Native Labour, in September 1916, the number of labourers being employed rose from 4,000 to 98,517 and their wage bill from £1,600 to almost £1,500,000 a month. At the same time British personnel responsible for these labourers rose from one officer and six other ranks to 253 officers and 1,061 other ranks. Labourers were paid daily, so the department devised a system which was both simple and efficient. Initially there was one pay office in Basra but as the number of labourers and locations grew, more offices were opened until 81 were in operation. Each corps and district had a pay clerk. To overcome a shortage of pay clerks, soldiers who had been detailed as supervisors of labour were trained to take over this role.

Labourers were sometimes used for unauthorised work or were badly managed. 20 Labour Corps, consisting of Punjabis and Pathans, were allotted to work on the railways in October 1919. In a report on the company the Director of Labour, Brigadier Frost, noted that once they had completed their allocated task they were employed on work which had not been laid down. Three companies were 'sent back in a special train for one day to build a station which had been forgotten between Imam Hamza and Dewaniyeh'.[16] Frost criticised a number of officers:

> Lieutenant Clifford, Commanding No 3 Coy, which is out in the desert 5 miles N of Dewaniyeh without an escort, apparently cannot perform his duties because he has a wife with him. He is reported as useless to the Corps [and] Indian Officers – Jemadar Maya Singh & Jaswand Singh and Subedar Issue Singh – are useless and I have ordered their dispatch to No 3 I.B.D. with a view to early demobilization. I am arranging to send 2 Pathan Officers and one Punjabi to take their place.[17][18]

The high levels of sickness amongst British troops hampered the work of the Directorate, as the DL noted: 'The casualties from sickness have been great especially among the B.O.R.s, but the extra work has been borne by the remainder with that wonderful cheerfulness which is characteristic of the British soldier.'[19]

Arab Labour

Local Arab labour was divided into two classes, casual labour and corps labour.

Casual Labour was made up of men, women and children who came into work daily and were not rationed or housed by the Government. They were generally from the poorer classes and did not have regular employment, except during harvest seasons. Labour officers recruited them through the village Mukhtars. The Mukhtar appointed his own Dubash who was responsible for 100 workers, these being split into 4 groups of 25. Each group of 100 had a supervisory British other rank who often held surprise musters during the day to ensure the numbers entered on the pay chit were still at work and, if necessary, correct the pay chit. During 1917 and 1918 approximately 24,000 casual labourers were employed throughout the occupied territories. By November 1919 numbers had dropped to 15,039 and to 3,947 by March 1920.[20]

Corps labour was divided into two different groups. South of Kut there were seven Arab Corps made up of tribal labour. Each sheikh, in consultation with the Political Department, provided a set percentage of the Corps and was responsible for keeping the numbers up to strength. North of Kut, nine Arab Corps were made up of volunteers recruited by the Labour officers.

Arab Corps were recruited under a 'shift' system, which resulted in the personnel changing every fortnight. If a tribe or village had 300 men available for work, 100 would work for a fortnight and were then released for a month, their place being taken by the second 100. These were then replaced by the third 100 two weeks later. By this method each man was only away from his land and family for a fortnight every six weeks. Recruiting the men was not without difficulties:

> The Arab comes into a corps and has to be taught sanitation, discipline of a rough sort and very often has to be trained to work that he has never dealt with before. He is generally frankly suspicious of the whole business and ready to bolt at anything he does not understand.[21]

Initially there were difficulties persuading the men to work on barges as they thought they would be taken away to become soldiers. However, they soon gained confidence in the British officers and other ranks and were 'moulded into very efficient labour'.[22]

During the winter of 1917/18 inadequate night shelter and a lack of blankets meant that many men deserted. The DL noted that 'the men sat up all night and shivered, some of them dying from exposure'.[23] As a result the authorities sanctioned the issue of two blankets per man. Early in 1918 typhus and fever broke out but this was largely solved by the introduction of delousing and disinfection.

Persian Labour

The first Persian (Kurdish) Labour Corps was recruited from volunteer Kurds, Persians and Lurs already in Basra in October 1916. Proving to be a success, four more corps were quickly formed at the base. Towards the end of 1916 almost all the Arab labour in Basra was employed by the Labour Department. As a result contractors in the area began to induce Persian labour to leave the corps and work for them. Being the subject of a neutral state the Persian was perfectly free to come and go as he wished and initially many left the corps. However, within a short time the Persians returned, preferring to work for the corps rather than private contractors.

The lack of tribal influence and discipline in the Persian corps made it difficult to handle successfully. As the DL noted: 'In the case of the Arab Corps, the Tindal or Dubash rules his gang firmly, but the Persian Tindal does not appear to have any control over his men.'[24] It was found that when employed by the day Persians averaged 1 ton per man each day, but when paid by piecework they could achieve between 6 and 9 tons a day.

With the advance during early 1917, and capture of Baghdad on 11 March, the demand for labour in the forward area resulted in the formation of further Persian Labour Corps who were mainly used on earthworks or porterage. The majority of Persian Corps were formed from men living in Mesopotamia, however in July 1917, when labourers were needed in the port of Nahr Umar, 39 Persian Labour Corps was formed from men imported from Bushire in Persia.

By November 1918, 24 Persian Labour units had been formed, employing 17,243 men. Whilst the establishment of a corps was 2,000 men, it appears that there was considerable variation in the size of individual corps.[25] In April 1919, for example, 44 Corps consisted of 895 men whereas 50 Corps had only 175 men.[26] During 1919, men were gradually repatriated and the number of corps reduced. Repatriation took place over a number of months, so when 6 Corps, which had been formed in October 1916, was disbanded, 300 men were sent home in September 1919 and during the following three months 150, 100 and 283 respectively.[27] There was discontent among men retained in 1919 and 1920, 1 Persian Labour Company, for example, had 359 deserters in four weeks in February/March 1920.[28]

Indian Labour

Prior to May 1918 Indian labour in Mesopotamia was not administered and controlled by the Directorate. This changed with the publication of GRO 540 which placed the control of all Labour Corps, both Indian and local, under the Labour Directorate from 15 May.

There were two distinct groups of Indians employed in Mesopotamia. The first group were men recruited from the various Indian districts. The second group consisted of men recruited from Indian jails.

Indian Free Labour

The Government of India failed to adopt a consistent policy regarding the recruitment of Indian labour. As a result men were recruited for variable terms ranging from six months to the duration of the war. The Labour Directorate found that six months was too short a period, incurring higher import and repatriation expenses. There was not enough time for the men to acclimatise and attain their full efficiency. The Directorate also found that recruitment of more than two years duration caused problems as there were additional costs associated with the granting of leave and the loss of efficiency through 'staleness'. A major difference from Arab labour was that the Indians were paid bonuses, 'which led to large increases in output'.[29]

As with the Indians in France, men came from different provinces and were found to be suited to different types of work. The Director of Labour described each group in his report:

Sontalis were described as 'slow but steady, of low intelligence and poor physique, extremely easy to control; and very little given to crime.'[30] They could not be used in cold climates.

Punjabis and Bombay Corps, 'all the men are of strong physique and fairly high intelligence. They are excellent workers but want strong officers who thoroughly understand them. The Bombay men are rather more given to intrigue than the Punjabis, in the Punjabis Corps the first intimation of a disagreement is a broken head.'[31] Both were suitable for the heaviest work and capable of working in cold climates.

Burmese were 'difficult to control and it is difficult to get officers; both British and Indian who understand their ways and language.'[32]

Bengalese and United Provinces 'are suitable for earthwork and should make fair builders, but unless recruited from hill areas have probably never seen stone and would be unsuitable for heavy rock cutting. Both are given to intrigue; a long-winded petition (often anonymous) is the general sign of disagreement in the camp.'[33] They were unsuitable for work in very cold climates.

Indian Jail Labour

Between October 1916 and February 1920 some 16,000 prisoners were sent from Indian jails to serve in the Jail Labour Corps (JLC). The Army preferred to use the term Disciplinary Labour Corps but this was rarely used, the usual term being either 'JLC' or 'Convict Corps'. The JLC cost less to employ than other Indians. The men were paid 10 Rupees a month with a bonus of 10 Rupees every six months, whereas the other Indian Labour Corps were paid 15 Rupees, which with allowances could rise to 20 Rupees a month. The JLC, unlike other Indian labour, were not entitled to wound or injury pensions nor to a family pension in case of death. A man whose jail sentence ended whilst he was in the JLC in Mesopotamia was retained in the corps and placed on a higher wage rate instead of being transferred to one of the free labour companies. When it was discovered that output was below expected standards a piecework system was introduced. This enabled prisoners to boost their wages.

Amongst the JLC were some companies that were raised to work as porters and some as labour units. There appears to have been little thought given as to which type of unit was established. The 12 (Burma) JLC, raised as a Porter Corps, was a failure since its men were of poor physique and unable to carry the necessary loads. Amongst its 1,000 men were 300 carpenters, 100 tinsmiths, 50 blacksmiths and 166 other tradesmen. When, in August 1918, men were urgently required to help build a camp at Baqubah, 500 men from the corps were sent as tradesmen. By November these men had proved so successful the Labour Directorate obtained permission for the corps to be re-designated as 148 (Burma) Jail Labour Corps. In January 1919 the corps again proved its worth when the demobilization of British artificers resulted in a shortage of skilled workers at the Advanced Mechanical Transport Depot and the corps was used to replace them.

In reviewing the work of this Corps Brigadier Frost reported: 'since its conversion to a Labour Corps it has been successful especially with skilled men'.[34] Despite this he was critical of their ability to undertake general labouring tasks on roads or earthworks and that they required more supervision than the free Corps in order to achieve the same output. In September 1919, on the recommendation of Lieutenant Colonel Lane, the Inspector of Disciplinary Labour, the JLC was reduced to 600 skilled tradesmen and used very successfully as an Artizan Company.

In October 1919 the Indian Government sent the British a telegram stating that they did not approve of Jail Labour serving in Mesopotamia and the last of the JLC were repatriated in February 1920.

Mauritius Labour Battalion

'Mauritius itself sent 1,700 men overseas in the Mauritius Labour Battalion to serve with Imperial forces fighting in Mesopotamia.'[35] The Battalion's War Diary indicates that the effective strength was around 1,000 from June 1917 until it was repatriated at the end of November 1919.[36]

One company of 252 tradesmen worked from June 1917 onwards at Magill for the Inland Water Transport (IWT). The company quickly earned a reputation for good work and a letter of appreciation for their work and discipline was received from the IWT's Director in October 1919. In addition to this skilled company, about 300 tradesmen were used for dockyard construction, on the light railways and general construction work.

The effectiveness of the Battalion was initially badly effected by illness. In June 1917, for example, of 554 men employed at Ashar, 200 were ill in hospital. Sickness reduced in 1918 as the men became more accustomed to the conditions under which they lived and worked. In September 1918, of the 1,031 men in the Battalion only 73 were unfit through illness. Discipline was generally good; there were two instances of men being charged with mutiny.

Chinese

On 6 October 1916 Sir John Jordan, British Minister in Peking, sent a telegram to Britain:

> General Officer Commanding at Singapore sending contractor there to recruit indentured Coolies for service in Mesopotamia. I have no information on the subject but there may be danger of schemes clashing with proposed recruitment at Wei-hei-We.[37]

It appears that these men formed part of the Chinese Labour Corps and they were skilled mechanics. In 1920 a note about the work of the Chinese in Mesopotamia records that 'small parties of skilled mechanics were also recruited for special work and numbers of these were also despatched from Shanghai to work in Mesopotamia'.[38] On 11 November 1918 there were 4,116 skilled mechanics and 214 unskilled Chinese labourers working for the IWT.[39] The CWGC records 227 unidentified casualties commemorated on the Tanooma Chinese Memorial in Basra War Cemetery.

A further 900 Chinese coolies were recruited in Shanghai by Major Manners RE and used to unload colliers at Basra. The IGC recorded that the first of these coolies arrived in August 1918 and appeared to be a good class of labour. In view of this he suggested that Major Manners recruit a further 500.[40]

PoW Labour

In May 1918 four PoW Labour corps were formed from Turkish prisoners then at the PoW Camp, Makina. One was sent to Kut and two to Nahr Umar to work as porters, with one remaining at Basra employed on railway work. These came under the control of the DL on 12 June and were immediately placed on piecework, their output of work trebling in all cases.

Three further PoW Labour corps were formed in the summer of 1918. The men were Turkish prisoners who were brought from prison camps in India. After the advance on Mosul in October 1918 a further eleven corps were formed from men captured during the advance. By November 1918 over 17,000 Turkish prisoners were employed on irrigation, canal work and bridge building.

Lieutenant Colonel Hartley, the Assistant Director of Labour, complained on 9 July 1919 about the way the Turkish prisoners were carrying out their work. He commented, 'on many occasions recently, after being told off … they simply sat down and a good number go off to sleep'.[41] He urged better supervision and additional disciplinary measures be introduced before the prisoners refused to undertake any work. Six days after writing this report an extra eleven British other ranks were added to each PoW company as guards.

---

1 Egan, E. F., *The War in the Cradle of the World,* p.103
2 Moberley, F. J., *The Campaign in Mesopotamia* Vol II, p.189.

3 ibid, p.279
4 ibid, p.280
5 It appears that, despite the numbering, these were the first two Arab Labour Corps units formed in Mesopotamia.
6 Three British officers, four Indian officers and twelve Indian other ranks administered each Porter Corps, which comprised of about 1,200 men.
7 Moberley, F., Vol II, p.359
8 Unlike other theatres the British other ranks in Mesopotamia appear to have been attached to the Directorate of Labour and not transferred to the Labour Corps.
9 Contractors were local suppliers of goods such as the supply of sheep, cattle and fruit, and services such as skilled tradesmen to the British forces.
10 NA WO 95/4992 Report of the Labour Directorate Mesopotamia Expeditionary Force p.6
11 ibid, p.7
12 ibid, p.10
13 Each local Labour Corps also has twelve British other ranks for supervision and clerical duties.
14 NA WO 95/4992 Report of the Labour Directorate p.33
15 ibid, p.13
16 ibid WO 95/4992
17 ibid WO 95/4992
18 ibid WO 95/4992
19 ibid WO 95/4992 Report of the Labour Directorate p.37
20 ibid WO 95/4992
21 ibid WO 95/4992
22 ibid WO 95/4992
23 ibid WO 95/4992
24 ibid WO 95/4992 p.21
25 In March 1920 the War Establishment was reduced to 1,500 men.
26 NA WO 95/4992
27 ibid
28 ibid
29 ibid WO 95/4992 Report of Labour Directorate p.13
30 ibid WO 95/4991 p.27
31 ibid WO 95/4991
32 ibid WO 95/4991
33 ibid WO 95/4991 p.28
34 ibid WO 95/4991
35 Jackson, A., *War and Empire in Mauritius and the Indian Ocean*, p.23
36 NA WO 95/5729
37 ibid WO 32/11345
38 ibid WO 106/33
39 Hall, J., *Inland Water Transport in Mesopotamia*, p.126
40 NA WO 95/5991
41 ibid WO 95/4992

EGYPT

When war was declared in 1914 Britain's influence in Egypt had been felt for over 80 years. In 1832 British forces had assisted the Ottoman Empire to put down

Muhammed Ali's attempt to declare Egypt an independent country. From this point on, British interest in Egypt grew and the opening of the Suez Canal heightened British concerns about French influence in the area. In 1875 the Khedive's financial difficulties allowed Disraeli to purchase a 40 per cent holding in the Suez Canal Company, making Britain the largest single shareholder. An uprising by Egyptian nationalists in 1881 was put down following their defeat by a British force at Tel-El-Kebir a year later. Although technically part of the Ottoman Empire in reality it was Britain rather than Turkey who now ran Egypt. With the signing of the *Entente Cordiale* in 1904 France recognised Egypt as within Britain's sphere of influence and Britain recognised Morocco, Tunisia and Algeria as France's areas of influence.

Turkey became involved in the First World War on 29 October 1914 when they assisted the German naval bombardment of Russia. General Maxwell, C-in-C of the British Forces in Egypt, declared Martial Law on 3 November outlawing nationalist activities and suppressing two nationalist newspapers. The following day Maxwell issued a proclamation which included the statement that 'Great Britain takes upon Herself the sole burden for the present war, without calling upon the Egyptian people for aid therein.'[1] In reality this assurance could not be kept and when Britain declared war on Turkey, Egypt was brought into the war. The Egyptian Army was used alongside British troops to defend the Suez Canal from Turkish attack.

Civilian Labour

Prior to 1916 the British recruited civilian labour as required, to work at the docks, on the road and railway systems and to move stores. If insufficient voluntary labour was available the Egyptian authorities made use of local troops and forced natives to work for the British. An example of this was recorded in November 1915: 'Work is being continued from Bir Saba on a metalled road and a Decauville Railway to El Allja, the road to run south of Khalassa. Large numbers of troops and civilian forced labour being employed, roughly 5,000 men and women.'[2] Military Labour Bureaux were established in 1916 in Alexandria, Port Said, Cairo and Ismailia, to recruit and administer all local sources of casual labour.

With the advance into Palestine in 1917, bureaux were opened at Jaffa and later at Jerusalem. Within a short time these two bureaux were employing 10,000 local labourers on work extending from Hebron to Jerusalem and Jerusalem to Jaffa. With virtually all able-bodied men in the area being employed, women and boys were also recruited for appropriate work. Other bureaux operating in the same way as Jaffa and Jerusalem were to be opened in 1918 at Tul Keram, Haifa and Beirut. The Military Labour Bureaux standardised rates of pay throughout Palestine and 'ensured that regular work was provided in Palestine for thousands of people who in many cases would otherwise have been destitute'.[3]

Some 1,500 skilled tradesmen were registered and employed on a casual basis. Two skills that were particularly successful were boatmen from Jaffa and stone dressers from Jerusalem.

Egyptian Labour Corps

At the beginning of 1916 the Egyptian Labour Corps (ELC) returned from their service in Gallipoli and became involved in supporting the Army in Egypt, Palestine and Syria. Initially, recruitment came from the larger cities and Upper Egypt. During 1916 the demand for men for both the ELC and the Camel Transport Corps meant recruitment moved to the Nile Delta area. Reception camps were opened at Sohag, Assyut, and Roda Island, Cairo, from which special trains conveyed 2,000 recruits at a time to the Base Depot at Kantara.

Early in 1917 a Directorate of Labour was established with Brigadier General R. C. Jellicoe, Director of Labour, based at GHQ. Two Assistant Directors (ADL), one for Egypt and one for Palestine and Syria, were responsible for both the ELC and locally recruited civilian labour. The ADL (Egypt) had 26 officers working from Alexandria to Aswan, to oversee recruitment. The Egyptian Ministry of the Interior appointed an Inspector of Recruiting to support the British.

Companies did not work under a Group system. Deputy Assistant Directors of Labour (DADLs) were appointed at the base ports, larger depots and at Jaffa, Haifa, Beirut, Tripoli and Alexandretta. They authorised labour from the pool under their control. The system in Egypt was a flexible one, with labour 'areas' being formed, when appropriate, to administer a number of companies undertaking a specific task or series of tasks.

The ELC worked under the RE on road and railway construction and maintenance, laying pipelines, well boring and quarrying stone. They worked at supply depots for the ASC, at ammunition depots for the AOC and as stretcher bearers. At Port Said, Alexandria, Suez and Kantara docks trained stevedore gangs worked under ELC officers unloading vessels as they arrived and loading vessels with stores and ammunition destined for Salonika.

Over 6,000 natives worked as skilled tradesmen; these included well borers, tinsmiths, saddlers, stokers, masons, carpenters and tent menders. As well as the skilled natives

> … certain companies, under selected Egyptian Labour Corps officers, reached such a high standard in connection with work on roads, railways, pipe-line, and other services, that they were able to make satisfactory progress without constant expert supervision.[4]

As the Army advanced into Palestine the ELC worked close to the front line

> … from the first day of operations the Egyptian Labour Corps has followed the troops as they advanced, working hard and successfully to improve the roads. On Sept. 19 companies were working on the roads in front of our original line, while our guns were still firing.[5]

British Labour

From the outbreak of war until 1917 men in the Garrison Battalions carried out the vast majority of employments in Egypt. By May 1917 the thirteen Garrison

Battalions stationed in Egypt consisted of 388 officers and 16,430 other ranks. The Garrison Battalions were composed of older soldiers and men who were medically downgraded. The majority of men were medical category B(i). In addition to employments they were used for guard duty and to release category A men.

The publication of ACI 837 on 23 May 1917, which created Area and Divisional Employment Companies in the Labour Corps, led to a change in the system.[6] Although this ACI only referred to France, Lieutenant General H. M. Lawson suggested in July 1917, that Employment Companies be created in Egypt in order to undertake work that could not be done by the ELC or civilian labour. Employment Companies consisted of 2 officers and 273 other ranks, the same establishment as existed in France. They were administered by the Director of Labour and became part of the Labour Corps. Lawson took the decision that the companies would be formed from men working in close proximity to each other even if they were from different battalions. The result of this decision can be seen in 809 Area Employment Company, which included men from the Northamptonshire, Cheshire, Middlesex, Lancashire Fusiliers, London Regiments and the Rifle Brigade.

The first sixteen Area Employment Companies, numbered 800 to 815, were formed at the end of September 1917. Four companies were placed in a group. Each group was allocated companies shown below.

Location	Group	Companies
Alexandria District	1	800, 801, 802, 803
Force in Egypt	2	804, 805, 806, 807
Palestine	3	808, 813, 814, 815
Palestine	4	809, 810, 811, 812

Table 10: Area Employment Companies – Egypt September 1917

None of the companies kept diaries and there are very few references to them in higher-level diaries. A few references indicate they were employed in detachments, as required in their area. On 3 November 1917, for example, 806 Company at Abbassia had 36 men at Boulac Convalescent Depot, 54 at Abbassia Convalescent Depot, 97 at three PoW camps, 20 at the School of Aerial Gunnery and 10 at the Citadel General Hospital.

At the end of December 1917 of the 230 men in 814 Company at Abbassia the largest detachment was 16 men at the AOC Depot. No fewer than 161 men were either working alone or in pairs in hospitals, canteens, at the YMCA or for other employers. Three further Employment Companies were formed during August or September 1918. Each was attached to a specific corps, 1000 Company to XX Corps, 1031 to XXI Corps and 1032 to the Desert Mounted Corps. These companies moved with their corps into Palestine and Syria.

The record of the advance of the Egyptian Expeditionary Force indicates that both the 52nd and 74th Divisions had Divisional Employment Companies during 1917. Neither of these companies appears in the Order of Battle of Divisions[8] nor has any record of them been found in the Army monthly returns.[9] It appears that these Employment Companies may not have become part of the Labour Corps.

1 Report on the Account of Army Expenditure for 1916–1917, p.78. The proclamation was issued on the instructions of the Foreign Office and with the approval of Lord Kitchener although the War Office was not aware that it was being issued.
2 NA WO 95/4360
3 Pirie-Gordon, H. A., *Brief Record of the Advance of the Egyptian Expeditionary Force,* p.110
4 ibid, p.109
5 ibid, p.36
6 NA WO 293/6
7 ibid 95/4493
8 Becke, Major A., *Order of Battle of Divisions Parts 2A and 2B*
9 NA WO 73/106 − 73/108

ITALY

On 24 October 1917 Austro-German forces attacked the Italians at Caporetto. By the end of the day the Austro-Germans had advanced 25 kilometres and within a week they had captured 300,000 Italian soldiers. With the Italian Army in danger of being defeated the Allies quickly sent French and British troops to the Italian Front. The first British fighting troops arrived in Italy on 4 November. These men were not the first British military personnel to serve in Italy, as Labour units had been employed there since June 1917. By the time British front line soldiers arrived 642 Labour Corps personnel and 2,009 Egyptians were already employed in Italy.[1]

Military labour was primarily used in two distinct areas; to the south around the port of Taranto which was on the overland supply route from Cherbourg to Salonika and Egypt; in the north, to support the British fighting troops at the front, in operations against Austria-Hungary. There was also a small Maltese Labour Corps mining company (see page 215) employed in Italy.

The North

196 Company had a detachment working at Faenza in June 1917 and the whole of 172 Company was at Faenza in September 1917. 16 Company is shown as serving in Italy in November 1917.[2] It has not been possible to identify where 16 Company was located but it is assumed they were supporting the operations of the British XI and XIV Corps against the Austro-Hungarian forces which started in November 1917.

As the corps and divisions arrived from France they brought with them Employment Companies to support them in the field. When XIV Corps arrived from France, for example, 273 Company was attached to them as their Employment Company. There was one exception, XI Corps, which served in Italy from November 1917 until March 1918. The Corps appears to have manned their Corps Employment Company from their own resources because their Employment Company, 271 Company, was not formed until April 1918 after they had returned to France.

In September or October 1918, 1034 Company was formed in Italy, from men unfit for front line service. Although it is not certain where the Company was employed it is known that there were detachments at Giavera and Montecchio Precalcino. In November 1918, as in France, men serving as PoW escorts were transferred to the Labour Corps.

A number of awards were made to British labour personnel for service in Italy; it has been possible to identify five MMs, nineteen MIDs and fifteen MSMs. The citation for the award of the MM to 657747 Private A. Rayner reads:

> For bravery and devotion to duty on the 27th and 28th October, 1918, when on traffic duty on the bridge at Lido. Although the bridge was heavily bombed by an enemy aeroplane, he continued at his post, and thus saved much confusion of traffic.[3]

Taranto

Taranto was the port in Southern Italy through which men and materials were transited to and from Salonika and Egypt. Taranto was chosen 'for its geographical situation, for railway reasons and for the other facilities obtainable there'.[4]

Plans were developed to use the Egyptian Labour Corps (ELC) at Taranto. On 3 July 1917, 85 Company ELC arrived from Egypt but as the request to retain them had not been approved by the Director of Labour at GHQ in France they were despatched to France.[5] Approval was received whilst they were en route, and on reaching Faenza they were ordered to return to Taranto. Arriving at Taranto on 14 July they were joined by 86 Company ELC. They worked at the docks and on camp construction.[6] The following month, 81, 82 and half of 80 Company ELC – 1,500 Egyptians – arrived at Taranto from France, bringing the total number of Egyptians at the base to 2,700.

By September 1917 the Egyptians were the primary source of labour at Taranto as General Wace recorded, 'the entire work at this Port was carried out by Egyptians, coaling, loading and unloading of ships, trains etc., building quays, making railways and erecting huts'.[7] They earned a good reputation for their work although there was wastage of labour due to poor organisation on the part of the employers.

On the night of 26 September 1917 there was discontent in 81 and 82 Companies about the finish date of their contracts. The men believed the six months dated from the date of enlistment whereas the authorities took it from the date of embarkation in Egypt. A disturbance started during the night and continued the following morning with stones thrown and threats made to both their officers and NCOs. A barbed wire fence was placed around the mutinous men and they were kept there for the whole day. The Base Commandant recorded that 'their ardour was considerably cooled by this and towards evening they were very penitent'.[8] The following day the men 'turned out to work as quiet as lambs and very penitent'.[9] From October 1917 the ELC were repatriated through Taranto, with 85 and 86 Companies being the last to leave in December.

The loss of the Egyptians put considerable pressure on the base and the Commandant complained, on 7 December 1917, that unless more labour was found, construction work would be seriously affected. Two days later orders were given to move the 11th Battalion, British West Indies Regiment (BWIR) from France to Taranto.

The Battalion arrived on 22 December and were joined during January by a further five BWIR Battalions. From the time they arrived at Taranto there were complaints from the Base Commandant about their work and poor attitude towards their officers and NCOs. Indiscipline resulted in restrictions being placed on the sale of alcohol, other than beer and cider, to the men. In March 1918 restrictions were placed on the number of BWIR men given leave to enter the town due to disagreements with the locals. These disagreements continued during April and May, culminating in a major clash on 15 May.

The BWIR continued to be employed at Taranto throughout the summer and autumn of 1918. Following the Armistice Taranto was used as the holding station for the BWIR before they were repatriated to the West Indies in 1919. The Fijian Labour Company arrived in Taranto in September 1918. As in France, they quickly obtained a positive reputation for their work. Lucas wrote in 1924, 'they leave behind them an appreciation of their general work with all those with whom they have come in contact'.[10]

1   NA CAB 27/14
2   Edmonds, J., *Military Operations Italy,* p.387
3   *London Gazette,* 6 December 1920, p.12036
4   Henniker, A., *Transportation on the Western Front,* p.290
5   NA WO 95/4006
6   ibid WO 95/4255
7   ibid WO 107/37 p.34
8   ibid WO 95/4255
9   ibid WO
10 Lucas, *The Empire at War* Vol III, p.395

TURKEY

With the end of the war both British and French troops moved to Constantinople (Istanbul) setting up an Allied military administration. The first British troops of what became the Army of the Black Sea reached the city on 13 November 1918.

Labour was to be provided primarily by British companies and the Black Sea Labour Corps. There was also a Maltese Employment Company although little is known about when it arrived or where it served.

British Labour

To support the Army, British and foreign labour units, administered by the Controller of Labour (Salonika) were employed in Constantinople, throughout the Black Sea area and the Dardanelles.

Initially, a detachment of 150 men from 202 Company, together with 80 labourers recruited in Constantinople, were employed clearing billets, offices, stables, hospitals and other buildings that would be used by the military authorities.[1] 201 Company was also sent to Constantinople so that in January 1919 there were some 400 British Labour troops in the city; their duties extended to include clerical work and guard duties. Neither 201 nor 202 Companies operated at their nominal strength of 273 other ranks. Between January and June 1919, 201 Company varied from 170 to 230 Category B men and 202 Company varied between 160 and 205 men. In July 1919, 202 Company was disbanded with its surplus men being sent to 201 Company.

Detachments from five other British companies, 97, 968, 982, 999 and 1036, also served in the Army of the Black Sea area during 1919 although no records of their location or employment have been found. As men were demobilised, the companies disbanded and surplus men were sent to 201 Company which, by August 1919, had 446 other ranks.

The CWGC records show sixteen men of the Labour Corps died in the Black Sea Army area between December 1918 and March 1920. Thirteen are buried in Haidar Pasha Cemetery, Istanbul and one at Chanak Consular Cemetery. Two men are commemorated on Haidar Pasha Memorial; 670039 Private Winch has no known grave, whereas 587490 Private Richardson is buried in South Russia, which means his grave cannot be maintained by the CWGC.

Black Sea Labour Corps

At the beginning of November 1918 the 1st Balkan Labour Battalion was formed in Salonika to work for the ASC and on sanitary work. By the end of the month it had grown to about 500 men of whom over half were skilled workers, including carpenters, chauffeurs, mechanics and interpreters. The Battalion moved to Constantinople, where by February 1919, it had grown to some 1,500 men. Unskilled labourers were employed at the docks and moving stores. The RE employed 400 skilled workers building a hospital, in place of sappers who had been demobilised.[2]

A second battalion, known as the 2nd Serbian Sentry Battalion, was formed in March 1919 from Serbian and Montenegrins, and replaced British guards in the Constantinople area. Initially 120 men were recruited although the Battalion grew to 345 by August 1919.

By June 1919 two further battalions had been formed. When the 1st Battalion reached 2,000 men and the 4th Battalion 2,760 men it was decided to form further battalions, and by August 1919 there were seven battalions. These varied in size from 345 in both the 2nd and 7th Battalions to 1,113 in the 4th Battalion. Most were used in or around the Constantinople area, the exception being the 5th Battalion which was based at Chanak.

Most battalions were used to unload and move stores at the docks and dumps, and to support the RE on road repairs at camps and provide water supplies. From June 1919 men of the Balkan Battalions were used to replace British personnel on employments; they were taken on the strength of the British unit to which they were attached. The 5th Battalion at Chanak provided nearly 400 men to work with the Graves Registration Unit establishing cemeteries on the Gallipoli Peninsula.[3]

On 27 June 1920 storekeeper Mehmet Ali, although fully dressed, dived into the sea at Feneraki Point and saved the life of another member of the Black Sea Labour Corps who had got into difficulties whilst bathing. This Act of Gallantry was recognised in Routine Orders on 16 July 1920.

1 NA WO 95/4820
2 ibid WO 95/4956
3 ibid

NORTH RUSSIA

There is little information about the labour used to support the British invasion of Russia in 1918. The Allied intervention in Murmansk and Archangel consisted of troops from Britain, France and other Allied nations (the North Russia Force) supporting the White Russian forces and defending Allied interests at the ports.

Major General Maynard, the C-in-C of the Allied Forces at Murmansk, recorded the need to use fighting troops for working parties in his second Despatch, which covered the period from 20 September 1918 to 28 February 1919: 'I was compelled to retain at the Port of Murmansk itself – a very considerable proportion of my troops for the purpose of furnishing the large permanent working parties necessitated by the lack of civilian labour.'[1]

It is known that men from the Russian companies of the Labour Corps were used to help form the North Russia force. 557385 Acting Sergeant M. Fredjohn, 9th Labour Battalion was attached to the Royal Fusiliers as an interpreter during the campaign and awarded the MSM for services in Russia.[2]

The campaign in North Russia included not only Allied troops sent from the west but a large number of local units. These created a number of problems as they had their own specific objectives and often contained men whose loyalty was questionable. One of the local units in the Murmansk area was the Karelian Regiment, which was commanded by a British officer, Colonel Woods. In the spring of 1919 intelligence reported that the Karelians were planning to revolt, demand separation from Russia, and wished to be incorporated into Finland. Whilst a revolt was avoided the Karelians refused to serve under Russian officers and it was decided to disband the regiment. The Karelians were offered the opportunity to serve in the Russian Army or as an unarmed labour battalion supporting the Russians. These alternatives were not implemented since, of the 3,700 men in the regiment, only 311 agreed to accept one of these alternatives. The option of the labour battalion was chosen by 11 of the 250 Karelian pioneers.[3]

The Slavo-British Legion, a fighting force, had been formed from Bolshevik prisoners and deserters under British and Russian officers. In July 1919 a mutiny in the 1st Slavo-British Legion resulted in the deaths of three British and four Russian officers. A number of men deserted and 26 were charged with mutiny. Twenty were found guilty, eleven being executed and nine sentenced to 10 years penal servitude. Following the mutiny the Legion was disarmed and turned into a labour unit to be used on the LoC.

A small number of Chinese were employed as labourers in North Russia, as Summerskill records in his work on the Chinese Labour Corps: 'on the Archangel Front 191 Chinese from the Corps served later with the Slavo-British Legion'.[4]

1 NA WO 95/4820
2 ibid WO 95/4956

3 ibid
4 Summerskill, *China on the Western Front*, p.196

EAST AFRICA

The campaigns in East Africa undoubtedly used more native workers than any other theatre. According to official figures there were 66,580 coloured labourers employed in East Africa on 23 November 1918 but the total number of natives employed between 1914 and 1918 exceeded 1,000,000.[1] Despite these huge numbers there is less recorded about the work of the natives in Africa than other foreign labour units. The majority, over 810,000, were employed as carriers. As one study states.

> ... although many Africans served as general labourers – clearing and building roads, constructing defensive positions – the vast majority were used for porterage on supply lines carrying military equipment and food to and from the front line or the scene of operations.[2]

In 1914 the movement of goods in East Africa was primarily borne by carriers since the bush was almost impassable to wagons. The tsetse fly produced sleeping sickness in oxen and mules used to pull wagons. With the coming of war the demand for labour led to the formation of what became known as the Carrier Corps (CC). Formed by Oscar Watkins, a District Commissioner in East Africa, in August 1914, there were initially five CCs each of about 1,000 men.

There were other military carriers that did not come under Watkins, and military railways had their own labour. From the start the use of native labour was beset with problems, with men moving from one group to another. Watkins faced the same problems that administrators of labour encountered in other theatres; that employers regarded the men as their personal property. In March 1915 the shortage of labour compelled Watkins to request the return of 238 men working for the RE. The RE officer in charge of the detachment objected as he needed them for another week. He complained to the GOC who, without consulting Watkins, agreed that the RE could retain them.

Recruitment

Recruitment in 1914 was on a voluntary basis although 'the working conditions of labour in military employ was a major deterrent to voluntary recruitment'.[3] Not only was the work potentially dangerous but the men were removed from their home areas. The term voluntary is misleading, as one porter, employed from 1914 to 1916, described:

> ... we came back one night from our yam farm. The chief called us and handed us over to a Government messenger. I did not know where we were going to, but the chief and the messenger said that the white man had sent for us and so we must go.[4]

Major General Sir Evan Gibb KBE CB CMG DSO. (Courtesy of RASC and RCT Institution)

Labour Corps' cap badge. (Authors' collection)

12 (Labour) Battalion Black Watch broadening a road, Fricourt, November 1916. (IWM Q4548)

Salvage, ammunition and equipment on the battlefield near Bapaume, January 1917. (IWM Q1795)

Men of a labour battalion repairing the road at Hamel, October 1916. (IWM Q1591)

Road repairs in ruined Bucquoy, 23 March 1917. (IWM Q5809)

Zonnebeke, 30 October 1917. Shell fire in the distance. (IWM E (AUS) 1172)

Officer and NCOs of 407 Agricultural Company, Richmond, Yorkshire. (Authors' collection)

ITISH SOLDIERS IN THE SOMME MENDING A ROAD.

Postcard issued by the YMCA Hut Fund. (Authors' collection)

Labour Battalion – possibly Berkshire Regiment – early 1917. (Authors' collection)

A dump of empty tins – to be melted down in kilns for the extraction of solder. Etaples, May 1918. (IWM Q8788)

Hazebrouck Road near Bailleul, June 1916. (IWM Q646)

172 Company, October 1917. (Authors' collection)

3rd Alien Company Middlesex Regiment. Captain Renwick MC is the officer with the stick and CSM Wiehl is seated on the front row holding the dog. (Courtesy of Kevin C. Dowson, grandson of Frederick Wiehl)

5 Southern Company, Non Combatant Corps. (Authors' collection)

184 Company Band 1917. (Authors' collection)

24 Company football team. (Authors' collection)

Men of the 46th Company, Labour Corps outside 'Leicester Lounge' Nesle, 22 June 1917.
(IWM Q2550)

Filling in trenches and tractor-ploughing at the Agricultural Directorate Farm at Roye, 9 March 1918. (IWM Q10281)

Remaking the Guillemont–Montauban road, September 1916. (IWM Q4250)

Indian jail labour at Sheikh Saad, Mesopotamia, October 1917. (IWM Q25227)

Railway Construction in Mesopotamia. (IWM Q24739)

9 PoW Company, Eawy Forest, January 1918. (IWM Q10236)

German prisoners employed at No 4 Heavy Workshops, salvage works, Rouen, 10 October 1918. (IWM Q29668)

Indian Labour Corps charcoal burning, Brottonne Forest, 22 January 1918. (IWM Q8494)

1 CLC at Tank Corps central workshops, Teneur. (IWM Q9862)

French postcard of Indian Labour Corps. (Authors' collection)

ELC at the Suez Canal, 1916. (IWM Q15871)

ELC moving a hut. (Courtesy of Stewarty Museum)

The BWIR in camp on the Albert–Amiens Road, September 1916. (IWM Q1202)

SANLC War Dance and Sports at Dannes, June 1917. Zulus ready for the war dance.
(IWM Q2393)

French women employed in an army laundry hanging out soldiers' shirts to dry. Poperinghe, 30 September 1917. (IWM Q2919)

Labour Corps headstones in CWGC cemeteries.

Captain S. Cohen, ELC, murdered 22 November 1919. Cairo War Memorial Cemetery. (Author's Collection)

542667 Private G.Y. Oddie, Ramleh War Cemetery, Israel. (Author's Collection)

Two of the four Labour Corps men murdered, 18 March 1919, buried in Cairo War Memorial Cemetery. (Authors' collection)

36059 CQMS Alfred Culyer.   549259 CQMS P.D. Peacock.

43758 Labourer Sung Te Chuan, Bourlon Wood Cemetery. (Authors' Collection)

Captain W. Greenhill, CLC, Hong Kong Cemetery. (Authors' Collection)

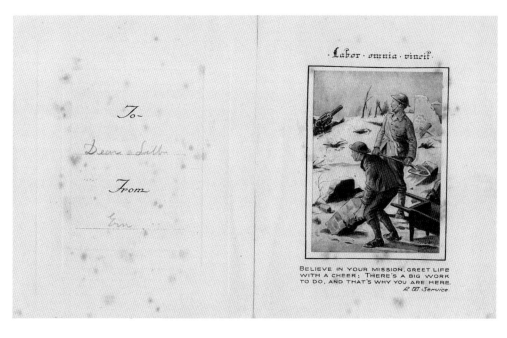

Interior 1917 Labour Corps Christmas card (Authors' collection)

Interior 1918 Labour Corps Christmas card (Authors' collection)

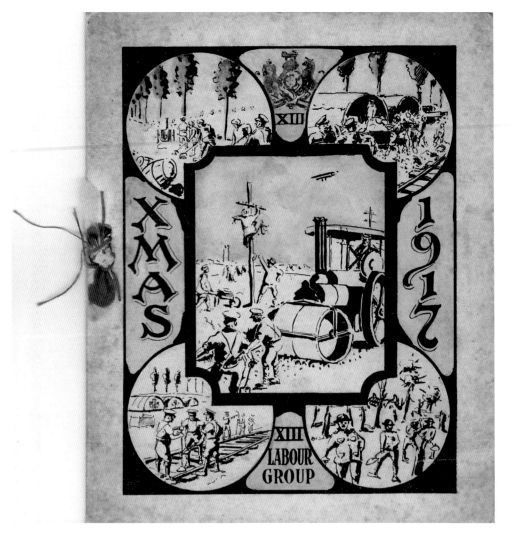

XIII Group Christmas card 1917 (Authors' collection)

707 Company Christmas card 1917 (Authors' collection)

XMAS 1917

Greetings From The 707th Labour Coy.

... B.E.F. FRANCE ...

ROYAL ENGINEERS

Labour Battalion returning in the evening after a day's work consolidating newly-won ground. Near Ypres, 6 September 1917. Photographer Lt E. Brooks. (IWM Q2992)

As the war continued it was found that insufficient natives were being 'voluntarily' recruited and in 1915 the Native Followers Recruitment Ordinance opened the way for compulsory service. By the end of 1915 the CC and other porter groups, which now amounted to around 70,000 men, was in need of one administrative system. The work of the CC had changed to include work on roads, bridges and pipelines.

Military Labour Bureau

In February 1916 Oscar Watkins, with the rank of captain, set up the Military Labour Bureau (MLB), which was to be responsible for all labour with the exception of Railway Labour. Watkins was allowed two officers and four NCOs for every 1,000 natives and began to set up what was an efficient administrative unit. British officers and NCOs, and Indian clerks supported Watkins in running the MLB. At its peak its staff amounted to 220 officers, about 600 NCOs and 120 clerks. Between 1916 and 1918, in addition to porters, a total of 218,411 natives were recruited as casual labour by the MLB.[5]

By 1917 Watkins had been promoted to major but was often in conflict with both employers and his superiors about what he considered were excessive demands being made of the CC. He was concerned that the authorities were 'bleeding the land of its manpower' and the effect this would have in the future. Watkins played a major role in persuading John Ainsworth, the Provisional Commissioner for Nyanza Province, to take on the role of Military Commissioner for Labour in March 1917.

With the rank of colonel, Ainsworth commanded the MLB, which was renamed the Military Labour Corps (MLC). Watkins remained as Director, subordinate to Ainsworth, and served as his right-hand man. Ainsworth faced the task of persuading settlers, particularly in Tanganyika, to recruit natives from their farms. He did this by introducing a system whereby natives were classed as fit for the MLB, fit for farm work and unfit for any work. At the same time he agreed to release for farm work men already recruited but subsequently found unsuitable for military work.

Ainsworth remained in the post until June 1918 when he was appointed Advisor on Native Affairs. Watkins, promoted to lieutenant colonel, was once again appointed to command the MLC.

Labourers

There is little information about the work of men recruited as labourers rather than porters. During 1916 a system was established whereby a line of permanent stations were set up, each of which housed a group of 50 labourers. These labourers were used to maintain roads, bridges and drainage systems, build huts and dig latrines. It is likely that the majority of labourers were employed in this manner. For example, a supply line of 180 miles would have 15 posts requiring 750 labourers.

On the coast the province around Mombasa included African, Indian and Arab labourers. Many skilled men, worked as motor drivers, grooms, officers' servants, tailors, saddlers, winch men, stevedores and canoe men lived. 'A growing demand for special workers fell mainly on Seyidie with its older technical traditions.'[6] Canoe men were used to move stores along rivers like the Rufiji and Rovuma. Many of the skilled labourers lived and worked at base workshops for the various Army departments. These were the highest paid of all the labourers, with Indian artisans earning between three and ten times the amount paid to Africans. Skilled labourers, carpenters, blacksmiths, masons and fitters were paid between 75 cents and 2 Rand a day compared to the 5 Rand a month paid to unskilled porters. Cooks, who were classified as amongst the most skilled porters, earned 25 Rand a month.

Carriers became 'builders of huge numbers of bandas or temporary shelters which were needed, made of poles, grass or coconut thatch'.[7] According to Watkins, 'the Royal Engineers were entirely relieved of building work'.[8]

Casualties

How many men died whilst employed by the British or as a result of illness is not known due to the lack of records. There are fewer than ten natives named in the CWGC records although one source puts the number of CC deaths at 95,000.[9] A second source puts the number who died at 23,311 with a further 25,695 missing, although it states that it is impossible to estimate how many died either on the way home or after reaching home.[10]

Compensation

In April 1915 King's African Rifles Regulations were amended to enable carriers and labourers to claim compensation in case of unclaimed pay, disablement or death. Applications for compensation were made through the District Commissioners, although few could be verified. Poor records and differences between African and European customs complicated the matter. Under African custom it was normal for compensation to be paid to both a man's widow and his male next of kin.

In 1918 the Director of Military Labour proposed that, where men had disappeared, money should be paid to the tribal organisations to which men belonged. Both civil and military authorities and the Colonial Office initially supported this. It appears the Colonial Office did not seek the consent of the War Office who withdrew their agreement since it was their responsibility to find the money. The Governors of Kenya and Tanganyika both objected to this decision but could not get it overturned.

In 1922 the War Office rejected a Colonial Office request to undertake a systematic search to trace those who had disappeared. Two years later the Governors of Kenya and Tanganyika once again sought approval for payment of compensation to the tribes. The British Government considered this in 1925. In December 1926 the Treasury announced that there was no obligation on the part of the British Government to pay the money.

The Colonial Office supported the views of the African Governments and stated, 'the military operations against German East Africa could not have been carried on without the assistance of these large bodies of native carriers, who rendered loyal and invaluable service in circumstances always arduous and often dangerous'.[11]

In 1934 the authorities in Kenya pointed out to the Treasury that they had passed an ordinance in 1918 that any outstanding money should be paid to the tribe to which the man belonged and that there were major grievances in the country that this had not happened. The Treasury again considered the matter, deciding that there were two problems. Firstly, the question of tribal recognition when there were no good records and secondly, the War Office view that overpayments and the pay of deserters would have to be deducted from the amount of money available. The Treasury decided not to pay money to tribal groups but to make an ex gratia payment of £50,000 to the Government of Kenya.[12] No payments were made to the Governments of Zanzibar, Uganda or Tanganyika.

1   *Statistics of the Military Effort of the British Empire During the Great War,* p.160
2   Killingray, D., *Labour exploitation for Military Campaigns in British Colonial Africa,* p. 484
3   ibid, p.492
4   Quoted in Killingray, p.484
5   Hodges, G., *The Carrier Corps,* p. 110
6   ibid, p.106
7   ibid, p.152
8   Watkins quoted in Hodges, p.152
9   Paice, E., *Tip and Run,* p. 392
10 Lucas, *Empire at War* Vol IV, p.215
11 NA CO 533/661
12 ibid T 161/666

SECTION FOUR: BRITISH AND DOMINION UNITS

ROYAL MARINE LABOUR CORPS

Unloading stores from ships at the ports was the responsibility of the Navy, with the Army taking over responsibility once the stores were on the quayside. With a decreasing supply of French labour the naval officers at the ports found it increasingly difficult to obtain the personnel they required. Military personnel assigned to the ports were constantly changing and had little experience of loading or unloading ships. The two ASC (Naval Labour) companies, comprising men experienced as stevedores, helped the situation but they were under the control of the Army.

Following lengthy discussions in 1916 it was decided that

> ... the Royal Marine system of organisation would best meet the case, for they would be subject to the standing orders and discipline of the ports under the local commanders, but would be entirely at the disposal of the Divisional Naval Transport Officers as regards the control and distribution of their work; a principle which had been settled many years before between the Admiralty and War Office.[1]

The Royal Marine Labour Corps (RMLC) was created on 2 February 1917 with the transfer of the two ASC (Naval Labour) companies to the Royal Marines. Recruiting for the RMLC was opened at ports in Britain, restricted to men with dock experience and over 41 years of age. At the time, men of this age were not eligible for combatant enlistment and there was no shortage of men, many between 50 and 60 years of age, who were keen to 'do their bit'. The officers of the RMLC were found from ex-Mercantile Mariners and dockworkers, including many men serving in the two ASC companies.

A divisional headquarters was established at Deal where recruits were clothed and equipped and at which the records of the Corps were kept. In France Lieutenant Colonel R. Cator RMLI commanded the Corps, which had a total strength of 56 officers, 117 WOs and sergeants, 531 corporals and 4,205 privates. Attached to the Corps were seven officers, seventeen WOs and sergeants and eight lance sergeants from the RMLI to assist in administration and discipline. Colonel Cator's headquarters was situated at GHQ where, in addition to

Lieutenant J. Carroll RMLI, the adjutant and quartermaster, he had a small staff of clerks.

Each port in France had its own detachment which was commanded by a RMLC captain assisted by a RMLI officer acting as adjutant. The size of the detachment varied depending on the amount of work, from 1,120 at Dunkirk, to 50 at St Valery. The number of RMLI also depended on the size of the port; larger ports each had a RMLI sergeant major (WO 1) and QMS (WO 2); the smaller ports had a RMLI company sergeant major (WO 2). Each port also had an RMLI sergeant and one or two lance corporals for policing and camp duties.

Administratively the Corps was in a strange position as the Army provided their accommodation, rations (for which the Admiralty paid) and medical attendance, whilst their stores were provided by the Admiralty and charged to the Royal Marines. In April 1918 it was suggested that the RMLC be amalgamated into the Labour Corps but the War Office rejected the idea.[2]

The men of the RMLC 'earned an excellent reputation for good work, particularly at Dunkirk and Calais where they were bombed almost nightly, but the RMLC stuck to their work in spite of casualties and damage.[3] Captain H.V. Fuller was awarded the Distinguished Service Cross following a bombing of the RMLC camp, the citation stating:

> On the night of the 6th–7th August, 1918, during an enemy air raid, in which several huts of the R.M.L.C. were demolished or severely damaged, his conduct was an example to all. He assisted in getting the men away from the wrecked huts, bandaging the wounded, rendering every assistance possible, and showed an utter disregard for his personal safety.[4]

In addition to Fuller's DSC, 7 men were awarded DSMs, 11 MSMs and 58 Mentioned in Dispatches.

Late in 1918 trouble occurred between men of the RMLC and the Inland Water Transport at Calais, and in 1919 discontent about demobilization resulted in strikes at both Dunkirk and Blangy. The authorities considered replacing the men at Blangy with members of the Chinese Labour Corps but the detachment returned to work after 25 men were charged with refusing to obey a lawful order.

In Britain, No. 1 (Home Service) Labour Company was formed in December 1917 specifically to handle the mines that the Navy were laying in the North Sea. Commanded by Major F. Athow RMLI, the company comprised one other officer with 4 sergeants and 226 other ranks as labourers. The men, who were affiliated to the Chatham Division, were over combatant age or of low medical category and paid at ASC rates. The unit was disbanded in 1919.

1 Blumberg, *Britain's Sea Soldiers,* p.450
2 NA WO 95/83
3 Blumberg, p.452
4 *London Gazette,* 14 January 1919, p.2

CONSCIENTIOUS OBJECTORS AND THE NON COMBATANT CORPS

Tribunals

The way the authorities dealt with conscientious objectors (COs) following the passing of the Military Service Act in January 1916 meant there was an overlap between those serving in the military and those employed in civil work. With the passing of the Act all eligible men were considered to have enlisted in any unit they were directed to by the military authorities. The Act did, however, give a man the right to apply for exemption on health grounds, because of his occupation or 'on the ground of a conscientious objection to bearing arms'.[1] This objection could be religious, moral or political and each local authority set up a tribunal to hear requests for exemption.

Instructions were given to local authorities by the local government Board that the tribunals should be fully representative of the whole community. However,

> Proven zeal in furthering recruiting was frequently rewarded by a Tribunal seat. Places were often offered to the parson and to an official of the local recruiting committee. A pro-war Labour man was considered a good catch, and a pro-war Quaker by no means beyond procurement – even better.[2]

Most tribunals took the view that Britain would lose the war if sufficient men were not recruited and that they should ensure cowards and shirkers did not get past them. At the Shaw Tribunal, in Manchester, one of the first men to claim exemption on religious grounds was told by a Councillor Hopwood, a member of the panel:

> I think you are exploiting God to save your own skin. It is nothing but deliberate and rank blasphemy. A man who would not help to defend his country and womanhood is a coward and a cad. You are nothing but a shivering mass of unwholesome fat![3]

Many tribunals included members who did not believe in the concept of conscientious objection. At the Wirral Tribunal in April 1916 the chairman told one claimant: 'I wish the Government had not put in this clause about conscientious objectors. I do not agree with it myself. Application refused.'[4]

The questions asked by the tribunals were intended to prove whether the man was a genuine CO or not. It was, however, common for questions to be put that doomed a man whatever his answer. When one claimant at Willesden responded 'Yes' to the question 'Do you believe the blood of Christ cleanses from all sin?' he was told: 'Then would you not be forgiven if you took part in this war?'[5] In Scotland one man was refused exemption on religious grounds because he repaired boots for miners who went down the pit to dig coals that were used by the Navy.

The Military Service Act stated:

> Any certificate of exemption may be absolute, conditional, or temporary, as the authority by whom it was granted think best suited to the case, the form of an exemp-

tion from combatant service only, or may be conditional on the applicant being engaged in some work which in the opinion of the tribunal dealing with the case is of national importance.[6]

Tribunals interpreted this in different ways. Some granted absolute exemptions to all claimants whereas others granted exemptions on the grounds of health or occupation but not to COs. At first it was up to individual tribunals to decide what constituted work of 'national importance'. At Brentford COs were refused exemption whereas the same tribunal granted it to workers at the local brewery on the grounds that they were undertaking work of national importance. At Market Bosworth exemption was granted to all the men employed by the local hunt and at Southwark 21 single men employed by Harmsworth Press on two magazines, *Home Chat* and *Comic Cuts*, were granted an exemption for six months.

In an attempt to clarify matters the Board of Trade set up the Pelham Committee which was charged with defining what work could be classed as being of national importance. The Committee decided there were eight areas: Agriculture, Forestry, Food Supply, Shipping, Transport, Mining, Education and Public Utility Services.[7]

If exemption was rejected the claimant could appeal to a Central Tribunal although this tended to support the view of the Local Tribunal. In March 1916 the Central Tribunal advised Local Tribunals that in its view, only religious objectors could legitimately claim exemption. Other genuine objectors, i.e. those with political objections to both combatant and non-combatant service, should be awarded conditional exemption as long as they undertook 'work of national importance'.

In February 1916 the Local Government Board pointed out that a man whose objection was on religious or moral grounds should be able to feel that his case was dealt with fairly and that the Act should be interpreted in an impartial and tolerant way. This liberal interpretation vanished when the number of applications grew.

Non Combatant Corps

As the number of applications for exemption on conscientious grounds increased, the Government looked for a way to overcome the problem of the high number being refused exemption but who would continue to refuse to bear arms. On 10 March 1916 Army Order 112 announced the formation of the Non Combatant Corps (NCC) for COs.[8] The NCC was to be an Army unit, subject to military law, but the men would not bear arms or fight.

The NCC was organised in companies with the same establishment as Infantry Works Companies. Each company was commanded by a captain or subaltern supported by a colour sergeant, two sergeants, four corporals and six lance corporals. The officer and NCOs were not COs, but men from regular infantry units unfit for general service. They were considered fit to serve abroad on the lines of communication. The 94 other ranks in each company were men who held a certificate of exemption from combatant service. The men wore uniform, were subject to military law and trained in squad drill but could not be armed or trained with arms of any description. Unlike most labour units the majority of men were category A and officers were instructed that COs were not to be given work which was lighter or more congenial than tasks given to men of British labour companies.[9] The badge and shoulder title for the corps were the letters NCC and the companies were numbered consecutively in each command in the order of formation, for example No. 1 Scottish Company NCC, No. 2 Eastern Company NCC.

Whilst the NCOs were entitled to working pay, NCC privates were not entitled to either working pay or civil rates but received a basic soldier's wage. A private could not be promoted and so, from the outset, the Army indicated that these men were to receive different treatment from other soldiers. By November 1916 it was decided that men in the NCC should, as far as possible, be employed on Army work and only lent to other government departments under exceptional circumstances, and they should not work for civilian contractors.[10]

In total, 34 NCC companies were formed, eight of which were to serve in France. In April 1916 the Corps had a strength of 203 men, which rose to 1,416 in June, 2,107 in August, 2,691 in October and 3,181 in December. Its highest recorded strength was 3,319 in August 1918.[11] In France the NCC repaired roads and railways, worked in quarries and forests, moved stores, provided huts and baths for soldiers coming out of the trenches, and cleared and burnt excreta. Men of the NCC were not paid the extra 4d a day that other soldiers received when employed burning excreta. Over three-quarters of the men in the NCC served at home although virtually nothing is known about the work of the NCC in Britain.

Some COs were willing to serve in the NCC or RAMC in non-combatant roles, some would not serve in the military but were willing to undertake civilian employment of national importance and some refused any kind of work, military or civilian.

The Tribunal did not always accept a CO's request to be employed in civilian work. Glen Hayler, a CO from Newcastle, had claimed exemption on religious grounds. Refused exemption he appealed and was again refused, following which he wrote to Pelham, chairman of the Committee established by the Board of Trade:

> I am ready to serve my country in any useful capacity under civil control. I am a gardener of some experience, and at the present time my work is finding food for some fifteen persons. I am ready to continue this work under my present employer, or to undertake similar work elsewhere for the Government, under civil control.[12]

Pelham replied informing him that they could only look at cases referred to them by a tribunal. Hayler was taken before the magistrate and handed over to the Army where he was posted to the 5th Battalion Royal Fusiliers and after refusing to obey orders was sentenced to six months detention by a court martial.

Military Law

Initially, men refused exemption who continued to refuse to serve in the military were handed over to the Army and dealt with through military law. A group of these objectors, who were being held in Landguard Fort, Harwich were attached to the 1st Eastern Company NCC and ordered to cart stones from the beach. Believing that the stones were to be used for military purposes they refused the order. On 7 May 1916 seventeen men were taken to France and told they were now soldiers and ordered to work. In France they were subject to abuse from their NCOs and threats of execution, as Howard Marten recalled:

> We were forever being threatened with the death sentence. Over and over again we'd be marched up and read out a notice: some man being sentenced to death through disobedience at the Front. Whether they were true cases I don't know. It was all done with the idea of intimidating us.[13]

On 10 May these men refused to march off the parade ground. It was decided that they should be split into a number of groups, one of which was sent to work in a quarry at Harfleur. The men in this group refused to handle the tools provided for them. Under military law their refusal resulted in them receiving 'Field Punishment No. 1' by which a man was kept in handcuffs, fetters or both and secured to a fixed object like a wheel or a gun carriage.[14] Four COs were tried by Field General Court Martial for disobedience on 2 June and again on 7 June.[15] Howard Marten recalled the situation on 15 June when they were informed of their punishment:

> Eventually we were taken out to the parade ground. There was a big concourse of men lined up in an immense square. Under escort we were taken out, one by one, to the middle of the square. I was the first of them, and until my verdict was known nobody knew exactly what was going to happen. Then the officer in charge of the proceedings read out the various crimes and misdemeanours refusing to obey a lawful command, disobedience at Boulogne and so on. Then 'The sentence of the court is to suffer death by being shot.'
>
> There was a suitable pause, and I thought, 'Well, that's that.' Then he said, 'Confirmed by the Commander in Chief,' which double sealed it. There was another long pause 'But subsequently commuted to penal servitude for ten years.'[16]

On 28 May a further sixteen men from the NCC base at Richmond Castle and on 29 May another eight from Abergele were taken to France. In the House of Commons on 22 June, George Barnes, Labour MP for Blackfriars in Glasgow, asked the Under Secretary for War, John Tennant, whether four COs had been sentenced to death in France. Tennant's response was that the majority of rumours about the treatment of COs were untrue and that he assumed that this was yet another unfounded rumour and promised an investigation. He told the House: 'There is no intention of dealing with them in any way harshly and there will be no question of them being sentenced to death.'[17]

Four days later Tennant had to tell the House that death sentences had been pronounced on these four and an additional 30 COs in France. He also told the House that he was not sure whether the sentences had been commuted and reminded them that wilful disobedience of orders was punishable by death when it occurred in a war zone. Whereas many MPs viewed COs as cowards, others took the view that if they were willing to face death for their convictions, their convictions must be genuine. Following pressure from both MPs and the Press on 29 June the Prime Minister pledged that this would never happen again: 'As far as I am concerned, and as far as the War Office is concerned, no soldier will be sent to France who we have good reason to believe is a conscientious objector.'[18] The men who had been sentenced to death were brought back from France and sent to various civilian jails. Their return was not without incident, being hissed at by French soldiers at Rouen and having tomatoes and eggs thrown at them when they arrived at Southampton.

The Adjutant General, Lieutenant General Sir Nevil Macready, was concerned about the Army becoming responsible for a large number of recruits who would be a potential threat to discipline. On 15 May he wrote a memorandum to Kitchener recommending that the Government establish a civil organization that would employ 'under conditions as severe as those of soldiers at the front' any COs who were considered useless for the Army.[19] Kitchener circulated the memorandum to the Cabinet and a week later informed the House of Lords that Government policy was to place the genuine CO under the civil power. On 25 May Army Order 179 directed that a CO found guilty of a military disciplinary offence should be sent to a civil prison and not placed under Army detention. A man in a civil prison, even when under military law, was the responsibility of the Home Office. This concept was more palatable to Liberal opinion. The authorities still faced the difficulty that once a man had served his sentence in a civil prison he was returned to the Army where he would again refuse to obey orders, be charged and brought before a court martial.

Brace Committee

By the end of June 1916 the Government had appointed a small committee under William Brace, one of the three Labour MPs in the Coalition Government, which announced that COs sentenced by courts martial would have their cases reviewed by the Central Tribunal. Those considered genuine would be released from prison to work under the Brace Committee, as part of what became known as the 'Home Office Scheme'. Men who refused to accept the Scheme, or not considered to be genuine COs, were returned to prison to complete their sentence. The Central Tribunal began interviews on 27 July 1916 and by the time of its last interview on 16 May 1919 it had reviewed 5,944 cases.

Following a Tribunal a man was placed into one of five classes (A to E):

Class A: Those to be treated as having a conscientious objection to all military service.

Class B: Those claiming to be a CO but whose convictions were not convincing enough to be placed in Class A.

Class C: Men politically opposed to the war but who would fight in a war if they approved of its purpose.

Class D: Those it was felt had no real conscientious objection to military service.

Class E: Those who refused to plead before the Tribunal or refused the Tribunal's conditions.

Initially, men in Classes A and B were released to work under the Home Office Scheme but after a few months the Brace Committee withdrew this option for Class B men. Men in Classes C and D (and later B) remained in prison and under military law. After a second court martial their case could be reconsidered if new evidence was submitted. In reality such reclassification was usually not as a result of new evidence but rather to avoid returning men, who would refuse to obey military orders, to the Army. Men in Class E were the absolutists – men who refused to recognise the tribunal or appear before it. This meant they could not be reclassified. Returned to the Army on completion of a prison sentence, the absolutists would refuse to obey orders, be charged, found guilty and sentenced again to prison. By the end of the war the Tribunal had classified 4,378 men as A, 196 B, 46 C, 267 D and 692 E.

Home Office Scheme

The first COs to be employed on the Home Office Scheme started work on 12 August 1916 and in total 4,126 were employed during the lifetime of the scheme. In theory the scheme enabled men who objected to military service to undertake work of national importance although it has been suggested that one reason for its introduction was to avoid the problem of the Army having to control thousands of men who had demonstrated their refusal to accept military discipline.[20] The first group of men employed were sent to one of three employers; the Road Board, the Home Grown Timber Committee or the Llanelli Rural District Council. The number of men being released by the Central Tribunal soon exceeded the requirement of these three employers and so 'work centres' were established at two disused prisons at Wakefield and Warwick. A large number of COs released to the scheme either could not or would not work and some actively caused problems from the start.

In the summer of 1916 a large work camp was established at Dyce, five miles northwest of Aberdeen. The camp was intended to hold several hundred COs who were to be employed under the Home Office Scheme in the quarry at Dyce and repairing and constructing roads in the area. The camp was set on a hillside with the men living in old army tents. These provided adequate accommodation in August but the autumn rain soaked through the tents onto the men's bedding, clothes and personal possessions. The ground became a mud bath with rivers of rain running through the tents. Many of the men at Dyce had previously been employed as schoolteachers or in sedentary occupations and were not used to heavy physical work. Some men had already suffered several weeks in the poor conditions of prison and as a result both their workload and morale were low. Walter Roberts from Stockport had arrived at Dyce exhausted after a sentence of four months prison with hard labour. Two weeks after his arrival he collapsed and died, some claiming his death was directly attributable to the conditions in the camp. At the end of October, ten weeks after Dyce camp opened, it was closed, the men being sent to other work centres or returned to prison.

Despite the failure of Dyce other centres were set up throughout Britain, including Chelsea, Grimsby, Lyme Regis, Loch Awe, Newhaven and at Knutsford Prison. At Knutsford, Lyme Regis and Wakefield, local people attacked the COs. In March 1917 several centres were closed down and 1,000 COs were moved to Dartmoor Prison.

Although this was a civil scheme, a man who caused difficulties for the authorities could be placed in the Army and face military law. W. E. Burns from Manchester was employed on the Home Office Scheme when he helped organise a strike and was sent back to the Army. He refused to obey orders and was court-martialled in November 1917, being sentenced to two years hard labour. He was sent to Hull Prison where his health rapidly deteriorated and by February 1918 he was so weak he could not stand up unaided. He requested the Home Office transfer him to the scheme or Manchester

Prison so his family could visit him. When he failed to hear from the Home Office he went on hunger strike. He was force fed for three days but on the fourth day the tube used was too short and the cocoa and milk was inhaled into his lungs and he choked to death. The inquest found that death was due to pneumonia accelerated by force-feeding, although the jury stated that no blame could be attached to the doctor.[21]

Refusing Military Service

Most men who were refused military exemption were placed in the NCC, although as illustrated by the following two examples, this was not always the case.

The service record of Alfred Catherall (ASC regimental number T4/216839) illustrates how a man could be transferred from military to civil and back to military service.[22] In September 1916 he was called up for service and arrested by the civil police when he failed to report, being handed over to the Army on 6 October. Charged with failing to obey a lawful command he was sentenced to 56 days in prison. In December he was transferred to class 'W' of the Army Reserve in order that he could be employed under the direction of the Brace Committee and was sent to the work centre at Wakefield Prison. Presumably something occurred whilst at Wakefield which led to him, in June 1917, being recalled to the Army where he again refused to obey instructions and was sentenced to 84 days in prison. On completion of this sentence he was taken to France where two further charges resulted in sentences of 84 days Field Punishment No. 1 and 112 days in prison.[23] He served in France until June 1918 and the House of Commons was informed on 15 July that he had been returned to Britain on 5 June.[24] On 3 April 1919 it was announced in the House of Commons that men who had served an aggregate of two years or more in prison as a result of offences committed against Army discipline, which they had pleaded was caused by conscientious objection, would have the remainder of their sentence remitted. The following day Catherall was dismissed from the Army on the grounds of misconduct.

Charles Cobb, a lay preacher, was called up in August 1916 but failed to report for military service. Taken before the magistrates he was fined £2 and handed over to the military authorities. When he refused to sign his attestation paper he was charged with disobeying a lawful command and remanded in Civil Custody to await a District Court Martial (DCM). Found guilty and sentenced to one year of hard labour, he was sent to Wormwood Scrubs on 13 September. On 15 December he was transferred to an Army unit, the 24th Training Reserve, where he was again charged with disobeying a lawful command and sentenced to two years of hard labour. The sentence was reduced to 112 days and on his return to the Army in March 1917 he faced his third DCM for which he was sentenced to two years. Between March 1917 and May 1918 his service record shows he was released from prison a further four times and on each occasion sentenced to between six months and two years at a DCM. On 23 May 1918 he was transferred to the Labour Corps and sent to Eastern Command Labour Centre. On 30 May at his eighth DCM he was sentenced to 6 months and sent to Winchester Prison. He remained there until 25 February 1919 when he was released on the order of the Home Secretary. He was released from the Army on medical grounds on the same day.[25] Charles Cobb was to die three weeks after his release from prison suffering from tuberculosis and curvature of the spine.

Absolutists

The 692 absolutists, the majority of whom were members of the Independent Labour Party (ILP) or Quakers, were to present particular problems for the authorities. The ILP condemned the war from its outset and in November 1914 formed the No Conscription Fellowship (NCF) in order to resist conscription. Clifford Allen, chairman of the NCF, was typical of the absolutists. Called up for service on 11 August 1916, he was posted to 7 Company Eastern NCC three days later and immediately charged with disobeying a lawful command. Found guilty and sentenced to one year hard labour he was placed in military detention. On 25 November he was sent back to his NCC Company and two days later was in detention again awaiting trial for refusing to obey instructions. Found guilty, he was sentenced to another year of hard labour and sent to Maidstone Prison. Refusing to co-operate with the prison authorities he was placed in solitary confinement on a diet of bread and water. Returned to the NCC in May 1917 a third court martial sentenced him to 2 years' hard labour. In an open letter to Lloyd George he gave notice that he would refuse any work in prison no matter what the consequences.[26] Allen served a total of 16 months in prison during which he lost three stone in weight and contracted tuberculosis. He was released on health grounds in December 1917.

Allen's letter caused difficulties for the NCF National Committee who were not only against works strikes by COs but actively tried to promote socially useful work under the Home Office Scheme. On 14 June 1917 the letter was published in full in the NCF's paper *The Tribunal* along with the statement that:

> Clifford Allen wishes it to be known that though he himself feels bound to refuse henceforth to do prison work whilst in custody under the Military Service Act, he entirely concurs with the view of the National Committee that it would not be right to organise a general refusal of work in prison.[27]

Despite protests from many supporters the NCF refused to organise a national prison strike. Even attempts by militant socialists to organise strikes in individual prisons, such as at Winchester in October 1918, failed as religious objectors would not support anything they considered to be indiscipline or rebellion. The hunger strike, which usually took place as a result of either brutal treatment or injustice, was another form of protest adopted in prisons. Again the NCF did not support what it considered a dangerous method of protest. Political objectors did organise hunger strikes in Newcastle, Maidstone, Winchester, Wandsworth, Carlisle, Canterbury and Hull Prisons during 1918 although they failed to get the support of religious objectors.

Demobilisation

At the end of the war the men of the NCC were not considered a priority when it came to demobilisation. On 6 January 1919 clerks at the Ripon Dispersal Unit refused to demobilise a member of the NCC. Following this the Director of

Mobilisation asked the Adjutant General for a ruling on whether this man should be demobilised pointing out that he was not a CO as he had not been sentenced by court martial for an offence which arose out of a conscientious objection to military service. Whilst it was confirmed that men of the NCC were not necessarily COs, it was decided at the beginning of February that those over the age limit for retention should be demobilised with others of their occupational class, but not until the others had passed through the dispersal station. Those under 37 years of age were to be retained in service whilst the Armies of Occupation were still in existence.

On 13 May 1919 Churchill told the House that he was not aware that any men eligible for demobilisation from the NCC were being retained unless the Army needed their services and that the same regulations applied to the NCC as other regiments or corps. Whilst this may have been the official Government position the reality appears to have been somewhat different.

In July 1919, 34 members of No. 3 Southern Company NCC sent a letter to their commanding officer. In the letter they pointed out that unlike other soldiers they continued to receive only 1s a day and were not entitled to work pay or a war gratuity. This meant that for many it was becoming increasingly difficult to support their families whilst retained in the Army. They also pointed out that many of them had employment waiting for them when they were demobilised and that requests for demobilisation had been turned down by order of Southern Command. It was their contention that they had

> Faithfully performed our duties as non-combatants, and that we are treated unjustly by being penalised for acting in accordance with an Act of Parliament which provided that those who could prove a conscientious objection to combatant service should be exempt.[28]

In September 1919 consideration was given to demobilising the NCC en bloc but the adjutant-general rejected this as 'extremely dangerous'.[29] At the time the NCC still comprised 1,609 men and only 300 were demobilised by the end of the year. During the first month of 1920 the NCC decreased from 1,321 to 455 men and these were demobilised the following month.

In 1921 the Conscientious Objectors Information Bureau compiled a list of 73 COs who they say died as a direct result of treatment they received in prison or at the hands of the military. Of these, ten are shown as dying in prison, in Home Office Centres, military custody or shortly after release. Of these ten men only three, Walter Bone, Percy Duxbury[30] and Charles Thompson, are among the 33 men of the NCC buried in CWGC graves.

1   Rae, J., *Conscience and Politics*, p.27
2   Boulton, D., *Objection Overruled*, p.124
3   ibid, p.125
4   ibid, p.9
5   ibid, p.125
6   ibid, p.48
7   The Committee further divided agriculture into farm labour, market gardening and fruit growing, seed raising, agricultural machinery making and repairs and agricultural

education and organisation; forestry – cutting, hauling and preparing timber; food supply – flour milling, sugar refining, and margarine production; shipping – merchant navy, shipbuilding and repairing; transport – railways and canals, docks and wharves; and Public Utility Services – sanitary services, local authorities, fire brigade, civil hospitals, workhouses, infirmaries and asylums.

8 NA WO 123/59
9 ibid WO 107/37 Report on Labour Appendix C
10 ibid WO 293/6 ACI 2090 – 6 Nov 1916
11 *Military Statistics 1914–1920*, p.226
12 The Case of Glen Herbert Hayler on http://www.creative-science.org.uk/glen.html
13 Arthur, M., *Forgotten Voices of the Great War*, p.173
14 The use of 'Field Punishment No. 1' was abandoned a few months later following publicity in Britain about its use on conscientious objectors in France.
15 Privates Howard Marten, Harry Scullard, Jack Foister and John Ring.
16 Arthur, pp.173–174
17 Boulton, p.174
18 Hansard 29 June 1916 vol 83 cc1013-8
19 NA CAB 37/147/35
20 Rae, p.163
21 NA WO 363/B2188
22 ibid WO 363/C76
23 Despite Asquith's assurance given in June 1916 at least ten objectors were taken to France between March and December 1917. Although it appears that, like Catherall, these men were not members of the NCC.
24 Boulton, p.175, states he was in British prison in February 1918 whereas his service record shows he was in France until June.
25 NA WO 363/C728
26 ibid WO 32/5472
27 Boulton, p.249
28 NA WO 32/5490
29 ibid
30 The COIB shows him as P. Dunbery.

MIDDLESEX ALIEN COMPANIES

Creation

The decision in June 1916 to form units from aliens of enemy parentage led to the formation of the 30th Battalion Middlesex Regiment.[1] Its officers and NCOs came from men serving in Northern, Western and Southern Commands. Originally located at Balmer Camp, Falmer, Sussex the Battalion moved to Pease Pottage Camp, Crawley, Sussex in August. When enlistments and transfers meant the 30th Battalion was above establishment, a second battalion, the 31st Middlesex, was formed at Mill Hill in September.

The decision to restrict those of alien parentage was a Government rather than an Army decision.[2] It met with opposition from a number of commanding officers who were unhappy at losing experienced men who had proved their loyalty to the Crown, many of whom had been wounded or awarded gallantry medals. As a result, on 18 August 1916 ACI 1613 enabled men whose parents were enemy aliens, had been brought up in Britain since infancy and who were 'considered by the Army Council to be entirely loyal to this country' to be considered for service in any regiment. Recruiting officers and commanding officers were informed that if it was not considered desirable to send a man to the Middlesex Regiment then the case was to be referred to the War Office.[3] As a result a number of men, like Sergeant Hermann Arlt, who had enlisted as a Territorial in the Norfolk Yeomanry in June 1909, were retained in their original units.[4]

Home Service

Initially, the two Middlesex battalions were used in Britain although no existing documents have been found outlining the work they undertook.

Early in 1917 the Army decided to send Alien Companies to France. This decision was raised in the House of Commons on the very day the first company left Britain. Philip Snowden MP asked the Under-Secretary of State for War:

> If the 30th Middlesex Regiment is an Infantry works battalion used for Home labour and is composed solely of men of enemy alien origin and naturalised enemy aliens; if these men were promised by the tribunals and the military authorities that they would be used for home labour only; if, in spite of these promises, these men have now been warned that they are to be sent for labour service in France; and, if so, will this instruction be revoked?[5]

The Under-Secretary's response was that the 'battalion is composed of men of enemy alien origin and of naturalised British subjects of enemy alien parentage and is employed on labour at home. Nothing is known of a promise that it should not be employed for labour in France'.[6]

The Liberal MP Joseph King raised the matter again on 21 March. He said that Lord Kitchener had enlisted the Battalion and given them a verbal assurance that they would not be sent abroad and that the Director of Recruiting had given a similar verbal assurance to the mother of one of the men in the Battalion. He described the Battalion as consisting

> ... very largely of men who think in German more than in English, and I am told that their conversation is largely carried on in German. They all have German names, they sing together German songs, and though I believe they are loyal subjects of the King and of our cause, undoubtedly they have strong German associations.[7]

He went on to say that they had been asked to volunteer for service overseas and that despite very few volunteering, a company of 500 had been sent to France. On arrival they had been issued with steel helmets and sent within a short distance of the front line. Something he saw as

> ... a double breach of the pledge, and very cruel and undesirable. Undoubtedly, according to German law, many of these men are still German subjects, and if they

were taken prisoners, as they might well be, there would be very little prospect for them of anything else but being shot after a court-martial.[8]

In replying to the MP, the Under-Secretary of State for War pointed out that the Battalion was formed several days after Kitchener had been drowned, saying: 'I am told, on the very best authority, that Lord Kitchener never gave any such pledge before his death.'[9] Unable to guarantee that other companies would not be sent to France he did confirm that they would not be sent into the fighting line but used for labour work behind the lines.

The two battalions remained in Britain to act as a receiving unit for the companies abroad and providing working parties from men unfit for service overseas and those no longer fit enough to serve in France. No records can be found about their work in Britain. As Home Service Battalions they do not appear to have kept War Diaries and neither the National Archives nor the National Army Museum hold any records of the two battalions.

France

As the men's parents were enemy aliens, there were concerns about sending the companies to France and it was decided that restrictions would be placed on where and how the companies could be employed. They were to be employed north of a line from Abbeville to Amiens. They could not be employed at or near a Base Port, in the Seine-Inferieure, at any location within 16 km of the front line, anywhere they could obtain valuable information or near to PoWs. They were not allowed to handle ammunition, and should ideally be employed in sparsely populated areas.

GHQ preferred the companies to be employed as a single unit. This was sometimes impracticable so the Labour Directorate, mindful of security issues, instructed that Alien personnel must 'never be employed as mess cooks, waiters, barbers, clerks or orderlies, or in officers' clubs or cinemas, or in any position in which they could obtain information useful to the enemy.'[10]

Alien companies were employed on road and rail work, in forests and quarries, at railheads, maintaining aerodromes, salvage, for hutting and in army workshops. General Wace commented they 'proved particularly useful in Hutting and Workshops'.[11] Men from the Alien companies had to obtain a pass to leave their camp and when a unit was moved from one location to another, details of the move had to be sent to Intelligence Branch at the Army Headquarters by the Assistant Director of Labour. Leave to Britain was permitted although the individual soldier had to inform his CO of the address where he would be staying and get his leave warrant stamped at the local police station within 24 hours of arriving.

In general, the concerns about the alien companies appear to have come more from GHQ than from either the Labour Directorate or officers dealing with them. The views of GHQ were expressed in November 1917 when they reminded officers of the restrictions placed on the alien companies: 'The restrictions are necessary as there have been cases where these men have expressed themselves as frankly disloyal and, in any case, as not one of them is purely British not one of them can be trusted.'[12]

When concerns emerged the matter was referred to Intelligence Branch. An example is the letter written by Private Herman Cook, 2 Company, which contained 'many coarse phrases and is evidently pro-German' the matter was referred to intelligence.[13] General Wace, in his Report on Labour, suggests that the number of men in alien companies with German sympathies was 'only about 4 or 5 per cent, and these men were known to their COs'.[14]

Concerns about the loyalty of men in Alien companies were largely unfounded and restrictions on men leaving camp were unofficially relaxed in many cases. Even some restrictions on where they were employed were relaxed in 1918. In September 1918, for example, 6 Company were sent to work in the Australian Corps area on a railway line, which was less than 16 km from the front.

On 7 October 1918 GHQ sent a letter to the War Office stating that the Alien companies were excellent labour and that no cases of sabotage had been notified to them. The letter also stated that the value of the companies was 'hampered by the limitations imposed on employment and it is intended to lift some of the restrictions and use the men in shelled areas'.[15] On 1 November GHQ was informed that the Army Council agreed to withdraw the restrictions that had been placed on the Alien companies.

There appear to have been few awards made to members of the Alien companies. In September 1917 recommendations were made for the award of the MC to the CO of 3 Company, Captain W. L. Renwick and for MSMs to G/35652 CSM F. Wiehl[16], G/31924 CQMS A. Korkhaus and G/45551 Cpl A. King.[17] The award of the MC to Captain Renwick was confirmed[18] and Corporal King was Mentioned in Despatches[19] but neither CSM Wiehl or CQMS Korkhaus appear to have been recognised.[20] In May 1918 MSMs were awarded to G/35438 Pte J. Malzer and G/31344 Pte J. Kriehn, both of 1 Company.[21]

1 NA WO 293/4 ACI 1209 Disposal of recruits of Enemy Alien Parentage
2 Messenger, C., *Call to Arms,* p.500
3 NA WO 293/6 ACI 1613 Aliens questions concerning 18 August 1916
4 Hermann Arlt served with the 2/1st Norfolk Yeomanry in Britain from 5 August 1914 until 1917 when he was transferred to the 6th Northamptonshire Regiment. Arriving in France on 13 April 1918 he was wounded fourteen days later and evacuated to Britain where he spent over four months in hospital. He was discharged on 26 February 1919.
5 Hansard, 5 March 1917
6 ibid, 5 March 1917
7 ibid, 21 March 1917
8 ibid
9 ibid
10 NA WO 107/37 Appendix C 'Notes for Guidance of Officers of the Labour Corps in France p.48
11 ibid WO 107/37 Report on Labour, p.66
12 ibid WO 95/36
13 ibid WO 95/430
14 ibid WO 107/37 p.66

15 ibid WO 95/83

16 Frederick Wiehl was born in Sunderland in 1891 of German parents. By December 1913 he was a policeman in Durham. He enlisted in the 28th Northumberland Fusiliers in July 1915. By the time the Alien companies were formed he had been promoted to Corporal. He arrived in France with the 3rd Alien Company on 14 March 1917 and was CSM in January 1918. Frederick Wiehl served with the Alien Company until demobilised in February 1919.

17 NA WO 95/358

18 *London Gazette,* 1 January 1918, p.44

19 ibid, 21 December 1917, p.1368

20 There is a photograph of the 3rd Alien Company on page 12 of the picture section that includes Captain Renwick and CSM Wiehl, who is seated on the front row holding the dog.

21 *London Gazette,* 6 Aug 1918, p.9256

MALTESE LABOUR CORPS

During the First World War approximately 20 per cent of the male population of Malta, some 15,000 men, served as part of the war effort. According to one source over 7,000 of them served in the Maltese Labour Corps although the Medal Rolls show the smaller figure of 5,621.[1] The Commonwealth War Graves Commission (CWGC) records show 128 died in service but this figure does not include the unknown number of men who died in Malta as a result of illness contracted whilst on active service in Gallipoli, Salonika, Italy and Turkey.

As with so many labour units the vital work of the Maltese Labour Corps is not recognised. The Official History of operations in Macedonia states only that in January 1918 there were some 2,000 Maltese employed on the lines of communication. A contemporary view gives a false impression of the Maltese Labour Corps; it failed to recognise the dangers and hardships these men faced: 'Almost from the very beginning Maltese labour battalions were doing splendid work. Gallipoli and Salonika knew well the lilting music of the swarthy gangs of broad-shouldered men who sang as tirelessly as they worked.'[2]

Gallipoli

According to the *Daily Malta Chronicle* of 2 September 1915 the initial call for men to serve as stevedores in Gallipoli quickly met its target.

It is generally known, although nothing has appeared in print, that a few days ago, there was a call in Malta for volunteers to serve as stevedores in the Gallipoli Peninsula. The result was most satisfactory, over 1,000 volunteers presenting themselves in less than a week. 864 were chosen, and they have now left in charge of Major J.V. Aspinall and Lieut J. L. Muscat, of the KOMRM.[3] The men are receiving an average pay of half a crown a day, besides rations, and a separate allowance of sixpence in favour of the wife, and a penny for every child.[4]

Emmanuel Attard, a 16-year-old from Gozo, was one of the men to answer this call and served in Gallipoli for five months. He later recalled that his widowed mother received a pension of half a crown a month, making the pay of the labourers excellent by Maltese standards. The men enlisted for a period of three months and many saw this as an opportunity to earn a substantial sum of money in a short period of time.

The men, having been told that they were to be located behind the troops, sailed from Malta to the Greek island of Mudros. During the trip there was rumour that they were going to be in the war zone and this caused some discontent among the men. On arrival in Mudros some 234 men, under the command of Captain Stivala, volunteered to serve in Gallipoli and sailed on 27 September together with Australian reinforcements for ANZAC.

> The ship was anchored close to a small jetty which the military engineers had built after they landed. When we got to our destination, our job was to unload barges from Egypt. Our first job was to erect two marquees. We had to erect them close to the hill for protection. We were ready to start work. We formed three gangs. Each gang worked on eight-hour shifts. All the days became alike, there was no Sunday or holidays, the only change was when the Turks sent a few shells over, but they either hit the top of the hill or landed in the water near the beach.[5]

Whilst there are no surviving records as to how the men in Mudros and Gallipoli were organised it appears that they worked in companies under the direction of a Maltese officer. Attard recalls that towards the end of the three month contract the men were asked to stay for a further three months and 'All of us agreed.'[6] The *Daily Malta Chronicle* reported on 29 November 1915 that 213 men out of the original 864 had returned to Malta early that month although it appears that many of them re-engaged for a further three months:

> We may say at once that the majority of them have only come to enjoy a short rest and to recoup previously to re-engaging and returning to the area of hostilities in which some 80 of them were wounded with shrapnel but quickly recovered and resumed work.[7]

With the approach of winter the Maltese were located with the British labour units on the northern side of Ari Burnu. Whilst here both shrapnel and machine-gun fire inflicted wounds on the men. One, 27-year-old Labourer Giuseppe Camilleri, was killed on 7 December 1915 and lies buried in Ari Burnu Cemetery, Anzac. It is likely that other men died as a result of injury or illness resulting from their service at Gallipoli.

The Medal Rolls indicate that a total of 1,088 men received the Bronze War Medal and the Victory Medal for service in Gallipoli.[8] The majority of the original contingent served from 1 September 1915 until 17 February 1916. Captain Alfred J. Gatt, Royal Malta Artillery, was awarded the Military Cross for his service with the Maltese Labour Corps at Gallipoli and six other officers were Mentioned in Despatches.[9]

On 13 November 1915 Lord Kitchener inspected the Corps at Gallipoli during his tour of the area. He congratulated them on their physique and thanked them for the valuable services they were rendering. In early December the Cabinet made the decision to evacuate the men from Gallipoli. Among the first to leave were the Maltese and Egyptian Labour Corps on 11 December.

The last of the Maltese Labour Corps who had served at Mudros and at Gallipoli, returned to Malta on 17 February 1916 where they were met by the Governor General and thanked for their service. Their work was also recognised by the C-in-C Mediterranean Forces in a letter sent to the Governor General, dated 23 January 1916:

> I have the honour to inform you that the need for the services of the Maltese Labour Battalion has now come to an end, and arrangements are being made for the Battalion to be sent back to Malta for disbanding.
>
> I wish to take this opportunity of expressing to you my personal thanks for the great trouble you took in raising this Battalion.
>
> I have much pleasure in informing you that the Battalion performed most excellent work, both at Anzac and elsewhere, and I shall be grateful if you will be good enough to express to the Commanding Officer, and through him to the NCOs and men of the Battalion, my high appreciation of the services they have rendered.[10]

Emmanuel Attard, like other members of the Corps, was discharged and paid the sum of twenty sovereigns, but in his words, 'After a few days idle, doing nothing, I got sick of it and decided to go to France'.[11] Arriving in Marseilles he initially worked with other Maltese at the docks but within a short time left for Australia where he joined the Army and returned to France as an Australian soldier.

Salonika

In August 1916 a call went out again for men to serve in the Maltese Labour Corps, this time in Salonika.

The 1st Maltese Labour Battalion, made up of 502 labourers, a dispenser, 6 hospital orderlies and 307 stevedores under the command of officers of the KOMRM, arrived in Salonika on 26 September 1916. A month later a further 216 men arrived from Malta, taking their strength to just over 900. The battalion suffered its first casualty on 2 November when Second Lieutenant E. Huber was killed in a traffic accident.

Labourers were recruited on a six month contract with a three month re-engagement option and the first group appear to have been repatriated at the end of nine months, in July 1917. Although the Battalion kept a War Diary it is only a record of the numbers arriving to join and those repatriated from the Battalion and records that the strength remained just under 1,000.[12] There are no details of the tasks undertaken by the Battalion. The Battalion's HQ was at the Ordnance Depot in Salonika. Detachments, ranging in size from 25 to 75 men, commanded by an officer, were sent to various locations on the Lines of Communications and Salonika docks.

By October 1917 the demand for labour resulted in the formation of a second battalion. In four days, from 13 October, some 750 labourers and farmers were recruited, mainly from Gozo. They were due to leave Malta on 20 October but a lack of transport meant they had to be sent home until 3 December. Whilst awaiting transport the Governor General agreed that the men should be paid at the rate of 6d a day rather than the half a crown a day they were to receive in Salonika. The 2nd Maltese Labour Battalion, now 1,000 strong, finally arrived in Salonika on 10 December 1917 and established their HQ at Janes about 40 km north-west of Salonika. Like the 1st Battalion they sent detachments to work throughout Salonika.

In March 1918 a detachment of 250 men was attached to 273 Company RE to work on the light railway at Stavros. The RE acknowledged the success of their work:

> The Director of railways directs me to convey to all officers and other ranks employed on the Stavros Line his appreciation of the celerity with which the work has been carried out. The Commander in Chief is very pleased with progress made.
> P. G. Douglas Major RE[13]

The decision to recruit farmers from Gozo appears to have been made with the intention of using their skills in Salonika. A detachment of the Battalion was employed unloading and stacking hay at Salmanli Hay Dump during April 1918 and others would have been used on the farms established in the area to provide food for the troops. The Diary records the men were used to load and unload stores for the RE, and for anti-malarial duties. Most entries are little more than details of the size of detachments and their location. Although initially paid at the same rate as other Maltese Labour Battalions, 2s 6d a day, this was increased to 3s a day during 1917.

An Employment Company was formed to support the Maltese Labour Battalions and British units on the LoC. On 9 February 1918, 14 cooks, 42 waiters and 63 servants were enrolled in Malta for a one year engagement. A week later these 119 men together with a CSM, 3 sergeants and 2 corporals left Malta under the command of Captain C. Brickdroff. On arrival in Salonika on 23 February the Company was located at the Labour Corps Base Depot that was situated on the Seres Road some 6½ km from Salonika. By 4 March, 66 men from the employment company had been tasked throughout the Salonika area and on 10 March the Company was brought up to full strength with the arrival of another officer, 3 NCOs, 18 waiters and 100 servants.

A second Employment Company served in Salonika.[14] One source says that they joined the Maltese labour battalions in Salonika in February 1918, the same time as the first Employment Company. 'Two Maltese Employment Companies of 325 men, including cooks, waiters and servants, joined them in February 1918.'[15] Another source dates the arrival of the second Employment Company as seven months later. 'Two Employment Companies left Malta (the first in February and the other in September 1918).'[16]

There are also contradictory references to the number of men that served in the Employment Companies. A War Office document written by Lieutenant Colonel Robert Wetherall in 1918 says the strength of the Maltese Employment Company was 419.[17] The Medal Rolls only show 267 names as members of the Maltese Employment Companies. This difference could be explained by the fact that some men were transferred to the employment companies from the Maltese labour battalions. CWGC records show that two men from the 2nd Employment Company are buried in Kirechkoi-Hortakoi Cemetery, 15 km north-east of Salonika.

64 men of the two battalions and the employment companies died whilst serving in Salonika and are buried in the region. They range in age from 17-year-old

Labourer E. Cassar who died of malaria on 15 September 1918, to 67-year-old Labourer A. Demetri who died on 19 December 1918.

A local labour company appears to have served on Malta although no records of this service can be found.[18]

Italy

From the summer of 1917 Taranto in Italy was a major depot on the Mediterranean LoC. It was a link between the fronts at Salonika and Egypt through Turin, Lyons and Le Mans to Cherbourg. In September 1917 there were 19,000 British and 5,000 native labour troops at Taranto but by December the base commandant was complaining that unless more labour was supplied construction would be severely restricted.[19] In addition to labour from the West Indies, Egypt, India and Italy, a detachment from the 1st and 2nd Maltese Labour Battalions was sent to Taranto in the spring of 1918. Records show that 23 Maltese labourers died between 25 July 1918 and 4 April 1919 and are buried in Taranto Town Cemetery Extension.

A mining company of the Maltese Labour Corps, about 110 strong, was involved in tunnelling work in the north of Italy.[20] The men were engaged on the same terms as the Maltese Labour Company, with the exception of skilled personnel who were paid 3s 6d a day.[21] Two members of the Company, Antonio Micallef and Giovanni Micallef, died of disease in November 1918 whilst serving with the Company and are buried in Montecchio Precalcino Communal Cemetery Extension.[22]

Turkey

The records of the CWGC indicate that a Maltese Labour Corps employment company was used to support the British troops stationed in Turkey after the war ended. Although there is no record of exactly where they served, the CWGC records show that two soldiers died, Private Grech on 31 October 1919, and Private Muscat on 31 July 1920. They are buried in Haidar Pasha Cemetery, Istanbul. It is known that a Maltese Employment Company served with the Army of the Black Sea. Labourer Buttigieg, died 31 May 1920, is commemorated on the Haidar Pasha Memorial, Istanbul.[23]

1 Lucas, Sir Charles, *The Empire at War* Vol V, p.11
2 *Times History of the War* ,Vol XVI, p.104
3 KOMRM – King's Own Malta Regiment of Militia
4 Quoted in Mizza, J., *Gallipoli The Malta Connection,* p.105
5 Caruana, M. and York, B., *Emmanuel Attard,* p.12
6 ibid, p.12
7 *Daily Malta Chronicle* quoted in Mizza, J., *Gallipoli The Malta Connection,* p.121
8 NA WO 329/2359
9 Major J.V. Aspinall, Captain F. Stivala, Second Lieutenants L. Samat and H. Curmi and Lieutenants J. Adair and G. Dandria.
10 *Daily Malta Chronicle* quoted in Mizza, J., *Gallipoli The Malta Connection,* p.122
11 Caruana, M. and York, B., p.13

12 NA WO 95/4944

13 ibid

14 Lucas, Sir Charles, *The Empire at War* Vol V, p.11

15 Mizzi, J., *Gallipoli The Malta Connection,* p.99

16 Zarb-Dimech, A., *Malta During the First World War,* p.109

17 NA WO 162/6

18 Lucas, p.11

19 NA WO 95/4255 7 December 1917.

20 The Medal Roll (NA WO 329) lists 112 names

21 Report on the Account of Army Expenditure for 1917–1918 p. 14

22 Montecchio Precalcino is a town in northern Italy, 17 km north of Vincenza

23 Commemoration on Haidar Pasha Memorial indicates that either Labourer Buttigieg
   has no known grave or is buried in a cemetery in South Russia and Transcaucasia
   whose graves can longer be maintained by the CWGC.

BERMUDA ROYAL GARRISON ARTILLERY

In 1895 enlistment started for the Bermuda Militia Artillery, a reserve force manned by the Island's black population under the command of white officers. Initially intended to be part of the Island's coastal defence force their role was to man 6" guns with a range of 6.25 miles.[1] At the outbreak of war the men were mobilized, but as part-time soldiers since there was also a need to maintain the Island's economy. Their military role, in addition to manning the guns, included construction of the Island's defences and other military employment at the wharfs in Saint Georges.

Towards the end of 1915 the authorities in Bermuda decided to raise a contingent of 3 officers and 196 men to serve in Europe. On 10 January 1916 the contingent, under the command of Major Thomas Melville Dill, began training at St David's. On 31 May they left Bermuda for France, arriving towards the end of June. They were attached to the Royal Garrison Artillery and known as the Bermuda RGA.

Employed on the Somme from June until December 1916 their role was primarily to work at the ammunition dumps to supply the heavy field guns and howitzers. They quickly earned themselves a reputation as good workers and a War Office letter of 6 August reported favourably on their role as an Ammunition Supply Company with the Heavy Siege Artillery. In view of the work of the Bermuda RGA the War Office suggested that two battalions of the British West Indies Regiment (BWIR) could be used in a similar role to replace British Artillery men.[2]

The first winter in Europe was difficult for the men, with several cases of trench foot and pneumonia, one of which resulted in the death of Gunner Rudolph George Wears. On 1 January 1917 the Bermuda RGA were moved to Bassins de Radoub south-east of Marseilles as replacements for 22 Company ASC. Once again they proved to be efficient workers and were rated by the DADL at Marseilles, on 6 February 1917, as good as ASC labour. In terms of efficiency they moved 4.92 tons per man in an eight-hour day compared to the BWIR's rate of only 1.12 tons per man.[3]

Although, as black soldiers, the Army would not use them in a fighting role they were prepared to use them to supervise other coloured workers. When 71 and 72 companies Egyptian Labour Corps arrived in Marseilles in March 1917, 20 members of the Bermuda RGA were attached to them as supervisors.

In April 1917 the Bermuda RGA moved north and were attached to the Canadian Corps at Vimy Ridge. They were stationed at Neuville St. Vaast where they stayed until 25 May. Their support for the Corps during the attack at Vimy was recorded in the 1st Army's Report on the Vimy Ridge Operation: 'The men of the Bermuda RGA, being accustomed to handle shells, made excellent working parties at Ammunition Railheads and Dumps.'[4]

The work at Vimy was also recognised by Field Marshal Haig in his report on the work of the Bermudans:

> They were employed on Heavy Ammunition Dumps, and great satisfaction was expressed with their work. Though called upon to perform labour of the most arduous and exacting nature at all times of the day and night, they were not only willing and efficient but also conspicuous for their cheeriness under all conditions. On more than one occasion the dumps at which they were employed were ignited by hostile shellfire and much of their work was done under shellfire. Their behaviour on all these occasions was excellent, and commanded the admiration of those with whom they were serving.[5]

The report did, however, raise a question about the employment of men from tropical countries in northern France:

> Neither the Bermuda RGA or the men of the West India Regiment were of much use in the cold weather experienced early in the year. The cold and wet seemed to numb their senses, and they became miserable and inert. Under these conditions they were unable to stand life in huts and tents, and it was found necessary to withdraw them to the rear areas and to billet them. The same remarks apply to all men from tropical climates.[6]

The Bermuda RGA took part in the attack on Messines Ridge on 7 June 1917 where they suffered several casualties due to wounds and gas. On 24 June they moved to the Ypres Salient where they were to remain until 16 January 1918, during which time several men were wounded and three died of their wounds.[7] Two members of the contingent, gunners Manders and Knight, were awarded Military Medals for their bravery during their time in the salient.

During June the contingent had been enlarged to some 240 men with the arrival of another small contingent from Bermuda.[8] During most of their time in the Salient Major Dill was able to command all 240 men as one unit. This was a rarity for the contingent, as during most of their time in France they tended to be used in small detachments. Consideration was given in September to them being moved south for the winter and GHQ recorded that: 'Bermuda RGA and BWI should be transferred to Mediterranean Command since they cannot be employed in Northern France during the winter.'[9] In the case of the Bermuda RGA this did not happen, although they were moved to Normandy for a rest in January 1918 before being sent back to the Front, seeing service at Lys, Steenworde, Bailleul and Menin. At the end of the war the contingent was sent to Hazebrouck and then Rouen before finally moving to Marseilles on 19 December 1918.

Throughout their time in France they gained a good reputation for their work and behaviour. Although working behind the trenches, like so many other labour units, they were frequently within view of the German observers and guns. They faced small arms, artillery and aerial bombardment for much of their time in France as well as illness and disease. Ten members of the Bermuda RGA never returned to their homeland, but lie buried in military cemeteries in France.

The positive comments about the work of the Bermuda RGA disguise the reality that, as the only coloured artillery unit in the British Army, they were treated in the same way as other coloured labour units, as second class men. The official report on the work of labour with the BEF has only one reference to these soldiers:

> Detachments of the Bermuda R.G.A. and 4 Battalions of the B.W.I. Regiment came out about the same time. They were nominally fighting troops but were employed in the handling of ammunition.[10]

The unit was awarded an MC, 3 MM and 1 MSM. The MC was awarded to Lt Lewis Wrigg, the citation stating:

> He was in command of a detachment working at Kruisecke forward ammunition dump, on the Ypres-Menin road on October 13th and 14th 1918, the spot being increasingly shelled by the enemy. By his disregard of his own safety and his good judgment and coolness he set a splendid example to his men, who remained at work offloading ammunition from light railway trucks and forwarding the same to near-by batteries.[11]

On 6 October 1918 Major Dill left France to return to Bermuda on leave. Arriving in December he was met at the dock by local dignitaries and well-wishers. They apologised that a Guard of Honour had not met him owing to the 'breaking up of the Bermuda Militia Artillery'. When the Bermuda Contingent RGA returned to Bermuda in July 1919 they were met by an enthusiastic crowd and accorded an honour guard made up of regular soldiers stationed on the island. Thirty of the men decided to temporarily re-enlist in the RGA for another year and the rest demobilized.

1 By 1914 battleships with a firing range of up to 16 miles meant that a ship safely firing from well out of their range could easily outgun the coastal defences.
2 NA WO 95/31
3 ibid WO 95/4040
4 ibid WO 95/184
5 Harris, Dr E., *Great War, 1914-18: Missing in action or in the archives.* A copy of the article can be found at http://www.aiipowmia.com/inter26/in071206wwi.html
6 NA WO 95/184
7 The contingent was stationed at St Jean from 22 October until 16 January unloading at Manners Junction.
8 On 6 May 1917 the second contingent of 60 men under the command of Lt Wrigg RGA left Bermuda for France.
9 NA WO 95/83

10 ibid WO 107/37 Report on Labour p.1
11 *London Gazette* 29 July page 9788

CAPE COLOURED LABOUR BATTALION

The idea of using coloured South African labour in France was first raised in early 1916 and discussions held with both the South African Government and the French allies. On 5 May the C-in-C reported that the French had no objections to such a scheme as long as the men were enlisted in labour battalions and were subject to military discipline.[1] Within the Army there were, however, mixed feelings about such a concept.

Two days later the IGC wrote to the QMG that he was aware of problems with employing 'that type' of labour as a result of his experiences in the Bechuanaland Expedition of 1884.[2] He was concerned at the Cape Boys' propensity to drink, the likelihood of trouble with French women and the probability of the Cape Boys demanding higher pay than British enlisted labour. He argued that if the idea were put into practice it would 'make it extremely difficult to carry on the work of the L of C,'[3] and he asked that his remarks 'may receive serious consideration before it is too late'.[4] The C-in-C responded on 11 May informing the IGC that, whilst he understood his concerns, the scarcity of labour meant that he could not refuse the offer of South African labour.

In July 1916 Louis Botha, the South African Prime Minister, agreed to the recruitment of a Cape Coloured Labour Battalion (CCL) for service in France.[5] The 1,000-strong battalion of enlisted soldiers, commanded by white South African officers who spoke the natives' language, was to serve in France under Imperial rather than South African command. Botha's decision to place the Battalion under Imperial command meant that expenses incurred running the Battalion would not have to be funded by South Africa, but by the British Government. More importantly it meant that Botha did not have to seek approval for the Battalion from the South African Parliament, as he knew that he would face opposition not only from the opposition but also many in his own party.[6]

The CCL Battalion, known as Cape Boys, was quickly recruited and by 12 August was ready to leave South Africa on the *Kenilworth Castle*.[7] The War Office took the decision that they should sail directly to Havre and not transit through England, claiming that this was due to there being no depot for them in England. Under the command of Lieutenant Colonel Van der Byl the Battalion arrived in France on 1 September 1916 and was employed at Rouen handling ammunition at Quevilly Wharf. They 'were handy, quick and intelligent and rapidly attained a very high pitch of efficiency at this work'.[8] The Battalion was made up of four companies, each of some 250 men, with Lieutenant Colonel Van der Bly assuming the role of advisor on Cape Boys Labour in addition to controlling the promotion of and overseeing the welfare of the men.

The Battalion had to be moved from Quevilly Wharf when the South African Native Labour Corps (SANLC) came to France. As enlisted soldiers the Cape Boys were not segregated and were allowed the same level of freedom as British soldiers in Rouen. The SANLC, however, were restricted to their compounds when not working. It was the fear that they would not be able to maintain discipline that caused the Army to move the Cape Boys to Cherbourg in June 1917, placing it under the control of the Mediterranean lines of communications.[9] The French authorities also expressed concern about the employment of South African natives in France. They sent the British a letter on 3 August 1917 informing them that coloured soldiers were to be banned from cafes, and another on the 19 November stressing the importance of ensuring native labourers employed by them did not come into contact with those working for the French.

A further 600 recruits arrived from South Africa during 1917 and in December 1917 the Battalion was taken on the strength of the Labour Directorate although they remained at Cherbourg.

The decision was taken in May 1918 for the Battalion to be formed into three companies, each of about 500 men, along the same lines as other labour companies. A major or captain commanded each company and was supported by four subalterns, a CSM, a CQMS and a medical officer, all white South Africans. In addition, each company had 26 black NCOs (8 sergeants and 18 corporals), 2 medical orderlies, 3 batmen and 6 drivers. The Battalion earned a reputation for its efficient handling of ammunition and so on 2 May 1918, when pressure on the Mediterranean Lines of Communications had eased, one company was moved to the 2nd Army at Ebblinghem specifically to move ordnance. A second company joined them later in the month and, although some platoons were later to return to Cherbourg, the Battalion maintained its work in the 2nd Army area until 16 November. On 19 June 1918 half a company was sent to Bayonne to load timber for the Forestry Directorate, where they appear to have remained until the end of the war.

Unlike the SANLC which had to be repatriated at the end of their contract, the Cape Boys, as enlisted soldiers, could be retained in service when the conflict ended. The 1st Company remained in the 5th Army Area. On 28 January 1919 the 2nd Company were sent to Dorignies in the 1st Army Area where they remained until 5 July and the 3rd Company to the 3rd Army Area. All three were involved in general salvage work and at the Animal Collecting Stations and Horse Staging Camps in order to facilitate the work of horse demobilisation. In the words of General Wace, 'Their special aptitude with animals proved of the greatest value in this work.'[10] In the late spring of 1919 Prime Minister Botha insisted that the men of the CCL Battalion be repatriated. The War Office ordered the repatriation on the 15 June 1919, and the following month the men left France.

The Medal Rolls held at the National Archives, Kew, shows 1,906 men served in France in the CCL Battalion although medals were only awarded to 1,267 men.[11] The South African Government decided that black men from South Africa would not be awarded medals. As far as can be ascertained only ten men in the Battalion were awarded either the MSM or Mentioned in Dispatches and, with one exception, they were all white officers or NCOs.[12] The only other award appears to be that of the *Croix De Guerre* to CSM Malcolm Leitch.

The Commonwealth War Graves Commission records show 29 men are buried in France and Belgium, four in South Africa and one on Ascension Island. One member of the Battalion, Private M. Abrams, who died on 16 April 1918, is commemorated on the Hollybrook Memorial, Southampton.[13] One of the Battalion's Officers, Lieutenant D. M. Tyndall, died on 18 June 1918 after a train hit the lorry in which he was travelling. The Medal Rolls also show the names of five men who died whilst serving with the Cape Boys but who do not appear to be in the CWGC records.[14] One of these, Private Johannes, is shown as having been murdered in France although no reference to this can be found in any of the War Diaries.

Three members of the Battalion were tried and executed for murder during 1919. On 12 May 1919 a French engine stoker, named Bekaert, found the body of Private Devries of the 1st Company CCL floating in the River Lys at Coutrai. The victim had his hands tied behind his back, a large stone had been attached to his body with telephone wire and he had head wounds, having been hit with a hammer. At the trials of two other members of the Company, Private P. Harris[15] and Private A. Davids,[16] evidence was given that Private Devries was killed because of an argument he had with Private Harris over a French girl, Anna Top. The two accused gave contradictory evidence, with Private Harris claiming that he had refused to hit Devries although he admitted helping to tie him up and roll him into the river. Private Davids claimed that it was Harris who had hit Devries. Both men were found guilty and executed at 05.35 hours on 26 August 1919. The medical officer present at the execution, Captain L. Gameson, recorded the event in his diary in which he describes being told that he could give the two men a heavy dose of morphine 'but the prisoners must be capable of walking with assistance and can on no account be carried'.[17] Captain Gameson was clearly badly affected by his role, which he described as the worst of the 'many distasteful professional duties, which have inevitably come my way'. He describes how he had to pin envelopes to the men's shirts: 'The envelopes were the targets. To do this while meeting these men's eyes looking into my eyes was humiliating and shocking.'[18]

Another Cape Boy to be executed was Private Freddie Alberts, a 19-year-old from Cape Town, whose real name was Boos. At the Field General Court Martial, held on 1 October 1919, Private Alberts was charged with five counts of murder. The first two counts related to the deaths of Madame Demassiet and her son Omer, shot dead at their home on 15 June 1919 during a robbery.

As part of the prosecution a statement made by Private Alberts to the Military Police on 26 July was presented to the court. In this Private Alberts said that on the day he had been out with a Private Stevens who had suggested they do a robbery. He admitted his part in the robbery, even to the extent of throwing Madame Demassiet to the ground, and that he had received about 1,000 Francs as his share of the proceeds, but said it was Private Stevens who had shot the woman and her son. The statement makes interesting reading as the language seems inappropriate for a man who said he could not write, but made a mark and thumb print at the end of the statement. At one point, for example, the statement reads: 'I followed the woman, and when I saw where she kept the money, and the amount she had in the box I signalled to Stevens, in a manner we had previously arranged between us'.[19]

The other three counts of murder relate to the deaths on 22 June of Monsieur and Madame Decaestaker and Private Stevens. The court heard from a Private de Beer who placed Private Alberts close to the farm where Decaestaker had been shot, and where Private Stevens' body was found. The court was also presented with two further statements given by Private Albert to the Military Police on the 26 and 28 June. Once again there is doubt that these are a true representation of what was said by Pte Alberts: 'Proceeding together to the farm of Decaestaker, we entered and ordered coffee ... I then went to Hazebrouck, but finding there was no train, I passed the night in that town.'[20]

In the statement of 26 June Private Alberts said that they had both been in the farmhouse, Private Stevens shot the couple, they had later quarrelled about the money and he had shot Stevens. In a second statement he said that he had been outside the farmhouse, heard shots and ran into the farmyard. He claimed that Private Stevens came out of the farmhouse and tried to shoot him but the gun was empty. Private Alberts admitted he had taken the gun and loaded it and when Stevens tried to stab him with a dagger he had shot him. Following this he went into the farmhouse, found the two dead bodies and saw a tin box on the table but it only contained letters so he went outside and searched Private Stevens, finding about 2,000 Francs, which he took.

Private Alberts gave no evidence at the court martial and called no witnesses to support him. His counsel said that he did not admit to the confessions and in miti-gation, that Private Alberts had killed Stevens in self-defence. Private Alberts was found not guilty on the charges of murdering Madame Demassiet and her son but guilty of the murder of Monsieur and Madame Decaestaker and of Private Stevens, and was sentenced to death. The death sentence was confirmed on 10 October and he was executed at Lille at 05.53 hours on 15 October 1919.[21]

Once again Captain Gameson was the medical officer present at the execution and his diary records how, not only did the firing squad fail in their allotted task, but how he came close to being shot himself:

> The squad's aiming had been bad. I dashed in immediately after the volley and at once told the sergeant on the opposite side of the moribund victim that the man still lived. With a revolver, he shot the man through the skull at its side's thinnest part. I repeat that I stood on the opposite flank of the victim. The sergeant fired before I had any chance to remove myself. The bullet went clean through and buzzed by my head. It was a messy, disturbing business. I told the sergeant it was much to his credit that he was so rattled by our sordid work as to be irresponsibly careless; perhaps the firing squad had been rattled. I kept the blindfolding bandage. In it were two bullet holes – not made by the revolver bullet. This was pretty wild shooting of presumably selected men. My target over the victim's heart had been plain to see at the prescribed short range.[22]

The bodies of these three executed soldiers now lie in graves in Y Farm Military Cemetery, Bois-Grenier France.

1 NA WO 95/3968
2 ibid
3 ibid
4 ibid
5 Clothier, N., *Black Valour*, p.11
6 Later, in September 1916, Botha was to use the South African Parliamentary recess in order to ensure the creation of the South African Native Labour Corps was undertaken without opposition.
7 NA WO 95/3968
8 ibid WO 107/37 Report on Labour p.18
9 Cherboug was the terminal point for the Mediterranean Lines of Communication.
10 NA WO 107/37 Report on Labour p.18

11 ibid WO 329/2346
12 Private E. Damaras appears to be the only other rank to have been Mentioned in Dispatches.
13 The CWGC have incorrectly shown Private Abrams as serving in the South African Native Labour Corps.
14 Three men, Privates Franke, Garrett, and Smith are shown as having died in France, Private Petersen as having died at sea and Private Johannes as having been murdered in France. To date no records of their death have been found.
15 NA WO 71/684
16 ibid WO 71/685
17 Diary of Captain L. Gameson quoted in Putkowski, J. and Sykes, J. *Shot at Dawn* p.267
18 ibid
19 NA WO 71/686
20 ibid
21 Putkowski and Sykes in their seminal work on executions, *Shot At Dawn*, attribute the death of Private Devries to Private Alberts and the murder of the French women to Privates Harris and Davids. This presumably arose from the information shown in the Battalion's Medal Roll as the authors did not have access to First World War capital trial documents which were not open to the public at the time.
22 Diary of Captain L. Gameson, quoted in Putkowski and Sykes, p.268

SOUTH AFRICAN NATIVE LABOUR CORPS

Origins

The idea of a South African Native Labour Corps (SANLC) to serve in France is credited to Josiah Wedgwood MP who, after service at Gallipoli, was attached in 1915 to the staff of General Smuts in East Africa where he had been impressed with the work of the black labour contingents.[1]

At the beginning of May 1916 the French agreed to the use of a Cape Boys Battalion on the condition that they were enlisted in a labour battalion and subject to military discipline. Having agreement from the French, the South African Government was asked whether they would be able to supply the battalion. Botha, the South African Prime Minister, ensured that they were under Imperial rather than South African command. Not only did this mean the cost of the unit would not fall upon his government but also, more importantly, that he did not have to seek approval from his own parliament.

The use of coloured labour, even when they had been recruited as soldiers like the Cape Coloured Boys, did not find favour with all senior officers. At the beginning of May the IGC expressed the view that using them would cause endless trouble on the lines of communication. The C-in-C responded that due to the scarcity of labour he was not prepared to refuse the offer of coloured battalions.[2]

On 12 June a letter was received at GHQ from the GOC Cape Town stating that the South African Government was prepared to raise 'Labour Battalions of Kaffirs for service in France'.[3] However, three days later the War Office wrote to the Colonial Office saying that they were willing to accept one battalion of the Cape Boys and that the South African Government would be notified of this. The question of raising labour battalions of Kaffirs was not rejected but was to be considered separately.

One source states it was on 7 September 1916 that Botha agreed to a British proposal to recruit black civilian labourers for service in France.[4] However Lieutenant Colonel Barnard, writing in 1918, says:

> In June of that year, suggestions to send Native Labourers from South Africa were put before the War Council, and an agreement was arrived at with the Government of the Union of South Africa whereby five battalions, each two thousand strong, including European Officers and Non-Commissioned Officers, were to be sent to France as an initial experiment. The Prime Minister, (The Right Honourable General Louis Botha P.C.) who also held the Portfolio of Minister of Native Affairs, took a keen interest in the movement, and at once appointed Colonel S.A.M. Pritchard C.M.G. Director of Native Affairs, to the Command of the Corps.[5]

There is no doubt that the decision had been made by August 1916. At a conference in France of senior officers[6] on 12 August General Woodward, Director of Organisation at the War Office, explained that the South African Government would have difficulties in recruiting more men for the Cape Boys and would 'find it easier to raise 10,000 kaffirs. They will be coming over in Battalions 2,000 strong, all under Col Pritchard and a small staff, he is to have the rank of Lt Colonel.'[7]

Although the South African Government agreed to natives being used in France they stipulated that the men should be segregated and housed within a closed compound. The Army agreed to this request but were concerned whether they had sufficient corrugated iron to ensure that the compounds were closed from view.

Recruitment and Contract

In South Africa a public announcement that native labour was to be recruited to work in France was made by Botha on 8 September 1916 and ten days later all magistrates, native commissioners and sub-commissioners received a circular outlining recruitment procedures. The circular explained that the Department of Native Affairs was responsible for recruiting five battalions, each of which was 2,000 strong. A battalion consisted of 59 white officers and NCOs, six black sergeants, two of them hospital orderlies, 64 corporals, 128 lance corporals, eight clerk interpreters and one chaplain, the remainder being native labourers.

The appointment of chaplains, interpreters and hospital orderlies had to be approved by the Secretary for Native Affairs. Native NCOs were to be appointed by battalion commanding officers at the depot although attesting officers could make recommendations for men to be appointed as NCOs. They were instructed not to inform a man that he was being considered. On attestation a man was required to carry one hundred pounds in weight over one hundred yards. If they passed this test they had a medical examination.

They were recruited on a twelve month contract, although they could re-engage if they wished. Part of their contract read:

> We, the undersigned Native Labourers, hereby agree to work as General Labourers in the Overseas Native Labour Contingent for the Imperial Government whenever called upon to do so for a period of twelve months from the date hereof and at the rate of pay of £3 per month.[8]

The contract included time for training in South Africa and travel to Europe so the men could serve as little as nine months in France.

When the scheme was announced the natives' rate of pay[9] led to some opposition in South Africa, as the *East London Daily Dispatch* pointed out, 'the Natives are to get £3 a month, the men of the infantry get 1/- a day'.[10] In fact this was not strictly accurate. Unlike white soldiers, natives were not entitled to any allowances for wives and families and their rate of pay was not increased during their service, whereas the rate for a white private was increased to 3s a day on 1 January 1917.

White officers and NCOs were recruited for the duration of the war plus an additional six months. They were selected from men unfit for front line units, who had knowledge of a Bantu language and experience of working with black labour. Command of the contingent was given to the Director of the Native Labour Bureau, Colonel Pritchard. Many of the officers were retired civil servants or men who were used to working natives in the mines or on the land. Among them were 61-year-old Lieutenant Samuel Emslie and 34-year-old Lieutenant Samuel Richardson, both of whom drowned in the sinking of the SS *Mendi*.

Within South Africa attitudes to the scheme varied considerably. The black press was generally favourable and appealed for blacks to volunteer. Reaction from the white press was mixed. Some, like the *Johannesburg Star*, merely reported the scheme whilst papers in the Eastern Cape and Natal were generally hostile. Many whites were afraid that blacks returning from France would expect equality with whites. This fear was voiced in the South African Parliament by J. B. Wessels MP during a debate in March 1917, 'Did they realise that the coloured man when he donned uniform, said to the white man: "I am now your equal, the equal of your wives and children".'[11]

Initial recruitment in Natal, Basutoland and the Cape was poor with most early recruits coming from the Transvaal. Where the tribal chiefs supported the scheme men enlisted in numbers, where they did not, few enlisted. Amongst the men who enlisted were many chiefs, sub-chiefs and the sons and grandsons of chiefs.[12] Most volunteers had received little or no education, which was the norm for natives at the time. There was, however, a minority of educated natives many of whom volunteered, an example being Joseph Tshite, a schoolmaster from Pretoria. It is likely that, like volunteers for the Chinese Labour Corps, educated natives saw service in France as an opportunity to broaden their horizons. Clothier, in his book *Black Valour* suggests that the 'elite of chiefs and educated men was disproportionately large'.[13] Missionaries with the SANLC supported this view calculating that one quarter of the men were from the black elite with teachers forming the largest group.[14]

To meet the men's spiritual needs 23 chaplains were recruited of whom 12 were black. White chaplains were ranked as captains whereas the black chaplains, whilst being the highest paid blacks at £6 a month, had no rank or status:

We found ourselves, in the great majority of cases, up against white officers who disliked 'educated natives' and who particularly disliked natives in clerical dress. Their whole attitude was an attempt to deny all privileges. Black was black, and a boy was a boy, however dressed, educated or entitled.[15]

Transport to France

The decision to bring natives to France appears to have been undertaken without involving or even notifying the Admiralty. On 19 September a telegram was received at the Admiralty from the Senior Naval Officer in South Africa saying that the contingent of 10,000 men were expected to be ready to leave by 20 October 1916 and asking whether their ships could carry a larger proportion of natives than troops. The next day the Admiralty contacted Searail, the body responsible for transporting troops, asking what was known of the proposal to recruit natives, as they had no previous notice of it. Searail responded two days later informing the Admiralty that the South African Government had notified them on 8 September of the decision to recruit the natives and that they expected to embark the first 2,000 men towards the end of October.[16]

On 30 September the South African Government indicated to the Colonial Office that it was essential that the natives should only be employed at ports on the south coast of France and that they should travel there direct, not via England. This request appears to have created some concern at the Colonial Office, as on 9 October, Bonar Law, the Secretary of State for the Colonies, sent a telegram to the Governor General of South Africa explaining that the natives could only be used in the British zone in northern France. The telegram suggests that he was concerned the South African Government might withdraw their offer of native labourers: 'should be glad to learn whether Ministers think it is possible to send any part of natives to North France, say one or two battalions selected men'.[17]

It is questionable whether the South Africans would want to withdraw their offer. Colonel Pritchard was already en route to France to discuss arrangements for the men, which suggests South Africa would not wish to avoid the commitment. Politically, the British wanted to accommodate the South African Government as much as possible as there was already considerable opposition to their involvement in the war.

Any concern Bonar Law may have had was put to rest on 19 October when the South Africans sent details of proposed sailing dates for the contingent. The first group of 1,500 men were due to leave South Africa on 24 October with a further 7,500 being transported in a further five sailings up to 23 November.

Accommodation and Employment

Soon after Colonel Pritchard arrived in France on 23 October a conference was held at GHQ to consider housing and employing the natives.[18] Any fear that the South African Government would object to the men being employed other than at the ports was immediately dispelled by Pritchard. He supported the idea of using them for road repairs, in forestry, in quarries, at ammunition dumps and railheads. His view was 'not only are the men more suited for such employment, but the difficulty of segregation anticipated to occur in towns would thereby be reduced'.[19] Pritchard explained that native sergeants would supervise the men when they were working and men from their own battalions would guard the men when they were working and in their compounds. The compounds, which were to be surrounded by a strong barbed wire fence, only had to be closed to view when located in a town.

The conference agreed that two hospitals manned by South Africans would be established at Dieppe (500 beds) and Boulogne (200 beds). The corps would manage the scale and type of clothing for the natives, their rations and, except for grave matters, discipline. Pritchard was keen that the ration scale[20] put forward by the South African Government was adopted so that 'the men will not be pampered through the addition of articles to which they are not normally accustomed'.[21] He did, however, agree to the addition of 1 oz of fat (margarine) a week.

The South African Government was anxious that natives should be segregated from other troops, labourers and the civilian population. Natives were not allowed outside their compounds unless accompanied by an officer or white NCO. They could not enter French houses and had to be escorted when visiting a shop. From January 1917 they were banned from entering any establishment which sold beer, wine or spirits, and it was an offence for another soldier to buy liquor for them. There was also a fear about possible relationships with women and advice given to their officers was 'under the conditions under which they are living in France, they are not to be trusted with white women'.[22]

SANLC Arrives

The first contingent of 20 officers, 47 white NCOs and 889 men left South Africa on 28 October on the *Kenilworth Castle*. They arrived at Plymouth on 15 November and bad weather meant they were there for four days, arriving in Havre on 20 November. They were sent to Eawy Forest near Dieppe and despite working in very cold weather they soon earned the praise of the forestry officers employing them. The second battalion left Cape Town on the *Benguela* on 5 November, a voyage that was to take 36 days. They soon ran into bad weather, which resulted in both the men and the boat's crew suffering severe seasickness. This was followed by further illness from which four natives died. When they reached the English Channel the ship's boiler broke down and they drifted for 9 hours. Despite all the problems the battalion finally arrived at Havre on 10 December and was employed on road making, at railheads and salvage work at Vaudricourt, Albert, Montauban, Fricourt and Meault.

Soon after the 1st Battalion arrived the decision was made to reform battalions into companies, each 497 strong. Commanded by a major or captain the company had 4 subalterns, 26 white NCOs, a native interpreter, a native clerk, 3 batmen and 462 natives. Among the men were a number of ruling chiefs and their relatives, as well as other natives of standing and influence. For the purposes of discipline, as well as for political reasons, it was decided that a superior position with distinctive badges of rank should be given to those natives who were suitable for employment as foremen and gangers. The rank of Induna was introduced for natives above the rank of lance corporal, each company having 1 Induna, Class I, and four Indunas Class II.

Whilst in France the natives were paid £1 a month, the remainder of their pay being paid to their family in South Africa or to them on their return home. They were able to spend their money at the canteen in their compound on items including food and Kaffir beer, which was brewed in France by the corps. Haig informed Botha on 4 January 1917 that the SANLC promised to be a great success. He noted that their conduct and work was good and that the sick rate was only 1½ per cent.

By the end of January 1917 the 3rd and 4th Battalions and half of the 5th Battalion had arrived, bringing the number in France to 52 officers and 8,000 other ranks. The other half of the 5th Battalion was left at Rosebank, South Africa awaiting a ship to take them to France. Their turn came on 16 January 1917 when they set sail on the SS *Mendi*.

The Tragedy of the *Mendi*

The *Mendi* had been chartered by the British Government in the autumn of 1916 and fitted out to transport troops. She was commanded by Captain Henry Yardley, who had fifteen years' experience as Ships Master. The ship had four holds with the two forward holds used as living accommodation for most of the natives. The white officers and NCOs' accommodation was in the cabins which were located amidships. A hospital was set up in what had been the second class accommodation, the medical orderlies and interpreters being quartered close by. The majority of the passengers were SANLC personnel consisting of five officers, seventeen white NCOs and 802 natives. There was also a small number of officers returning to Europe after leave or recovered from wounds, and a group selected for service with the Royal Flying Corps.

On leaving Cape Town the *Mendi* joined a convoy of South African and Australian troop ships. The voyage turned out to be a fairly quiet one with the natives involved in boxing matches, singing and dancing and ensuring their kit and the ship was kept clean. En route to West Africa the SANLC's CO, Captain John McLean, became ill with appendicitis. The medical officer, Captain L. Herslet was so concerned that the whole convoy was stopped to enable the convoy's senior medical officer to come onboard to see McLean. The two doctors decided the best course of action was to delay operating until they reached England, which meant McLean could no longer command the SANLC, his place being taken by Lieutenant Richardson. Their route took them to Lagos in Nigeria and then to Freetown in Sierra Leone. From Freetown the *Mendi* continued to Plymouth, arriving 34 days after leaving Cape Town.

At Plymouth all military personnel except the SANLC disembarked and Captain McLean was taken to hospital. The next day, 20 February 1917, the *Mendi* sailed again for Havre accompanied by the destroyer HMS *Brisk*. The weather was overcast with mist threatening and the sea calm. Initially the *Mendi* sailed with one lookout in the crow's nest, two on the forecastle head and several natives stationed round the ship looking for submarines. At about 7.30 pm the ship's oil sidelights and its stern light were lit and the mast head light was lit and put in its cage so that it could be hoisted if needed.

That evening the SS *Darro* left Havre bound for Britain. The *Darro* was been built in 1912 and was capable of carrying 1,177 persons. She had been in dry dock at Havre since 8 February, having a hole in her starboard side repaired. She left France with virtually no cargo, no passengers and a crew of 143 men. The lack of cargo meant she was sailing bow high. When she left Le Havre the weather and sea were similar to the conditions the *Mendi* had found on leaving Plymouth. The weather cleared and her captain, Henry Stump, wanting to make the English coast before daylight, ordered her to sail at full speed, 13 knots.

At about 11 pm the *Darro* encountered fog but did not cut her speed nor use her whistle. With the fog coming in patches, the *Mendi's* speed varied depending on the weather. At 3.45 am, in thick fog, the *Mendi's* engines were put to slow and her whistle sounded continuously. The fog was even thicker at 4.30 a.m. when Yardley left the bridge to go to the chartroom, leaving Second Officer Raine and Fourth Officer Trapnell on the bridge. Despite the fog the *Darro* continued at full speed and did not sound her whistle.

It was Trapnell who first saw another vessel, which was on a collision course with the *Mendi*. Second Officer Raine rang 'Full Speed Astern,' ordered 'Hard-a-starboard' and blew another three short warning blasts of the whistle. The *Darro* responded with three or four blasts of siren and orders were given to put the engines full steam astern but no instruction was given to the helmsman. Yardley, hearing the warning signal, returned to the *Mendi's* bridge only to see another vessel bearing down on them.

At 4.57 am on 21 February 1917, at a point eleven miles south south-west of St Catherine's Point, Isle of Wight, the *Darro* slammed into the smaller ship with tremendous force. The *Darro's* bow struck between two forward holds, causing a cut of about 20 feet in the *Mendi*.

With the *Darro's* engines at full astern she pulled out of the *Mendi* and the sea poured in through the hole. The collision would have killed a number of SANLC who were asleep in the holds and damaged at least one of the exit ladders. 'A large number (one estimate was 140) never made their way to the deck and drowned in the blackness of the hold as the water rose quickly.'[23]

Yardley ordered the engines to be stopped, sent for the wireless operator, ordered the lifeboats to be lowered and gave four blasts on the whistle, which was the signal for all hands to go to boat stations. The wireless operator never arrived, nor was he seen again, so no SOS was sent out. Lieutenant Richardson, together with the other officers and those men who had been lookouts, tried to assist men to get out of the flooded forward holds. It is suggested that around 750 survivors managed to get to the deck and 'there was now a struggle in the darkness to lower the boats, those seven boats which could take a total of 298 men'.[24]

As water poured into the *Mendi* she began to list heavily to starboard and it became increasingly difficult to get out the port side boats. Of the seven boats, one on the port side jammed and could not be lowered, two were overloaded and capsized and one smashed against the ship's side and was holed. The fate of a fifth is unknown but does not appear to have been launched. There were also 46 rafts, each of which could hold 20 men. Ropes that secured these should have been cut, but in the confusion time was lost as men tried to undo the ropes.

Within ten minutes of the collision Yardley, realising the ship would not stay afloat much longer, ordered everyone to leave the ship. Both the crew and men of the SANLC carried out these orders in a disciplined manner. Men began to jump into the sea, making for the rafts. A large number of the black men were too afraid to jump into the sea and there are reports of white NCOs staying and encouraging them to jump overboard.

According to oral tradition, just before the *Mendi* sank Reverend Isaac Wauchope Dyobha addressed the natives on the deck:

> Be quiet and calm, my countrymen, for what is taking place is exactly what you came to do. You are going to die … but that is what you came to do … Brothers, we are drilling the death drill. I, a Xhosa, say you are my brothers. Swazis, Pondos, Basutos, we die like brothers. We are the sons of Africa. Raise your war cries, brothers, for though they made us leave our assegais back in the kraals, our voices are left with our bodies.[25]

After the address the men are said to have taken off their boots and stamped the death dance on the deck of the sinking ship.

This story has become the most famous incident in the tragedy although no survivor's or official accounts have confirmed it.[26] It has been suggested that this and other 'such unlikely accounts of the actual events of that fateful day were in circulation during and shortly after the Second World War.'[27] The *Mendi* disaster assumed 'mythological dimensions with nationalist overtones, in African group memory'.[28]

Shortly after 5.30 am there were about 120 men in the two lifeboats and hundreds more on rafts, clinging to wreckage or supported by lifebelts in the freezing water. Lieutenant Lawrens van Vuren SANLC described seeing natives collapsing because of the freezing water. 'The *Darro* however lowered no boats and made no effort to save us. She was only 200 yards away from the *Mendi* and must have seen us and heard our cries as the seas were very calm.'[29] The *Darro* did pick up about 120 men in the two lifeboats and three natives on a raft but did not lower any boats or search for other survivors. One of the last to leave the *Mendi* was Yardley who remained on the bridge until the sea was level with it. He then walked into the sea where he floated for about an hour and a half before being picked up.

Survivors and dead bodies were picked up by HMS *Brisk*, the minesweeper *Balfour* and the steamer *Sandsend* and landed at Southampton, Portsmouth and Newhaven. Of the 802 SANLC natives on the *Mendi* 607 died, together with two of their officers, 7 white NCOs and 31 of the ship's crew. The names of 550 natives, two officers and six NCOs who have no known grave, appear on the Hollybrook Memorial, Southampton. Bodies recovered and men who died after reaching land are buried in Britain, France and Holland. The only reference to the sinking of the *Mendi* in the Report on Labour is: 'On February 21st 1917 HMS 'Mendi' came into collision with another ship in the channel and the loss of life to Officers, Non-commissioned officers, and Natives totalling 616 is deeply regretted.[30]

Towards the end of July 1917 a Court of Inquiry was held by the Board of Trade. Evidence was heard from the masters of the two ships, their chief officers and members of their crews. The only evidence from members of the SANLC was sworn statements from Lieutenants Hertslet and van Vuren, both of whom were now serving with the Corps in France. The court found that the collision, loss of life, loss of the *Mendi* and damage to the *Darro* were the fault of Henry Stump, master of the *Darro*. He was criticised for failing 'to send away a boat or boats to ascertain the extent of the damage to the *Mendi*, and to render her, her master, crew and passengers such assistance as was practicable and necessary.'[31] Stump's punishment was to prohibit him from commanding a vessel for twelve months.

The SANLC in France

In January 1917 the SANLC were employed loading and unloading wagons at the railheads in Army Areas with the exception of one company employed on quarrying at Arques and two companies at Dieppe Docks.

The camps of those working near Albert came under shellfire during January and the companies sustained a number of casualties: 'The Natives became nervous and some of the companies presented a petition stating that they wished to be removed from the danger zone and representing that their contracts stated they were to be employed on Dock work.'[32] Colonel Pritchard advised GHQ that it would cause political problems in South Africa if there were reports the natives were being used near the fighting and that it was almost impossible to ensure segregation of the natives in Army Areas. In view of this it was decided to remove all SANLC Companies, including those working in the Eawy Forest, to the LoC. Colonel Pritchard insisted on segregated camps and it was not until the middle of March 1917 that enough camps could be prepared on the LoC for the withdrawal from Army Areas to be undertaken.

It was found that the SANLC were most efficient when used as unskilled labour loading and unloading stores. In July 1917

> ... a party of the SANLC working on ammunition at Martainville created a record. Fifty Natives, with 4 NCOs and 1 White NCO man-handled 700 tons of ammunition, loading if from dump to lorry and from lorry to [railway] truck in 345 man hours, an average of 2.03 tons per man hour.[33]

In South Africa it had been suggested that the different tribes should not be put together in the same company. The British ignored this advice and when different tribes were mixed there was no racial tension. It was 'found beneficial to mix them together because they were easier to handle and friendly competition in the work resulted'.[34]

SANLC Companies were separated from other labour and, in particular, from British labour. The authorities were worried that if the natives worked alongside British labour of a lower medical category it would lead to slackness among the SANLC. The South African authorities were particularly worried about natives picking up political or social aspirations that they would bring back to South Africa.

The Report on Labour states one reason for not mixing the SANLC with other labour units was 'Trade Unionism is not indulged in by the Natives at present'.[35]

The attitude of the majority of their officers and NCOs to the natives can be summed up in the remarks of one officer to a group at Rouen docks after French women had served tea to some black dock workers: 'When you people get back to South Africa again, don't start thinking you are whites just because this place has spoilt you. You are black and will stay black.'[36]

On 10 July 1917 King George V, accompanied by the Queen, Prince of Wales and Field Marshall Haig, inspected the SANLC at Abbeville. The King's speech was translated into Zulu, si-Xhosa and Sesuto.

> Then the native troops, led by Corporal Alfred Tsingane, nephew of the last Zulu Chief Dinuxulu, gave the Zulu Royal Salute 'Bayete!' The Basuto, not to be outdone, shouted 'Khotso! Khotso! Khotso! (Peace! Peace! Peace!), in which all the men of the other tribes also joined.[37]

In keeping with South African tradition the King presented the men with a white ox, and also presented a gramophone and records to each of the two Native Hospitals.

In general the SANLC had a good disciplinary record although two incidents did occur during July 1917. At Dieppe members of 22 Company attempted to release natives who had been arrested. During the incident two white NCOs were injured and the armed guard fired on the rioters, killing two and wounding eleven. GHQ Diary recorded that, 'the riot was quickly quelled and the Natives returned to duty'.[38] The other incident occurred at Dannes when men broke out of their camp; 'One of these was accidentally shot. The incident did not give rise to any further trouble.'[39]

South African archives record six cases involving insubordination or drunkenness, all occurring during 1918. On 19 April Private Jacob was sentenced to 12 months and 91 days for drunkenness at Rouen, offering violence to his section officer and attempting to strike Second Lieutenant J. Roos. Three other men received the same sentence for similar offences and two men received lesser sentences. All six were returned to South Africa to serve their sentences and were released on 25 December 1918.[40]

The question of enforcing discipline was addressed in *The Times* in December 1917:

> Is there any trouble in enforcing discipline in these strange and novel surroundings? I was told that there was none so long as the native was kept under control. But the control must be stringent. It would not do to allow these gullible people to range freely among the French and Flemish villages and liquor-shops. They might, find too many civilized temptations there.[41]

The GOC LoC recorded acts of courage by two members of 8 Company:

> At 5.45 p.m. on the 25th September 1917, Second-Lieutenant Brownlee was waiting for the Transbordeur Bridge at Rouen, when a man was seen to fall off the bridge into

the River Seine, Second-Lieutenant Brownlee immediately dived into the river, and although fully dressed and wearing field boots, succeeded in effecting a rescue.

About 9 p.m. on the 6th October 1917, No 479 A/Sergeant A. Tibbits courageously jumped into the Seine in the dark and rescued Lieutenant DA Cave R.N.R., who had been knocked into the river between the landing stage and a ship.[42]

In December 1917 consideration was given to changing recruitment from twelve months to 'duration of the war'. When it was realised that this would not be possible the decision was taken to cease recruitment altogether. On 17 January 1918 General Botha issued a public statement announcing that recruitment would cease immediately and no further contingents would be sent to France. Re-engagement was offered to the natives, 222 deciding to remain in France.

Repatriation

On 20 September 1917 the AG informed the War Office that the first contracts expired on 4 October 1917 and advised, 'shipment should commence in September to allay a feeling of uncertainty amongst the men as to their repatriation'.[43] Lack of shipping caused delays in repatriation, the first group from 1 and 2 Companies leaving France on 6 October 1917.

On 14 October there was unrest among 5, 6, 7 and 9 Companies at Abancourt as their contracts had expired. Two days later 50 men of 7 Company went on strike and there were strikes among 8 and 18 Companies at Rouen. The most serious incident appears to have been in 18 Company where sixteen ringleaders were charged with mutiny and sentenced to three years penal servitude, later commuted to two years hard labour.

In general there was little unrest over expired contracts. One of the reasons may have been as a result of instructions given in November that as natives became due for repatriation they were drafted from their companies to a concentration camp at Havre.

From France men were sent to Plymouth. On arrival they marched to their camp at St Bedeaux in Devonport and were 'enthusiastically welcomed by local residents, including women, who cheered and greeted the "gallant" forces of the Empire'.[44] The camp at Devonport was not a closed one. Following attempts by some to make contact with local women the CO of the Devonport area issued the following statement:

> It is absolutely essential that the Kaffir should regard white women as unapproachable; the mischief that can be done by merely good-natured familiarity – apart from anything worse – is incalculable: and the people who will suffer from this levity on the part of white women at home, are the wives and daughters of our settlers in South Africa.[45]

On 15 November 1917, whilst sailing to South Africa on the vessel *Miltiades,* a mutiny occurred. The mutineers objected to taking orders as their contracts had expired. During the incident one man was killed, another wounded and eight ringleaders arrested. The ringleaders were court-martialled at Cape Town in December after a petition to the South African Supreme Court that they were not subject to military law had been turned down. One man, Corporal Mukubedi, was sentenced to 12 years hard labour and the others to 10 years. The South African Prime Minister and the Governor General both considered these sentences excessive and after they contacted the War Office the men were released in May 1918.

Before the last contingent left France on 26 September 1918 a message from Field Marshall Haig was translated into Zulu, si-Xhosa and Sesuto and read to the men:

> Will you please convey to the remaining Units of the South African Native Labour Corps who are leaving for South Africa tomorrow my warm appreciation of the good work done by them for the British Army during their stay in France. They have rendered loyal and excellent service wherever they have been employed and I send them my heartiest thanks and all good wishes for a prosperous journey home. Haig.[46]

Health, Casualties and Honours

The natives appeared to have coped with the weather in northern France far better than had been anticipated. Reports suggest that the two native hospitals were never more than half full.[47] During the severe winter of 1916/17 there were several cases of loss of limbs due to frostbite. Anti-frostbite precautions were issued to the companies and no further cases reported during the following winter. Men sent to hospital who were unlikely to recover within three months were repatriated to South Africa. Most fatalities through illness were caused by tuberculosis and bronchial catarrh, the most common complaint at sick parades.

Of the 20,887 natives who embarked from South Africa 1,107 died during service. Of these 607 died on the *Mendi*, 25 from accidents and 475 through illness. Among the white personnel six officers died, two on the *Mendi*, two in France[48] and two on returning to South Africa. Of the 966 white warrant officers and NCOs 21 died, seven on the *Mendi*, six in France, two before leaving South Africa, one on repatriation and five who drowned when the *Galway Castle* was torpedoed.

The vast majority of honours and awards were made to white personnel of the SANLC. Colonel Pritchard was made a Companion of the Order of St. Michael and St. George, five officers and one of the SANLC's chaplains, Reverend John Lennox, were awarded OBEs, one officer an MBE and there were fourteen MSMs and 26 MIDs.

On his return to South Africa, Colonel Pritchard produced a report on the work of the SANLC in which he listed 92 black men, whose names were 'submitted with the recommendation that appropriate recognition of their service may be granted them'.[49] From an examination of the *London Gazette* it would appear that the MSM was awarded to only five or six natives, including Native Chaplain Dambuza.

The white personnel were entitled to the British War Medal in silver for service in France. The black personnel, as with other coloured labour units, to the medal in bronze. However, the South African government decided that it would not be given to men from the Union. The medal was given to black personnel from what were then High Commission Territories (Basutoland, Bechuanaland and Swaziland).

Summary

The SANLC were most efficient when under instruction from the officers and NCOs who had come from South Africa with them. At Dannes, when their own officers supervised them, the ammunition depot they built was completed ahead of time and saved the Army 'hundreds of thousands of pounds'.[50]

At Havre the efficiency of labour determined the amount of grain that could be unloaded from moored vessels. In June 1918 the SANLC earned praise from both the Deputy Controller of Labour and the civilian engineering company who were testing a new grain elevator. In a letter to the OC of 14 Labour Group the engineering company explained that two platoons of 31 Company had unloaded nearly 170 tons per hour describing their work as

> … an absolutely unique achievement and in spite of a great deal of experience of what can be done in handling sacks, we were ourselves utterly astonished at the result.
>
> It is clear from the reports we have received that the success of this demonstration was due in the main to the splendid exertions of your boys and the keenness of their officers and NCOs to demonstrate the capacity of native labour. Undoubtedly, the work was done throughout with an energy far in excess of what we should ourselves have expected of white labour and with an intelligence which speaks highly for the possibilities of the South African Labour Groups.[51]

Three things hampered the work of the SANLC. Firstly, the journey time to and from France being included as part of the twelve month contract. As General Wace noted, 'the natives had to be sent back just when they had reached their highest pitch of training'.[52] Secondly, that they could not be used near the front because of the political implications in South Africa, and thirdly, having to segregate the natives meant they were too immobile to use in Army Areas and they had to be restricted to the LoC.

1 Clothier, N., *Black Valour*, p.12
2 NA WO 95/3968
3 ibid WO 95/30
4 Clothier, p.12
5 NA WO 107/37
6 Those present were the Adjutant General, Inspector General Communications, Quarter Master General, Deputy QMG and the Director of Organisation.
7 NA WO 95/31
8 Clothier, p.13
9 Lance corporals received £3.10s, corporals £4, orderlies £4.10s, clerk interpreters and sergeants £5 and chaplains and senior interpreters £6 a month.
10 Quoted in Clothier, p.16
11 Quoted in Clothier, p.17

12 Clothier, p.19, identifies six chiefs and sub-chiefs
13 Clothier, p.24
14 Grundlingh, A., *Fighting Their Own War,* p.77
15 Keable 'African Priests in France' quoted in Grundlingh, p.104
16 NA MT 23/630
17 NA MT 23/630
18 ibid WO 95/32
19 ibid
20 The authorised ration scale for a week was 1lb frozen meat (or 9 ozs preserved meat), 1lb mealie meal, 1lb bread, 1 oz coffee, 1 oz sugar, ½ oz salt, 8 ozs fresh vegetables, 2 ozs English tobacco or cigarettes (or 3 ozs S African tobacco and 1 box matches).
21 NA WO 95/32
22 ibid WO 107/37
23 Clothier, p.53
24 ibid, p.57
25 ibid, p.59, variations of the words are to be found in other sources.
26 ibid, p.59
27 Grundlingh, p.140
28 ibid
29 Affidavit of van Vuren quoted in Clothier, p.60
30 NA WO 107/37 Appendix F
31 Report of Board of Trade Investigation quoted in Clothier, p.90
32 NA WO 107/37 Appendix F
33 ibid WO 95/83
34 ibid WO 107/37 Appendix F
35 ibid
36 Perry (ed), *Jingoes,* p.92 quoted in Grundlingh, p.103
37 Clothier p.141
38 NA WO 95/83
39 ibid
40 Clothier, p.160
41 *The Times,* 'An Army of Labour', 27 December 1917
42 NA WO 123/200
43 ibid WO 95/35
44 Grundlingh, p.111
45 *Western Morning News,* 22 October 1917, quoted in Grundlingh, p.112
46 NA WO 107/37 Appendix F
47 Clothier, p.156
48 Second Lieutenant Robert Sharps was killed in action with the Machine Gun Corps on 19 April 1918 having been transferred from the SANLC.
49 Quoted in Clothier p.166
50 NA WO 107/37 Report on Labour, p.27
51 ibid WO 107/37 Appendix H
52 ibid WO 107/37 Report on Labour, p.29

SEYCHELLES LABOUR BATTALION

A contemporary report on the role the Seychelles played during the war described it as 'small', stating, 'they did their best with enthusiasm, nevertheless, and succeeded in raising several Labour Corps, which did excellent service in the strenuous campaign in East Africa'.[1] What this does not reflect is the sacrifice made by the men of Seychelles. The contribution from the Seychelles has been referred to in different sources as a battalion, corps, contingent and carrier corps. A 1918 Army report uses the term battalion,[2] *The Times* refers to a Labour Corps, the Medal Roll uses contingent and the Commonwealth War Graves Commission refers to it as a carrier corps. These four variations reflect the limited information about this labour unit.

Formed for service in East Africa after General Smuts found that he had almost exhausted the supply of local labour, men were recruited for a period of twelve months, with the first recruits being available in December 1916.[3] In terms of its population the Seychelles made a significant contribution to the war effort. In 1916 the adult male population was about 5,000, of whom about 500 were white officials and the remainder illiterate coloured labourers with little or no knowledge of the world outside their islands. Over fifteen per cent of the population of the Seychelles served in the contingent.

The force comprised 791 officers and men and it is recorded that 'they did good work at the base' in Dar-es-Salaam.[4] The Seychelles contingent was badly affected by malaria and bacillary dysentery and was repatriated after six months. Almost half the contingent, 341 men, died during service or soon after returning to Seychelles as a result of illness acquired in East Africa. Of these, 289 have no known grave and are commemorated on the Mont-Fleuri Memorial, Victoria, Seychelles.

It has been suggested that despite the high death rate it was finance that prevented a further contingent being formed in the Seychelles: 'Many others would willingly have gone on active service, but the very slender finances of the colony would not admit of assisted passages.'[5]

1 *The Times History of the War* Vol XVI, p.106
2 NA WO 106/33
3 ibid CO 323/757
4 Lucas, C., *The Empire at War* Vol IV, p.553
5 ibid

BRITISH WEST INDIES REGIMENT

The declaration of war resulted in an upsurge of patriotism amongst West Indians, and on all the islands the Colonial Governments were inundated with offers to enlist in the Army. Whilst the Colonial Office was anxious to encourage West Indian participation in the war, it supported the view of the War Office that black West Indians should not be used against white forces.

On 28 August 1914 the Colonial Office asked the War Office about the possibility of a British West Indian contingent serving overseas.[1] The War Office held the view that the fighting quality of black West Indians was suspect and that they would be better used in a hot climate. The War Office's response was that such a contingent would be of more use in the West Indies in a defensive role and 'maintaining order, if necessary, in the islands'.[2]

The War Office's refusal was passed to the governors of the various islands and resulted in a number of West Indians travelling, at their own expense, to England to enlist in the British Army. However, as the following extract from the *Stratford Express* shows, their efforts were in vain:

THE DOCKS – Black Men for the Front At West Ham Police Court to-day (Wednesday).

Nine black men, natives of Barbados, West Indies, were charged with being stowaways on the SS *Danube*. Mr J.W. Richards, who prosecuted for the Royal Mail Steam Packet Company, said that the SS *Danube* made a voyage from Trinidad to England, and the day after leaving Trinidad the ship called at Barbados. It was presumed that the men came aboard there for the day. Afterwards they were found on the vessel. Mr Gillespie: In a dark corner, I suppose? (Laughter). Mr Richards continued that the men were put to work, and they did not cause any trouble. He was told that the men were desirous of enlisting in the Army. Mr Gillespie: What, do they want to enlist in the Black Guards? (Laughter). Det. Sergt. Holby said he had made enquiries at the local recruiting office and they told him they could not enlist because of their colour, but if application was made to the War Office no doubt they could enlist in some regiment of black men. Remanded for a week.[3]

Towards the end of November 1914, Lord Dundonald, a major landowner in the West Indies, wrote to Lewis Harcourt, the Colonial Secretary, to report that he had been informed the 'lighter coloured' volunteers had been accepted for the Army but the black volunteers had been rejected.[4] Whilst Dundonald did not support the introduction of blacks into British regiments he recognised that a failure to make use of the black population of the West Indies could be harmful to the Empire.[5] He went on to suggest the formation of a West Indian contingent for service in Egypt as part of the war against Turkey, or in a temperate climate.

Harcourt sent Dundonald's letter to the War Office on 8 December in a further attempt to get a West Indian contingent accepted. In a supporting note he stressed that offers from the West Indies could not be continually rejected. He also acknowledged that it was impracticable for a West Indian contingent to serve in France for a number of reasons. The only reason stated in his note was the difficulty of colour. Once again the War Office turned down the suggestion saying that the Army Council felt the West Indians would not be suitable for employment against the Turks in Egypt nor the Germans in East Africa.

By the end of 1914 there appeared to be no prospect of forming a West Indian contingent to serve overseas. Despite this, active steps were being taken in Barbados, Jamaica, British Guiana and Trinidad to raise a contingent for overseas service whether the British Government acceded to their request or not.

Royal Intervention

The personal intervention of George V in April 1915 changed things. Lord Stamfordham, the King's Private Secretary wrote to Harcourt on 17 April explaining that the King had received a request for the employment of a West Indian contingent. He added that the King felt such a contingent could be usefully employed in Egypt and that he was aware of the political importance of not turning down the offer of men from the West Indies. Harcourt replied to Stamfordham on 20 April explaining the correspondence that had already taken place between the War Office and his department. He pointed out that the War Office had turned down all the ideas put to them and expressed his concern that continued rejection would affect the loyalty of the black population of the West Indies.

George V met with Lord Kitchener, the Secretary for War, on 22 April. At this meeting Kitchener was shown Harcourt's letter but told the King that not only had the War Office never refused the offer of a West Indian force but that he would be happy to accept such a unit as long as there were no conditions about where it could serve.[6] As soon as the meeting ended Lord Stamfordham contacted Harcourt and informed him of Kitchener's remarks. Harcourt was clearly angered by the remarks for that same day he wrote to Kitchener stating that on 2 September and again on 14 December 1914 the War Office had turned down his offers of a West Indian unit. The following day the Colonial Office sent a copy of this letter together with copies of the letters they had sent to the War Office in September and December to George V.

BWIR Formed

Whether Kitchener had misled the King or been badly briefed by his advisors is not known, but the effect was that the War Office could no longer continue to refuse the offer of a unit from the West Indies and their formal acceptance came on 19 May. The War Office would not allow these volunteers to be enlisted into the British Army as this would entitle them to the same pay and rights as a British soldier. Instead they suggested that the unit be formed as a single contingent in the West Indies and that the Colonial Governments be responsible for pensions, care of the men's families and dependants, including separation allowances, and other costs.[7] The Colonial Office was unhappy with the financial liabilities being placed upon the Colonial Governments. It pointed out that in May Harcourt had indicated to the West Indian Governments that separation allowances would be paid from Imperial Funds. In addition, Bonar Law, who had replaced Harcourt as Colonial Secretary, was concerned that the Islands would not have the financial resources to cover pensions and other charges. This would be a particular problem if there was a high rate of casualties amongst men from one of the smaller islands, which would be least able to meet pension demands. Bonar Law suggested that each colony be asked to contribute a fixed percentage of the costs and the Colonial Governments would cover the costs of transporting the men to France.

The War Office accepted Bonar Law's suggestions and it was agreed that the men would be paid at British rates while separation allowances were at the same rate as those paid to men in the West India Regiment. The unit would be known as the British West Indies Regiment (BWIR). About 1,000 men had already tried to enlist and the original intention was to form one battalion. The War Office requested a draft of a further 150 men to maintain the battalion's strength.

In September 1915 the War Office decided there should be two battalions, 2,000 men, and this would require a draft of 300 men a month. Each battalion required 300 men as reinforcements. The War Office, still opposed to the use of the BWIR, hoped the West Indian Islands would be unable to recruit these men and this would stop the Regiment but the Colonial Governments immediately responded, promising over 2,100 men as shown below.

Bahamas	130		Jamaica	500–550
Barbados	123		Leewards	about 120
British Guiana	272		St Lucia	110
British Honduras	110		St Vincent	55
Grenada	200		Trinidad	500

Table 11: Response to War Office request for BWIR men – September 1915

The first contingent arrived in England in October 1915 and was sent for training at Seaford, Sussex. Command of the BWIR was given to Colonel A. E. Barchard, a Jamaican who had served in the West India Regiment. The men, who came from all the islands except Jamaica where recruitment was still taking place, were formed into four companies based on their origin – A Company: British Guiana; B Company: Trinidad; C Company: Trinidad and St Vincent; and D Company: Grenada and Barbados.

On 26 October 1915 the formal announcement of the formation of the BWIR appeared in the London Gazette. The notice was reproduced in the battalion orders of the contingent on 6 November and three days later a detachment of 42 men of the BWIR, under Major Golding and Captain Cavenaugh, took part in the procession for the Lord Mayor's display in London. According to the Daily Chronicle:

> Every newspaper which published an account of the procession noted the fact that a very special cheer greeted the appearance of the British West Indies Regiment. And the pleasure of the occasion was reciprocal. The dusky faces of the smiling West Indians made one forget that colour had ever been a racial barrier.[8]

The question of race was still an issue with the War Office. The Colonial Office had informed the authorities in British Guiana that the War Office did not want them to enlist East Indians (personnel of Indian descent) living in the colony. However, other colonies had not been informed of this decision and amongst the men who arrived in England from Trinidad were 41 Indian volunteers. The War Office stated they were unacceptable as soldiers because they did not speak English and there would be problems regarding their food. Their immediate repatriation was demanded. The War Office had no objections to creoles of Indian descent as long as they were British subjects who had been born in the colonies, could speak English and accept standard British rations.[9]

Soon after the first contingent arrived in England the War Office revised their requirements for reinforcements from 300 to 1,000 men for each battalion.

On 30 October they asked Bonar Law whether it would be possible to obtain 2,000 men during the coming year so that two battalions could be maintained. A week earlier the Governor of Jamaica had offered the Colonial Office an additional 1,000 men together with a further 1,000 reinforcements, and Bonar Law immediately replied that this could be achieved. Shortly after this the first contingent from Jamaica arrived in England, 736 men rather than the 550 that had been expected. By the end of 1915 the BWIR in England consisted of 48 officers and 2,448 men. A further 1,000 men had been promised by Jamaica and there were plans for future drafts which would maintain not two but three battalions.

On 8 January 1916 the Jamaican *Daily Gleaner* published a list of 25 officers and 1,096 men, the second contingent to leave for England. The third contingent, a further 25 officers and over 1,115 men, left Jamaica on 6 March. On 4 April news of the tragedy that had befallen this third contingent reached Jamaica.

Death at sea

The third contingent sailed on the SS *Verdala*[10] on a route that took them to Halifax in Nova Scotia,

> Unfortunately those who made the arrangements in England never considered that those to be conveyed from Jamaica to Halifax, at an extremely cold time of the year, were men who had lived all their lives in a tropical colony and were therefore an easy prey to cold.[11]

Just before reaching Halifax, the ship, which was unheated, ran into a blizzard. The effect of the blizzard was exacerbated by the fact that the men had not been supplied with clothing suitable for such conditions and the contingent suffered badly from frostbite.

Reports in the Jamaican *Daily Gleaner* on 5 April 1916 indicated that 106 men suffered from frostbite, four had to have a leg amputated and five died as a result of the cold. The exact number of casualties is uncertain; J. H. W. Park suggests that the figure was around 400[12] whereas Glenford Howe puts the figure at approximately 600.[13] On 29 September the Jamaican Acting Colonial Secretary reported to the Colonies Legislature that 118 men of the third contingent had returned to Jamaica on 30 May and a further 273 on 8 September having been rejected because of the 'effects of cold'.[14] He also reported that no communication had been received from the Imperial authorities regarding the contingent that had been frostbitten in March and therefore was unable to give an exact number of men that had been incapacitated.

Recruiting continues

Despite the casualties suffered by the third contingent, the long-term effect on recruiting seems to have been minimal. In early September it was reported in Jamaica that transport for a fourth contingent would become available within a few weeks. At the time some 600 men had been enlisted and a call was made for more men. The fourth contingent of 36 officers and 726 men sailed from Jamaica on 30 September 1916. Recruitment for the BWIR continued until October 1917. Jamaica raised a further five contingents:

30 March 1917   30 officers and 1,656 men
1 June 1917   33 officers and 1,656 men
20 July 1917   22 officers and 851 men
26 August 1917   31 officers and 1,304 men
2 October 1917   18 officers and 985 men[15]

Egypt

By the end of April 1916, the 1st, 2nd and 3rd Battalions had been moved from Seaford to Alexandria in Egypt where the 4th Battalion joined them in mid-August. In June consideration was given to converting the BWIR into pioneer battalions for service on the railways in Mesopotamia. The GOC Egypt thought they would be no better at coping with the heat of the desert than the British territorials under his command and rejected this idea. He pointed out that the battalions and the people of the West Indies would resent the BWIR being turned into labour troops, even if disguised as pioneers.[16] The War Office response, decided by the Army Council on 9 July, was to stop recruitment for the BWIR and to reduce the opportunity for the four battalions to fight as one unit in Egypt. Five hundred men from the 1st, 2nd and 3rd Battalions were transferred to East Africa in July to help bring the West India Regiment up to strength. 100 men from the 2nd Battalion were sent to Mesopotamia as support troops to the Indian Expeditionary Force.

At a meeting on 23 January 1917 the War Cabinet received and endorsed a report submitted by the War Office, which had come from the GOC Egypt. The report stated that the BWIR had done well as ammunition carriers on the lines of communications but that as front line troops they had not received good reports.[17] The implication was that they were poor front line soldiers when, in fact, they had not been used in this role.

Whilst the BWIR, as front line soldiers, is not within the scope of this work it would be wrong not to acknowledge the role they played. Throughout 1916 and into 1917 the BWIR in Egypt continued to work on the lines of communications despite attempts by Lt Colonel Wood Hill, CO 1st Battalion, to persuade HQ to allow them to serve in a combatant role. In July 1917 he was given permission to attach his machine-gun section to the 1st/5th Bedfordshire Regiment and they were involved in a raid at Umbrella Hill on the night of 20/21 July.[18] In August the 1st Battalion became part of XXI Corps and from then on began to take a more active part in the fighting in Egypt and Palestine. In November 1917, following their part in an attack on the Gaza–Beersheba line, Lt Colonel Wood Hill was awarded the Distinguished Service Order (DSO), Captain Fink the Military Cross (MC) and Lance Corporal Johns and Privates Hyndman and Pullar Military Medals (MM). They became part of Major General E. W. C. Chaytor's Force in September 1918 serving with distinction in the Jordan Valley. As the report of the Commander in Chief Egyptian Expeditionary Force states: 'during the operations they displayed great steadiness under fire, and dash in the attack, and gave proof of marching power of a high order'.[19]

France

The vast majority of the BWIR were employed in France as labour troops. The first to arrive were the 3rd and 4th Battalions who left Egypt on 28 August 1916 bound for Marseilles. They proceeded to the Somme where they were primarily used to move ammunition.

On 28 September 1916 the War Office informed the Colonial Office that they would need some 10,000 labourers to build light railways in France during the coming winter and requested the use of men from the West Indies. The Colonial Office replied, on 4 October, pointing out the health problems BWIR men had encountered whilst stationed at Seaford during the winter of 1915, when eighteen men had died. It was thought unwise to send men to France during the winter. Bonar Law questioned whether the BWIR men already in France could continue to be employed there during the winter period. He did, however, ask the Governors of the West Indian Islands if it was possible to obtain men who could do the work and withstand the climate.

On 31 October 1916, the War Office requested a further two BWIR Battalions, which would initially be sent to Egypt and then transferred to France when required for work at the ammunition dumps.[20] At a conference in Egypt at which the BWIR was represented by Lieutenant Colonel Wood Hill, it was agreed that the BWIR should be used in warmer climates and that they should be used in a more active role. Wood Hill suggested 'using the 3rd and 4th Battalions more or less as labour troops was doing untold harm to recruiting in the West Indies'.[21]

When the COs of 3rd and 4th Battalions in France were informed of the Egyptian conference they held their own meeting, which resulted in a letter being sent by them to the War Office in which they rejected the suggestion that the officers and men of their battalions objected to carrying shells and that on no account did they wish to be returned to Egypt. It has been suggested that, 'this want of unanimity practically killed the Regiment,' losing any chance of it serving as a fighting brigade in Egypt.[22] The War Office decided that the 1st, 2nd and 5th Battalions would remain in Egypt whereas the 3rd, 4th and any future battalions would serve in France at the ammunition dumps.

A photograph of the BWIR on the Albert–Amiens road taken in September 1916[23] shows the men with rifles and 'there are reports of West Indies Regiment soldiers fighting off counter-attacks'.[24] A former member of the 4th Battalion, George Blackman, is quoted as remembering trench fights in which he fought alongside white soldiers:

> The Tommies said, 'Darkie, let them have it.' I made the order: 'Bayonets, fix,' and then 'B company, fire.' You know what it is to go and fight somebody hand to hand? You need plenty nerves. They come at you with the bayonet. He pushes at me, I push at he. You push that bayonet in there and hit with the butt of the gun – if he is dead he is dead, if he live he live.[25]

It has not been possible to find evidence of the BWIR being involved in fighting in France, one author states, 'black Bermudan and West Indians were never actively engaged in the fighting on the western front'.[26]

There is uncertainty about the degree to which the BWIR in France were issued with arms. A year after the IWM photograph was taken, on 5 September

1917, the QMG issued a Routine Order specifically about arming the BWIR. In the order it was stated that rifles and ammunition should not be issued to untrained men and the commanding officers of the battalions were to be consulted about how many of their men were sufficiently trained in the use of rifles and issue made accordingly.[27]

The 3rd and 4th Battalions were the only ones employed in France during 1916. Initially used as ammunition supply companies they were moved to Marseilles during the winter of 1916. On 23 January 1917 there was trouble with men of the 3rd Battalion who were employed at Marseilles docks coaling the SS *Megantic*. The Provost Martial arrested several 'ringleaders'. The objection to coaling appears to have continued throughout January; the Regiment is shown as having only 139 men working on 8 February. At the time the work rate of the BWIR was shown as unsatisfactory when compared to the Bermuda RGA. The Bermuda RGA moved 4.92 tons per man during an 8 hour day whereas the BWIR were only managing 1.12 tons per man.

With the warmer spring weather the men were moved north to the 1st and 5th Army Areas. Both the BWIR and the Bermuda RGA were used to move ammunition at the railheads and ammunition dumps in support of the Canadians during the Vimy Ridge operations. The work was often carried out within range of the German guns and the actions of Captain Robinson on 10 July 1917 in rescuing wounded men and saving ammunition when the railhead came under shellfire resulted in the award of a MC. The 1st Army report on the Vimy operations noted: 'The men of the West Indies Regiment, being strong and powerful, did well on similar work, so soon as they became accustomed to handling shell and awkward loads.'[28]

However, the Report on Labour expressed concern about using men from the tropics in cold weather:

> Neither the Bermuda RGA nor the men of the West India [Indies] Regiment were of much use in the cold weather experienced early in the year. The cold and wet seemed to numb their senses, and they became miserable and inert. Under these conditions they were unable to stand life in huts and tents, and it was found necessary to withdraw them to the rear areas and to billet them. The same remarks apply to all men from tropical climates.[29]

The 6th, 7th and 8th Battalions arrived between April and July 1917 bringing the BWIR in France to almost 5,000 men. On 1 August the War Office decided they would suspend recruitment of the BWIR during the winter months. On 4 September it was recommended to the Adjutant General that both the BWIR and Bermuda RGA be sent to Egypt for the winter as it was thought they would be very little use as labour in France. Three days later GHQ decided they should be transferred to the Mediterranean Command during the winter months, sending 4,000 to Taranto and 500 to Faenza.

In a 1918 report the work of the BWIR in France was described as 'of considerable value in handling ammunition in warm weather, but practically useless in wet and cold weather. On the whole however this labour was not a success.'[30]

Taranto

On 22 December 1917 the 11th Battalion arrived at Taranto, the Camp Commandant reporting a week later that they paid little attention to their officers and NCOs and showed a strong disinclination to work.[31] By the end of February he suggested that the BWIR be moved from Taranto and replaced with Italian labour. His suggestion was rejected and over 3,000 more men of the BWIR arrived during March and April 1918. On 15 May a disagreement between men of the 10th and 11th Battalions and Italian labourers resulted in the death of 14388 Private Hall. A Carabinieri opened fire on a BWIR detachment commanded by the CO of the 10th Battalion. A Court of Enquiry found that both the BWIR and the Italian workmen were responsible for the disturbance and that the actions of Carabinieri Martina, the man who fired the shots, were 'calculated to increase the disturbance'.[32]

With the Armistice several battalions of the BWIR were moved to Taranto from France, other parts of Italy and Egypt. On 6 December 1918 the CO of 9th Battalion, Lieutenant Colonel Willis, ordered his men to clean the latrines used by Italian labourers. The men refused, attacking their officers and NCOs. Although these men dispersed, the dissatisfaction spread to other battalions. On 8 December a mutineer was shot dead by a sergeant of the 7th Battalion who was later sentenced to four months of hard labour for negligently discharging his rifle. Disturbances, strikes and insubordination continued until 12 December when a battalion of the Worcestershire Regiment was sent to Taranto in case they were needed to quell the mutiny. A decision was made to disarm the BWIR Battalions and to increase the rate of repatriation. There is contradictory evidence about the mutiny at Taranto, which appears to have been glossed over at the time, as the following entries from the Camp Commandant's Diary show:

6 December	Disturbance in 9th Bn BWIR. Col Willis injured
7–12 December	Reports of disaffection and refusal to work in BWIR
9th & 10th	Bns are disarmed
8 December	Sgt of 7th BWI shoots a Private and is badly mauled by his comrades[33]

A number of sources[34] state that one mutineer was executed but it appears that the execution was that of Private Albert Denny 8th Battalion. Denny was executed on 20 January 1919 for murdering Private Agard Best whilst committing robbery on 5 September 1918.[35]

The mutineers were arrested:

Forty-nine men were found guilty of mutiny and sentenced to between three and five years imprisonment with hard labour; one man received fourteen years and a Private Sanches, apparently the ringleader, received a death sentence, commuted to twenty years imprisonment.[36]

Black BWIR NCOs were unhappy that they could not be commissioned and that white NCOs were often promoted before black soldiers. In October 1917 permission was sought to offer commissions to men 'not of pure European descent'.

The Secretary of State replied: '... [the] War Office have no objection to the grant to slightly coloured gentlemen of temporary commissions in British West Indies Regiment provided the candidates are British subjects and are considered in every other respect suitable to undertake the leadership of men'.[37]

On 17 December 1918 sergeants of the BWIR held a secret meeting at which they formed the Caribbean League. The purpose of the League was to promote closer co-operation between the West Indian Islands. During the next few weeks, at further meetings the men discussed blacks having the freedom to govern themselves and the idea of a general strike for higher wages once back in the West Indies. The League came to an end after one of the 8th Battalion sergeants reported the meetings to his CO. Information that the League may have been formed to promote disorder on the islands was passed from the Colonial Office to the Governor of Jamaica.

In 1919 veterans of the fighting in the Middle East began to arrive at Taranto and were subjected to the same treatment as the Labour Battalions. They were rigidly segregated from white soldiers and employed on fatigues and labouring tasks despite being assured this would not happen. Major Thursfield, 5th Battalion, protested to the Taranto Camp Commandant, Brigadier General Carey Bernard, about the men's treatment. Bernard's response being:

> ... the men were only niggers and ... no such treatment should ever have been promised to them ... they were better fed and treated than any nigger had a right to expect ... he would order them to do whatever work he pleased, and if they objected he would force them to do it.[38]

Concerned that a mutiny would take place, GHQ in Egypt was asked in May 1919 to ensure the three battalions did not arrive at Taranto en masse.[39]

Honours, Awards and Casualties

Most of the higher honours and decorations were made to white officers and it has not been possible to completely separate awards made in Egypt from those made in France. One report, written in 1923[40], gave the awards in all theatres as:

Distinguished Service Order	5
Military Cross	9
Military Cross with Bar	1
Membership of the OBE.	2
Distinguished Conduct Medal	8
Military Medal	37
Military Medal with Bar	1
Meritorious Service Medal	13
Royal Humane Society's Medal	4
Medaille d'Honneur	1
Mentions in Dispatches	49

Table 12: Awards to BWIR

Of the 37 MMs, nine were awarded for two incidents. On 7 November 1917 five members of the 7th Battalion were awarded MMs when an incendiary bomb was dropped near the centre of Harengo Dump, Bosinghe. 10686 Private Thomas saw the bomb explode and alerted 10799 Lance Corporal Walker, 9621 Lance Corporal Archer, 9741 Lance Corporal Boyce and 10619 Private Smith. Although under heavy bombing the four men extinguished the flames and saved the dump.[41] Corporal Walker was later awarded a bar to his MM.

The other incident took place on 2 July 1918 when aircraft bombed La Bezeque Farm dump. One bomb scored a direct hit on a stack of shells. It was only as a result of the gallant actions of 500 Sergeant Miller, 4136 Sergeant McDonald, 5781 Corporal Evans and 14997 Lance Corporal Cummings of 3rd Battalion that the dump was not destroyed.[42]

Over 15,200 men served in the BWIR in France and Egypt, 185 were killed or died of wounds, 697 wounded and 1,071 died due to sickness.[43] They were not treated as well as white troops. When ill they were sent to a native hospital and several men died of neglect at No. 6 Native Labour Hospital.[44] In August 1918 nineteen men of the BWIR were detained as lunatics in the Marseilles Stationary Hospital. It is suggested that they were held there until early in 1919, not because they were lunatics, but because they were thought to be a threat to military order.[45]

The BWIR also encountered racism in Britain. In November 1918 some 50 injured or ill BWIR soldiers were patients at Belmont Road Auxiliary Hospital, Liverpool. When white soldiers in the concert room taunted black soldiers the room was placed out of bounds to the black men. Later a fight broke out between about 400 white soldiers and the 50 black soldiers. During the melee a nurse was knocked down, went into shock and later died of pneumonia. A number of white soldiers assisted the black soldiers as a contemporary report said:

> When the Provost Martial arrived on the scene with a number of military police to restore order, there were many white soldiers seen standing over crippled black limbless soldiers, and protecting them with their sticks and crutches from the furious onslaught of the other white soldiers until order was restored.[46]

Execution and Mutiny

The 6th Battalion arrived from the West Indies on 17 April 1917. They arrived in Poperinghe on 24 June where they were primarily employed moving ammunition. The Battalion's diary records that men were being killed or wounded on a daily basis between 7 and 13 July and again between 16 and 19 August. One man affected by the shelling was 17-year-old 7429 Private Herbert Morris. On 16 July he absented himself from his detachment, being apprehended in Boulogne the following day. For this offence he was awarded 14 days Field Punishment No. 1

Herbert Morris absented himself again on 20 August and was charged under section 12 (1a) of the Army Act that:

When on active service deserting His Majesty's Services in that he, in the field, on 20th August 1917, when warned for duty in the neighbourhood of the front line absented himself from his detachment until apprehended by the Military Police at Boulogne on the 21st August 1917.[47]

Lieutenant Marshall, the platoon commander, testified that Morris was one of 60 men detailed to move ammunition for the 80-pounder guns at Essex Farm, which was about 3,500 yards from the front line. Morris made a statement to the court saying: 'I am troubled with my head and cannot stand the sound of the guns.'[48] Found guilty of the charge he was executed at Poperinghe on 20 September 1917.

War diaries suggest it was whilst at Taranto that the most serious incidents of insubordination or mutiny occurred. From May to December 1917 not one account of insubordination is recorded in the 7th Battalion diary. On 5 January 1918 the Battalion arrived in Taranto and by the end of March four men had been tried by court martial for striking an officer, offering violence and disobeying a lawful command.

Between January and May 1919 eight men were found guilty of mutiny at Taranto, receiving sentences of between 6 months and 3 years. Discontent was not confined to Taranto; in February 1919 four men in the BWIR were found guilty of mutiny at Plymouth and sentenced to 2 years detention.

Conclusion

The BWIR had proved itself both as a fighting force in Egypt and as a labouring unit in France. Following the war a number of the men who had served in the BWIR played important roles in the growth of the working class movement, the organisation of trade unions and the demand for representative government in the West Indies. Captain A. Cipriani, 5th Battalion, served as Mayor of Port of Spain, Trinidad and a member of the island's Legislative Council.

1 The Colonial Office's request came on the same day that the Cabinet decided that an Indian force of two divisions and a cavalry brigade should serve in France.
2 NA CO 318/33 2 September 1914
3 *Stratford Express* (London), 19 May 1915, page 3 quoted on website http://website. lineone.net/~bwir/bwi_regt.htm
4 NA CO 318/33 23 November 1914
5 Dundonald's view was the black population's loyalty to Britain was vital in stopping any proposal to exchange 'the Stars and Stripes for the Union Jack'.
6 The reference to there being no conditions about where they could serve suggests that Kitchener was aware of the correspondence that had already taken place between the War Office and the Colonial Office At the end of 1914 the War Office had suggested that they would allow a battalion of West Indians to be used as garrison troops in the Cameroons. The Colonial Office had rejected this suggestion as the role was a non-combatant one and because of fear that the men would be at too great a risk of malaria.
7 NA CO 318/336 25 June 1915
8 *The Times History of the War* Vol XVI, p. 86
9 NA CO 318/336 25 October 1915
10 Different sources show the name as the SS *Verdalla* and SS *Verdula*

11 *Daily Gleaner* 5 April 1916 quoted on web site http://www.rootsweb.com/~jamwgw/3contin.htm

12 http://jamaicanfamilysearch.com/Samples2/who19_01.html

13 http://www.bbc.co.uk/history/worldwars/wwone/west_indies_04.shtml

14 *Daily Gleaner* 30 September 1916 quoted on website http://www.rootsweb.com/~jamwgw/3contin.htm

15 In total Jamaica supplied some 300 of the 400 officers of the BWIR and 10,000 of the 15,000 other ranks.

16 NA CO 318/339 29 June 1916.

17 ibid CAB 23/1

18 Lance Corporal Alexander from British Guiana was awarded the MM for 'exceptional coolness and devotion to duty' during the raid.

19 NA CO 318/350 17 December 1918

20 ibid CO 318/340 31 October 1916

21 Joseph , C. L. , The British West Indian Regiment 1914–1918 *Journal of Caribbean History* 1971 Vol 2 p.107

22 Joseph, p.108

23 See picture section

24 Rogers, S., 'There were no parades for us' ,the *Guardian,* 6 November 2002

25 ibid

26 Joseph, p.113

27 NA WO 95/858

28 ibid WO 95/184

29 ibid

30 ibid WO 106/33

31 ibid WO 95/4255

32 ibid

33 ibid

34 James, L. *Mutiny* p. 259, Howe, G. *Race, War and Nationalism* p, 165 also Jamaica and the Great War at http://www.jamaica-gleaner.com/pages/history/story0014.html, The British West Indies Regiment at http://website.lineone.net/~bwir/bwi_regt.htm#Introduction

35 NA WO 71/675

36 Smith, R., *Jamaican Volunteers in the First World War,* p. 131

37 NA CO 28/292/37

38 Cipriani, *Twenty Years After*, p. 62 quoted in Smith, p. 134

39 NA WO 95/4373

40 Lucas, Sir Charles., *The Empire at War* Vol II, p.335

41 NA WO 95/409

42 ibid

43 Lucas, p.335

44 Joseph, p.119

45 Smith pp.123-124

46 'The Belmont Hospital Affair', *African Telegraph* I/8 December 1918 quoted in Fryer, P., *Staying Power* p. 297

47 NA WO 71/594

48 ibid

ANZACs

Australian and New Zealand soldiers were paid at a higher rate than the British and this led to concerns that it would be uneconomical to use them as labour troops. In October 1916 the War Office proposed sending all ANZAC Permanent Base (PB) men in France back to Britain for repatriation.

On 4 January 1917 Haig wrote to the War Office suggesting ANZACs could be retained for labour duties:

> There are at present no Australian or New Zealand Labour Units serving with the force. It is probable that there are similarly many Australians and New Zealanders who might be employed in France on Labour duties, and that Australian Labour Companies could be organised in England and sent out to France at an early date.[1]

The matter was discussed at a meeting of the Standing Committee on the organisation of PB men on 15 February 1917. The Committee, which had been set up at the suggestion of the Director of Labour, acted as a link between the Labour Directorate and the AG Branch.

Colonel Whitehead, the AAG, brought to the Committee a proposal from the GOC ANZAC Corps that

> … most 'PB' men from the Corps should be sent to England, to be returned to Australia and New Zealand, on the grounds that the high rate of pay of the ANZAC personnel rendered their retention with the Force uneconomical, when they could no longer perform the duties for which they enlisted. A small number per Division would be kept for the performance of 'PB' duties.'[2]

In accepting this proposal the idea of using ANZACs as labour troops was rejected.

This resulted in the vast majority of work within the ANZAC Corps being undertaken by either British or foreign labour who worked under the labour group system. When Divisional Employment Companies were created in May 1917 none were allocated to the ANZAC Corps who continued to use their own PB men for regimental employment.

During May 1917 a New Zealand 'Special Service Company' was formed at Codford, Hampshire under the command of Captain R. Quinn. Its duties were to be salvage, baths and laundries and the Company arrived in France at the end of the month. In June 1917 New Zealand Routine Order 352 announced the creation of two Employment Companies. No. 1 Company was a Divisional Employment Company and No. 2 Company an Area Employment Company. Commanded by a captain or major the companies comprised a lieutenant, a CQMS, an orderly room clerk, a batman and 270 NCOs and privates.

Captain Quinn's company was renamed as No. 1 Divisional Employment Company. On 7 July No. 2 Area Employment Company was formed at Codford under the command of Lieutenant Huggins. Arriving in France on 10 July it was sent to Bailleul where 100 other ranks were transferred to No. 1 Company. It appears that PB men were sent to No 2 Company where they were assessed before being retained, sent to infantry units or to Britain. On 29 November 118 Class B men joined No. 2 Company taking its strength to 372 other ranks. The following day 82 Class C men were sent to Britain and 19 Class A men to the reinforcement centre.

In January 1918, No. 2 Company was located at XXII Corps Headquarters and its strength had risen to 398 men. The men were employed as cooks, waiters, batmen, guards, office workers, telephonists, on construction work and for general duties.

During the German spring offensive a Corps HQ Company was formed in XXII Corps, the men coming from Corps Schools and No. 2 Company, which was disbanded. The HQ Company was made up of 100 New Zealanders and 100 British troops and existed until the beginning of May 1918. Armed with both Vickers and Lewis guns it was to dig shelters at Rosignol Wood and man trenches north of Vierstraat Crossroads.

No. 2 Company was reformed when the Corps HQ Company was disbanded and continued in existence until March 1919. The Company war diary records that in October 1918 they were within five miles of the line at Cambrai.[3] No. 1 Company was located at Divisional HQ at Poperinghe, Ouderdom and then Orville. Whilst at Poperinghe in December 1917 the HQ was bombed with four men killed and twelve wounded. In July 1918 the Company strength had grown to 455 other ranks, which included 28 on salvage, 53 on traffic control, 30 in canteens, 50 at the YMCA, 25 in the band and 63 in pierrot troupes.

The New Zealanders used PB men to support front line troops. Private N. Ingram became ill with trench fever late in 1917. After a spell in hospital in England he returned to an entrenching battalion in France in March 1918 where he was employed digging trenches and then 'loaned to a Canadian Railway Construction Battalion, excavating and laying down a light railway track'.[4]

The Australians did not form an employment company until 1 November 1917. The company had a total establishment of 517 Class B men, was made up of one Corps detachment and five Divisional detachments. The detachments provided men to run baths, laundries, canteens, cinemas and theatres, for sanitary duties, traffic control, as cooks, waiters and batmen, at the YMCA and for general duties. They appear to have followed a similar pattern to the New Zealanders; men were sent to the company where they were assessed before being retained, sent to infantry units or to Britain.

In March 1918 the Australians also formed a company of one officer and 70 other ranks from PB men and under-aged boys who were being held at the divisional reinforcement depots. It was called K Working Company and was employed on roads, working for the RE. Little is known about this Company other than that they were located at Meteren at the end of March, at Querrieu in the beginning of June and Bussy Chateau from June to August 1918.

1   NA WO 95/33
2   ibid
3   idid WO 95/1039
4   anon, Anzac Diary, p. 106

CANADIANS

There are few references to Canadian labour in Canadian Histories. Nicholson[1] makes no reference to them in the Official History, and Love[2], in 'A Call to Arms,' includes information about labour but incorrectly states that in 1916 the 1st and 4th Labour Battalions were absorbed into the Canadian Engineers.[3]

Labour Units

By late 1916 a large number of Canadian soldiers in England were, on arrival from Canada, deemed to be unfit for service in the front line in France because of their age or medical defects. Additionally, there were men who had served in France and been sent to England following illness or injury and were unfit to be returned to their units.

It was decided to form these men into four Canadian Infantry Labour Battalions, each composed of 50 per cent B(i) and 50 per cent B(ii) men. The original idea was that these Battalions would be attached to the Canadian Corps, one to each division, as second line pioneers. This did not happen and they were allotted to the Imperial Force to be employed on Light and Broad Gauge Railways working for the RE Railway Construction Companies. In the spring of 1917 the Canadians asked for these Battalions to be reallocated to the Canadian Corps but this was turned down as they had become so effective at railway work.

The creation of the Labour Directorate saw Major A. Wilby, 7 Infantry Battalion, appointed Deputy Assistant Director of Labour (DADL) for the Canadian Corps. Following his appointment, Canadian Corps Routine Order 1234 was published on 18 May 1917.[4] This stated that labour attached to the Canadian Corps would be in a labour group, under the direction of the DADL. It also made it clear that no movement of labour units were to be ordered by employers, or to take place without the knowledge of the DADL.

In November 1917 there was a reorganization of the Canadian labour battalions which resolved the question of the Canadian corps seeking direct control of these battalions rather than their being always employed on rail work. The 2nd and 3rd Canadian Labour Battalions became 12th and 11th Canadian Railway Troops working directly for the Director General Transport. The 1st and 4th Canadian Labour Battalions came under the control of the DADL Canadian Corps becoming the 1st and 2nd Canadian Labour Battalions.

In line with the British Army's change from Labour Directorate to Labour Control on 1 March 1918, Major A. Wilby was appointed the Canadian Labour Commandant with the temporary rank of colonel. The new organization gave the Labour Commandant direct command, instead of administration, of the labour troops and 'proved a big advantage over the old Order of things'.[5]

Colonel Wilby, on becoming Labour Commandant, became responsible for the two Canadian Labour battalions, three Canadian Employment Companies and 23 Labour Group, which was made up of six British labour companies. The number of men commanded by the Labour Commandant varied according to the size of the sector in which the Canadians were operating. This was never fewer than 6,000 and as many as 14,000.

The Canadian corps operated a different system from their British counter-parts, with units being, as far as possible, concentrated rather than working in small detachments. It was felt that this approach gave the OC better control over his men, improved discipline and produced units that were capable of carrying out all types of work. There were some companies, which after working for a long period of time on one particular type of work, became skilled in that task and were always allocated similar employment. There was often a shortage of transport and efforts were made to use the labour closest to the work and to give units clear and explicit movement orders.

There were concerns both at HQ level[6] and amongst the soldiers serving in the labour battalions about the use of the title 'Labour' as the men had either enlisted voluntarily for front line service or had already served in France. In March 1918 authority was given to change the names of the two battalions to the 1st and 2nd Canadian Infantry Works Battalions.

With the German Spring Offensive each battalion was armed with rifles and four Lewis guns. When the Canadian Corps was withdrawn to reserve positions in May 1918 the labour battalions remained, working first in XVIII Corps then in VIII Corps. They continued in this role until July when the Canadian Corps, now in the Amiens area, requested their return. In August the Canadian Corps moved to Arras and for a short time the two Battalions worked for III Corps. In September they rejoined the Canadian Corps, being employed on roads, ammunition and tramways.

Unlike British labour units the Canadians retained the battalion structure during 1917 and much of 1918 but this proved to be uneconomical. In April 1918 the Labour Commandant had recommended the battalions be reorganised to form a Canadian Works Group HQ and four Infantry Works companies, similar to the British system. Approval for this was given on 14 September and the next day Lieutenant Colonel J. McKinery became OC of the Canadian Works Group with the 1st Canadian Infantry Works Battalion becoming the 1st and 3rd Canadian Infantry Works Companies, and the 2nd Canadian Infantry Works Battalion the 2nd and 4th Canadian Infantry Works Companies. The Labour Commandant thought the group system was not necessary.[7] For much of the time there was only one Group within the Corps and, when it did have two, there was not sufficient work for both of them.

As the Canadian Corps advanced during the last two months of the war, the Works Companies accompanied them with the 1st and 3rd Companies being allot-ted to roadwork and the 2nd and 4th to tramways. Three companies accompanied the Canadian Corps on its march to the Rhine as part of the Army of Occupation, reaching a few kilometres south of Bonn on 16 December 1918. Soon after they arrived the decision was taken to demobilise all Canadian 'B' men as soon as possible and the companies were sent to Aubin St Vaast. The 4th Works Company was the first to be demobilised in January 1919, the other three Companies remained in France for three more months, the 3rd Company being used primarily for burial duties.

Employments within the Corps, which included routine tasks such as guards and clerks, were undertaken by nine Employment Companies. The 1st to 4th Companies were divisional companies moving with their respective division. The 5th Employment Company was the Corps HQ Company and moved with the Corps. The 6th, 7th and 8th were Area Employment Companies and usually remained in a fixed location within the Corps area. They provided personnel for Town Majors and at establishments including laundries, baths and canteens. The 9th AE Company had a larger establishment of one officer and 435 other ranks. This company moved with the Corps providing all personnel for YMCA work and the chaplains services. The 6th to 9th AE Companies were administered directly by the Labour Commandant and not the Labour Group.

In addition to the Works and Employment Companies the Canadians had a Corps Labour Reinforcement Pool. The Reinforcement Pool received category B men direct from England and men whose medical category dropped whilst in France. These men were used for temporary employments whilst awaiting despatch to a labour unit. The Labour Commandant complained that these reinforcements were 'very often not satisfactory, as it was found that a certain percentage, while supposedly fulfilling all requirements medically, were nevertheless unable to carry out the work required'.[8]

In his report in 1919, on the work of Labour with the Canadian Corps,[9] the Labour Commandant identified a number of matters which he believed affected the efficiency of the labour under his command. These included the fact that the Labour Battalions were not attached to the Canadian Corps from the outset and the units were referred to as 'Labour' which associated them with 'other classes of labour, such as conscientious objectors and the hired blacks and Chinese'.[10] He also felt that co-operation and liaison between the various services and the Labour Commandant could have been better. In his view 'a clear co-operation with the Branches of the Staff and various services would at times have given much better results, or would at least have made the results less difficult to attain'.[11] Through close contact with employers the efficiency of Labour was improved during 1918, with companies being given both more responsibility and a freer hand. However 'the habit of employers always asking for more men than were needed had always to be carefully checked'.[12]

He believed there was a lack of appreciation of Labour's work and that this disheartened the men and lead to slackness. He attributed this to the Corps always having at its disposal a large Pioneer or Engineer Establishment and a lack of understanding about both the amount and diverse nature of the work. The men worked and lived in areas subject to shelling and bombing. He suggests 'that much better results would have been attained had the units been treated more like Engineering and Pioneer Units and less like a purely Labour Organisation trying to do so many hours work a day for so many days a week'.[13]

It appears that it was not only in the Canadian Corps that the work of the Canadian Labour units was unappreciated. In General Wace's Report on Labour the work of the Canadians is almost ignored, his only comment being:

> The work of these Canadian Units was excellent, though there was a tendency on the part of their COs to keep too many men in camp. The personnel was of a type that adapted itself well to the varied requirements of work, containing as it did so large a proportion of 'handy men,' and men used to railway and bridge construction.[14]

War Graves

In May 1919 the Canadians formed two War Graves Companies under the command of Major W. Piper, formerly 31st Battalion. The eight officers and 1000 other ranks were men who had been in England and volunteered for the work.

The unit moved from Etaples to Neuville St Vaast on 24 May. On 2 June No.1 Company commenced work on Maroc British Cemetery and No. 2 Company in the Courcelette area. On 12 June Major Piper recorded that the work of the two Companies was being hampered by a lack of transport.[15] On 18 June 3 American soldiers and 2 Nursing Sisters visited the Headquarters about the location of graves and on 21 June two French soldiers were attached to No. 1 Company, which suggests that they were finding bodies from these countries as well as British and Canadian soldiers.

Forestry Units

As skilled units the Canadian Forestry Companies are outside the scope of this history. It would, however, be wrong to exclude them in view of not only their importance but as major employers of unskilled labour.

In February 1916 the British Government sent a telegram to the Governor General of Canada asking whether a battalion of Canadian lumbermen could be formed to work in forests in France and Britain. Within nine days the 224th Battalion was formed and the first detachment, complete with portable saw mills, arrived in Britain on 12 April.

In May 1916 the Army Council asked the Canadians for a further 2,000 lumbermen and in November another 5,000. 'The transfer of skilled Canadian woodsmen across the Atlantic continued throughout the war, and the Armistice found 12,127 Canadian foresters in France and 9967 in England.'[16]

The Canadians produced their first lumber at Windsor Great Park on 13 May 1916. A Base Depot was set up at Windsor on 6 January 1917. As operations expanded the country was divided into six Districts, numbered 51 to 56 as shown below.

District	Headquarters (date established)
51	Edinburgh (May 1916), Nairn (July 1917), Inverness (November 1917)
52	Carlisle (November 1916)
53	London (November 1916), Egham (November 1917)
54	Southampton (August 1917)
55	Stirling (November 1917)
56	East Sheen (August 1918)

Table 13: Canadian Forestry Corps Districts in Britain

A colonel was in charge of each District with work being carried out by companies of 165 men commanded by a major. District 56 was set up to build aerodromes for the RAF with small detachments working throughout Britain.

Work was supported by unskilled or semi-skilled labour provided by Finns, Portuguese, surplus seamen and PoWs. In September 1917 it was decided that the

Canadian Forestry units could have up to 2,000 Finns, 2,000 Portuguese and as many PoWs as could be provided. Where PoWs were used the Canadians built camps for them, with the British supplying the guards. The Portuguese were tried in Scottish forests but the climate proved unsuitable for them. 'Eventually it was found that the Finns and prisoners of war were the most satisfactory forms of attached labour, and the Portuguese were largely transferred to other work.'[17]

In France the first Forestry units arrived during the autumn of 1916. In November 1916 the Canadian Forestry Corps was established under the command of Colonel (later Brigadier General) A. McDougall. The Corps was organised into a Corps Headquarters, a Technical Warehouse at Havre, Group Headquarters, District Headquarters and Companies. Each Group administered two Districts and each District two or more Companies in its area.

By the end of May 1917, 22 Companies had arrived in France with this rising to 55 by October. At the same time Numbers 1 and 2 Forest Parties, Canadians who had been working under the direction of the British, were added to the Forestry Corps as No. 1 and 2 Companies. More companies arrived during 1918 with a total of 65 employed in France by the Armistice.[18]

Support for companies in the Army Areas came primarily from the Indian Labour Corps:

> No. 76 (Kumaon), No. 27 (Lushai) and No. 28 (Lushai) Indian Labour Companies all doing particularly good work – the latter Company being considered by their Employers, after working for several months in the Foret de Lyons as excellent.[19]

Other labour employed by the Canadian Forestry Corps was found from the South African Native Labour Corps, Chinese Labour Corps, PoW companies and British Labour companies. Among the Chinese and PoW companies were several made up of skilled men, such as 118 and 125 Chinese Companies. The scale of support can be seen in March 1918 when there were 7,322 PoWs, 1,025 Indians and 2,189 Chinese being employed in support of the Forestry Companies outside of the Army Areas.[20]

No. 2 Construction Battalion

On 2 July 1916 authorisation was given for the formation of No. 2 Construction Battalion at Pictou, Nova Scotia. Lieutenant Colonel Daniel Sutherland, a railroad contractor from Nova Scotia, was appointed Commanding Officer. The Battalion was to be made up of black men and permission was given for it to recruit in all provinces, wherever black people were residing. 'Despite previous rejections and the segregated status of the Battalion, Black men and boys throughout the country immediately volunteered for duty.'[21]

Numbers appear to have been small as in August 1916 there were only 180 recruits at Pictou. Recruitment continued to be a problem and in the spring of 1917, 165 black Americans were recruited for the Battalion. In December 1916 Sutherland was told that the Battalion was needed overseas. The Battalion, with a strength of nineteen officers and 605 other ranks, sailed from Halifax on 28 March 1917 arriving in Liverpool ten days later.

In early May the Battalion's status was changed to a Company and it was sent to France where it was attached to the Canadian Forestry Corps as unskilled labour. The majority served at Lajoux in the Jura Mountains, with smaller detachments at Peronne and Alencon. Early in 1919 the unit returned to Canada where it was officially disbanded on 15 September 1920.

1   Nicholson, G., *Canadian Expeditionary Force 1914–1919*
2   Love, D. A., *Call to Arms*
3   ibid p.255
4   NA WO 95/1068
5   ibid
6   ibid
7   ibid
8   ibid
9   ibid
10 ibid
11 ibid
12 ibid
13 ibid
14 ibid WO 107/37 p.66
15 Library and Archives Canada RG9, Militia and Defence, Series III-D-3, Volume 5053, Reel T-10945 Headquarters, Canadian War Graves Detachment
16 Nicholson, p.499
17 Bird & Davies, *The Canadian Forestry Corps* p.30
18 Bird & Davies (p.37) give this as the figure whereas Nicholson (p.500) puts the figure at 56.
19 NA WO 107/37 p.42
20 ibid WO 95/64
21 Ruck, C. *The Black Battalion* p.15

INDIAN LABOUR CORPS

Indian labour units were referred to as corps, rather than battalions, each comprised of about 2,000 men. They served in both France and Mesopotamia.

France

In September 1915 the Indian Corps in France recommended the formation of a working battalion. It appears that the men serving in the Battalion were either temporarily unfit for front line service or could be spared from other duties. Under the direction of the DAG 3rd Echelon the Battalion was formed without addition to the establishment of the Indian Corps and on condition that men would be released for the front line when required.[1]

There is also evidence that Indian troops were used in a labour role in January 1916 when 1,000 dismounted men from the Indian Cavalry Corps were used to replace a Labour battalion working on the 3rd Army Defences[2] and to move stores in Marseilles.[3]

Formation of a Labour Corps

In 1916 Britain turned to India to supply a civilian labour corps in an effort to meet the labour requirements in France. However, the needs of the Army in France were not appreciated by the Indian administration either in London or India. The Indian Government's instructions to the six provinces[4] were to recruit, locally, a corps commanded by a lieutenant colonel as commandant, with two assistant commandants. Each corps was to be made up of four sections, of 480 men, each under a supervisor with 'Warrant Rank'. The vagueness of the instructions to the provinces created difficulties for the authorities in France as each corps had a different establishment and terms of engagement.

In Manipur the Maharaja, Churachand Singh, offered to recruit 2,000 Nagas and Kukis immediately and a further 2,000 at a later date. However some of the Kuki chiefs in the outlying hill areas objected to this recruitment and a small military force had to be sent to stop them interfering with the recruitment. The 2,000 men, made up of 1,200 Nagas and 800 Kukis, under the command of Lieutenant Colonel H. W. G. Cole, who had been the province's Political Agent, left for France in May 1917[5]. An attempt to raise the second 2,000 later in 1917 saw the Kukis rise up in a rebellion that lasted for three years.

Formation of Labour Companies

On 19 May 1917, a month before the arrival of the first of the ILC in France, Lieutenant Colonel Lord Ampthill became the Indian Advisor. Recognising that a Corps of almost 2,000 men under the command of only three officers would not fit in with the requirements of the Labour Organisation in France the decision was taken two days later that each ILC Corps would be reorganised into four companies of 500 men, each with its own officer establishment comparable to the British Labour companies.

The 23 United Provinces contingent with 2 British, 4 Indian supervisors and 6,370 men arrived at Marseilles on 16 June on the SS *Aragon* and over the next five weeks some 40 officers and 20,000 other ranks were to arrive at Marseilles or Taranto. It was discovered that the Indian Government's vague instructions concerning the formation of the Corps meant that, in effect, there were ten different contingents rather than a single labour corps.

Lord Ampthill encountered difficulties with the officers. Some of the commandants were highly placed civil servants, some regular Indian Army soldiers who had been seconded to administrative appointments and some had no military experience at all.

Since these commandants held the rank of lieutenant colonel they were too senior to command one of the newly formed companies and they were appointed to command Labour groups. However, 'Officers who had no previous military experience found great difficulty in mastering the many problems which present themselves to a Labour Group Commander in the Field'.[6]

Age does not seem to have been a barrier to appointment as an officer. Captain Herbert Cunningham Clogstoun, a former policeman and farmer in India, was 60 years and 7 months old when he arrived in France in August 1917. He commanded

55 (Khasi) Company until August 1918 when he became an instructor at the Indian Base Depot.

Supervisors, who had been recruited from different groups in each province, also presented difficulties for the British. In Assam, for example, they were recruited from white planters and Government officials whereas in the United Provinces most supervisors were drawn from the 'domicile community'[7] or well educated Indians. Not only were the British faced with both white and native supervisors but even the term supervisor presented problems as they were described as holding 'Warrant Rank'. In fact, they held no such rank, which meant they were not enlisted in either the British or Indian Army. Eventually, after a visit to France by Lieutenant General Sir H. Cox, Military Secretary at the India Office, it was decided to grant temporary commissions in the Indian Army Reserve of Officers to British or Anglo-Indian supervisors, and temporary commissions in the Native Indian Land Forces to those supervisors of pure Indian birth.

There was considerable variation in the number of men in each contingent, the greatest being 6,370 men and the fewest 417. The men were recruited from some twelve different tribes, many of whom would not work together. When each corps was split into companies these factors had to be taken into account.

Experience of coloured labour in France had shown that close supervision by white officers and NCOs was absolutely necessary if the best results were to be obtained from the labour. Arriving with only seven officers and supervisors for 2,000 men, when divided into companies, no company could have had more than two officers. The War Office was asked to supply officers from Britain who had knowledge of Indian dialects. Although there were few serving officers who could be spared for this role the situation was eased through the recruitment of retired Indian civil servants living in Britain. Attaching three British staff sergeants to each Indian company, when it was required for work, provided additional supervision.

In August the Indian contingents were reorganised into nine Corps,[8] based on their home provinces, and the companies renumbered from the 21st (United Provinces) ILC to the 51st (Ranchi) ILC.[9] Each corps was made up of four companies with the exception of the 22nd (Manpuri) and 26th (Khassi) Corps each of which had only two companies and 24th (NWF) Corps, which had three companies. The majority of the ILC was initially sent to the 3rd Army Area and employed on salvage work where they 'with perhaps the exception of the Pathans, who never would work unless in their own interests, carried out some very good work'.[10]

Employment

Concerns were expressed that the physique of the Indians fell far below that of the South Africans and Chinese coolies. It was believed they would not be able to move ammunition and supplies fast enough to keep up with demand. These fears were soon dispelled and, as Table 14 shows, over a period of four months in 1917 the Indians equalled or bettered the South Africans and Chinese. It was recorded that when there was an urgent demand for supplies, the Indians, with their desire to help beat the enemy of their King and Emperor, could be relied upon to turn out even when they had already completed a day's work.[11]

	Indian	Chinese	South African
Ammunition	1.22	1.25	1.22
Supplies (general)	.49	.46	.49
R.E. Stores	.89	.78	.88
Ordnance Stores	.93	.79	.92
Timber	.79	.99	.84

Table 14: Tons per Man Hour Loading and Offloading at an Advanced Depot.[12]

A number of companies soon proved themselves proficient at certain tasks and were repeatedly used for the same type of work. 76 (Kumaon), 27 (Lushai) and 28 (Lushai) Companies were very effective in forestry work and charcoal burning; Forestry officers noted that the men of 27 ILC were better than the Prisoners of War previously employed and put it down to the belief that 'they stand the heat better than white men'.[13] 65 and 66 (Manipur) Companies carried out semi-skilled work on camp construction and making trench boards. 24 (United Provinces), 77 (Kumaon) and 66 (Manipur) Companies were noted for road making, brick making and in quarrying.

The one area where the ILC was not successful was when they replaced the British West Indies Regiment and Egyptian Labour Corps on dockwork at Marseilles. They were of little use, solely on account of their physique, and they were withdrawn and replaced by Prisoners of War.

During the German Offensive of March 1918 many ILC Companies were praised for their work and excellent behaviour when forced to leave their camps at a moment's notice.

> This withdrawal was effected with admirable steadiness, and there was no panic, although in some cases the Companies had to endure shell fire and attacks by Aeroplanes with bombs and machine guns, both by day and by night. Whenever called upon, they halted and even turned back to work at the loading of stores on trains, lorries and wagons. One Company assisted the wounded with a hospital train and performed this work – for which they had no training – in such a manner as to win high praise from the Medical Officers.[14]

Illness greatly affected the work of the ILC. In October 1917 there were concerns that the Indians would not be capable of dealing with the harsh winter weather in France.[15] The ILC's Senior Medical Officer advised GHQ that men from the Indian Plains should not be sent from Marseilles to northern France during the winter months of 1917. On 21 December 1917 GHQ decided that until April only Indians recruited in the hills of northern India would be employed in northern France.[16] It is clear that the ILC did suffer because of the weather in France and in March 1918 the ILC Advisor expressed concern at the number of men having limbs amputated due to frostbite.

Almost 1,500 natives of the ILC died during service in France, the majority through illness. In general, discipline amongst the ILC was good during 1917, although 25 (United Provinces) Company went on strike and refused to turn out for work on 17 August.

Rumours began in India, in the autumn of 1917, that the men were to be issued with steel helmets and that they would then be employed in the front line. Officers who had been involved in recruiting the natives, or responsible for bringing them to Europe, were asked about the terms of engagement. GHQ found that the terms varied not only from province to province but also within districts in a province. The Nagas, for example, were told they would not be called upon to fight, but the men fully understood they would be in the danger zone, whereas Garos had received a definite pledge that they would not be employed within 40 miles of the front line.

Contract Termination and Repatriation

Unrest grew in the ILC during 1918 over their contracts. The men had been recruited for one year or the duration of the war (whichever was less).[17] There was uncertainty about whether the contract commenced when the man was engaged in India or when he arrived in France. In some cases men had been engaged in India some five months before they arrived in France. Allowing for the time it would take to travel to India for discharge at the end of the contract, men might only serve five months in France.

The question of repatriation was complicated by a lack of shipping to transport the men to India. In February 1918 a letter was sent to all companies asking for the number of men they expected to re-engage, explaining that it was hoped men would re-engage up to 31 October 1918. As an incentive the men were offered a bonus of 25 Rupees if they remained in France beyond the date they should have left for India, extra duty pay of 10 Rupees per month for the 1st, 2nd and 3rd months during which the men were kept at work beyond the date of their contract and 15 Rupees a month beyond that. They were also offered other inducements such as the opportunity for leave in London and Paris.[18] At the same time a decision was made to repatriate the ILC as soon as shipping became available with the intention that everyone would be repatriated by the end of October.

At the beginning of March Lieutenant General Cox visited each company to explain the terms of re-engagement and the problems with the lack of shipping. Whilst most companies accepted the terms, between March and December 1918, there are twelve recorded instances of ILC Companies going on strike in protest at not being repatriated. Whilst the ILC Companies undoubtedly carried out good work in France the Report on the Work of Labour in the BEF questions whether they were value for money:

> Indian Labour, as a whole, cannot fairly be said to have justified the expense involved in transport and maintenance. The Contract was too short, the organisation was confused, and the men did not stand the winter in Northern France well.[19]

Mesopotamia

Indian Labour was used in Mesopotamia from early in 1916 although it only came under the control of the Directorate of Labour in May 1918. It played a vital role in the expansion of the ports and the construction of railway lines.

In Britain an idealistic view of the work of Indians in Mesopotamia appeared in newspapers. In 1917 Edmund Chandler, a correspondent for *The Times,* wrote of the Santals in Baghdad:

> They were scurrying like a flock of sheep, not because they were rushed, I was told, but simply for fun. Someone had started it, and others had broken into a jogtrot. One of them, with bricks balanced on his head, was playing a small reed flute – the Pipe of Pan. Another had stuck a spray of salmon-pink oleander in his hair. The full round cheeks of the little men made their black skin look as if it had been sewn up tightly and tucked under their chin. They were like happy golliwogs.[20]

Initial recruitment was on a voluntary basis although, as with recruitment for France, it is likely that many men were encouraged or even coerced into service. In 1916 'Mesopotamia was a name of terror to the unenlightened Indian'[21] and recruiters found it difficult to find suitable men for the ILC. As news reached India that conditions were better than had first been feared recruitment increased, although in 1918 the Director of Labour reported, 'the skilled and clerical classes are of indifferent quality'.[22]

When insufficient men volunteered the idea of conscription was considered. The Indian Government rejected this, fearing it would cause unrest, and instead looked to jails as a source of labour. From 1916 onwards there were two distinct groups of Indian Labour employed in Mesopotamia. The ILC made up of free men and the Jail Labour Corps (JLC). There were at least 26 Corps in Mesopotamia. Each JLC was divided into two sections, the first being for convicts still serving their sentence and the other section was for 'free' men who had completed their sentence and were in the receipt of pay.

In theory, prisoners volunteered to serve in the JLC for two years or the duration of the war. Prisoners serving sentences for murder, military or political offences, and adolescents, were barred from joining the JLC. Enrolled as a 'follower' under the Indian Army Act, the un-expired part of a man's sentence was suspended whilst he was in Mesopotamia and remitted on his return to India.

It is likely that many, if not most of the men, were coerced into volunteering. Samandarkhan Samankhan from Bombay 'volunteered' to replace a prisoner who had died even though he only had some six weeks of his sentence left to serve. Four prisoners from Bihar and Orissa had already completed their sentences when they joined the JLC.[23]

There is no doubt that the JLC had advantages for the authorities in Mesopotamia. It was a flexible corps that could be used wherever and whenever needed. Prisoners were already used to receiving and obeying orders from their warders, and to being punished if they disobeyed. When local Arab labour refused to work and demanded higher wages the 11th Bombay JLC was used to break the strike.

Both the JLC and the free Labour Corps were subject to military law. This caused some conflict between the Labour Directorate and Lieutenant Colonel Lane, the Inspector of Disciplinary Labour. Lane, together with the officers who had come from India, tended to support the summary use of flogging for breaches of discipline. The British authorities pointed out that the men were enrolled under the Army Act and therefore punishment should only be administered as a result of the findings of a court martial. To overcome this problem Lane started a Disciplinary Camp at Kut where Labour Corps offenders were kept under a harsh regime making bricks.

At the end of November 1918 the men in 11 (Bengal) JLC gave notice that they would not work from 1 December as they had completed their two years and should be returned to India. On 4 December their strike commenced and men broke out from their camp. Soldiers of the South Wales Borderers surrounded the camp and 24 ringleaders were placed under armed guard. They were charged with either causing or joining a mutiny. Tried by Special General Court Martial they were sentenced to terms of rigorous imprisonment ranging from one to eight years. A further 204 men were returned, with an escort of 100 Royal Welsh Fusiliers, to serve their original sentences in India.

Many of the JLC Corps were found to be good workers. The 10 (Punjab) JLC, for example, made 608,000 bricks, dug 12,000 yards of water channel and built six unloading ramps at Khirr Railway Depot during July 1919.[24] Even when the war in Europe ended the authorities in Mesopotamia continued to recruit and employ Indian labour. In February 1919 Headquarters in Delhi wrote to Baghdad stating that there were four Labour Corps in India available for work in Mesopotamia and that if they were disbanded it would save money but it would be difficult to replace them in the future. It was also suggested that there were Indians currently in Mesopotamia 'whose early repatriation requires sympathetical consideration'.[25]

Demobilisation started but was suspended with the outbreak of hostilities in Afghanistan in July 1919. By February 1920 all men in the JLC had been repatriated. At the same time over 18,800 Indians were still employed in Mesopotamia.

1 NA WO 95/3960
2 ibid WO 95/3964
3 ibid WO 95/3969
4 United Provinces, Bihar and Orissa, Assam, North–West Frontier, Burma and Bengal.
5 It has been suggested that these men were sent against their will to France in May 1917. See A Brief History of Manipur at http://www.manipurforum.com/2007/10/02/a-brief-history-of-manipur/
6 NA WO 107/37 Report on Labour p.40
7 The domicile community often referred to, as 'poor whites' was originally those born in India of parents who were of British and/or European descent although by 1900 included those of mixed Anglo-Indian birth.
8 The Burmese and Kumaon ILC being added following their arrival in September.
9 ILC companies in France were numbered from 21 onwards to avoid confusion with the ILC companies serving in Mesopotamia.
10 NA WO 107/37 Report on Labour p.43
11 ibid WO p.42
12 ibid WO
13 ibid WO 95/378
14 ibid WO 107/37 p.45
15 ibid WO 95/42
16 ibid WO 95/83

17 Four Companies, the 33 (Bihar), 55 (United Provinces) 78 (Burma) and 85 (Kumaon) were recruited for the duration of the War. Although the 78 (Burma) Company were to question whether this was correct in December 1918.

18 On 25 July 1918 the King inspected a party of the ILC from the United Provinces under the command of 2nd Lt Bull at Buckingham Palace.

19 NA WO 107/37 p. 45

20 *The Times* 'The Model Coolie in Mesopotamia' 20 June 1917

21 NA WO 95/4992 Report of the Labour Directorate Mesopotamia Expeditionary Force p.26

22 ibid

23 Singha, R. *The Jail Porter and Labour Corps* p.428

24 NA WO 95/5037

25 ibid WO 95/4991

FIJIAN LABOUR CORPS

The story of the Fijian Labour Corps is not one of the British Government seeking help from a colony but that of a colony wanting to help Britain. At the outbreak of war Fiji had a population of about 150,000 living on some 250 islands.[1] In January 1915 the 'First Fiji Contingent', some 60 white men, was sent 'home' (Britain), where most of them were immediately attached to the King's Royal Rifles. By the end of the war some 600 white Fijians had answered the call to arms.

The native population of Fiji were equally eager to serve, but initially, prejudice about employing 'blacks' meant that any idea of using them was rejected. In August 1914, Ratu Joseva Sukuna, a Fijian high chief was studying Law at Wadham College, Oxford. Despite both his education and breeding he was rejected when he tried to enlist with the British. He went to France where he joined and fought with the French Foreign Legion and later served in the Fijian Labour Corps.[2]

For a time there were similar obstructions in Fiji to the use of natives, however, the Governor, Sir E. B. Sweet-Escott, came to recognise that 'there was even greater difficulty in keeping them back from going "home" to England to serve'.[3] He therefore approached the British Government and offered a contingent of natives for transport work. The War Office wrote to the C-in-C on 30 January 1917 informing him that the Governor's offer had been accepted. The Fijians had agreed to enlist at ordinary rates of pay and, as such, would be soldiers rather than civilian labour.

The Company, 2 officers, 5 NCOs and 96 other ranks arrived at Boulogne on 6 July 1917, having travelled to Europe through Canada. They were immediately sent to Calais where their first task was to carry flour at the Calais bakery. The following week a case of mumps in the Company caused them to be kept apart from other men and they were sent to the sand-siding where they loaded sand into trucks.

The Fijians were affected by the prejudice displayed by both the French and British authorities. As coloured troops the French banned them from cafes[4] and expressed concern when their work brought them into contact with Chinese Labourers: 'From 1 August to 23 September they were employed loading supplies, but contact with Chinese at this work necessitated their removal to the Detail Issue Store.'[5] No reason can be found for this separation. It may have been in view of concerns in Fiji about the Chinese that: 'During World War 1, the colonial government suspected the Chinese of undermining Fijian confidence in the British.'[6]

Alternatively the British authorities may have been concerned that the Fijian's work rate, which was significantly higher than the Chinese, would decrease.

In the 'Notes for Officers of the Labour Corps' the Fijians are shown as being treated the same as British soldiers in respect of pay, accounting, discipline, medical arrangements and accommodation[7] but when it comes to canteens the prejudice of the time prevailed and they were restricted to the 'dry side' of British canteens. Their positive qualities were recognised in the section 'General Remarks':

> The contingent contains a few winch-men. All are good boatmen and good wharf labourers, with a proportion of stevedores. There are a few good clerks among them. They are educated and intelligent. They are well behaved and well disciplined.[8]

Quickly earning a reputation for hard work and positive discipline the Company formally became part of the Labour Corps on 26 August 1917 as its Fijian Section, the only coloured unit to be afforded such a status.

Their patriotism and high standard of work was reported to the British public in an article published in *The Times* towards the end of 1917 under the title 'An Army of Labour':

> Lastly, it may be noted that there is a small body of labourers from that most sequestrated and remote of all our dependencies, the island group of Fiji. These men have joined the corps not so much for love of gain, but out of patriotism and a sense of duty. If they could have had their way the Fijians would gladly have raised a contingent for the fighting ranks. This was not deemed desirable; so at the instance of the High Commissioner and the leading chiefs they decided to help the Empire in other ways. They have sent money and supplies, according to their limited resources, and now this picked company of labour recruits – splendid men they are, with the lithe muscular forms, the olive skin, and the chiselled features of the true and noble Polynesian type – these aristocrats of the Pacific are putting their strength into trundling trucks and hauling bales at a base port. It is no mean sacrifice; for in his island home the Fijian is not a manual worker, but a landowner, a fisherman and hunter, or, at the best, an agriculturist in a casual, leisurely fashion. Here in France he has been taught to labour diligently, and does his share in handling the 20,000 to 40,000 tons of goods that are landed weekly at this one harbour alone. To watch these children from the sun-kissed South Seas toiling in the cold and grimy sheds is to gain a new conception of the meaning of Empire; and you marvel afresh at the strange magic which enables Englishmen, cold and stiff, and unsympathetic as they seem, to gain the loyalty of so many diverse and sundered peoples. Perhaps it is the magic of faith. These coloured men trust the Englishmen who have brought them across the oceans to work as so many other natives have learnt to put their trust in the British officers who lead them into battle.[9]

As winter approached the incidence of ill health, particularly pneumonia and bronchitis, increased as they found it difficult to cope with the cold climate. In view of this the decision was taken that they should be moved to Marseilles. The Company arrived in Marseilles on 24 January 1918 where they were employed at the docks.

Mr (later Sir) C. H. Rodwell, who became Governor of Fiji in October 1918, paid a visit to the Company on 6 June 1918 and two days later met with the Controller of Labour at HQ. Although there is no surviving record of this meeting it is likely that one aspect was the Royal Warrant, which was published as Army Order 228 on 1 July 1918 stating: 'OUR WILL AND PLEASURE is that the Fijian Labour Corps shall be deemed a corps for the purposes of the Army Act.'[10] The Fijians were no longer merely a section of the Labour Corps but a Corps in their own right.

The Fijians gained a reputation for excellent work at Marseilles and this was recognised in the Official Report:

> The men were great strong fellows, all volunteers who could earn with ease in their own country considerably more than their army pay. Their employment resulted in the saving of some 25% of Labour on work they undertook. The coaling of ships and the dust at Marseilles had serious effects, however, on the health of the contingent.[11]

In addition to health problems caused by working in dusty conditions there were concerns that the winter of 1918, even in southern France, would be too harsh for the Fijians. GHQ Diary noted on 7 August that 'Fijians are susceptible to respiratory diseases particularly pneumonia and bronchitis hence they should not remain in France during the winter.'[12] As a result they were moved, on the orders of the War Office, to Taranto, Italy on 17 September 1918 where they remained until repatriated. The work of the Fijian Labour Corps was acknowledged by the King when, in August 1918, he inspected a contingent of fifteen men under their Commanding Officer Captain Allardyce at Buckingham Palace.

The Corps returned to Fiji without ten of their men who had died whilst in service, six being buried in France, three in Italy and one in New Zealand. Captain Allardyce was awarded the MBE in 1919 and two members of the Corps, Sergeants Colata and Lala, were awarded the MSM.

The Medal Roll shows that the three white NCOs were awarded Silver British War Medals and Victory medals but that the native Fijians, as coloured troops, were issued Bronze British War Medals. These Bronze medals all appear to have been either returned or lost and in 1932/33 the native members of the Corps were issued with Silver British War Medals and Victory Medals. Perhaps it is fitting that the final recognition of the work of the Fijians was the award of the same medal as white soldiers.

1 About two-thirds of the population were natives, 50,000 East Indians and 4,000 white.
2 He enlisted in the Foreign Legion on 8 January 1915, as an African. He served at Arras and was awarded the *Croix de Guerre* and *Medaille Militaire*. After being wounded at Champange in September 1915 he returned to Fiji and was commissioned into the Defence Force although the Governor decreed that Europeans need not salute him. He resigned his commission to serve overseas in the Labour Corps, in which he was a Quartermaster Sergeant. He returned to Fiji where he became the Speaker in the Legislative Council. He was made a CBE in 1942, a KCMG in 1946 and died in 1958.
3 *The Times History of the War* Vol XVI p.98
4 NA WO 95/83 3 August 1917
5 ibid WO 107/37 Report on Labour p.34
6 Ali, *Chinese in Fiji* p.53
7 Although it was recognised that huts with stoves in winter were essential.
8 NA WO 107/37 Report on Labour Appendix C
9 *The Times* 27 December 1917

10 NA WO 123/60
11 ibid WO 107/37 p.34–35
12 ibid WO 95/83

MAURITIUS LABOUR BATTALION

The Times History of the War, published in 1918, devotes less than 30 words to the Mauritius Labour Battalion (MLB): 'several Labour Corps, which subsequently did excellent service under difficult conditions in Mesopotamia, were quickly raised, and frequent later drafts were sent to maintain their strength.'[1] 'War and Empire in Mauritius and the Indian Ocean' published in 2001 is equally brief: 'Mauritius itself sent 1,700 men overseas in the Mauritius Labour Battalion to serve with Imperial forces fighting in Mesopotamia. The Battalion consisted of coloured Mauritians officered by white Franco-Mauritians and British regulars.'[2]

There is contradictory information as to when the Battalion's service in Mesopotamia commenced. An article in French written in 2003, on the website 'Mauritius and its Environments' states that the Battalion was set up following a Proclamation of the Governor, Sir Hesketh Bell, in November 1915, with the first group of men leaving Mauritius for Mesopotamia on 10 January 1916.[3] However, a report written in 1918 by Lieutenant Colonel R. Wetherell, Adjutant General's Department states the first contingent sailed on 12 May 1917.[4]

The first reference to the Battalion in a Diary[5] does not occur until 1 June 1917 when the HMT *Benefactor* arrived at Basra. It has not been possible to confirm whether there were men of the MLB in Mesopotamia before June 1917. The Diary records that on 1 June Lieutenant Colonel A. Grantia was appointed Officer Commanding and on 4 June the Battalion, consisting of 8 officers and 675 men, was reformed into four companies.

The Battalion had a high number of tradesmen.[6] On 6 June, A Company, some 252 tradesmen under Captain Hyde and Lieutenant Upton, were attached to the Inland Water Transport Depot at Maqil. Although the original officers were transferred to Arab Labour Companies in October 1917, A Company remained with the IWT until October 1919. They were employed at the dockyard using their trades in boat building and repair work. In October 1919 the Battalion received a letter of appreciation for their work from Brigadier Hughes, the Director of the IWT.

The other three companies were used as required by the Director of Works, the IWT or the Directors of Labour at Maqil, Makina, Shaiba and Ashar. The IWT tended to make use of the skilled tradesmen on dockyard and boat construction. Unskilled men were used for basic labouring tasks at the docks, on the Basra light railway, as hospital orderlies and on regimental duties as cooks and batmen. At times tradesmen were attached to other units in order to utilise their specific skills. For example, on 23 January 1918, 30 carpenters and masons were attached to 5 Labour Corps; on 21 June 1918, eleven trained mechanical transport drivers were sent to 1056 MT Company; and on 12 May 1919, 25 carpenters and 15 fitters were sent to Baghdad to work for the Director of Labour. Specialist training was available and 25 men were trained as motor boat drivers and 30 men as mechanical transport drivers.[7]

Unlike local and Indian labour, the MLB did not come under the command of the Director of Labour, Brigadier F. D. Frost, and their work is almost completely ignored in his Diary. The only reference is on 17 July 1919[8], which gives the Battalion's strength as 1,062 with 50 men employed on the railways, 100 at central depots and 912 at other depots. The MLB is not mentioned by name in the Report of the Directorate of Labour.[9] There is a reference in the section on skilled labour to 200 Ford van drivers having been enrolled in the Mechanical Transport unit, relieving a considerable number of British personnel. The MLB Diary records that there was a Mauritian Ford Van Company of some 208 men. From 22 February until 27 October 1919 it operated at Khanaquin and Mosul and it appears likely that these were the 200 men referred to in Brigadier Frost's report.

The work of the MLB suffered due to illness. 123 men were invalided to India between 6 June and 3 July 1917. On 1 July, of the 951 men in the Battalion, 276 were unable to work because of illness. By August repatriation had reduced the Battalion to 770 men and a further draft of 251 men arrived on 10 October. Nine days later 50 of the draft were in hospital due to the heat. A further draft of 174 men arrived on 16 August 1918, the Diary recording that five men had died and four absented themselves en route.[10] A number of deaths were caused by pneumonia and flu, and records show an outbreak of plague at Asher in May 1919 although there are no details of any casualties. There were only two deaths, which are attributed to causes other than illness. On 1 October 1918 Private Agathe died from burns and 15 March 1919 Private Bardeau drowned whilst working on a barge at the IWT dockyard, the Diary noting that he had 'been in dispute with an NCO of IWT'.[11]

The MLB Diary gives little detail regarding discipline within the Battalion. The entry for 12 May 1918 records '5 men FGCM – all sentenced to between 2 years and 6 months HL'[12] with Private Viellese receiving 2 years hard labour.[13] A mutiny occurred on 6 January 1919 when A Company at Maqil refused to work on the grounds that the war was over and that they wanted to return to Mauritius. The Diary records that 'They had been lectured on demobilisation. CO proceeded to warn the men of the seriousness of the offence and arrested 2 NCOs and 5 men and detained in Makina Detention Barracks. Company paraded and marched to work.'[14] Five of the men were sentenced to 84 days detention, Private Green to one year's hard labour and Acting Corporal Sophie to 2 years' hard labour.[15]

From April 1919 onwards fewer demands were put upon the Battalion. On 31 August Captain H. Coombes, who had taken command of the Battalion in May 1918, commented, 'work is dying down and 500 men could be returned home'.[16] There was only enough work for half the Battalion.

The Battalion left Mesopotamia on 31 November 1919 leaving 48 men buried in Basra War Cemetery with four more commemorated on the Basra Memorial. The Commonwealth War Graves Commission records that the MLB suffered 68 casualties. There is no record of how many men, who were repatriated due to illness, later died and are not recorded as casualties.

In 1920 the Treasury agreed to pensions being awarded in cases of death or disability. Depending on the degree of disability and the man's status the pension ranged from 6d to 3s a week. In case of death, wives were awarded between 7s and 10s, unmarried partners 5s and children 2s 6d until they were 14 years old.[17]

1 *The Times History of the War* Vol XVI p.105
2 Jackson, A. *War and Empire in Mauritius and the Indian Ocean* p.23
3 Article available at www.intnet.mu/iels/13avril03_ww1.htm.
4 NA WO 162/6
5 ibid WO 95/5279
6 The trades included carpenters, fitters, masons, blacksmiths, painters, electricians, and mechanics.
7 NA WO 95/5279 22 July and 5 August 1918
8 ibid WO 95/4992
9 ibid WO/95/4991
10 Only three of these men can be identified Labourers Gamille and Juddoo who are buried in Suez War Memorial Cemetery and Labourer Antonie who is commemorated on the Heliopolis (Aden) Memorial.
11 NA
12 ibid
13 ibid WO 90/7/151
14 ibid WO 95/5279
15 ibid WO 90/7/169
16 ibid WO 95/5279
17 ibid T 161/23

Section Five: Foreign Labour Units

EGYPTIAN LABOUR CORPS

The creation of the Egyptian Labour Corps (ELC) came about because of the Army's need for labour in Gallipoli. From the 3,000 men employed in Gallipoli the ELC grew to several hundred thousand men who were employed in Egypt, France, Mesopotamia and Salonika.[1]

Numbers and Casualties

The ELC has, in common with so many of the foreign labour units, been largely ignored in War Diaries and official documents. There is, for example, no accurate record of how many Egyptians served in the ELC. Official statistics quote 82,000 but this only relates to those employed in Egypt in November 1918.[2] This is contradicted by another official source which gives a figure, for this date, of 100,002[3] and the Australian Official History, which states that by August 1918, 'the hard-working, singing Egyptians of the Labour Corps now numbered nearly 135,000'.[4]

An article published in *The Times* in 1918 refers to 'several hundred thousand'.[5] Another article by Sir Valentine Chirol, in 1920, says that the Egyptians put the number who served in the ELC at about one million.[6] This figure probably relates to the total number of enrolments for the ELC. It is known that many men re-enrolled more than once so the figure was at least 250,000 and could have been in excess of 500,000.

Even in death there are no accurate records, as *The Times* reported: 'No information is available as to the casualties of the Egyptian Labour Corps. Though they must have been considerable, if only from sickness and exposure, they appear never to have been notified to families.'[7] The CWGC records show 260 Egyptian natives are buried in graves administered by them, none of which are in Egypt. It is estimated that over 10,000 men died whilst serving in the ELC.[8] When, in July 1918, questions were raised in Egypt about the accurate reporting of ELC deaths and registration of graves, the Deputy Assistant Director of Graves Registration explained that he would need more men if full registration was to take place. He pointed out that: 'The relatives of the deceased ELC personnel apparently take no interest in the graves and so far as can be ascertained have not requested any information about them.'[9]

As a result most natives lie in unidentified graves, like the 198 men buried in the Bab Sitna Mariam Cemetery, Jerusalem, the 966 men commemorated by a memorial at the CWGC Cemetery at Ramleh and the 192 men buried near Dayr Sunayd, Israel.

Gallipoli

Four Works Companies of the Egyptian Army were sent to the peninsula to support the RE in May 1915. It was soon apparent that more labour was required and the following month the decision was made to recruit civilians on a three month contract to work on Lemnos and at Gallipoli.

The authorities appear to have had little difficulty in getting men to volunteer for this work and the first men of the ELC arrived on Lemnos at the beginning of July where they were used primarily for 'making roads and clearing the ground for huts and camps'.[10] Contemporary reports suggest that they were not the most efficient workers. Fred Garrett, an Australian soldier, recorded the work of the Egyptian's road building on Lemnos:

> Two rows of them standing facing the leader, who stands facing towards them. They are supposed to be ramming the metal down. 'Halyar heyli' says the leader and swinging the rammers across in front of the other foot they drop them with a 'Unmendahlah' all together and so on chant and chorus. They don't put any weight behind the rammers but merely let them drop with their 'unmendahlah'. Its heart breaking to watch them.[11]

There also appears to have been a feeling amongst the British sailors at Lemnos that the ELC were not being used effectively:

> We felt strongly that they should be employed coaling the enormous transports instead of our own sailors. Whenever I saw these Egyptians they were either chanting some mournful dirge or attending a funeral.[12]

A shortage of labour on the peninsula led to the Egyptians being sent, on 17 July, to both Helles and Suvla Bay. By 15 August the company at Suvla had to be moved back to Mudros as they would not work under shellfire.

In September a company of 165 men was sent to ANZAC and another of 195 men to Suvla. The Official History notes: 'these civilian workers were of little use if employed under shell fire'.[13] Military labour could not be spared from the trenches and the C-in-C was averse to using soldiers on fatigues when they were already tired from trench duties. The only alternative was to use the civilian labour and so more men of the ELC were sent to ANZAC, Suvla and Mudros during October and November.

With the onset of winter the Egyptians had difficulty coping with the cold weather: 'Unfortunately, the wild, bitter climate of these Aegean Isles proved too much for the sun-nurtured Egyptians, and a large amount of sickness prevailed in their ranks.'[14] With the absence of a properly organized medical system to treat the ELC 'their sick and death-rates mounted inconveniently high'.[15]

Casualties were also caused by accidents and shellfire. Fred Garrett records one accident in his diary:

> A yarn from Anzac. One of the Egyptian labourers stole a jam tin bomb and took it to his dugout. That night he lit it in their cookhouse, full of expectation. Half a dozen others were gathered around and they took the bomb to be a new sort of lamp. Presently stretcher-bearers were much in demand and 6 damaged Gipoes were carried to Hospital.[16]

There are no accurate records of how many men of the ELC died during this campaign. There are three labourers buried on Lemnos and there are none on the peninsula itself.

When the labour units serving on the peninsula were withdrawn at the beginning of December 1915 the majority of the ELC returned to Egypt. One detachment, known as the 'Naval wing'[17] remained at Mudros on Lemnos where they loaded and unloaded ships.

Recruitment

During 1915 the requirement for labour in Egypt was met by the use of British troops, supplemented by Egyptian civil labour. In 1916 the demand for more labour to support the Army in Egypt led to the recruitment of native labourers and British officers to command them.

A shortage of British officers led to Europeans living in Egypt being recruited as officers. These men lacked military experience and their 'local and temporary' rank entitled them to serve on the safe western side of the Suez Canal. To overcome officer shortages the British began to commission men serving in Egypt who were unfit or too old for front line service. Of the 500 officers of the ELC, 400 came from the ranks. In Europe native labour units had a ratio of one officer to 100 natives but in Egypt it was only possible to recruit at a ratio of 1 to 200.

The lack of officers meant the NCOs took on more responsibility. The majority of NCOs were Egyptian subjects of European descent and many of them proved unsuitable. They lacked military experience and were often more interested in what they could gain personally from their position. In order to overcome these problems British NCOs were attached to the ELC.

From the outset the British encountered difficulties with recruitment. Whether the recruitment problem was due to reports of poor medical treatment on Lemnos and Gallipoli, the lack of British civil servants to supervise recruitment, or the contract itself, is uncertain. Initially, men were recruited for just three months but this soon changed to a six month contract for labourers, and the duration of the war for NCOs and the ELC Police. The Egyptians disliked contracting themselves for a greater period than three months.[18] When insufficient men came forward, rather than introduce conscription, as was the norm for the Egyptian Army, the British turned to the Egyptian village system to increase voluntary enlistment.

Egypt had 3,600 village areas, each with an Omdeh (Mayor) who was both a local landowner and Government official. The British asked the Omdehs to organise recruitment in their area. Unfortunately a high proportion of them were little more than petty tyrants who terrorized their neighbours and ensured their own wealth and that of their superiors increased. Recruits often came from those who had annoyed the Omdeh or failed to pay a bribe to avoid service. Many Omdeh saw recruitment as a way of gaining kudos with the British. Some people began to flee from their villages and soldiers and police were sent to scour the country to bring the 'volunteers', under escort, to the labour depots.

In 1919 E. M. Forster wrote to *The Times:* 'as the supply of recruits ran low a compulsory system was gradually introduced. This system was absolutely secret, and the districts which suffered most were the country ones, where public opinion could least express itself'.[19] Compulsory recruitment was gradually extended to the towns so that by November 1918 only Cairo and Alexandria were exempt.

On recruitment a man underwent a medical examination; those that passed had their hair closely clipped, their armpits and pubic hair shaved and were introduced two at a time into a large bath of fluid consisting of 'a solution of cresol, soft soap, paraffin and sulphur – a combination which can be relied upon to put to an end any insect-plague in or out of Egypt'.[20] Many failed at the medical stage. Between November 1916 and April 1917 some 130,000 men were examined of which 30,000 were rejected, mainly for eye trouble.[21] The men, who were paid 5 piastres (about 1s) a day, were then issued with an army blanket and their uniform, a loose khaki tunic, knee-length trousers, a camelhair skull-cap and a short cotton turban. The recruits were placed in gangs of 50, 49 labourers under a rais (supervisor) who would usually know all the men in the squad since he often came from the same village. A single company, 600 strong, was formed from 12 gangs and a double company from 24 gangs. In November 1918 there were 75 single companies and 24 double companies.

Following the lessons learnt in the Gallipoli Campaign a separate section of the RAMC was set up to deal with the medical needs of the ELC. As labourers moved around Egypt and Palestine 17 tented hospitals were set up to cater for them. Hospital beds consisted of a waterproof ground sheet and blankets laid upon the sand. There were also two semi-permanent tented hospitals at Ismailia and Kantara. Kantara started in April 1916 with 150 beds and increased to between 1,200 and 1,500 beds by November 1918.

Egypt and Palestine

In 1919 Anthony Bluett wrote: 'Little is known outside the country of this admirable corps, yet it is scarcely too much to say that they saved the situation here as elsewhere.'[22] It has also been noted that, 'the official military history from the British government only sporadically mentions the ELC'.[23] References are in general terms, like the one about the defence lines that were built at Bir el Abd and

Salmana, 'The construction of these two latter positions would be the task of the Egyptian Labour Corps'.[24]

By the end of June 1917 the ELC in Egypt had grown to 32,000 men of whom 1,600 were sick in hospital. About half the force was employed by RE on defences or other works in Egypt and on the Palestine LoC. Other employers included the ASC (5,000), RAMC (2,000), AOC (2,000), at the Docks (2,000) and in the ELC Police (1,000).[25] Contemporary articles about the ELC in British newspapers gave the impression that the men were eagerly and voluntarily recruited and were child-like. An article published in *The Times* under the sub-heading 'A Busy Band of Children,' stated: 'they give as much trouble as would so many children. And children, they are, in good sooth, though there be grey heads among them.'[26] This concept of being childlike was almost certainly the view the British had of the Egyptian native at the time: 'The pure-blooded Egyptian is at heart a child; and a child of, in many ways, very attractive and lovable qualities into the bargain.'[27]

The vast majority of the ELC were fellaheen, recruited from villages, who had little or no experience of modern life. Captain Teichman, a Medical Officer with the 52nd Division recorded in his diary the lack of understanding of modern weapons amongst the natives. He also stated that: 'The Egyptian Labour Corps ... when thoroughly frightened always collected into large groups, which were a very easy target for Fritz when he was flying low.'[28]

Most British officers were not used to the fellaheen and had little idea of what the natives expected of them. The fellaheen were used to harsh treatment, which included brutal beatings for the most minor of matters, from their own police. The British use of corporal punishment was lenient by Egyptian standards and, at times, taken by the natives as a sign of weakness. Lieutenant E. K. Venables, OC 39 Company, wrote one of the most comprehensive accounts of the ELC.[29] He described the fellaheen as 'usually of no great mental capacity, their muscular limbs are developed to their occupation on the land'.[30] He found many of the locally recruited NCOs inept, often unreliable and 'much inclined towards gaining piastres as "baksheesh" by theft and sale of stores or other shifty means.'[31] The fellaheen had great faith in their officers showing 'an almost childlike reliance on their officers, especially in difficulty or emergency'.[32] British officers soon learnt that they should not use Arabic to reprimand an offender as this was taken as a personal insult.

Without the road and rail network that the ELC helped to build it would have been impossible for the advance into Sinai and Palestine. Sir Archibald Murray, Commander of the Forces in Egypt wrote: 'It is interesting to note that the road constructed was first made by the Romans, repaired by Napoleon, and remade by the Egyptian Labour Corps.'[33] Working under the RE, the ELC built the water pipeline from Kantara to El Arish by February 1917. As the Allies advanced into Palestine the pipeline was extended for over 230 miles, with pumping stations built at twenty mile intervals. This pipeline allowed water to be brought from the Suez Canal to the troops at the front.

During the second battle of Gaza in April 1917 men of the ELC were used as stretcher-bearers, 'a duty which they carried out with remarkable skill and sympathy'.[34] As the British advanced through Gaza and Palestine the ELC played a major role in reconstructing roads and the rail network. As soon as stores arrived the ELC would unload them and take them to front line soldiers. As the winter approached the ELC faced a new problem, illness due to the weather. Venables refers to his men suffering from bronchial problems and one source states 'death from illness became a common theme for the ELC in the Palestine campaign'.[35]

Following the capture of Jerusalem, the work of the ELC was recognised in General Allenby's Special Order of the Day: 'the work of the Egyptian Labour Corps has been of the greatest value in contributing to the rapid advance of the troops and in overcoming the difficulties of the communications'.[36] On at least one occasion the ELC was used to create a diversion.

> During attack on Gaza defences ELC used on 1 November 1917, day before actual attack, to make enemy think there was a landing taking place behind his right flank at Deir el Balah. Starting at 4.30 pm men of the ELC were disembarked from motor launches, trawlers and tugs and marched down to the beach in fours in view of the enemy.[37]

The majority of British civil servants in Egypt had been commissioned into the Army, and consequently, civil records about recruitment, casualties and discipline were poorly kept and often inaccurate. Captain Teichman, for example, recorded that on 7 January 1917 enemy aircraft killed 29 and wounded 30 natives working at a railhead near El Arish.[38] There is no official record of these deaths or where the men were buried.

It appears that even serious incidents of indiscipline may not have been recorded. Fred Mills, a Sapper in the RE, noted in his Diary on 9 March 1918: 'An Egyptian Labour Corps private shot at 6 am for killing an English Egyptian Labour Corps officer. All the E.L.C. paraded to see it done.'[39] In researching this reference no evidence was found in the Field General Court Martial (FGCM) records at the National Archives (class WO 71) or in any other source about men executed during the war.[40] Initially, it was thought that the entry might have been one of those 'myths of war' until proof was discovered in the service record of 2nd Lieutenant P. A. Cooney, ELC. At Kantara ELC Camp on 23 February 1918 Lieutenant Cooney ordered one of his company, Ahmed Tewfik, to be detained for insubordination. Tewfik became violent and his wrists were bound. Later Lieutenant Cooney visited Tewfik and found his wrists unbound. Tewfik said he had untied himself and, when Lieutenant Cooney called him a liar, he stabbed him in the neck with a clasp knife. Tewfik was tried by FGCM and executed at 6.05 am on 9 March 1918.[41]

France

The C-in-C wrote to the War Office on 24 January 1917 requesting 1,000 Egyptian labourers to work at Marseilles from 1 April and 10,000 for northern France a month later. Pointing out that battalion organisation was quite unsuitable for labour units he asked for them to be formed in companies and for an early indication of when and how many Egyptians would be available.[42] Six days later he received a reply, which confirmed that in Egypt companies of 600 natives had proved successful and would be used in France. On 15 March a conference was held at GHQ at which it was decided that the Base Depot for the ELC in France would be Marseilles. Arrangements were made for their equipment, rationing, accommodation, discipline and medical care.

Six days later GHQ received details from the War Office of rates of pay and compensation in case of injury or death. The men would be contracted for six months if employed in northern France and seven months in Marseilles. GHQ was also informed that the officers coming with the ELC had been 'carefully selected as being those accustomed to work with the Corps in Egypt and as being the most suitable obtainable locally for the purpose'.[43] In 1918 General Wace noted the officers of the ELC in France were 'handicapped by a lack of military experience, and some also by a complete ignorance of the Arabic language'.[44]

Lieutenant Colonel Malcolm Coutts, an officer with wide experience of working with Egyptian natives, was appointed Egyptian Labour Advisor. General Wace described him as 'invaluable in advising both the Director of Labour and Base and Administrative Area Commandants.'[45] GHQ was informed that the NCO foremen (sergeants and corporals) were 'as a rule, recruited from civilians who have a good knowledge of Arabic, and are generally either British or subjects of Allied Powers, approved by General Staff (Intelligence).'[46] Lieutenant Colonel Coutts considered the NCOs the weakest part of the organisation with the majority incapable of performing the duties expected of them. He wrote:

> They have had no Military experience and are, for the most part drawn from a class incapable at any time of inspiring in, or commanding any respect from, natives or others. They are mostly low class Europeans and Refugee Jews, with a sprinkling of Egyptians. Egyptians will not work for, or obey, this class of European; and Jews they utterly despise.[47]

Accompanying the Egyptians was Captain G. F. Foster Smith RAMC who was placed in charge of their medical facilities. A hospital was set up at Marseilles with separate sections in other hospitals where the men were employed. If a man was likely to be in a local hospital for more than three weeks he was transferred to Marseilles. Trachoma was a problem amongst the Egyptians, the worst cases being repatriated and minor cases segregated to prevent the spread of the disease. Whilst generally fit they were badly affected by the cold weather, with a large number of pulmonary complaints and rheumatism.

The ELC was accommodated in tents or huts depending on locality. Towards the end of their contract men were housed in huts because of the weather. They were restricted to camp when not working. Small groups of up to eight men could go out if granted a pass and escorted by NCOs. Most natives were Muslims and special arrangements were made to ensure that burials were performed in accordance with religious beliefs. They were allowed to celebrate religious festivals with one live sheep provided for every 200 men on such days. 71 and 72 Companies arrived at Marseilles on 24 March 1917. 73, 74 and 75 Companies arrived on 30 April, 76, 77, 78 and 79 Companies during May and a further nine (80 to 88) during June and July. 71 Company remained at Marseille to coal vessels, their work being described as 'very satisfactory' by the DADL on 30 March.[48] The other companies were sent to Dunkirk, Calais, Boulogne, the 4th Army and Taranto.

On 26 May four bombs fell on the ELC camp at Dunkirk killing 4 Egyptians and wounding 24. The remainder stampeded and fled into the nearby fields and village. After another air raid on 4 June the men refused to stay in camp, armed themselves with sticks and stones, and threatened their officers. Breaking out of camp they attempted to enter Dunkirk but were stopped by the guard. As a result the companies were moved from Dunkirk, 72 and 76 Companies to Rouen and 75 Company to Havre. Following this incident the ELC appears to have worked well during June, July and August. The only incident of any note occurring in June when the ELC at Fournier Camp, Marseilles had to be isolated, probably due to trachoma, and replaced by Indian Labourers.

Following an air raid on the night of 4 September at Boulogne the men of 73 and 78 Companies refused to work on the grounds that their contract had expired. Colonel Coutts met with the men on the evening of 5 September but they refused to return to work. Coutts intended to meet with the men again on the morning of 6 September but Colonel Wace, the DDL, took the view that the dispute was not a matter for negotiation. It was a disciplinary issue to be settled by force if the strike continued. A detachment of the Garrison Battalion was sent to the camp and the men instructed to return to work. When the men attempted to break out of the camp the guard fired upon them, killing 23 and wounding 24. A similar incident occurred on 10 September when 74 Company at Calais refused to work, saying their contract had expired. The following day British troops opened fire on the mutineers, killing four and wounding fifteen. The question of the length of contract was cleared up on 14 September. A telegram from Cairo HQ stated that the contract was for six months in France and not 'village to village'. Officers of the ELC explained this to their men in order to defuse unrest.

Before the information could be sent to all companies another mutiny occured on 16 September 1917 involving 71 Company at Fournier Camp, Marseilles. During the unrest Labourer Mahmoud Mahomed Ahmed 'struck on the head and wounded with a stick 2Lt A. G. Turley ELC his superior officer whilst in the execution of his office'.[49] Ahmed, who had previously received fifteen lashes for insubordination in April and ten lashes for causing a riot in May, being subject to military law, was tried by FGCM.[50] Found guilty of striking his superior officer and mutinous conduct he was executed by firing squad on 10 October.

The question of the contract surfaced again on 25 October when the men in 74, 75 and 76 Companies all refused to work. On this occasion the British took a more conciliatory approach and moved the companies to a rest camp until they could be repatriated. Repatriation was completed by the end of the year, the ELC Depot at Marseilles being closed on 23 February 1918. In June 1918 consideration was given to raising another two ELC companies to work at the docks in Marseilles but the labour situation in Egypt prevented this.

Mesopotamia

The first contingent of the ELC to work in Mesopotamia arrived in Basra in March 1916.[51] In October 1916 a further six officers and 2,512 men arrived to work for the Director of IWT.[52] By June 1917, 5,224 men of the ELC were employed in

Mesopotamia.[53] It has not been possible to identify the total number of Egyptians that worked in Mesopotamia, although one source puts the figure at 8,000.[54]

The most successful Egyptians appear to have been those housed at Keshla Camp and employed by the IWT. Their work included land reclamation and slipway construction around Basra and building the Basra Light Railway, which 'greatly facilitated the supply of coal to otherwise awkwardly placed units'.[55] One special-ised area of their work is referred to in Sir Archibald Murray's Despatches: 'It is interesting to note that in Mesopotamia Egyptian Labour Corps men have been selected, trained and formed into a police force for policing Baghdad.'[56]

Salonika

One company of the ELC served in Salonika, from March 1916. Following a request for a specially trained company for railway construction, the authorities in Egypt selected and trained 70 Company.[57] Two members of the company, one of whom was attached to the 7th Mounted Brigade, died on 2 August 1917 and are buried in Mikra British Cemetery. In October 1918 consideration was given to sending a further 7,000 labourers to Salonika but this does not appear to have taken take place due to the Armistice.[58]

Armistice and Nationalism

Following the Armistice Egypt saw the rise of nationalism, which included attacks upon British troops. It has been suggested that one of the reasons for this nationalism was the way the fellaheen had been compulsorily recruited into the ELC and the poor medical treatment they received from the British.[59] Four members of the Labour Corps were among seven British military personnel and an Egyptian Inspector of Prisons attacked and murdered by a mob on 18 March 1919.[60] They were travelling on a train from Assyut towards Cairo. At Dairut a mob boarded the train and three of the men, all of who were unarmed, were attacked and murdered. The train managed to get to Dier Moes where others, armed with stones, sticks and knives, joined the natives still on board the train and murdered the other five British personnel. On the evening of 22 November 1919 Captain Simon Cohen, ELC, was shot and killed in Cairo.[61] Although his assailants were never found it is almost certain that they were Arab nationalists. A Court of Enquiry into his murder was told that the lamp on the other side of the road had been put out making the place quite dark with the 'assailant prob-ably hiding round side of house in the dark with intention of firing at anyone in British uniform'.[62] The following day, shots were fired at five British sol-diers wounding one of them and on 26 November another two were wounded by gunfire.

Recognition of the work of the ELC came not from the British Government, but the Imperial War Graves Commission. Built by the IWGC as a memorial to those who died in service, the Giza Memorial Ophthalmic Laboratory, Cairo was completed and handed over to the Egyptian Government on 26 January 1925.

1 Lucas, Sir C., *The Empire at War* Vol V p.43
2 *Statistics of Military Effort* pp.160–161
3 Pirie-Gordon, H., *A Brief Record of the Advance of the Egyptian Expeditionary Force* p.108
4 Gullet, H., *The Australian Imperial Force in Egypt and Palestine* p.678
5 'The Egyptian Labour Corps A Busy Band of Brothers' *The Times* 17 August 1918
6 'The Blunder of the E.L.C.' *The Times* 1 January 1920
7 ibid
8 Fuchs, R., *Sites of memory in the Holy Land: the design of the British war cemeteries in Mandate Palestine* p650 in Journal of Historical Geography Vol 30 (2004)
9 NA WO 95/4391
10 Hargrave, J., *At Suvla Bay* p.25
11 Fred Garrett's Diary 13th October 1915 at http://www.grantsmilitaria.com/garrett/html/oct1915.htm
12 Denham, H., *Dardanelles A Midshipman's Diary* p.156
13 Aspinall-Oglander, *Military Operations Gallipoli* Volume II p.395
14 'Serjeant-Major, R.A.M.C.' With the R.A.M.C. in Egypt p.278
15 ibid p.279
16 Fred Garrett's Diary 8th December 1915
17 Murray, A. *Sir Archibald Murray's Dispatches* p.206
18 NA WO 158/985
19 *The Times* 13 November 1919
20 'Serjeant-Major, R.A.M.C.' p.298
21 ibid p.297
22 Bluett, A., *With our Army in Palestine* p.22
23 Shihadeh, I., *They Also Serve* p.3
24 Macmunn, Sir G., Falls, C. *Military Operations Egypt and Palestine* Vol 1 p.249
25 NA WO 158/985
26 *The Times* 'Egyptian Labour Corps' 17 August 1917
27 Sergeant-Major R.A.M.C. p.293
28 Teichman, Captain O., *The Diary of a Yeomanry M.O.* p.96
29 Venables, *They Also Served* IWM Document 10416
30 ibid p.2
31 ibid p.8
32 ibid p.11
33 Murray A., p.206
34 Venables, p.24
35 Shihadeh p.22
36 quoted in Massey, W., *How Jerusalem was Won* Appendix IX
37 Falls, C. *Military Operations Egypt and Palestine* Part I p.66
38 Teichman p.96
39 Pryor, A. and Woods, J., *Great Uncle Fred's War* p.33
40 See Oram, Putkowski & Sykes and Corns & Hughes-Wilson
41 NA WO 339/108546
42 ibid MT 23/761
43 ibid WO 95/33
44 ibid WO 107/37 Report on Labour p.36
45 ibid WO 107/37 p.32
46 ibid WO 95/33
47 ibid WO 107/37 p.36
48 ibid WO 95/404
49 ibid WO 95/4040

50 ibid WO 71/600
51 Moberley, F. *The Campaign in Mesopotamia* Vol II p.359
52 Hall, L. *Inland Water Transport in Mesopotamia* p.14
53 NA WO 158/985
54 Lucas p.44
55 Hall p.48
56 Murray, Sir A., p.210
57 ibid p.210
58 Pirie-Gordon H., p.108
59 *The Times* 'The Blunders of the ELC' 1 Jan 1920
60 The four Labour Corps men were 360529 CQMS A. Culyer, 361171 CQMS A. Summergill, 362433 CQMS G. Field and 549259 CQMS D. Peacock. Their bodies were recovered and reburied in Plot P at Cairo War Cemetery.
61 See picure section for a photographs of Captain Cohen, CQMS Culyer's and CQMS Peacock's headstones
62 NA WO 339/109981

JEWISH LABOUR

The role played by Jews in labour units cannot be explained without considering the place of the Jewish community in Britain, the influence of Zionists and the formation of Jewish battalions of the Royal Fusiliers.

Expelled by Edward I in 1290, Jews did not begin to return to England until 1656. From then on there was a slow but steady stream of immigrants, and by 1800 the Jewish population of Britain had risen to about 25,000. The population rose steadily throughout the century and by 1880 more than half the 60,000 Jews in Britain had been born in the country.[1] By this time Anglo-Jewry, whilst retaining its religious heritage, was a stable community that had integrated well into British society.

It was the pogroms and anti-Jewish laws passed in Russia following the assassination of Tsar Alexander II in 1881 that resulted in more than 2,000,000 Jews leaving Russia between 1880 and 1914. Whilst America became the homeland for the majority of these immigrants, at least 120,000 settled in Britain. These new immigrants to Britain were very different from Anglo-Jewry; most arrived penniless, spoke Yiddish but not English, had little, if any, formal education and many were not used to living in a big city. Both Anglo-Jewry and non-Jews saw them as un-English and alien.

When war broke out there were only about 400 Jews in the Army and 600 in the Territorial force. The *Jewish Chronicle* immediately urged Anglo-Jewry to join up, although an attempt to recruit a Jewish Pals battalion in London in October 1914 failed to attract enough men. Prior to the introduction of conscription in 1916 some 10,000 Anglo-Jews had volunteered for active service, 1,140 as officers.[2]

Whilst Anglo-Jewry responded to the call, the same was not true in 1914 for the new immigrants. For many immigrants whose families had come from Russia, the thought of fighting to support the Tsar who had persecuted them was an anathema. Service in the Russian Army was compulsory and there was a fear that service in the British Army would result in the same ill treatment, humiliation and anti-Semitism that had been experienced in Russia. Many immigrants supported the anti-Tsarist revolutionary movement and opposed the war on political grounds.[3]

When German and Austrian immigrant Jews were interned in 1914, the Board of Deputies of British Jews, the representative organisation of the Jewish population, refused to support them at appeal tribunals, taking the view that they were interned as aliens, not as Jews. During 1915, particularly after the sinking of the *Lusitania*, anti-German feeling intensified in Britain, leading to attacks on establishments owned by those of German ancestry and even those with German sounding names. Whilst these attacks were not anti-Semitic there were several instances of Jewish property being attacked.

Amongst Jews throughout the world there were the Zionists, a group whose aim was the creation of a Jewish state in Turkish ruled Palestine. It was the influence of Zionists that helped create the Zion Mule Corps, which led the way to the creation of the Judean Battalions of the Royal Fusiliers and the 'Russian' Companies of the Labour Corps. In September 1914 Pinhas Rutenberg, a Russian Jew who had fled to Italy, came to Britain and suggested to Chaim Weizmann the idea of a Jewish force fighting on the side of the Allies.[4] Although at the time British Zionists were advocating a neutral stance to the war the meeting did sow the seed of the idea in their minds. Rutenberg also took his idea to other Zionists including Ze'ev Jabotinsky, who helped form the first Jewish unit, the Zion Mule Corps (ZMC), in Egypt in March 1915.

Throughout 1915 there were concerns amongst Anglo-Jewry that more of the immigrant community could and should be serving in the forces. In order to encourage more Jews to enlist a Central Jewish Recruiting Committee, chaired by Edmund Sebag-Montefiore, was established in December 1915. Both the Committee and the War Office were aware that there were potentially many more recruits among the immigrant population. The War Office reminded Recruiting Officers: 'a man born in this country is a British subject, although he may be of alien parentage, and consequently, if otherwise suitable and acceptable, is eligible for enlistment in the Army'.[5]

In the case of British born Jews with a German or Austrian name, reference had to be made to the Jewish Recruiting Committee before the man could be accepted. Where a man was British born of enemy alien parentage he could still be accepted if he could speak English, had lived continuously in Britain since his birth and was vouched for by the Jewish Recruiting Committee. In a further attempt to encourage recruitment in areas where there were considerable numbers of eligible Jews, Recruiting Officers 'should arrange with COs of units so that Jews who enlist may be enabled as far as possible to serve with their friends'.[6]

Jabotinsky arrived in London in August 1915 and tried to persuade the War Office to expand the ZMC into a Jewish Brigade for service in the Middle East. He estimated that there were some 20,000 Russian subjects living in Britain, France, Switzerland, Italy, Holland and Scandinavia and a further 40,000 Jews in Egypt and 50,000 in Tunisia; from which the Brigade would be recruited. The Chief of the Imperial General Staff asked the Quarter Master General whether the ZMC could be spared and whether 'it is desirable to enrol a foreign legion of this nature'.[7]

The QMG's response appears to have been formulated as much from an Anti-Semitic viewpoint as a military one:

> If it desired to form a Zion Fighting Corps, I am rather at a loss to understand as to why it should be necessary to interfere with the Zion Mule Corps, as I was rather under the impression that the Jews of the world were as numerous as the herrings of the sea, so that, therefore, they could form both a Zion Fighting Corps and a Zion Mules Corps, the latter which, after all, only consists, so far as I can make out, of some six to seven hundred men, and is, so far as I can ascertain, performing good transport work.[8]

So despite support from Colonel Patterson of the ZMC, General Birdwood and the Russian Ambassador in London, the War Office rejected the idea suggesting Jabotinsky should ask the Foreign Office to allow the formation of a Foreign Legion to fight for the Allies.[9]

When compulsory conscription was introduced in 1916 immigrant Jews were eligible for conscription, although there is evidence that many applied for exemption for a variety of reasons.[10] In addition, about 20,000 Russian-born Jews of military age, as aliens, were ineligible for service. This became an issue for Anglo-Jewry who were concerned that the British public would view all Jews as shirkers and this would lead to more incidents of anti-Semitism.

On 26 May 1916 Major H. L. Nathan, who was serving with the 1st London Regiment in France, wrote to the Secretary for War in an attempt to persuade the War Office to raise a Jewish Battalion for General Service:

> Since I have been home on leave from France I have been much struck, on visiting the East End, by the fact a large number of young men of eligible age and suitable physique are excluded from service in the Army, though themselves willing and anxious to serve on the grounds they are not British subjects. They are, for the most part Russian and Polish Jews, whose parents brought them here in their childhood in order to escape religious persecution in their own country. There are large numbers of such young men in London, Manchester and other centres, forming a considerable reserve on which to draw upon.
>
> It seems unfortunate that, at a time when the need for men is so insistent those who are British in everything save the technical sense of the term, should be denied the opportunity of serving with the permission and the assistance of the War Office. I am prepared to endeavour at once to raise a full Battalion (with necessary reserves) for general service, and think that such an attempt would be likely to succeed. I shall be glad to hear if the War Office will grant its authority.[11]

Whilst Nathan's offer was rejected his letter was forwarded from the Secretary of War to the Director of Recruiting with the comment: 'You may like to see this. If these men would enlist in various corps – perhaps we might be able to utilize the services of some of them.'[12]

Within three weeks the Army Council had introduced two measures aimed at enabling aliens to enlist for service. On 8 June it was announced that both friendly aliens and men born in Britain whose parents were enemy aliens could serve in the Army. Any unit could contain up to 2 per cent friendly aliens. In the case of Russian Jews they were accepted on production of a certificate from Jews Work Services' Committee and 'if they so desire, may be posted in batches to serve together in the same unit'.[13]

A further announcement, nine days later, affected men born in Britain or who were naturalized British subjects of enemy alien parentage. On enlistment they were placed in the 30th (Works) Battalion Middlesex Regiment (see page 207) from which Alien Companies were formed. Despite these changes, recruitment amongst the immigrant community remained relatively small and the Home Secretary, Herbert Samuel, who was a Jew, announced the threat of compulsory deportation to Russia unless numbers increased. Whilst the Board of Deputies supported this threat there was major opposition from a new organisation, the Foreign Jews Protection Committee against Deportation to Russia and Compulsion, and the threat was withdrawn.

Jabotinsky, in a letter to *The Times* acknowledged that voluntary enlistment had been a failure. He suggested the formation of a Jewish Legion made up of foreign Jews for service in Egypt: 'The appeal must be made to their own enthusiasm and not fear of "deportation". They should be given the privilege of serving in units which bear the Jewish name and of knowing that their merits will be recorded for the glory of their race.'[14] This view was supported in an Editorial, which stated: 'There is much force in these contentions. They deserve the earnest attention of the Government.'[15]

Following the abdication of the Tsar in March 1917, an Anglo-Russian Convention on Military Service was signed, by which Russian subjects living in Britain became liable for conscription under the Military Service Act of 1916. Despite this Convention it appears that the number of immigrant Jews called up between March and November 1917 was relatively small. The Bolshevik Revolution in November ended the Convention.

The military authorities also appear to have faced difficulties with high numbers of men failing their medical examinations. In November 1917, for example, the Commissioner for Medical Services for the Director of Recruiting, North Western Region wrote to the Ministry of National Service expressing concern about the medical examination of Russian Jews at Hulme Town Hall, Manchester. He referred to nearly 50 medical sheets where the candidates were being categorised as unfit for service, with medical notes, which contained the words 'states he has', or equivalent. His letter expressed concern that a Dr Saul 'may be looking sympathetically towards Jews'.[16] The Ministry instructed that the men concerned should be called up and medically re-examined.

Jabotinsky and his fellow Zionists continued to press for a Jewish Regiment although their idea was not supported by some of Anglo-Jewry who considered the immigrant Jews as lower class citizens. On 8 August 1917 *The Times* reported that the former commandant of the Zion Mule Corps, Colonel Patterson, was to take command of a Jewish Regiment for service in Palestine.[17] However on 30 August a deputation of Anglo-Jewry met Lord Derby, the Secretary of State for War, to argue against the formation of a Jewish Regiment and on 3 September it was reported in *The Times* that Lord Derby had abandoned the formation of the Jewish Regiment. Instead the War Office agreed to the formation of Jewish Battalions in the Royal Fusiliers.[18]

In his definitive work on British Regiments, James states that three service Battalions (38th to 40th Battalions Royal Fusiliers) and two Reserve Battalions (41st and 42nd Battalions) were formed at Plymouth in January 1918.[19] However the War Office Monthly Returns shows 152 other ranks in the 38th Battalion in September 1917, rising to 1,352 in December 1917.[20] Patterson, the CO 38th

Battalion, complained it took four months instead of a few weeks to recruit the Battalion since Anglo-Jewry placed every obstacle possible in the way even to the extent of sending people to the East End of London and provincial cities to urge young Jews not to enlist.[21] The 38th Battalion left Southampton on 5 February 1918 arriving in Alexandria on 1 March.

Testimonials given by veterans of the 38th Battalion to the Beit Hagudim Museum, Israel would suggest that a high proportion of the Battalion were British subjects rather than 'Friendly Alien Jews'.[22] A high proportion of the 39th Battalion was made up from the 2,000 Zionist Jews recruited in America for the Jewish Battalions and the 40th Battalion primarily of Jews recruited in Palestine.[23] Whilst there are no accurate figures it does appear that the Jewish Battalions of the Royal Fusiliers did not attract high numbers of Russian Jews.

Russia's withdrawal from the war also raised concerns about the loyalty of Russians serving in the British Army. In March 1918 General Allenby cabled the CIGS expressing concern that there were a number of Russian Jews in the 38th Battalion whose loyalty might be in question. As a result, the War Office decided it was undesirable to enlist any further Russian Jews for the Battalion[24] and from April 1918 Russian Jews were to be posted to their own labour units.[25] The War Office rescinded this decision on 8 August although after this date most Russian Jews were posted to the Labour Corps rather than the Royal Fusiliers.

Zion Mule Corps

Technically the Zion Mule Corps (ZMC) was an armed transport unit, however its importance in relation to Jewish Labour units warrants its inclusion in this book. The story of the ZMC is, in many ways, the story of three men, Ze'ev Jabotinsky, Joseph Trumpeldor and Colonel John Patterson.

In December 1914 the Turkish authorities in Palestine began arresting Jews and then, as non-Turkish citizens, deporting them. Between December 1914 and September 1915 over 11,000 Jews expelled from Palestine arrived in Alexandria, over 1,200 in December alone. Jabotinsky[26] travelled to Alexandria in December where, whilst working in the refugee camps he met Joseph Trumpeldor.[27]

Jabotinsky and Trumpeldor advocated creating a Jewish Legion from the refugees to fight alongside the British and help liberate Palestine from the Turks. Along with 200 refugees they offered their services to General Sir John Maxwell, Commander of the British Forces in Egypt, on 15 March 1915. Maxwell pointed out that there was no plan for action in Palestine and that British regulations did not allow foreign nationals to be recruited into the Army. Instead he suggested the formation of a mule transport unit for service alongside the Allies. Whilst Maxwell could not tell Jabotinsky and Trumpeldor of the campaign that was about to start in the Dardanelles he must have known that there was barely time to put together a mule transport unit let alone train the men as fighting troops.[28]

Jabotinsky felt this was unacceptable and left Egypt to pursue the Zionist cause in Western Europe and America. Trumpeldor, however, felt it would help towards achieving a Zionist state in Palestine. His view was 'to get the Turk out of Palestine we've got to smash the Turk. Which side you begin the smashing, north or south, is just technique. Any front leads to Zion.'[29] As a former soldier he also realised that the unit would be working alongside the fighting soldier and that there was every chance that their role would be more than just one of moving supplies. As he explained in 1917 when he gave evidence to the Dardanelles Commission:

> They told us that in the British Army it is just the same, transport or fighting unit, just the same conditions … they offered us to accept service in this transport unit and to organise it. After they told us that it was the same honour and just the same conditions we accepted it.[30]

Major General Godley, Commander of the New Zealand Expeditionary Force recommended Lieutenant Colonel John Patterson DSO to command the ZMC. General Maxwell confirmed the appointment on 19 March 1915.[31] Patterson later recorded:

> It certainly was curious that the General's choice should have fallen upon me, for, of course, he knew nothing of my knowledge of Jewish history, or of my sympathy for the Jewish race. When, as a boy, I eagerly devoured the records of the glorious deeds of Jewish military captains such as Joshua, Joab, Gideon and Judas Maccabeus, I little dreamt that one day I, myself, would, in a small way, be a captain of a host of the Children of Israel![32]

Maxwell, accompanied by Godley, Patterson and Trumpeldor, addressed a meeting of several hundred of the refugees and on 23 March the Grand Rabbi of Alexandria swore in about 400 volunteers. As a locally recruited unit the men signed contracts of twelve months duration, were issued with Mauser rifles which had been captured from the Turks, British Army uniforms, and a cap badge made up of a Shield of David. Five British and eight Jewish officers assisted Patterson although Trumpeldor was the only officer with previous military experience. Despite the lack of military background Patterson acknowledged the role played by his officers:

> I was, indeed, lucky in getting such good men who loyally seconded me in everything and quickly mastered the details necessary for the running of the Corps; nor did they spare themselves during those four weeks of slavery which we together put in while getting the men ready for active service.[33]

On 17 April the ZMC sailed for Mudros, the HQ and A and B Troops on the Transport *Hymettus* and C and D Troop on the Transport *Anglo Egyptian*. At Mudros Patterson was informed that they were to be split into two groups, Patterson with A and B Troops were sent to serve with 29 Division in southern Gallipoli and C and D Troops to ANZAC.

Patterson protested that half the ZMC were removed from his direct command:

> I greatly feared that the half away from my own personal supervision would not prove a success, for officers, NCOs and men were entirely new to soldiering, and it was too much to expect that they could go straight into the firing line, after only some three weeks' training, and come through the ordeal triumphantly without an experienced commander.[34]

His fears proved to be correct. C and D Troop, some 213 men and 196 mules, disembarked at ANZAC between 28 April and 3 May and were tasked with moving water, food and ammunition to the front line, primarily at night. However their lack of training and the inability of most of the men to speak English soon resulted in the decision to use them on board transports to look after the Divisional Train Mules, replacing Army Service Corps drivers.[35] By 17 May the Indian Mule Corps had been brought in to replace C and D Troop who were returned to Alexandria. On arrival in Egypt they were both demoralised and in poor physical condition. By 11 June only 20 were available for duty, 62 were discharged on medical grounds, 57 placed under arrest for refusing to obey orders and 51 had deserted when they were refused permission to visit their families in the refugee camps.[36] As a result, the decision was taken five days later to disband C and D troop.

The decision of the Director of Transport to split the ZMC into two groups was to be criticised by General Hamilton in a letter to Maxwell on 15 July: 'I have been very much annoyed by the stupidity of a very stupid man, my Director of Transport.'[37] Hamilton says that he had intended to remove them from ANZAC and join them to the Helles group who were both happy and doing well. He was also concerned that returning discontented men to Egypt would kill further recruiting.

The ship Patterson and his half of the ZMC were on ran aground on a sandbank as they were leaving for Gallipoli. This delayed their departure; they were transferred to the *Dundrennon* and finally reached V Beach on the night of 27/28 April. Some 200 of the mules and their handlers were taken to W beach about a mile to the west where they were immediately put into service taking supplies to the front line. According to Watts, in his history of the Jewish Legion, the ZMC suffered their first casualty during their first night ashore when Private David Muscovitz went missing during the move to W Beach.[38] This is contradicted by the CWGC who record the date of his death as 20 May.

Patterson recalls how French soldiers suspected one man, tasked with guarding supplies on V Beach, of being Turkish, and were about to execute him. He was only saved by his own sergeant who, fortunately, spoke French and could explain that the man was speaking Hebrew and Russian, not Turkish, and why he was armed with a Turkish rifle. As a result of this incident Patterson would only allow his men out of camp when accompanied by an interpreter or if they spoke English.

On 1 May Second Lieutenant Claude Rolo was in charge of a supply party near Gully Ravine when Turkish guns opened fire. Falling shrapnel caused some of the mules to break free and stampede in the direction of the Turkish line. Unbeknown to the British, three lines of Turks were creeping towards the British line. They presumably thought they were facing a British cavalry attack and opened fire on the mules. The ZMC Muleteers instantly lined the trenches and opened such an intense fire that the Turks were utterly routed, and those of them that were left alive fled back to the cover of their own trenches. Although shot through both arms, Private Groushkousky held on to his panicking mules and successfully delivered his ammunition to the front line. For his bravery Patterson promoted him to corporal and recommended him for the DCM which was awarded.[39] Following this incident some 50 men petitioned Patterson for permission to be involved in the fighting. Patterson took their request to General Hunter-Weston who turned it down on the grounds that they were performing invaluable service keeping the men in the trenches supplied with ammunition and food.

The ZMC was made up primarily of two groups; those who had emigrated from Russia to Palestine, supported the Zionist cause and were generally better disciplined; and Sephardic Jews from Alexandria who were generally unsuited to military life and ignorant of the Zionist movement. By early June, sickness and low morale resulted in men refusing to work and an armed guard was placed over them.[40] Patterson ordered three ringleaders to receive twelve lashes each, be tied to wagon wheels for three hours and placed on bread and water for three days. His action achieved its objective and military discipline was restored.

By the end of July, eight men had been killed and about sixty wounded but illness meant the ZMC's strength was reduced to less than half the number who had landed on W Beach in April. Hamilton ordered Patterson back to Egypt to recruit replacements and establish a base depot. The experiences of C and D Troop meant that after nearly two months he was only able to recruit some 150 men, primarily Sephardic Jews from Cairo. He formed them into what he called his 'Cairo Troop' with their own NCOs so that he could keep them separate from the established troops. Patterson and the 'Cairo Troop' arrived in Gallipoli at the beginning of October.

Towards the end of August the ZMC base at Helles was inspected by the Assistant Director of Transport, MEF. His report, which only covered the men and mules actually at the base, confirmed that the Alexandrian men were of little use, being troublemakers in the camp and reporting sick when needed for work.[41] He considered the Russians to be far better and noted that the majority of them were on detachment with regimental units. Personnel at the base tended to be men who did not want to be in Gallipoli. Patterson was taken ill at the end of November and sent first to hospital in Alexandria and then to England. Trumpeldor took over command of the ZMC and on 19 December received a bullet wound in his left shoulder. Despite this he remained in command, overseeing the evacuation of the ZMC from Gallipoli on 31 December.

The ZMC arrived in Alexandria on 10 January 1916 and for the next few months Trumpeldor continually pressed the authorities to use them in Palestine. His request was rejected; the only offer made was for them to be used in Ireland following the Easter uprising, an idea firmly rejected by Trumpeldor. Lack of activity meant that men returned to their families and on 26 May the ZMC was disbanded. Around 120 men, including Trumpeldor, managed to remain attached to the British Army and served in a number of different units including many in the 38th–40th Battalions, Royal Fusiliers.

Jewish Labour Corps

The Russian Companies of the Labour Corps were not the first Jewish Labour units to be formed. In April 1915 the Jewish Labour Corps (JLC) was formed in Egypt, although it only existed for about six weeks. Little is known about the JLC although some information is to be found in the JLC Medal Roll at the National Archive, Kew.[42] Mosche Liberman (Labourer 264) wrote to the War Office about his medal entitlement in 1927. The War Office had no information about the JLC and enquiries were made with the authorities in Egypt. This resulted in the decision, on 3 March 1928, to award the men the British War Medal in Bronze. On 14 May 1928 a nominal list of personnel who served in the JLC was created and placed in the Medal Roll.

Attached to the Medal Roll are a few War Office documents, dating from 1921 and 1927, which give a little background. A letter, dated 27 February 1921, from Aaron Cohen, Secretary, Commission Zion Mule Corps, Alexandria to Rev Michael Adler is a request for the ZMC to be included in the British Jewry Book of Honour that Adler was compiling. The letter indicates that Cohen had included a list of the '1st Battalion' of the ZMC and that a '2nd Battalion' had been formed later but no records were left. Cohen goes on to say that the 2nd Battalion was only in existence for a few months and did not take any active part in the campaign. The inclusion of this letter suggests that the War Office may have considered the JLC was the '2nd Battalion' of the ZMC. However two factors indicate that this was not the case. Firstly, the members of the ZMC were locally recruited soldiers and served under military ranks whereas the members of the JLC were locally recruited labourers. Secondly, Patterson refers to the time when he, accompanied by Claude Rolo, Trumpeldor and Groushkousky returned to Egypt and recruited his 'Cairo Troop' of some 150 men who 'after a brief training, they found themselves before the enemy in Gallipoli'.[43] It is possible that this recruitment drive was what Cohen referred to as the '2nd Battalion', however, Patterson did not leave for Egypt on this mission until 25 July, almost two months after the JLC had been disbanded.

A letter from the Ministry of Finance in Cairo to the British Army HQ in Cairo dated 6 December 1927 explains that the only reference that can be found to the JLC is a ledger, which contains some 189 names. The ledger indicates that the men were enlisted from 15 to 22 April 1915, and they were all discharged between 22 and 28 May 1915. The letter also indicated that the rates of pay were 1s a day for labourers, 1s 6d a day for gangers, 2s a day for foremen and £12 10s per month for the superintendent.

Another letter from the GOC British Troops in Egypt, to the Under Secretary of State, War Office, dated 10 December 1927, states that 'a careful search has been made in the Zion Mule Corps files in my possession to trace some record of the Jewish Labour Corps without result'.[44] The GOC went on to say that he had obtained the pay certificate books of Mosche Liberman and Hirsch Rabinovitch, which showed that they had been discharged on 'Completion of Service'. The GOC stated that from the statement given by Mr Mosche Liberman it would appear that the Jewish Labour Corps did proceed to the Dardanelles shortly after the formation of the Corps.

There is evidence that the IGC Mediterranean Force endeavoured to raise a further corps along the lines of the Zion Mule Corps during April 1915. He sent officers to Cairo for this purpose, with hardly with any success: 'they managed to collect a few of quite the wrong class and incidentally caused a small riot, the Jews imagining they were being commandeered and forcibly impressed'.[45]

The embarkation records for HMV *Trevillard* when she left Alexandria on 17/ 19 April 1915, include Major S. Hutchins, Lt. F. Hodsell and 148 labourers of the Jewish Labour Corps.[46] One source suggests this is proof that the JLC participated in the Dardanelles Campaign. The source, however, incorrectly refers to them as a unit that 'fought in Gallipoli' when they were labourers and not a fighting unit.[47] There is a record on 21 April of the Director of Supply and Transport visiting the *Ramazon* at Lemnos and inspecting the Jewish Labour Corps.[48] There are, however, no records of them sailing to Gallipoli nor of them working on Lemnos.

The fact that the War Office decided to award these men only the Bronze War Medal suggests that they may never have arrived in Gallipoli, as the ZMC were awarded the 1914–15 Star.

It is unknown when the JLC left Lemnos and returned to Egypt. It is known that the *Anglo-Egyptian* arrived in Alexandria on 21 May carrying Jewish troops or labourers. Since nearly two-thirds of the JLC were discharged on 22 or 23 May it is possible that they were also on this ship.

Russian Labour Battalions and Companies

In April 1918 the War Office decided to form two Labour Corps Battalions which would be made up of Russian recruits, with officers and NCOs from existing army units.[49] The 8th Labour Battalion at Sevenoaks for recruits from Eastern and Southern Command and London District and the 9th Battalion at Fort Scoveston near Neyland in Pembroke for those from Northern, Western and Scottish Command.

The 8th Battalion consisted of a headquarters and three companies and the 9th a headquarters and two companies. From these two battalions a number of overseas Labour Corps Companies were to be formed and the Company numbers 1001–1020 were allocated to the 8th Battalion and 1021–1030 to the 9th Battalion. The allocation of 30 company numbers, a company being 500 men strong, suggests that the War Office anticipated that as many as 15,000 men were eligible for service with them.

Accurate figures do not exist for the total number of Russian Jews who served in the Labour Corps. Sir Auckland Geddes, Minister of National Service, informed the House of Commons on 9 July 1918 that about 22 per cent (about 5,500) of the Russians liable for service under the Anglo-Russian Convention had been enlisted in Labour Battalions. When asked why the figure was so low he replied that many were medically unfit, many had received exemptions from tribunals and there was also a high percentage of absenteeism. Service records show men were still being conscripted into the 8th and 9th Battalion in the autumn of 1918 so it is likely that the total number enlisted was about 6,000.

According to the War Office Monthly Returns the 9th Battalion was the first to be established with 231 men enlisted by the end of April.[50] A month later the 8th Battalion and 1021 Company had been formed and there were now 1,081 other ranks. The July Return shows 1001, 1021 and 1022 Companies had been formed for service overseas. The units reached their peak strength in December 1918 when there were a total of 3,046 other ranks of whom 1,620 were serving in France.

The 8th Battalion was disbanded in January 1919 and the 9th Battalion retained to provide drafts for the companies overseas. The 9th Battalion rapidly decreased from 938 other ranks in January 1919 to 354 in March and then maintained about 300 men throughout 1919. Almost all men had been demobilized by December 1919 and the final return for the 9th Battalion in February 1920 shows a mere 26 other ranks.

As with other Home Service Labour Companies the 8th and 9th Battalion did not keep War Diaries and little is known about their employment in Britain. One problem was the poor physique of the men. In December 1918, for example, of the 972 men in the British Battalions 326 were unavailable for service on medical grounds and a further 400 were of medical category B(ii) or lower. Over two-thirds of the men were only fit for the lowest category of work.

In many cases men were called up but within a relatively short time at their battalion, were found medically unfit for service and discharged. One of the most extreme cases is that of 557034 Private Hyman Zablotsky, a 31-year-old ladies tailor who enlisted at Whitehall on 15 April 1918. Called up for service on 20 April and posted to the 8th Battalion, he was admitted to Fort Pitt Military Hospital the following day with general disability. At his Medical Board at the hospital on 25 June it was recorded that his medical history included two attacks of rheumatic fever prior to enlistment and that there was a family history of consumption. He was discharged from service ten days after enlisting as no longer fit for military service.

The authorities faced a problem, as many Russian immigrants did not want to serve in the Army. Concern that, having been medically examined and attested, men would fail to report when called up, led in December 1917 to the decision that aliens should be handed over to Military Authorities immediately after medical examination and attestation.[51] Some, like 557988 Private Joseph Lebarsky, tried to persuade the Army that they were medically unfit. Called up on 18 June 1918 he was posted to the 8th Battalion on 24 June. Two days later he was charged with the offence of 'wilfully producing the appearance of disease in a man belonging to His Majesty's Forces, calculated to lead to the belief that the said man was unfit for duty'. This was an offence under the Defence of the Realm Regulations. Lebarsky was tried by District Court Martial at Devonport on 13 August and sentenced to 2 years hard labour. He was discharged from the Army on 1 September 1919.[52]

The poor physique of the men meant that it was some time before the companies could be sent to France. The first 1001, Company, primarily comprised of Jews from the East End of London, did not arrive until 10 June and was considered unfit for purpose. It appears that the need for labour in France resulted in the Company being sent before it was ready for service. Initially, 5 officers and 355 other ranks, some 145 below strength, arrived at Havre and were sent to Marieux in the IV Corps area on 15 June to replace 149 Company Chinese Labour Corps. On arrival the Labour Commandant noted that they were of poor physique and had no military knowledge.[53] The officers were considered unsatisfactory and the Company was 'badly disciplined and of poor physique. It will be 2 months before the coy becomes effective. Only moving 30 cubic/feet/man per day.'[54]

Such was the concern that a Conference was held at 3rd Army HQ and it was decided

… to obtain an instructor in Physical Drill to train the Officers and 2 men of each platoon to give instruction for ½ hour a day before work. This should improve fitness and discipline whilst some working time may be lost. It was generally agreed that the benefits would outweigh the costs.[55]

Captain J. H. Rogers, 60 Company, was attached to the Company on 14 July to instruct in drill and improve discipline. On 20 July 114 reinforcements arrived to bring the Company up to strength. Unfortunately, the War Diaries do not give any further information about the tasks undertaken by 1001 Company which was to remain in France until September 1919. However, in common with other labour companies, they would have been used for general labouring tasks and in clearance and salvage work after the war ended.

If the men in 1001 Company were not initially fit for service the same was not true for 1021 Company, the second Russian company to arrive in France. Comprising primarily of Jews from Manchester, Leeds and Glasgow the 5 officers and 340 other ranks arrived in Boulogne on 22 June and were sent to work on defences at Saulty. Here they were described as 'well organised and moving 70 cubic feet/man/day of "rooted" soil'.[56] By 22 August their work was considered satisfactory enough for them to be used to replace 11 Company Labour Corps repairing the Broad Gauge railway near Mondicourt. By October they were also used to move stores and ammunition at the railheads, ammunition dumps and at the canals in the Ribecourt area. With the end of the war they were moved to the Solesmes area where, as far as is known, they remained until amalgamated with 1002 Company in September 1919. Their work must have been satisfactory as in March 1919 there was a request made to GHQ by the 3rd Army to retain the Company in XIII Corps area.

The third Russian company, 1002, arrived in August and was initially put to work on the LoC. In September they moved to the Bailleul area to work for XV Corps' Salvage Officer. On 15 September the Company had its first casualty; 557816 Private Wenger was killed when a grenade he was holding exploded. The Company was employed on roadwork in late September, woodcutting in November and then returned to salvage work in December in the Steenvorde area. They remained here until March 1919 when they were moved to the Ypres area undertaking salvage and clearance work at Zillebeke.

The last Russian Company to be sent to France, 1022 Company, did not arrive until December 1918. They would have been used for battlefield clearance and salvage work. On arrival in France they were sent to Esquerchin and are known to have been in Neuville St Vaast in July 1919 but there is no record for earlier in 1919. The companies in France reached their peak of 1,963 other ranks in February 1919. Numbers had dropped to 1,485 by May, to 1,032 in September and to 887 in November 1919.

1 Bermant, C., *Troubled Eden* p.15
2 Adler ed, *The British Jewry Book of Honour* p.3
3 The majority of these Russian socialists were to become conscientious objectors following the introduction of conscription in 1916.
4 Weitzmann a research scientist at Manchester University solved the Ministry of Munitions acetone supply problem. The British Government's Balfour Declaration of

1917, which laid the way for a Jewish state in Palestine, is often seen as a direct result of Weitzmann's acetone work. He was later to become the first president of Israel.

5   NA WO 293/3 ACI 206 Enlistment of Jews – 18 Dec 1915
6   ibid
7   ibid WO 32/11349
8   ibid
9   ibid FO 371/2835/18995
10 Bush, J. *Behind The Lines East London Labour 1914–1919* p.172 and Hyman, J. *Jews in Great Britain During the Great War* pp.23–40
11 NA WO 32/11351
12 ibid WO 32/11351
13 ibid WO 293/4 ACI 1156 Enlistment of Friendly Aliens – 8 June 1916
14 *The Times* 15 July 1916
15 ibid
16 NA NATS 1/718 Medical Examination of Jews at Hulme Town Hall
17 Patterson's appointment as Commanding Officer of the Jewish Regiment appeared in the *London Gazette* on 24 August 1917.
18 NA WO 293/7 ACI 1415 Formation of Battalions for the Reception of Friendly Alien Jews 12 September 1917
19 James, E. A., *British Regiments 1914–18* p.50
20 NA WO 73/107 and WO 73/108
21 Patterson, J. *With the Judeans in the Palestine Campaign* p.25
22 Watts, M. *The Jewish Legion and the First World War* pp. 130–135
23 *British Jewry Book of Honour* p.10
24 NA WO 32/11353
25 ibid WO 293/8 ACI 414 Formation of Labour Battalions and Labour Companies composed of Russian Subjects – 19 April 1918
26 Jabotinsky was a Russian Zionist and journalist. At the outbreak of war the Odessa newspaper he worked for sent him to the West as its correspondent. He saw Turkey's entry into the war as an opportunity for the establishment of a Zionist state in Palestine. He urged Zionist organisations to move from their neutral stance to support for the Allies.
27 Trumpeldor was one of those expelled from Palestine. A former soldier in the Russian Army, uniquely for a Jew, he had been promoted to an officer, decorated and lost an arm during the Russo-Japanese War.
28 Watts p.24
29 Jabotinsky, *The Story of the Jewish Legion* p.42
30 NA CAB 19/33 Report of the Dardanelles Commission
31 Patterson was an Irish Protestant with both considerable knowledge of Jewish history and sympathy for the Jewish race. He joined the Army as a private in 1885 at the age of 18. After 12 years service he left to work as a railway engineer in Africa only to re-enlist at the outbreak of the Boer War in 1899. During the Boer War he was Mentioned in Despatches no less than three times, awarded the DSO and rose from 2nd Lieutenant to Lieutenant Colonel in a mere eight months. In 1907 he was appointed Chief Game Warden for East Africa but his Army career appears to have ended following the death of a soldier under his command and he appears on the list of retired officers in 1908. In 1913 he resigned his commission in protest of the Liberal Government's policy in Ulster. As a result, when war was declared in 1914 he initially found it difficult to gain an appointment. Patterson had a number of influential friends from the Boer War, including the man who was later to command the Egyptian Expeditionary Force and become Field Marshall, Edmund Allenby and with their help was finally accepted at his previous rank of Lieutenant Colonel.

32 Patterson p.33

33 ibid p.36

34 ibid p.52

35 NA WO 95/4350

36 Watts p.33

37 Hamilton Papers File 5/12 quoted in Watts p. 32

38 Watts p.35

39 Patterson dates this incident as 1 May although Watts (p.36) dates it as 5 May.

40 NA WO 95/4269

41 ibid

42 ibid WO 329/2359

43 Patterson p.236

44 NA WO 329/2359

45 ibid WO 95/4360

46 ibid WO 25/3541

47 Sugarman, M., *The Jewish Labour Corps* available at http://www.jewishvirtuallibrary. org/jsource/History/sugar9.html

48 NA WO 95/4269

49 ibid WO 293/8 ACI 414 Formation of Labour Battalions and Labour Companies composed of Russian Subjects – 19 April 1918

50 ibid WO 73/108 to WO 73/112

51 ibid WO 293/7 ACI 1793 Recruitment & Posting of Aliens and Alien Parentage – 9 Dec 1917

52 ibid WO 363 L326

53 ibid WO 95/736

54 ibid WO 95/384

55 ibid WO

56 ibid WO

GREEK, MACEDONIAN AND SERBIAN LABOUR

Greek Labour

The first use of Greek civilian labour on the islands of Imbros and Lemnos followed the arrival of the British and French fleets of almost 90 vessels, at Mudros in February 1915. At that time Mudros had no piers or wharves and very few warehouses to store the supplies that had to be brought from Alexandria. To speed up the unloading of ships the Navy used local civilian workers to build a few small piers and landing stages.

The Director of Supply and Transport, who was responsible for the provision of labour to support the Army during the Gallipoli campaign, recorded on 19 April that consideration was being given to the recruitment of about 1,000 Greek labourers from Mitylene and surrounding islands.[1] They were to be paid about 2s a day plus rations but not be issued with clothing. There would be no allowances for the families although arrangements would be made for a proportion of a man's wages to be paid directly to his family. Ten days later it was confirmed that these men would be recruited from Telendos and Mitylene.[2] The men appear to have been recruited on a six month contract although it has not been possible to confirm this. It is believed that these men became the Greek Labour Corps (GLC). The role of the GLC covered three locations: Lemnos, Helles and ANZAC.

Very little is known about employment of the Greek labourers on Lemnos. In July 1915 Greeks were making roads and clearing the ground for huts and camps.[3] It has not been possible to confirm whether these were locally employed civilians or members of the GLC. Greek labour was also used to unload ships: 'Vice Admiral asks for 200 Greeks to work on board supply ship. He is informed that IGC has already been asked to place Greek working parties on all supply and store ships.'[4]

There is no record of when the Greeks arrived at Helles but on 25 May the Reverend Creighton, Chaplain of the 29th Division, recalled: 'I explored a road being made at the foot of the cliffs to "X" beach and beyond. There are corps of Egyptians and Greeks doing this.'[5] Not all labourers proved satisfactory and at the end of May arrangements were made to send 200 undesirable Greek labourers at Lancashire Landing, Helles, back to Mitylene. They were replaced by a fresh supply of men.[6]

By the end of August the physical condition of the labourers employed at Helles meant they were not capable of undertaking heavy fatigues. Preparation for the coming winter, which included increasing stocks of ammunition and stores, required fresh labour. On 10 September it was decided that a further 800 labourers should be recruited for Helles.[7] The OC GLC saw no difficulty in recruiting another 800 men as soon as accommodation was available. On 30 September it was suggested that if the housing for the Greek labourers could not be arranged they could be replaced with Egyptian labourers who would bring their own tents. As a temporary measure the Greeks were housed on Lancashire Landing until dugouts could be provided. On 9 December a request was made for marquees to accommodate Greek labourers.

By the end of October 1,255 Greek Labourers were employed on Helles, with a further 21 arriving in November. The GLC, some 1,290 men, left Helles on 29 December 1915.

There is very little information about the work of the GLC in the ANZAC area. The Official History of the Gallipoli campaign's only reference is, 'to Suvla were allotted 800 civilian labourers of various kinds'.[8] In June 1915 Army fatigue parties were doing all work at ANZAC.[9] It is not known when the GLC arrived at ANZAC, but on 11 August an unspecified number of the GLC arrived from Imbros.[10] The area was subject to heavier Turkish shellfire than Helles and this badly affected the Greek labourers. The DQMG noted at the end of August 'the Greek Labourers are quick to cease work when shelling commences and it is difficult to get them to start again'.[11] At the beginning of September the commander at ANZAC requested more working parties for use at night but was informed that no further civilian labour was available. Another 60 labourers were sent from Imbros to Suvla on 25 September and 61 from Mudros to ANZAC on 24 November. It has not been possible to determine how many Greek labourers served at Suvla or ANZAC or when they were evacuated.

On 9 December 1915 the War Office wrote to the Treasury asking for approval to pay a gratuity, not exceeding one year's pay, in case of injury or death:

This Corps consists of about 2,000 Greeks working under British Officers and Non-commissioned officers and has been employed continuously at Helles in connection with the Expeditionary Forces. The pay of unskilled men varies from 2/- a day, for a labourer to £8 a month for a head foreman, with rations, clothing and extra pay for good work. The pay of skilled men has not been definitely fixed, but will be somewhat higher.[12]

The request was approved on 16 December. In case of death or total disablement a widow would be awarded up to one year's pay and children up to six months. It was also agreed that up to two months pay could be awarded in case of temporary disablement.[13]

Although the GLC was evacuated from Gallipoli in December 1915 it appears that they were still in existence on Lemnos in February 1916. The Royal Naval Division's Diary noted on 14 February that: 'There was a disturbance in the Greek Labour Corps this morning. A Guard from the Cyclist Company was sent for and order was restored.'[14] The GLC do not appear to have been awarded the 1914–15 Star for their service. The Medal Roll contains the names of only three Greek members of the Corps, none of whom are shown as being awarded a medal. One of the men died on 8 June 1915, the second claimed compensation in April 1931, and the third made a claim to be awarded the 1914–15 Star. The medal request was forwarded to Egypt although there is no indication of any response being received.

Macedonian Labour Battalions

The Macedonian Labour Battalions (MLB) were formed in 1917 from the Civilian Labour units that had been in existence since the arrival of the Allies in Salonika in 1915. The labourers, both male and female, were used to build defences, for road and rail work, to move stores, at quarries, on agriculture and anti-malarial work. Skilled personnel were used for a wide variety of tasks including brick making, baking, masonry, carpentry, mining and as herdsmen. Labourers were paid 4 drachmas a day and skilled workers between 5 and 10 drachma depending on their trade and skill level. The highest paid were steamroller drivers and vehicle mechanics. Foremen could earn up to 10 drachmas a day if they had the ability to manage men and speak a number of languages.

The British found that many recruits were medically unsuitable, often due to malaria or venereal disease. Personnel were medically examined before being engaged and then every three months during their service in the MLB. It was common for deserters from the Greek Army to enlist in the MLB. If found they were handed over to the Greek authorities. In July 1918, for example, this was the fate of 100 men in the 3rd Battalion.[15] The decision to hand men over to the Greeks had a detrimental effect with many men deserting the MLB rather than risk being forced into the Greek Army.

In April 1918 instructions were issued that no Greeks of any age should be enlisted in the MLB 'since a number are trying to avoid service in the Greek Army.'[16] The following month all Macedonian labourers in the Greek Reserve were transferred to the Greek Army.[17] Local police tried to force MLB men to join the Greek Army. They frequently harassed or even deported to adjacent islands the families of men, particularly those classed as Turks, in an attempt to force men to leave the MLB and join the Greek Army. Labourers were issued with exemption certificates, although, as happened in Liana in July 1918, the police often ignored them and forced the men into service in the Greek Army. The Turks appear to have been particularly badly treated by the Greek police and the CO 23rd Battalion noted that desertion was worse among the Turkish employees.[18]

1st Serbian Sentry Battalion

In Salonika, Serbians initially served in the Macedonian Labour battalions where the British found them reliable and hardworking. Given the opportunity, in November 1917, to guard hay stores their role was soon extended to include stores depots, hospitals and camps. By March 1918 there were over 500 Serbians employed as guards and the decision was made to issue them with rifles and bayonets. In April Captain Malcolm Burr was given the opportunity to create and command a Serbian Battalion. A British QM, clerk and batman and a Serbian sergeant major, who also acted as interpreter, supported him. Issued with British uniforms, the recruits were men too old or unfit for service in the Serbian Army, students living outside Serbia and boys. By the end of May the battalion had grown to 653 Serbian other ranks and included a mounted section of 45 men. The battalion supplied guards at 67 different locations around Salonika, with a detachment of 70 men working at XVI Corps Farm at Kilo 74½, Seres Road.[19]

On 14 June 1918 Private Alexander Petrovich saw a fire in a truck full of shells. Having sent for help he jumped into the wagon and stamped out the fire. He received a letter of commendation from the Base Commandant. The work of the Battalion did not go unnoticed. As Burr recorded:

> I am glad to say that I was able to testify publicly to their services by recommending three of them for the Meritorious Service Medal, with the result that on the list of that award, issued on October 20, 1919, there appear the following Serbian names: No. 192, Private Alexander Petrovich; No. 693, Sergeant Major Mihajlo Rachkovich; No. 5, Sergeant Kosta Shapera.[20]

1   NA WO 95/4269
2   ibid WO 95/4266
3   Hargrave, J. *At Suvla Bay* p.18
4   NA WO 95/4266
5   Creighton, Rev O., *With the Twenty-Ninth Division in Gallipoli* p.111
6   NA WO 95/4266
7   ibid WO 95/4275
8   Aspinall-Oglander, Brigadier-General C. F., *Military Operations Gallipoli Volume* II p.395
9   Bean, C. E. W., *The Story of Anzac* Volume ll pp. 264–5.
10 NA WO 95/4275
11 ibid
12 NA T 1/11988
13 ibid
14 NA ADM 137/3084
15 NA WO 95/4944
16 NA WO 95/4826

17 NO WO 95/4826
18 NA WO 95/4944
19 ibid
20 Burr, M. *Slouch Hat* p. 273

CHINESE LABOUR CORPS

The Chinese Labour Corps (CLC) was the largest foreign labour force employed by the British on the Western Front. In June 1915 Liang Shih-Yi, a close associate of the Chinese President, suggested that China could supply 300,000 military labourers, and 100,000 rifles, who could serve under British officers. The idea was described to the Foreign Secretary by the British Minister to China, Sir John Jordan, as 'hardly practicable,' a view supported by the War Office.[1]

The idea of using Chinese labourers to support the British, had been discussed and rejected by the French Ministry of War in March 1915. Liang suggested their use to the French in June 1915 although only as labourers rather than military labourers. On 11 November the French War Ministry decided to recruit Chinese labourers and sent Georges Truptil, a retired Army lieutenant colonel, to China.[2] The French recruited about 43,000 Chinese labourers, the first group arriving in France on 24 August 1916.[3]

The British considered using Chinese labourers on 11 July 1916 when the War Office informed the IGC that there were a number of Chinese accustomed to port work presently unemployed in Britain who could be sent to work at the French ports. The IGC rejected the idea on the grounds that they would have to be despatched as a body and wear uniform. He suggested they be employed in Britain and release British subjects who could serve in labour battalions.[4]

In August 1916 David Lloyd George, the Secretary of State for War, was authorised to discuss with the French the use of Chinese labour. The reason for this decision is not clear but may be as a result of the casualties the British suffered following the Somme offensive.[5] A letter from the War Office to the Colonial Office states the reason was to enable 'the British labour now being employed in France be released for work at home to mitigate the existing shortage of men in agriculture and industries'.[6]

In France, on 12 August, Major General Woodward, the Director of Organisation, informed the AG, QMG and IGC that Chinese and black labour would be used in France to enable unfit men to be returned to Britain to work in munitions or on the land. The IGC continued to voice his disapproval of the idea, and was supported by the AG and QMG:

> They expressed their conviction that until there was a definite assurance that the Trade Unions, Tribunals, etc, at home would agree to release a corresponding number of men for active service at the front, no steps should be taken to replace by Chinese and Black labour, those men now working on the LofC in France who are not fit for the front.[7]

The British Military attaché in China, Lieutenant Colonel David Robertson, had seen both political and military advantages in using Chinese when it was first suggested in 1915. When the decision was made to recruit Chinese it was Robertson who decided that Wei-hai-wei in Shantung would be used as the departure point, and later played a pivotal role in the decision to open a second base about 150 miles south-west at Tsingtao. On 1 September the French notified the British that they would allow them to recruit Chinese labourers, as long as they were subject to military law. Before recruitment began instructions were sent to China stating 'it is desirable that 5 per cent of the men should be skilled labourers of the following trades – Blacksmith, Carpenter, Glazier, Mason, Bricklayer, Painter, and Plasterer'.[8]

At the beginning of October 1916 the General Officer Commanding (GOC) in Singapore began to recruit Chinese labourers from Amoy to serve in Mesopotamia. Amoy is about 1,200 miles south of Wei-hai-wei and Jordan sent a cipher to Britain, on 6 October, pointing out that the scheme could clash with recruitment at Wei-hai-wei. The Amoy recruitment continued and between 5000 and 5,500 were recruited and sent to work for the Inland Water Transport and as colliers at Basra.

By the end of October Thomas Johnstone Bourne, a railway engineer who had 28 years experience of working in China, had arrived from Britain to head the recruitment mission. Bourne has been described as 'dedicated, hard working and extraordinarily able' in his dealings with the Chinese, the British diplomats in China and his superiors in Britian.[9] Bourne found agents to recruit the men, including many who had previous experience recruiting Chinese for work in South African gold mines. He also made use of missionaries in China, a number of whom became officers in the CLC.

Bourne may have been sent from England to head the recruitment mission but the importance of the role played by David Robertson cannot be underestimated. Michael Summerskill, in his seminal work on the Chinese Labour Corps, states: 'it is to David Robertson more than any other single man that credit must go for the creation of this particular scheme'.[10]

Recruitment

Recruitment was initially slow, with only about 40 men recruited in the first month. Jordan sent a telegram to the Foreign Office on 12 November 1916 stating that the scheme 'appears to me to be assuming too military a character and I fear this may further militate against it'.[11] On 14 November it was announced in the *London Gazette* that Captain Bryan Fairfax, Reserve of Officers, was appointed Commander of the CLC with the temporary rank of lieutenant colonel.

Jordan's concerns appear to have been heeded and on 18 January 1917 the first contingent of 7 officers and 1,086 coolies left Wei-hai-wei bound for Havre via the Cape of Good Hope. By the end of April 1917, 19,392 coolies had left China bound for the Western Front. The numbers rose to 45,848 by August 1917, 82,876 by the end of 1917 and 94,580 by March 1918.[12] Two main factors contributed to the success of the recruitment mission. Firstly, there was close co-operation between the War Office and the Foreign Office. Secondly, there were 'widespread British interests in China and the enormous experience of the British minister Jordan also played some role in the success of the recruitment program.'[13]

The Army Council wanted 13 officers for each battalion of 1,000 men. The C-in-C Home Forces was asked to find six captains and six subalterns to serve with the CLC, the criteria for selection being that the 'officers selected should have former military experience, and should be good disciplinarians'.[14]

At the end of November 1916 the Foreign Office wrote to the Army Council pointing out that in China there were

> … only 260 British subjects qualified as interpreters and therefore suitable to act as officers and of these 158 are missionaries. An outside estimate was that if half available as officers and if Army Council finally had a force of 50,000 coolies they would need 650 Officers but there were likely to be less than 100.[15]

The Army Council's response was that not all officers needed to be interpreters so more officers should be found in China. From the shipping data it appears that about 350 of the 950 CLC officers were recruited in China.[16] Men being recruited into the CLC first had to pass a medical examination. They were then sent to the depot at Wei-hai-wei where their clothes were discarded and those with pig-tails had them cut off by the barber. They then showered and were issued with blue overalls, padded with cotton wool, and a fur lined cap.

The Chinese were recruited as labourers but not all of them were from traditional labouring classes. Many, particularly the interpreters, were educated men who saw service in France as a way to broaden their horizons and earn, by Chinese standards, a good wage. As a correspondent of *The Times* put it:

> I talked to one of these, a suave, dapper little man in a neat blue uniform, who could write English as well as speak it, and had seen the world in Hong-kong, Singapore, and the Philippines. I asked him if the coolies knew anything about the war or, were interested in it. He thought not, though he politely said that he was himself glad to be of service to the nations which were the allies of China.[17]

Some of the Chinese had little or no education. Morris Cohen, an NCO with the 8th Battalion Canadian Railway Troops, was seconded to the CLC because of his previous experience of working with Chinese in Canada. He did not find educated Chinese: 'these were just plain coolies, illiterate, unskilled and completely ignorant'.[18]

The Contract

On recruitment each labourer signed a contract with his two thumb prints. The contract was between the labourer and the Emigration Bureau, a British Government agency. The labourer was officially described in the contract as a 'coolie': 'I, the undersigned coolie recruited by the British Emigration Bureau, declare myself to be a willing labourer under the following conditions, which conditions have been explained and made clear to me.'[19] Each man had an identity card that was completed in both English and Chinese. It included his name, height and any identifying marks together with a photograph of the man, his thumb-prints and the number assigned to him. His number was also stamped on a brass identification bracelet in English and Chinese. It was by this number and the thumb print that the coolie was identified in France. A team of fingerprint experts maintained personnel records at the CLC Depot at Noyelles.

Recruitment was for a period of three years, the British having the right to terminate the contract at any time after one year by giving six months' notice or at any time in the case of misconduct or inefficiency on the part of the labourer. At the end of the contract the British provided free passage back to China. The man was entitled to free food, clothing, housing, fuel, light and medical attention. The contract stated that work could be on 'railways, roads, etc., and in factories, mines, dockyards, fields, forests etc.'[20] None of the coolies recruited by the British worked in factories or mines and there is no explanation why these two employments are specifically mentioned. They may have been included to allow coolies to work in privately owned French run factories or mines, or be employed in Britain to support the war effort. From April 1917 there was a camp at Shorncliffe, Kent that housed South African and Chinese labourers on their way to, or returning from, France. The Chinese built huts at the local military camp and also helped build the flood defence known as the 'Chinese Wall' at the aerodrome at Orford Ness, Suffolk.[21]

An average of ten hours work a day, seven days a week was stipulated in the contract although 'due consideration will be given to Chinese Festivals'.[22] This was modified, with the normal working day being eight hours, excluding the time marching to and from work and meal times, six days a week. One seventh of the men were rested each day.

In addition to labourers, men were recruited as gangers, dressers and interpreters. Each of these roles was divided into either two or three classes, depending on a man's responsibility and skill level. There were three levels of gangers, who were responsible for overseeing the work of the labourers. Dressers, who worked for the medical officer, varied from those who had worked in missionary hospitals and had elementary nursing knowledge to men with no nursing training or knowledge. Interpreters were divided into two classes, the interpreter clerk who worked at the company headquarters, and field interpreters who acted as the link between the Chinese and European soldiers.

The original contract set out the daily rate of pay at 1 Franc for a coolie and 1.5 Francs for a Class One Ganger. Dressers and interpreter clerks were paid from the time they arrived at their depot in China, other men receiving pay from the time they left for Europe. Having only two rates of pay proved unsatisfactory and a new scale was introduced. The interpreter clerk was the highest paid at 5 Francs a day, other men being paid between 1.25 Francs and 3.5 Francs a day depending on their position.

Whilst the men were overseas their families received a monthly allowance of between £1 8s and £8 a month, according to the man's position. Compensation of up to £10 was payable in case of partial disablement and up to £20 in case of permanent disablement or death. For interpreters this was increased to £20 and £27 respectively. In January 1918 the War Office wrote to Jordan proposing that in case of death by accident or disease a man's widow would receive a regular payment for eighteen months, and his children for nine months. In the case of disablement, payment was for twelve months. The Treasury confirmed these proposals on 28 June 1919.[23]

Omitted from the contract was the fact that the coolie would be subject to military law once in France. As such he could be court-martialled and subject to military punishment including the death penalty. As Summerskill points out 'it seems doubtful whether the proposed application of military law was put to the men on recruitment'.[24] It was almost certainly not until the coolie arrived at the CLC Depot at Noyelles that it was explained that he was subject to military law.

Probably the most contentious part of the contract was that they were 'not to be employed in military operations'.[25] German propaganda in China informed them that they were going into action, and to their deaths. From the outset there was fear amongst the Chinese that this was the case. The first contingent was so concerned that 'a mutiny took place on board the ship before she was far on her way, an absurd rumour upsetting them to the effect that they were walking into a death-trap.'[26] Following this incident the officers in China assured each group that they were not being used as soldiers before they departed.

To the Chinese 'military operations' included being shelled or bombed. An air raid at Dunkirk on the night of 4 September 1917 killed 15 and wounded 21 Chinese. At 9.00 am the following day the Chinese refused to return to work saying that their contract stipulated they would not be placed in danger and the bombing of Dunkirk endangered them. A further air raid occurred on 6 September, which resulted in 2,163 Chinese hiding in the dunes west of St Pol. The British moved the Chinese further inland from Dunkirk. Four days later 104 Chinese were still absent from their camps, which had armed guards posted around them. At times the Chinese complained that the dangerous nature of their work broke their contract. At Arras they 'organised protests when some of them were hurt by explosions while clearing dangerous debris. They knew that they were not to be involved in military operations.'[27]

Transport to Europe

The second and third contingents of Chinese both arrived at Devonport and travelled by rail to Folkstone before crossing the Channel to Boulogne. The fourth contingent arrived in France at Marseilles after being transhipped in Egypt. Many more contingents were shipped to Boulogne during 1917. From February 1918 most men sailed from China to the west coast of Canada, crossed to the east coast by rail, and then travelled by ship to Britain, the vast majority arriving at Liverpool.

Daryl Klein wrote one of the best descriptions of the journey from China to France in 1918.[28] Klein joined the CLC in December 1917 and left Tsingtao on 26 February 1918 together with another 12 officers and 4,171 coolies. Their first port of call, two days later, was Nagasaki, which some coolies decided was England or France. After loading coal they sailed, the following day, for Vancouver. On arrival they disembarked and were accommodated in a tented camp on Vancouver Island where the officers appointed company cooks. 'This was a simple matter, for every coolie is a potential cook. But, as company officers were later to learn, not every cook makes a company cook.'[29] They spent the next ten weeks in camp where there was little to do other than split wood for the kitchens. The party then divided into two groups, five companies being transported in sealed trains for the week-long journey across Canada to Halifax from whence they sailed to Liverpool.

The other group, including Klein's company, remained in camp until 23 May when they embarked on HMT *Empress of Asia* bound for England via the Panama Canal. Once through the Canal they stopped at Jamaica and New York, although neither officers nor men were allowed to go ashore at either port, before crossing to England.

In France

On 29 December 1916 a conference was held at GHQ to discuss the employment of the Chinese who were being sent to France. Colonel Fairfax stated that 'labour from China can be obtained in large quantities if the conditions of employment are satisfactory and if the labour are contented'.[30] To this end he recommended that baths should be provided at the same rate as for British troops and that a canteen, where the men could buy comforts, be set up at the Base Depot. Their own cooks would prepare the meals and it would not be necessary for British troops to guard camps, as the Chinese would provide their own police to maintain order. The conference also agreed that a hospital should be set up at the depot.

'The heart of the Chinese Labor Corps was the individual company.'[31] A CLC Company, commanded by a major or captain, had four subalterns and eighteen European NCOs. As with other native units the War Office view was that the European officers and NCOs should speak the language of the natives but this frequently was not the case. To overcome difficulties, Colonel Purdon, Advisor on Chinese Labour, produced a phrase book of common phrases in English, with Chinese characters and phonetic pronunciation. Although the phrase book was approved in October 1917 it was not until March 1918 that copies were issued to companies. There were 473 Chinese, who did not hold a military rank, 443 of whom were labourers. The other 30 consisted of an interpreter clerk, interpreters, gangers and dressers.

There was a clear attempt to separate the white members of a company from the Chinese. Instructions were given that in 'the interests of discipline, sleeping, accommodation, latrines, ablution rooms, and cook-houses for Officers and white personnel must be well removed from, and outside, the Chinese enclosures'.[32] On arrival in France a man's thumbprints were taken and compared to those on his identification card. This resulted in a number of impersonators being discovered. Most were youngsters under age for service or men who had failed the medical examination in China. Impersonators were not sent back to China but found suitable employment. As a result of recruiting in northern China many of the Chinese were strong, as tall as Europeans, and of good health. They were described in *The Times* as, 'a sturdy lot, of good physique, who are not likely to suffer much from the mild rigours of the French winter'.[33]

The first contingent, arriving at Havre on 19 April 1917, was sent to the Depot at Noyelles which could accommodate 35 officers, 200 NCOs and 3,000 coolies. By May 1917 the Depot was already full when a sudden rush of new recruits arrived from China and there were insufficient tents. Fourteen men had to sleep in a tent designed for ten. A lack of British uniforms in China meant that many officers arrived in civilian clothes. GHQ informed the depot that: 'Officers arriving from China in "mufti" should be sent to the depot in Shorncliffe to obtain uniforms.'[34]

Cases of unrest amongst the Chinese started soon after their arrival in France. Number 4 Company CLC, employed at Calais docks from 4 May, had 40 cases of trachoma diagnosed on 17 May. Two days later the men complained that they were not getting sufficient rice. On 23 May there was a clash between men of the Company and Egyptians at the docks. On 28 May 200 coolies refused to work, stating they were not getting enough to eat. The following day, after the ring leaders had been punished, Captain Peil, RAMC, visited the company and found 60 men were undernourished due to a lack of rice. He instructed that their daily allowance be increased by ½ lb to 2 lbs a day.[35]

Complaints about the shortage of rice from all companies, continued throughout May and into June. A lack of understanding on the part of their OCs and other British officers did not improve matters. On 15 June one OC suggested that the way to deal with complaints was to withhold the tobacco ration and only give tobacco as a reward. The following day in Dunkirk the Labour Commandant suggested reducing the rice ration, the idea only being rejected when the company OCs informed him that they 'could not guarantee that the coolies would work'.[36]

A decision was taken on 20 June 1917 to allow men to undertake trade tests which would enable them to become skilled workers and receive additional pay. On 26 July the Chinese establishment of a company was changed with the creation of a Head Ganger. Under the Head Ganger, who was equivalent to a CSM and responsible for discipline, there were seven Class One Gangers (equivalent to sergeant) each responsible for just over 60 men. Each company also had eight Class Two Gangers (corporals) and sixteen Class Three Gangers (lance corporals).

White officers and NCOs, even when they spoke the requisite Mandarin Chinese, did not instruct the coolies. The normal practice was for gangers to issue instructions. 'The elevation to ganger appears to have been an unpopular one, for it meant translating and implementing the orders of the British officers and seeing that production quotas were met.'[37] Equally the British had to be careful to ensure that the ganger did not lose face among his men. If a British officer or NCO publicly humiliated a ganger the men under him would refuse to obey his orders.

From 4 August 1917 Dunkirk suffered air raids for several weeks. By the end of the month 12 Chinese had been killed and 32 wounded during these raids. On 4 September a further 15 were killed and 21 wounded which led to strikes and over 2,100 men fleeing to the sand dunes near Dunkirk. The Chinese were also reported as 'wandering all over the place, doing a considerable amount of damage, breaking into houses and generally misbehaving'.[38] With so many Chinese not working the 3rd Canadian Labour Battalion and the British 74 Company had to be urgently moved to Dunkirk to replace them at the docks.

As with other foreign labour, restrictions were placed upon the Chinese. British soldiers were forbidden from supplying them with alcohol. Chinese speakers, other than members of the CLC, were not allowed into canteens or recreation huts at their camps. The Chinese could, with passes, visit towns but like all coloured labourers were banned from cafes and *estaminets*. Towns were often made out of bounds to the Chinese, unless they were part of a working party, as happened at Poperinghe in August 1917. The French would not allow the British recruited Chinese to mix with their Chinese.

On 1 October 1917 a letter was sent from GHQ to the War Office stating that some Chinese had earned considerable amounts of money and that 'arranging for the remittance of money by the Chinese to their homes or alternatively of enabling them to save up their earnings until their return has now become a matter of urgency'.[39] It appears that instituting a banking scheme took some time, as it is not until the publication of General Routine Order 4574 on 23 July 1918 that reference is found to a Savings Bank being opened at the CLC Depot.

Discontent and Crime

Many instances of discontent amongst the Chinese led to them taking a stand about what they saw as their rights according to their contract. An example being that on 22 October 1918 there was unrest among 174 Company due to the lack of a canteen at Cambrai where they were working. Records rarely give more than brief details of incidents. On 16 December 1917, at Fontinettes, armed guards fired on men in 21 Company killing four and wounding nine. In the incident a Canadian ASC private was hit by a stray bullet and died. The Calais Diary merely describes it as a serious incident without giving any indication of its cause.[40]

Moving from the relative comfort of the Noyelles Base Depot to tented accommodation in 3rd Army Area led to unrest in 38 Company on 17 January 1918. The incident appears to have been handled badly by Major Terry, their CO, as he was replaced and the Company was sent away for two weeks to reorganise.

Poor relationships between the men and their white officers and NCOs also led to protests as happened on 3 September 1918 when 22 Company refused to eat, as they disliked the quartermaster sergeant.

The Chinese had little opportunity to spend their money and gambling featured heavily in their lives. This often led to problems that resulted in violence and even murder. Coolie 53497 Tseng Sung Kung, 60 Company, was executed on 23 July 1918 for the murder of coolie 53512.[41] At his trial he claimed that the victim owed him money and it is likely that this was as a result of gambling.

Visiting a town gave the Chinese the opportunity to buy items, including wine, although there appears to have been few instances of drunkenness. Theft from the local population and colleagues was a greater problem. Of the fifteen Chinese sentenced to death, thirteen were as a result of murder either during a robbery or due to an argument over money. Two labourers, 4976 Yu Lung His and 5884 Wang Fa Yu, for example, were sentenced to death following the murder of Madame Boulanger during a robbery at her shop in Rouen on 7 December 1918. Wang Fa Yu's sentence was carried out on 15 February 1919, Yu Lung His committing suicide before the sentence could be carried out.[42]

Religious differences and membership of secret societies also led to disagreements and even death. In 112 Company, on 13 June 1918, 42476 Labourer Hui I He murdered 42532 Labourer Ni Shan. At his trial the accused claimed that he was frightened of the deceased who had asked him for money. In his evidence Captain Swallow CLC, who had been sent from the depot to investigate the incident, explained that he had found it difficult to get the Chinese to speak out. He told the court that the accused, the deceased and at least three others, all with the same name, came from a village known in China as the Robber Village. He also explained that they were all Muslims and part of a secret society or gang led by Ganger 42483. Evidence from 38088, the company interpreter, was that he had heard gossip that Ganger 42483 made the accused commit the crime. Hui I He was found guilty of the murder and executed at Calais on 12 September 1918.[43]

Honours and Awards

The work and bravery of the Chinese coolies was rarely recognised. Of the 52 MSMs awarded to members of the CLC only five have been identified as Chinese. 66475 First Class Ganger Liu Dien Chen, 108 Company, was recommended for the Military Medal. The Labour Commandant of XV Corps recorded that:

> On Wednesday 13 March 1918, he was in charge of a party of 60 coolies in No 1 CRE Yard, LA GORGUE. During the morning the enemy began to shell the town at some distance beyond the yard. As the shells passed directly over the yard the Chinese coolies became panicky and only by constant effort were kept at their work. Early in the afternoon the range was shortened and the shells began to burst near the yard. The Chinese immediately scattered, some of them running right into the danger zone. These he followed and led out of danger, then bringing all the others back he set them to work. They continued to work for a short time, but as the range was again shortened they disappeared for a second time. Again he persuaded them to return and going among them, by his fearlessness and disregard for his own safety set such an example they remained at their work and completed it.[44]

However, at this time Chinese personnel could not be awarded any honour. Following this recommendation it was decided that they would be eligible for the immediate award of an MSM and Liu Dien Chen's award of MSM was confirmed. Two other MSMs were awarded in April 1918 to 30828 Coolie Chao Wen Te and 30064 Coolie Wang Chen Ching, both of 57 Company, although it has not been possible to find the citation for these awards. During 1919 two further MSMs, one to 91085 1st Class Ganger Yen Teng Feng (see page 157). The other MSM was to 15333 Coolie Wang Yu Bhan[45]. On 6 June 1919 he saw a fire in ammunition, close to a collection point. He ran to the dump and threw two buckets of water on the fire. He then picked up a burning bomb, threw it away from the ammunition and put out other fires that had started close to other ordnance.

Managing the work

The original idea of importing Chinese Labour was that they should work on the railways. In view of this the Director General of Transport (DGT), Sir Eric Geddes, claimed the first 7,000 Chinese for his department. The QMG decided that it was not practical to hand these men permanently to the DGT and agreed that he would be allocated fourteen of the first 20 companies to arrive in France. Numbers 1, 4 and 6 Companies were allocated to port construction and formed from men with suitable skills.

Using the specific skills of the Chinese was a feature of the way the CLC was administered. On arrival at Noyelles each man's trade was recorded, with the first of these reports being sent to GHQ on 19 April 1917, the day the first contingent arrived in France. The system helped produce the skilled companies that were to earn high praise from their employers. The downside was that many of the unskilled companies were made up of men with little education. Unfortunately, poor management in the field often negated the positive administration and organisation of the companies. The Report on Labour states: 'most of the defects of discipline in Chinese Labour Companies were in great measure due to the inexperience of the officers and NCOs of whom only a very small proportion had ever handled Chinese Labour before'.[46] Many officers from China did not have previous military experience but were missionaries, merchants, civil servants or administrators.

Colonel Fairfax attempted to ensure British officers and NCOs were instructed in their duties before sending them to a company. However, the rapid arrival of the Chinese and the slow influx of officers and NCOs at Noyelles meant that companies were often formed with two or three officers and seven to nine NCOs instead of the five and nineteen on the establishment. This reduced establishment had a major effect on maintaining discipline.

Some British officers and NCOs were transferred to the CLC because they had experience of working with Chinese and others at their own request. There were also those transferred for other reasons: 'Some of the officers in those units didn't know much about the Chinese; in fact they'd only been posted to them because they weren't well liked in their own regiments.'[47]

When Morris Cohen was seconded to the CLC he found officers who

> ... didn't know how to handle Orientals and they showed it. Some lost their tempers and tried to throw their weight about, others were frankly frightened. I know it sounds silly to feel frightened of a Chinese coolie, but that's the way it was with them. The coolies knew it at once, and they also knew that their officers weren't much good anyway. So they just slacked and chiselled and when they found that they could get away with it, they slacked and chiselled some more till they were doing darned little work at all.[48]

To overcome the problem he introduced task work.

> Next morning I was out early with the field-surveyors and we put in marking posts to cover twice the length of grading they'd averaged before. Then I lined up the labourers and told them that that was the work to be done that day and as soon as they'd finished they could knock off and cook their suppers. They worked like beavers and it was completed soon after four o'clock.[49]

An inadequate officer, or one who was too strict, risked losing the respect of his men, which inevitably led to poor work. In the case of Captain H. Taylor, OC 53

Company, it may have cost him his life. A merchant in civilian life, he arrived from China in May 1917. Captain Taylor was a strict disciplinarian and was not liked by the bad characters in his company who called him 'Great Tiger'. On the night of 10 September 1918 he left the mess to visit the company as an air raid was taking place. The next morning his body was found in the local river. A post mortem showed that his head had been under the water whilst he was still alive. At the Court of Inquiry Captain Mowatt, an officer sent from Noyelles to investigate, stated that a coolie had told him that there had been foul play. Evidence was not taken from any of the coolies in the company. The finding of the Court was:

> … having further investigated the case and considered the evidence are of opinion that although a motive of foul play exists there is no proof that foul-play occurred. Consequently the Court consider that they must come to the conclusion that Capt H Taylor met his death by misadventure.[50]

Skilled Companies

A letter sent to the War Office on 6 August 1917 proposed that the Chinese be paid for skilled work. This was approved on 29 August. Procedures were laid down for Chinese labourers to be tested by RE officers. This proved unsatisfactory 'due to slackness on the part of Officers conducting the tests, and numbers of Chinese were brought on to skilled rates of pay who either did not deserve promotion or were not required to work as tradesmen'.[51] To overcome the problem GHQ produced a list of 32 trades for which tests were authorised. These included blacksmiths, tinsmiths, crane drivers, masons, shoemakers, tailors and bricklayers.

When a man arrived from China, and was known to be a skilled tradesman, he was placed in an appropriate company and undertook a trade test. Chinese speaking technical officers from Noyelles also visited companies at work to identify men who were likely to be useful tradesmen. These men were transferred to 103 RE Works Depot Company where they were tested. If a man passed the test he was sent to a company where his skills could be used or if he failed he was returned to his company. By the beginning of 1918 there were 4,726 certified skilled tradesmen in the CLC.

In July 1918 GHQ recorded that 'a considerable number of Chinese are now engaged on skilled work, such as port construction, railway maintenance and workshops'.[52] Examples of skilled companies include 1, 4 and 6 Companies employed on port construction at Dunkirk, Calais and Dieppe; 113 Company in the Railway Wagon Repair Shops at Audruicq; 114, a Motor Transport Repair Company, at Bergues; 128, a Forestry Company, in the Foret d'Eu; and 135, a Works Company, at Etaples. Two companies, 51 and 69, were formed for work in the tank workshops at Erin and Teneur. At Erin the fitters and riveters of 51 Company brought 127 mud-choked tanks, salvaged from Flanders, back to fighting condition.[53] The 1,856 skilled Chinese working in seven railway maintenance companies were particularly successful. The chief railway construction engineer giving 'the whole of the Railway Maintenance "on contract" to Chinese Labour.'[54] A total of 21 skilled companies were formed but there were numerous other companies that, at some time, were employed on skilled work. In July 1918, for example, a detachment of skilled workers from 183 Company was sent to No. 2 RE Workshop at Abancourt to assist 163, a skilled Works Company.

Chinese labourers had also been employed as crane drives at Dunkirk since August 1917 when, at the end of 1918, demobilisation of British troops resulted in a shortage of crane drivers. Further Chinese were trained to assume this role at Rouen, Havre, Dieppe, Zeneghem, Calais and Dunkirk.

Health and Death

A Hospital was established at Noyelles by April 1917. Initially it could accommodate 300 men but was enlarged throughout 1917 and by early 1918 could accommodate 1,500 men. Under the command of Lieutenant Colonel Douglas Gray, formerly medical advisor to the British Legation in Peking, many of its doctors, and the medical officers serving with individual companies, were mission doctors from China. Following complaints from the medical officers, recruitment of dressers was stopped in China in July 1917 and suitable men selected and trained from those serving in France. Another hospital was opened at Havre during 1918.

Hospitals often accommodated more men than those suffering from illness or injury. Officers were instructed, 'when casualties or accidents occur, one or two friends should always be allowed to accompany the man to hospital; this is specially important in the case of a serious accident, as if the man dies on the way suspicion is aroused.'[55] As with all other nations they suffered badly from the influenza outbreak in 1918 although it is not known how many died.

The most common illness was trachoma, an infectious eye disease that could spread rapidly through the shared use of towels and blankets. The medical examination carried out in China was supposed to identify men with trachoma. Anyone found to have the infection would be rejected but this did not always happen. There was also the danger of impersonators suffering with the disease. Mindful of the danger of trachoma spreading to other native labourers or to Allied soldiers, as far as possible men with the disease were put into separate companies and were accommodated and employed away from other units. Where a full company could not be formed trachoma sufferers would be placed in the same section. Amongst the first contingents to arrive in France the trachoma rate was about thirteen per cent and instructions were sent to China that the medical examination needed to be more stringent. This was applied and the rate dropped to around three per cent. At the same time, in France, the Chinese were regularly examined and, when found, treated for trachoma.

In August 1917 a scheme was inaugurated whereby three different types of companies were formed. 'X' Companies, which contained clean men and could be sent anywhere, 'Y' Companies whose men might have trachoma or conjunctivitis and 'Z' Companies whose men had trachoma. As treatment took place in the man's own time, not when he was working, inspections for trachoma were normally held on the day the man was resting. Once posted to a 'Z' Company the man stayed in that company even if he was later declared clear of trachoma. In October 1917 each man was issued with a second towel in an attempt to avoid men sharing towels. From January 1918 onwards 'Y' and 'Z' Companies were provided with an additional 40 lbs of coal, or its equivalent in wood, each day 'for the purpose of maintaining a cauldron of boiling water for disinfecting and cleaning towels'.[56]

Six trachoma treatment centres were established at Boulogne, Calais, Dannes-Camiers, Seigneville, Vendrouz and Abancourt each with a full time ophthalmic specialist. Between four and six 'Z' Companies were posted in the vicinity of each centre. All Chinese, whether infected or not, received daily eye drops of boric acid and zinc sulphate in order to minimise the disease. By May 1918 some 4,700 men had been formed into 9½ 'Y' Companies and 7,750 into 15½ 'Z' Companies.

The exact number of CLC men who died is not known. The Commonwealth War Graves Commission states: 'nearly 2,000 men from the Chinese Labour Corps died during the First World War, some as a direct result of enemy action, or of wounds received in the course of their duties, but many more in the influenza epidemic that swept Europe in 1918–19.'[57] Summerskill suggests a slightly higher figure: '1,834 died in France, 279 died at sea on the way home, and 32 could not be traced.'[58]

Arrangements were made for Chinese to be buried according to their traditions. Ideally, to drive away evil spirits the cemetery was on sloping ground with a stream below or a gully down which water flowed. Graves were not dug parallel to one of the cardinal points. Where possible the Chinese were buried in their own cemeteries. When this could not be done they were buried in a section of a cemetery in such a way that the graves were not completely surrounded by the graves of Europeans. There are CLC cemeteries at Noyelles, which contains 800 graves and a memorial to 40 who died on land or at sea and have no known grave, and Ruminghem, which contains 75 graves. Three other cemeteries in France with large numbers of CLC graves are St Etienne-au-Mont Communal Cemetery (170), Les Baraques Military Cemetery (200) and Arques-la-Bataille British Cemetery (70). In Britain there is a Chinese section to the military cemetery at Shorncliffe.

Repatriation

The first men to be repatriated left France in November 1918, although the War Office was keen to retain as many as possible to assist with clearing the battlefields and salvage work. By the end of August 1919 about 15,000 had left France and this rose to 59,300 by the end of the year. Repatriation continued into 1920; the final group 'of 73 labourers arrived at Tsingtao on 13th September 1920'.[59]

A number of Chinese returned home by eastward passage through the Indian Ocean but the majority, about 75,000, returned to China via Canada. A holding camp was built at Coquitlam, British Columbia for men awaiting ships to make the final part of the journey to China. Among the vessels was the *Empress of Asia*, which made three trips during 1919 and 1920, carrying nearly 7,000 coolies. The coolies became frustrated with the wait in Canada and it was inevitable that trouble occurred: 'One of the worst coolie riots took place in far-away Victoria, British Columbia, where over 8,000 coolies waited in March 1920 for the transport in which to continue the tedious journey home.'[60]

The last group of the CLC arrived back in China 'on 13 September 1920, and were paid off the following day, four years after the British Government had adopted the scheme'.[61]

1 NA WO 106/35
2 Xu Guoqi, *China and the Great War* pp.116–120
3 Xu Guoqi calculated by this figure based on his research of the 'messy' French records (pages 126–129).
4 NA WO 95/3969
5 Xu Guoqi p.123
6 NA WO 32/11345 8 Aug 1916
7 ibid 12 Aug 1916
8 ibid 22 Sept 1916
9 Griffin, N., *Britain's Chinese Labour in World War 1* p.103
10 Summerskill, M. *China on the Western Front* p.48
11 NA WO 32/11345
12 ibid
13 Xu Guoqi p.126
14 NA WO 32/11345 6 Nov 1916
15 ibid 25 Nov 1916
16 Of the forty-seven sailings of the CLC from China thirteen do not record the number of officers.
17 *The Times* 27 December 1917
18 Drage, C., *Two Gun Cohen* p.68
19 Summerskill p.80
20 ibid p.86
21 National Trust web site: http://www.nationaltrust.org.uk/main/w-global/w-localtoyou/w-eastengland/w-eastengland-news/w-eastengland-news-orford-ness-ninety-years-of-remembrance.htm
22 Summerskill p.96
23 NA T 1/12343
24 Summerskill p.83
25 ibid p.88
26 Klein, D., *With the Chinks* p.18
27 ibid p.145
28 Klein, D., *With the Chinks*
29 ibid p.167
30 NA WO 32/11345
31 Griffin p.105
32 NA 107/37 Notes for Officers of Chinese Labour Companies p.14
33 *The Times* 27 December 1917
34 NA WO 95/83
35 ibid WO 95/4174
36 ibid WO 95/4025
37 Griffin p.105
38 NA WO 95/83
39 ibid WO 95/36
40 ibid WO 95/4018
41 ibid WO 71/651
42 Oram, G. *Death Sentences Passed by Military courts* p.130
43 NA WO 71/665
44 ibid WO 95/929
45 *London Gazette* 30 March 1920, Page 4017
46 NA 107/37 Report on Labour p.52
47 Drage p.67

48 ibid p.67
49 ibid p.68
50 NA WO 339/108221
51 ibid WO 107/37 p.49
52 ibid WO 95/83
53 Campbell, C., *Band of Brigands* p.310
54 NA WO 107/37 Appendix K
55 ibid 107/37 Notes for Officers of Chinese Labour Companies p.21
56 ibid WO 95/527
57 CWGC, The Chinese Labour Corps at the Western Front
58 Summerskill p.195
59 ibid p.199
60 Griffin p.106
61 Summerskill p.199

PORTUGUESE LABOUR

On 30 November 1916 the War Office sent the C-in-C a telegram informing him that the Army Council was considering a proposal to raise Portuguese Labour Battalions and asking him to ascertain whether the French authorities would have any objection. He responded on 5 December saying that provided any such battalions were under military discipline there were no objections from the French. He also offered his recommendation that if these battalions were raised, they should be organized in companies of 250 men with 3 officers per company. Additionally, personnel should be selected who had qualifications for work in wood cutting, quarrying, road work and general labour and individual companies be formed from men with similar skills.

The first Portuguese troops arrived in France on 2 February 1917 and were integrated into the BEF. On 23 June approval was given to the formation of a Portuguese Pioneer Battalion in each Portuguese Division, the men being provided by the pioneer platoons in their infantry battalions.[1]

In September 1917 there is a reference in the 1st Army Diary to the Portuguese working 'steadily, but slowly, on the small Cemeteries in their area' but it is unclear whether this was work being carried out by a specific labour unit or front line soldiers on fatigues.[2] XV Corps Diary does not mention Portuguese labour but refers to 176 Company Labour Corps being employed on tramways in the Portuguese Area in December 1917.[3] This suggests that Portuguese labour units were supplemented with British labour.

Almost from the beginning there were problems with the Portuguese Expeditionary Force. In the main, the soldiers were of peasant stock and illiterate, hated British rations and did not feel they were fighting for their homeland. Leave for other ranks, when granted, was for a short period in case they failed to return. Officers were granted leave, although, of the 1,920 officers who went on leave, 822 failed to return to their unit.[4] A change of Government in Portugal in December 1917 meant that reinforcements were not forthcoming to replace men lost though injury or ill health, a factor that further reduced morale.

On 4 April 1918 the Commander of the Portuguese Expeditionary Forces informed Lisbon of the first of the mutinies that occurred amongst his men.

The British decided to relieve the Portuguese at the front and two days later the 55th (West Lancashire) Division replaced the 1st Portuguese Division. The 2nd Portuguese Division was due to be replaced on 9 April but before this could take place, the Germans launched the Lys Offensive, otherwise known as 'Operation Georgette.' The 2nd Portuguese Division was quickly overcome and retreated in disarray with 398 men killed and 6,585 taken prisoner.

Withdrawn from the Front, a new Portuguese HQ was established at Ambleteuse on the coast, about 20 kilometres south-west of Calais. Although the 1st Division returned to the Front later in 1918, many of the men were 'used as labour for digging trenches and road repairs as 'punishment' for what the British perceived as their "cowardice"'.[5] The Portuguese were placed under the command of the GOC LoC. No Portuguese officers or other ranks were permitted outside the bounds of the Portuguese Area unless granted a pass. Portuguese camps were out of bounds to British troops. British camps, and British installations within the Portuguese Area, were out of bounds to Portuguese troops.[6] Water, electric, telephone, and stores were all maintained and run by the British. The first reference to a Portuguese Works Company is to be found in a War Diary.[7] On 12 April 1918 the Company, which comprised 6 officers, 1 British NCO and 563 other ranks, joined I Corps at Noeux Les Mines. A Portuguese Guard of 37 other ranks supported the Company.

On 23 April the 11th (Pioneer) Battalion of the King's Liverpool Regiment were employed on the GHQ defence line at Molinghem.[8] Their Diary records 3 officers and 292 other ranks of the '29th Portuguese Infantry Regiment now organized as a Labour Company, attached to the Battalion for work'.[9] It has not been possible to ascertain whether this company was a detachment from the Portuguese Works Company based with I Corps or was an additional company. This record supports the suggestion that the Portuguese infantry were being 'punished' by conversion into labour units. Further support comes in one diary, which states that on 25 April 1918 'All Portuguese are employed on construction or rear defences.'[10] There is reference to a Portuguese company being attached to X Corps, moving from L'Omlois to La Lacque on 8 June but no indication of when they joined the Corps.

One of the most intriguing references to the Portuguese is to be found in GHQ AQ Diary[11] on 15 July 1918, which states that 1,200 Portuguese Labourers moved from Havre to Southampton. It has not been possible to confirm if these were soldiers, or why they were moved to Britain.

A visit by the Director of Medical Services to the Portuguese HQ on 16 May points to poor management on the part of the Portuguese officers. He found the whole camp was becoming very unsanitary with men not using latrines. In some cases no latrines had been dug. He also found soldiers were watering horses, drawing water for drinking, and washing themselves and their clothes anywhere in the streams. He advised that not only should the facilities be kept separate but that they should also be kept under close police supervision. The British Mission to the Portuguese immediately passed these concerns on to their CO in a strongly worded note: 'You will wish to receive this letter early, and take action upon it, before a letter on the subject arrives from HQ, LofC Area'.[12]

During June consideration was given to using the Portuguese on a quiet sector of the French Front, or repatriating them. Both plans were rejected since a move to the French Front could allow the French to undermine British influence with the Portuguese Government. Equally, repatriation could result in the British/ Portuguese alliance being broken.

On 30 June the British Mission reported that only half the Portuguese were available for work with high numbers reporting sick without real cause. They were also critical of the leadership of the Portuguese officers:

> The task set for each man is 140 cubic feet – employed on preparation of defences for the 1st Army. The soil is easy and the task is completed in 4 hours, this work is not organized by the Portuguese but by the formation they are supporting.
>
> The Portuguese are good labourers and capable of sustained effort in the hands of a competent director and unhampered by the presence of their own officers.[13]

Discipline amongst the Portuguese was an ongoing problem and on 24 May Portuguese Punishment Camp No. 1 was attached to I Corps.

On 25 October 1918 the Portuguese Corps ordered No 1 Labour Company back to their Corps area, stating it was no longer part of the 1st Portuguese Division.[14] There is no indication of why this decision was made. There is little reference to the Labour Company until the end of operations when, on 10 November, it was at Lesquin near Lille attached to III Corps. It remained there until 14 December when it moved to Ligne, finally coming under the direct administration of the Portuguese Corps.[15] Six days after the end of the War GHQ requested employment of the Portuguese Punishment Battalion and they were allocated to salvage work at Laventie on 19 November. The Portuguese were repatriated from Cherbourg in January 1919.

1 NA WO 95/5488
2 ibid WO 95/185
3 ibid WO 95/929
4 Philippart, J. L., *L'entrée du Portugal dans la Grande Guerre* (9 Mars 1916–11 Mai 1917) at http://www.grande-guerre.org/Articles/Portugal.htm
5 Rodrigues, H., *France at War Portugal in the Great War* at www.worldwar1.com/france/portugal.htm
6 NA WO 95/5489
7 ibid WO 95/622
8 Molinghem is only 26 km from Noeux Les Mines
9 NA WO 95/1890
10 ibid WO 95/3922
11 ibid WO 95/39
12 ibid WO 95/5489
13 ibid
14 ibid
15 ibid

ITALIAN LABOUR

On 19 January 1918 a meeting took place in Rome between the Italian Government's representative, Colonel Commandant Vacchelli, and the French

Government's M. Planche. At the meeting an agreement was reached whereby the Italians placed at the disposal of the French 60,000 soldiers to be used for defence work within France. These men were already serving in the Italian Army and comprised some 40,000 men who were unfit for front line service. The other 20,000 soldiers were fit men although within three months they were replaced by an equivalent number of unfit men.

The commander was Major General Commandant Joseph Tarditi with the title Inspector General of Auxiliary Service in France. He had four colonels from the Italian Artillery or Engineering Services, each responsible for a 'regroupement' made up of twenty Noyaux. A Noyau, commanded by either a major or captain, was made up of ten companies. Each company, commanded by either a captain or senior lieutenant, comprised three centuries (100 men strong) under a subaltern and were known as Auxiliary Companies. General Tarditi and the four colonels were provided with the administrative and sanitary personnel required for normal working of the various services.

Under the agreement between the Italians and the French the men were to be employed in grouped units. The Italian colonel in charge of the group was responsible for allotting the grouped units to a specific area of work. He was under the command of the OC of the French unit he was supporting. This organisation was, in the view of the British, 'in-elastic and therefore unsuitable'.[1]

The Italian Government agreed to provide each man with his personal equipment and two blankets; the French providing all other equipment and accommodation. Whilst serving in France the men were entitled to the same rations and medical facilities provided for French soldiers. They were paid at the same rate as French soldiers, this being funded by the Italian Government. The first contingent of 1,500 men arrived at Chambery on 21 January 1918 and four days later 600 of them arrived at Brie to support the British Cavalry Corps. By 8 February there were seven Italian companies working on the rear lines of defence in the 5th Army Area, two with the Cavalry Corps at Brie and Doingt, two in VII Corps at Tincourt and Nurlu and three in XVIII Corps at Cugny and Foreste.

As the Italian labourers arrived in France more were transferred to the British 5th Army. By 23 February the 7th, 17th, 19th and 20th Italian Noyaux were supporting the Cavalry, VII, XVIII and III Corps respectively; a total of 12,255 men. The British placed all Italian Labour under the command of the Labour Commandants within the Army HQ.[2] Colonel Zombelli OC Italian Auxiliary Forces arrived at 5th Army HQ on 27 February 1918. The Labour Commandant in the 5th Army Area had seen the number of labourers under his control increase from 26,567 on 22 December 1917 to 67,967 on 16 March 1918.[3] Almost half of these were foreign labourers who spoke little or no English. The French failed to honour their part of the agreement to supply the Italians with accommodation; rationing and the additional equipment they required exacerbated these difficulties. Within six weeks over 12,000 Italians arrived with nothing more than their personal equipment and two blankets. It is not surprising that on 12 March the conditions in the Italian's camps were described as 'unsatisfactory'.[4]

By the 18 March all 12,000 Italian labourers were working on the Green Line's (Reserve Line) defences under the direction of the CRE. Three days later at 05.35 the Germans launched their major offensive and arrangements had to be made to quickly withdraw the Italian labourers. The Labour Commandant of III Corps, Colonel Sir Eric Swayne, in his report on labour during the German offensive, commented:

> There was great difficulty in keeping [in] touch, owing to the disconnection of tel-ephonic communication and to the scarcity of horses and bicycles, and the congested condition of the roads. This was especially the case when withdrawing the 13 Italian Companies from their advanced positions at Flavy, Cugny, Jussy, Autreville.[5]

Colonel Swayne personally extracted two Italian companies on 21 March down the Flavy-Cugny-Neuville road, the first part of which, from Flavy to Cugny, was under shellfire. The two companies were initially moved to Murancourt and the next day to Noyon. With the Germans advancing on Noyon the decision was made at midnight on 23 March to move all labour units to Estrees-St Denis. Arriving on 25 March, the two Italian companies were handed over to the French Army.

In XIX Corps British officers guided the companies in 7 Noyau to safety, as the Italians had not been instructed on the action to take in case of a German attack.[6] The Corps War Diary notes 'panic was avoided'[7] and the companies marched to Abancourt where they were joined by 17 and 19 Noyau and a few companies from 20 Noyau. The situation in VII Corps appears to have been confused. On 22 March rather than being withdrawn, 17 Noyau were placed under the control of the CRE to work in areas not being shelled. The following day, however, they were moved from Peronne to Bray-sur-Somme and then on 24 March to Boves.

In XVIII Corps the initial withdrawal of all labour was to Nesle where they arrived on 22 March. The following day a rumour spread that the Germans were close to Nesle and at 16.40 seven companies of 19 Noyau[8] left the area without permission. They were later found in Amiens and turned back. The War Diaries record how three days after the start of the German offensive the situation was still one of considerable confusion. At GHQ the decision was taken on 24 March that all Italian and Coloured labour was to be evacuated to base using empty supply and ammunition trains. This order was recorded and implemented in XIX Corps. In XVIII Corps the Italians were sent to Moreuil, where they arrived on 25 March, only to be moved on arrival to Boves.

The German offensive in March ended the use of Italian labourers in the British sector. 7, 17 Noyaux and seven companies of 20 Noyau were transferred from the 5th Army to the LoC on 26 March, moving to the newly opened Labour Emergency Camp at Abancourt. The experience of the Italians, 110 officers and 7,340 men, who arrived at Abancourt, was not a good one. The day after they arrived there was a fire in their camp and on 29 March an outbreak of mumps resulted in an isolation camp being set up at Cullere. On 29 March 19 and 20 Noyau transferred to the LoC. French officers arrived at Abancourt on 2 April to assume responsibility for the Italians and arrange for their repatriation, which took place on 18 April.

The Italians were used to support the British sector for less than two months and it was not a great success. They were not supplied with the basic tools required for the work they were asked to undertake; they were expected to survive on British rations which were unsuited to the Italians and 'their discipline was poor and the work indifferent'.[9] Despite all the criticisms, in June 1918, the War Office revisited the idea of using Italian labour although they decided not to proceed.

1 NA WO 107/37 Report on Labour p.40
2 ibid WO 95/83
3 Shaw Sparrow, W., *The Fifth Army in March* 1918 p. 17
4 NA WO 95/537
5 ibid WO 107/37 Report on Labour Appendix CC
6 Evacuation plans for labour in case of a German offensive had been issued on 7 March 1918 although these do not appear to have been communicated to the Italians in XIX Corps.
7 NA WO 95/844
8 168, 169, 181, 182, 183, 184 and 190 were the Italian companies that left the area. The other three companies, 185, 186 and 187 remained on station.
9 NA WO 107/37 p.40

GERMAN PRISONERS OF WAR

The history of Prisoner of War companies has two parts; the prisoners and their work; and the British officers and men who administered and guarded the companies.

During the first two years of war, PoWs were sent to camps in Britain rather than be retained in France and Flanders. On 4 February 1916 the QMG wrote to the IGC stating that the shortage of labour in France would not be solved until sufficient men had been found for the munitions industry in Britain and suggested the use of PoWs in France on 'work of a nature which they would be best fitted'[1] in forests and at the ports. On 16 February the Director of Works informed the IGC that he could employ 2,600 PoWs at Dieppe, Havre, Rouen, Calais and Abancourt. The IGC's response to these suggestions was that employing PoWs to unload military stores would contravene the Hague Convention, that employing them in the forests was too risky and that in his view 'the proper place to employ Prisoners of War is in England thus releasing personnel for France'.[2]

On 11 March the IGC was informed that the War Office wanted all able-bodied prisoners to be retained in France. However, the existing PoW camp at Havre was unsuitable for long-term detention and three days later the War Office decided that until there were secure camps and suitable work in France, prisoners would continue to be sent to Britain. At the same time, the QMG was suggesting that PoWs could be employed in both quarries and forests and in April 1,000 PoWs, four groups of 250 men, were assigned to work in forests.

During the Battle of the Somme the decision was taken to retain PoWs in France and use them for tasks in the rear area, replacing fighting soldiers. On 27 July 1916 the AG informed Army commanders that they could apply to GHQ to form PoW companies, each of 425 men, to be employed on road maintenance, at railheads, in quarries and on railway construction. They were not to be employed on defence work or within the range of enemy artillery. The following day five companies were formed. Each company was intended to be self-supporting with the 400 labourers organised into four groups of 100. Support came from 25 other prisoners (ten NCOs, six interpreters, two tailors, two shoemakers, four cooks and a medical orderly). Labourers were paid 4d a day,[3] and the NCOs and interpreters 6d a day, which they received in token form, the possession of French or British currency being forbidden. The concept of self-supporting was, in October 1917, extended to growing their own vegetables.

Each PoW Company was commanded and administered by a British captain or major supported by a CSM, a CQMS and a clerk. In addition, one officer, four sergeants, eight corporals and forty other ranks were appointed as escorts. Six ASC soldiers were attached to each company to drive the GS Wagon, the water cart and the supply wagons. Both the AG's department at GHQ and individual Escort Officers thought the role of the escorts was solely to prevent escapes. The escorts failed to ensure the prisoners worked efficiently. In August 1916 a request by the C-in-C that British based PoW companies be returned to France for forestry work. The War Office rejected the idea and suggested forming forestry companies from PoWs in France.

There were two important changes in November 1916. The first was the formation of a company of PoW mechanics to work for 320 Company ASC at their Heavy Repair Shop. This made use of skilled PoWs rather than employing them on general labouring tasks. The second was the Director of Works being given approval to work PoWs at night. There was indignation in the House of Commons, in November, when it was confirmed that PoWs in Rouen were being accommodated in huts with bedsteads whilst nearby British units were in tents with boarded floors and blankets.

By the start of 1917 there were over 18,600 prisoners in 47 PoW companies in France, working on the roads, in quarries, in forests and building huts. PoWs were also involved in the construction of ammunition depots although this ended in March 1917 when it was realised that intelligence could be passed to the enemy by sick PoWs being repatriated. The Labour Directorate was formed in January 1917 and assumed responsibility for the allotment and distribution of PoW Companies.

The work of the company attached to the ASC Heavy Repair Shop, having proved successful, led to a change in the way companies were set up. From June 1917 PoWs were sorted into trade groups consisting of one NCO and twenty men, and were sent to a collecting station at Abbeville.[4] At Abbeville the Labour Directorate was then able to create companies with personnel suited for the work they were to undertake. When a company was formed, a record was made of the number of each tradesman in the company. This record was then used to allot a company to appropriate work. Skilled companies of engineers and electricians worked at RE and ASC workshops, and for the Ordnance Department. Semi-skilled companies, which contained a mix of tradesmen and general labourers, were allocated to work for the Director of Works.[5] Semi-skilled companies of miners and quarrymen worked at the quarries at Rinxent under the Director of Roads. General labour companies were formed from unskilled PoWs. At times, semi-skilled companies were used as general labour. For example on 17 December 1917, when snow blocked roads in the 3rd Army Area, all PoW companies were used to clear the roads.[6] In the same month a request was made for 4,000 PoW skilled ploughmen to be sent to Britain to work for the Board of Agriculture. 1,000 appear to have been sent in January 1918.[7]

The Labour Directorate continued to face problems with the efficiency of PoW companies despite the attachment, in July 1917, of one sergeant and four corporals to each PoW company to supervise work parties. Officers of the Labour Corps were also attached to companies to ensure efficient work was achieved through the maintenance of good discipline. Restrictions on where PoW companies could be employed caused further problems. Prior to February 1917 PoWs were employed within 8 km of the Front. Following an agreement with the French this was raised to 20 km, and the British Cabinet increased it to 30 km in April 1917. There were many tasks for which it was considered inadvisable to use PoWs. These included handling supplies, for fear of sabotage; and unloading of ships, for fear of escapes and sabotage.

Although PoW companies were not allowed to work within 30 km of the front they did suffer casualties. At Rinxent, on the 4 September 1917, a German air raid killed 9 escorts and 39 prisoners and wounded 6 escorts and 40 prisoners from No. 5 and No. 20 PoW Companies. In June 1918, 11 PoW Company at Wail were bombed despite being over 50 km from the Front and in a marked PoW camp. Following the German offensive in March 1918 arrangements were made to evacuate PoWs to Britain, and 28 companies with over 12,200 prisoners were evacuated during April.

On 30 March 1918

> ... the interdependence of discipline and working efficiency was at last recognised and instructions were issued by A.G. to the effect that all PoW Company Officers and the escort were responsible for obtaining the full working efficiency of their units.[8]

The following month, officers serving with PoW companies were transferred to the Labour Corps, which meant that command, escort duties and supervision of efficient working came under the control of the Labour Directorate.

In June 1918 a revised establishment was introduced with five officers per company. This revision also introduced three scales of escort depending on the type of work being undertaken. Scale 'A' companies employed in workshops and on other tasks where supervision was relatively easy, had twelve NCOs and 40 other ranks as escorts. Scale 'B' companies, which included general labouring duties, had 15 NCOs and 62 other ranks. Scale 'C' companies, which included work like forestry where prisoners were employed over a large area, had 18 NCOs and 84 other ranks. In July 1918 these NCOs and other ranks were transferred to the Labour Corps.

180 and 206 Companies had been formed primarily of Poles but with a small group of Germans. In September 1918 GHQ instructed that Polish PoWs were to be separated from German PoWs because it was believed the Polish were unwilling conscripts in the German Army and therefore assumed that they would work better on their own. The Germans were transferred out of the companies and the level of escorts was reduced from 1:10 to 1:15.

The Franco-British offensive, which began on 8 August 1918, resulted in large numbers of new PoWs. Eleven companies (157–167) were formed on 11 August and a further 31 over the next three weeks. To administer and guard these new companies required over 200 officers and nearly 3,500 men and 'necessitated considerable readjustment of Labour to make use of these Companies'.[9] During

September and October a further 126 companies were formed, making it difficult to find enough guards. The Controller of Labour suggested reducing the number of escorts for each company but GHQ rejected this idea. Instead, more prisoners were evacuated to Britain, with 10,000 being sent at the beginning of October.[10]

Supervision of the prisoners was still giving cause for concern since employers were providing extra supervision. On 22 October it was decided that five additional Labour Corps NCOs would be added to each company to ease the burden on employers. Ensuring a high work output from PoW companies was a continuing problem. The PoWs had no incentive to work hard as a man was working against his own country and no matter how hard he worked he could not improve his daily rate of pay. The PoWs' pay could be withheld but this was so small it had little effect. The OC could withhold rations, but a poorly fed man was not capable of good work. In theory the German NCO supervising a working party was responsible for its efficiency but, as a fellow captive, he would rarely do more than 'take a man's name' when instructed to by an escort.

The OC of one company maintained that the only way to achieve a good result was by creating an esprit de corps amongst the prisoners. When he took over his company he called the German NCOs together and pointed out to them that, in effect, they were still a company of the German Army but under the command of a British officer. As such he expected them to uphold the best traditions of the German Army including smartness, cleanliness and discipline within their own ranks. The NCOs responded to this and whenever a new draft arrived their NCOs told them that they had two options, behave like a German soldier or face court martial for disobeying a superior.[11] This approach was not always successful and there are several recorded instances of companies refusing to work and going on strike.

In October 1918 an incentive scheme was introduced whereby men who worked well were awarded with an increased ration of 2 oz of edible fat and this appears to have had a positive effect in those companies where the OC understood its purpose.

The OC of a company might have eight or ten parties working several miles apart. Since he could spend little time with any particular working party he relied on the escorts to ensure the POWs worked efficiently. It was not uncommon for a working party to increase its work rate when an officer was approaching, to create a good impression. The escorts, who were men of low medical category, were not always up to the task. The OC of one company described the class of man usually sent to PoW companies for escort duties as 'practised lead-swingers, degenerates and physical and mental deficients'.[12] He maintained the lack of work rate and indiscipline within the companies 'arose from the slack talk as well as the slack ways of the British personnel with whom they worked'.[13]

Towards the end of the war the 372 companies were insufficient to accommodate the number of prisoners being captured. Three days after the Armistice the size of PoW companies was increased from 400 to 550 men. Despite the repatriation of PoWs the Labour Corps still did not have sufficient escorts and in February 1919 it was announced that infantry soldiers could be used as escorts. These escorts were not transferred to the Labour Corps but retained in their Infantry Regiments.

Using PoWs to remove mines and delayed action fuses was approved on 16 November and four days later the 4th Army Diary recorded that 'The handling of German ammunition in the Army Area will be done by German prisoners of war.

In no circumstances will British troops or labour be employed on the handling of unsafe German ammunition.'[14] Restrictions on the employment of PoWs were lifted so they could unload ships, move stores, carry out salvage work and exhume and bury the dead. PoWs were not allowed to work at petrol installations, with British ammunition or handle hay.[15] The final restriction to be lifted on 2 July 1919 enabled them to work on light railways.

With the Armistice, men who had been prisoners for 18 months or more were to the first to be repatriated. By August 1919 2,000 men a day were being repatriated and, with a few exceptions, all were repatriated by the end of October 1919.

1   NA WO 95/3965
2   ibid
3   From December 1917 skilled prisoners in 'Work' Companies at the workshops received a higher rate of trade pay.
4   According to the 1st Army AQ Diary (WO 95/184) there were pens at Abbeville and St Omer. However the Report on of Labour (WO 107/37) only refers to the pen at Abbeville.
5   Men were organised into eight trade groups – mechanics and workers in iron, tin etc; engineers and electricians; miners and quarrymen; sawyers, woodcutters and lumbermen; joiners and carpenters; painters, bricklayers and masons; tailors, shoemakers and saddlers and farmers and agricultural workers.
6   NA WO 95/378
7   NA WO 95/537
8   NA WO 107/37 p.58
9   NA WO 95/83
10 NA WO 95/89
11 NA WO 107/37 Appendix M
12 ibid
13 ibid
14 NA WO 95/445
15 The restriction on handling hay was removed on 26 December 1918.

SECTION SIX: RESEARCH

RESEARCHING AN ANCESTOR

Researching the service of any First World War soldier is difficult as German bombing in 1940 destroyed the majority of service records. This section outlines the most common questions asked when searching for an ancestor's Labour Corps service.

Why was a man transferred to the Labour Corps?

Men were transferred to the Labour Corps because illness or injury meant they were not fit to serve in a Front Line unit. Men were not transferred because they had a specific skill or trade. A man's previous trade was taken into account when he was transferred to the Corps, for example an agricultural worker could be used in an Agricultural Company.

How can I find out about my ancestor's service in the Labour Corps?

The surviving records of other ranks are held at the National Archives, Kew in classes WO 363 and WO 364. The records have been transferred to microfilm, which can be viewed at Kew. Both these sets of records are being made available online through www.ancestry.co.uk. Officer's records are held at the National Archives, Kew in classes WO 339 and WO 374. It is possible to search online for the file number of a specific officer but the actual file can only be viewed at Kew.

Can you tell which company a man was in from his Labour Corps number?

When the Labour Corps was formed in 1917 the numbers from 1–170140 were allocated to specific companies (see page 325). However, more numbers were allocated to each company than they needed. Unused numbers were returned and then issued to men joining the Corps at a later date.

This pattern continued throughout 1917 and 1918. As an example, most men with numbers around 275000, like 275294 Private W. Cosh, became members of the Labour Corps in May 1917. However 274160 Private P. Cahill, who has a lower number, was not transferred to the Labour Corps until 1 February 1918, by which time most men were allocated numbers around 520,000.

Another difficulty is that men were frequently transferred from one company to another for the benefit of the service. 340763 Private C. Negus was transferred to the Labour Corps on 30 July 1917 and posted to 439 Agricultural Company. On 17 November he was posted to 656 Agricultural Company and in February 1918 to 396 Agricultural Company. He retained the same Labour Corps number, which could differ significantly from that of other personnel in 656 and 396 Companies.

Can you tell when a man joined the Labour Corps from his regimental number?

As indicated in the previous question it is not possible to give a definitive date based on the regimental number. In general terms:

Regimental Number	Approximate Date joined Labour Corps
Up to 170140	April/May 1917
170141 to around 357600	June to September 1917
357680 to around 362500	September 1917 in Egypt
362600 to around 364000	September/October 1917
364250 to around 364700	Early 1918 in Irish Command
364700 to around 388200	September to November 1917
388300 to around 389500	October/November 1917 in Salonika
390000 to around 393400	September to November 1917
393460 to around 394300	October/November 1917 in Salonika
394500 to around 484900	October 1917 to January 1918
485000 to around 489600	November/December in Salonika
489600 to around 533000	October to February 1918
533200 to around 534100	January/February 1918 in Salonika
534100 to around 542000	February/March 1918
542000 to around 543000	March/April 1918 in Egypt
543000 to around 547800	February/March 1918
547900 to around 549850	May to September 1918 in Egypt
549900 to around 555600	May to September 1918
555600 to around 559100	May to September 1918 – Russian Companies
559200 to around 587450	May to September 1918
587500 to around 588200	May to September 1918 in Salonika
588200 to around 602800	May to September 1918
602800 to around 603400	July 1918 – Graves Registration Working Parties
603400 to around 603700	May to September 1918
603700 to around 621000	May to August 1918 – mainly PoW Companies
621000 to around 622800	October/November 1918 in Egypt
622800 to around 649400	July to September 1918
649400 to around 655100	October 1918 – mainly PoW Companies
655100 to around 694400	September to December 1918
694400 to around 711000	Primarily men who enlisted in 1919 for exhumation and reburial duties in France
711000 to around 995500	Various dates mainly from 1919 onwards

Table 15: Labour Corps Regimental Numbers

Can you tell where a man served from his regimental number?

The table of regimental numbers gives some idea of whether a man served initially in a Labour Company in Egypt or Salonika. However even this should not be considered a definitive answer since it was common for men to be returned from France, Salonika or Egypt to Britain if their medical category dropped.

I know an ancestor served in the Labour Corps but cannot find a Medal Card entry for him.

It is possible that there was an error and his card was not completed. It is more likely that he served only in Britain. Medals were only awarded to men who served overseas.

Will the Medal Card tell me which company he was in?

Most Medal Cards do not record a company number.

My ancestor's Medal Card shows he served in xxx regiment and the Labour Corps. Why are there two different numbers shown?

During the First World War a man was issued with a new number when he moved from one regiment or corps to another. If a man served in two regiments he would have two different numbers.

It was possible for a man to have two Labour Corps numbers if he left the Corps and then returned for further service, as the record for William Bedford illustrates. From 24 March 1915 he served in France as 91613 Corporal Bedford 19th Yorkshires. On 15 July 1918 he became 573779 Corporal Bedford Labour Corps when transferred to 151 PoW Company. Demobilised on 3 February 1919 he re-enlisted on 19 May 1919. Volunteering for one year of service in the Labour Corps on exhumation and burial duties. His new Labour Corps regimental number was 690692. On 8 June 1919 he arrived in France and was posted to 725 Company on burial duties, serving with them until demobilised due to ill health on 8 November 1919.

The Medal Cards can be accessed online at www.nationalarchives.gov.uk. The original Medal Cards sometimes recorded a man's address. These have been photographed and can be accessed at www.ancestry.co.uk. The Medal Cards have a reference to the Medal Rolls. These are books in which a man's details are recorded. Medal Rolls are available at the National Archives in class WO 329. The National Archives have a guide to the Medal Index Cards at www.nationalarchives.gov.uk/documentsonline/medals.asp.

My ancestor served in the Labour Corps.
Why are his medals engraved xxx Regiment?

The 1914–15 Star, War and Victory medals were engraved with the details of the first regiment or corps a man served in when he went overseas. For example, Samuel Slinger first went overseas as 42988 Private Slinger, 5 Infantry Labour Company King's Liverpool Regiment. On the formation of the Labour Corps he became 41790 Private Slinger, 70 Company Labour Corps. His medals are engraved Pte S Slinger 42988 King's Liverpool.

My ancestor was awarded a Military Medal.
What would be engraved on his medal?

Decorations like the Military Medal and MSM are engraved with the unit a man was serving in when the award was made. For example, Thomas Munnery was awarded the MM whilst serving in 112 Company Labour Corps and his medal is engraved with '66895 Lab Cps'. Because his first unit was 4 Infantry Labour Company Queen's Regiment, his War and Victory medals are engraved '35448 Pte T Munnery Queens Regt'.

My ancestor was awarded a Silver War Badge,
why did he get this badge?

Men who were discharged during the war as no longer fit for military service were awarded the Silver War Badge (SWB). This badge would be worn in the lapel to show people that the man had served his country and was not a shirker or conscientious objector. The SWB was awarded to all men, whether they had served in Britain or overseas.

Each badge had its own unique number engraved on the reverse. By consulting the SWB Roll this number can provide further details about a man's service. The SWB Roll records some or all of the following details: name; rank; regimental number; unit he was discharged from; dates of enlistment and discharge; cause of discharge. The SWB Roll is available at the National Archives in class WO 329.

For men discharged from the Labour Corps the SWB Roll often includes both his previous regiment and the Labour Corps company he was in when discharged.

My ancestor died and is buried in a cemetery
in France. When I visited his grave it did not say
he was in the Labour Corps.

In 1919 it was decided that the headstone of a member of the Labour Corps, 'who has previously served in any other unit, should record his connection with his previous regiment'.[1] If a man had been in more than one regiment before the

Labour Corps the headstone should have the details of the last regiment in which he served before transferring to the Labour Corps. The headstone will not show his original regiment.

For example, Samuel Slinger's headstone in Bard Cottage Cemetery shows the badge of the King's Liverpool Regiment and his King's regimental number. It does not have details of his Labour Corps service.

There are examples where a headstone gives details of more than one regiment. An example is to be found in Cairo War Memorial Cemetery. 3788 Private Alfred Cuyler enlisted in 1st/7th Essex Regiment. He transferred to the Labour Corps, regimental number 360529, where he became a CQMS. Cuyler was murdered on 18 March 1919 (see page 278). His headstone is engraved with the badge of the Essex Regiment but with the number 360529. His rank is shown as CQMS and under his name is engraved 'Essex Regiment and Labour Corps'.

Where can I find the Diary for a Labour Corps company?

There are no existing Diaries for any of the companies that were stationed in Britain or Egypt. Only a very small number of companies in France kept Diaries. Those that survive are kept at the National Archives, Kew in class WO 95 although most cover a period of less than three months. There are Diaries for most of the Infantry Labour Battalions and a few Infantry Labour Companies covering the period prior to the formation of the Labour Corps in April 1917. The period covered by these Diaries varies considerably. For example, in WO 95/430, the Diary for the 12th Labour Battalion West Riding Regiment covers the period March 1916 to April 1917, whereas the Diary for 7th Labour Company Devonshire Regiment covers only one month, March 1917. There are a number of Diaries for the RE Labour Battalions but these cease with their transfer to the Labour Corps in July 1917. Labour Group Headquarters did keep Diaries from April to October/November 1917. The quantity and quality of information contained in them varies considerably.

Generally, information about individual companies in France is to be found in Diaries kept at Corps, Army or GHQ level. However these rarely contain more than the location(s) of a company. Diaries for Salonika (95 to 98 and 201 Companies) are in WO 95/4944. The period covered by these Diaries varies. In general they run from June 1917 to June 1918.

1 NA WO 293/10 ACI 68 30 Jan 1919

BRITISH LABOUR COMPANIES

The only surviving list of regimental numbers was published in ACI 611 in April 1917. This details the numbers allocated to Companies 1 to 203 and Labour Groups 1 to 42 overseas, and to Companies 295 to 358 and seven Labour Battalions in Britain. In 1940 the building holding the nominal rolls of the Corps was bombed and these records destroyed.

The transient nature of the Labour Corps means that a regimental number only indicates the first company a man was posted to and not that he remained with the company. The information below has been included to assist the genealogist researching an ancestor (where the number of a man's company is known or for a regimental number below 186,240).

Overseas

France

Table 16: Companies formed from Labour Battalions and Infantry Labour Companies – May 1917

Coy	Regimental Numbers	Created from
1	1–600	19th Bn Royal Scots
2	601–1200	19th Bn Royal Scots
3	1201–1800	14th Bn Cameronians
4	1801–2400	14th Bn Cameronians
5	2401–3000	12th Bn Black Watch
6	3001–3600	12th Bn Black Watch
7	3601–4200	9th Bn Cameron Highlanders
8	4201–4800	9th Bn Cameron Highlanders
9	4801–5400	1st ILC R Scots Fusiliers
10	5401–6000	2nd ILC R Scots Fusiliers
11	6001–6600	3rd ILC R Scots Fusiliers
12	6601–7200	1st ILC Seaforth Highlanders
13	7201–7800	2nd ILC Seaforth Highlanders
14	7801–8400	3rd ILC Seaforth Highlanders
15	8400–9000	4th ILC Seaforth Highlanders
16	9001–9600	12th Bn Lincolnshire
17	9601– 10200	12th Bn Lincolnshire
18	10201–10800	22nd Bn West Yorks
19	10801–11400	22nd Bn West Yorks
20	11401–12000	13th Bn Leicester
21	12001–12600	13th Bn Leicester
22	12601–13200	16th Bn Yorkshire
23	13201–13800	16th Bn Yorkshire
24	13801–14400	12th Bn West Riding
25	14401–15000	12th Bn West Riding
26	15001–15600	12th Bn South Staffs
27	15601–16200	12th Bn South Staffs
28	16201–16800	20th Bn Notts and Derby
29	16801–17400	20th Bn Notts and Derby
30	17401–18000	17th Bn Yorks & Lancs
31	18001–18600	17th Bn Yorks & Lancs
32	18601–19200	1st ILC DLI
33	19201–19800	2nd ILC DLI
34	19801–20400	3rd ILC DLI
35	20401–21000	4th ILC DLI
36	21001–21600	5th ILC DLI
37	21601–22200	6th ILC DLI
38	22201–22800	7th ILC DLI
39	22801–23400	8th ILC DLI
40	23401–24000	1st ILC Lincoln
41	24001–24600	2nd ILC Lincoln
42	24601–25200	3rd ILC Lincoln
43	25201–25800	4th ILC Lincoln
44	25801–26400	5th ILC Lincoln
45	26401–27000	6th ILC Lincoln

46	27001–27600	7th ILC Lincoln
47	27601–28200	8th ILC Lincoln
48	28201–28800	9th ILC Lincoln
49	28801–29400	10th ILC Lincoln
50	29401–30000	11th ILC Lincoln
51	30001–30600	12th ILC Lincoln
52	30601–31200	13th ILC Lincoln
53	31201–31800	14th ILC Lincoln
54	31801–32400	15th ILC Lincoln
55	32401–33000	16th ILC Lincoln
56	33001–33600	18th Bn Cheshire
57	33601–34200	18th Bn Cheshire
58	34201–34800	19th Bn Cheshire
59	34801–35400	19th Bn Cheshire
60	35401–36000	20th Bn Cheshire
61	36001–36600	20th Bn Cheshire
62	36601–37200	21st Bn Cheshire
63	37201–37800	21st Bn Cheshire
64	37801–38400	22nd Bn Cheshire
65	38401–39000	22nd Bn Cheshire
66	39001–39600	1st ILC King's
67	39601–40200	2nd ILC King's
68	40020–40800	3rd ILC King's
69	40801–41400	4th ILC King's
70	41401–42000	5th ILC King's
71	42001–42600	6th ILC King's
72	42601–43200	7th ILC King's
73	43201–43800	8th ILC King's
74	43801–44400	9th ILC King's
75	44401–45000	10th ILC King's
76	45001–45600	11th ILC King's
77	45601–46200	12th ILC King's
78	46201–46800	13th ILC King's
79	46801–47400	14th ILC King's
80	47401–48000	15th ILC King's
81	48001–48600	16th ILC King's
82	48601–49200	17th ILC King's
83	49201–49800	18th ILC King's
84	49801–50400	19th ILC King's
85	50401–51000	20th ILC King's
86	51001–51600	21st ILC King's
87	51601–52200	22nd ILC King's
88	52201–52800	23rd ILC King's
89	52801–53400	24th ILC King's
90	53401–54000	25th ILC King's
91	54001–54600	26th ILC King's
92	54601–55200	27th ILC King's
93	55201–55800	13th Bn The Queen's
94	55801–56400	13th Bn The Queen's
99	58801–59400	33rd Bn Royal Fusiliers
100	59401–60000	33rd Bn Royal Fusiliers
101	60001–60600	34th Bn Royal Fusiliers
102	60601–61200	34th Bn Royal Fusiliers
103	61201–61800	35th Bn Royal Fusiliers
104	61801–62400	35th Bn Royal Fusiliers
105	62401–63000	36th Bn Royal Fusiliers
106	63001–63600	36th Bn Royal Fusiliers
107	63601–64200	37th Bn Royal Fusiliers
108	64201–64800	37th Bn Royal Fusiliers
109	64801–65400	1st ILC The Queen's
110	65401–66000	2nd ILC The Queen's
111	66001–66600	3rd ILC The Queen's

112	66601–67200	4th ILC The Queen's
113	67201–67800	5th ILC The Queen's
114	67801–68400	6th ILC The Queen's
115	68401–69000	7th ILC The Queen's
116	69001–69600	8th ILC The Queen's
117	69601–70200	9th ILC The Queen's
118	70201–70800	10th ILC The Queen's
119	70801–71400	11th ILC The Queen's
120	71401–72000	12th ILC The Queen's
121	72001–72600	13th ILC The Queen's
122	72601–73200	14th ILC The Queen's
123	73201–73800	15th ILC The Queen's
124	73801–74400	16th ILC The Queen's
125	74401–75000	17th ILC The Queen's
126	75001–75600	18th ILC The Queen's
127	75601–76200	19th ILC The Queen's
128	76201–76800	20th ILC The Queen's
129	76801–77400	21st ILC The Queen's
130	77401–78000	22nd ILC The Queen's
131	78001–78600	23rd ILC The Queen's
132	78601–79200	24th ILC The Queen's
133	79201–79800	25th ILC The Queen's
134	79801–80400	26th ILC The Queen's
135	80401–81000	27th ILC The Queen's
136	81001–81600	28th ILC The Queen's
137	81601–82200	29th ILC The Queen's
138	82201–82800	30th ILC The Queen's
139	82801–83400	1st ILC Northants
140	83401–84000	2nd ILC Northants
141	84001–84600	3rd ILC Northants
142	84601–85200	4th ILC Northants
143	85201–85800	5th ILC Northants
144	85801–86400	6th ILC Northants
145	86401–87000	7th ILC Northants
146	87001–87600	8th ILC Northants
147	87601–88200	9th ILC Northants
148	88201–88800	10th ILC Northants
149	88801–89400	11th ILC Northants
150	89401–90000	12th ILC Northants
151	90001–90600	13th ILC Northants
152	90601–91200	12th Bn Devonshire
153	91201–91800	12th Bn Devonshire
154	91801–92400	14th Bn Devonshire
155	92401–93000	14th Bn Devonshire
156	93001–93600	12th Bn DCLI
157	93601–94200	12th Bn DCLI
158	94201–94800	10th Bn Berkshire
159	94801–95400	10th Bn Berkshire
160	95401–96000	11th Bn Berkshire
161	96001–96600	11th Bn Berkshire
162	96601–97200	12th Bn Berkshire
163	97201–97800	12th Bn Berkshire
164	97801–98400	13th Bn Berkshire
165	98401–99000	13th Bn Berkshire
166	99001–99600	1st ILC Devonshire
167	99601–100200	2nd ILC Devonshire
168	100201–100800	3rd ILC Devonshire
169	100801–101400	4th ILC Devonshire
170	101401–102000	5th ILC Devonshire
171	102001–102600	6th ILC Devonshire
172	102601–103200	7th ILC Devonshire
173	103201–103800	8th ILC Devonshire

174	103801–104400	9th ILC Devonshire
175	104401–105000	10th ILC Devonshire
176	105001–105600	11th ILC Devonshire
177	105601–106200	12th ILC Devonshire
178	106201–106800	1st ILC Hampshire
179	106801–107400	2nd ILC Hampshire
180	107401–108000	3rd ILC Hampshire
181	108001–108600	4th ILC Hampshire
182	108601–109200	1st ILC R Irish
183	109201–109800	2nd ILC R Irish

Table 17: Companies formed from PB and Bantams – May 1917

Coy	Regimental Numbers
184	109801–110400
185	110401–111000
186	111001–111600
187	111601–112200
188	112201–112800
189	112801–113400
190	113401–114000
191	114001–114600
192	114601–115200
193	115201–115800
194	115801–116400
195	116401–117000
196	117001–117600
197	117601–118200
198	118201–118800
199	118801–119400
200	119401–120000

Table 18: Labour Group Headquarters – May 1917

Group Number	Regimental Numbers
1	121,801–121,820
2	121,821–121,840
3	121,841–121,860
4	121,861–121,880
5	121,881–121,900
6	121,901–121,920
7	121,921–121,940
8	121,941–121,960
9	121,961–121,980
10	121,981–122,000
11	122,001–122,020
12	122,021–122,040
13	122,041–122,060
14	122,061–122,080
15	122,081–122,100
16	122,101–122,120
17	122,121–122,140
18	122,141–122,160
19	122,161–122,180
20	122,181–122,200
21	122,201–122,220
22	122,221–122,240
23	122,241–122,260
24	122,261–122,280
25	122,281–122,300

26	122,301–122,320
27	122,321–122,340
28	122,341–122,360
29	122,361–122,380
30	122,381–122,400
31	122,401–122,420
32	122,421–122,440
33	122,441–122,460
34	122,461–122,480
35	122,481–122,500
36	122,501–122,520
37	122,521–122,540
38	122,541–122,560
39	122,561–122,580
40	122,581–122,600

Table 19: Companies formed from RE and ASC Labour units – June 1917

Coy	Original RE Labour Battalion	Regimental Numbers
700	1st	289501–290100
701	2nd	290101–290700
702	3rd	290701–291300
703	4th	291301–291900
704	5th	291901–292500
705	6th	292501–293100
706	7th	293101–293700
707	8th	293701–294300
708	9th	204301–294900
709	10th	294901–295500
710	11th	295501–295100
711*	12th	348240–348500

*711 Company was formed in Salonika

Coy	Original ASC Labour Company
712	1st
713	2nd
714	3rd
715	5th
716	6th
717	7th
718	8th
719	9th
720	10th
721	11th
722	12th
723	13th
724	14th
725	15th
726	16th
727	18th
728	19th
729	20th
730	24th
731	25th
732	27th
733	28th
734	31st
735	32nd

The original companies formed from ASC Labour Companies had regimental numbers in the range 296701–310800. Companies were formed primarily from the ASC Companies shown above but it is not possible to state exactly the numbers allocated to a Company.

Other companies in France

Labour Companies: 968–969, 990–991, 1001–1002 and 1021–1022
Divisional Employment (DE) Companies: 204–254, 771–773, 924–925 and 984–985.

Area Employment (AE) Companies: 255–294, 736–779, 783–784, 787–789, 794–799, 821–827, 835–847, 850–851, 854–862, 870–871, 883–892, 897–905, 911, 926, 930, 946–949, 992–995 and 1043

Artizan Companies: 780–782, 828–830, 834, 849, 919–923, 927–929, 936–945

Garrison Guard Companies: 785–786, 790–793, 831, 848, 852–853, 863–869, 872–882, 893–896, 906–918, 931–935, 950–967, 986 and 989

Agricultural Companies: 987–988, 996 and 1037–1042

Italy

173, 196, 208, 223, 238 and 273 Companies

Salonika

Table 20: Labour Companies – Salonika May 1917

Companies:

Coy	Regimental Numbers	Created from
95	56401–57000	14th Bn The Queen's
96	57001–57600	14th Bn The Queen's
97	57601–58200	15th Bn The Queen's
98	58201–58800	15th Bn The Queen's
201	120,001–120,600	14th Bn The Queen's

Divisional Employment Companies:

202	120601–121200
203	121200–121800

Labour Group Headquarters:

Group No.	Regimental Numbers
41	122601–122620
42	122621–122640

Other Divisional Companies: 816–820, 968–983, 997–999 and 1035–1036

Egypt

Area Employment Companies: 800–815, 1000 and 1031–1032

Home Service

The tables below include the type of company and, where known, its location. An entry like Thetford/Sutton indicates the company moved location. During 1918 a number of companies were changed to Agricultural Companies these are indicated by XXX/AGR. Where two locations are shown for these companies the first related to their work as an Employment company and the second as an Agricultural Company.

Table 21: Labour Corps Companies in the UK – May 1917

Coy	Regimental Numbers	Type	Location
295	122641–123240	RCOY	Blairgowrie
296	123241–123840	RCOY	Blairgowrie
297	123841–124440	RCOY	Ripon

298	124441–125040	RCOY	Strensall/Ripon
299	125041–125640	RCOY	Oswestry
300	125641–126240	RCOY	Oswestry
301	126241–126840	RCOY	Thetford/Sutton
302	126841–127440	RCOY	Thetford/Sutton
303	127441–128040	RCOY	Plymouth
304	128041–128640	RCOY	Plymouth
305	170141–170440	WORKS	Chester
306	170441–170740	WORKS	Crosby
307	170741–171040	WORKS	Aldershot
308	171041–171340	WORKS	Bordon
309	171341–171640	WORKS	Farnbrough
310	171641–171940	WORKS	Yatesbury
311	171941–172240	WORKS	Southampton
312	172241–172540	WORKS	Bulford
313	172541–172840	WORKS	Bristol
314	172841–173140	WORKS	Shirehampton
315	173141–173440	WORKS	Fovant
316	173441–173740	WORKS	
317	173741–174040	WORKS	Canterbury
318	174041–174340	WORKS	Winchester
319	174341–174640	WORKS	Sutton Veny
320	174641–174940	WORKS	
321	174941–175240	WORKS	Gourock/Invergordon
322	175241–175540	WORKS	Edinburgh
323	175541–175840	WORKS	Turnhouse
324	175841–176140	WORKS	Kinross
325	176141–176440	WORKS	
326	176441–176740	WORKS	Thetford
327	176741–177040	WORKS	Norwich
328	177041–177340	WORKS	Northampton
329	177341–177640	WORKS	Orford
330	177641–177940	WORKS	Felixtowe
331	177941–178240	WORKS	Ipswich
332	178241–178540	WORKS	Chelmsford
333	178541–178840	WORKS	Hounslow
334	178841–179140	WORKS	Hounslow
335	179141–179440	WORKS	
336	179441–179740	WORKS	Woolwich
337	179741–180040	WORKS	Chatham
338	180041–180340	WORKS	Sheerness
339	180341–180640	WORKS	Shoreham
340	180641–180940	WORKS	
341	180941–181240	WORKS	Hythe
342	181241–181540	WORKS	Hythe
343	181541–181840	WORKS	Dover
344	181841–182140	WORKS	Boldon Colliery
345	182141–182440	WORKS	Newcastle
346	182441–182740	WORKS	W Hartlepool
347	182741–183040	WORKS	W Hartlepool
348	183041–183340	WORKS	Northumberland/Blyth
349	183341–183640	WORKS	Hull
350	183641–183940	WORKS	
351	183941–184240	WORKS	York
352	184241–184540	WORKS	Catterick
353	184541–184840	WORKS	Stafford
354	184841–185040	WORKS	
355	185041–185340	WORKS	Grantham
356	185341–185640	WORKS	
357	185641–185940	WORKS	Ripon
358	185941–186240	WORKS	Lincoln

Table 22: Labour Battalions – May 1917

Bn Number	Regimental Numbers	Created from
1	128,641–132,640	23rd Bn Liverpool
2	132,641–134,640	27th Bn Liverpool
3	134,641–146,640	13th Bn Devonshire
4	146,641–149,640	10th Bn Royal Scots Fusiliers
5	149,641–162,640	29th Bn Middlesex
6	162,641–164,640	33rd Bn Middlesex
7	164,641–170,640	25th Bn Durham Light Infantry

Table 23: UK Companies formed autumn 1917

Coy	Type	Location
359	REMP	Blairgowrie
360	REMP	Strensell
361	REMP	Tipperary
362	REMP	Oswestry
363	REMP	Thetford/Sutton
364	REMP	Plymouth
365	REMP	Aldershot
366	REMP	Peckham
367	LAB	Aldershot
368	LAB	Roehampton/City Road
369	LAB	White City
370	LAB	Hampstead
371	LAB	West Ham
372	LAB/AGR	London/Aberdeen
373	LAB	Blairgowrie
374	LAB	Blairgowrie
375	LAB	Oswestry
376	LAB	Kinmel Park
377	LAB	Rugeley Camp
378	LAB	Catterick
379	LAB	Winchester
380	LAB	Salisbury Plain
381	LAB	Didcot
382	LAB	Didcot
383	LAB	Weymouth
384	LAB	Portsmouth
385	LAB	Devonport
386	LAB	Colchester
387	LAB	Charlton
388	LAB	Shoeburyness
389	LAB	Folkstone
390	LAB	Hythe
391	LAB	
392	LAB	Whitechurch
393	LAB	Pembroke Dock
394	AGR	Hereford
395	EMP	Randalstown
396	EMP/AGR	X/Oxford
397	EMP	Norwich
398	EMP	Cambridge
399	EMP	Uckfield
400	EMP	Hemel Hempstead
401	EMP	Hounslow
402	EMP	Northampton
403	AGR	Perth
404	AGR	Ayr
405	AGR	Hamilton
406	AGR	York

407	AGR	Richmond
408	AGR	York
409	AGR	Lincoln
410	AGR	Leicester
411	AGR	Derby
412	AGR	Newcastle
413	AGR	Lichfield
414	AGR	Beverley
415	AGR	Halifax
416	AGR	Lancaster
417	AGR	Carlisle
418	AGR	Chester
419	AGR	Wrexham
420	AGR	Brecon
421	AGR	Warrington
422	AGR	Cardiff
423	AGR	Shrewsbury
424	AGR	Worcester
425	AGR	Guildford
426	AGR	Canterbury
427	AGR	Hounslow
428	AGR	Norwich
429	AGR	Norwich
430	AGR	Norwich
431	AGR	Bury St Edmunds
432	AGR	Bedford
433	AGR	Bedford
434	AGR	Chichester
435	AGR	Warley
436	AGR	Northampton
437	AGR	Maidstone
438	AGR	Mill Hill
439	AGR	Reading
440	AGR	Bristol
441	AGR	Winchester
442	AGR	Devizes
443	AGR	Dorchester
444	AGR	Exeter
445	AGR	Bodmin
446	AGR	Warwick
447	AGR	Devizes
448	AGR	Exeter
449	AGR	Taunton
450	EMP	Edinburgh
451	EMP	Edinburgh
452	AGR	Aberdeen
453	EMP	Stirling
454	AGR	Inverness
455	EMP	Kinghorn
456	AGR	Inverness
457	AGR	Perth
458	EMP	Edinburgh
459	AGR	Stirling
460	AGR	Ayr
461	EMP	Edinburgh
462	EMP	Invergordon
463	AGR	Berwick
464	EMP	Dunbarton
465	AGR	Glencoe
466	EMP	Dunbarton
467	AGR	Hamilton
468	EMP	Blairgowrie

469	EMP	Dumbarton
470	EMP	Richmond Yorks
471	EMP	Newcastle
472	AGR	Nottingham
473	EMP	Ripon
474	AGR	York
475	EMP	Ripon
476	EMP	
477	AGR	Lincoln
478	EMP	Ripon
479	AGR	Lincoln
480	EMP	Catterick
481	EMP	Edinburgh
482	AGR	Leicester
483	EMP	Scarbrough
484	AGR	Derby
485	EMP	Rugeley
486	EMP	Clipstone
487	AGR	Newcastle
488	EMP	Brocton
489	EMP	Rugeley Camp
490	AGR	Litchfield
491	EMP	Rugeley Camp
492	AGR	Beverley
493	EMP	Cannock Chase
494	AGR	York
495	EMP	W Hartlepool/ Middlesborough
496	AGR	Lincoln
497	EMP	Newcastle
498	EMP	Newcastle
499	EMP	Sunderland
500	EMP	Sunderland
501	AGR	Derby
502	EMP	Cullercoats
503	EMP	Cullercoats
504	EMP	Louth
505	AGR	Richmond
506	EMP	Grimsby
507	AGR	Beverley
508	EMP	Patrington
509	EMP/AGR	York
510	EMP	Hornsea
511	EMP/AGR	Leicester
512	EMP	Newark
513	EMP	Grantham
514	AGR	Perth
515	AGR	Cupar
516	AGR	Ayr
517	EMP	Halifax
518	EMP	
519	EMP	
520	EMP	York
521	EMP	
522	EMP	Sheffield
523	EMP	Lichfield
524	EMP	Derby/Nottingham
525	EMP	Lincoln
526	EMP	Blyth
527	EMP	Nottingham
528	EMP	Catterick
529	EMP	

530	EMP	
531	EMP	
532	EMP/AGR	Preston
533	EMP/AGR	Carmarthen
534	EMP/AGR	Cardiff
535	EMP	Oswestry
536	EMP/AGR	Carlisle
537	EMP	Oswestry
538	EMP/AGR	Carlisle
539	EMP	Oswestry
540	EMP	Prees Heath
541	EMP/AGR	Preston
542	EMP	Press Heath
543	EMP/AGR	Preston
544	EMP	Kinmel Park
545	EMP/AGR	Chester
546	EMP	Kinmel Park
547	EMP/AGR	Chester
548	EMP/AGR	Wrexham
549	EMP	Pembroke Dock
550	EMP/AGR	Wrexham
551	EMP	Liverpool
552	EMP	Grest Crosby
553	EMP/AGR	Shrewsbury
554	EMP	Altcar
555	EMP/AGR	Shrewsbury
556	EMP	Prescot
557	EMP	Cardiff
558	EMP	Shrewsbury
559	EMP/AGR	Hereford
560	EMP	Chester
561	EMP	Manchester
562	EMP	Heaton Park
563	EMP	Preston
564	EMP/AGR	Carmarthen
565	EMP	Conway
566	EMP	Blackpool
567	EMP	Barrow-in-Furness
568	EMP	Bettisfield Camp
569	EMP/AGR	Brecon
570	AGR	Cardiff
571	AGR	Cardiff
572	AGR	Maidstone
573	AGR	Warley
574	AGR	Oxford
575	EMP	Halton/Harwich
576	EMP	Crowborough/Hastings
577	EMP	Tunbridge Wells
578	EMP	Tunbridge Wells
579	EMP	Felixstowe
580	EMP/AGR	Peterborough
581	EMP	Felixstowe
582	EMP/AGR	Preston
583	EMP	Dover
584	EMP	Dover
585	EMP	Dover
586	EMP	Bedford
587	EMP	Bedford
588	EMP	Houghton Regis
589	EMP	Woolwich
590	EMP	Woolwich
591	EMP	

592	EMP	
593	EMP/AGR	Taunton
594	EMP	Shirley
595	EMP	Luton
596	EMP	High Wycombe
597	EMP	Warley
598	EMP/AGR	Reading
599	EMP/AGR	Bristol
600	EMP	Chatham
601	EMP	Chatham
602	EMP	Sheerness
603	EMP	Scocles Minster
604	EMP	Sittingbourne
605	EMP/AGR	Winchester
606	EMP	Bury St Edmunds
607	EMP	Shoreham
608	EMP	Newhaven
609	EMP/AGR	Bexhill/Dorchester
610	EMP	Eastbourne
611	EMP/AGR	X/Bodmin
612	EMP	Shoreham
613	EMP	Maidstone
614	EMP	Thetford/Sutton
615	EMP	Salisbury
616	EMP	Winchester
617	EMP/AGR	Reading
618	EMP	Winchester
619	EMP	Winchester
620	EMP/AGR	Aldershot
621	EMP/AGR	St David's
622	EMP	Swanage
623	EMP	Southampton
624	EMP	Rolleston
625	EMP	Sutton Veny
626	EMP/AGR	Taunton
627	EMP/AGR	Worcester
628	EMP	Sutton Veny
629	EMP	Portsmouth
630	EMP	Hilsea
631	EMP	Parkhurst
632	EMP	Wareham
633	EMP	Tidworth
634	EMP	Tidworth
635	EMP	Larkhill
636	EMP	Bulford
637	EMP	Weymouth
638	EMP	Reading
639	EMP	Oxford
640	EMP	Worcester
641	EMP	Devonport
642	EMP	Plymouth
643	EMP	Exeter
644	EMP	Devizes
645	EMP	Boyton
646	AGR	Oxford
647	AGR	Warwick
648	AGR	Bristol
649	AGR	Winchester
650	AGR	Bodmin
651	AGR	Devizes
652	AGR	Taunton
653	EMP	Dublin

654	AGR	Exeter
655	EMP	Curragh
656	AGR	Bedford
657	EMP	Kildare
658	EMP	Athlone
659	EMP	Cork
660	AGR	Norwich
661	AGR	Norwich
662	EMP	Cahir
663	EMP	Fermoy
664	EMP	Belfast
665	AGR	Bury St Edmunds
666	EMP	Newtonards
667	AGR	Warley
668	EMP	Enniskillen
669	AGR	Peterborough
670	EMP	Aldershot
671	EMP	Aldershot
672	EMP	Aldershot
673	EMP	Aldershot
674	EMP	Aldershot
675	EMP	Aldershot
676	EMP	Aldershot
677	EMP	Aldershot
678	EMP	Aldershot
679	EMP	
680	EMP	Guildford
681	EMP	Hounslow
682	EMP	Northampton
683	EMP	Peterborough
684	EMP	Warley
685	EMP	158 City Rd
686	EMP	158 City Rd
687	EMP	158 City Rd
688	EMP	158 City Rd
689	EMP	158 City Rd
690	EMP	Ballyvonare
691	AGR	St Edmunds
692	AGR	Ipswich
693	AGR	Bedford
694	AGR	Guildford
695	AGR	Chichester
696	AGR	Lewes/Chichester
697	AGR	Maidstone
698	AGR	Maidstone
699	AGR	Canterbury

HONOURS AND AWARDS

It is impossible to provide a completely accurate listing of awards made to the Labour Corps. There are two main reasons for this. Firstly, there are changes in spelling as many errors occur in transcription; and secondly, the transient nature of many personnel in the Labour Corps, particularly officers who only served for short periods before rejoining their parent Regiment, makes identification difficult. Officers are often shown in the *Gazette* as General List, Special List or Reserve of Officers and there is no indication of the unit they are attached to.

The following list is based on the *London Gazette* but other documents have been consulted including Corps and Army Routine Orders that notify immediate awards. Personnel marked ★ indicates a person named in Routine Orders or in a diary/citation but not identified in the *London Gazette*.

Distinguished Service Order (3 UK, 3 Empire)

Name		Rank	Unit
Gibson	Thomas	Maj	Canadian Bn
McKinery	John William Herbert	Lt Col	Canadian Bn
Morgan	David Watts	Maj	LC
Neeland	Robert Henry	Lt Col	Canadian Bn
Paul	John William	Lt Col	LC
Vaughan	Arthur Owen	Lt Cpl	LC

Distinguished Service Cross (1 UK)

Name		Rank	Unit
Fuller	Henry Vincent	Capt	RMLC

Military Cross (50 UK and Empire, 4 LC detached and 14 attached)

Name		Rank	Unit
Barnes	Thomas Percy	2Lt	137 Coy
Bowman	Thomas Walter	2Lt	
Boyes★		Capt	
Brown	Arthur Kirkhill	Lt	40 Coy CLC
Browning	Ernest Frederick	Capt	122 Coy
Carhart	Stanley	A/Capt	BWIR
Cauldwell	Harry	Capt	Canadian
Collier	Alan Arthur	2Lt	
Collier	William	2Lt	175 Coy
Cooper	William Bernard	A/Capt	Canadian
D'Arcy	Norman Joyce	Lt	Canadian
Dore	William Charles Henry	2Lt	
Driver	Godfrey Rolles	Capt	Graves Unit
Dunlop	Allan Aloysius	2Lt	BWIR
Ellis	Herbert Moats	Capt	
Fink	Ralph Havelock Lewis	ACapt	BWIR
Furst	Lionel Alfred	2Lt	
Groom	Gerald Baxter	Capt	BWIR
Hervey	Eric Falkenburg	2Lt	Mil LC (East Africa)
Hoepner	Arthur William	Capt	ELC
Humphries★		Capt	35 *Gp*
Jennings	Sydney	Capt	4 Bn Canada
Jones	Arthur Ellis	Capt	Canadian
Kelly	Michael	A/Capt	
Kirkbride	Alexander Smeath	A/Capt	ELC
Livingstone		Capt	35 *Group*
Lunn	Reginald Owton	2Lt	
MacDonald	Murdo Bayne	2Lt	
McCashin	J. W.	Capt	
McEnuff	William	Capt	
McKenzie★		Lt	
Mullholland	William	A/Maj	Lab Bureau
Myatt	Percy Edward	2Lt	
O'Conner	John	2Lt	145 Coy
Pomeroy	Robert Arthur	A/Capt	21 Gp
Renwick	Walter Lancaster	Capt	3 Alien Coy
Robb	J.	Capt	35 Group
Robinson	C. D. A.	Capt	BWIR

Rose	Richard	Lt	15 Coy (Indian Army)
Russell	Alexander	Capt	Lab Bureau
Shairp	William	2Lt	
Spalding	Lester Lewis	Lt	Canadian
Taggart	William Alexander	2Lt	Mil LC (East Africa)
Thomas	Basil Walter	Capt	Graves Unit
Thomas	Thomas Charles	Capt	55 Coy
Topley	William Frederick	Capt	
Turner	Arthur Robert	Lt	
Wild	Percy	2Lt	108 Coy
Wrigg	Lewis	Lt	Bermuda RGA
Youles	Frank Louis	2Lt	79 Coy

Dickerson	Samuel	2Lt	Attached to RE
Pearce	Richard	Lt	Att 23 Bn Lancashire Fusiliers
Smiles	Stanley	2Lt	Att 13 Bn Inniskilling Fus
Worrall	James Fletcher	A/Capt	Attached 8 Bn Liverpool

Beckett	Albert Caleb	A/Capt	RE attached 67 Gp
Clarke	George	Lt (QM)	Gen List att 43 Group
Deane	Charles Gordon	Capt	RAMC attached BWIR
Gatt	Alfred J.	Capt	Royal Malta Artillery
Gladwell	Clarence William	A/Capt	RE attached 109 Coy
Healy	Maurice	A/Capt	Dublin Fusiliers attached
Kerr	Duncan Campbell	2Lt	Gen List attached ELC
Page	Arthur Frederick	2Lt	Warwickshire Regt attached
Pomeroy	Herbert	Lt	Cheshire Regt attached
Rawlings	George William	A/Cpl	RE attached
Richardson	Robert Liddle Thomson	Lt	Royal Scots attached 7 Coy
Rogers	Louis	Rev	RAChD attached 38 Gp
Sykes	Alfred Theodore Knowles	A/Capt	DWR attached 38 Coy
Weatherdon	Henry Buckland	2Lt	RFA attached

Distinguished Service Medal (6 UK)

Name		Number	Rank	Coy
Boyd	M.	Deal/13644	Pte	RMLC
Cook	J.W.	Deal/9790	Sgt	RMLC
Doull	B.	Deal/9820	Sgt	RMLC
McIntosh	R.	Deal/9531	Sgt	RMLC
Mace	J.W.		Sgt	RMLC
Rate	J.J.	Deal/1008	Pte	RMLC

Distinguished Conduct Medal (24 UK, 16 Empire)

Name		Number	Rank	Coy
Bellamy	C.E.	2947	Sgt	BWIR
Blacktin	E.	614997	Sgt	
Briggs	B.	12604	Sgt	22
Broom	J.H.	33001	A/RSM	35 Gp
Butcher	H.E.	2465	Pte	BWIR
Coutts	J.	6235	SM	BWIR
Downie	T.	4207	Sgt	8
Duckworth	E.	376141	A/Sgt	760
Dudley	E.W.	104404	Sgt	175
Edwards	J.P.	33246	CSM	56
Gazeley	G.W.	46147	Cpl	1 Bn Canadian
Goldsworthy	W.T.	12770	LCpl	22
Gough	A.	104419	Cpl	175
Grant	A.	3953	Sgt	BWIR
Halligan	J.R.	16806	Sgt	29

Hope	J. C.	1040	Pte	BWIR
Hosker	T. G.	619054	Cpl	
Jordan	L.	5062	Sgt	BWIR
Kennedy	J.	109373	Sgt	183
Knight	U.	6493	Pte	BWIR
MacFarquhar	J.	4014	CSM	Indian LC
McAllister	A.	7813	Sgt	14
McArdle	P.	114738	Pte	192
Mill	G. A.	443302	CSM	97
Morgan	W.	42607	Sgt	72
Murphy	G.	79201	CSM	133
Osborne	E.	5575	Sgt	BWIR
Playford	A. E.	319203	Pte	
Powell	A.	3525	Sgt	BWIR
Reid	H.	6475	LCpl	BWIR
Richards	D.	79210	Sgt	133
Riding	W.	34597	Pte	58
Roper	G.	2406	Sgt	5
Simpson	M.	6124	Cpl	BWIR
Smith	J.	6083	Pte	BWIR
Thomas MM	G. J.	64018	Cpl	107
Walker	A. M.	90615	Cpl	152
Warren	P.	28201	CSM	48
Weir	C.	3099	Sgt	BWIR
Wright	R.	6398	LCpl	BWIR

Bar to Military Medal (2 UK, 1 Empire)

Name		Number	Rank	Coy
Ellison★	J.	39159	Pte	66
Pirie	A.	4243	LCpl	8
Walker	J.	10799	Pte	7 Bn BWIR

Military Medal (400 UK, 44 Empire)

Name		Number	Rank	Coy
Alderman	F. G.	102008	Pte	171
Alliss	C. W.	6001	CQMS	101
Allum	G. C.	85801	Sgt	144
Ambrose	H. J.	116903	Sgt	5 Bn RE
Anderson	F.	4475	Pte	8
Anderson	F. S.	45010	Pte	76
Appleyard	F. H.	18644	Cpl	31 Gp
Archer	H.	293167	Sgt	706
Ashcroft	S.	50411	Cpl	85
Avent	J.	293159	Pte	706
Bailey	J.	479413	Pte	144
Baker	J. H.	9604	Pte	17
Baldwin	J.	13869	Pte	24
Bancroft	F.	13874	Pte	24
Bannister	J. H. A.	85277	Sgt	143
Barlow	A.	608247	Sgt	199
Barnes	F.	27014	Sgt	46
Barnes	T.	34283	A/Sgt	58
Basquill	J.	27048	Pte	46
Batchelor	T.	67203	Sgt	113
Bateman	W.	87666	Pte	147
Bates	F.	84062	Cpl	141
Beadle	H. G.	495022	Pte	728
Beer	G.	108060	CSM	181
Bessler	C. H.	33876	Sgt	57

Bickell	P. J.	64244	CQMS	108
Binch	H.	206494	Pte	84
Blundell	A. H.	97813	Cpl	164
Bond	A. T.	445277	Pte	34
Boon	A.	67265	Cpl	113
Booth	J. E.	224274	Pte	246
Bourne	V. J.	104413	Cpl	175
Bridges	F. E.	603602	Sgt	76
Briggs	B.	12604	Sgt	22
Briggs	J.	205336	Pte	731
Brindle	R.	446500	Pte	714
Brooks	G.	258311	Pte	223
Brooks	J.	449511	Pte	822
Brown	A. G.	59441	Sgt	100
Brown	W. J.	24646	Pte	42
Bryce	J.	123350	A/Sgt	38
Buckley	P.	101403	Sgt	170
Burgess	G. H.	239196	Pte	738
Butler	C. S. F.	479417	Pte	144
Cameron	J.	575985	Pte	
Careless	C. H.	61329	Cpl	103
Cassidy	M.	377065	Pte	763
Castle	W.	91209	A/Sgt	153
Chadwick	W.	34920	Pte	59
Chance	T. J.	487720	CQMS	
Chapman	J.	385533	Pte	106
Chisnall	R. H.	38460	Sgt	781
Clarke	G.	31293	Pte	53
Clee	T.	34226	Sgt	58
Cobner	T.	39008	Sgt	66
Cole	C. R.	510858	Pte	930
Collier	F. T.	22325	LCpl	38
Collingwood	F. A.	81614	Sgt	137
Coneyworth	W. R.	632492	Cpl	244
Connell	E.	369895	Pte	285
Connolly	T. J.	445464	Cpl	113
Cook	J.	566484	Pte	
Cooper	G.	14561	Pte	25
Cowell	J.	384605	Pte	19
Cox	C. S.	64815	Sgt	109
Cramplin	A.	225233	Sgt	226
Crane	H.	90014	Cpl	151
Crosby	J.	450098	Pte	823
Cullen	H.	30009	Sgt	51
Daniels	J.	91350	Cpl	153
Dauncey	E. J.	224587	LSgt	251
Davies	E. M.	211847	Pte	246
Davies	J.	293526	Pte	706
Davies	W.	49816	A/Sgt	84
Davison	W. H.	64305	Sgt	108
Davitt	T.	513917	Pte	206
Dawson	A.	15331	LCpl	80 Gp
Deeley	B.	290123	Sgt	701
Dickinsen	H.	12008	Sgt	718
Dingle	G. L.	81753	Pte	137
Dougan	J.	372221	Pte	293
Dove	J.	71550	Pte	120
Drant	J.	23552	A/LCpl	40
Du Four	A.	291378	LCpl	703
Dunn	P.	382639	Pte	84
Earl	E. W.	64319	Pte	108
Eastwood	F.	246456	A/Sgt	40

Eayrs	W.	109988	Pte	184
Edwards	J.	291328	Sgt	703
Eldridge	W. T.	76335	Cpl	128
Elkes	G.	34360	A/Cpl	58
Ellis	R	479348	Sgt	143
Ellis	T. S.	224973	LCpl	220
Ellison	J.	39159	Pte	66
Emler	H. E.	296720	Sgt	712
Emmett	J.	107519	Pte	180
Ervine	A.	364683	Pte	145
Evans	H. J.	24737	L/Cpl	42
Eve	A. H.	293593	Pte	706
Farley	J.	206418	Cpl	85
Fernely★			Pte	58
Finch	J. W.	419552	Pte	136
Finch	T.	34965	Pte	59
Fordham	F. C.	64338	Cpl	108
Fothergill	O.	14616	Pte	25
Foy	J.	37448	Pte	63
Freeman	H. A.	30186	Pte	832
Fuller	F. A. O.	63780	Pte	107
Garner	S. A.	85402	Cpl	143
Garnett	R. J.	85406	Pte	143
Garrard	R.	451438	A/LCpl	946
George	W.	51178	Sgt	86
Gibson	W.	292678	Cpl	781
Gilbert	J.	34833	Pte	59
Goch	J. F.	376953	Sgt	763
Goddard	J.	478091	Cpl	90
Goldson	W. S.	14422	A/Sgt	25
Gore	J.	39190	Pte	66
Gray	A.	14432	Sgt	25
Gray	E. E.	567297	Pte	65
Green	G.	425178	Pte	63
Grewcock	A.	22386	Pte	38
Grierson	R. W.	380282	Cpl	24
Hadfield	F.	34429	Pte	58
Haley	F.	37371	Cpl	63
Halford	E. T.	104589	Pte	175
Hannah	A.	3490	A/LCpl	6
Harbour	S. A.	55929	Pte	94
Hardwick	W. H.	76389	A/LCpl	128
Hardy	W. H.	9949	Cpl	17
Hardy	W. P.	68631	A/LCpl	115
Hargreaves	F.	20008	Pte	34
Harrison	J.	632338	Pte	229
Harrop	W.	346093	A/LCpl	239
Hart	B. J.	31215	Sgt	53
Harvey	W.	69198	Cpl	116
Hawthorne	W.	60149	Cpl	101
Haynes	S. E.	10212	Cpl	18
Heath	W.	382780	Pte	113
Henderson	E. H.	67430	Sgt	113
Hicks	F.	4802	CQMS	9
Higginson	J.	37389	Pte	63
Hill	A.	289844	Pte	700
Hing	G. L.	888	Pte	2
Hinton	A. J.	95615	Pte	173
Hitchins	C. G.	102189	Pte	171
Hodgson	J.	292532	Sgt	705
Holmes	J. H.	111750	Sgt	187
Hoof	W.	38000	Pte	64

Hornbuckle	F.	473373	Pte	53
Hoskin	W.	91460	Pte	153
Howard	J.	104434	Cpl	175
Hughes	R.	102190	Pte	171
Humphries	W.	514682	Pte	949
Hussey	F. H.	424385	Pte	80
Hutchinson	J. O.	116401	Sgt	195
Jackson	A.	403595	Pte	113
Jackson	H.	39016	A/Sgt	66
Jackson	T. W.	27234	Pte	46
Johnston	A. C.	224458	Sgt	249
Johnstone★			Cpl	33
Jones	C.	396517	Pte	107
Jones	F. L.	34806	Sgt	59
Jones	R.	632339	Pte	229
Joynes	G. A.	11113	Cpl	19
Karle	F.	93302	Pte	156
Kavanagh	C.	169257	A/Sgt	174
Keenan	W.	3607	Sgt	7
Kellett	W.	223562	A/Sgt	232
Kelly	W.	41070	Pte	69
Kenny	S.	593721	Pte	
Kent	J.	424980	Sgt	36
Kerr	R.	4203	Sgt	8
King	C.	84245	Pte	141
King	D.	12260	Pte	21
Kingsworth	W. F.	276702	A/Cpl	762
Kirkland	W.	15834	A/CSM	188
Kirkum★	H. J.	6535	Pte	
Knight	F. R.	62690	Pte	105
Knowles	A. R.	473375	Pte	53
Laing	G.	888	Pte	2
Lang	S.	90273	Pte	151
Latham	J. E.	78008	Sgt	131
Lawrence★	G.	42147	Pte	
Lawrence	G.	22236	Sgt	38
Leah	J.	49821	LSgt	84
Leonard	A. T.	54258	Pte	91
Leonard	M.	4339	Pte	8
Lewis	E. I.	67222	Sgt	113
Lewis	H.	92421	Sgt	154
Lockett	F.	80415	Sgt	135
Lomas	A. D.	30018	Sgt	51
Long	J.	90273	Pte	151
Louden	A. E.	45641	Pte	
Lucas	C. J.	90299	Pte	151
Lucas	W. J.	84269	Pte	141
MacMullin★	R.	45328	Pte	76
Magee	G.	51292	Pte	86
Makin	J. D.	64453	Sgt	108
Maney	H. J.	375551	Sgt	198
Manners	J. W.	29420	A/Sgt	50
Martin	J.	27874	Pte	47
Mason	G.	81900	Pte	137
Masters	W.	421041	Pte	38
Maton	E.	86714	A/Cpl	145
Maylor	J. H.	34541	Pte	58
McBride	S.	482488	Pte	14
McGahey	J.	290139	Cpl	701
McGhee	A.	115968	Pte	194
McGillivray	J.	115519	Pte	193
McGowan	W. F.	51280	Sgt	86

McGuire	J.	421148	Pte	195
McKay	R.	49473	Sgt	83
McLeod	D.	7823	A/Cpl	14
McMullen	R.	45328	Pte	76
McQuade	J.	115814	Sgt	194
Meadows	A.	34537	Pte	58
Meiklejohn	J.	4807	Sgt	9
Mennie	A.	90007	Sgt	151
Metcalfe	T.	22206	CSM	38
Miller	A. E.	86082	Cpl	144
Miller	F. D.	94496	Pte	109
Mills	A.	4205	Sgt	8
Miskell	T.	35105	Pte	59
Mitchell	H.	91214	Sgt	153
Moffatt	J. T.	632343	Pte	229
Moorhouse	J.	376819	Pte	762
Mott	C. V.	64820	Cpl	109
Moulds	J.	28213	Cpl	48
Munnery	T.	66895	Pte	112
Munro	J.	632345	Pte	229
Needham	J.	425681	Pte	239
Nelson	J.	42601	CSM	72
Nicholson	A.	419748	Pte	54
Nicholson	H. H.	27603	A/CSM	47
Norman	C. P.	25535	A/LCpl	43
Norman	M.	8150	Pte	14
O'Connell	J.	947	Pte	34
Oddie	G. T.	116559	Pte	195
Oddy	A.	106208	Sgt	178
Oliver	F. J.	72320	A/Cpl	121
Owen	R.	47665	Sgt	80
Painter	W. H.	9731	A/LCpl	17
Palfrey	W.	77089	Cpl	129
Palmer	A.	87932	Pte	147
Parish	W.	189562	Pte	
Parker	C.	27004	Sgt	46
Parker	J.	90364	Pte	151
Parry	A. L.	102323	Pte	171
Parsley	C.	51337	Cpl	86
Pass	T.	54292	Pte	91
Paterson	G. N.	4395	Pte	184
Payne	W.	56094	Pte	94
Pemberton	E.	102318	Pte	171
Perkins	G.	4641	Pte	8
Pettifer	A.	378581	Pte	763
Phillips	F.	34574	Pte	58
Pipet	W.	75006	Sgt	126
Pirie	A.	4243	LCpl	8
Pirie	W.	2414	Sgt	5
Pittom	T.	108329	Pte	181
Poacher	W.	476307	L/Cpl	69
Poole★	C. G. W.	49006	Sgt	
Pope	T. R.	62405	A/CSM	105
Portsmouth	E.	102312	Sgt	171
Potter	G. S.	12609	Sgt	22
Powell	F.	81608	Sgt	137
Poyner	T.	34558	Cpl	58
Prangley	A. H.	107693	Cpl	180
Price	C. A.	39922	A/CSM	67
Pullen	E .A.	64535	Cpl	108
Rafter	W. J.	479299	Sgt	45
Ramsey	G.	14429	Sgt	25

Rawe	G. J.	19202	CQMS	33
Raynor	A.	512783	Pte	223
Raynor	A.	657747	Pte	223
Reaney	M.	281152	Pte	738
Redding	A .J.	66976	Cpl	112
Reekie	A.	34601	Pte	58
Ribchester	G.	42945	A/LCpl	92
Rice	F.	10714	Sgt	18
Richards	F.	92018	Pte	154
Richards	S. H.	39049	A/Cpl	66
Rigden	J. W.	72607	Sgt	122
Roberts	J.	60453	Sgt	101
Robinson	S. J.	59583	Sgt	100
Roderick	W.	35161	Pte	59
Rodges	T. A.	116780	Sgt	195
Ross	J.	13810	Sgt	24
Rowe	W. W.	104408	Sgt	175
Rowland	F. W.	85594	Cpl	143
Ryder	J. T.	21007	Sgt	36
Sanders	R. L.	75997	Cpl	127
Saxby	E. J.	74729	Sgt	45 Gp
Scott	C. S.	101189	Cpl	169
Sears	C.	293571	Cpl	706
Senoir	R. L.	67601	A/LCpl	113
Sergeant	J.	3003	Sgt	Bermuda RGA
Sewell★	J.		Cpl	18 CLC
Shand	A. T.	76206	Sgt	128
Sheeter	M. H.	397093	Pte	949
Shelly	J.	1122	Pte	19
Shipcott	W. J.	224312	Pte	264
Simmons	G.	60027	Cpl	101
Simpsom	M.	346356	A/LCpl	226
Sims	A.	31594	Pte	53
Singleton	H.	42976	Pte	72
Skyrme	W. E.	50785	Pte	85
Slade	S. W.	222163	Pte	207
Slade	W. C.	128063	Sgt	196
Smale	A.	632583	Pte	252
Small	J. S.	7819	Cpl	14
Smith	A.	51404	Sgt	86
Smith	G.	5206	A/LCpl	9
Smith	H. N.	15026	L/Cpl	26
Smith	J.	632378	A/LCpl	234
Sneddon	J.	223201	Pte	226
Snowball	H.	10846	Cpl	19
Spark	J. B.	5809	Pte	10
Spencer	T.	28220	Sgt	48
Sporle	T.	62406	Sgt	105
Stansfield	N.	111785	L/Cpl	187
Stanton	F. W.	56130	Cpl	94
Stark	J.	30962	Cpl	52
Steel	A. A.	86171	Sgt	144
Stephen	U.	377074	Pte	763
Stewart	R.	4232	LCpl	8
Stockdale	A. E.	47817	Pte	80
Stokes	A. J.	102392	Pte	171
Strong	S.	110042	Pte	184
Strowbridge	A. E.	102391	Pte	171
Sullivan	S.	43003	Pte	72
Summers	H.	129798	CQMS	226
Summers	W.	297930	Sgt	714

Sutherland	C.	515064	A/LCpl	245
Tarney	P.	419736	A/Sgt	54
Tattersall	C.	425057	L/Cpl	63
Taylor	H.	450229	L/Cpl	823
Thomas	G. J.	64018	Cpl	107
Thomas	L.	38088	Cpl	37 Bn RF
Thomas	T.	47401	CSM	80
Thomas	W.	107178	Cpl	947
Thompson	J.	551815	Pte	79
Thompson	W.	15006	Sgt	26
Thorogood	J. J.	75632	Cpl	127
Thorpe	F. W.	478450	Sgt	144
Threlfall	W.	91206	Sgt	153
Till	W. R.	290121	CSM	701
Town	F. A.	80613	Cpl	135
Town	P. A.	224596	A/Sgt	252
Trainer	A.	36999	Cpl	62
Turnbull	A.	116793	Sgt	195
Turner	H.	100808	Sgt	169
Turner	J. T.	15265	Sgt	26
Tyler	A.	568941	Pte	175
Tyler	T.	513499	Sgt	226
Underwood	W. H.	14450	Cpl	25
Vickers	J.	372479	Sgt	294
Victor	M. C.	64820	Cpl	
Vizard	A. T.	309132	Pte	732
Vowles	E.	301266	Pte	738
Wainwright	S.	47245	Cpl	59
Waldron	G.	293495	Cpl	706
Walker	R. D.	297931	Sgt	714
Waller	A.	64636	Pte	108
Wallis	G. T.	92049	Cpl	154
Walters	W. H.	104410	CQMS	175
Ward	A. E.	34219	Sgt	58
Warn	H. H.	97418	A/Sgt	163
Wass	W.	15231	Pte	832
Watson	F.	11281	Pte	19
Watson	J. W.	38121	Sgt	37 Bn RF
Watson	L.	59284	A/CQMS	99
Weeds	W.	62796	Pte	105
Welch	J. F.	450235	Sgt	823
Whalley	J.	53879	Pte	90
Wheatley	E.	290146	Cpl	701
Wheeler	L. J. K.	43050	Pte	72
Wheelhouse	T. H.	116818	A/LCpl	195
White	F.	14433	Sgt	25
White	H.	297950	Cpl	714
Whitehead*			Pte	152
Whitfield	F.	116603	Pte	195
Whitham	W.	91835	A/Cpl	
Wigham	A. S.	116752	Pte	195
Wild	J.	40030	Sgt	67
Wilkin	T.	85661	Cpl	143
Wilkinson	W. D.	21048	A/LCpl	36
Williams	J.	87615	Sgt	147
Williams	J. T.	40682	Sgt	68
Williamson	A.	4204	Sgt	8
Willmore	V.	425183	Pte	63
Willoughby	T.	64663	Pte	108
Winder	F. G.	214786	Cpl	762
Wingate	H. B.	419971	Cpl	931
Winter	H.	425201	Pte	
Winter	T.	64831	Sgt	109

Wood	T. H.	13064	Pte			22
Wright★	W.	43983	LCpl			762
Yallop	E. C.	55689	Sgt			93

Attached personnel:

Carter	W.	T4/14156	Dvr			ASC
Chadwick	J.	23820	Pte	213		11th Manchester
Chapman	H. W.	307876	Pte	243		1/7th W Riding
Goater	C. H.	19259	CQMS	4	BWIR	Devons
Jackson	G.	C/12756	ASgt	238		21 KRRC
Tyler	A. J.	394222	Sgt	249		2/9 London

Dominion Personnel:

Name		Number	Rank	Unit
Allan	L. M.	4025	Pte	BWIR
Archer	G.	9621	A/LCpl	3 BWIR
Bailey	T. A.	7268	Pte	6 BWIR
Barton	S.	4736	Pte	4 BWIR
Boyce	J.	9741	A/LCpl	7 BWIR
Conway	A.	23/2554	Pte	NZ
Cummings	C.	14997	LCpl	7 BWIR
Davis	J.	5777	Pte	4 BWIR
De Pas	A.	5766	Pte	4 BWIR
Donnelly	T. K.	623216	A/Sgt	4 Cdn
Ellacott	J. H.	681287	Pte	4 Cdn
England	P. A.	3266	Sgt	BWIR
Evans	R. B.	5781	Cpl	4 BWIR
Ferguson	H.	6260	Pte	4 BWIR
Francis	T.	734589	A/Sgt	4 Cdn
French	D. L.	4368	Pte	BWIR
Gordon	W. R.	1081746	A/Sgt	4 Cdn
Henry	A. L. McL	1960	LCpl	BWIR
Highland	A. P.	907456	Cpl	1 Cdn
Holland	F. W.	3970	Sgt	4 BWIR
Houston	H. K.	150122	Cpl	2 Cdn
Hyndman	C. A.	368	Pte	
Irish	W.	1188	Pte	
Janniero	V.	12254	Pte	
John Apa		16/1321	A/Cpl	
Jones	V. E.	2441	L/Cpl	
Knight	H.	1037	Gnr	Bermuda RGA
Lamoureux	A.	624408	A/Sgt	
Lowe	W. B. A.	6473	Pte	
Mais	D. C.	3110	Sgt	
Manders	A.	1041	Gnr	Bermuda RGA
McDonald	D. G.	4156	Sgt	
Miller	L. N.	4675	Sgt	
Nichols	T. W.	16/164	Cpl	
Parr	F. L.	190053	Pte	
Rollins	E.	690928	LCpl	
Smith	D.	10619	Pte	
Sparks	A.	16/739	Cpl	
Stevenson	W. T.	407022	Cpl	
Tangatake	W.	16/1275	Pte	
Thomas	J.	10686	Pte	
Thompson	J. W.	823427	Pte	
Walker	J.	10799	Pte	
Williams	E.	8292	Pte	

Order of St Michael and St George – 3rd Class (5 UK)

CBE (4 UK)

OBE (93 UK, 4 Empire, 6 attached)

MBE (23 UK, 22 Empire, 1 attached)

Meritorious Service Medal (1115 UK, 155 Empire)
1270 MSMs have been identified as having been awarded to Labour Corps Personnel (including 38 for Gallantry). Apart from British Units the following Empire awards were made both to Colonial soldiers and British NCOs.

Chinese: 52 (including Ganger Yen Teng-Feng and Coolies Wang Chen Ching, Wang Yu Bahn, Chao We Te, and Liu Dien Chen)
Canadian: 28
East African: 28
BWIR: 14
SANLC: 20 (including Native Chaplin Dambuza)
Cape Coloured: 4
New Zealand: 5
Fijian: 2
Maltaese 1
Bermuda RGA: 1
Two Aliens were awarded the MSM for Gallantry G/31344 Pte A. Kriehn and G/35438 Pte J. Malzer.
The last award seems to have been to 693664 Sgt C. Skinner on 11 Aug 1952.

Mentioned in Dispatches
1,106 MIDs have been identified to British and Canadians.

Long Service and Good Conduct Medal
76 awards were made to the Labour Corps but personnel will have served in other units prior to joining the Labour Corps.

Overseas Awards
These are even harder to identify, especially French and Belgian awards. Although listed in the *London Gazette* a number have been missed. For example, Lt E. Barron has a *Croix de Guerre* on his records but no *London Gazette* entry can be found. The award seems to have been issued during his attachment to the French 109 Labour Battalion.

Country	Award	Number
France	Legion d'Honneur – Chevalier	2
	Croix de Guerre	19
	Medaille Militaire	4
	Medaille d'Honneur avec Glaives (en Vermeil)	8
	Medaille d'Honneur avec Glaives (en Argent)	18
	Medaille d'Honneur avec Glaives (en Bronze)	74
	Medaille des Epidemies (en Argent)	1
	Ordre de Merite Agricole–Chevalier	1
Belgium	Ordre de Leopold avec Croix de Guerre–Chevalier	1
	Ordre de la Couronne – Office	1
	Croix de Guerre	26
	Order de Leopold Chevalier	10
	Decoration Militare avec Croix de Guerre	3
	Decoration Militare	2
	Decoration Militare – 2nd Class	7
Italy	Croce di Guerre	2
	Bronze Medal for Military Valour	1
Portugal	Military Medal for Good Service (Copper)	1
Romania	Order of the Star (Chevalier)	1
	Order of the Crown (Chevalier)	2
	Crois De Virtute Militara (2nd Class)	2
	Medaille Barbatie si Credinta	1
	Medaille Barbatie si Credinta (2nd Class)	2
	Medaille Barbatie si Credinta (3rd Class)	7
Egypt	Order of the Nile – 3rd Class	1
	Order of the Nile – 4th Class	7
Serbia	Gold Medal for Valour	2
	Silver Medal for Zealous Service	1
China	Order of the Golden Grain (or Excellent Crop) – 2nd Class	1
	Order of Wen-Hu – 2nd Class	1
	Order of Wen-Hu – 3rd Class	1
	Order of Wen-Hu – 4th Class	15
	Order of Wen-Hu – 5th Class	58
Greece	Order of the Redeemer 5th Class	2
Hedjaz	Order of El Nahda – 4th Class	2
Salonika	Order of St Michael and St George – Member 3rd Class	1
Russia	Russian Orders of St Stanislas – 2nd Class	1

POSTSCRIPT

On 17 October 1939 the Auxiliary Military Pioneer Corps (AMPC) was formed to provide labour for the British Expeditionary Force.[1] The title Pioneer was selected because troops were too proud to be described as 'Labour.' The initial organization mirrored that of the early Labour Corps, with Groups and Companies. The command structure consisted of Labour Advisors and not Controllers. The original force consisted of 6 Group HQs and 48 Companies, each having an establishment of between 300 and 500 men. The officers were mostly retired from the infantry and cavalry and had battle experience in The Great War. Plans were made in 1939 for the importation of 30,000 Chinese labourers from Hong Kong to arrive in France by the end of August 1940 but these were cancelled because of concerns about antagonizing the Japanese.[2]

On 22 November 1940 the name of the AMPC was changed to Pioneer Corps.[3] It was felt the 'Auxiliary' suggested a non-fighting Corps and the Pioneers had proved an effective fighting force in numerous actions including Boulogne.

During 1941, Pioneer officers travelled to many parts of the world enlisting and training volunteer native Pioneers. There were Swazis, Basutos and Bechuanas from the High Commission Territories of South Africa, East and West Africans, Mauritians, Rodriguais and Seychellois, Indians of all classes, Singhalese, Syrians, Cypriots, Palestinians, Maltese and Arabs.

The Pioneer Corps was a combatant unit which included specialized troops, for example Civil Labour Units and Smoke Companies. During the War over 10,000 Aliens served in its ranks, many later transferring to the SOE, Commandos and Airborne Forces. On D Day 6,000 men, in 23 Companies, landed in Normandy and numbers increased to over 125,000 men. By the end of the War the Corps consisted of a military force of 12,000 officers, 166,000 British personnel and about 400,000 Pioneers from other parts of the Empire. Pioneers were responsible for a civilian labour force of 1,074,000 and for a prisoner of war force of 173,000.

The Corps was bestowed the honour 'Royal' in 1946 and became the Royal Pioneer Corps.[4] After the War the Corps reduced in size but continued to supply both Military and civilian Labour to all operations and peacetime garrisons. On 3 April 1993 the Royal Pioneer Corps was amalgamated into the Royal Logistic Corps and 23 Group became 23 Pioneer Regiment Royal Logistic Corps.

1   NA WO 123/82 Army Order 200
2   ibid FO/371/23537
3   ibid WO 123/83 Army Order 200 22 Nov 1940
4   Elliott, E., *Royal Pioneers* p.51

Appendix I

Transport Workers Battalions – October 1917

16th York and Lancaster	17th Cameronians	13th Bedfordshire
Aire & Calder Navigation (Canals)	Alloa	Brentford
Barrow	Ayr	Chatham
Bolton (Canals)	Coatbridge	Chelsea
Bradford (Railways)	Dundee	Erith
Cargo Fleet	Falkirk	Folkestone
Dinsdale	Glasgow	Greenwich
Gateshead	Greenock	Heyes
Glasgow	Leith	Ipswich
Grangetown	Muirkirk	Littlehampton
Greenock	Newmains	Newhaven
Horbury (Railways)	Rochdale (Canals)	Northolt
Jarrow	Stevenston	Rotherhithe
Middlesborough	Wishaw	Sittingbourne
Port Clarence		Southall (Canals)
Redcar		Stroud
Rochdale (Canals)		Tring (Canals)
Sheffield & S Yorks (Canals)		Agriculture★
Stockton		
Sunderland	**15th South Lancashire**	**15th Worcestershire**
Tyne Dock	Barrow & Ulverston	Birmingham (Canals)
West Hartlepool	Liverpool & Birkenhead	Bristol
	Manchester	Manchester
	Midlands (Canals)	Newhaven
	Newhaven	Southampton
	Sheffield (Railways)	Agriculture★
	Farming★	
16th Cameronians	**16th South Lancashire**	**16th Worcestershire**
Ardrossan	Manchester	Barrow
Ayr	Midlands (Canals)	Bebington
Georgetown	Fleetwood	Cardiff
Glasgow	Farming★	Didcot (Railways)
Glengarnock		Fishguard
Greenock	**12th Bedfordshire**	Manchester
Kilwinning	Birmingham (Canals)	Milford
Mallaig	Chatham	Newhaven
Paisley	Devizes	Reading (Railways)
Renfrew	Midlands (Canals)	Steventon (Railways)
	Newhaven	Swindon (Railways)
	Rochdale (Canals)	Agriculture★
	Rochester	
	Sittingbourne	
	Waford (Canals)	
	Weymouth	
	Agriculture★	

★ No locations shown

APPENDIX II

Allocation of Labour – August 1916

Employer	Units
IGC	13th Battalion Queen's
	10th Battalion Berkshire
	16th Battalion Yorkshire
	35th Battalion Royal Fusiliers
	36th Battalion Royal Fusiliers
	Cape Coloured Labour Battalion
	29 ASC Companies
Director of Works	12th Battalion South Staffords (on forestry)
	14th Battalion Cameronians (on forestry)
	19th Battalion Royal Scots (on works)
	12th Battalion Berkshire (on works)
	12th Battalion Lincolns (on works)
	37th Battalion Royal Fusiliers (in quarries)
	10th Labour Battalion RE (on forestry)
	8th Labour Battalion RE (½ forestry, ½ quarries)
	6 Companies NCC (2 works, 4 quarries)
Railway Directorate	12th Battalion West Riding
	19th Battalion Cheshires
	20th Battalion Cheshires
	5th Labour Battalion RE
	20th Railway Battalion RE
1st Army	33rd Battalion Royal Fusiliers (roads)
	½ 1st Labour Battalion RE
	17 PoW Company
2nd Army	½ 1st Labour Battalion RE
	4th Labour Battalion RE
	7th Labour Battalion RE
	11th Labour Battalion RE
3rd Army	3 Labour Battalion RE
	4, 6, and 9 PoW Companies
4th Army	12th Battalion Devonshire
	12th Battalion DCLI
	11th Battalion Berkshire
	12th Battalion Black Watch
	22nd Battalion West Yorkshire
	18th Battalion Cheshire (railways)
	2nd Labour Battalion RE
	1, 2, 7, 11, 13, 14 and 19 PoW Companies
Reserve Army (5th Army)	34th Battalion Royal Fusiliers
	6th Labour Battalion RE
	9th Labour Battalion RE
	3, 8, 10, and 12 PoW Companies

APPENDIX III

A Company Diary

There are very few diaries for individual labour companies. Those that do exist tend to cover only two or three months during 1917. Most of the information about the work of an individual company was provided in the daily and weekly returns companies sent to Labour Groups Headquarters. These returns no longer exist; they were among the material destroyed by German bombing in 1940.

In May 1916 the 19th (Labour) Battalion, Cheshire Regiment was formed. It was, on the formation of the Labour Corps in April 1917, to become 58 Company (the old A and C Companies) and 59 Company (the old B and D Companies). The Battalion Headquarters became Headquarters 56 Group.

From its formation, C Company 19th Cheshire Regiment was commanded by Capt T. C. Thomas OBE MC. With the creation of the Labour Corps he became OC 58 Company. He remained the Company's OC until January 1919. Thomas was to maintain a record of 58 Company, which he published at the end of the war under the title *With a Labour Company in France*. Thomas's record has been supplemented by information about the Company in GHQ, Army and Corps Diaries and details of individual officers and men from the *London Gazette*, the Commonwealth War Graves Commission and service records.

One of the main differences between this unit and other companies is that the majority of their time was spent on railway construction and maintenance compared to other units which would have undertaken more general tasks such as operating rail-heads, road-heads, road maintenance and constructing defences.

Where possible, locations are named – grid references are given using the grid system in use at the time. Some grids vary between diaries. In some instances, where a location has no name the grid reference is given. No individuals, except the commander are named in diaries.

1916	
May	Formed as 19th Battalion the Cheshire Regiment under Lt Col O'Sullivan DSO Northern Rhodesia Police at Chadderton from men of lower physical category.[1] Unit commences two weeks military training.[2]
26 May	Moves to Southampton by train.[2]
28 May	Arrived Le Havre from Southampton on SS *Arundel* and SS *Bellerophan*, 12 officers & 1,016 other ranks.[1]
29 May	A and C Companies move to Ville to construct gun positions and ammunition dumps.[1] They are 3,000 yards from the line, which contravenes a recent statement in Parliament that no Labour was employed within 20 miles of the line.[2]
2 Jun	A and C Companies supply 300 men to make gun pits.[1]
6 Jun	PH (Phenate Helmets) helmets issued.[1]
19 Jun	Whole Battalion moves to Bailleul. A and C Companies, 400 men, working on road repairs on the La Clytte ring road.[1]

18 Jul	Battalion moves to 93 High Street, Meaulte for work on Broad Gauge Railway with 110 Company RE.[2] Numerous small working parties, each consisting of 1 NCO and 11 men, working between Albert and Fricourt.[1]
22 Jul	Tents issued since men had been sleeping in the open.[1]
20 Aug	Air raid by fourteen planes.[2]
22 Aug	C Company moved to tents at Bazentin Le Grand to build Bazentin Station Yard.[2]
30 Aug	A and C Companies resting.[1]
11 Sep	Moves from XV Corps to XIV Corps.[1]
21 Oct	Battalion moves to Bazentin Le Grand and camped at 57C/S.15.c. The main task is building Meaulte–Martinpuich railway line with 110 Company RE.[1]
20 Nov	C and D Companies, 390 men, building a new railway station at Longueval with 109 Company RE.[1]
4 Dec	C Company moves to Le Sars for rail work.[2]
31 Dec	110 Company RE handed over task to 120 Company RE.[2] The following casualties suffered by the Battalion since arriving in France: one accidentally killed, two died of wounds, two died in hospital, thirteen wounded and thirteen returned to Britain. Strength now 11 officers and 959 other ranks.[2]
1917	
1 Jan	Headquarters located at Bazentin.[1] A Company undertaking railway ballasting at Bazentin Station whilst B, C and D Companies constructing a rail extension to High Wood with 120 Company RE.[1]
5 Jan	Joined III Corps.[3]
25 Jan	A Company moves to a new camp at Willow Avenue to supply 155 men on Meaulte Guillemont[2] meter gauge line maintenance.[1]
11 Feb	C Company undertaking re-alignment of the Willow to Caterpillar line with 120 Company RE.[1]
19 Feb	C Company moves to Beaussart for railway construction following German retreat.[2]
28 Feb	HQ moves from Bazentin to Meaulte (62D/E.11.d.3.1).[3] A Company constructing Becourt–La Boiselle line.
1 Mar	A Company supplying 140 men for the construction of La Boiselle to Pozieres extension.[1]
23 Mar	Joined V Corps from 1 ANZAC Corps.[4]
25 Mar	Battalion move to Beaussart, A and C Companies, 320 men, on rail line construction between Colincamps and Achiet Le Petit.[1]
18 Apr	C Company moves to Bihucourt doubling Achiet Le Grand to Bapaume line.[2]
13 Apr	In accordance with ACI 611, 58 Company Labour Corps formed (from old A and C Companies) Capt T. C. Thomas commanding. Men re-numbered with numbers between 34,201 and 34,800.[5]
21 Apr	Working on line construction between Bapaume and Achiet Le Petit.[1]
12 May	56 Group consists of 9, 18, 58, 59, 67, 129 and 145 Companies.[4]

21 May	Company moves to Velu to work on Fremicourt to Havrincourt line and joins 60 Group.[2]
26 May	Joined 57 Group but remains at Velu.[6]
30 May	Overall command changes from 5th Army to 2nd Army.[7]
30 May	Company moves to Swiss Cottage, Ypres (28/A.8.c.8.2)[8] along with 101 and 152 Companies, to build light rail east of International Corner[2] with VIII Corps.
5 Jun	58 Company move from 28/A.8.c.8.2 to 28/A.8.c.9.2 but the new location is no nearer to their work.[8]
6 Jun	Two wounded.[2]
7 Jun	34292 Pte T. Bilsborough drowned whilst bathing.[2]
14 Jun	Joins 32 Group.[9]
19 Jun	Joins the newly formed 65 Group.[4]
27 Jun	24238 LCpl J. Walsh, 34255 Pte W. H. Atkinson, 24417 Pte W. Hughes, 34595 Pte J. Rushforth and 34596 Pte O. W. Richards killed and seven wounded by shellfire on Woesten Road.[10] [11] 54761 Pte H. Mason, 34506 Pte A. F. Morton 34679 Pte J. A. William were to die from wounds.
24 Jul	Under command 67 Group, XIV Corps, still on Light Railway work.[12]
28 Jul	34204 Sgt A. Ellis killed and 12 wounded when a truck full of shells explodes due to enemy fire. Pte Fernely, Stretcher Bearer, commended for working to save 11 wounded although wounded himself[2]
17 Aug	58 Company moves to 28/A.12.b.5.9, 67 Group, working for Assistant Director Light Railways[12]
17 Aug	Camp moves to Woesten from Duffield Woods 28/A.12.b.5.9 still working on A1/A8 Light Railway line[2]
10 Sep	3 wounded by shellfire[2]
10 Sep	Now under Canadian Corps [13]
16 Sep	Line shelled 18 breaks repaired but 1 man wounded [2]
17 Sep	1 man wounded[2]
20 Sep	3 men wounded[2] 1 x DCM and 5 x MM awarded 34597 Pte W. Riding – party leader – DCM (London Gazette 6 Feb. 1918).[14] For conspicuous gallantry and devotion to duty. He was in charge of a party repairing a light railway. He was under fire the entire time, but by his splendid example and courage kept his party at work until the repairing was completed. This line was urgently needed for the passage of ambulance train. 34537 Pte A. Medows, 34541 Pte J. H. Maylor, 34574 Pte F. Phillips, 34601 Pte A. Reekie and 34429 Pte F. Hadfield – MM.[2] At Tamworth, on 20 September 1917, were members of a party detailed to repair several breaks in the light railway line, such repair being urgently needed for the passage of ambulance trains.

	The party were under very heavy shellfire from the time the work was started, and one shell blew up one of our guns 10 yards away, and ignited some ammunition lying between the party and the guns, causing the gunners to retire. Every man in the party showed the greatest coolness and bravery, remaining at work and taking out damaged rails, until a shell burst alongside them and compelled them to retire temporarily. They immediately returned to work, however, and completed the repair. While still under shell fire, and in great danger from the burning ammunition, the party went to another break close by, and after carrying rails some 2 hundred yards, removed the damaged rails, and placed the others in position, being compelled to complete the bolting up while lying flat on their stomachs owing to the heavy shellfire and their exposed position.
21 Sep	Move from 28/A.12.b.5.9 to 28/A.12.d.1.6 but remain 67 Group.[12]
24 Sep	Twelve casualties and twelve breaks repaired.[2]
30 Sep	GHQ Diary notes that 58 Company are considered above average working on Light railways.[15]
7 Oct	Extract from letter from Director Light Railways:[2] The magnificent work done by the following officers of your Company while working with Light Railways has been brought to notice:- CAPTAIN T. CHARLES THOMAS. 2ND LIEUT. JAMES F. WORRALL. I wish to express to you personally my appreciation of the valuable help rendered by your Company to Light Railways as a whole.' (Signed) J. H. WARREN, Brig. General, G.H.Q., D. L. R.
13 Oct	67 Group consists of: 58, 74, 101, 165, 164 and 184 Companies and one other unidentified Company.[16]
2 Dec	Company to work forward at Pilkem Ridge but camp to remain in old location because of heavy shelling of Pilkem. Working towards Houlthrust Forest.[2]
13 Dec	Two wounded.[2]
30 Dec	During the month six men were wounded.[17]
1918	
16 Jan	Move to Agadir Farm (28/B.30.a.5.1.) and join 43 Group, II Corps, located in tents.[18]
17 Jan	½ Company move to work on Steedbeeck to recover a train and carriages lost when a bridge collapsed in a flood.[2]
26 Jan	Entire Company at Agadir Farm.[2]
30 Jan	2Lt C. Lewis wounded. He only joined two days earlier.[2]
26 Feb	Company moves to Nissen Huts at Morocco Farm (28/C.19.c.8.5, West of Yser Canal) as Agadir too muddy.[2]
22 Mar	491615 Pte J. Clark killed and 34368 Pte R. Ellis died of wounds and four wounded at Stoke.[2, 11]
28 Mar	34490 Pte T. H. Lye, 170206 Pte W. H. Miller, 384790 Pte P. C. Stephenson killed and 34442 Pte A. Hart died of wounds and seven wounded in camp by artillery 'short'.[2, 11]
9 Apr	Heavy shelling – no casualties.[2]

13 Apr	Move to 28/A.3.b.7.1. join 32 Group still working on light railways.[19]
13 Apr 1	Company move to Bailey Farm, International Corner[2] (20/S.26.d.2.3), a Hutted Camp built by the Chinese, the main task is demolishing the rail lines to slow the German advance.
14 Apr	100 rifles issued.[2]
6 May	Recovered an abandoned 8' Howitzer at Bochcastle.[2]
8 May	Company moves to 27/E.17.b.8.5 and joined 59 Group to work on ammunition supply.[19]
12 May	Join VIII Corps for Light Railway work.[19]
16 May	Pte Ryan the mess cook is wounded by bullet.[2]
19 May	Extract from letter from Lieut. Colonel J. K. Cornwall, Commanding 8th Battalion Canadian Railway Troops:[2]

I am enclosing for your information copy of letter from Major Barber, D.S.O., Chief Engineer, in which special mention is made of the workmanship of the 58th Labour Company.

    This Company has specialised in grading and is a particularly well-balanced Company for this class of work. They are fortunate in being commanded by an officer who has taken great pains and pride in bringing his Company up to this high state of efficiency, and he certainly must have had the hearty and whole-souled co-operation of his officers, NCOs and men. The work of this Company has been a good object lesson to the 8th Battalion, C.R.T. While we may excel in all round railroad work we do not mind admitting that the grading performance of the 58th Labour Company beats anything we have been able to do in this Battalion in the grading line.

    The L. 6 line was constructed for the French, and was completed seven days under the time limit, which is the cleanest, fastest and most complete operation of its kind that has been done in this part of France, and your Company is entitled to its full proportion of credit.

(Signed) J. K. CORNWALL, Lieut. Col.,
Commanding 8th Battalion C. R. T. |
| 26 May | Company move to Ledringham (27/C.26.d.2.3) to build railways to the ammunition dumps. The following is a note by Capt Thomas:

These two years had been spent continuously in the forward areas except for March 1917, when the Boch retired on the Somme, so fast we could not follow him, during the whole period we had never either worked or lived out of reach of the German Field Guns. We were heartily glad of a chance to escape from it all for a time; the strain had really been an exceedingly heavy one. Our battle casualties were nearly 100, and a large number had returned to the UK suffering from illness. Yet despite all, I never had a single case of malingering or reporting sick without a cause. The men worked well and cheerfully.[2] |
5 Jun	66 Group consisting of 58, 118, 126 and 134 Companies and detachments from 192 and 705 Companies. Join VII Corps[20]. Working on Light Railways but have a defence responsibility in Le Peuplier Sector.[19]
25 Jun	Detachment of 2 officers and 164 men move to Abeele (27/L.27.cent).[18] Support to No 1 Company Canadian Railway Troops, constructing a new line between Abeele past Boeschepe to near Reninghelst.[2]
30 Jun	Command passes to XIX Corps.[18]
7 Jul	Detachment of 2 officers and 164 men move to 27/L.21.a.9.1.[18]
14 Jul	Location HQ 27/K.26.d.3.4. and detachment at 27/L.21.a.9.1.[18]

17 Jul	34219 Sgt A. E. Ward recommended for MM whilst leading a detachment, 1 Sgt and 15 men, salvaging rails in the vicinity of Zevecoten Dump for 'bringing in 7 wounded from another Company out of the "Brick Spur" whilst under fire. After being shelled out himself, he saw others in difficulties, brought out the slightly wounded, returned and assisted the walking wounded. Brought up his tractor and dispatched the badly wounded to hospital'.[2]
30 Jul	Detachment rejoins HQ at 27/K.26.d.3.4.[18]
6 Aug	King visits the area and some men are able to view him.[2]
3 Sep	Now part of 30 Group, XIX Corps, with HQ at 27/K.26.d.2.3. and detachment at 27/K.21.c.3.4.[18]
23 Sep	Detachments at 27/X.21.b.5.1. and 27/W.3.b.5.8.[21]
24 Sep	Move to Meteren (27/X.21.b.5.1)[21] with ½ Company at Caestre (27/W.3.b.3.8).[21] Join 33 Group XV Corps.[22] Working on light railways.[19]
30 Sep	Company complete at Meteren then moves to Hell Fire Corner (28/I.16.a.8.7) for re-ballasting Broad Gauge line to Roulers including Zonnebeke Station and Passchendale[2]. Part of 32 Group, II Corps.[22]
7 Oct	Company moves forward to Neuve Eglise (36/C.2.a.6.6) working on lines leading to Ploegstreet Woods in support of 8 Company Canadian Railway Troops,[2] now in 5 Group, XV Corps.[19]
9 Oct	Company move to Beythem (28/K.24.a.3.5) over Passchendale Ridge.[22] 199140 CSM A. N. Baker killed in train derailment.[2, 11]. Task involves relaying the German 1m line to river Scheldt as a 60 cm line (over 6 miles).
18 Oct	Now under II Corps.[21]
25 Oct	Company moves to Courtrai (29/H.33.a) rebuilding bridges over the Lys[2] as part of 66 Group, XIX Corps.[18]
28 Oct	Extract from letter from 2nd Army Light Railway Chief Engineer:[2] For many months, the 58th Labour Company has been under my direct supervision and they have invariably done the tasks allotted to them with such speed, intelligence and scientific finish that I place them amongst the very best who have been on Light Railways in the Second Army. Captain Thomas is well qualified to take over any railway work and he has trained his officers, N.C.O.'s and men in such a manner that they have become highly skilled railway troops.
5 Nov	Move to 29/I.29.b.9.6, 32 Group, still with XIX Corps, with a detachment of 1 officer and 50 men at Vichte (29/I.24.d.) working Audenarde Line.[2]
16 Nov	32 Group now under 2nd Army consists of 19, 25, 31, 40, 43, 58, 91, 126, 130, 140, 143, 184 and 188 Companies.[19]
19 Nov	MC Awarded to T/Capt Thomas Charles Thomas.[23] The citation states: Near Courtrai, from the 19th to 23rd October 1918, he displayed fine leadership, and made excellent dispositions of his company, which was engaged in converting meter gauge to light railway 60cm track under considerable enemy shell fire and without proper tools for this work. Chiefly owing to his personal effort and example his company completed the 5½ miles of track required for corps ammunition supply by a voluntary effort of 11½ hours work under hostile shell fire.[14]
21 Nov	Move to Sottegham (30/I.13.a.)[24] to repair the large railway junction destroyed by Germans.[2] Join 38 Group.
28 Nov	38 Group, Headquarters at Hal, transferred from XIX Corps to III Corps. Units consist of 10, 19, 40, 52, 58, 91, 111, 133, 140, 144, 147, 151, 179, 186, 719 and 759 Companies.[24]

1919	
4 Jan	Leave 38 Group, III Corps[25] and move to 32 Group, XV Corps.[24]
14 Jan	Under command of 87 Group, Headquarters in Le Gorgue.[24]
20 Apr	Move from La Gorgue to Templeuve, 80 Group.[24]
22 Apr	Undertaking salvage operations in Lille Area as part of 80 Group.[26]
26 Apr	Working at Templeuve on salvage alongside 91 PW Company.[27]
10 Jul	Move from Templeuve to Baisieux and join 68 Group.[27]
27 Aug	Move from Baisieux to Meaulte, No 3 Area, still on salvage but soon to be disbanded.[27]

Honours and Awards

Below are the Honours and awards, that it has been possible to identify, gained by the unit.

Number	Rank	Forename	Surname	Award	London Gazette	
34283	A/Sgt	Thomas	Barnes	MM	20 Aug 19	p. 10579
34226	Sgt	Thomas	Clee	MM	20 Aug 19	p. 10579
34226	Sgt	Thomas	Clee	CdeG (F)	14 Jul 19	p. 8959
34226	Sgt	Thomas	Clee	CdeG (B)	4 Sep 19	p. 11217
34243	Sgt	Albert	Clements	MSM	3 Jul 19	p. 6895
34360	Pte	George	Elkes	MM	20 Aug 19	p. 10580
34429	Pte	Frank	Hadfield	MM	12 Dec 17	p. 13012
34541	Pte	Joseph H	Maylor	MM	12 Dec 17	p. 13016
34504	Cpl	Roland	McIlwain	MID	10 Jul 19	p. 8749
34537	Pte	Albert	Meadows	MM	12 Dec 17	p. 13017
34574	Pte	Frederick	Phillips	MM	12 Dec 17	p. 13018
34558	Cpl	Thomas	Poyner	MM	20 Aug 19	p. 10579
34601	Pte	A	Reekie	MM	2 Dec 17	p. 34601
34597	Pte	W	Riding	DCM	19 Nov 17	p. 11956
	Capt	Thomas C.	Thomas	MC	8 Mar 19	p. 3247
	Capt	Thomas C.	Thomas	OBE	1 Jan 19	p. 10
34219	Sgt	Albert E.	Ward	MM	13 Nov 18	p. 13400
	Lt	James F.	Worrall	MC	29 Nov 18	p. 14270

Lt (A/Capt) James Fletcher Worrall Labour Corps was attached to 8 Battalion Liverpool Regiment from 58 Coy on 14 October 1917, he was to be awarded the MC (citation *London Gazette* 29 Nov 18 page 14270):

> For conspicuous gallantry and resource during three days' operation. He made several reconnaissances under heavy fire and obtained important information. On one occasion he rendered valuable service in guiding companies to their positions in the dark to meet a counter-attack. His devotion to duty and determination were a splendid example to the men.

Casualties

The following 58 Company casualties have been identified:

Number	Rank	Name	Date of Death	Remarks
34263	Pte	Ashworth, John Robert	12 Nov 18	Disease
34255	Pte	Atkinson, William Henry	27 Jun 17	KIA
199140	CSM	Baker, Alfred Nelson	19 Oct 18	Accident
34292	Pte	Bilsborough, Thomas	8 Jun 17	Drowned
491615	Pte	Clark, John	22 Mar 18	KIA
505680	Pte	Costello, Augustine	11 Jan 20	
34332	Pte	Davis, Henry	16 Sep 17	DoW
34368	Pte	Ellis, Robert	22 Mar 18	DoW
24204	Sgt	Ellis, Alfred	28 Jul 17	
34359	Pte	Evans, David	10 Jul 18	
150916	Pte	Gibbs, Harry	14 Feb 19	Pneumonia
34442	Pte	Hart, Albert	3 Apr 18	DoW
34417	Pte	Hughes, Walter	27 Jun 17	KIA
50655	Pte	Jones, William	16 Feb 18	
34490	Pte	Lye, Thomas H.	28 Mar 18	KIA
58553	Pte	Mason, Harry	28 Jun 17	DoW
170206	Pte	Miller, Henry William	28 Mar 18	KIA
36519	Pte	Morris, E.	14 Dec 18	Died UK
34506	Pte	Morton, Arthur Francis	28 Jun 17	DoW
34596	Pte	Richards, Owen W.	27 Jun 17	KIA
34595	Pte	Rushforth, John	27 Jun 17	KIA
384790	Pte	Stephenson, Percival Cade	28 Mar 18	KIA
34698	Pte	Tracey, Ralph	17 Feb 19	
34238	LCpl	Walsh, John	27 Jun 17	KIA
34679	Pte	Williams, John A.	27 Jun 17	DoW

1   NA WO 95/571 Bn War Diary
2   Thomas, *With a Labour Company in France*
3   NA WO 95/442 4th Army AQ Diary
4   ibid WO 95/524 5th Army AQ Diary
5   ibid WO 293/4 ACI 611 1 April 1918
6   ibid WO 95/4173 60 Group Diary
7   ibid WO 95/724 IV Corps AQ Diary
8   ibid WO 95/823 VIII Corps AQ Diary
9   ibid WO 95/571 57 Group Diary
10 ibid WO 95/571 65 Group Diary
11 Commonwealth War Graves Commission
12 NA WO 95/914 XIV Corps AQ Diary
13 ibid WO 95/611 I Corps AQ Diary
14 *London Gazette*
15 NA WO 95/185 GHQ AQ Diary
16 ibid WO 95/526 5th Army AQ Diary
17 ibid WO 95/964 XIX Corps AQ Diary
18 ibid WO 95/965 XIX Corps AQ Diary
19 ibid WO 95/283 2nd Army AQ Diary
20 ibid WO 95/753 VII Corps AQ Diary
21 ibid WO 95/924 XV Corps AQ Diary

22 ibid WO 95/929 XV Corps Diary

23 ibid WO 95/650 II Corps AQ Diary

24 ibid WO 95/530 5th Army AQ Diary

25 ibid WO 95/688 III Corps AQ Diary

26 ibid WO 95/530 5th Salvage Area Diary

27 ibid WO 95/4036 Commandant Lille Area Diary

APPENDIX IV

A Divisional
Employment Company

225th Divisional Employment Company

The work of 25th Division's Employment Company (225 Company) was described by the Company's OC in August 1917. His report survives in the GHQ Diary (National Archives – WO 95/83) and has been reproduced in full below.

Summary of work executed by 225th Divisional Employment Company

The Institutions and Organisations mentioned below, are administered by the O.C. 225th Divisional Employment Company and the whole of the staffs necessary are drawn from the personnel of the Company whilst all accountancy and clerical work involved by these institutions is carried out by special clerks of the Company.

1. DIVISIONAL BATHS.
When the Division moves into an area where there are no permanent baths, the Pioneers of the Company erect sets of Portable Baths usually in the proportion of one to each Infantry Brigade and one for the Divisional Artillery, in all, 4 sets. The staffs necessary to work these are drawn from men of the Company.

The issue of clean clothing is also carried out by these men, who collect all dirty clothing and sort out all clothing unfit for further use, and clothing necessary to be washed and disinfected. The latter is taken to the Foden Disinfector, and former to the Divisional Salvage section for disposal. All new underclothing from D.A.D.O.S. is sent to the baths instead of being taken direct to the units, and is distributed as occasion arises which materially affects a great saving in clothing, which compensates to a great extent for the extra labour involved in the handling of the new clothes.

2. FODEN DISINFECTOR.
The whole of the soiled underclothing of the Division is dealt with by this machine, and with the exception of the 2 drivers, this work is carried out by a staff of the Company men. The whole of the clothing is counted here and tied into bundles of ten and sent to either the Laundry or Salvage.

3. DIVISIONAL LAUNDRIES.
These are instituted in conjunction with Baths, and civilian female labour is employed on the actual washing and mending, but the administration and counting is done by staffs of the Company. The clothing upon its arrival from the Disinfector is sorted out and issued to the women, who take it to their homes where all the washing and

ironing is carried out. Upon its return to the Laundry depot it is counted and checked as to its cleanliness, and stored or dispatched immediately to the Baths for re-issue.

4. SOCK DEPOTS.

These are established with each Infantry Brigade. H.Q. during the Winter months, and staffs from the Company are engaged on the work of receiving wet socks from the men in the trenches, sorting them, and all that are fit for re-issue are taken to specially constructed drying rooms and dried. The dirty and torn socks are counted and put into bags, and dispatched to the Laundry for attention and return. Units send down daily all socks for disposal, and clean dry socks are issued in return.

5. DIVISIONAL CANTEENS & RECREATION ROOMS.

These Canteens and Recreation Rooms—at the present time 10 in number—are established in the forward area for the benefit of units of the Division.

The work in connection with these institutions includes the buying in of stocks from the E.F.C., the distribution to branch canteens together with constant checking and supervision.

6. SOUP DEPOTS.

Hot soup and other hot foodstuff is issued to the troops in the line by the staffs of these depots, which are established in the forward area.   These institutions are a great boon to the men in the line during the Winter months

7. FORWARD DEPOTS FOR MEDICAL COMFORTS SUPPLIES.

These are established for active operations. Through the agency of these Depots a constant supply of Medical Comforts is kept up to the troops in the line. During recent operations, 20,000 tin boxes were made by the Company Pioneers from old tin collected from different sources. These were filled with chocolate, biscuits, cigarettes, etc. and sent forward to the troops Just before the attack.

8. DIVISIONAL SODA-WATER FACTORY.

This machine is placed in the most convenient place in the Divisional area, having regard to the best water supply and most central position. This also is supervised and worked by men of the Company.

9. DIVISIONAL STORES.

These stores are maintained for the purpose of storing material not required at the moment, and men of the Company are responsible for the receiving, checking and issuing; of such stores.

The entertainments for the Division are under control of the O.C. Company, who is responsible for the drawing up of weekly entertainment programmes and the supervision of same. The following is a list of the institutions which provide these entertainments:-
1 – Divisional Band and 2 Divisional Orchestras.

2 – Divisional 'Pierrot' Troupe.

3 – 2 Divisional Cinemas.

4 – Divisional Sports.

Upon the Division moving into a new area, there is naturally a great deal of work to be done in connection with fitting up staging and lighting for these entertainments, and men of the Company along with the Pioneers carry out this work.

The staff for the Cinema is drawn from the personnel of the Company.

Whenever possible Divisional Sports are arranged and carried out, under the direct superintendence of the O.C. Company.

DIVISIONAL PIONEERS

To carry out the varied duties of the Company, a number of tradesmen of the Company have been, formed into a Pioneer Section, and the whole of the technical work required to be done is carried out by these men under a capable N.C.O. The duties of this section may be summarised under the following headings:

1 – The construction of Bath Houses, Drying Rooms, Office Furniture, etc.

2 – Divisional Sign Boards.

3 – Carpentry in connection with Divisional Entertainments, etc.

4 – Divisional Headquarters Tailoring.

5 – Divisional Barber.

6 – Electric light installation.

7 – General repair shop.

DIVISIONAL DISTINGUISHING PATCHES.

In addition to his usual duties, the Tailor is also responsible for the cutting out of all distinguishing patches for the Division. These patches consist of red cloth in the shape of a horse-shoe, with nail holes, and a lozenge in different coloured cloths to distinguish between the different Brigades, etc. in the Division.

Men are provide from the Company to act as Water Guards, Cemetery Wardens, Caretakers, etc. as directed by Divisional Headquarters.

The Company is also responsible for the maintenance and supervision of the Divisional Reinforcement Guides, their duty being to direct reinforcements to units of the Division; men returning from leave; and men discharged from hospital rejoining their units; to their respective Battalions. During active operations, man are posted for duty at the Divisional Rest Station to deal with men (convalescents and slightly wounded cases) who on discharge from the Rest Station rejoin their units.

A Sanitary Detachment has been formed within the Company to supervise the general Sanitation of the Division. Each unit is visited daily - the NCOs i/c Areas reporting on the general condition, and sanitary requirements put in hand where necessary to keep up the sanitation to the standard required. Where units are not able themselves to carry out any necessary requirements, the Divisional Pioneers are called upon to execute the work.

DIVISIONAL REST BILLET.
An institution designed to give six days rest and recreation for 200 to 250 men each week, such men being selected by Medical Officers as being in need of a change.

DIVISIONAL LIBRARY
This library is run from a central store, and supplies forward Canteens and Soup Depots with a constant change of books, etc.

DIVISIONAL ACCOUNTS.
The Officer Commanding the Company is entirely responsible for the safe custody of Divisional Funds, and for the transaction of all business purchases, etc. in connection with the Divisional Funds.

APPENDIX V

The March 1918 Retreat

The following compiled from the 3rd Army[1] and V Corps[2] Diaries and a Report[3] by the Corps Labour Commandant, Colonel J. A. Smith, illustrates the stages of retreat in March 1918 and the speed with which the Labour Corps returned to work.

21 March	4.45 a.m. German Offensive began. Order 'Concentrate' issued to all Groups. Haplincourt heavily shelled – 34 Group to retire to Beaulencourt. Ytres railhead heavily shelled – 42 Company heavily bombed, although casualties were sustained the company maintained its steadiness and continued to load ammunition.
22 March	29, 34 & 46 Companies, Indian Labour Corps in forward positions ordered to fall back to 68 Group at Montauban. 34 and 39 Groups ordered to retire to Geudecourt and Manancourt.
23 March	Colonel Smith visited and spoke to every Company Commander, taking charge of several companies who had become detached from their group and come into his area. 39 Group shelled out of Manancourt – ordered to Le Transloy. 42 Company began work on ammunition at Trones Wood. 34 and 40 Groups safely at Geudecourt and Montauban. Colonel Smith assumed command of 36, 54 and 68 Groups who had come into the area.
24 March	34 and 39 Groups ordered to Pozieres and Meaulte. 54 and 68 Groups ordered to Talmas.
25 March	Colonel Smith visited all Groups and ordered 36 to Hedauville, 39 to Contay, 40 to Heilly, and 54 and 68 to remain at Talmas.
26 March	Colonel Smith visited all Groups to inform them that they should be prepared to change orders and retire to the North West moving to Saulty, Humbercourt and Lucheux.
27 March	As situation had changed again Colonel Smith is asked to move Labour as soon as possible to dig a defence line (Louvencourt – Lealvillers – Vadencourt).
28 March	800 men working on the Defence Line, a further 4,000 were available but waiting for tools.
29 March	1,400 men now digging Defence Line and railhead companies at Puchevillers and Belle Eglise. 34 and 36 Groups handed over to IV Corps to work on their defensive line.
30 March	4,000 men on Defence Line. Colonel Smith takes command of personnel from all Army and Corps Schools to dig defences.

1   NA WO 95/384
2   NA WO 95/760
3   NA WO 107/37 Appendix BB

APPENDIX VI

Exhumation and Reburial

When the war ended concentration cemeteries were formed from existing battlefield cemeteries. This brought together bodies from small battlefield cemeteries and those found on the battlefields. Searching for bodies, their exhumation and reburial started at the beginning of 1919 and continued well into the 1920s. Even today, individuals or groups of bodies are found and buried in CWGC Cemeteries. In order to create a concentration cemetery it was often necessary to search the existing cemetery if, like Hooge Crater Cemetery, it had been subject to shelling. Once this had been done bodies were brought from other cemeteries or the battlefield.

The 7th Division Burial Officer started Hooge Crater Cemetery in October 1917. The land was lost to the Germans in April 1918 and regained on 28 September 1918. By November 1918, the

> ... area had been under shell fire perhaps more consistently intense than in any other area of the war and that the crosses originally erected to mark the grave on the battlefield may have been blown from its place many times and each time replaced over a spot that was further and further away from the original grave.[1]

Procedures used by the Labour Corps Exhumation Squads and Cemetery Parties were based upon the instructions written by Captain Crawford, the OC of 68 Company in July 1919. His Company pioneered exhumation and re-burial procedures. They created Hooge Crater Cemetery as a concentration cemetery between January 1919 and April 1920.

The following notes are taken from Captain Crawford's written procedures. All this work was under the control of the Director Graves Registration and Enquiries (DGR&E) and his staff.

The Survey Officer

The Survey Officer laid out the area to be searched and instructed the Burial Officer where searches and reburial should take place. He placed flags at each corner of the land to be searched. He was also responsible for the layout of the concentration cemetery. He pegged out the cemetery site into rows of graves according to plans agreed with DGR&E Staff and ensured the burial parties kept to the plan. When a cemetery was completed he prepared a final plan and a comprehensive report that was sent to the DGR&E.

The Army Burial Officer

He was responsible for the exhumation of all remains found, and for their transport to the site of the new burial ground. He had to ensure that any effects found with the body and the original cross, where one existed, were also transported to the new site. At the concentration cemetery, following the Survey Officer's plans, he was responsible for re-internment of the body. He also had to complete the paperwork, which included the map reference where the body was found, the name of the cemetery, plot, row and grave number where reburied, whether a cross was found together with the regimental particulars on it and whether any effects were forwarded to the Base.

Exhumation Squads

Exhumation squads of 32 men worked for the Army Burial Officer. Each squad was supplied with stakes to mark the position of bodies, rubber gloves, shovels, canvas and rope in which the bodies were wrapped, stretchers, cresol and wire cutters. The squad would search a 500-yard square of land looking for signs of a burial. Graves could be identified by a rifle or post bearing a helmet or equipment, or a stake with the letter 'E' burnt into it which indicated where a British soldier had been buried by the Germans.

All too often it was the experience of the squad that determined where they should dig. The men looked for signs like remains of equipment on or protruding through the surface of the ground, and rat holes, as rats often brought small pieces of bone or equipment to the surface. Men were also trained to look for grass that was a vivid bluish green colour and earth or water that was either greenish black or grey as these often indicated where bodies were buried.

Should the exhumation squad search a battlefield cemetery containing 40 or more burials it would be marked with a blue flag. Smaller cemeteries were marked with a yellow flag. These were left untouched until further orders were received from DGR&E. Once the area had been searched and staked the unpleasant task of exhumation began. Care had to be taken not to dig too close to the burial site in case more than one man had been buried in the grave. The exhumed body or bodies were placed on canvas soaked with cresol and the task of identification began. A careful examination was made of pockets for personal effects and the neck, wrists and braces for identification tags. All personal effects were placed in a ration bag and sent, attached to the body, to the concentration cemetery.

Once the examination was complete the remains were wrapped in canvas, which was tied up and labelled. The Exhumation Officer completed and signed the label. The label detailed:

1 Sheet number of map used
2 Map reference where body was found
3 If a cross ha been found
4 Number and rank of deceased
5 Name

6 Unit

7 List of effects found and sent with body, mentioning particularly where pay-book is found, whether there is a will

8 Whether a committal service is required. This will depend upon whether, in the opinion of the officer present at the exhumation, the body has previously been properly committed or not.

9 Religion, if possible

10 Signature of the officer responsible

When more than one body was found in a grave the remains were kept together and the labels marked so that the bodies would be buried side by side. It was often possible to identify unknown bodies from unit records that had details of men being buried together. The final task of the exhumation squad was to place any equipment not needed for identification back into the empty grave, pour cresol on it and fill in the grave.

The company clerk kept details of the officers and men involved and the squares they worked. Details were also kept about the number of bodies registered as buried in the area. The exhumation squad usually had an idea of the minimum number of bodies in an area. Crawford stated the officer 'should not be content to leave the square as soon as the number has been exhumed but should satisfy himself that the area is cleared.'[2]

Crawford recommended that, in the summer, the work be done in the early hours of the morning. Men on exhumation work were instructed to thoroughly wash their hands and rubber gloves with cresol after handling bodies or effects. By July 1919 grass and nettles covered much of the battlefields, which meant signs of burials became more difficult to find. For this reason companies were instructed to check and recheck the ground before declaring it clear of graves. As French and Belgians began to return to their homes and cultivate the ground, bodies were found in areas that had not been searched or that had been missed earlier. To cope with such finds and for other isolated bodies it was recommended that each company have a 'Flying Squad' under the charge of an officer.

Cemetery Parties

A cemetery party consisted of the Chaplain attached to the company, one officer, a clerk, (who ensured all effects were taken from the bodies, and checked the particulars given upon the label), an NCO or NCOs in charge of the digging party, a sanitary man and the digging party. The size of the digging party depended on the number of bodies being received on the day. They dug a trench 4 feet 6 inches deep. Between 10 and 12 men were expected to dig a trench sufficient for 20 bodies, and carry out the re-burials, during a normal working day.

PoWs were used to dig trenches but were not allowed to bury men and had to be outside the cemetery during the burial service or when the ground was being consecrated. On arrival at the cemetery all effects were carefully examined. A magnifying glass was used to help read the identity tags and any query had to be discussed with the Exhumation Officer who reported to the cemetery each day. Bodies were buried according to plans provided by the DGR&E Surveyor. Each grave was marked either with the cross which had been sent in by the exhumation squad or with a stake. The sanitary man's job was to wash stretchers in cresol once the bodies had been removed and return them to the transport.

Transport

Bodies were transported to the cemeteries in either GS wagons over rough ground, or motor ambulances where exhumation occurred near a main road. One man from the exhumation squad walked behind the GS Wagon when it was loaded with bodies to ensure there were no problems on the way to the cemetery. Each body was carried on a stretcher; a GS wagon carried five loaded stretchers, four on top and one underneath. GS wagons and ambulances also carried a Union Flag that was used to cover the bodies at reburial.

Identification

Crawford's instructions emphasised the importance of identification:

> It has been found advisable to impress upon reinforcements that their extra pay is not given them because the work is dangerous, but because it is of vital importance, having regard to the number of men still missing, many of whom can be found and identified if the work is carefully done. Furthermore, it is found that the greater the stress laid upon the need for identification, the greater the interest the men take in the work.[3]

1 CWGC DG R&E48 *Report of Committee of Enquiry* 13 January 1921
2 ibid
3 ibid

Gallipoli and Salonika

Western Front

BIBLIOGRAPHY

Primary Sources

Library and Archives Canada RG9, Militia and Defence, Series III-D-3, Volume 5053, Reel
    T-10945 Headquarters, Canadian War Graves Detachment
Commonwealth War Graves Commission
Imperial War Museum
National Archives
Classes ADM; CAB; CO; FO; MT; MUN; NATS; T;
WO 107/37 Report on the Work of Labour with the B.E.F.;
Unit Diaries in WO 95
Also WO 32; 73; 106; 123; 129; 162; 293; 339; 363; 364; and 374

Newspapers

Banffshire Herald
Blairgowrie Advertiser
Bolton Journal
London Gazette
Southport Guardian
The *Guardian*
The Times

Secondary Sources

Adler, M., *British Jewry Book of Honour* (London 1922)
Alexander, Major M. H., *On Two Fronts* (London)
Ali, Bessie Ng Kumlin, *Chinese in Fiji* (Suva, 2002)
Arthur, M., *Forgotten Voices of the Great War* (London 2002)
Arthur, M., *Last Post* (London 2005)
Aspinall-Oglander, Brigadier-General C. F., *Military Operations Gallipoli Volumes I & II* (London
    1992)
Barker Brown, *The History of the Corps of Engineers Vol V* (Chatham 1922)
Barthorp, M., *War on the Nile* (Poole 1984)
Bean, C. E. W., *The Story of ANZAC Volume II* (Sydney 1924)

Becket, I., 'The Nation in Arms 1914–1918', in I. Becket and K. Simpson (eds.), *A Nation in Arms: A Social Study of the British Army in the First World War* (Manchester 1985)

Becket, I., *Home Front 1914–1918* (London 2006)

Bell, J., *We Did Not Fight* (London 1935)

Bermant, C., *Troubled Eden* (London 1969)

Blacker, J., *Have You Forgotten Yet?* (Barnsley 2000)

Bluett, A., *With our Army in Palestine* (London 1919)

Bond, B., *Look to Your Front* (Staplehurst 1999)

Bird, C. W. & Davies, J. B., *The Canadian Forestry Corps* (London 1919)

Blumberg, General Sir H., *Britain's Sea Soldiers* (1927)

Bluett, A., *With our Army in Palestine* (London 1919)

Boulton, D., *Objection Overruled* (London 1967)

Buchan, J., *The History of the South African Forces in France* (London 1920)

Burr, M., *Slouch Hat* (London 1935)

Bush, J., *Behind The Lines East London Labour 1914–1919* (London 1984)

Campbell, C., *Band of Brigands* (London 2008)

Canada in the Great World War (Toronto 1920)

Carlyon, L. A., *Gallipoli* (London 2003)

Caruana, M. & York, B., *Emmanuel Attard* (Canberra, Australia 1994)

Cassar, G. H., *The Forgotten Front: The British Campaign in Italy 1917–1918* (London, 1998)

Clothier, N., *Black Valour* (Pietermaritzburg, South Africa 1987)

Commonwealth War Graves Commission, *The Chinese Labour Corps at the Western Front*

Cooksley, P., *The Home Front* (Stroud 2006)

Corns, C. & Hughes-Wilson, J., *Blindfold and Alone* (London 2001)

Crawford, T. S., *Wiltshire and the Great War* (Reading 1999)

Creighton, Rev O., *With the Twenty-Ninth Division in Gallipoli* (London 1916)

Crozier, Brigadier General F. P., *A Brass Hat in No Man's Land* (London 1930)

Dallas, G. & Gill, D., *The Unknown Army* (London 1985)

DeGroot, G., *Blighty* (London 1996)

Denham, H. M., *Dardenelles A Midshipman's Diary* (London 1981)

Dewey, P., 'Agriculture Labour Supply in England and Wales during the First World War', in *Economic History Review* 1975

Dewey, P. *British Agriculture in the First World War* (London 1989)

Dewey, P., 'Military Recruiting and the British Labour Force During the First World War' in *Historical Journal* 1984

Dewey, P., 'The New Warfare and Economic Mobilisation' in J. Turner (ed.), in *Britain and the First World War* (London 1988)

Drage, C., *Two Gun Cohen* (London 1954)

Dunn, Captain J. C., *The War The Infantry Knew* (London 1987)

Edmonds, J., *Military Operations France and Belgium 1916 Vol 1* (London 1932)

Edmonds, J., *Military Operations France and Belgium 1918* (London 1935)

Edmonds, J., *Military Operations Italy* (London 1949)

Edmonds, J., *The Occupation of the Rhineland 1918–1929* (London 1987)

Egan, E. F., *The War in the Cradle of the World* (London 1918)

Elliott, E. R., *The Royal Pioneers 1945–1993* (London 1993)

Elliston R. A., *Eastbourne's Great War 1918–1918* (Seaford 1999)

Ernle, *English Farming Past and Present* (London 1927)

Falls, C., *Military Operations France and Belgium 1917* (London 1940)

Falls, C., *Military Operations Egypt and Palestine* (London 1930)

Falls, C., *Military Operations Macedonia* (London 1935)

Ferguson, N., *The Pity of War* (London 1998)

Ferguson, N., *The War of the World* (London 2007)

Fewster, K. Basarin V., Basarin H. H., *Gallipoli The Turkish Story* (Sydney, Australia 2003)

French, D., *British Economic and Strategic Planning 1905–1915* (London 1982)

Fryer, P., *Staying Power The History of Black People in Britain* (London 1984)

Fuller, Major-General J. C. F., *The Conduct of War 1789–1961* (London 1961)

Fuchs, R., 'Sites of memory in the Holy Land: the design of the British war cemeteries in Mandate Palestine' in *Journal of Historical Geography* 2004 Volume 30 pp. 643–664

Gibson, C., 'The British Army, French Farmers and the War on the Western Front' in *Past and Present* 2003 Volume 180 pp. 175–239

Gleeson, I., *The Unknown Force* (Rivonia 1994)

Gliddon, G., *Norfolk and Suffolk in the Great War* (Norwich, 1988)

Gough, General Sir H., *The March Retreat* (Cassell 1934)

Grace, R., *The Obligation Of Service: The Jewish Chronicle and the Formation of the Jewish Legion during World War 1* (M.A. Thesis Florida State University 2006)

Graubard, S. R., 'Military Demobilization in Great Britain Following the First World War' in *Journal of Modern History* 1947

Grieves, K., *The Politics of Manpower, 1914–18* (Manchester 1988)

Grieves, K., 'The Liverpool Dock Battalion: Military Intervention in the Mersey Docks, 1915–1918' in *Transactions of the Historic Society of Lancashire and Cheshire for the year 1981* Volume 131 pp. 139–158 (Liverpool 1982)

Griffin, N. J., 'Britain's Chinese Labour in World War 1' in *Military Affairs 1976* Pages 102–108

Griffin, N. J., 'Scientific Management in the Direction of Britain's Military Labour Establishment During WW1' in *Military Affairs 1978* Volume 42 pp. 197–201

Grundlingh, A., *Fighting Their Own War* (Johannesburg 1987)

'G.S.O.', G.H.Q., *(Montreuil-Sur-Mer)* (London 1920)

Gullet, H., *The Australian Imperial Force in Egypt and Palestine* (Sydney 1941)

Hall, J., *Inland Water Transport in Mesopotamia* (London 1921)

Hamilton, Sir I., *Gallipoli Diary* (London 1920)

Hamilton, J. A. B., *Britain's Railways in World War 1* (London 1967)

Hammerton, Sir J., *A Popular History of the Great War* (London)

Harding, B., *On Flows The Tay* (Dunfermline 2000)

Hargrave, J., *At Suvla Bay* (London 1916)

Hargrave, J., *The Suvla Bay Landing* (London 1964)

Haslam M. J., 'The Chilwell Story' (*RAOC Corps Gazette*, Nottingham, 1982)

Henniker, A. M., *Transportation on the Western Front*, (London 1992)

Holmes, R., *Tommy* (London 2004)

Hodges, G., *The Carrier Corps* (London 1986)

Holt, T. & V., *Battlefield Guide Somme* (London 1996)

Holt, T. & V., *Battlefield Guide Gallipoli* (Barnsley 2000)

Horn, P., *Rural Life in England In the First World Ward* (New York 1984)

Howe, G., *Race, War and Nationalism: A Social History of West Indians in the First World War* (Oxford 2002)

Hughes, C., 'The New Armies', in I. Becket and K. Simpson (eds.), *A Nation in Arms: A Social Study of the British Army in the First World War* (Manchester 1985)

Hughes, J. M., *The Unwanted* (University of Alberta Press, Edmonton 2005)

Ingram, N. M., *Anzac Diary A Nonentity in Khaki* (Christchurch, New Zealand)

Jackson, A., *War and Empire in Mauritius and the Indian Ocean* (London 2001)

Jabotinsky, V., *The Story of the Jewish Legion* (New York 1945)

James, E. A., *British Regiments 1914–18* (London 1993)

James, L., *Mutiny* (London 1987)

Joseph, C. L., 'The British West Indian Regiment 1914–1918' in *Journal of Caribbean History 1971* Volume 2 pp. 94–124

Killingray, D., 'Labour Exploitation for Military Campaigns in British Colonial Africa 1870–1945' in *Journal of Contemporary History 1989* Volume 24 pp. 483–501

Kinvig, C., *Churchill's Crusade* (London 2006)

Klein, D., *With the Chinks* (London 1919)

Leigh, M. S., *The Punjab and the War* (Lahore 1997)

Lindsay, Lord, 'The Organisation of Labour in the Army in France During the War and Its Lessons' in *Economic Journal 1924* Vol XXXIV Part 13 pp. 69–82

Love, D., *A Call to Arms* (Calgary 1999)

Lucas, Sir C., *The Empire At War Vol I* (Oxford 1921)

Lucas, Sir C., *The Empire At War Vol II* (Oxford 1923)

Lucas, Sir C., *The Empire At War Vol III* (Oxford 1924)

Lucas, Sir C., *The Empire At War Vol IV* (Oxford 1924)

Lucas, Sir C., *The Empire At War Vol V* (Oxford 1926)

Lloyd George D., *War Memoirs of David Lloyd George* (London)

Maclean, M., *Farming and Forestry on the Western Front* (Ipswich 2004)

MacMunn, Sir George & Falls, C. *Military Operations Egypt Vol I* (London 1966)

MacMunn, Sir George, *History of the Sikh Pioneers (23rd, 32nd, 34th)* (London 1936)

MacPherson, Sir W. *Medical Services Volume 2* (London 1923)

Mansfield, N., 'Class Conflict and Village War Memorials, 1914–24' in *Rural History* 1995

Masefield, J., *Gallipoli* (London 1916)

Massey, W., *How Jerusalem was Won* (London 1919)

McMillan, Rev. A. W., *The Indian Labour Corps in France* (London)

Messenger, C., *Call to Arms The British Army 1914–1918* (London 2005)

Middlebrook, M. & M., *The Somme Battlefields* (London 1991)

Middlebrook, M., *Your Country Needs You* (Barnsley 2000)

Middleton, T. H., *Food Production in the War* (Oxford 1923)

Mitchinson, K. W., *Pioneer Battalions in the Great War* (London 1997)

Mitchinson, K. W., *Defending Albion Britain's Home Army 1909–1919* (London 2005)

Mizzi, J. A., *Gallipoli The Malta Connection* (Luqa, Malta 1991)

Moberley, F., *The Campaign in Mesopotamia Vol II* (London 1924)

Moberley, F., *The Campaign in Mesopotamia Vol IV* (London 1927)

Montgomery, J., *Agricultural Labour Supply in England and Wales* (Rome 1922)

Morgan, J. C., 'A Labour Company at Ypres' in *True World War 1 Stories* pp.130–135

Murray, A., *Sir Archibald Murray's Dispatches: June 1916–June 1917* (London 1920)

Nasmith, Sir George, *Canada's Sons and Great Britain in the Great War* (Toronto 1919)

Nevinson, H. W., *The Dardanelles Campaign* (London 1918)

Nichols, B., *The Unforgiving Minute* (London 1978)

Nicholson, G., *Canadian Expeditionary Force 1914–1919* (Ottawa 1962)

Norris, K. P., 'Porton Military Railway' in *Industrial Railway Record* 1997

Northcliffe, Lord, *At the War* (London 1916)

Oram, G., *Death Sentences passed by military courts of the British Army 1914–1924* (London 2005)

Paice, E., *Tip & Run* (London 2007)

Pakenham, T., *The Boer War* (London 1979)

Parker, H. M. D., *Manpower A Study of War-time Policy and Administration* (London 1957)

Pedley, J. H., *Short Account Of Some Of My Experiences During The Slight Disturbance That Occurred In Europe During The Years 1914–15–16–17–18 and 1919* (Chelmsford 1920)

Pirie-Gordon, H. A., *Brief Record of the Advance of the Egyptian Expeditionary Force* (London 1919)

Pocock, G., *Outrider of Empire The Life and Adventures of Roger Pocock* (Edmonton, Alberta 2007)

Pocock, Captain R., 'My Labour Company at Ypres' in *I Was There* ed. Sir John Hammerton pages 992–1000 (London)

Pryor, A. & Woods, J., *Great Uncle Fred's War* (Whistable 1985)

Putkowski, J., *British Army Mutineers 1914–1922* (London 1998)

Putkowski, J. & Sykes, J., *Shot at Dawn* (Barnsley 1999)

Rae, J., *Conscience & Politics* (London 1970)

Report of the Board of Agriculture and Fisheries on Wages and Conditions of Employment in Agriculture (London 1919)

Rhodes-Woods, E. H., *A War History of the Royal Pioneer Corps* (Aldershot 1960)

Rothstein, A., *The Soldiers Strikes of 1919* (London 1980)

Ruck, C., *The Black Battalion* (Halifax, N.S. 1987)

Bibliography

'Serjeant-Major, R.A.M.C.' *With the R.A.M.C. in Egypt* (London 1918)

Scott, P., 'Chinese in France in WWI' in *War Monthly* No. 76 May 1980

Scott, P., 'The German Companies of the BEF' in *The Great War* 1991 Vol 3 No.2 pp. 44–53

Seligman, V., *The Salonica Sideshow* (London 1919)

Shaw Sparrow, W., *The Fifth Army in March 1918* (London 1921)

Sheffield, G. & Todman, D., *Command and Control on the Western Front* (Spellmount Staplehurst 2004)

Sparrow, W. H., *The Fifth Army in March 1918* (London 1921)

Simkins, P., *Kitchener's Army* (Manchester 1988)

Singha, R., 'Finding Labour From India for the War in Iraq: The Jail Porter and Labour Corps 1916–1920' in *Comparative Studies in Society & History* 2007 pp. 412–444

Smith, R., *Jamaican Volunteers in the First World War* (Manchester 2004)

Stewart, T., 'With the Labour Corps' in *Journal of the Royal United Services Institute 1929* Vol 74 pp. 567–571

Story, H., *History Of The Cameronians Scottish Rifles 1910–1933* (Aldershot 1957)

Strachan, H., *The First World War in Africa* (Oxford 2004)

Sullivan, D., *Navvyman* (London 1983)

Summerskill, M., *China on the Western Front* (London c1982)

Swinton, Sir E., *Twenty Years After* (London n.d)

Teichman, Captain O., *The Diary of a Yeomanry M.O.* (London 1921)

Terraine, J., *Impacts of War 1914 & 1918* (London 1970)

The Times History of the War (1914–1920)

Thomas, T. C., *With a Labour Company in France* (Birmingham 1920?)

Travers, T., *Gallipoli 1915* (Stroud 2001)

Tugwell, W. B. P., *History of the Bombay Pioneers* (London 1938)

Van Emden, R. & Humphries, S., *All Quiet on the Home Front* (London 2004)

Voigt, F. A., *Combed Out* (London 1929)

Ward, G. Kingsley, & Gibson, E., *Courage Remembered* (London 1995)

Ward Price, G., *The Story of the Salonica Army* (London, 1918)

War Office, *Statistics of the Military Effort of the British Empire During the Great War 1914–1920* (Naval & Military Press 1999)

Watts, M., *The Jewish Legion and the First World War* (Basingstoke 2004)

Whally-Kelly, Captain H., *Ich Dien* (Aldershot 1935)

Wilks, J. & Wilks, E., *The British Army in Italy 1917–1918* (Barnsley 1998)

Williams, J., *The Other Battleground* (Chicago 1972)

Whitehouse, C. J. & G. P., *A Town for Four Winters* (Brocton 1996)

Wolfe, H., *Labour Supply and Regulation* (Oxford 1923)

Woodward, D. R., *Forgotten Soldiers of the First World War* (Stroud 2007)

Xu Gouqi, *China and the Great War* (Cambridge 2005)

Young, D., *Forgotten Scottish Voices from the Great War* (Stroud 2005)

Young, M., *Army Service Corps 1902–1918* (Barnsley 2000)

Zarb-Dimech, A., *Malta During the First World War* (Malta 2004)

Internet Sources

Algazy, J., 'Silent Testimony of Cruelty' at www.haaretz.co.il

Fred Garrett's Diary at http://www.grantsmilitaria.com/garrett/html/oct1915.htm

Hyman, J., 'Jews in Britain during the Great War' (Manchester 2001) at http://www.arts.manchester. ac.uk/subjectareas/history/research/manchesterpapers/files/Fileuploadmax10Mb,125118,en.pdf

Shihadeh, Iyad, They Also Served: The Untold Story of the Egyptian Labour Corps in the Great War at http://cujh.columbia.edu/2008/09/iyad-shihadeh-they-also-served-untold.html

Stratford Express at http://website.lineone.net/~bwir/bwi_regt.htm

Sugarman, M., 'The Jewish Labour Corps' available at http://www.jewishvirtuallibrary.org/ jsource/History/sugar9.html

Thomas Cook www.thomascook.com/about-us/thomas-cook-history/

INDEX

Index